A HIDDEN CHURCH

Michael,

I hope you enjoy the read, your one of the best in the diocese

Love

Liam Swords.

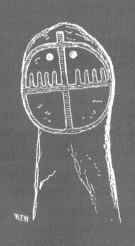

Liam Swords

A HIDDEN CHURCH

The Diocese of Achonry 1689–1818

the columba press

First published in 1997 by
the columba press
55A Spruce Avenue, Stillorgan Industrial Park, Blackrock, Co Dublin

Designed by Bill Bolger
Originated by The Columba Press
Printed in Ireland by Colour Books Ltd, Dublin

ISBN 1856072045

Title page picture: Dance before Midnight Mass (Carleton, *Traits and Stories*)

Copyright © 1997, Liam Swords

CONTENTS

List of Illustrations *page* 8
Abbreviations *page* 10
Preface *page* 11
Introduction *page* 13

Chapter One Political Events 1689–1758 *page* 17
Achonry diocese – Land Settlements – The Jacobite War 1688–91 – Repercussions – The Wild Geese – Dillon Regiment – Colonel Oliver O'Gara – Andrew McDonagh – Ambrose O'Higgins – The Stuart Connection – The Penal Laws: The Banishment Act 1697 – Friars – Staid Nua na hÉireann 1697 – Returning Friars – Registration Act 1704 – Sureties – Registered Priests – The Oath of Abjuration 1710 – Priest-hunting – Bishop Hugh McDermot – Returning Priests – Report on the State of Popery 1731 – The Stuart Scare 1744 – Gavelkind – O'Dowds – MacDermot, Prince of Coolavin

Chapter Two Dismantling the Penal Laws 1758–1818 *page* 49
Charles O'Conor of Belanagare – The Oath of Allegiance – The Catholic Relief Acts – Maynooth College – The Volunteers – Ulster Migration to Connacht – United Irishmen – The Orange Order – Scapularism – The French Landing at Killala – Henry O'Kane – Occupation of Killala – James O'Dowd – Ballina – Castlebar – March to Collooney – Battle of Collooney – Relief of Killala – James Little – Reprisals – Aftermath – Rebels on the Run – The Act of Union 1800 – The Veto Controversy

Chapter Three Life on the Land *page* 83
Population – Towns – Landlords – Absentees – The O'Haras – The Dillon Family – First Tenants – Rundale – Cottiers – Spalpeens – Rents – Linen – Ballymote – Tradesmen and Servants – Servants – Poteen (Póitín) – Sheebeens (Síbín) – Famine and Distress – Crop failures – Depression 1815 – The Farming Year: Spring – Ploughing – Sowing the Crops – Cutting Turf – Road-making – Migrant Labourers – Beggars – Harvest – Barley and Oats – Bringing Home the Turf – Picking the Potatoes

Chapter Four Living and Leisure *page* 109
Food – Fish – Meat – Health – Teeth – Gout – Inoculation – Longevity – Cabins (Cabáin) – Furniture – Clothes – Home-wear – Sunday-wear – The Great Coat – Womenswear – Barefoot – Brogues – Improvements – Fairs and Markets – Faction fights – Sport – Dancing – Singing – Úna Bhán – Music Playing – 'O'Carolan Country' – Raiftearaí – Story-telling – The Friars of Urlaur – Character of the people

Chapter Five 'By Law Established' *page* 137
Bishops – Deaneries – Vicarages – Protestant Population – Churches – Vicars – Glebes – Tithes – Tobias Caulfield – James Neligan – John Wesley – Catholic-Protestant Relations – Conversions – 'The Second Reformation' – William Moore (1752–1839) – Bartley Hart and Family

Chapter Six 'Hedge-Schools' *page* 165
Illiteracy – Schools – Hedge-Schools – School-houses – Pupils – Schoolbooks – Pay Schools – Free Schools – Schoolmasters – Private Tuition – Charter Schools – The Roman Reaction – Evangelical Societies: APCK – Kildare Place Society – London Hibernian Society – Baptist Society – Irish Society – Latin Schools – Novitiates – Lay Classical Schools – The 'Poor Scholar' – Clerical Relations – Standard of Education

Chapter Seven Educated Abroad *page* 197
Irish College, Rome – Other Colleges – Salamanca – Ordinations – Going abroad – Travel – The Irish College, Paris – Community of Priests – Community of Students – The great dispute – Donlevy's Catechism – University – Homeward Bound – Coming home

Chapter Eight The People's Priest *page* 219
Culture-shock – Mass-rocks – Terence O'Gara Snr – Mass-houses – Sunday Mass – Mass Attendance – Chapels – Priests' Lodgings – Pastoral Life – Parishes – Levitical Families – Friars – Augustinians – Dominicans: Straide – Urlaur – Friaries – Decline – Priests' Dues – Clerical Incomes – Clerical Dress – Clerical Vices – 'Saggart Aroon'

Chapter Nine The Cradle to the Grave *page* 241
Christenings – Churching – Confirmation – Stations – Confessions – Weddings – Match-making – Dowries – Dispensations – Marriage Banns – The Sick and Dying – Last Anointing – Wakes – The 'Irish Cry' – Wake Games – Funerals – Cairns – Cemetries

Chapter Ten Prayers and Patterns *page* 265
Feastdays – St Brigid's Day – St Patrick's Day – Lent – Lady Days – St Martin's Eve – Secular Feasts – Christmas – Holy Wells – Patterns – Balla Holy Well – Prayers – Superstitions – Hospitality – Courtesy – Modesty – Swearing – Drunkenness – Stealing

Chapter Eleven Occasional Visitors *page* 287
Hugh MacDermot, Apostolic Vicar, 1683–1707 – Hugh MacDermot, Bishop 1707–1725 – Dominick O'Daly 1735–1735 - consecration – Vicar general – Cathedratics – Accusations – John O'Hart 1735–9 – O'Carolan – The Priest of Collooney – The Gallaghar Affair – Walter Blake 1739–1758 – Non-Residency – Relatio Status – Synod of Balla – Blake's Will – Patrick Robert Kirwan 1758–1776 – Synod of Bunninadden – The Gallagher Affair – A Clerical Conspiracy – Administrator of Clonfert – Kirwan's Will – Philip Philips 1776–1785 – Tuam Meeting – Dunmore Affair – The Oath of Allegiance – Philips to Tuam – Boetius Egan 22 Nov 1785–3 Dec 1787 – Mensal Parish – Thomas O'Connor 3 Dec 1787–18 Feb 1803 – Relatio Status 1792 – 'Calamitous Times' – The Costello Affair – Tuam Succession – O'Connor's Will – Charles Lynagh 13 May 1803–1808 – The Costello affair again – Lynagh's Will

Chapter Twelve 'All this for Achonry!' *page* 329

Postualtions – 'Taking time by the forelock' – Stuart Nomination – Irish Network – Appointment of Philips 1776 – Egan's appointment 1785 – Irish Agents – Valentine Bodkin – Thomas Costello's appointment to Clonfert 1786 – John Fitzmaurice – Lynagh's appointment 1803 – O'Flynn's appointment 1809

Chapter Thirteen The Last Straw *page* 349

Bishop John O'Flynn 1809–17 – Patrick Grady – The Coadjutor Campaign – New Roman Regulations – The Four Banada Resolutions – James Filan – Address to the Clergy of Achonry – Patrick McNicholas – The Dalton Campaign – The 'Forgery' – Factions and Parties – McNicholas' Letter – The Counter-Postulation – The Lay Postulation – McNicholas' appointment – Epilogue: The Filan Affair – The Grady Case – Towards a New Age

Appendices *page* 375

Bibliography *page* 437

Index *page* 446

Ballisodare Church
(Grose, *Antiquities*)

LIST OF ILLUSTRATIONS

Dance before Midnight Mass *Title page*
Ballisodare 7
Court Abbey 9
Achonry diocese showing baronies and parishes 16
Ballymote Castle 20
Battle of 'Green Fort' 22
Kean O'Hara 23
Nicholas Lord Taaffe 24
Ms. *Staid Nua na hÉireann 1697* 32
An Act for Registring the Popish Clergy 34
Bishop Hugh McDermot's letter to Kean O'Hara 31 May 1704 35
Bishop Robert Clayton 42
Myles McDermot, Prince of Coolavin and wife Bridget 48
Charles O'Conor of Belanagare 50
Sligo Volunteer 1780 55
Bishop Joseph Stock 63
Map of Humbert's Route 68
Collooney Medal 69
Bartholomew Teeling 70
Surrender of General Humbert at Ballinamuck 71
Lady Morgan 77
Markrea Castle 84
Annaghmore House 85
Charles O'Hara senior 86
Alexander Percival 87
Spinning-wheel 93
Girls beetling linen 94
Scalding the thread 95
The Still 98
Beggar group 105
Woman with turf 107
Slide-cart 108
Potato pot, potato-basket, piggin, stool, bodhrán 110
Young woman in cabin 113
Hovel near the foot of the Reek 115
Better sort of Connacht cabin 116
Four-handled madder 117
Three-legged armchair *117*
Worst sort of Mayo stone cabin 117
Rush-light holder 118
Interior of one of the better kind of Irish cottages 119
Peasant girl 122
Faction fight 125
MacDermot's Castle, Lough Key 129
Irish piper 130
Turlough O'Carolan 131
Anthony Raftery 133
Urlaur Abbey 135
Bishop John Porter 139
Protestant church, Collooney 144
Foxford church 145
Neligan's Glebe House 146
Brabazon House 156
A Memoir of William Moore 159
Authentic Narrative 160
Common sort of Mayo mud cabin 170
Urlaur Abbey 188
Thady Connellan 190
Kirwan's Latin Letter 195
Corpo Santo, Lisbon 196
Street sign, Rome 199
The Continental Colleges 200
Sailing Ships 1757 205
Chapel of Collège des Lombards 208
Collège des Irlandais, Paris 210
O'Gara's letter 211
Donlevy's *Catechism* 213
The Sorbonne 216
St Anthony's, Louvain 218
Altar and stones, Toormour 220
'Four Altars' 221
Mass-rock in Masshill, Tourlestrane 222
Keash Chapel, aerial view 225
Plan of St Kevin's Church, Keash 226
Banada Abbey 231
Sculpted tomb, Straide 232
Court Abbey 235
The Station 245
'Bringing home the bride' 251
Wake 255

Irish Wake 256
Bean caointe 258
Musical notation of the keen 259
Funeral procession of a farmer 261
Tobacco pipes in churchyard in the West of Ireland 263
St Brigid's Cross from Co Sligo 266
Brídeog 267
Ballisodare river and mills 270
Map of Holy Wells in Achonry Diocese 273
St Attracta's Well, Clogher 274
St Patrick's Well, Tullaghan 276
Tobar Cuimhne 278
Pattern Day 279
Ancient Cross at St Attracta's Well, Kilturra 285
Irish College, Prague 286
Sculpted Bishop from Straide Abbey 289
Eighteenth-century Pectoral Cross 293
Athenry Abbey 294
O'Carolan's Harp 297
Doorway in Ballisodare church 299
O'Gara's Castle 301
Relatio Status of Killala 303
Ballisodare village 308
Bishop Boetius Egan 317
St Mary's Cathedral, Tuam 318
Urlaur Abbey 319
Bishop Thomas O'Connor 323
Dr Charles O'Conor 325

Meemlough Castle 328
Lay postulation of Hugh MacDermot 1683 330
Postulation by the clergy of Philip Philips 331
Letter of Boetius Egan 333
Papal Tiara in Ballymote Friary 334
Old Irish College, Rome 339
Irish College, Paris 340
Archbishop Troy 342
Castlemore 345
Dr Charles O'Conor 346
Eighteenth-century Pectoral Cross 347
The Radical Anti-Veto 350
Pamphlet on Champs-de-Mars incident 1790 352
Banada Abbey 357
RC College Maynooth Founded 1795 358
Archbishop Oliver Kelly 363
St Isidore's, Rome 365
Collooney waterfall 367
Ballincarrow chapel 373
'A Swineford Car' 374
Templehouse 389
Urlaur Chalice 414
Kilbarron Protestant church 418
Banada chalice 424
Ballymote chalice 432
Haran chalice 434
Straide Abbey 445

Court Abbey
(Grose, *Antiquities*)

ABBREVIATIONS

AGOP	General Archives of the Order of Preachers, Santa Sabina, Rome
AICR	Archives of the Irish College, Rome
AN	Archives Nationales, Paris
APF	Archives of the Congregation de Propaganda Fide, Rome
Arch. Hib.	*Archivium Hibernicum*
ASV	Archivio Segreto Vaticano, Vatican City
Coll. Hib.	*Collectanea Hibernica*
CP	Congregazioni Particolari, APF
DDA	Dublin Diocesan Archives
HO	Home Office, London
IFC	Irish Folklore Commission, University College Dublin
KPS	Kildare Place Society
LHS	London Hibernian Society
Nat. Arch.	National Archives, Dublin
NLI	National Library, Dublin
Nunz. di Fiandra	Nunziatura di Fiandra, ASV
OCD	O'Conor Don Papers, Clonalis House, Castlerea
PRO	Public Record Office, London
PRONI	Public Record Office, Belfast
RIA	Royal Irish Academy
R.S.A.I.Jn.	*Journal of the Royal Society of Antiquaries of Ireland*
SC Irlanda	Scritture riferite nei Congressi, APF
SCAR	San Clemente Archives, Via Labicana, Rome
SOCG	Scritture Originali riferite nelli Congregazioni Generali, APF
TA	Archives of the Irish Dominican Province, Tallaght, Dublin
TCD	Trinity College Dublin
UCD	University College Dublin

Preface

The diocese of Achonry is one of the smaller dioceses in Ireland. It incorporates parts of three counties, extending from the sea at Ballisodare Bay through south county Sligo, north west Roscommon and east Mayo as far as Foxford and Straide. It is a rural diocese with a number of small towns. These include Collooney, Ballymote, Tubbercurry, Ballaghaderreen, Charlestown, Swinford, Foxford and Kiltimagh. The cathedral today is located in Ballaghaderreen.

The diocese takes its name from the village of Achonry which is five miles north of Tubbercurry on the road to Sligo. There Saint Finnian founded a monastery in the sixth century and left a local monk in charge when he returned to his own monastery in Clonard. That local monk was Nathy who is founder and patron of the diocese. In later times, the diocesan bishop lived there and had his cathedral there, until the death of Bishop Eugene O'Harte in 1603. After that, the site passed into Protestant hands and the Church of Ireland cathedral is now located there.

The diocesan boundaries date from the Synod of Kells in 1152 and bear no relation to present-day county or civil units. These latter came at a much later date.

This volume of Fr Swords' history gives us a great insight into the lives and beliefs of our ancestors. That history is part of what we now are. It has helped to mould our attitudes, to fashion our outlook, to ground our faith and to understand who we are. It gives us our roots and our sense of place. Without that consciousness of belonging, we can lose our sense of security and of being at home in our own land. How often do we find divisions between families and communities, the origins of which are long forgotten and lost in history? Understanding their origins can help to resolve them.

Most of the sources for the history of the Catholic Church in eighteenth century Ireland are not readily available in Ireland but must be researched on the mainland continent of Europe. Fr Swords was ideally suited to carry out this research because of his extensive knowledge of European languages, his sharp eye for scanning manuscripts, his ability to spend hours pouring over old half-faded documents in rarely-opened files, and his dedication to a work he loved. We owe him a deep debt of gratitude.

While this volume is a history of the diocese of Achonry, it reflects in a very vivid way the lives and experiences of many people in rural Ireland in the eighteenth century. *A Hidden Church* tells the story of a people who, though persecuted and impoverished, developed a vibrant religion. Their lives are minutely described – their dress, food and cabins, their passion for music and dancing, holy wells, their pilgrimages and patterns, hedge-schools and poor scholars, station Masses, fairs, faction fights and poteen-making. This is an authentic history and written in a very attractive style. In its pages the lives of our ancestors spring to life again and we can walk with them in their struggles and celebrations along a road long forgotten and hidden from us. I have found it a very rewarding experience and I am grateful to Fr Swords for making it possible.

✠ *Thomas Flynn,*
Bishop of Achonry
24 October 1997

Introduction

The title *A Hidden Church* was chosen as Ireland in the eighteenth century was until very recently regarded as the 'hidden' Ireland. Achonry was a very small diocese and then somewhat remote from Dublin, the centre of political and social life. Relatively few of the foreigners who toured the country in the eighteenth century ventured as far as Achonry. The Catholic Church had little or no infrastructure, no churches, no presbyteries, no schools or other institutions. No documents have survived from this period in the diocese. What scanty sources still exist are to be found mainly in Rome and to a lesser extent in Paris. The information gleaned from these is supplemented with similar material on the neighbouring dioceses of Killala, Elphin and the archdiocese of Tuam. Unfortunately, no reliable histories of these dioceses have yet been written. Local histories are rare and interest in the subject is a very recent phenomenon. Terence O'Rorke's *Ballysadare and Kilvarnet*, and *Sligo: Town and County*, published over a hundred years ago, are more reliable on the nineteenth than the eighteenth century. Besides, O'Rorke gives few references to sources. More recently, John C. McTernan's *Sligo: Sources of Local History* provides a useful comprehensive guide which should prove invaluable for local historians.

A Hidden Church is a social rather than a purely ecclesiastical history. The people played a paramount role in the religion of the period. No clear picture of that church could be attempted without a detailed description of their lives and times. Priests were close to the people and heavily dependent on them for their maintenance. Bishops were often distanced by their class and, in the case of Achonry, by their residences which were usually in other dioceses of the province of Connacht. The history of the diocese is told thematically rather than chronologically. The early chapters set the political and social background of the period. Other topics include education, the training of priests, their pastoral ministry and the religious and spiritual lives of the people. Bishops, their selection and ministry, receive special attention. On this topic Roman documents are generally copious and revealing. No history of the diocese would be complete without a description of the other Christian religions. In particular, the Established Church merits its own chapter. Chapter headings are in Irish in recognition of the sole language spoken by the majority of the people then.

To facilitate the reader we have made a number of editorial decisions. The language used in quotations was generally modernised, e.g. 'ye' was changed to 'the', and abbreviations were expanded. Proper names presented a special problem. People in the eighteenth century sometimes spelt their own names differently and often omitted or added the O-prefix at will. One form of each surname is adopted throughout this book, e.g. 'MacDonagh' is rendered 'Mc Donogh'. 'Mac' is changed to 'Mc' except in the case of the ancient family of MacDermot of Coolavin which preserves its present spelling. Another exception applies where original documents are reproduced as in the case of the Registration of the Clergy in 1704 (Appendix 7). Placenames often presented an even greater problem. Urlaur was often written as Urlar or Orlar, while Ballisodare was spelt Ballysadare until relatively recently. The present postal spelling is adopted except where the name occurs in the title of a book, as in O'Rorke's *Ballysadare and Kilvarnet*.

Aware that I was venturing into somewhat uncharted territory, I took the precaution of asking widely recognised experts to read early drafts of this work and alert me to possible pitfalls. Professor Thomas Bartlett of UCD advised me on the political background of the period and Professor L. M. Cullen of TCD was similarly helpful on the social history. An tOllamh Pádraig de Brún of the Dublin Institute for Advanced Studies provided valuable information on education as well as his expertise on the Irish texts quoted in the book. Dr Hugh Fenning OP was my mentor and guide on the Roman archives and I drew heavily on his pioneering work on friars during the period. Another old friend, Dr Réamonn Ó Muirí, helped me greatly with the section on the spiritual life of the people. To Dr Nollaig Ó Muraíle of the Celtic Department in Queen's University, Belfast, I am indebted for the translations of the Gaelic poetry of Seán Ó Gadhra as well as biographical information on the poet. Fr James Finan, Keash, helped me with the translation of Bishop Kirwan's Latin letters.

Above all, I owe an enormous debt of gratitude to Bishop Thomas Flynn who originated the idea of a history of his diocese and was always generous and encouraging throughout the project. It is hoped that this volume will remain a fitting monument to his episcopacy and inspire other bishops to follow his enlightened lead. It was also my good fortune to have entrusted the production of this book to two friends of long standing. The creative talent of Bill Bolger never ceases to surprise me but in the design of this book he has surpassed himself as I think the reader will agree. Nothing will ever recompense him for the long hours he spent designing individual pages and transforming what were often drab originals into little masterpieces. His labour has only been exceeded by that of the publisher, Seán O'Boyle of Columba Press. There is scarcely a comma in the book which he did not pick over several times. Both he and myself have long since lost count of the number of times the proofs have been read. If time means money this book will certainly not figure among his profitable publications. Many a manuscript could have been prepared for printing in the time we both spent compiling the index alone .

My thanks are also due to Archbishop Michael Neary for the reproduction of the portrait of Boetius Egan and to Madame Felicity MacDermot of Coolavin, Dermot O'Hara of Annaghmore House and Mr and Mrs Percival of Templehouse for permission to reproduce family portraits, as well as the photograpers, Jack Ruane, Ballina, Patrick Glynn, Castlerea, Sean MacEntee, Dublin, and Fr Andrew Johnson, Foxford. A special word of thanks goes to Mr and Mrs Pyers O'Conor Nash of Clonalis House for the reproduction of their portraits as well as access to their extensive archives. I wish also to acknowledge the assistance of the director and staff of the National Archives, Dublin, the Royal Irish Academy, Dublin, Archives Nationales, Paris, Archives de Paris, Archives de Versailles, the Vatican Archives and the Archives of Propaganda Fide, Rome, the Public Record Office, London, the Public Record Office of Northern Ireland, Belfast, and the libraries of the University of London and Trinity College, Dublin. I would like especially to acknowledge the assistance I received from Gerard Lyne, Dónal Ó Luanaigh and Colette O'Daly of the National Library, David Sheehy of the Dublin Diocesan Archives, Raymond Refaussé of the Representative Church Body Library, Dublin, Mgr John Hanly and Mgr John Fleming of the Irish College, and the prior of San Clemente, Rome. I am particularly grateful to the director as well as Déirdre Hennigan and Bairbre Ní Fhloinn of the Irish Folklore Commission, UCD, who always made my frequent visits there pleasant as well as profitable. Others whose assistance was greatly appreciated are acknowledged in the appropriate sections of the book.

Achonry diocese, showing baronies and parishes

CHAPTER ONE[1]

Dlithe na nGall

Political Events 1689–1758

Achonry diocese has twenty-two parishes, half of them situated in east Mayo and the other half in south-west Sligo. It comprises one-third of Co Sligo and one-fifth of Co Mayo, with one single parish, Ballaghaderreen, partially situated in Co Roscommon. Oddly enough, Ballaghaderreen is now the episcopal seat of the diocese. Like all Irish dioceses, Achonry has access to the sea, at Ballisodare Bay. The Ox Mountains, stretching from Ballisodare to Bonniconlon, forms the northern boundary of the diocese. On the sea-side of the mountains, the narrow coastal strip, extending from almost Sligo town to Ballina, belongs to Killala diocese. The eastern, southern and western boundaries are formed partially by waterways, rivers and lakes, such as the river Moy at Foxford, separating it from Killala, and Lough Urlaur and Lough Gara in the south. It is bordered on the east and south by Elphin diocese and on north, west and south by Killala diocese and the archdiocese of Tuam. The diocese extends 36 miles from east to west and 24 miles from north to south.

Achonry diocese

In size and population, it was, and is, one of the smallest dioceses in Ireland. In this period there was no town in the diocese. The nearest sizeable towns were Sligo in the north-east and Ballina and Castlebar in the west. The diocese was divided into baronies, parishes and townlands.[2] Three of the six baronies of Co Sligo, Leyny, Corran and Coolavin, were in the diocese. Of the other three, one, Tireragh, was in Killala diocese and the other two, Carbury and Tirerril, were in Elphin. Two baronies, Gallen and Costello, comprised the Mayo section. Coolavin, usually described as a 'half-barony', had only three parishes, Gurteen (Kilfree and Killaraght) and part of Kilcolman (Ballaghaderreen). Leyny had five, Tourlestrane (Kilmactigue), Achonry, Coolaney (Killoran), Collooney (Kilvarnet) and part of Ballisodare.[3] The parishes in Corran barony were Ballymote (Emlefad and Kilmorgan), Keash

1 I am indebted to Prof Thomas Bartlett, Department of Modern History, UCD, for reading an early draft of chapters 1 & 2 and offering suggestions.
2 Parishes referred to here are civil parishes and not identical to ecclesiastical parishes. National Archives, Townland Index, Landed Estate Court Rentals; NLI Ms. 5628, pp. 90, 96, 97, 100: see Appendix 50
3 A portion of Ballisodare was in Tirerril barony.

(Drumrat and Toomour), Bunninadden (Cloonoghill, Kilturra and Kilshalvey). The Mayo barony of Gallen had ten parishes, all of which, except one,[4] were in Achonry. The other nine were Bonninconlon (Kilgarvan), Attymass, Killasser, Foxford (Toomore), Straide (Templemore), Bohola, Kiltimagh (Killedan) and Swinford (Kilconduff and Meelick). Costello had eight parishes, half of them in Achonry and the other half in Tuam. The Achonry parishes were Charlestown (Kilbeagh), Ballaghaderreen (Castlemore) and Kilmovee.[5] In the eighteenth century Achonry was very remote, particularly from Dublin, which was two to three days journey away and up to the end of the century there was no mail-coach route from Dublin to Sligo. The diocese of Achonry, like the county of Sligo, was 'not on the way to anywhere else, except from Donegal to Mayo.'[6] Only the diocese of Killala in the west of Ireland, which in the Protestant church was united to Achonry, was more remote.

Land Settlements

Considerable changes in land-ownership took place in Co Sligo as a result of the Cromwellian settlement in the middle of the seventeenth century.[7]

Originally the county was designated part of the province of Connacht to which Catholics were to be transplanted. However, the amount of land available for soldiers who served in the Cromwellian campaign was not sufficient to meet the demand and Co Sligo was withdrawn from the transplantation scheme. Many Cromwellian supporters, such as Cootes, Coopers, Gores and Ormsbys, were given grants of lands there. Some further changes occurred with the act of settlement on the restoration of Charles II. A Catholic, Theobald Taaffe, the Earl of Carlingford, was restored to about 11,000 acres of land, mainly in the vicinity of Ballymote. The Crofton family of Beltra, then Catholic, also had their Sligo lands restored.

In 1688 ninety per cent of the land in the county was owned by Protestants, making it the most Protestant part of Connacht. There were then about eighty-five landlords in the county. Half of them had owned land there before the 1641 rebellion and Cromwellian war. A few like Taaffe, and Richard Coote, Lord Collooney, held estates of over 10,000 acres. Others, like Kean O'Hara, held over 4,000 acres. The O'Haras of Annaghmore were the only Gaelic landowners to survive. They had converted to Protestantism early in the seventeenth century. The Taaffes in Ballymote were the only substantial Catholic landlords to survive. Others, like O'Connor Sligo and the O'Garas

4   Ballavary (Kildacommogue), which was in the archdiocese of Tuam.
5   The Tuam parishes were Aghamore, Knockmore, Annagh and Beakan.
6   J. G. Simms, 'County Sligo in the eighteenth century', *Royal Society of Antiquaries of Ireland Journal*, vol. 91, p. 153
7   see Mary O'Dowd, *Power, politics and land: Early Modern Sligo 1568–1688*, pp. 11-40

of Moygara, were irrevocably dispossessed and disappeared from the history of the region. Some Gaelic families stayed on as tenants on their former possessions and re-emerged again during the Jacobite War.

The other half of the landowners were newcomers who had joined the army in the 1640s or were Cromwellian soldiers. Their war-service earned them their lands and insured that they would become the dominant political influence in the county. Many brothers and members of the same family had received grants of land. Richard Coote, Lord Collooney, was the brother of Sir Charles Coote. There were six members of the Ormsby family, three Gore brothers, three Nicholsons, and two King brothers. Their position and influence was consolidated by inter-marriage. The Mayo section of Achonry diocese was in the part of Connacht reserved for the Irish under the Cromwellian transplantation scheme. There, the great landlord, Viscount Dillon of Costello-Gallen, was a Catholic.

In spite of its remoteness, the diocese of Achonry figured in the only two major military engagements of the period, the Jacobite war at the beginning and the Humbert expedition at the end. Sligo was of strategic importance in the Jacobite War, commanding the road to Connacht from Ulster, where the Williamites were particularly powerful.[8] With the accession of the Catholic, James II, in 1685, Protestants became alarmed at the prospect of Catholics recovering their lands. In 1689 a Protestant association was formed in Sligo under Lord Kingston and the Hon Chidley Coote.[9] Troops of horse and foot were organised and occupied Sligo and a number of other strong points, including Collooney, where the Coopers had their seat at Markrea.

The Jacobite War 1688–91

Some of the garrisons in the county, such as Bellaghy and Ballymote, had been occupied by the Jacobites. Captain Arthur Cooper of Markrea led a patrol of troopers against the Taaffe castle in Ballymote, where the Catholic garrison was commanded by Counsellor Terence McDonogh. McDonogh was the head of one of the Sligo McDonogh septs and an eminent Catholic barrister.[10] He drew up his men in front of the castle. They were fired on by Cooper's men who killed one, wounded five others and the rest were driven back into the castle. A more serious engagement took place at Longford Castle which was Henry Crofton's seat at Beltra. Crofton had been raised a Catholic and his home was believed to be a base for the Jacobites. The castle was stormed

8   see J. G. Simms, 'Sligo in the Jacobite War, 1688–91', *Irish Sword*, vol. 7 (1965-66), pp. 124-35
9   M. Ó Duigeannáin, 'Three seventeenth-century Connacht documents' in *Galway Arch. and Hist. Journal*, xvii, pp. 154-61 (1936)
10 J. C. MacDonagh, 'Counsellor Terence MacDonagh' in *Studies*, xxxvi, p. 310

Ballymote Castle
(Grose, *Antiquities*)

by a patrol commanded by William Ormsby and Francis Gore and a number of arms were seized.

But the main Protestant strong-point was Sligo town itself. Colonel Lundy, the Protestant commander at Derry, urged Lord Kingston and his Sligo men to join the Derry forces as the Catholic viceroy, Tyrconnell, was then threatening to send troops from Dublin against them. They decided to leave Sligo and burn whatever stores they could not take. The Protestant exodus began on 24 March 1689 in bad weather, some going by boat from Sligo harbour, but most going overland. A contemporary wrote a graphic account of their journey.

'And God knows the hardships poor gentlewomen with their children suffered that night at Grange, it being the forerunner of what they were to suffer soon after, and what they had endured the next day in their march by the extreme badness of the weather and the difficulty in passing over rivers especially Bundrowis which did sweep the loads of the horses backs very often down the river; and a great many of the enemy appearing to fall on the stragglers that were not able to keep up, but they were pursued and driven to the bogs and woods.'[11]

By the time they reached Ballybofey in early April, the Jacobites had already cut off the approach to Derry. Kingston left for Scotland to join King William and the others made their way to Enniskillen.

Meanwhile the Jacobites had occupied Sligo. King James appointed Henry Luttrell as governor of Sligo, which was now an important Jacobite base. It was the centre of operations for Patrick Sarsfield, who was one of the leading

---

11   Ó Duigeannáin, M., op. cit., p. 159

commanders in the north-west region. Thomas Lloyd of Croghan near Boyle, known to his followers as 'little Cromwell', was leader of the Williamites in the area. He routed the Jacobites near Belleek on the Erne and captured Terence McDonogh, who was exchanged soon afterwards for some Williamite prisoners captured by Sarsfield. The main Jacobite force fell back on Sligo. Meanwhile, the siege of Derry was raised and the Jacobite position in the north-west was threatened. Francis Gore, at the head of a small Williamite force, approached Sligo. He had taken an Irish prisoner and threatened to hang him. He agreed to spare his life if he carried a message to Sarsfield's camp in Sligo, warning him that the whole Williamite force from Derry and Enniskillen were marching on Sligo and that 20,000 men would reach it the following day. This was early in August 1689. In the face of this overwhelmingly superior force Sarsfield decided to retire from Sligo. Gore and his small force entered Sligo and were reinforced shortly afterwards by Sir Albert Conyngham with a regiment from south-west Donegal.

Thomas Lloyd later took command in Sligo and succeeded in dislodging the Jacobites from Boyle. His success in Boyle was short-lived and Lloyd was forced back into Sligo, which was once more threatened by Sarsfield and his Jacobite forces. The French Huguenot, St Sauveur, tried to hold Ballisodare for the Williamites, but was forced back into Sligo by Sarsfield. St Sauveur and Lloyd took up their positions on two forts, the Stone Fort and the Green Fort, on a hill overlooking the town. They put up a gallant fight but ran out of provisions and water and were obliged to surrender on honourable terms to Sarsfield. It was said that when the garrison was marching out over the bridge, Sarsfield stood there with a purse of guineas and offered anyone who would fight for King James a horse and arms and five guineas advance pay, but they all answered they would never fight for the Papishes (as they called them), except one who took the horse and arms and guineas and deserted the following day.[12]

It was now the end of October 1689 and the Jacobites continued to hold Sligo for almost two years, nearly as long as the war lasted. By the summer of 1690 things were looking bleak for the Jacobites. They lost their last stronghold in Ulster when Teague O'Regan had to surrender Charlemont. O'Regan was put in charge of Sligo. In spite of appearances – he was a hunchback, wearing an old weather-beaten wig – O'Regan from Cork was a talented soldier. He reinforced the Green Fort. With their defeat at the Boyne in July, the Jacobites suffered a severe setback and the Williamites advanced towards the

---

12 G. Story, *Impartial history of the affairs of Ireland*, p. 34, recounted in Simms, p. 129

Battle of 'Green Fort' (Wood-Martin, *Sligo*)

Shannon. Athlone held out and the war was discontinued at the outset of winter.

The Williamites re-opened their campaign in June and it was mainly directed at Athlone, with Sligo a subsidiary target. On 21 May, Kean O'Hara had received a requisition order signed by Sarsfield, 'that the several gentlemen of counties Sligo, Mayo, Galway and Roscommon should send one or two or more of their servants, tenants or followers well-armed and clothed to save his Majesty under Lt Col John Bodkin.' Bodkin himself renewed the demand on 3 June.[13] At Aughrim the Jacobites suffered another severe blow in July. The Williamites renewed their pressure on Sligo and gained an important success at Ballisodare bridge when a party of horse and dragoons beat back O'Regan on 23 July. Michelburne, the Williamite commander, wrote to O'Regan on 26 July demanding his surrender. He sent 'a bottle of usquebaugh and some good London snuff' with his letter. Terms were drawn up to hand over Sligo and the garrison was to march out on 15 August with the honours of war.

The day came and went without the surrender of Sligo. Teague O'Regan had written to Hugh Baldearg O'Donnell, who commanded the Ulster Jacobite division, explaining that he had agreed to surrender, unless he was relieved within ten days. O'Donnell, a direct descendant of the chieftains of Tír Chonaill, who had been in the Spanish service, moved to the neighbourhood

---

13 O'Hara Papers, PRONI T. 2812 / 25 / 26

of Sligo with the result that the Williamites retired. O'Regan now regarded himself as freed from the undertaking to surrender. Michelburne was severely criticised for the fiasco and relieved of his command which was given to the Earl of Granard. On 12 September Lord Granard wrote from his camp in Ballisodare to Kean O'Hara 'that you would applott upon the several baronies of your county as many fat beeves, muttons, meal bread and all other provisions ... to supply their (Majesties') camp before Sligo ...'[14]

Meanwhile, O'Donnell who was convinced that the Jacobite cause was lost, switched sides. In spite of the unwillingness of many of his followers, he decided to help the Williamites against Sligo. He suffered a setback at Collooney, where Sir Albert Conyngham was captured and killed. But the superiority of the Williamite forces left no doubt about the final outcome. O'Donnell was reinforced, pushed the Jacobites back into Sligo and was sent to take Ballymote. Sligo was surrendered on the terms originally arranged. On 13 September they marched out with the full honours of war. Those who wished made their way to Limerick, which was then in the last stages of its final siege. Many of them joined Sarsfield and later went with him to fight in France. The townsmen who stayed behind in Sligo were to be protected in their lives, liberties and goods. The clergy were also to have full liberty to exercise their functions, terms which were not to be honoured in later years.

Repercussions

Very little change in the ownership of land took place in Co Sligo as a result of the war. A cloud of suspicion hung over Kean O'Hara for a while. 'Some said you were turned papist and in King James' army,' his step-sister, Mary Aldworth, wrote to him from Reading in January 1692, 'I did not give much credit to what I heard, believing you were well grounded in the Protestant religion which I hope in God we shall all live and die in, which no doubt is the true religion.' She left little doubt about the strength of the O'Hara's attachment to their Protestantism. 'I am mightily satisfied that you have preserved your life, religion, fortune and reputation which were all in danger.'[15] There was no doubt about her own religious convictions and she regarded King William's victory as 'proof of God's providence'. It had preserved them from the cruel mercies of 'priests and Jesuits' when 'the poor Protestants (were) ready to be devoured by these inhuman beasts'. Both sides had plied Kean with requests for provisions during the conflict but he appeared to have followed a 'policy of cautious and prudent

Kean O'Hara
(Annaghmore House)

14 O'Hara Papers, PRONI T. 2812 / 29
15 O'Hara Papers, PRONI T. 2812 / 4 / 40

neutrality'.¹⁶ In October 1691 Roger Jones, with fourteen other Protestants, signed a letter to Kean acknowledging his 'kindness and readiness to serve the Protestants of your county during the late troubles'.¹⁷

The Taaffes retained their estates in Ballymote, though the head of that family, Lord Carlingford, had been killed fighting for King James at the battle of the Boyne. His brother and heir was a celebrated soldier in the Austrian army of the Holy Roman Emperor, who was then King William's principal ally. Lord Carlingford was given a posthumous pardon as a result and the Taaffes remained in possession of their estates, though they continued to live abroad in Austria. Nicholas, the sixth Viscount Taaffe, who was born in Co Sligo in 1677, reached the rank of lieutenant general in the Austrian army. He failed to obtain the Taaffe estates when he succeeded to the viscountcy. An act of the British parliament on 16 June 1742 ordered the lands to be sold.

Nicholas Lord Taaffe (National Library of Ireland)

In the Mayo section of the diocese, the Dillons also managed to retain their extensive holdings in the baronies of Costello and Gallen. Theobald, the seventh Viscount of Costello-Gallen, was a lieutenant-colonel in the Jacobite army and was killed at the battle of Aughrim on 12 July 1691. Though outlawed by the Williamites, his son, Henry, succeeded in having the act reversed and managed to hold on to the Dillon estates. Henry himself had been a colonel in the Jacobite army and governor of Galway. Nevertheless, he succeeded as the eighth Viscount. Thus for much of the eighteenth century, two of the greatest landowners in the diocese, the Taaffes and the Dillons, were Catholics.

The Wild Geese

Some 12,000 soldiers sailed to France a fortnight after the treaty of Limerick was signed. In 1697 the poet, Seán Ó Gadhra, lamented their going:

Mo thruaighe stáid nua na hÉireann,
Tá a huaisle marbh sa bhFrainc 's i n-Éirinn,
Acht fuigheall beag air atá craidhte créachtach
Dá mbocadh ó thuinn go tuinn mar éanlaith

(Alas the new state of Ireland,
Her nobility are dead in France and in Ireland,
Save a few survivors from battle, miserable and wounded,
Pushed from wave to wave like birds)¹⁸

16 Thomas Bartlett, 'The O'Haras of Annaghmore c.1600–c.1800: Survival and Revival', in *Irish Economic and Social History*, vol. ix, p. 39
17 O'Hara Papers, PRONI T. 2812 / 4 / 31
18 An tAthair Mac Domhnaill, ed., *Dánta is Amhráin Sheáin Uí Ghadhra*, p. 20

Irish regiments were established in the French army, and of these the Dillon regiment was one of the most famous and durable. Arthur Dillon, who was born in Co Roscommon, was the second son of the seventh Viscount of Costello-Gallen and colonel of the Dillon regiment when it went to France. Under him the regiment played an important role in the successful defence of Cremona against Eugene of Savoy in 1702. One of those who distiguished themselves at Cremona was Captain Andrew McDonogh from Sligo. Later Dillon's regiment was stationed in Spain, where its achievements were chronicled by Richard Gaydon.[19] Arthur Dillon retired from active service in 1730 and his son, Charles Dillon, became the colonel-proprietor of the regiment from 1730–41. Charles succeeded to the family estate in Costello-Gallen and his brother James became colonel of the regiment. During the war of the Austrian succession the Irish regiments were actively engaged in several of the principal battles. With five other Irish regiments of foot, the Dillon regiment made a significant contribution to the French victory at the battle of Fontenoy in 1745. The Dillon regiment in particular suffered heavy casualties and their colonel, James, was killed. The Irish, who fought with special fury, were reputed to have cried out *'Cuimhnigí ar Luimneach agus feall na Sasanach'* (remember Limerick and the treachery of the Saxons). Another brother, Arthur Richard, became a priest and later a bishop. Prior to the French Revolution he served as archbishop first of Toulouse and later of Narbonne and was one of the most powerful ecclesiastics of the *ancien régime*.

Dillon Regiment

The regiment continued to be commanded by successive Dillons up to the French Revolution. The last colonel proprietor was Arthur Dillon, the younger brother of Charles (1745–1813), the twelfth viscount of Costello-Gallen. At the outbreak of the French revolution, many of the Irish regiments joined the royalists against the revolutionaries. Some, including the Dillon regiment, remained to serve the revolutionary government. In 1791 the Irish brigade as such was abolished by the national assembly and the regiments were absorbed into the French army and given regimental numbers. Arthur Dillon protested strongly against the proposed merger. He himself served in the revolutionary forces as chief of the army of the north and played an important part in the successful battle of Valmy. He participated in a banquet in White's Hotel in Paris in November 1792, which included among others, Lord Edward Fitzgerald, the Sheares brothers and some students from the Irish college. Dillon proposed a toast to 'the people of Ireland', offering to place his own sword at their service. However, later, when French xenophobia

---

19 Translated by Liam Ó Briain, in *Irish Sword*, iii-vi (1958-54)

became rampant during the reign of terror, Dillon was suspected as a foreigner, arrested and guillotined on 13 April 1794. His cousin, Theobald, who was a cavalry general in the revolutionary army, was killed by his own men who panicked after a skirmish with Austrian troops in 1792.

Colonel Oliver O'Gara

Others with ancestral connections to the diocese who joined the French service included Colonel Oliver O'Gara. He was a grandson of Fergal O'Gara of Moygara, the patron of *The Four Masters*. He had fought at Athlone and Aughrim and was present at the signing of the treaty of Limerick. From there he went to France where he was given command of the Queen's Dragoons and became governor of Montega in Spain in 1705. His father and the father of Charles O'Conor of Belanagare were first cousins. He died at St Germain-en-laye, where the Irish Jacobites had their base. One of his sons, Oliver, also became a colonel and was in a languishing state of health in 1769. Another son, Charles, became a count of the Holy Roman Empire and was living in Brussels in 1774. The French O'Garas left a legacy to Charles O'Conor.[20] O'Conor had other relatives, including a brother, in the French service. In 1727 one of them, also called Charles, received a certificate from the superiors of the Irish Collège des Lombards in Paris. Here he was described as 'descended from a very illustrious and ancient house of Ireland, being of the same name as the last king of Ireland, Roderick O'Connor'. His father had lost a considerable amount of his property as a result of the Jacobite war and three of his brothers were at present officers in the French service.[21]

Andrew McDonogh

Andrew McDonogh was a nephew of his namesake who fought at Cremona. He was born in Sligo in 1738 and later joined the Dillon regiment in France. No fewer than forty-two members of this family served as officers in France between 1690 and 1770. When Andrew's regiment was stationed at Lille he fell in love and secretly married Rose Plunkett, who was at school in a convent there. Her family had him imprisoned in the Bastille, from where he was later transported to Ile Sainte Marguerite. There he was imprisoned for almost thirteen years in the cell that had been occupied by the Man in the Iron Mask. On his release he returned to Paris where he resumed his military career and in 1796 took part in the Hoche expedition to Bantry Bay.[22]

Ambrose O'Higgins

One of the more colourful figures among the Irish émigrés of the period was the Sligo-born Ambrose O'Higgins. He went to Spain to work for an Irish firm in Cadiz and in 1761 joined the Spanish army as an engineer officer.

20 Ward, Wrynn, Ward, *Letters of Charles O'Conor*, pp. 16, 235
21 Micheline Walsh, 'Irish Soldiers and the Irish College in Paris 1706–1791' in Swords, *The Irish-French Connection*, pp. 73–4
22 Hayes, *Biographical Dictionary of Irishmen in France*, pp. 176–7

From there he went to Chile, where he helped to establish a postal route across the Andes. After returning to Spain, he wrote a description of Chile, in which he proposed the establishment of colleges where missionaries and officials could learn the native languages and customs. He was sent back to Chile where he became a field marshall in 1776. Later in 1795 he became viceroy of Peru. His illegitimate son, Bernardo, is celebrated as the emancipator of Chile.[23]

Perhaps the most notable legacy of the Jacobite war was the continuing allegiance of Irish Catholics to the house of Stuart. Louis XIV continued for a short period to recognise James II as the legitimate king of England and provided him with a home in the chateau of St Germain-en-laye. By the treaty of Ryswick in 1697 Louis recognised William as king of England. But the Stuarts continued to retain one royal prerogative, the right to nominate Catholic bishops to vacant Irish dioceses. Rome adopted the device of issuing double briefs. One mentioned the Stuart nomination and was sent to the Jacobite court; the other, with no reference to that nomination, was sent to the new bishop.

The Stuart Connection

Two consequences resulted from the exercise of this royal prerogative by the Stuarts. Candidates for bishop used their intermediaries on the continent to lobby in their favour at the Stuart court. More importantly, it aggravated the conflict between the Irish Catholic Church and the Protestant government and provoked waves of persecution against the Catholic clergy. The poet, Seán Ó Gadhra, alluded to this in 1697:

> *Is é Rí na ríghthe is Rí Séamus,*
> *An Pápa na bráithre 's an tréadhnus,*
> *Rí Laoiseach chuir an chríostaigheacht fo réiteach,*
> *Do chuir an bann so ar Chlainn Mhilésius.*

(Attachment to the King of Kings and King James
To the Pope and the penitential brothers,
To King Louis and to our Christianity,
Which caused the oppression of the Children of Milesius)[24]

The priests who registered in 1704, were later required in 1709 to take an oath abjuring the Stuart pretensions. Most refused, which rendered them liable to arrest and banishment. James III, the 'old Pretender', continued to exercise this prerogative. Charles O'Conor of Belanagare (1710–90) became convinced as early as 1736 of the harmful effects of the Stuart pretensions in

---

23 J. G. Simms, 'The Irish on the Continent, 1691–1800' in *A New History of Ireland*, vol. IV, p. 639; Brian de Breffny, 'Ambrose O'Higgins' in *Irish Ancestor*, ii (1970), pp. 81–9
24 Loose translation by the author.

Ireland: 'As for the Pretender, I neither like nor detest his cause. I am of opinion the affairs of this Kingdom may be well enough administered with or without his presiding over them; and as the present disposition runs, I believe the Government would be safer in any other hands than his.'[25]

After the death of James III in 1766, the Pope refused to recognise his son, Charles Edward, as king of England. The Stuart nomination ceased and the way was paved for a settlement between the Irish bishops and the government, based on mutual recognition. Finally, an oath of allegiance was devised which was acceptable to the bishops and the government, and when the bishops and clergy took this oath, it paved the way for a relaxation of the penal laws.

The Penal Laws
The Banishment Act
1697

The first article of the treaty of Limerick, signed on 3 October, guaranteed that 'the Roman catholics of this kingdom shall enjoy such privileges in the exercise of their religion, as are consistent with the laws of Ireland, or as they did enjoy in the reign of Charles II.' Though this article may have been open to various interpretations, the laws enacted by the Irish parliament against Catholics in the following years were in direct violation of the treaty. In 1697 an act was passed 'for banishing all Papists exercising any ecclesiastical jurisdiction, and all regulars of the Popish clergy out of this kingdom.' The act was directed against bishops, deans and vicars-general as well as all friars such as Franciscans, Dominicans and Carmelites. They were to quit the country before 1 May 1698. If they were discovered in the country after that date, they would be transported abroad. Should they return again they would be guilty of high treason and subject to the appropriate penalties. Each revenue district had to make returns of the numbers of diocesan and religious (friars) in each area. There were forty revenue districts in the country, each with a collector of taxes, who was expected to know every home and person in his district. While their returns, with the exception of Dublin, have been lost, a summary has survived. In this the district of Foxford, which covered Mayo, returned forty-nine diocesan priests and forty-two friars and that of Sligo thirty-three diocesan priests and twenty-nine friars. The incomplete list for the country contained 838 diocesean and 399 religious clergy.[26]

There was no bishop in Achonry then. The diocese was governed by an apostolic-vicar, who was Hugh MacDermot, an Elphin priest. He had been appointed in 1683. Though included under the terms of the act, he remained in the country, acting as a simple parish priest in the diocese of Elphin. James

25 quoted in Síle Ní Chinnéide, 'Díalann Í Chonchuir', *Galvia*, iv (1957), p. 6
26 W. P. Burke, *Irish Priests in the Penal Times*, pp. 127–8; see Ambrose Colman OP, 'The General Exile of 1698', in *Irish Ecclesiastical Record*, v, 4th series (Jan–June 1899), pp. 19–21

Lynch, the Archbishop of Tuam, had already left the country and was living in the abbey of St Amande near Louvain. Apart from Hugh MacDermot, the only other prelate in the western province was the elderly Bishop Donnellan of Clonfert. Phelim O'Hara, who had been dean of Achonry at the end of 1684, might well have been dead by now. His successor, if any, is not known.

The Banishment Act was also directed against friars and it had potentially far more substantial consequences for the diocese.[27] There were then in the diocese two Dominican friaries, Urlaur and Straide, as well as two Franciscan, Ballymote and Court, one Augustinian at Banada and one Carmelite at Knockmore near Gurteen. In addition, the diocese had a close association with the Dominican abbey in Sligo. There would have been a total of about thirty friars in the diocese. An international diplomatic effort was made to avert the banishment of the friars but it came to nothing.

Friars

Many, if not most, of the friars did leave. The Dominicans in Sligo 'were forced to break house and home by act of Parliament and leave the Kingdom'. Sligo had been at the centre of the Jacobite conflict. The friars there would have been well known to the authorities. Besides, they had suffered financially by the loss of many of their benefactors and protectors as a result of the Williamite settlement. Patrick McDonogh, the former prior, now in Bilbao, Spain, wrote in 1703:

> It is certain that the friars of Sligo lost all their goods and effects in the unhappy wars of Ireland only their chalices and ornaments and were very poor, and though they came to a head in the country, they lived in a mean condition having but from the hand to the mouth by reason we could benefit nothing by our mortgage, and the country and our benefactors were reduced and charity was very cold in the heart of Christians.[28]

Before they left they disposed of some of their chalices as they 'found it more proper and lawful before God and the world to make use of them than to perish in foreign countries, not knowing to what part of the universe would they be driven nor what reception they would get amongst strangers'. One of their chalices was acquired by James O'Connell, parish priest of Ballisodare, on 'condition that the convent of Sligo could redeem it'.[29]

Some left before 1 May 1698, as did the Dominican community of Galway, late in the previous March. Others left after the appointed date including a large group, numbering one hundred and twenty-six, who sailed from Galway on 17 June. In all one hundred and ninety priests and religious were

27 See Appendices 38–41
28 quoted Fenning, *The Irish Dominican Province*, p. 6
29 O'Rorke, *Ballysadare and Kilvarnet*, p. 474

shipped from Galway, almost forty more than left from Dublin. Seventy-five left from Cork and only twenty-six from Waterford.[30] Some, like the Athenry Dominican community, may have profited from the act to send their novices abroad for further studies. Each ship's captain was paid three pounds for every person he transported to Europe. Among the four Athenry novices who embarked in Galway was Dominick O'Daly, a future bishop of Achonry. They put in at Nantes and made their way to Paris, where O'Daly and the other novices were placed in the general novitiate in faubourg St Germain.[31] By January 1699 there were about four hundred Irish religious in Paris. There were then three Dominicans from the Sligo convent studying at San Sisto in Rome.[32] One of them, Peter Cluane, later became parish priest of Collooney (Kilvarnet).[33]

Some friars may have decided to stay and risk the consequences. Urlaur was remote and the friars there could easily have melted into the isolated countryside at the first rumours of danger. Besides, they enjoyed the protection of a powerful Catholic landlord, Henry Dillon, Viscount of Costello-Gallen. Six friars remained at home 'because there is hardly a Protestant in the whole barony of Costello and besides it is a very mountainous and boggy tract of country'. Their names were recorded there in 1706. Two of the friars, Donald McDonnell and Thomas Costello, did go into exile. Costello, a former prior of Urlaur, went to Rome and from there to Louvain where he died in 1702.[34] The same was true to a lesser extent about the Dominicans in Straide. A little over four years later, there were six friars there when it was visited by Ambrose O'Connor. Urlaur had five friars in 1703. It seems a relatively short period for the friars to have gone into exile abroad, returned home and regrouped in their various convents. The risks they ran by remaining in the country were no greater than those incurred by returning.

One friar who did remain in the country was Patrick O'Connor, a Dominican from Sligo. He was captured and indicted at the Sligo Assizes on 6 March 1702. He was ordered to be kept in gaol without bail until he was transported out of the country. Mr Justice Macartney reported in October 1703 that 'some gentlemen of the County of Sligo desired me to move the Government to have the said Patrick Connor transported.' This was in marked contrast to Macartney's experience in Galway, where another Dominican, Daniel McDonnell, was found guilty of returning to the country.

30   Burke, p. 132
31   Fenning, p. 22
32   ibid, p. 37
33   Burke, p. 438
34   O'Heyne, *Irish Dominicans*, pp. 229-31

Here Macartney was asked by McDonnell's friends 'to speak to the Government that he might not be transported because he was very sickly.'[35]

It is also possible that some older friars and those in poor health would have remained at home rather than face the hardship and uncertainties of foreign travel. But the case of Francis Dillon, a Franciscan friar from Athlone, suggests that the regime showed no compassion towards the unfortunate. Dillon was in 'great infirmity and distressed condition going on crutches and for the most part bed rid'. From gaol in Dublin Castle where he had been committed, he petitioned the Lords Justices in October 1698 to release him. They ordered that he be examined by the state physician and surgeon. They duly reported that 'notwithstanding that lameness which he complaineth of, he may be transported beyond seas without any damage of his life or health.' The Lords Justices ordered the sheriffs of Dublin on 'the first opportunity to cause the said Francis Dillon to be put on board ship bound from hence to some port beyond seas out of his Majesties Dominions.' They added rather vindictively: 'You are to take particular care to see the same effectually done.'[36]

Seán Ó Gadhra, the Kilshalvey poet, painted a bleak picture of the state of Ireland in 1697.[37]

Staid nua na hÉireann 1697 (The new state of Ireland, 1697)

Is fada atá an aindeise ar Ghaedhluibh
Faoi mhasla ag gach aicme dhá thréine;
Ní bhfuair a dhaoine ag Maoise ar éanchor
Leath a ndaoirse thríd an tréan-mhuir.

Leathrom tíre, is díth na laechradh;
Gan cead airm ná sailm cléire ...

Is cosmhail a gcás le pláigh na hÉigipt
Nó leis an mbroid do chuir Turgésius
Maor Lochlann, sa(n) bhfothrom dá gcéasadh,
Nó an connradh do chuir Cromaill is Értoin.

(The Gaels have been long in misery,
Being insulted by every strong party.
The people of Moses never suffered
Half their slavery going through the strong sea.

---

34 Burke, pp. 158, 161
35 Burke, pp. 146–7
37 An tAthair Mac Domhnaill ed., *Dánta is amhráin Sheáin Uí Ghadhra*, pp. 19–21. I am indebted to Nollaig Ó Muraíle for the English translation.

The country is unjustly treated and the warriors wiped out,
There is no permission for arms or the psalms of the clergy ...
Their plight is like the plague of Egypt,
Or like the oppression of Turgesius
The Viking lord, who tortured them in conflict,
Or the treaty Cromwell and Ireton imposed)

In 1697 Ó Gadhra was apparently aware of the act of banishment.

*Níl cead ag neach a dhul as talamh na hÉireann,
Acht mar urraim go gcuirfeam an chléir as.*

(No one is permitted to leave the land of Ireland,
Save that we are supposed to put the clergy out.)

Ms. *Stáid nua na hÉireann 1697* (Royal Irish Academy)

His anger became palpable when he described the oppressiveness of the new regime:

*Cíos ríogh cíos tíre cíos cléire,
Cíos sróna cíos tóna cíos téighte,
Airgead ceann i gceann gach féile,
Airgead teallaigh is bealaigh do réidhteach.*

(Tax to the king, to the country, to the clergy,[38]
Nose tax, arse tax, heat tax,
Head tax on every feastday,
Hearth tax and roads being cleared.)

Worse was to come in the following years.

Returning Friars

By September 1699 the Lords Justices were aware that many of the banished friars were already returning to the country. In November 1701 a proclamation was issued charging the revenue officers in the kingdom 'in the several ports, creeks and harbours thereof, to take an exact account of all passengers coming in any ship, vessel or boat and on suspicion to carry or convey such suspected person or persons before the next magistrate or justice of the peace, who is hereby required to deal with him according to the known laws'.[39] Rewards were offered for all arrests made, one hundred pounds for bishops, thirty pounds for deans and vicars-general and ten pounds for friars. These rewards led to the emergence of bounty-hunters in the form of priest-catchers. Yet in spite of the severity of these measures many friars returned. Donald McDonnell from Urlaur returned almost immediately from exile but was detected while the ship was at anchor and he was thrown into prison. After fourteen months in chains he was transported to France. He made another attempt to return but was captured and had spent almost six years in prison by 1706. In November 1705, Peter MacDermot, prior of San Sisto in Rome, petitioned Propaganda on behalf of Peter Cluane and two other Dominicans from Sligo for missionary faculties, religious books in English and money for their journey to Ireland.[40] Some of them showed a surprising lack of fear or discretion. There is a chalice in the possession of the present Bishop of Achonry, dating from 1703 and inscribed with the name of Thomas Haran of the Sligo convent. Whether Haran brought the chalice back with him from exile or had it made and inscribed in Ireland, it was a very incriminating article for somebody whose presence in the country was illegal.

So far the diocesan clergy, with the exception of bishops, vicars-general and deans, remained untouched. An act was passed in 1704, obliging all of them to register, giving their names, places of abode, age, parish, when, where and by whom they were ordained.[41] One thousand and eighty priests country-wide registered, of which two hundred and fifty-nine were in Connacht, and twenty-six in the diocese of Achonry. The total figure was almost two-hun-

Registration Act 1704

38 Probably tithes paid to the Protestant ministers.
39 Burke, op. cit., p. 149
40 Fenning, p. 37
41 See Appendix 7

dred more than that found in the returns of five years previously, suggesting that some friars may have registered themselves as parish priests.

The distribution of Achonry priests between the Mayo and Sligo parts of the diocese was surprisingly uneven. Only seven or at most eight registered for the Mayo half, while twenty registered for the Sligo half. In Mayo, nobody registered for Charlestown (Kilbeagh), while one priest registered for the two parishes of Kiltimagh (Killedan) and Bohola, and another for the parishes of Bonniconlon (Kilgarvan) and Attymass. Foxford (Toomore) was absorbed, half into Straide (Templemore) and the other half into Killasser. Terence O'Gara registered in Sligo for Ballaghaderreen (Kilcolman). With the omission of O'Gara, nineteen priests registered in the Sligo end. Three priests registered for each of the three parishes, Achonry, Tourlestrane (Kilmactigue) and Ballymote (Emlefad and Kilmorgan). It is difficult to explain how more than one priest registered for these parishes as the act expressly stated that 'no popish priest shall have any popish curate, assistant or coadjutor'. Kilfree and Killaraght (now Gurteen) were then separate parishes, each with a priest, as was Ballisodare. Medieval parishes which had been long united such as Kilturra and Kilshalvey (now Bunninadden), Drumrat and Toomour (now Keash), were revived and a priest registered for each. Hugh MacDermot, apostolic-vicar of the diocese and as such illegal, registered as parish priest of Ardcarne (Cootehall) in his native diocese of Elphin.

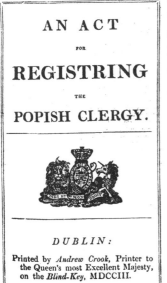

Sureties

In order to register, each priest had to produce two sureties, each for fifty pounds 'that such popish priest shall be of peaceable behaviour and not remove out of such county into any other part of the kingdom'. Fifty pounds was then a considerable sum and the guarantors had to be people of means. Finding such guarantors could have posed problems in the depressed state of Catholic landowners in the aftermath of the Williamite settlement. About five weeks before 11 July 1704, the date fixed for the registration, Hugh MacDermot, then apostolic-vicar of the diocese, wrote to Kean O'Hara, a Protestant, apparently requesting him to act as guarantor for one of his priests.

'My request is about Dr Charles O'Hara, who now stands in need of some friend, of which he will inform you at large, so that I beg you will privately work that a man of his name in the County of Sligo should not be postponed to others; I do not doubt, but Capt Gethings will be his friend, for I have some interest in that Gentleman, who I am sure will second what may be just and honest.'[42]

42 O'Hara Papers, Ms. 20,384 (iv)

If such was the purpose of MacDermot's letter, it was not successful. Kean O'Hara or Capt Gethings did not act as guarantors for Charles O'Hara or any other priest of the diocese. Nor is there any clear evidence that any of the other guarantors were Protestants with the possible exception of Francis King, junior, and Thomas Jones of Rathmore in the parish of Coolaney (Killoran) who provided sureties for the parish priest of that parish. The guarantors for Charles O'Hara were Thomas Corcoran and Patrick Duany, two Catholic merchants in Sligo town.

There were five such merchants, four from Sligo and one, James Dolan, from Collooney, who acted as guarantors for Achonry priests. Corcoran and Duany also went guarantor for Teige Brennan of Cloonoghill (Bunninadden).

Bishop Hugh MacDermot's letter to Kean O'Hara, 31 May 1704 (O'Hara Papers)

Another Sligo merchant, John Maley, acted for Thady Higgins of Ballymote (Emlefad). Two members of the Crean family of Sligo, John and Stephen, were also guarantors. John, a merchant, gave a surety for James O'Connell of Ballisodare and Stephen, who may also have been a merchant, was Thady Higgins' second guarantor. John Crean and John Maley gave sureties also for priests of their own diocese of Elphin and Maley also acted guarantor for the parish priest of Skreen and Dromard in the diocese of Killala.

There were a total of thirty-nine guarantors for the Achonry priests. Fifteen went guarantor for more than one priest, such as Morgan McDonogh of Rosgrib in the parish of Keash (Toomour), who produced sureties for no less than five priests which amounted to £250.[43] Only sixteen of the guarantors were identifiably natives of the diocese.[44] One, Edward Braxton, Ballisodare, was guarantor for the parish priest of Templeboy and Dromore-West (Kilmacshalgan) in the diocese of Killala. Only five priests found guarantors among members of their own families or at least shared the same surname with their guarantor. James and Phelim O'Gara acted as joint guarantors of Terence O'Gara of Ballaghaderreen (Kilcolman). James Mullruniffin of Keash (Toomour), lived in Templevanny as did one of his guarantors, Owen.[45] Three McDonogh priests, William, parish priest of Collooney (Kilvarnet), Teige of Bunninadden (Kilturra) and John of Keash (Drumrat), all received sureties from Morgan McDonogh of Rosgrib in the parish of Keash.

Apart from the five merchants and one doctor, Francis MacLea of Kilteenane,[46] all the others were apparently landholders. All twelve guarantors in the Mayo section were designated as 'gent.' This term was used in the early eighteenth century to describe middlemen, 'frequently holding a large amount

43 The others were Andrew Brown, Breaghwey (Breaffy) (5), Theobald Burke, Urlure (3), Neal O'Neal, Carrowrory (3), Mark Lynch, Garachloon (2), John Gallagher, Sessuegarry (2), Charles Philips, Ogham, Bunninadden (Kilturra) (3), Miles Philips, Ballindoon (3), Manus O'Donnell, Roseturke (4). O'Donnell was guarantor for one Achonry priest and three others in the dioceses of Killala and Tuam. Similarly with Brown, Burke, Charles Philips and Neal O'Neal.
44 Dudley Costello, Cully, Achonry; John Gallagher, Sessuegarry, Achonry; Francis King, junior and Thomas Jones, Rathmore, Coolaney (Killoran); Denis MacAlaster, Coolrecul, Tourlestrane (Kilmactigue); Charles Philips, Ogham, Bunninadden (Kilturra), barony of Corran; James Dolan, Collooney; Bartholomew Hart, Banada; Roger Horohy, and George Enerist, Ballymote; James O'Gara, Lomecloon, Gurteen (Killaraght) and Francis O'Gara, Lishocunian, both in the barony of Coolavin; Dr Francis MacLea, and Phelim O'Gara, Kilteenane; Owen Mullruniffin, Templevanny, Keash; Terence O'Donnell, Ellagh, Bonninconlon (Kilgarvan).
45 The Mulrooney Fin family had a long association with Templevanny in the parish of Keash. They were tenants on church lands there in the sixteenth century. Grady, *The Radical Anti-Veto*, Appendix, p. ii
46 Mac an Leagha was a Gaelic medical family who ministered to the O'Gara family. One of the MacLea family attended the O'Garas in Killaraght in 1509.

of land'. They sublet some of it to smaller tenants. 'Having tenants under them on some of their holdings was crucial to their social standing, as it confirmed their gentlemanly status.'⁴⁷ Only one of the twelve guarantors in the Mayo section, Terence O'Donnell of Ellagh in Bonniconlon, was a native of the diocese. Lack of lay guarantors there may explain the relatively low number of priests who registered. Though it was not expressly stated, the majority of the guarantors in the Sligo section of the diocese probably belonged to the same class of middlemen. The term 'Esq' was reserved for landlords. None of these acted as guarantors in Achonry diocese. Neither did the Viscount of Costello-Gallen or any other member of the Dillon family, although they were Catholics and their vast holdings covered much of the Mayo section of the diocese. Neither did the other Catholic landlords, the Taaffes of Ballymote or the MacDermots of Coolavin, act as guarantors for priests. Having evaded confiscation in the recent Williamite settlement, they may have thought it expedient to keep a low profile in matters relating to their co-religionists.

There is little biographical information available on the individual guarantors. The Sligo merchant, Thomas (known as 'Galda') Corcoran, may have been reared or educated in England. He belonged to an old Sligo family. Early in the eighteenth century, he demolished a portion of Sligo abbey, while the friars still lived there, and used the material to build a row of houses. Corkran's Mall and Thomas Street today are named after him.⁴⁸ The Creans, John and Stephen, belonged to an old and distinguished Sligo family which ranked second only to the O'Connor Sligo family. Their residence was known as O'Crean's Castle and between the 15th and 17th centuries they were a 'family of great wealth and high station and foremost among the merchant princes of that era'. They lost much of their property as a result of the 1641 rebellion.⁴⁹ Charles Philips probably belonged to the Philips family of Cloonmore, who later provided a bishop to the diocese. A story is recorded of him during this period, coming to the rescue of a Franciscan friar from Ballymote, who was being pursued by priest-hunters.⁵⁰

A law had already been introduced forbidding foreign education. Priests educated abroad were not permitted to enter the country after 1 January 1704. Thus with the bishops banished and priests forbidden to study abroad and return to the country, it was confidently expected that the clergy would

Registered Priests

---

47 Louis M. Cullen, 'Catholic Social Classes under the Penal Laws' in Power and Whelan, *Endurance and Emergence*, p. 68
48 John C. McTernan, *Olde Sligoe*, pp. 90–91, 99
49 McTernan, p. 22
50 O'Rorke, *Ballysadare and Kilvarnet*, pp. 476-7

disappear in time by natural wastage. In Achonry this could have happened within a relatively few years. The average age of the priests who registered was high. Of the twenty-nine priests, nineteen were over fifty. One of these, Peter Nelly of Ballymote, was seventy-three and four others were sixty or over. Only two were in their thirties and the youngest, William McDonogh, the parish priest of Collooney (Kilvarnet), was twenty-eight.[51] All the others were in their mid or late forties.

By 1712 two of the seven priests, John Roddy of Meelick and Maurice Frain of Swinford (Kilconduff), who had registered in the Mayo section of the diocese, were dead. Two others in Co Sligo were also dead. James O'Connell, parish priest of Ballisodare, died in April 1710 and Thady Higgins of Ballymote (Emlefad) died some time before 1712. There may well have been more deaths but only these were reported.[52] Peter Nelly would have been in his eighties by then.

The Oath of Abjuration 1710

In 1708 registered priests were faced with a new challenge when there were rumours of a projected Jacobite invasion of Scotland and Ireland. A proclamation was issued 'for seizing and committing all popish priests to gaol until further orders'. Before the scare subsided a new act was passed in 1709. 'All popish priests who have been registered in pursuance of the former act for registering the popish clergy shall take the oath of abjuration before the 25th day of March 1710.' After the death of James II, his son assumed the title of King James III and was recognised as such by the Pope. Now the priests were required to take an oath to 'renounce, abjure and refuse any allegiance or obedience to him'. Only thirty-three priests throughout the country, out of 1,080 who had registered, took the oath. One of them was John Durkan, parish priest of the united parishes of Kiltimagh (Killedan) and Bohola. Durkan was the only priest in Co Mayo to take the oath. He was 'turned out of his parish' and replaced by Dominick Berne, who had registered but for no particular parish.

As a result of their refusal to take the oath, all priests were now illegal and liable to arrest and deportation. To avoid arrest they were compelled to leave their homes as these were known to the authorities since the registration act. Their situation was further complicated by an outbreak of agrarian trouble in Connacht in 1711–12. The priests were suspected of being the fomentors of these troubles. Early in 1712 instructions were issued to have them arrested. Warrants were issued at the end of February by the Co Sligo magistrates. In March Colonel Chidley of Collooney was instructed to commit them to jail.

51 His date of ordination, which is given as 1670, is obviously wrong.
52 Burke, op. cit., pp. 431, 436

But they could not be found. Dublin Castle was informed from Sligo that 'most of the popish priests are fled from their dwelling houses and their usual places of abode'. A proclamation was issued calling on all priests to surrender themselves before 28 March. No priest came forward.

Later in the year laymen, such as the Sligo merchants Thomas Corcoran and John Maley, were summoned and obliged to make a deposition under oath, stating where they last attended Mass and who was the officiating priest. Examined under oath, Bryan McDonogh declared that he heard Teige Davey 'celebrate mass in the parish of Ballysodar in this County at Carrigbanaghan'. Another, William Burke, stated that 'he did see one Rourke who is reputed to be Bishop of Killala travelling on the road in the barony of Curren (Corran)'. In December 1712, Sligo informed Dublin Castle, 'No priest yet brought in.'

Laymen and schoolmasters were also required to take the oath of abjuration. Among those summoned to do so in Sligo in June 1714 were Morgan McDonogh, Naughten O'Donnell and John Maley, who had acted as guarantors of Achonry priests in 1704. However, they all refused to appear and take the oath.

The application of the law very much depended on individual county authorities. Gilbert Ormsby was an energetic Leitrim magistrate, who reckoned 'that all our unhappiness and misfortunes proceed from the Priests'. 'Nor do I believe we shall ever be safe or quiet,' he informed the government in 1711, 'till a wolf's head and a priest's be at the same rate.'[53] The pursuit of priests achieved greater success in Co Roscommon than in either of the counties of Mayo or Sligo. On 5 March 1711 the high sheriff of the county, Hugh Kelly, informed Dublin Castle that he had arrested eight priests who were now lodged in Roscommon gaol.

Priest-hunting

Heading the list was Hugh MacDermot, parish priest of Cootehall (Ardcarne).[54] MacDermot, who had been apostolic-vicar of Achonry since 1683, became the bishop of the diocese on the last day of April 1707. He was the first bishop to occupy that post for more than a hundred years. In August 1710 he had informed Rome that the situation in the province of Connacht was relatively quiet. 'We cannot but acknowledge gratefully that the authorities who govern show us much moderation and seem rather sympathetic to our condition.'[55] Less than a year later he was languishing in Roscommon gaol.

Bishop Hugh MacDermot

MacDermot, with the other prisoners, petitioned the Lords Justices to

53 Burke, p. 440
54 Burke, p. 447
55 SOCG, vol. 573, f. 590r

release them 'or to order them subsistence during their confinement'. Prisoners while in gaol were expected to provide their own food. In this case, the priests claimed that 'most of them if not all being so poor and at so great a distance from such friends as would in charity relieve them, that they cannot long subsist of themselves'. It appears from the petition that MacDermot and the other priests had given themselves up voluntarily, when orders had been issued to arrest the clergy because of the agrarian troubles. They insisted 'that no cattle were houghed in the parts where they were registered and that their Protestant neighbours can give a favourable account of their entire submission to the Government'. At the end of March the assizes were held in Roscommon but no evidence was presented against the priests and they were released on bail after spending a month in gaol.[56]

The authorities seemed unaware that they had in their hands the Bishop of Achonry in the person of Hugh MacDermot. This they learned a year later from the notorious priest-catcher, Edward Tyrrell. Tyrrell was the son-in-law of the eminent scholar Roderick O'Flaherty of Parke, Co Galway. Early in 1711, he visited the Irish Franciscan college in Louvain, posing as a friend. Here he learned that Hugh MacDermot had been made a bishop, about the same time that Thady O'Rorke became Bishop of Killala. He included this information in a detailed statement he made to the government in March 1712.[57] But no action was taken and MacDermot was not re-arrested.

He continued to minister as a bishop. With few bishops in the country and these mostly in Connacht, MacDermot was much in demand, particularly for administering the sacrament of ordination. On such occasions the ordaining bishop provided the newly-ordained with a signed certificate in Latin which served as a passport to one of the Irish colleges in Europe. Should he be apprehended before he left the country, the certificate provided incriminating evidence against the bishop. In September 1713 MacDermot ordained John O'Connor from the diocese of Limerick and provided him with a certificate of ordination. O'Connor subsequently became parish priest of Newcastle in his own diocese. Eight years later he was arrested in Dungarvan, Co Waterford, preparing to take ship for Spain. MacDermot's certificate was found on his person as well as another one signed by the vicar general of Limerick. Warrants were issued for the arrest of MacDermot and the vicar general.[58] There is no evidence that the warrants were ever executed. Mac Dermot was now almost seventy and died three years later in 1725.

56 Burke, pp. 447–8
57 Burke, pp. 227, 228
58 Burke, pp. 365–7

Attempts to arrest priests were sometimes foiled by the people. 'The Papists of this county are so numerous,' the mayor of Sligo informed Dublin Castle in October 1714, 'that without the assistance of the army there is no good to be done.'[59] Women sometimes played leading roles in helping priests evade the authorities. In October 1715 a Franciscan was rescued when he was being brought to Roscommon gaol. A proclamation was issued offering a reward for the capture of four people, two of them women, who took part in the rescue. The two were named as Una McManus and Margaret Tristan. A third, Mary Baken, was arrested 'in the dead time of night'. She was tried in Roscommon in 1716, found guilty and fined twenty pounds. Another woman was sent to Sligo gaol in 1715 for harbouring 'two non-juring popish priests and had one of them in bed in her house' when the search party arrived.[60]

In fact very few priests were arrested and even less transported abroad. An attempt was made in 1719 to stiffen the penalties against them. It was proposed by a committee of the House of Commons that every unregistered priest or friar found in the country after 1 May 1720 should be branded on the cheek with a hot iron. The Privy Council, regarding that proposal as too lenient, recommended instead that all priests returning from abroad should be liable to castration. This bill never became law.

In spite of all the efforts of the authorities, priests continued to function, new priests were ordained, went abroad to be educated and many returned to minister in the diocese. John O'Hart, who later became bishop of the diocese, was in Paris in 1707 when he took his M.A. He was still there in the Irish Collège des Lombards in 1711 when he gained a baccalaureate in theology.[61] In 1714 he was reported to have returned. At the same time, Michael Mc Donogh from the barony of Corran, who had also 'been educated abroad beyond sea' was stated to have returned.[62] James Tymon, who later became parish priest of Keash, was also in the Collège des Lombards in 1711 and gained a baccalaureate in canon and civil law in 1715.[63] Another Achonry priest, Thomas Moore, was there between 1715 and 1718 but his subsequent career is unknown.[64] Andrew Donlevy, the author of the catechism, who registered in the university of Paris in 1718, was one of those who did not re-

Returning Priests

---

59 Burke, p. 436
60 Burke, pp. 436, 450–1
61 Brockliss and Ferté, *Irish clerics in France in the seventeenth and eighteenth centuries: a statistical survey*, no. 1019 (unpublished typescript in RIA); Swords, *The Irish-French Connection*, p. 67
62 Burke, p. 436
63 Swords, p. 66; Brockliss and Ferté, no. 1024
64 Brockliss and Ferté, no. 1022

turn.[65] In 1721 there were at least three Achonry priests in Paris, Edmund Jordan and John Duffy in Collège de Navarre and Edmund Costello in Collège des Lombards.[66] John Duffy later became parish priest of Ballaghaderreen and dean and vicar general of the diocese.

By 1711 the authorities were already alarmed by the numbers of priests returning from abroad. The Grand Jury of Mayo reported to the Lords Justices in April 1715: 'We find and believe that great numbers of Popish Friars and other Ecclesiastics of the Romish persuasion have come into this kingdom these four years last past and that several have also been ordained within that time in this County.'[67] The story was the same from Sligo, where 'the popish clergy of all ranks and orders were never more numerous nor active'.[68] All the government legislation aimed at the suppression of the clergy proved to be ineffective in the end as it was not or could not be effectively enforced.

Bishop Robert Clayton *(National Library of Ireland)*

65 ibid, no. 1016
66 AN MC et / XVII / 614
67 Burke, op. cit., p. 430
68 Burke, op. cit., p. 436

A 'Report on the state of Popery' countrywide was compiled in 1731. The Protestant Bishop of Killala and Achonry, Robert Clayton (1729–35) submitted the information on Achonry diocese.[69] He probably used the seven Protestant ministers then resident in the diocese, to collect the details.[70] The report stated that there were twenty-six 'popish priests' (of which eight were named), and thirteen friars, all of them named, in the diocese. The figures given in the report were probably approximate rather than exact.

Report on the State of Popery 1731

However, the total number of friars given was not even approximate. Only three friaries were mentioned, one in Achonry (Court Abbey) with three Franciscan friars, another in Ballymote (Emlefad), with seven Franciscans and a third in Bunninadden (Cloonoghill) with three friars. The latter is difficult to explain as there was no friary historically established there. It may have been the Carmelite friary of Knockmore in the neighbouring parish of Gurteen. In 1744 it was reported to have three friars.[71] The Augustinian friary in Banada is not mentioned. Over ten years later one friar was reported to be living there and later in the century there were two or three friars there. More importantly, the report failed to take account of the two Dominican friaries of Urlaur and Straide. Three years later, when they were visited by the provincial, he found eleven friars in Straide and eight in Urlaur, not counting some absentees.[72] On these figures, the total number of friars in the diocese would have been about thirty-six, instead of the reported thirteen.

The report stated that there were twenty-six diocesan priests. This is probably a fairly accurate figure. Four of these had registered in 1704. Teige Davey, parish priest of Ballymote and mentioned by name in the report, was then aged sixty. The three others who were parish priests in 1704, were James Howley of Tourlestrane (Kilmactigue), now seventy-three years old, David Henry of Gurteen (Kilfree), now seventy-seven and William McDonogh, now fifty-five. All four were still alive four years later.[73] The report also revealed that the uneven distribution of priests in the two halves of the diocese so notable in 1704 was now corrected. There were now thirteen in the Mayo section as against only seven or at most eight in 1704. Most parishes there, such as Foxford, Straide, Killasser, Kiltimagh and Bohola, were independent

---

69 *Arch. Hib.*, vol. 3 (1914), pp. 128–9; see Appendix 8
70 Tobias Caulfield, Ballisodare (1695–36); Robert Faussett, Tourlestrane (Kilmactigue) (1722–60); Thomas Vesey, Ballaghaderreen (1724–43); James Sotheby, Swinford (Kilconduff) and Straide (Templemore) (1729–51); and possibly Charles Maturin, Ballymote (?–1751); the other two are not known.
71 Burke, p. 438
72 Fenning, p. 197
73 ASV, Nunz. di Fiandra, vol. 131, f. 107rv: see Giblin, *Collectanea Hibernica*, vol. 9, pp. 48–9

units now with a separate priest in each. Charlestown (Kilbeagh) for which no priest registered in 1704, now had two priests. Ballaghaderreen also had two, one in Kilcolman and one in Castlemore. Only Attymass and Bonniconlon remained united with one priest serving the two parishes.

In the Sligo section, Keash which included Kilmurragh, Drumrat and Toomour, had four priests. James Tymon was parish priest and his assistants were named as Nich O'Hara, John Henry and Edwd Mullruniffin.[74] Gurteen had two priests, one in Killaraght and the other in Kilfree. There were two also in Bunninadden, one in Kilshalvey and the other in Kilturra. Cloonoghill (now part of Bunninadden) appeared to be linked with Achonry as the report commented: 'These three Fryars officiate as assistants to O'Hara in the Parish of Cloonoghill.' The said Thady O'Hara, described as the parish priest of Achonry and conducting a school for philosophy there, himself presents a problem. There is no record elsewhere of a Thady O'Hara. It may have been Dr Charles O'Hara, who registered for that parish in 1704 at the age of forty-two and would now be sixty-nine. The last reference to Charles was in September 1725, when the Archbishop of Tuam applied for faculties for him as vicar capitular on the death of Bishop Hugh MacDermot.[75]

Ballisodare, Coolaney (Killoran) and Collooney (Kilvarnet) were bracketed in the report with the observation: 'These parishes mostly inhabited by British Indentures. The Priests here have a Custom of Alternative Services so that one Priest does not serve above two years successively in one place.' The report listed no priests in these three parishes. John O'Hart, the future bishop, was then the parish priest of Ballisodare. William McDonogh, who had registered as parish priest of Collooney (Kilvarnet) in 1704, was still alive and in fact only fifty-five years old. In 1743 Henry Prendergast, the Carmelite prior of Knockmore near Gurteen, was listed as parish priest of Coolaney (Killoran). Adding these three to the number given in the report the total comes to twenty-nine parish priests, which is exactly the same as the number of those who registered in 1704.

However, when the number of friars is taken into account the total number of priests in the diocese in 1731 was approximately sixty-five. The legislation which had been designed to wipe out the clergy within a few generations was a spectacular failure by 1731. Natural wastage by then would have left only four or at most five priests in the diocese of Achonry. The 1731 report summed up the situation in the diocese: 'This Country swarms with a new

---

74 Probably the same person as Edmd. Mullruniffin mentioned in Kilturra.
75 Acta, vol. 95, f. 533v: SOCG, vol. 649, ff. 558–9

Set of Priests who live dispersed so that the Poor groan under their Burthen.' In fact the great numbers of priests were posing a problem for the Irish Catholic Church. Over the next twenty years it gave rise to a lively debate between the bishops, the religious orders and Rome, which led to Rome suppressing novitiates in Ireland in 1750.[76]

The Stuart Scare 1744

While the penal laws against the clergy remained on the statute book, no further serious effort was made to enforce them. In 1739 the Lord Lieutenant, referring to priests, commented: 'It has been the maxim here, while they give no disturbance to the Government, to let them alone.'[77] Only threats from abroad caused the laws to be re-activated. Such a threat surfaced in 1744. The previous year England became involved in the War of the Austrian Succession against their traditional enemy France. There were fears of a French invasion to restore the Stuarts. A French fleet set out for England but was dispersed by a storm. In March 1744 the Lord Lieutenant of Ireland issued a proclamation 'commanding all justices of the peace and other magistrates, strictly to put into execution the several laws against all Popish archbishops, bishops and other Popish ecclesiastical persons.'[78]

Two detailed returns were made for Co Sligo on 9 March, giving the names of some of the clergy.[79] The first list resulted from an examination of Ambrose Gilligan, a Dominican friar from Sligo Abbey. Ten bishops were named including the primate and the Archbishop of Tuam. The Bishop of Achonry is named as 'Bleak'. This was Walter Blake who was the bishop of the diocese from 1739 to 1758. Six vicars-general were named including Patrick Henican, who was dean and vicar general and parish priest of Ballisodare. The list also contained the names of nine friaries, seven in Sligo and two in Mayo, with the names of the friars in each. These friaries included the Franciscans in Ballymote, the Carmelites in Knockmore and the Augustinians in Banada. A total of eight friars were named, one Augustinian, John O'Hara in Banada, three Carmelites, of whom the prior was also parish priest of Killoran and four Franciscans.[80]

The second list which was compiled by twenty-six Protestant jurors under oath, comprised thirty names. Only two bishops, Elphin and Kilmore, are named. Seven Achonry priests and friars are mentioned, including the vicar general, Patrick Henican, whose residence is said to be in Ballisodare. Two

76 see Fenning, *The Undoing of the Friars Minor in Ireland*
77 Wall, *Catholic Ireland in the 18th Century*, p. 48
78 Brady, *Eighteenth-century Press*, p. 65
79 Burke, pp. 437–9
80 Ballymote: Michael Conian, Guardian, Francis McDonogh, Anthony McDonogh, Francis Davey. Knockmore: Henry Prendergast, Prior, – Hart, James Nangle.

other parish priests were named, Peter Clewane (Cluane) of Collooney (Kilvarnet) and Murtagh (O') Hara of Achonry. Cluane, a Dominican belonging to the Sligo convent, had spent seven years on the mission in Scotland, some time after he returned from studying in Rome, but he was back in his convent in Sligo by 1735.[81] He was probably a native of Coolaney. Richard Cluane had been parish priest of Coolaney (Killoran) and Collooney (Kilvarnet) in September 1684.[82] He registered in 1704 as parish priest of Coolaney (Killoran) and was then aged fifty. He could well have been Peter's uncle. The Cluane family had a long association with that parish, where they had been tenants on the bishop's lands in the sixteenth century.[83]

The others mentioned on the 1744 list consisted of three friars and Patrick Keregan, vicar of Achonry.[84] The bishop, Walter Blake, his vicar general, Patrick Henican, and other priests may have gone underground briefly until the crisis passed. There is no evidence that any of them was ever arrested. In any event Walter Blake seems to have been a rather elusive figure in the diocese. His name occurred on only one of the lists and this merely as 'Bleak'. He was mentioned in 1755 in a list drawn up in Galway, again without his christian name and here he was described as 'Titular Bishop of Killala'.[85] Walter Blake died in 1758.

Gavelkind

The most enduring part of the penal code was not that dealing with the clergy but with property. The 'popery act' of 1704 prohibited a Catholic from buying land or from leasing it for more than thirty-one years. At his death his estate had to be gavelled, that is, divided among all his sons, unless the eldest turned Protestant, in which case he got the whole estate. Further amendments to the act in 1709 introduced the 'discoverer', that is, a person who claimed the act was being evaded could be given possession of the estate.

While the results of the act have been greatly exaggerated, Catholic ownership diminished from fourteen per cent in 1702 to five percent in 1776.[86] This diminution varied widely from one region to another. A Catholic gentry continued to flourish throughout this period in Mayo. In Galway there was a large number of Catholic gentry. This explains why many of the Achonry

81 Fenning, pp. 146, 197
82 CP, vol. 30, f. 242rv
83 Patrick Grady, *The Radical Anti-Veto*, Appendix, p. ii. Peter Clewane is probably the Dominican friar, Peter Clowan, mentioned in the first list as a member of the Sligo community.
84 The friars named were John Henry, in Collooney (Kilvarnet), – McCoye, in Achonry and Henry Brett, in Ballymote (Kilmorgan).
85 Burke, p. 421
86 see Louis M. Cullen, 'Catholics under the Penal Laws' in *Eighteenth Century Ireland*, vol. 1, pp. 23–36

bishops, such as Dominick O'Daly (1725–35), Patrick Robert Kirwan (1758–76), Boetius Egan (1785–88) and Thomas O'Connor (1788–1803) were all chosen from Galway Catholic propertied families. O'Connor had a sizeable estate in the neighbourhood of Tuam.

O'Dowds

Elsewhere in Connacht only a handful of families with small hereditary estates survived. These included the MacDermots of Coolavin, the Philips in Cloonmore and the O'Dowds in Bonniconlon, within the diocese, and the O'Conors of Belanagare just outside it. They successfully evaded or avoided the law of gavelkind by dispatching younger sons abroad to seek military careers and thus keeping their small estates intact. When Dominick O'Dowd died in 1739 he was succeeded by his eldest son David. Two younger sons, James and Thady, had gone abroad. James saw service in the army in France where he died. Thady went to Austria where he followed a military career. He married the daughter of an Austrian baron and their son, James, was born in Austria. When David died, James resigned his commission in the imperial army and returned from Austria in 1788 to take possession of the family estate in Bonniconlon.

MacDermot, Prince of Coolavin

The MacDermots of Coolavin are well documented.[87] Charles MacDermot (c.1670–1758) had four sons. Terence studied medicine in France and later practised in Co Roscommon. In 1753 Roger became an officer in the Hibernia regiment in Spain where he later died. Hugh, the youngest son, joined the Bengal Army of the East India Company and he died in Calcutta in 1787. Myles (c.1720–1793), the eldest son, who took over from his father in Coolavin, married Bridget, the only daughter of Charles O'Conor of Belanagare. They had five sons, Hugh, Charles, Terence, Roderick and Henry, and a daughter Kitty. Hugh, who succeeded Myles in 1793, had studied medicine in Paris and Edinburgh prior to the French Revolution. Charles was educated in Rome and later sailed to South America where nothing further was heard of him. Terence went to work on a sugar plantation in Jamaica and never returned. Roderick became a land agent for the Brownes of Cloonfad. Henry, who was educated in Rome, followed a career in the army. He fought with the Connaught Rangers in Spain in the Peninsular War and was killed at the battle of Orthez in 1814.

Such Catholic families were under considerable pressure to conform to the established religion and some did. Henry and Mary O'Hara of Tullyhugh in the parish of Achonry conformed in 1738.[88] They may have belonged to the same family as Dr Charles O'Hara of the same address who was elected

87 Dermot MacDermot, *MacDermot of Moylurg*, pp. 254–5, 263–5
88 *Convert Rolls*, p. 223

vicar capitular of the diocese the following year. Others of this class who conformed were James Philips of the parish of Bunninadden (Kilturra), Christopher Taaffe of Ballynaglogh, Robert Plunkett of Collooney and George Brabazon.[89] The Taaffes of Ballymote, then in Austria, lost their estate in 1753 when it was claimed by a Protestant relation.[90] Charles Dillon, twelfth Viscount of Costello-Gallen, conformed to the established church in 1767, when he was in his thirties.[91] He was an absentee landlord with a mansion in Oxfordshire. He expected to die in England but on a visit to his estates in 1813 'subtle death, more rogueish than a fox, took him in the mountains of Mayo, and put an end to his pious existence.'[92] He was buried in the Augustinian abbey in Ballyhaunis.

Myles MacDermot, Prince of Coolavin and wife Bridget *(Madame Felicity MacDermot)*

---

89 ibid, pp. 20, 229, 231, 265
90 O'Rorke, *Sligo*, vol. 2, pp. 166–7
91 Máire McDonnell-Garvey, *Mid-Connacht*, p. 29
92 *Recollections of Skeffington Gibbon from 1796 to 1829*, p. 88

CHAPTER TWO

Dóchas

Dismantling the Penal Laws 1758–1818

The first Catholic organisation, the Catholic Association, was set up in Dublin in July 1756. The prime mover was Charles O'Conor of Belanagare (1710–90). The O'Conors of Belanagare were a Catholic family who managed to hold on to their estate and their religion after the confiscations of the seventeenth century. 'I enjoy 800 acres still of the old family estate,' Charles wrote in 1767, 'the plank on which we came on shore after our great shipwreck.'[1] By a technicality of the law, the family retained the use, if not the ownership, of the holdings, because they had been mortgaged to Protestant neighbours, the Frenchs of Frenchpark, to whom they paid a rent of about £80 a year. The estate was in Co Roscommon, not far from the boundary of Achonry diocese. Throughout the eighteenth century they increased their holdings by acquiring leases, one of which was in the diocese of Achonry in the neighbourhood of Banada.

Charles O'Conor of Belanagare

O'Conor was descended from the last High King of Ireland, of which he was extremely proud. He received his early education at home under the supervision of his maternal uncle, Thady O'Rorke, Bishop of Killala. Later he was sent to Dublin, where he spent two years at an academy run by an elderly priest, Walter Skelton, and learnt French and science. He became a formidable Irish scholar, historian and antiquarian and his studies inspired an interest in politics and particularly in the amelioration of the plight of Catholics and the removal of the penal legislation against them.[2] He lived in the style of most country landlords, dividing his time between Belanagare and Dublin. 'I spend one half of the year reading, scribbling and improving my grounds. The other half I spend in our capital city where I mix with men of all descriptions.'[3] He was himself a devout Catholic and one of his brothers, Matthew, was the parish priest of Roscommon. His daughter Bridget was married to Myles MacDermot, the 'Prince of Coolavin'.

To propagate the Catholic cause, O'Conor decided to enlist the support of the Sligo-born Viscount Taaffe, who had been obliged in 1753 to relinquish

---

1 Ward, Wrynn, Ward, *The Letters of Charles O'Conor*, p. 205
2 see T. Bartlett, *The Fall and Rise of the Irish Nation*, pp. 51–5
3 Ward, Wrynn, Ward, p. 10

his ancestral estate in Ballymote. Taaffe spent most of his life in Austria where he had become a fieldmarshal and a count of the Holy Roman Empire. O'Conor believed that Taaffe's eminence and influence would advance the Catholic cause in English court circles. In the summer of 1761 Taaffe visited O'Conor in Belanagare and O'Conor acted for a while as his secretary.[4]

Charles O'Conor of Belanagare (Clonalis House)

The Oath of Allegiance

About mid-century there was a noticeable thaw in Protestants' hostility towards Catholics. This spirit of toleration resulted from a variety of factors. The French enlightenment was beginning to make an impact on Irish Protestants and the writings of the *philosophes* were enthusiastically received by the Dublin intellectual elite. It was fashionable for members of the Protestant ascendancy to make 'the grand tour' and they were impressed by the sophistication of Catholic capitals, such as Paris and Rome. The term 'Roman Catholic' began to replace the term 'papist' in Irish parliamentary debates. Besides, after the death of James III in 1766, Rome refused to recognise the claims of his successor to the English throne and no longer accorded him the right of nomination of Irish Catholic bishops. The way was now open to bring that influential body within the ambit of the law.

4   Ward, Wrynn, Ward, pp. 108, 110

Frederick Augustus Hervey, Protestant Bishop of Cloyne, who had travelled extensively on the continent, put forward a proposal that Catholics should take an oath of allegiance to the English crown. In February 1774 he suggested to Charles O'Conor that he draw up an oath of allegiance acceptable to Catholics. O'Conor did so and a bill was introduced into the Irish House of Commons enabling Catholics to take the oath. The new oath had some variations from the formula put forward by O'Conor and he was opposed to it for a while. There were also reservations among a section of the clergy about it. In July 1775 Bishop Troy of Ossory wrote to Propaganda warning that 'if the Pope did not proscribe the oath, many Irish bishops would take it.'[5] Rome issued no condemnation, preferring to reserve judgement. Some Munster bishops and the Bishop of Kildare and Leighlin led groups of their clergy in taking the oath in December 1775.

But the debate continued elsewhere. On October 1778 O'Conor wrote to a Dublin parish priest: 'On Tuesday last there has been a meeting of our Prelates in the county of Galway on the subject of the Test, but nothing of what they have done has as yet transpired, and I doubt much of unanimity among them.'[6] In that same month the nuncio in Paris wrote to Cardinal Pallavicini enclosing a letter from Archbishop Richard Dillon of Narbonne. His brother, Lord Dillon, and other Catholic peers had met in Dublin where they had decided that Archbishop Dillon should approach the French nuncio and impress on him the desirability of blocking any decision by Rome to condemn the oath.[7]

O'Conor himself overcame his scruples and took the oath in 1778 and by 1780 it was estimated that some 6,500 Catholics had sworn allegiance. Philip Philips, Bishop of Achonry, (1776–85) led thirteen of his parish priests and two friars in taking the oath. The exact date is uncertain.[8] The two friars who swore allegiance on that occasion were William Hurly, the Augustinian prior of Banada and Lewis Williams, the Franciscan guardian of Ballymote. The parish priests of Foxford, Straide, Attymass, Charlestown, Collooney, Coolaney, Ballisodare and Gurteen, were not recorded as taking the oath. Two priests were listed for each of three parishes, Achonry (including Tubbercurry),

---

5 ASV, Nunz. di Fiandra, vol. 135, ff. 53v, 54r–56v
6 Ward, Wrynn, Ward, p. 368
7 ASV, Nunz. di Fiandra, vol. 135, ff. 61r, 62r–63v; see Giblin, *Collectanea Hibernica*, 11 (1968), pp. 62–9
8 *Arch. Hib.*, vol. 1 (1912), pp. 70–1; see Appendix 18. It was 1779 or later as Francis Donlevy, parish priest of Bunninadden (Kilshalvey) was described, in the document recording his oath, as being ordained in that year. It was most likely 1782-3 as Lewis Williams who took the oath was then guardian of Ballymote.

Ballaghaderreen (Kilcolman and Castlemore) and Bunninadden (Cloonoghill and Kilshalvey).

The Catholic Relief Acts

The oath of allegiance for Catholics set the scene for the first Catholic relief act which was passed in 1778. This act gave Catholics the right to purchase land on equal terms with Protestants and to bequeath their estate without having to gavel it. 'The Catholics of this kingdom now begin to breathe,' Edward Barry, Catholic curate in Fermoy informed Rome.[9] Up to now, landed Catholic families were under pressure to have one of their members conform to the Established Church in order to preserve the family estate intact. This pressure was removed by the 1778 act. Of some fifteen people in the diocese known to have conformed in the eighteenth century, almost a third of them did so after 1778 apparently for social or poitical reasons.[10] The only real advantage to be gained now by conforming was the acquisition of the vote in parliamentary elections.

Attempts were made in 1779 by Charles O'Hara, junior, M.P. for Sligo, to introduce further relief measures but they ran into opposition from an unexpected source. One of the provisions of O'Hara's bill envisaged the banishment of the regular clergy (friars) from Ireland. Archbishop Troy, himself a Dominican, took strong exception to the bill and orchestrated opposition from the rest of the hierarchy. Troy claimed that the bishops 'all dislike the intended bill'. He was assured that O'Hara's bill would be replaced by 'a less complicated and more agreeable' substitute and that nothing would be introduced without consultation with the Irish bishops.[11]

In 1782 a much more sweeping Catholic relief act was enacted. The diocesan clergy were given legal recognition provided they took the oath of allegiance and registered with the authorities. However, some restrictions remained. They were forbidden to officiate in any 'church or chapel with a steeple or bell' or at a funeral in a church or churchyard. Furthermore, they could not 'assume any ecclesiastical rank or title whatsoever', nor perform 'the rites or ceremonies of the popish religion or wear the habits of their order' in any place other than their usual places of worship or private houses. The 1782 act removed most of the remaining restrictions on Catholics holding property. 'The Catholics of this kingdom are now almost on the same footing as that of the rest of the king's subjects,' Barry from Fermoy informed

9   SC Irlanda, vol. 13, f. 216rv
10 Rowland Carter, Ballisodare, 1781/1784; Neal Lawry, Rathbarron, 1782; Mary McCormack, Nymphsfield, 1782; Roger O'Hara, Achonry, 1779; Robert Plunkett, Collooney, 1780; Bryan Murrin, Toolany (Coolaney?), 1790. *Convert Rolls*, pp. 43, 161, 173, 223, 231, 293
11 Dáire Keogh, 'The French Disease', pp. 21–2

Rome in April 1783.[12] Some other obsolete penal laws were also repealed, such as the ban on Catholics owning a horse worth more than £5. An act was also passed in that year which permitted a Catholic 'to keep school' provided he obtained a licence from the Protestant bishop.

The 1782 act inaugurated the great era of chapel-building throughout the country which continued into the early decades of the next century. In his report to Rome in 1792, Bishop Thomas O'Connor (1788–1803) enclosed an attestation signed by the canons of Achonry, stating that O'Connor had had seven new chapels built in the five years since he became bishop and subsidised the reparation of many others.[13] In 1822 when Bishop Patrick McNicholas (1818–52) made his first report to Rome, he stated that there were twenty-three parish chapels, five of which had been built in the four years since he became bishop.[14]

Up to now the legal position of English Catholics lagged behind that of their Irish counterparts. Early in 1791 a bill was introduced in the English parliament making Catholics there free to practise their religion without hindrance. This had an immediate impact on Ireland. A new more widely based Catholic Committee was elected who were no longer content with composing occasional humble addresses of loyalty from Irish Catholics to the English monarch. The climate of the times was radically altered by the French Revolution and the United Irishmen were forging an alliance between Irish Catholics and Presbyterians. The result was a new Catholic relief act which was passed in 1792. Catholics were now permitted to become barristers and attorneys. The obligation on a Catholic schoolmaster to get a licence from the Protestant bishop was abolished. The act removed the limitation on the number of apprentices a Catholic might keep and the restrictions on intermarriage and foreign education.

On the same day that the act was passed, Charles O'Hara, junior, presented a petition from the Catholic Committee requesting the vote for Catholics. Charles junior, unlike his father, Charles senior, had a reputation for being sympathetic to the Catholic claims. It did not endear him to some members of his family. O'Hara introduced the petition on 25 January but was obliged to withdraw it on a point of order. In April he received a stern letter from his cousin, Frances Jones in Bath:

> Permit me my dear Cousin and friend in return for your attention to my interest to mention what makes me quite unhappy about yours. It is to

12 SC Irlanda, vol. 15, f. 346r
13 Fondo di Vienna, vol. 28, f. 37v
14 SC Irlanda, vol. 23, f. 611r

hear from various quarters 'that you have injured it in the opinion of many by presenting the R.C. Bill'. I trust it is not true and am so averse to saying anything unpleasant and would not mention it, but think by knowing it you may efface evil impressions by explaining your motive of action.[15]

What O'Hara's reply (if any) was, is not known.

The request in O'Hara's aborted petition was granted a year later when the final relief act was passed. The 1793 act granted Catholics the vote in parliamentary elections. It also permitted Catholics to hold all offices under the crown with a number of important exceptions, such as judges in the superior courts, law officers, king's counsel, generals on the staff, privy councillors and a number of higher state offices. Catholics could take degrees in Trinity College and, with certain property qualifications, keep arms as Protestants did.

Maynooth College

In 1795 a bill was introduced for the foundation and endowment of Maynooth College, which opened its door to seminarians before the end of that year. The outbreak of the French Revolution led to the suppression of the Irish colleges, first in France and later in the Low Countries and Italy when the victorious revolutionary armies conquered these countries. Throughout the eighteenth century the great bulk of the Irish priesthood had been educated in France, mostly in the two Irish colleges in Paris and another one in Nantes. Lesser numbers studied in the Irish colleges in Bordeaux and Toulouse. Their suppression posed a major potential crisis for the Irish church. The government, relieved at the closure of these colleges, was happy to endow Maynooth in the hope that home-trained priests were more likely to be loyal citizens uncontaminated by revolutionary ideas.

But the loss, particularly of the Irish College, Paris, was acutely felt in Achonry and continued to have consequences there for almost two decades. When Patrick McNicholas became bishop in 1818, he found no less than fifteen priests who had received no theological training whatsoever.[16] The situation was similar in the neighbouring Killala diocese. Maynooth was expensive and though it accepted for a while a small number of ordained priests as students, the majority of entrants were seminarians. The Irish College, Paris was well endowed with burses by the end of the eighteenth century and there was a long tradition there of priest-students paying their way with Mass-stipends. Bishop McNicholas had to establish an ad-hoc seminary in the diocese to qualify those uneducated priests.

The Volunteers

The timing of these relief acts was largely dictated by international events.

15 O'Hara Papers, Ms. 20, 291 (10)
16 SC Irlanda, vol. 23, f. 611v

The American war of independence began in 1775 and this war 'directly and drastically influenced the course of Irish politics.'[17] When France entered the war on the side of the American rebels in 1777 the danger of a French invasion of Ireland became obvious. Troops had been withdrawn from Ireland and to fill the gap local volunteer corps spontaneously sprung up for home defence. These consisted exclusively of Protestants who had a long tradition of forming armed associations for the protection of peace in their localities. Local landlords took the initiative in forming corps. Charles O'Hara junior played a major role in setting up the Loyal Leyny Volunteers.[18]

The Volunteers sometimes acted as special constables, controlling crowds and occasionally suppressing riots. Many of the corps became debating clubs where Protestants could discuss the new radical ideas coming particularly from France. But above all in rural Ireland it satisfied another human instinct:

> A Volunteer could parade in public in a resplendent uniform, and for some, indeed proportionately rather many, there were the glories of Volunteer rank, captains and colonels soon abounding in Irish society. The Volunteers seem to have thoroughly enjoyed adding colour and purpose to Irish life by their parades, marches, and great reviews when a few thousand Volunteers assembled, each corps in its distinctive uniform, for an inspection, manoeuvres, or even a sham battle with much expenditure of powder. Then there was the social side of the movement – cheerful gatherings, dinners and other festivities.[19]

Sligo Volunteer 1780 (Wood-Martin, *Sligo*)

Volunteer corps, such as the Loyal Leyny Volunteers, whose uniform was scarlet faced with blue, distributed their commissions liberally and many of the recipients, such as Colonel Joshua Edward Cooper, Colonel Percival and Captain and later Major Charles O'Hara, proudly carried their military titles for the rest of their lives. Cooper and O'Hara were among the Sligo delegates to the national convention of the Volunteers in Dungannon in 1783 and O'Hara had also represented the county at the meeting of the Connacht Volunteers at Ballinasloe on 15 March 1782, where fifty-nine volunteer corps assembled.[20]

---

17   R. B. McDowell, 'Colonial nationalism', in *A New History of Ireland*, vol. IV, p. 215
18   O'Hara Papers, Ms. 20, 282
19   McDowell, op. cit., p. 223
20   see O'Rorke, *Sligo*, vol. I, pp. 361–4; Wood-Martin, *Sligo, 1691–1891*, pp. 9–10

In 1796 the government proposed the establishment of corps of yeomanry to replace the Volunteer corps. In Sligo these consisted again, like the Volunteers, almost exclusively of Protestants although a Catholic, James O'Dowd of Bonniconlon, became a captain in the Tyrawley Cavalry. Three infantry and four cavalry corps were raised in Co Sligo at the end of 1796. Two of them, the Ballymote Infantry and the Corran, Leyny and Coolavin Cavalry, were in the diocese. The officers of these district corps were commissioned by the crown, rather than elected as was the case with the Volunteers. Charles O'Hara was commissioned captain of the Corran, Leyny and Coolavin Cavalry.[21]

Ulster Migration to Connacht

1796 also saw an unusual phenomenon which was to leave its mark on the diocese, an immigration to Connacht of a large number of Catholics from the North, who were flying from persecution by the Protestant Peep O'Day Boys.[22] From early 1795 armed groups of Peep O'Day Boys were breaking into the homes of Catholics in the North and looting them. The Catholics formed an oath-bound secret organisation called the 'Defenders'. On 21 September 1795 they clashed with Protestants at a crossroads between Portadown and Loughgall, in the so-called 'Battle of the Diamond', in which thirty Catholics were killed. This became the pretext for the massive expulsion of Catholics, most of whom took refuge in Connacht.

By the end of 1796 Lord Altamont of Westport House estimated that there were nearly 4,000 such immigrants (including children) in Co Mayo.[23] Most of them settled in the districts of Westport, Ballina, Crossmolina and Foxford. Denis Browne, Lord Altamont's brother, named 950 of the immigrants in the district of Westport. Lord Altamont was deeply touched by their plight and was determined to do what he could to alleviate it, to the tune of £1,000, 'provided a sum of two thousand pounds is added to it from the public funds, towards building houses for those unhappy sufferers who have been obliged to fly from their own homes by a merciless and unheard of persecution and have taken refuge on my estate.'[24]

James Cuffe, a sizeable landowner in Crossmolina, listed 167 such persons in the Foxford, Crossmolina and Ballina districts, 'almost all of them weavers'. Nineteen northern families comprising a total of seventy-one persons, settled in Foxford.[25] 'I found them all decent and well-behaved,' Cuffe, who met

21 Wood-Martin, pp. 12–13
22 Patrick Hogan, 'The Migration of Ulster Catholics to Connaught, 1795–96', in *Seanchas Ard Mhacha*, vol. 9, no. 2 (1979), pp. 286–301
23 Altamont to Cooke, 27 Nov 1796, Nat. Arch., Rebellion Papers, 620 / 26 / 82
24 Altamont to Pelham, 27 June 1796, Nat. Arch., State of Country Papers, 1015 / 21
25 Rebellion Papers, 620 / 26 / 145; see Appendix 43

them in Ballina, wrote in December 1796, 'and much more intelligent than the natives of the place.' Of the 167 persons Cuffe met, only three or four of them had been plundered and a similar number ordered to leave their homes. Most of them left the North of their own free will. The reason they gave for migrating was that the Protestant Peep O' Day Boys had become too powerful 'and likely to worst them at Fairs and other public places where they must meet them'. Fourteen of the families who settled in Foxford were from Armagh, two from Down and one each from Antrim and Derry. The most numerous were the McConvills, consisting of four families comprising sixteen persons. There were thirteen Branigans, twelve McNeas (McVeas?) and five McCanns. All except two were described as weavers. Smaller groups settled elsewhere in the county, in places identifiable today only by a concentration of northern names, such as Brady, McCann, Quinn, Hughes, Lynsky, Cassidy, etc. It is believed that one such area was in the neighbourhood of Swinford near Barnacuaige, where the immigrants cleared the stony mountainous ground to provide themselves with the necessary potato-patch.

If they inspired in their new neighbours a hatred and terror of Orangemen, it was not as a result of any great injuries they themselves had personally suffered at the hands of the latter. Nevertheless the rumours circulating in 1798, notably in the Foxford area, of an imminent masscacre of Catholics by Orangemen, were probably originated by the new immigrants.[26] 'Be assured that no circumstance that has happened in Ireland for a hundred years past,' Denis Browne had warned the government on 5 November 1796, 'has gone so decidedly to separate the mind of this country from the government as this unfortunate and untimely business.'[27] On the other hand he believed the overtures made by the United Irishmen to the French were not well received by the natives in his part of the country.

> The inhabitants of this part of Mayo have connected the French and the Presbyterians of the North who they hear have invited the French over. Consequently they have transferred a portion of their hatred to the enemy who they are persuaded are coming with their Northern allies to drive them from their inhabitations and propertys and so strongly does this operate that I am persuaded they would beat the French out of this country with stones.[28]

The fall of the Bastille in Paris on 14 July 1789 caught the imagination of people all over Europe. The ideas which underpinned the French Revolution

United Irishmen

---

26 Musgrave, *Memoirs of the Different Rebellions in Ireland*, p. 560
27 Denis Browne to Pelham, 5 Nov 1796, quoted in Hogan, op. cit., p. 301
28 Browne to Pelham, 30 Dec 1796, Rebellion Papers, 620 / 26 / 184

received an enthusiastic reception among radicals, particularly in Dublin and Belfast. Thomas Paine's manifesto, *Rights of Man,* had an immediate impact on Ireland, when its Irish edition appeared there early in 1791. In July of that year the second anniversary of the fall of the Bastille was celebrated by the Dublin Volunteers who paraded to St Stephen's Green under the command of Colonel James Napper Tandy. Belfast held a large procession and meeting where the citizens carried portraits of Mirabeau. In the address which followed, the Belfast Volunteers looked forward to seeing 'all civil and religious intolerance annihilated in this land'. A meeting of Catholics held in Elphin on 14 August passed a motion of thanks to the Belfast Volunteers for this declaration against the penal laws.

In August Theobald Wolfe Tone, the son of a Dublin coach maker, published a pamphlet entitled *An Argument on behalf of the Catholics of Ireland,* which became the radical Irish manifesto. In October he took part in Belfast in the foundation of the Society of United Irishmen. Shortly afterwards the Society was established in Dublin. Dr Charles O'Conor, who had studied for the priesthood in Rome, was the grandson of Charles O'Conor of Belanagare and now parish priest of Castlerea. Early in 1792 he wrote to Rome informing them of the founding of the Belfast United Irishmen 'to which men of all creeds are admitted to destroy the harm caused by religious difference leading to political division'. He went on to comment 'that in this way little by little a kind of political union between the two great bodies in the nation begins to take shape against the government'.[29] Archbishop Troy was also in communication with Rome about the Society of the United Irishmen, but he did not share the young O'Conor's enthusiasm for it and neither was he happy with O'Conor taking it upon himself to keep Rome informed about political developments in Ireland.[30]

The Defenders were a secret oath-bound association which preceded the United Irishmen in Co Sligo. They seemed to have spread rapidly and outrages were on the increase there in 1794 when a number of them were convicted at the assizes. The government sent the Earl of Carhampton to ascertain the scale of disorders in Sligo. He found the leader of the disturbances was known under the assumed name of 'Captain Stout', who was so intimidating that victims were afraid to prosecute. One magistrate in the county was advised by the priest of a certain parish in Sligo to remain a 'passive spectator' of the outrages lest he be murdered. Mr Percival of Templehouse was given the same advice.[31]

29 Fondo di Vienna, vol. 28, ff. 23rv, 24rv
30 ibid, ff. 25rv, 26r
31 Wood-Martin, *Sligo,* p. 12

The United Irishmen found fertile ground among the Defenders. The society spread throughout the country but penetrated into Connacht later than elsewhere. 'This association has been going on for a long time,' Charles O'Hara informed a correspondent in 1795, 'but it is much extended of late and is very formidable to every Protestant.'[32] Though O'Hara does not mention the United Irishmen by name they may well have been the subject of his letter.

> I will venture on a few lines and give you the best idea I can of the disaffected particularly in this county. Those bordering Co Mayo seem to me to differ very much from the Defenders of Co Roscommon and to be much more dangerous. They do not tender oaths indiscriminately but rather to persons who appear fit for their purpose; to no Protestant, nor to any one connected with a Protestant. As far as I can collect they talk of friends at Dundalk and look to a foreigner as their leader. Their secrecy is astonishing. I authorized a person in that neighbourhood these four (?) months past to offer a considerable reward to any one who would give information upon oath that any of them might be apprehended but in vain.

O'Hara named Foxford, Bellaghy, Banada and Tubbercurry as the villages 'in the centre of this business' and believed that 'that part of this County will for some time require a military force'. Outrages occurred nightly, with arms taken, places set on fire and cattle destroyed. O'Hara did not attribute these outrages to the Society but regarded them as consequences of it. 'I take it the views of that sworn party go much further,' he concluded.

At the beginning of 1797 an insurrection act was passed which authorised the Lord Lieutenant, at the request of the justices of the peace, to proclaim a county to be 'in a state of disturbance'. In a proclaimed area the magistrates could search for arms and impose a curfew. In May 1797 the whole of Co Sligo was proclaimed. The magistrate in Ballina was Rev James Neligan who later became the Protestant vicar of Kilmactigue.[33] In the summer of 1798 Neligan and a few friends were aware of a considerable amount of underground activity in the vicinity 'but they were conducted with such secrecy as to elude their vigilance'. Neligan believed that 'petty shop-keepers, mechanicks and servants of the popish persuasion used to hold meetings at the low tippling houses in Ballina (for treasonable purposes)'. He succeeded in having a pedlar called Reynolds, who frequented Boyle, arrested and after Reynolds received a few lashes, he 'discovered the whole plot'. Neligan was astonished 'at the number and respectability of those involved'.[34]

32 O'Hara Papers, Ms. 20, 283 (1). The letter is a rough draft scrawled on the back of a letter from Charles Williams, London to O'Hara, 28 April 1795.
33 On Neligan see chapter 5, pp. 150–1
34 Richard Musgrave, *Memoirs of the Different Rebellions in Ireland*, vol. 2, pp. 120–1

On 7 August 1798, William James MacNeven was questioned by Lord Dillon before the Secret Committee of the House of Lords in Dublin. Dillon asked him whether the United Irishmen had extended much into Connacht and MacNeven replied: 'It has, very considerably.' He went on to add that the extent of the organisation there was 'less perhaps than in other places' as it came later into Connacht, but nonetheless, 'very great numbers have taken the test'.[35] Rev James Little, the vicar of Lackan, noted that 'a considerable degree of fermentation prevailed among the Inhabitants of the Co Mayo'. This unrest 'had been long manifest in the nocturnal robberies that were almost everywhere committed'.[36]

One of the measures taken by the authorities to prevent the spread of sedition among the people was to persuade the Catholic clergy and their congregations to take an oath of allegiance. Early in June 1798 Joseph Stock, Protestant Bishop of Killala and Achonry, held a meeting in Ballina and formed a committee for administering the oath of allegiance. It was alleged that many of the parish priests in the counties of Mayo and Sligo collected their congregations and swore the oath of allegiance before a magistrate.[37] Sectarian bitterness was virtually non-existent in Co Mayo 'where the Protestants and Roman Catholics had long lived together in a greater degree of harmony than in most other parts of the kingdom.' James Little described the situation there on the eve of the French invasion:

> No nocturnal meetings or cabals were discovered or suspected, no open display of rebellious or armed force, nor could the public vigilance fasten upon anything obnoxious except a few profligate persons of the lower order charged with administering the United Irishmen's oath to a few others of their own description: it was indeed suspected that many had taken this oath and this was confirmed afterwards but for anything discoverable in the public demeanour, it seemed as if they regarded it as little as they did the oath of allegiance and had been equally well content had no occasion ever called upon them to fulfill either one or the other.[38]

The Orange Order

From the early months of 1798 rumours were circulating in the counties of Mayo and Sligo 'that the Orangemen had combined and were determined to massacre the Roman Catholicks'. The Orange Society had been established at

---

35 Gilbert, *Documents relating to Ireland, 1795–1804*, p. 167
36 'Little's Diary of the French Landing in 1798', ed. Nuala Costello in *Analecta Hibernica*, no. 11 (1941), p. 63
37 Musgrave, op. cit., pp. 567, 569
38 Little, op. cit., pp. 68, 69

the end of 1795.[39] Their activities were sectarian and it was believed that their oath pledged Orangemen to extirpate Catholics. 'The name of Orangemen had but just begun to be heard in Connaught,' Bishop Stock wrote later, 'and much it were to be wished that no such society had ever appeared among us, to furnish to the Romanists too plausible a pretext for alarm and hostility against their Protestant brethern.' He 'opposed their establishment with all his might' because the Orange Society 'some years before had disgraced itself by an infamy new to Protestants, an actual expulsion of Roman Catholics from their homes'.[40]

The rumours of the intended massacre of Catholics was widely believed. The parish priest of Foxford was approached in July 1798 by a magistrate (probably Neligan), who 'recommended him to undeceive his flock by assuring them from the altar that they were false and groundless'. The parish priest declined to do so 'alleging as an excuse, that it would offend some of his most respectable parishioners'.[41]

Another phenomenon which appeared ominous to Protestants, at least in hindsight, was what was known as 'scapularism'. Priests enrolled people in confraternities by conferring scapulars on them. Popular assemblies, except those for religious worship, were now prohibited by law. Confraternities could provide a pretext for evading the law. 'God forbid,' James Little protested, 'I should mean to insinuate that every individual who connected himself with the Scapulars was influenced by sinister motives.' But he did believe that the confraternity 'was designed by its authors to constitute not a religious, but a factious or anti-Orange association'.[42]

Scapularism

A clergyman of the Established Church (probably Neligan) wrote later: 'Thousands of these (scapulars) were made and consecrated by the Roman Catholic Clergy at the time of the late rebellion and sold for one shilling each to the poor deluded Irish, under an assurance of protecting them from evil. Many of the Rebels, who were taken or killed at that time, were found to have had these blessed preservatives about them.'[43] The same author described the scapular as 'a small piece of cloth doubled and stitched together, with strings fastened to it, and worn round the neck by those who are called Carmelites.' When the French arrived in Killala they found the practice of

39 There was an Orange lodge in Sligo in December 1793. An advertisement appeared in the *Sligo Journal,* 20 December 1793 placed by the 'Knights Templar and Royal Orange Lodge, No. 626'. O'Rorke, *Sligo,* vol. 2, pp. 543–4
40 *Narrative,* pp. 66–7
41 Musgrave, op. cit., vol. 2, p. 118
42 Little, op. cit., pp. 66–7; see Musgrave, op. cit., p. 565
43 *An Authentic Narrative of the Recent Conversion of Twelve Roman Catholics named Hart,* p. 51

scapular-wearing widespread among the natives. *'Tous, hommes et femmes, portent suspendu a leurs cous, de larges, sales et crasseux scapulaires, ainsi que des chapelets ou rosaires'* (All, men and women, wear round their necks, large, dirty and disgusting scapulars, as well as beads or rosaries).[44] The fact that they also wore rosaries suggests that the practice had only a religious significance. Besides, the widespread wearing of the *Leabhar Eoin* by the country people was very much in the same tradition.[45] However, as James Little observed, 'considering the time and circumstances of its introduction' it acquired some degree of political significance. In 1799 Archbishop Dillon of Tuam issued a pastoral against scapulars, not only because they were objects of superstition but also because they had been worn as emblems by the rebels.[46]

The French Landing at Killala

Things were relatively quiet in the province of Connacht in the summer of 1798 while the three other provinces were still in ferment after the recent rebellions there. 'It gives us great pleasure to hear your province is tranquil,' Thomas Carpendale of Armagh wrote in June to Charles O'Hara.[47] On 7 August William James MacNeven warned Lord Dillon before the Secret Committee of the House of Lords: 'From the misery of the poor people, and the oppressiveness of landlords in many parts of that province, we have no doubt but if the French ever land in force there, they will be joined by thousands, probably by the whole of its population.'[48] Two weeks later his prediction was put to the test.

On Thursday 23 August Bishop Joseph Stock was holding his first visitation for the clergy of the united dioceses of Killala and Achonry, which mainly took the form of a dinner where the bishop entertained the clergymen and their wives. Stock, the eldest son of a Dublin hosier, had only been consecrated bishop the previous January in the chapel of Trinity College by the Archbishop of Tuam.[49] 'The company was preparing to join the ladies, between seven and eight on a fine summer's evening, when a terrified messenger entered the room with the news that the French were landed, and that 300 of them were within a mile from the town.'[50]

The French in fact had arrived in the bay on the previous morning, when they were spotted by two visitors who informed Rev James Little, vicar of Lackan. All three rode to the hill of Lackan near the vicar's house, where Little

44 Jobit, *Journal de l'Expedition d'Irlande*, in *Analecta Hibernica*, no. 11 (1941), p. 16
45 see chapter 9, p. 254 and chapter 10, pp. 281–2.
46 Keogh, p. 125
47 O'Hara Papers, Ms. 20, 280 (6)
48 Gilbert, p. 167
49 J. B. Leslie, *Biographical Succession list of the Clergy of Achonry and Killala*.
50 Bishop Stock's *Narrative*, p. 5

Bishop Joseph Stock
(*Trinity College Dublin*)

studied them through his telescope. There were three frigates, one of which was flying the English flag.[51] The English colours also fooled Bishop Stock's two teenage sons, Arthur and Edwin, who persuaded James Ruttledge, the port-surveyor, to row them out to the ships where they were promptly arrested by the French.

The French expedition, under General Humbert, had left La Rochelle on 6 August. It comprised 1025 men, 3000 guns, 400 pistols, three cannons, 30 *milliers de poudre,* 66,000 cartridges and 1,000 French uniforms. They were transported on three frigates, *La Concorde, La Franchise* and *La Medée* under the command of Admiral Savary. The voyage, which should have taken six or seven days, lasted sixteen, as they were becalmed for three days and took a more circuitous route to escape English detection.[52] Savary's instructions were to land at Achill Island or Mullet Island, or if the wind was northerly to put in somewhere on the coast of Donegal.[53]

51 Little, pp. 73–4
52 Jobit, op. cit., p. 12
53 Desbriére, *Projets et Tentatives de Débarquement aux Iles Britanniques,* pp. 78 ff

August that year was hot and sultry and the sea was calm. The French had the good fortune to capture a little Irish trading boat, whose owner gave them valuable information which helped them make a successful landing. Shortly after four o clock they disembarked on Lackan strand. James Little got the first view of them: 'we could see from my house (which is on a very high hill), a column of soldiers which the telescope shewed to be armed with Musquets, & dressed in blue & green uniforms marching down from the head land of Kilcummin'. He also recorded the first reactions of the local people to the arrival of the French:

> The common people, many of whom live very near me, ran out to view them and tho' I watched their countenances with suspicion, I could not read in any of them, any mark of agreeable surprize, or of hope or expectation realized, on the contrary they viewed them with looks of wonder and apprehension; which is the more remarkable, as I have been informed that some of them were sworn (as they call it) i.e. had taken the United Irishmen's Oath. [54]

Little, who had no knowledge of military affairs, was still unaware of the nationality of the invaders. Shortly afterwards, a Protestant neighbour galloped up and blurted out, 'My dear Mr L., we are undone, they are French!', and handed Little a copy of the proclamation which the French were distributing among the Irish. Little and his neighbour decided to try and make their escape immediately, taking with them the other members of their families.

Henry O'Kane

Among those who arrived with the French were a small number of Irishmen. One of them was Wolfe Tone's brother, Matthew. Another was Bartholomew Teeling, who was aide-de-camp to Humbert. Teeling had gone to France in 1796 and had served with General Hoche in La Vendée. Perhaps the most interesting Irishman on the expedition was a local man, who was the first to reach the shore. Henry O'Kane, a native of the barony of Tyrawley, was born near Ballina in 1742, where his father and two brothers still lived. He was ordained a priest for the diocese of Killala and was sent to France to be educated, probably at the Irish College, Nantes. In any case he was working there as a *curé* at the outbreak of the revolution.

In November 1789 the National Assembly issued a decree nationalising all church property in France and this was followed some months later by the Civil Constitution of the Clergy which split the French church and drove many of the priests underground. O'Kane quit the priesthood 'when the revolution, stripping him at once of profession and livelihood, forced him to become a

---

54 op. cit., pp. 74–5

soldier for bread'.[55] However, his sympathies may well have lain with the revolutionaries as in 1776 he had been a member of an Irish freemason club called *L'Irlandaise du soleil levant* (The Irish (club) of the rising sun).[56] Bishop Stock, with whom O'Kane dined occasionally with the other French officers, gave a pen-portrait of him: 'He was a fat, jolly looking man, with a ruddy countenance that carried nothing forbidding in it, except that his black thick eyebrows ran into each other, as they often do in aboriginal Irish faces. Of the English tongue he retained enough to be quite intelligible; and being also expert in Irish as well as French, he was able to render considerable service to his cause.' From their conversation the bishop 'conceived a good opinion' of O'Kane whose 'language breathed nothing but mildness and liberality'.[57]

The first challenge facing the French was the capture of Killala. Estimates vary as to the size of the garrison in Killala – between fifty and two hundred – but it was probably closer to the former than to the latter. Their encounter with the French advance party was sharp and decisive when they 'were seized with a panic and fled'.[58] The French had 'made a running charge at the enemy, who immediately took flight'.[59] Two of the yeomanry were killed. A number of prisoners, about twenty-three, were taken, including two officers, one of whom, Lieutenant Sills, an Englishman, was conveyed to the French frigate to be transported to France.

Occupation of Killala

The French established their headquarters in the bishop's palace which was known locally as 'the castle'. General Humbert assured the bishop, who 'was tolerably fluent in French', that no harm would come to him or to his property, which Stock later acknowledged 'was most religiously observed'. The three-storeyed palace was occupied, with three hundred French soldiers taking over the lower part, as well as the courtyard and offices. On the second floor, the prisoners occupied the drawing-room, while the two adjoining bedrooms were reserved for Humbert and his principal officers. The top storey, which contained a library and three bedrooms, 'continued sacred to the bishop and his family'.

The first priority for the French was to unload the three frigates, and this was achieved with remarkable speed, thanks to the use of the little Irish brig which had been captured. Much of the material was transferred to the brig and conveyed directly to Killala. 'All was so well arranged that in less than 12 hours, the frigates were ready to hoist sail and return to France.'[60]

55 Stock, p. 47
56 AN FM 2 18
57 Stock, pp. 47–8
58 Stock, p. 5
59 Jobit, p. 15
60 Jobit, p. 15

The first French impressions of the people they had come to liberate were those of astonishment at their extreme poverty:

> *Nous fumes fort étonnés de l'extreme pauvreté qui s'offrit partout à nos yeux, dans le commencement de cette contrée d'Irlande. Jamais pays n'a présenté une perspective plus malheureuse; les hommes, les femmes, les enfants presque nus n'y ont d'autre azile qu'une étroite et mauvaise chaumière qui ne les met à couvert des rigueurs des saisons. Encore partagent-ils cette chétive habitation avec toute leur base-cour!'* (We were very astonished by the extreme poverty of Ireland, which from the very beginning was to be seen everywhere. There was never a country which presented a more unhappy appearance; men, women and children, almost naked, had no other shelter than a poor narrow cabin, where they found protection from the rigours of the weather. This they share with all the farmyard animals).[61]

Uniforms and arms were issued to the Irish recruits who rushed to join the French. These were fairly numerous. Bishop Stock estimated them at over two thousand. Once in uniform the Irish rebels made an impressive sight:

> The uncombed, ragged peasant, who had never before known the luxury of shoes and stocking, now washed, powdered, and full dressed, was metamorphosed into another being, the rather because the far greater part of these mountaineers were by no means deficient either in size or person. 'Look at these poor fellows,' said Humbert to the bishop, 'they are made, you find, of the same stuff with ourselves.'[62]

According to Stock, a thousand of the Irish were completely outfitted. Others were given everything but shoes and stockings, while the rest were given only arms.

James O'Dowd

One of the first to join the French was James O'Dowd of Bonniconlon. In 1788 he inherited what remained of the family estate in Bonniconlon and came to Ireland to take up residence there. He was informed by Thomas Dillon of Loughglynn House in January 1795 that he had been left 'a handsome sum of money' by a relation in Austria. This may have been Baron Vippler who was the father of O'Dowd's mother.[63] In 1798 O'Dowd was a captain in the Tyrawley Cavalry. On hearing of the French arrival he resigned his captaincy and led his tenants in Bonniconlon and Attymass to join the French. O'Dowd was very much the exception among his class. 'Indeed, no Catholic of sense, character or property in the province,' Hugh MacDermot of Coolavin informed his brother Henry in 1798, 'none but the lowest rabble and a few gentlemen of desperate fortune and unprincipled character joined the

61 Jobit, op. cit., pp. 15–16
62 Stock, p. 18
63 J. F. Quinn, *History of Mayo*

French.'64 General Humbert raised O'Dowd to the rank of colonel. Bishop Stock, who was not impressed by O'Dowd, described him as 'a man of some estate, and almost the only gentleman who took arms with the rebels'.65

From Killala the French marched on Ballina, where the government troops, reinforced by some yeomanry, presented as little resistance as the French had experienced at Killala. 'As soon as they sniffed our approach, the enemy made haste to evacuate. We entered Ballina without any obstacle and without firing a shot.'66 One of those who had special reasons for making a hasty escape from Ballina was its energetic magistrate.

Ballina

> The reverend Mr Neligan of Ballina, a gentleman of elegant taste and extensive learning and an active and intelligent magistrate, narrowly escaped from that town with some more loyalists; and after having passed through a country infested by banditti, who were roaming in quest of Protestants, and after much peril and difficulty, arrived at Seaview, the seat of Mr Hillas in the county of Sligo. On his arrival there, some of the popish servants of Mrs Hillas informed her that she would run a great risk of having her house demolished by harbouring a Protestant clergyman.67

On Sunday 24 August Humbert left Killala and marched towards Castlebar via Ballina, Crossmolina and Lahardane. He took this little-used road across the mountains as General Taylor, who had marched from Sligo with 1,200 men, had occupied Foxford where he prepared to meet the French advance. Humbert took the bishop's eldest son with him as a hostage. Behind him he left two French officers, Charost and Ponson, with two hundred soldiers to secure Killala, as well as Colonel O'Dowd with his Irish rebels.68 He also left another officer, Truc, 'with a few French and a rabble of the Irish to retain possession of Ballina'. Henry O'Kane remained with this group. Horses and harnesses were so scarce that the Irish rebels were drafted to pull the heavy baggage-carts and two cannons. 'This operation required an enormous effort, because of the length of the journey and the high mountains between Killala and Castlebar.'69

Castlebar

The English force in Castlebar was estimated to be between 4,000 and 6,000 troops, with sixteen cannons, which considerably outnumbered the French-Irish contingent. It was as Jobit described *'un morceau dur à digérer*

---

64 quoted in Dermot MacDermot, *MacDermot of Moylurg*, p. 257
65 Stock, p. 82
66 Jobit, op. cit., p. 16
67 Musgrave, vol. 2, pp. 126–7
68 Stock, pp. 32, 82; Jobit stated that 100 French were left. Jobit, op. cit., p. 19
69 Jobit, op. cit., p. 25

pour une petite armée telle que la notre' (a hard morsel to swallow for a little army like ours).⁷⁰ The battle lasted four hours, during which it was alleged that the Irish broke and fled at the first sound of the English cannon. After some fierce fighting, the French put the English to flight. Casualties, particularly on the English side were high, though figures vary considerably depending on the sources.⁷¹

Not surprisingly, great numbers of Irish flocked to join the French after this victory. Among those who volunteered their services to the French was a thirty-six year old Castlebar-born priest, Michael Gannon, who had been educated in France and returned to Ireland at the beginning the revolution.⁷² Described as 'a tall, handsome man, with dignified agreeable manners', Gannon was employed as a commisary to the French army. A government informer, Michael Burke, described Gannon as a very superstitious priest who went about Castlebar with holy oils promising the people 'that if any were

Map of Humbert's Route (Hayes, *Last Invasion*)

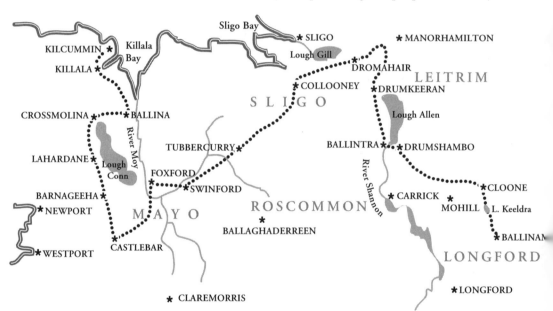

wounded he would anoint them so that they would go to heaven'.⁷³ The parish priest of Castlebar was Boetius Egan, a nephew and namesake of the former Bishop of Achonry. He was said to have served on Humbert's municipal town council, though his involvement with the revolutionaries seemed

70 op. cit., p. 20
71 Jobit gave 480 English killed or wounded and 186 French.
72 AN MC et / XLV11 / 564: *La Montagne Sainte-Geneviève et ses abords*, no. 192 (Oct 1976) p. 56
73 Miles Byrne, *Memoirs*, vol. 3, p. 62; Richard Hayes, *Last Invasion of Ireland*, p. 66

somewhat out of character.[74] Irish rebels took control of Westport and Newport and in his dispatch to France, Humbert informed the Directory that he now controlled Killala, Ballina, Foxford, Castlebar, Newport, Ballinrobe and Westport.[75]

Bishop Stock could not understand 'by what means a handful of men continued so long to brave the force of a whole kingdom' and suspected treason on the part of some of the government forces. This idea was reinforced by the arrival in Killala of a number of deserters.[76] He was greatly alarmed when Humbert ordered the French remaining in Killala to join him in Castlebar. 'All the horrors, that had been acted at Wexford,' he wrote, 'now stared the loyalists in the face.'[77] It was finally agreed that Charost and two other French officers with two hundred Irish insurgents would remain to guard Killala and its Protestant inhabitants. In return, Stock was obliged to send another of his three sons to Castlebar as a hostage. Lots were drawn and Arthur, a lad of just sixteen, was chosen.

Inexplicably, Humbert waited eight days in Castlebar. He had sent an account of his victory at Castlebar to the French Directory in Paris, urgently impressing on them the necessity of sending him fresh reinforcement and he may have delayed his departure from Castlebar until he had received an answer. Finally, on 3 September, he set off marching his army towards Sligo via Foxford. The glorious weather, which they had enjoyed since their arrival, gave way to heavy rainfall. They halted briefly at Swinford for refreshments and then continued on to Bellaghy where they camped for the night. General Lake, with 16,000 government forces, was camped at Ballaghaderreen, only eight miles away. On the following morning, Humbert continued his advance towards Tubbercurry.

Tubbercurry had just been occupied by the Corran, Leyny and Coolavin Cavalry under Captain Charles O'Hara M.P.. They attacked Humbert's advance party and in the encounter two of their officers were killed, several of the soldiers taken prisoner and O'Hara and the others fled back to Sligo. Humbert was now joined by a party of insurgents who were led across the Ox Mountains from Ballina by Colonel O'Dowd. A tradition recorded in Killasser claimed that the French were joined in Killasser by Father O'Brien and a party of local boys.[78] O'Dowd's contingent probably passed through Killasser on their way to Tubbercurry.

March to Collooney

Collooney Medal (Wood-Martin, *Sligo*)

74 Hayes, p. 59
75 Jobit, op. cit., p. 24; J. Jones, *The Irish Rebellion*, pp. 288 ff
76 op. cit., p. 31
77 ibid, p. 33
78 IFC Ms. 117, p. 90

Battle of Collooney

The Franco-Irish army continued its march towards Collooney. Riding in front of the advance party on a broken-down horse was the dejected figure of Captain Knott of the Corran, Leyny and Coolavin Cavalry who had been taken prisoner. 'Beside him on a splendidly groomed horse of fine proportions was a handsome French woman, who had come with the expedition from France and fought in the various engagements up to this with much bravery. From her belt hung pistols, while in her hand she carried a sword.'[79]

Meanwhile, O'Hara had informed Colonel Vereker, commander of the Sligo garrison, of Humbert's advance towards Collooney. Vereker set out with two field guns and three hundred men of the Limerick Militia, passed through Ballisodare and stopped at Carrignagat a short distance from Collooney. The ensuing battle lasted for about an hour. Bartholomew Teeling is credited with displaying extraordinary bravery, riding up to one of the enemy cannons and shooting the gunner.[80] Vereker and his troops were forced to retreat. Their casualties numbered seven killed and twenty-seven wounded. In spite of his victory, Humbert's casualties were somewhat higher. Limerick Corporation ordered a silver medal to be struck 'to the heroes of Collooney' in honour of Vereker and his Limerick Militia and a street in Limerick city was named Collooney.[81]

Bartholomew Teeling (National Library of Ireland)

Humbert decided to by-pass Sligo and head towards Longford, where he was informed that the United Irishmen had risen. He crossed into Co Leitrim. By now General Lake, who had been joined by Colonel Crawford with a corps of dragoons in Tubbercurry on 4 September, was in hot pursuit. The final outcome was no longer in doubt. It happened on Saturday 8 September. The French with the Irish insurgents were surrounded at Ballinamuck by the English force which vastly outnumbered them and after an engagement lasting an hour and a half, they were forced to surrender. The French were taken prisoner, while the Irish were killed or executed on the spot. Among the latter was James O'Dowd. A fervent Catholic, he requested the assistance of a priest but was refused.[82]

79 Hayes, p. 90. Two women in disguise had come with the expedition as stowaways. Desbrière, pp. 82 ff
80 Hayes, op. cit., p. 93
81 Ironically, it was subsequently renamed Wolfe Tone Street. Hayes, 'A Limerick Medal of 1798' in *North Munster Antiquarian Journal*, vol. 1, no. 2 (1944), pp. 77–8; George James Hewson, *Royal Hist. and Arch. Association of Ireland Jn.*, ser. 4, vol. 3, part 1 (1874), pp. 241–3
82 Hayes, *Last Invasion of Ireland*, p. 158

Surrender of General Humbert at Ballinamuck *(National Library of Ireland)*

Surprisingly, it took another two weeks before Killala was re-taken. 'How astonishing!' Bishop Stock wrote in his diary on 17 September, 'that no effort is making by our Govt to deliver us from perpetual pillage and daily and nightly expectation of murder.'[83] However, in Killala the bishop and his family continued to enjoy the protection of Charost and the other two French officers. 'The commandant and the bishop, finding each other to be honest men and above the meanness of deceit, soon came to a mutual good understanding.'[84]

Relief of Killala

83 Killala Diary, p. 21, TCD., Ms. 1690
84 Stock, p. 39

They also enjoyed the best fare that the neighbourhood could provide.

> The choicest beef and mutton from grazing grounds that feed the boast of the markets of Dublin, excellent wines and spirits extracted from the cellars of his very good friends the neighbouring gentry, made their visits in due order to the castle, and were received, at first with groans and lamentations over the times, and at last with great equanimity, as a misfortune that could not be helped. At times the company at the castle even felt a disposition to be merry on the arrival of one of those felonious cargoes.'[85]

Henry O'Kane, who had been left with another French officer in Ballina, joined them occasionally for dinner.

James Little

James Little, vicar of Lackan, suffered an altogether different experience. Having failed to effect his escape with his wife and daughter in the first hours after the French landing, he found himself trapped in a very hostile environment. He believed that he and his wife and daughter would be murdered.

> When night approached in which we were to be burned, I bolted the doors, and we sat together till near midnight intending not to quit the house, or strive to conceal ourselves, and to suffer death together without resistance; ... yet could we not account for our having remained till midnight unmolested: we began to grow sleepy, having for three preceding nights sat up later and rose earlier than usual, and it seemed absurd to go now to rest. I began to lose my patience ... Under the impulse of these sentiments, right or wrong, I took three pair of pistols, one of which I put in my pocket, fastened another in a belt, and kept a third in my hands, and taking my station below stairs, after I had placed behind me a gun and a sword cane, I intended if attacked to use the weapons as long and as well as I could.'[86]

Little tried to make his way to Killala to ask protection for himself and his family. On the way he was captured by a band of insurgents who had robbed him the previous night and he was escorted under armed guard back to Lackan:

> I was brought guarded in the manner I have mentioned, till we came to the Church of Lackan wherein I officiated, which stands close to the road, and is very near the Parsonage house in which I lived; and when we were opposite to the Church, the fellow who was captain of the band, about twelve in number, half of whom went before my horse, and the rest behind me, called out to them to halt and charge their musquets, which they accordingly did: and their doing so without any apparent necessity, as nobody was with them but myself, and they knew nobody would at-

85 Stock, pp. 60–1
86 Little, p. 90

tempt my rescue, made me imagine they had chosen this spot before the Church as the fittest place to sacrifice the Minister: I expected the next word of command after the musquets were charged would be to present and fire at me with them; and I recommended myself to the Divine Mercy.'[87]

He was in fact spared on this occasion by his assailants, who were in search of plunder rather than blood. Finally, after his house and church had been ransacked and he had spent a night hiding in the fields, he resolved to get himself and his family to the relative safety of Killala. He sent a note to Bishop Stock begging him to have a French escort sent to Lackan to bring him and his wife and daughter to Killala. As a result the Littles and a neighbouring Protestant family were conducted to Killala on 31 August. In Killala Little mentioned in the presence of O'Dowd that he feared his house in Lackan would be destroyed. O'Dowd promptly sent some of his men there to protect it, which they did until they and O'Dowd were ordered to rejoin the French army on its march to Collooney.[88]

Almost three weeks later relief was finally on its way to the loyalists in Killala. On Saturday 22 September, the rebels brought Stock and other Protestants to the top of a hill 'in order to be eye witnesses of the havoc a party of the king's army was making,' as it advanced from Sligo. 'A train of fire too clearly distinguished their line of march, flaming up from the houses of the unfortunate peasants. "They are only a few cabins," remarked the bishop; and he had scarcely uttered the words when he felt the imprudence of them. "A poor man's cabin," answered one of the rebels, "is to him as valuable as a palace."'[89]

On Sunday morning Henry O'Kane and the remaining French officer in Ballina took refuge in the bishop's palace. Meanwhile, the Irish insurgents, numbering about eight hundred, were preparing to make their last stand. The royal army numbered about twelve hundred with five pieces of cannon. The ensuing battle lasted about twenty minutes after which the rebels broke and fled, pursued by the enemy. About four hundred of the rebels were killed. Killala 'exhibited almost all of the marks of a place taken by storm. Some houses were perforated like a riddle, most of them had their doors and windows destroyed, the trembling inhabitants scarcely escaping with life by laying prostrate on the floor, as at the castle.'[90]

The four French officers surrendered and were treated as prisoners of war. *Reprisals*

---

87 op. cit., p. 101
88 Little, p. 98
89 Stock, op. cit., p. 87
90 Stock, p. 98

So did Henry O'Kane, whose plea that he was a naturalised Frenchman was disregarded. He was courtmartialled in Castlebar in November and faced execution for treason. However, he escaped with his life 'with the help of an attestation in his favour from the bishop among many others'.[91] He returned to France where he continued his military career and was later awarded the Legion of Honour for his services in the republican army. Other priests, such as Michael Gannon, went on the run after the French surrender. Gannon was said to have been imprisoned by the French before they left Castlebar because 'he wished to desert'.[92] He was seen in January 1799 in Ballynakill in Connemara in the company of Myles Prendergast, the Augustinian prior of Murrisk and other rebel fugitives.[93] He made his way to Lisbon and from there, with the help of Lucien Bonaparte, to Paris. Later he became a parish priest in the diocese of Versailles where he served in several parishes.

Two priests, James Conroy of Adragool in the diocese of Elphin and Manus Sweeney of Newport in the archdiocese of Tuam, were subsequently executed. The latter was betrayed by Michael Conway, parish priest of Ardagh (Killala) for which he was paid fifty pounds by the government. James Jennings, parish priest of the Neale (Tuam), received a similar reward after he had 'apprehended and lodged in jail several desperate ruffians'.[94] Rewards were offered for a number of other priests including Owen Cowley, Castleconnor,[95] David Kelly of Ballysokeary, Fr McGowan of Crossmolina, Phelim McDonnell of Easkey and Fr O'Donnell of Dromore-West, all from Killala diocese, but they eluded capture. Thomas Monelly of Backs was arrested but later escaped to the United States. Bernard Dease of Kilglass, Co Mayo, was arrested near Ballina on 4 September 1798 and later that month in Sligo informed on Kelly, Monelly, Conroy and Cowley. He also accused the Bishop of Killala, Dominick Bellew.[96] Bellew was probably implicated by his brother, Matthew, who had been appointed a commander by the French, and was subsequently executed. The bishop went personally to the Boards of Commissioners to protest his loyalty. Lord Tyrawley also wrote on his behalf to Dublin Castle.[97] Only one Achonry priest, Fr Browne of Foxford, was said to have been involved with the rebels but his identity is shrouded in mystery.[98]

91 Stock, p. 48
92 Examination of Michael Burke, Rebellion Papers, 620 / 52 / 125
93 Examination of John Burke, Galway, 29 March 1799, Rebellion Papers, 620 / 46 / 83
94 Rebellion Papers, 620 / 47 / 28
95 Rebellion Papers, 620 / 46 / 74
96 Rebellion Papers, 620 / 40 / 58
97 Rebellion Papers, 620 / 56 / 200
98 Hayes, *Last Invasion*, p. 197; The name of Browne occurs in none of the contemporary lists of Achonry clergy. O'Rorke refers to 'Rev Mr Brown, Parish Priest of Swinford' at this period. *Ballysadare and Kilvarnet*, pp. 485–6

Aftermath

The rebellion left scars, particularly on the relationship between the two religious communities. Before the rebellion Protestants and Catholics in Co Mayo 'had long lived together in a greater degree of harmony than in most other parts of the kingdom'.[99] There is some evidence to suggest that the Irish rebels regarded the rebellion as a religious crusade. 'The Common People talked much about Religion and made it very much a religious business'. The reason given by soldiers of the Longford and Kilkenny regiments for deserting was 'to serve the cause of religion'.[100] Bishop Stock made a similar observation: 'It astonished the French officers to hear the recruits, when they offered their services, declare, "that they were come to take up arms for France and the blessed Virgin."' Bishop Stock found the religious contrast between the French and their Irish allies 'extremely curious'. He thought it incredible that 'the zealous papist should come to any terms of agreement with a set of men who boasted openly in our hearing, "that they had just driven Mr Pope out of Italy, and did not expect to find him again so suddenly in Ireland".'[101]

'That enmity to the Protestant religion entered into the motives of devastation of Connaught,' Bishop Stock wrote, 'cannot without any shew of reason be denied.'[102] Bartholomew Teeling was greatly incensed when a party of rebels were brought before him for plundering and 'justified themselves as having attacked only Protestants'.[103] During the rebellion Protestant churches were sometimes the targets of attack by the rebels. 'There was scarcely another Protestant place of worship throughout the united diocese that did not quickly bear evident marks of the religious intolerance of the rebels.'[104] However, there is only documented evidence for damage inflicted on one church, Kilmactigue, in Achonry diocese. The perpetrators were named by informers as James O'Hara of Banada, whom they saw with a mob 'breaking' Kilmactigue church and later bringing an iron bar of the church home with him, and one Beatly of Tullycusheen, 'who broke the inside windows of the Church'.[105] Ironically, it fell to Rev James Neligan, the energetic magistrate of Ballina, to repair it when he became vicar of Kilmactigue shortly afterwards. He claimed that several other churches in the two dioceses 'were the object of popular fury and fanaticism'.[106]

99 Little, op. cit., p. 68
100 Statement of Michael Burke, Rebellion Papers, 620 / 52 / 123
101 op. cit., p. 63
102 op. cit., p. 76
103 Statement of Michael Burke, Rebellion Papers, 620 / 52 / 123
104 Stock, op. cit., p. 68
105 O'Hara Papers, Ms. 20, 280 (6)
106 Neligan, 'Parish of Kilmactige', in W. S. Mason, *A Statistical Account or Parochial Survey of Ireland*, vol. 2, p. 358

Rebels on the Run

Some names of Achonry rebel leaders have survived, such has Thomas Farrell of Coolcarney who led sixty men to Killala to join the rebels and Pat O'Hara from Tubbercurry who brought in seventy men.[107] Other names are more difficult to confirm.[108] A list of 'Persons supposed to have been engaged in the Late Rebellion or United Irishmen' gave the names of nineteen people all from the diocese.[109] Two of them, Michael Scanlon and Pat Kearen, were severely wounded fighting with the French. Five of them, Tim Killoran, Patrick and Michael Davey, James Killalea and John Finan, had followed the French to Ballinamuck. It appears that Killoran, Killalea and the two Daveys were released on bail 'for want of prosecution'. Dudley Scanlon was accused of attempting to swear in John Anderson, the constable in Ballymote, on 3 September. Martin Doyle, Curry, was 'represented to be a fellow of infamous character, a swearer in of United men and Captain of Rebels'. The compiler of the list added: 'I am inform'd there is a Denis O'Hara now a recruiting serjeant in Sligo, bred at Achonry and made a serjeant thro' the interest of Mr Gore, who after confessing his own guilt did inform against most of them before some magistrate of the county. Since my last I am informed there is another nest of rebels about Carrickbanagher.'

Some rebels took refuge in the mountains, between Barnageeha and Lough Conn near Foxford. Major-General Trench Power sent a detachment of soldiers from Castlebar to flush them out. The rebels dispersed and one of them, Captain Kinlan, 'a most active rebel leader and notorious for the Robberys and acts of cruelty he has committed', was discovered near Foxford with another rebel of the same name, both well armed. They were pursued to Balla, where they were apprehended after an exchange of gunfire. A young lad called Clark was shot dead. Kinlan, who had deserted from the King's Life Guards, was taken to Castlebar. He was tried and, dressed in a French uniform, was executed two hours later. 'He made no discovery and died extremely hardened.'[110]

The Act of Union 1800

The events of 1798 brought home to the English government the realisation that Ireland was the Achilles' heel of the empire. It resolved to impose a permanent solution in the form of a union of the two kingdoms. After eighteen

107 Rebellion Papers, 620 / 40 / 58
108 Hayes mentions a tradition about a United Irish group in Swinford which included Anthony Curley, innkeeper, William Brabazon (a natural son of Sir Anthony Brabazon), Seamas Duv Horkan and Patrick Brennan, a blacksmith, as well as three young women named Larkin, Ryan and Brennan. They were said to have successfully ambushed a party of three hundred dragoons on the road between Swinford and Bellaghy. *Last Invasion*, pp. 274–5
109 H. Thomson to Charles O'Hara, O'Hara Papers, Ms. 20, 303; see Appendix 44
110 Rebellion Papers, 620 / 46 / 112, 3 April 1799, Trench Power to –?

months of hectic activity, lobbying and bribing the Irish members of parliament and making vague promises to Catholics of full emancipation, a bill was introduced into the House of Commons on 21 May 1800. The Act of Union was passed by 158 to 87 votes. Among those who vigorously opposed the act was the seventy-year-old Joshua Cooper of Markrea. He died a mere six months later. Dominick Bellew, Catholic Bishop of Killala, 'without any previous communication or solicitation', sent Lord Tyrawley an address from the Roman Catholics of the baronies of Tyrawley and Tireragh in favour of the union with England.[111] Bellew's action was probably inspired by his eagerness to establish his loyalty with the authorities, after he had been accused by one of his priests of being involved in the 1798 rebellion.

The Act of Union meant little to the ordinary people in the west. 'A few days back,' Lady Morgan wrote in Co Sligo, 'I met with two peasants who were making complaints of the oppression they endured. A gentleman asked them if they thought they were worse off since the union. They replied, "they had never heard anything about the union and did not know what it meant."' She commented: 'So full is the heart of an Irish peasant of his own grievance, and so little is his head troubled about publick affairs.'[112]

Among the grievances most deeply felt by the country people were the tithes they had to pay to the Protestant ministers and the fees charged by their own priests for their various services. Prices rose sharply during the Napoleonic Wars resulting in an increase in prosperity among the country people. It appears that priests took advange of this to raise their dues, claiming it was necessary for them to offset the rise in their cost of living. The country people in Co Sligo fought back by organising in the autumn of 1806 an oath-bound secret society called the Threshers.[113] They wore white shirts over their coats and white bands round their hats and were 'for the most part well mounted',[114] which suggests that they were the better-off tenants or farmers, that very class to which the priests themselves generally belonged. The Threshers assembled at night in large numbers, sometimes several hundreds, administered the oath and it was alleged used strong-armed methods to induce others to join and give them firearms. Those who took the oath undertook 'to pay no Tithes except to the Minister of the Parish, not to admit of Tithe proctors, to give their Priests but certain reduced fees for the various

Lady Morgan (1783?–1859) alias Miss Sydney Owenson was the daughter of Robert Owenson, an actor born into a poor family near Collooney. Lady Morgan stayed for some time with the Croftons in Longford House, Beltra, Co Sligo where she wrote *Patriotic Sketches* and her first novel *The Wild Irish Girl* (1806) where she modelled the hero, Prince of Innismore, on the Prince of Coolavin. Her description of the social conditions of the period is based on her observations in Co Sligo. In 1812 she married Sir Thomas Morgan.
(Picture: National Library of Ireland)

111 Lord Tyrawley to Dublin Castle, 27 Sept 1799, Rebellion Papers, 620 / 56 / 200
112 *Patriotic Sketches*, vol. 1, p. 121n.
113 The name was apparently derived from the practice of 'threshing' the stacks of corn of those who refused to cooperate with them, i.e. 'violently throwing them down and destroying them in mud or dunghill'. PRO HO 100 / 136 36303 f. 113
114 PRONI, T 3725 / 26; PRO, HO 100 / 136 36303

duties, to be ready at all times to obey Captain Thrasher's orders, and accompany him in his nightly excursions'.[115] They also posted notices on chapel doors listing the reduced fees to be paid to priests and sometimes obstructed the services on Sundays in these chapels.

Lady Morgan, who was then 'residing in that part of Ireland, where the association of the Thrashers (sic) first arose', claimed that the Threshers also promulgated other laws to curb 'rustic vanity'. 'One of their manifestos fixed on the door of a chapel, interdicted the use of shoes in favour of *brogues,* except to such as did not speak Irish, they being considered equally unworthy of the national character and national dress. The Irish *kirchiff* and *binogue* were also to be worn, on the penalty of having any more modern covering taken from the wearer.'[116]

The local gentry and magistrates at first took a fairly lenient view of the activities of the Threshers. That Catholic priests had become the targets of their own followers would not have particularly perturbed them. The innate anticlericalism of the gentry made them less than sympathetic to the plight of even their own clergymen. But other political figures were not so complacent. The Marquis of Buckingham, who lived at Stowe but had large estates in Co Longford, wrote a lengthy letter on the subject of the Threshers to the Prime Minister, Lord Grenville, on 11 December.[117] By now the Threshers had reached that county from where Buckingham had just been informed by his agent that all his tenants had taken the oath. 'During the whole of this time,' Buckingham informed the Prime Minister, 'the magistrates have shown little inclination to interfere.' Meanwhile, the list of Threshers' grievances had extended to letting of lands to stranger occupants, to county rates, to wages and to absentees, 'and latterly they have gone the lengths of "a cheer for Bonaparte, who is to set all this right".' Writing again a week later, Buckingham expanded on the role he believed France was playing in the Thresher movement. He claimed to have the names of two men who had been very active in the late rebellion, had taken refuge in France and had returned recently loaded with money. 'Both of them have latterly been seen very openly in different parts of the north-west of Ireland, and are universally considered from their language as very active and dangerous agents from France.' Lord Dillon of Costello-Gallen held the same view. 'I do not hesitate to declare,' he told the Prime Minister, 'that it is the same spirit and the same people who produced the late

115 PRO HO 100 / 136 36303
116 *Patriotic Sketches*, vol. 2, pp. 129–30n; vol. 1, pp. 102, 118–19. The *binogue (beannóg)* was a headscarf traditionally worn by country women. See chapter four, p. 121
117 Irish Manuscripts Commission, Fortescue Mss., vol. VIII, pp. 463–67. Buckingham had been Lord Lieutenant in Ireland from 1787 to 1789.

rebellion, and are now endeavouring to create another, aided by the French.'[118]

Buckingham implored the Prime Minister not to be diverted 'from your intention of proclaiming the county of Sligo, where those disturbances originated'.[119] Recent trials in Sligo had only produced two convictions from twenty-seven Threshers arrested on capital charges. There had been twelve convictions at Castlebar but Buckingham felt that this was not enough to 'check the flame that is running like a wildfire'. He informed the Prime Minister that there were then ships in Portsmouth destined for Botany Bay and that they should be availed of for the transportation of convicted Threshers. If the Prime Minister hesitated on proclaiming Sligo, Buckingham warned him, he risked 'a general rebellion in Ireland'.[120]

Buckingham blamed the outbreak of lawlessness in Sligo and Mayo on the absenteeism of the powerful landlords, Lords Tyrawley, Dillon and Lucan. Dillon, through his agent in Ireland, Mr Wyatt, had offered to raise a corps of yeomanry at his own expense to police the baronies of Costello and Gallen, but his offer was declined by the Irish administration. Now, in December 1806, after receiving from his son and others 'the most melancholy accounts of the situation in Ireland', he told the Prime Minister that he was ready to go over there. However, the Irish government could not see what advantage could be gained from Dillon's presence in the country 'when he manifests so evident a dissatisfaction at the conduct of the Irish Administration'.[121]

Two of those convicted by a special commission in Sligo, Jack Killraine and Tom Kilmartin, were sentenced to be flogged through the streets of Sligo.[122] They had been captured at Lugawarry in the parish of Ballisodare by Colonel Irwin and a party of yeomen and in the encounter a third Thresher, Jack Cassidy, was fatally wounded. Flogging was the usual punishment for those convicted. In March 1807, Alexander Percival sent Charles O'Hara a chilling description of a flogging he presided at:

> Last Wednesday I flogged a Thrasher, he was sentenced by the Court Martial to a thousand lashes, two hundred of which he received when I winked to the Doctor to have him taken down as if he was not able to bear more for I could not do so myself without forgiving him, and I preferred keeping him in suspense with 800 men staring him in the face in hopes he

118 ibid, Viscount Dillon to Lord Grenville, 6 December 1806, p. 480
119 op. cit., p. 475
120 op. cit., p. 479
121 ibid, The Duke of Bedford to Lord Grenville, 19 December 1806, p. 480
122 For the names of those charged as Threshers in Mayo and Sligo see Appendix 46.

might confess and discover but he still holds out tho' as clearly proved a Thrasher as could possibly be; the Drummers, his Executioners, exacted themselves, even the Drum-Major volunteered his services, and a desperate fellow he is. The officers all said they never saw 200 better bestowed with more determination. I have another flogging ordered tomorrow...'[123]

Percival believed that even more drastic measures were required to put down the Threshers in Co Sligo. 'I am in great hopes,' he told O'Hara, 'that hanging those men the Papers say are to be hanged will help to quiet it.'

The names of some of the Achonry priests who clashed with the Threshers were remembered locally. James Henry, who had only recently become parish priest of Ballisodare and Kilvarnet, was said to have had to take refuge in Co Mayo for a few weeks, because of his opposition to the Threshers in his parish.[124] Mark Rush, parish priest of Bunninadden, was also supposed to have come into conflict with them.[125] Patrick Grady, parish priest of Ballymote, was one of their more formidable opponents. It was said that one Tom Quigly of Rathnarrow, who had been recently married in Ballymote, paid Grady a guinea for his services. Shortly afterwards, Quigly was visited by the Threshers who threatened to 'card'[126] him for paying in excess of the rates set by them. Quigly blamed Grady and he was spared on condition that he return to Grady and demand his money back. Quigly did as he was ordered but Grady retorted that if the Threshers wanted the money back, let them come themselves to demand it. Grady, as his subsequent career showed, 'was not a man to be trifled with.'[127] Memories of the Threshers themselves also survived in parts of the diocese.[128]

In spite of government repression, the Thresher agitation continued for a number of years. In October 1810 the Bishop of Elphin issued a printed notice against the Threshers. It offered a reward of 100 guineas for anyone providing information leading to the conviction of Threshers and promised a pardon to Threshers themselves who confessed and informed on their accomplices.[129] The Thresher agitation in the diocese of Achonry was to re-emerge in the immediate pre-Famine period in the form of the Penny Boys.

The vague promises made by the English government to grant Catholic emancipation in the aftermath of the Union never materialised. Catholics

123 O'Hara Papers, Ms. 20, 338
124 O'Rorke, *Ballysadare and Kilvarnet*, pp. 486–88
125 O'Rorke, *Sligo*, vol. 2, p. 198
126 A card was an insrument studded with spikes for combing flax.
127 O'Rorke, *Ballysadare and Kilvarnet*, p. 265
128 A song was recorded in the parish of Bonniconlon c.1938 from Mrs Cunny, aged 75, Coolcarney, Bonniconlon. IFC Ms. 114, p. 394:

continued to press their claims by way of petitions to the English parliament. These petitions met with no success and in 1811 and 1812 were rejected by large majorities. Charles O'Hara, who had earlier espoused the Catholic cause, had now apparently abandoned it. On 14 October 1810 he received a letter from J. Everard, Sligo, who was politically active on O'Hara's behalf.[130] 'I thought you had unequivocally promised to support Catholic Claims and exultingly told them (Catholics) so,' Everard wrote, 'as my object was to secure to you and to your family the future representation of this county. You may guess my surprise and mortification at being bearded and taunted with a speech in which it is reported (I hope falsely) that you said further Catholic concessions were inconsistant with the safety of the Protestant Establishment.' O'Hara's support for further Catholic concessions had indeed waned as is clear from the draft of a letter he wrote to an unknown correspondent concerning a petition to the English parliament.[131] 'I was convinced no minister would propose or support the Roman Catholic petition in England and preserve his situation,' he wrote, 'My mind has been made up upon that subject ever since the act of 1793 which I have considered as final.' He believed that 'the landed gentlemen of this Co Sligo are unanimously of the same sentiments'.

The Veto Controversy

As early as 1799 Lord Castlereagh had met Archbishop Troy to sound him on Catholic reaction to a proposal of some sort of state payment of the Catholic clergy in return for the government having a say in the appointment of bishops. The archbishop's response was encouraging and at a meeting of the bishops later in Maynooth, it was agreed, with some qualifications, that the government might be given such an input into the appointment of bishops 'as may enable it to be satisfied of the loyalty of the person appointed'.[132]

> A Sunday morning as carelessly I took my way
> To the chapel of Coolcarney,
> Where I thought I'd spend the day.
> My mind being soon altered
> By a guard that did me embrace.
> He swore I was a chief Commander
> Of Coolcarney over these threshing blades.
> For three weeks and three days
> I was in confinement
> Until a neighbour and I did make free.
> May the heavens above preserve my love
> And raise her dignity.

It appears that on this occasion the Thresher was released by the turnkey's daughter who had fallen in love with him.

129 O'Conor Don Papers, 9. 1. H. 261; see G.W. and Janet Dunleavy, ed., *The O'Conor Papers: a descriptive catalog and surname register of the materials at Clonalis House*, p. 150
130 O'Hara Papers, Ms. 20, 280 (21)
131 O'Hara Papers, Ms. 20, 280 (24)
132 T. Bartlett, *The Fall and Rise of the Irish Nation*, pp. 250–1

This government veto on the appointment of bishops caused considerable controversy in Catholic circles in the early decades of the nineteenth century. When the bishops met in 1808 they decided that it would not be expedient to make any change in the manner of appointing bishops. 'From this point on, a furious controversy broke out in which allegations of bad faith, lies, heresy, disloyalty and even insanity were bandied about with increasing but depressing facility.'[133] Most of the priests were opposed to granting a veto to the English government.

Among those who rushed into print on the veto controversy was Patrick Grady, parish priest of Ballymote. In 1814 he published a pamphlet in Dublin entitled *The Radical Anti-Veto*. Part of the 57-page pamphlet is a measured and reasoned rejection of the veto, drawing heavily on history and canon law, with a penchant for some colourful language. 'As for the Veto itself, it is in its nature an absurdity,' Grady wrote, 'as the head of one religion to nominate and that of another to institute, would be a system capable of producing a religious mongrelism, a kind of Mule-Bishops, neither Catholic nor Protestant, unfit to propagate the Catholic Religion in its purity, beyond their own day.'[134] The rest of the pamphlet was an undisguised attack on Troy, whom Grady believed was prepared to concede a veto to the government.

> If such an attempt may chance to be made, let it be recorded to posterity as the labour in vain of the illustrious Dr Troy. What a pruriency for policy in a Prelate, who, by his monastic vows, has long since most solemnly engaged himself to the Almighty God, to forsake all such concerns for ever! Yet this is the Prelate, this is the Politician who, by his influence, can thrust any sort of head he pleases into an Irish mitre. Look sharp, Ireland! 'Romane caveto.' Aye, Dr Troy having crept forth from his humble cell, has soared to the lofty regions of church and state power, from both (of) which he has derived an accumulated mass of influence.[135]

In 1814 Cardinal Quarantotti had sent a rescript to Ireland suggesting that a negative veto could be given to a Protestant king. By now Troy and the Irish bishops were firmly opposed to granting any such veto and the controversy eventually petered out.

Perhaps the most enduring legacy of the veto controversy was the extent to which it politicised the Irish priesthood, as Grady's pamphlet illustrates. It also brought into prominence a young Catholic barrister called Daniel O'Connell. He was to harness these new political priests into a cohesive force which culminated in winning emancipation in 1829.

133 Bartlett, p. 292
134 op. cit., pp. 26–7
135 op. cit., p. 12

CHAPTER THREE

Ó Rí go Rámhainn
Life on the Land

Sligo was very thinly populated at the end of the Jacobite war. In 1693, Kean O'Hara complained that landlords were having difficulty finding tenants 'for there is not half enough people in it to take half the land that is (here).'[1] Estimates of the population in Ireland in the eighteenth century vary.[2] A contemporary, basing himself on the Hearth Money collectors, estimated the total number of houses in Co Sligo in 1733 at 6,233.[3] A modern historian put the population of the county for that year at about 48,000.[4] As approximately half of the diocese of Achonry occupied one-third of Co Sligo the population of the whole diocese in 1733 could be estimated at about 32,000, remarkably similar to its present level.

Population

According to Charles O'Hara, there were about 6,000 houses in Co Sligo in 1744. With the subsequent famine in 1745–6, that number fell to 4,000. By 1751 it had increased to 4,624. By then O'Hara believed that 'the County of Sligo compared with the whole Kingdom is sufficient for double the number of its present inhabitants' which he put at 55,488. In 1756 he wrote that 'the number of souls in this County continues to lessen'. In 1757 the number of houses began to increase again and in 1762 was 5,970, which was about the same as the pre-famine figure of almost twenty years earlier.[5] The population continued on an upward curve for the rest of the century.

1   Thomas Bartlett, 'The O'Haras of Annaghmore, c.1600–c.1800: Survival and Revival' in *Irish Economic and Social History*, vol. ix, p. 41
2   It is suggested that in 1712 there were 2.8 million, and 3.5 million in 1767. K. H. Connell, *The Population of Ireland 1750–1845*, p. 24; on population see L. M. Cullen, 'Economic development 1750–1800', in *A New History of Ireland*, vol. IV, pp. 161–4. Charles O'Conor of Belanagare stated that the 1731 returns gave the number of Catholics in the country as 1,309,768. Ward, Wrynn, Ward, op. cit., p. 251
3   William Henry, 'Hints towards a natural and topographical history of the counties of Sligo, Donegal, Fermanagh and Lough Erne', Nat. Arch., Ms. 2533
4   J. G. Simms, 'County Sligo in the Eighteenth Century' in *Royal Society of Antiquaries of Ireland Journal*, vol. 91, pp. 155–6
5   O'Hara Papers, Ms. 20, 397

While it may be difficult to be precise about overall figures, there is no doubt that the population grew rapidly in the second half of the century. In 1758, John Wesley travelled from Boyle to Sligo via Ballymote, Collooney and Ballisodare and counted eight villages within seven miles. He described the county of Sligo as 'the best peopled I have seen in the kingdom'.[6] Lord Altamont of Westport informed Arthur Young in 1776 that the increase in population was 'very great' and that the numbers on his estate had doubled in twenty years.[7] Joshua Cooper of Markrea Castle told him that the population of Co Sligo was increasing 'very fast'. Young attributed this increase to inoculation which had been introduced about ten years earlier.[8]

Markrea Castle (O'Rorke, *Ballysadare*)

Apart from inoculation, Young attributed the considerable growth in population to five main reasons: the absence of Poor Laws, habitations, early marriages, desire for children, and the potato.[9] As parishes in England had to pay rates to support the poor, positive steps were taken to limit their number. Housing was not a problem in Ireland as a mud cabin could be erected with two days' labour so that 'the young couple pass not their youth in celibacy for want of a nest to produce their young in'. Marriage was a popular institution among the poorer classes and there was no economic or other reason for delaying it. 'Their happiness and ease,' Young said of the country people, was 'generally relative to the number of their children and nothing considered as great a misfortune as having none.' The potato formed the staple diet of the people and was produced 'by as small a space of land as possible'.

While the overall effect of the growth in population throughout this period was generally positive, the accelerated growth at the end of the eighteenth and the early decades of the next century was ominous. From an estimated population of 32,000 in the diocese in 1733 it almost quadrupled in a hundred

6   *Journal*, vol. 4, pp. 267–8
7   *A Tour of Ireland*, p. 83. Arthur Young was born in Suffolk in 1741, the son of a clergyman. He became one of the greatest of English writers on agriculture, publishing his *Farmer's Letters to the People of England* in 1767 and his *English Tours* between 1768 and 1771 and his *Political Arithmetic* in 1774. He arrived in Ireland on 20 June 1776 and began to travel throughout the country. He reached Ballymote on 23 August and Markrea Castle a few days later. He spent the rest of August in Sligo and Mayo. His observations were published as *A Tour in Ireland* which remains a major source for Irish economic conditions for the latter part of the eighteenth century. The edition quoted here, unless otherwise stated, is by Constantia Maxwell (1925).
8   ibid, pp. 75, 77
9   op. cit., pp. 198–9

years, standing at 115,877 in 1731.[10] People were forced further up mountains and out into bogs in search of potato-plots. The exploding population then strained to the limit, and sometimes beyond, the available tillage land and living standards deteriorated rapidly. Sligo became one of the most overcrowded and poverty-stricken counties in Ireland.

Towns

Economically and socially, life in the eighteenth century was hierarchically structured. The landlord occupied the top of the pyramid. The economy was completely rural. The estates of landlords marked the important social and geographical centres. Travellers, like Arthur Young, went from one country seat to another. There were no towns in Achonry. In 1802 six were listed in the Mayo section of the diocese, Aclare, Ballaghaderreen, Carracastle, Foxford, Straide and Swinford, but the author added 'the only right they can claim to the name town (from their smallness and insignificance) is merely being the place where fairs are held.'[11] Foxford was described as 'a very poor town' in 1752 and 'a rather miserable village' in 1791. Collooney, a place 'for which God had done much and man nothing', was described by a visitor in 1791 as 'a decayed place' which recalled Goldsmith's *Deserted Village*.[12] Even such 'towns' did not exist in the barony of Costello in 1776, where Young found that there was no 'post-house, market town or justice of the peace'.[13] What local roads existed often radiated from the big house and were constructed for the convenience of the landlord. The importance of a county was determined by the wealth and prestige of its landlords. These county families inhanced their standing and consolidated their position by marriage alliances with other similar aristocratic families.

Annaghmore House (O'Rorke, *Ballysadare*)

Landlords

The landed families of Achonry may have played little or no role on the national stage but they were all but omnipotent in local affairs. The O'Haras of Annaghmore, the Coopers of Markrea, and the Wynnes of Hazelwood occupied the chief political and administrative positions in the county of Sligo.

---

10 *Parliamentary Papers*, vol. 35, pp. 60d-63d. In 1791 the population of County Sligo was estimated to be about 90,000 and growing rapidly. It had almost doubled since 1733. It was to double again to 180,000 by the census of 1841.
11 McParlan, *Statistical Survey of Mayo*, p. 85
12 *Bishop Pococke's Tour in Ireland in 1752*, p. 81; *Recollections of Skeffington Gibbon*, p. 142; Síle Ní Chinnéide, 'A Frenchman's Tour in Connacht in 1791' in *Galway Arch. Soc. Jn.*, vol. 35, pp. 60, 64
13 op. cit., p. 79

Absentees

Other important landed families in the diocese who held lands in the same county included the Taaffes, the Jones, the Percivals, the Croftons, the Mac-Dermots of Coolavin and the Irwins. The Mayo baronies of the diocese were dominated by the Dillon family who were viscounts of Costello-Gallen. Other families of lesser importance included the Costellos of Edmondstown and the Brabazons of Swinford. Some, like the O'Haras and the Coopers, had their seats in the diocese. Others had their seats just outside like the Dillons at Loughglynn, the Wynnes at Hazelwood, and the Croftons at Longford in Beltra.

Absentee landlords were a feature of the period. Charles O'Hara, senior, of Annaghmore, himself a resident landlord, estimated that over half the rents of the county were sent out of it. £20,460 was paid annually from Co Sligo in the middle of the century to absentee landlords, while only £15,267 remained in the county. The figure paid to absentees had risen to £70,000 early in the nineteenth century which reflected the increase in rents over the period.[14] The Viscounts of Costello-Gallen and the Taaffes, Earls of Carlingford, were the most notable absentees. The Protestant Bishop of Killala and Achonry was another.

Charles O'Hara, senior (*Annaghmore House*)

Even those, like Charles O'Hara, who claimed to be resident, spent only the summer months on their estates. They spent the rest of the year living in their town houses in Dublin. O'Hara, who was a keen racing man, divided his time between the Curragh and Newmarket, London and Dublin, spending only about two months in Nymphsfield, his country seat. Supposedly resident landlords, who commuted seasonally between their town house in Dublin and their country seat, imposed a further drain on local resources. Even while at home 'the first rank of people send their money abroad, for wine, groceries, wearing apparel etc,' Charles O'Hara admitted.[15] He had a somewhat inflated opinion of the contribution made locally by his class: 'If gentlemen are what gentlemen should be, by their example to teach the great political virtues of temperance, economy and justice, and with moderation and steadiness to enforce the laws, the good they do is beyond the reach of calculation.'

The O'Haras

The O'Haras of Annaghmore were descended from the O'Hara Boy branch who adopted Protestantism early in the seventeenth century to preserve their lands. Kean O'Hara (1685–1719) astutely avoided taking sides during the Jacobite occupation of Sligo, 'notwithstanding,' as he later declared,

14 O'Hara Papers, Ms. 20,313 (7)
15 O'Hara Papers, Ms. 20,397

'the many threats and persuasions that were used to me in the late times to change that religion in which I was bred'. Nevertheless in 1701 he married a Catholic, Eleanor Matthew, of a wealthy Co Tipperary family. She was not by any means his first choice. Of the few Protestant ladies suitable, to whom he made overtures, none relished the prospect of country life in Co Sligo. Eleanor brought with her a dowry of £1,000. Kean's son, Charles (c.1705–76) married Lady Mary Carmichael, a sister of William who later became Archbishop of Dublin. His son, also Charles, became M.P. for Co Sligo.

At the other end of the diocese, the Dillon family had extensive holdings. Later on in the century they issued leases on over twenty thousand acres in the baronies of Costello and Gallen.[16] Richard, the ninth Viscount, built the family home in Loughglynn in 1715 and married a daughter of the Earl of Clanrickard. He died in 1737, leaving only a daughter who married a cousin, Charles Dillon, the colonel-proprietor of Dillon's regiment in France. Shortly afterwards, he died and was succeeded as Viscount by his brother Henry. His eldest son, Charles, succeeded him as twelfth Viscount and conformed to the Established Church in 1767.

The Dillon Family

'Not one papist has a freehold in the county,' one contemporary wrote of Co Sligo in 1739, 'except Baron Taaffe, that valiant German officer, who is a native of this county.'[17] Though most landlords in the diocese were Protestant, apart from the Taaffes, one other major landowner, the Dillons, were Catholic for most of the period. There were other smaller landowners, like the MacDermots of Coolavin and the Philips of Cloonmore, who were also Catholic. Protestant landlords, like the O'Haras, Coopers and Percivals, preferred to lease their lands to Protestants. They even encouraged immigration from the north of Ireland to fill tenancies on their estates. The Dillons, on the other hand, had no such preferences and thus there existed a striking dichotomy between the eastern and western ends of the diocese.

Alexander Percival
(Templehouse)

Landlords often let their lands in large portions to first tenants, who in turn sub-let it to others. In the middle of the century Charles O'Hara estimated that the profit rent of first tenants was £35,727 which was equal to that

---

16 Dillon Papers, Oxfordshire County Record Office, XII / b / 7. I am indebted to Nollaig Ó Muraíle for providing me with a list of the Dillon leaseholders. In 1666 Dillon held 68,804 acres in the barony of Costello, of which 23,388 were profitable and 45,416 unprofitable.
17 Rev William Henry, *Account of Co Sligo*, M. 2533, National Archives, Dublin.

of the landlords, residents and absentees combined. Arthur Young described these middlemen as *Terney begs*, i.e. *Tiarnaí beaga*, 'little landlords', and he was scathing in his comments on them: 'your fellows with round hats edged with gold, who hunt in the day, get drunk in the evening, and fight the next morning.'[18] Landlords often preferred such tenants as their rents were paid more punctually. The lower class of tenants were prone to exploitation by these middlemen. Such was the situation that Young found in the neighbourhood of Westport, which led to the oppression of the poor 'who have a strong aversion to renting of these *terney begs*'.[19] Here the farms of first tenants were surprisingly large, ranging fom 500 to 5,000 acres.

First Tenants

In the eastern portion of the diocese first tenants were almost exclusively Protestants. In 1775 Charles O'Hara, senior, wrote to Joseph Meredith of Cloonamahon protesting against one of his tenants selling his lease to a Catholic. 'If he uses me so ill as to sell his tenure under a lease to a papist, I shall not facilitate his getting lands from any other person.'[20] O'Hara's cousin, Frances Jones, an absentee landlord, informed him in 1784 that she preferred Protestant to Catholic tenants. However, she had 'an established dislike to letting land to half-gentry'. She shared Young's antipathy to middlemen. 'For I think the superior prosperity of English yeomanry is owing to their not having the sort of being which too frequently exists here between landlord and the real occupier of the land'.[21]

An analysis of the lease-holders on the Dillon estate at the end of the century reveals a number of sizeable tenants.[22] In 1798 Walter Plunkett leased over 278 acres in Ballaghaderreen (Castlemore) and James Hughes over 272 acres about the same time. In the parish of Kilmovee James Taaffe had over 277 acres in 1791, Anthony Madden had over 103 acres and in Kilkelly, Edmund Taaffe had over 208 acres. In Bunninadden (Kilturra) parish Tim MacDermot had over 195 acres in 1798.[23] There were many other tenants with

18 op. cit., (1970) vol. 2, p. 155
19 ibid, p. 83
20 O'Hara Papers, Ms. 20, 280 (1)
21 ibid, Ms 20, 291 (3)
22 Oxford, DIL. xii/b/7
23 These were 'plantation' acres which were larger, with two such acres equal to three ordinary ones. Other sizeable tenants included Patrick Taaffe with over 66 acres, Michael Grady, over 96, Keadh McDonnell, almost 60, Edward Philips with two separate leases, one of over 65, and the other of 71 acres, Edmund Kelly, over 168, and John Thomas, over 102 acres in the parish of Charlestown (Kilbeagh); Eneas McDonnell with over 99 acres and Christopher Taaffe, over 102 acres in the Kilmovee.
24 Michael Grady had over 16 in Kilmovee. Margaret McDonnell had 48 and Patrick Taaffe 35 in Charlestown (Kilbeagh), James Dillon, 24 in Ballaghaderreen (Castlemore), both Garret and Thomas Dalton, 29 each in Kilmovee.

leases ranging from ten to fifty acres.[24] All over the diocese there were many such Catholic tenants who were fairly prosperous. When famine occurred in 1816 a committee was established in Coolaney to relieve the distress suffered by the poor. It was decided to solicit contributions from those the parish priest, Daniel O'Connor, described as 'in easy circumstances'. There were thirty-three such persons in the parish listed, all with Irish Catholic names.[25]

At the beginning of the nineteenth century a tenant in Tourlestrane (Kilmactigue) with ten acres, three of which were unproductive, produced one and a half acres of potatoes and divided the remaining tillage between oats and flax. 'He keeps a brood mare and two cows, and is enabled (with the assistance of two sons) to cultivate his ground, to pay his rent punctually, and to feed and clothe his family, consisting of a wife and six children, decently and comfortably.'[26] He paid £12 a year rent from the sale of butter, some flax or yarn, a pig or two and a few small sheep. He also sold a calf and a foal each year. He fed his family with his own potatoes, saved his own turf and his wife spun their own wool and yarn to clothe the family.

Small occupiers held their leases in partnership following the rundale system. There were many hundreds of this class of tenants in Tourlestrane: 'The townlands are divided into three or four portions, and each of these occupied by a certain number of tenants who hold in common, dividing the arable in equal parts, and appropriating the coarse ground and pasture to grazing; each having a right to put on a certain number of cattle, reckoning by their ages and kinds.'[27] Here, the holding was ten acres shared by four tenants, having two and a half acres each. The land was of variable quality which generally produced for each, three roods of potatoes, one rood of flax and an acre of oats, with half an acre of pasture for grazing a single cow. In 1776 Arthur Young found the rundale system in the Cooper and O'Hara estates. He gave the subdivisions as five or six acres. On the Dillon estate the average holding was between twenty and forty acres which, assuming four in the partnership, gave five to ten acres each. There were, however, some much larger holdings of up to a hundred acres, held in common.[28] Such holdings would have provided four occupants with fifteen to twenty acres each, though there may have been a higher percentage of waste ground.

Rundale

25 O'Hara Papers, Ms. 20, 313 (7)
26 Neligan, 'The Parish of Kilmactigue' in W. Shaw Mason, *A Statistical Account or Parochial Survey of Ireland*, vol. 2, p. 387
27 ibid, p. 384
28 Martin Towey and Co had over 96 acres in the parish of Ballaghaderreen (Castlemore) in 1799. Peter Cannon and Co had over 73 acres, Patrick Carroll and Co over 68 and Patrick Quinn and Co over 86 in Charlestown (Kilbeagh). In 1789 Charles Carroll and Co held over 86 acres in the parish of Kilmovee.

Because these farms were not enclosed, they gave rise to frequent disputes and quarrels among the occupants. 'The system of running in common is a great evil, and produces much mischief among them.'[29] In the early nineteenth century, the occupants tended to enclose their respective portions.

Most of those who held their leases under the rundale system were known as village tenants as their cabins were normally grouped together in 'clusters'. This continued even after the rundale system was abandoned at the turn of the century.[30] In the 1720s, village tenants were moved off the lowlands to make way for cattle and some of them took mountain farms. By 1728 the demand for beef began to abate, the price of land fell and many of the village tenants returned. With the introduction of flax growing and spinning, their economic situation began and continued to improve throughout the rest of the century. In the 1750s Charles O'Hara estimated the annual income of a village tenant as £24.

Cottiers

'There is no knowing,' Charles O'Hara wrote, 'what proportion the labouring men bear to the village tenants.' Cottiers were labourers who were given a site for their cabin and a potato plot on a farm and in return they worked for the farmer at the usual daily rate. They were not paid in money but their labour was computed against the rent of their plot. The working days of such a labourer was reckoned as 250 in a year. Arthur Young settled on this figure by subtracting Sundays, thirty holydays, ten days for bad weather and twenty days which the cottier devoted to cultivating his own potato patch.[31] O'Hara, who described cottiers as 'the lowest species of slaves', estimated their family income in the middle of the century to be worth £13 a year, allowing £6 for the cottier's day labour for his landlord, £3 for labour on his own plot and £4 earnings from his wife's spinning. Such cottiers were not notably worse off than the smaller rundale tenants.[32]

Young regarded the Irish cottier system as better than the system in England where labourers were paid money. The Irish cottier was given the means of

29 Neligan, p. 382
30 McParlan, *Statistical Survey of Co Mayo*, (1802), pp. 85–6
31 ibid, (192? edition), vol. 1, pp. 445, 456
32 In Tourlestrane (Kilmactigue) early in the nineteenth century one gentleman paid his cottiers fourpence a day. He also gave them an acre of land for thirty shillings and the grazing of a cow for the same amount. Thus the cottier had to work for 180 days. He also gave them one meal a day, consisting chiefly of potatoes and milk or herrings. He offered them sixpence without food, which would have reduced their working days to 120, but they preferred to be given food. The Protestant vicar, James Neligan, paid them sixpence in winter and eight pence in summer without food, and with two acres of land at sixty shillings rent. He subsequently changed that to tenpence throughout the year, and 1s. 1d. during spring and harvest. op. cit., pp. 283–4

living, i.e. the potato plot and the cow's grazing, instead of money. Thus he was not subject to fluctuations in the price of food. He had an abundance of potatoes for most of the year to feed his family and enough milk at least for the younger children. The English cottier had to buy bread, cheese and meat to feed his family and on his wages could only provide them very sparingly. Besides, the Irish cottier could not spend his wages in the alehouse on a Saturday night as was commonly done by his English counterpart.[33]

At the very bottom of the social order were landless labourers called spalpeens who were paid money for their labour. In places like Tourlestrane (Kilmactigue), they were seldom hired except during spring and harvest. They moved from place to place in search of work and threw up their mud-cabins usually on the roadside. In the summer spalpeens from Connacht went to Leinster, while their wives and children took to the roads at home begging. Later on in the century, they crossed to England and returned home at the end of the harvest with two to six guineas, depending on their success in finding work there. In 1776 Arthur Young found that spalpeens were on the decline in Co Sligo but with the huge growth in the population they re-emerged later on. Small-under tenants, cottiers and spalpeens were not rigid social classes. One easily descended from one class to another, tenants dissolving into cottiers and they in turn into spalpeens.

Spalpeens

'In the beginning of this century the whole country was covered with cottage tenants who mostly paid their rents in kind, in duties and in work.'[34] There was little or no money in circulation and the economy was not based on cash. It was a time when, as Charles O'Conor of Belanagare informed Edmund Burke, 'the price of labour and the value of land held a reasonable proportion'. Up to 1720 a labourer was paid a groat (fourpence) a day and paid twelve shillings a year for the grazing of a cow and the same for an acre of tillage. With the expansion of the colonies and the development of navigation, demand for beef grew, particularly in the south of Ireland. Graziers from there came to Connacht fairs, such as at Ballinasloe, in search of store cattle. As a result more and more of the land was stocked with cattle and the cottage tenants were moved off it to more mountainous holdings. The price of land soared and, though village tenants later returned, land prices continued to rise for the rest of the century. In 1765 O'Conor estimated that rents had almost tripled. 'Where the father paid 24 shillings in dear times,' he told Burke, 'the son pays 70 in the dearest.' Meanwhile, the labourers' wages remained at four or at most five pence a day. In 1776 wages had only risen an

Rents

33 *A Tour of Ireland*, p. 184
34 O'Hara Papers, Ms 20, 397

average of a penny and three farthings during the previous twenty years. In Tourlestrane (Kilmactigue) in 1814 there were some families paying £2. 4s. an acre and wages were tenpence a day. These families 'live but very poorly, and find great difficulty in making up the rent for the landlord'.[35]

Those who could not pay their rent on time usually had their cattle impounded. They were often more harshly treated by first tenants or middlemen than by the original landlord to whom they sometimes turned to seek redress where 'they find relief and assistance they never can expect as under tenants'. The absentee landlord, Frances Jones, claimed lofty aspirations with regard to distressed tenants. 'To make poor people content and happy is most surely the only blessing of oppulence.'[36] The widow Regan, a mother of seven, appealed to Charles O'Hara against her 'landlord', Peter McCormack. She was in arrears with her rent and O'Hara allowed her another year for which no doubt the widow and 'seven orphans' were eternally grateful. Peter McCormack, whose name suggests he may have been a Catholic, was particularly harsh in his treatment of his under-tenants. 'I wish to save O'Connor and his wife at Coolaney,' Charles O'Hara instructed his agent in 1803, 'from being distressed at present by Peter McCormack, their landlord.'[37]

Linen

'About the years (17)17 and (17)18 the better sort of people introduced the sowing of flax seed, and made their tenants' wives spin the produce, which they had wove into coarse linens for their own use. This industry descended, and the lower sort of people had their linen made at home.' Thus Charles O'Hara described the origin of the linen industry in Co Sligo.[38] It took off rapidly there as in the neighbouring county of Mayo. The people were given flax seed, spinning wheels and reels by the Linen Board and the women manufactured the flax into yarn which, from about 1735 on, was sold for cash to northern buyers. In the middle of the century bounties were given for the exportation of linen and great quantities of cloth were made. There was a temporary hiccup in the trade when English demand fell between 1753 and 1755 but it revived again in 1756 and the price of yarn rose towards the end of 1757 and continued to rise the following year. By 1760 the linen business was booming and it continued to thrive.[39] 'The linen manufacture makes great strides,' Charles O'Hara wrote in 1763, 'and the lower people are growing rich.'

35 Neligan, op. cit., p. 388
36 O'Hara Papers, Ms. 20, 291 (2)
37 O'Hara Papers, Ms. 20, 280 (11)
38 O'Hara Papers, Ms. 20, 397; see especially J. C. McTernan, 'The Linen Industry in Co Sligo' in *Olde Sligoe*, pp. 154–172
39 Robert Stephenson, *Reports and Observations 1760–61*, pp. 62, 69

By 1766 the money earned from yarn was sufficient to pay the rent, turning the women folk into important contributors to the family economy. 'Three pence a day, the most that can be made by spinning, was an inducement fit only to be held out to women so educated. The earning was proportioned to their mode of living and became wealth to the family.'[40] The price of yarn continued to rise until the end of 1769, but the failure of some Dublin banks in 1770 caused the yarn to fall to one-third of its value and it remained low until the end of 1773. When Arthur Young visited Sligo in 1776 he found the yarn trade thriving there with £80,000 worth of yarn exported to Manchester and Liverpool from Sligo port in 1775. Spinning was now established as the main source for paying the rent in Sligo and Mayo. 'In their domestic economy, they reckon that the men feed the family with their labour in the field, and the women pay the rent by spinning.' This was the situation Young discovered in Westport and in Joshua Cooper's estate at Markrea.[41] The people as a result were 'infinitely better off than twenty years ago'.

Spinning-wheel
(Mr & Mrs S. C. Hall, *Ireland*)

Spinning also improved the social life of women as they often gathered together in groups in barns, each bringing their own flax and spinning wheel, and sang together while they worked. Lady Morgan described how she was attracted by the sound of music coming from a barn 'where a group of young females were seated round an old hag who formed the centre of the circle; they were all busily employed at their wheels, which I observed went merrily round in exact time with their song'.[42]

Bleaching and weaving inevitably followed and in 1776 there were six bleach greens in Co Sligo. John Petty Fitzmaurice, first Earl of Shelburne, introduced linen manufacture into Ballymote shortly after he acquired the Taaffe estate there. By 1760 Shelburne had advanced £3000 to establish a large factory. After his death, his widow brought in a Mr Wakefield from London

Ballymote

40 O'Hara Papers, Ms. 20, 397
41 op. cit., pp. 75, 83
42 She wrote that 'these conventions of female industry, so frequent in many parts of Ireland, are called *Ouris*' (possibly *abhras*, a parcel of wool or flax for spinning; *mná abhrais*, women spinners). Sometimes these gatherings amounted to a hundred women and girls together. *The Wild Irish Girl*, vol. 1, pp. 60, 61n, 62n. Where the girls gathered, the boys often followed: 'Every evening of the week throughout the winter season, a party of young females went successively to the houses of their respective parents, with their spinning wheels, and dedicated a great part of the night to the double purpose of industry and innocent amusement. Hither they were generally followed by their lovers: the song and the tale went round, and labour ceased to be toil.' Robert Bell, *A Description of the Conditions and Manners of the Irish Peasantry 1780–1790*, pp. 20–21; see also Shaw Mason, op. cit., vol. 2, p. 169

to manage the enterprise and during the five years of his management the number of looms was increased to sixty. In 1765 a Dublin newspaper advertised for weavers, 'particularly those who have large families', assuring them wages as good as anywhere in the province.[43] In 1776 Young found in Ballymote one of the finest bleach mills in the country. It had been constructed two years earlier by Thomas Petty Fitzmaurice, Shelburne's son, who took over the management of the project after Wakefield's death. He had brought in weavers from the north of Ireland who now numbered eighty. In addition he employed a further eighty women and forty children, quilling, warping and winding. He built stone and slate cottages for the northern weavers at a cost of £50 each. He had other grander ambitions for Ballymote which included a large market house, a handsome inn, a mansion house for himself in the style of a castle and 'to pull down all the old cabins in the town and rebuild them in regular streets of good houses for weavers and mechanics'.[44]

The manufacture of linen continued to increase up to the early decades of the nineteenth century. In the neighbourhood of Foxford the French consul, Coquebert de Montbret, observed in 1791 'a large amount of flax cultivated in all this district'.[45] There were over 300 acres of flax grown in Co Sligo in 1796. That year the Linen Board offered a prize of a spinning wheel for each rood of flax sown between March and June. Almost 1,000 growers in the county qualified for the prize and about 90% of them cultivated a rood each.[46] By 1809 the acreage under flax had more than doubled to 684

Girls beetling linen (Mr & Mrs S. C. Hall, *Ireland*)

43 *Faulkner's Journal*, 12 / 2 / 1765 ; Robert Stephenson, op. cit., quoted in McTernan, p. 157
44 Young, pp. 71–74
45 Charles-Etienne Coquebert de Montbret was appointed French consul in Dublin in January 1789. He had previously been consul general for the Hanseatic Towns and was based in Hamburg. During his two and a half years stay in Ireland he made three long journeys through the country. In May 1791 he set out on his third journey to explore the west and the north. He recorded his impressions in four notebooks, *carnets de voyage*, three of which are in the Bibliothèque Nationale, Paris and one in the Municipal Library, Rouen. They are also available on microfilm in the National Library of Ireland. His notes on his Connacht tour have been edited by Síle Ní Chinnéide in the *Galway Archaeological & Historical Journal*, vols. 25, 35, 36. op. cit., vol. 35, p. 61
46 Most of the acreage under flax was in the parishes of Achonry, Ballisodare, Coolaney (Killoran), Collooney (Kilvarnet), Tourlestrane (Kilmactigue) and Ballymote (Emlefad). Strangely, there was no flax grown in the parishes of Bunninadden, Keash, Curry or Gurteen. *List of Persons to whom Premiums for sowing flax-seed in the year 1796 have been adjudged by the Trustees of the Linen Board*, Dublin 1796

with 5,192 growers. Two years later there were almost 2,000 acres sown and this was increased by almost 1,000 acres more in 1817.

This increase in acreage was not matched by an increase in the money a woman made from spinning. In 1776 Young estimated that a woman made twopence halfpenny a day in the Collooney area. Almost forty years later it was estimated that a woman in Tourlestrane (Kilmactigue) earned only twopence a day if she had to buy the flax, which was not 'sufficient to buy tobacco for herself and her husband'. However, for the half year when she had her own flax, she could, with the help of a daughter or two, earn considerably more, which amounted to about half the rent.[47] It was suggested that landlords should provide their tenants with a sufficient supply of flax seed in spring at cost price so that 'the female part of the family would be able by their work, to pay half the rent of the ground from that article, and have a saving to procure necessaries for themselves'.[48] In 1811, the linen inspector for Connacht descibed Sligo as the principal linen county in the province and many of the landlords promoted the industry. Charles O'Hara had a bleach-mill constructed at Greenville in Coolaney. Colonel Percival of Templehouse, John Armstrong of Chaffpool and James Bridgeman, John Motherwell and Rev John Garrett of Ballymote, were all active in promoting it on their estates. Weavers, who wove cloth for themselves or their neighbours or to sell at local markets, were to be found dispersed throughout the villages. There were large weekly markets in Sligo and Ballina, and smaller ones in Collooney and Ballymote. The latter also held an annual linen fair.[49]

Scalding the Thread (Mr & Mrs S. C. Hall, *Ireland*)

A list of trades and professions was recorded in 1814 for the parish of Fuerty near Roscommon in the diocese of Elphin.[50] It could be taken as representative of most parishes in the neighbouring diocese of Achonry. Some twenty-two trades and professions were listed. Weavers were the most numerous at thirty. There were twelve blacksmiths, eleven carpenters, ten masons and ten tailors. The number of shoemakers was five, while mantuamakers, sawyers, and wheelwrights numbered four each. The others were all single tradesmen, such as millers, butchers, coopers and cabinetmakers. The 1749 census of Elphin painted a similar picture of the same parish.[51] There were then twelve

Tradesmen and Servants

47 Neligan, pp. 385, 387
48 ibid, p. 392
49 McParlan, *A Statistical Survey of Co Sligo*, pp. 26–29
50 Shaw Mason, op. cit., vol. 1, p. 413
51 National Archives, M. 2466

weavers. Shepherds numbered eight. Next came masons at five. There were four each of smiths, tailors and brogue-makers, three sawyers and gardeners and two joiners. The rest had single representatives, one butcher, ale-seller, miller, maltster, tanner, turner, slieve-maker and schoolmaster.

The parish of Fairymount (Tibohine) then bordered two Achonry parishes, Ballaghaderreen and Kilmovee, and was presumably more representative of these parishes. In 1749 weavers were the most numerous at twenty, followed by eleven blacksmiths, and seven each of innkeepers, sergeants, car-men, and tailors. There were six masons, five millers, four merchants and three joiners and coopers. There was a distinction between brogue-makers, of which there were two, and the single cobbler.[52]

Servants

The greatest source of employment outside the home was domestic service. The parish priest of Tourlestrane (Kilmactigue) gave the number of Catholic families there in 1814 as twelve hundred and there were ten Protestant families. 'Many of these families keep a servant boy or girl, and sometimes both, for three, six, or nine months in the year, to assist them in their work.'[53] Charles O'Hara made a similar observation some sixty years earlier. 'The common people of this county are for the most part very poor, so that when their children grow up, they commonly leave them to look for service.'[54]

Landlords, such as O'Hara, were the greatest employers of servants and in many of the better-off Protestant homes, servants were numerous. In 1749 Thomas Mahon of Strokestown Park had twenty servants, half of them Protestant and the other half Catholic. Gilbert King of Boyle, a magistrate and father of three children, had fourteen servants. Robert Waller of Kilmore in the diocese of Elphin had twenty-two servants, eleven of them Catholic and eleven Protestant. Edward Synge, the Protestant Bishop of Elphin, who only resided there for a few months each summer, had seventeen servants, all Protestants. His vicars, who were fully resident, usually employed about five servants, some Protestants and some Catholics. The medical doctor and the apothecary in the parish of Elphin, both of whom were Catholics, had each four servants, all of whom were Catholic.

Catholic priests probably kept one or two servants, one of whom acted as groom or horse-boy. In 1749 Peter Corr, a parish priest in the diocese of Elphin, had two servants, one male and the other female. The parish priest of Boyle had then one male servant, while the parish priest of Fairymount (Tibohine)

52 Other occupations listed included carpenters (2), cord-winders (2), nailors (2), pump-makers (2), clothiers (2), schoolmaster (1), glazier (1), clerk (1), physician (1), and horserider (1).
53 Neligan, op. cit., p. 259
54 O'Hara Papers, Ms. 20, 397

had one female servant. In the same parish there was a friar, A. Duffy, who had four servants, two male and two female. This was probably Andrew Duffy, who was prior of the Dominican friars of Urlaur in 1756, and parish priest of Kilmovee in Achonry in 1758. The four servants employed may have been for the upkeep of the friary where there were usually six to ten friars. Only the prior may have been present when the census was taken, the others dispersed on various errands as was customary.[55]

The parish of Fairymount (Tibohine) shared boundaries with the parishes of Kilmovee and of Ballaghaderreen in Achonry. Presumably it shared many other sociological features as well. In the 1749 census servants were the second most numerous profession listed in Fairymount. Two hundred and sixty-four persons were so designated or almost 16% of the total adult population of the parish. Servants there were only outnumbered by labourers (393). Even labourers had servants and some had two. Blacksmiths, judging by the number of their servants, seemed to have been relatively prosperous. One Catholic blacksmith in the parish of Fairymount had no less than seven servants, five male and two female, while he had only two children under the age of fourteen. The five male servants were probably employed assisting him in his forge. Another Catholic blacksmith in the parish had two Protestant male servants. The sergeant, who was also a Catholic and had only one child under fourteen, had five servants, two males and three females.

While spinning may have paid one half of the rent, some families made up the other half by distilling whiskey or poteen-making. 'Private distillation is the only feasible means the poor people here have of paying their rents, and supporting their families.'[56] Such was the situation in Tourlestrane in 1814 where 'every man understands the trade, and carries it on, as opportunity may serve'. Though illegal and subject to severe penalties, this activity was widely practised throughout the diocese. Every townland had at least one family, and sometimes several, constantly employed in distilling. Some of them bought small stills, partly for their own use and partly to let out on hire to others.

Poteen (Póitín)

Malted barley was used in the distillation in the barony of Costello which was great barley country, as was the sea-side of the Ox mountains.[57] But there was no barley grown in Tourlestrane and people there had to buy it from neighbouring parishes. There they sometimes mixed the barley with malted

---

55 Fairymount (Tibohine) had no friary while the Dominican friary of Urlaur was only a short distance away on the other side of Lake Urlaur.
56 Neligan, p. 394
57 McParlan, op. cit., p. 30

The Still
(Mr & Mrs S. C. Hall, *Ireland*)

oats which produced the greatest quantity of spirits, but most often it was distilled from oats alone. With the collapse of prices following the end of the Napoleonic War, the price of barley and oats fell by almost two-thirds which made poteen-making even more profitable. In Tourlestrane a barrel of oats sold at a market more than ten miles away would only make fourteen shillings, while the same barrel could produce eight gallons of whiskey at seven or eight shillings a gallon.

Distilling generally took place at night in a secluded spot to avoid detection by the revenue officers.[58] One traveller in a remote part of Mayo had a mishap late at night when his horse got stuck in the mud. Luckily for him 'a parcel of men passed on their way to an illicit still', pulled out his horse and 'with that charming suavity of kindness, which so conspicuously identifies the Connacht peasant', escorted him in safety for about a mile.[59] It was the function of the revenue officer to detect and seize these illicit stills. It could be a dangerous occupation: 'no revenue officer would venture to approach the places where they were, without a strong military guard; and numerous detachments of cavalry were stationed all over the country for no other purpose than that of still hunting.'[60] People often had to bribe the constables employed by the revenue officers and some constables were even paid protection money to warn distillers of an impending raid. Though lookouts were usually posted to warn of their approach, raids were sometimes successful. Often the search

58 Bell, op. cit., p. 29
59 McParlan, *A Statistical Survey of Co Mayo*, p. 94
60 Bell, op. cit., p. 29

party fanned out over a wide expanse of land and the discovery was eventually made by a single individual who was then bribed to leave without exposing them. On one occasion a number of soldiers, after becoming separated from their revenue officer, discovered a still in operation. They were duly bribed and happily departed. The illicit distiller subsequently reported them to their commanding officer for extortion and had his money restored.[61]

The quality of this locally distilled whiskey was probably superior to that of the poteen of later times. It was certainly good enough to satisfy some refined tastes. The bottle of whiskey served at the priest's breakfast after a station Mass in Tourlestrane (Kilmactigue) was most likely a local product. Priests were certainly among the clientele of local distillers. One carrier from Tubbercurry, who was apprehended, stated in evidence that he went to Collooney and called at the priest's house, 'whom he had heard wanted a keg of spirits'.[62] There was a constant demand for it among all classes, especially for christenings, wedding and wakes and it was estimated that 'perhaps ten gallons or more' were consumed at weddings in Tourlestrane.'[63]

Sheebeens (Síbín)

Sheebeens were numerous throughout the countryside. 'There was hardly one cabin in ten on an average throughout the interior of Ireland, in which an inferior kind of ale or whiskey was not sold.'[64] Lady Morgan has left a description of one of these sheebeens: 'This hut they call a sheebeen house, and is something inferior to a certain description of a Spanish inn. Although a little board informs the weary he is only to expect "good dry lodgings", yet the landlord contrives to let you know in an *entre nous* manner, that he keeps some real Inishone (or spirits, smuggled from a tract of country so called) for his particular friends.'[65] It was reported to Rome that Thomas Costello from Ballaghaderreen, one of the candidates recommended to be Bishop of Clonfert, came from a good family which 'had been much degraded by the profession of his father' who 'kept a country inn and sells beer on the public street'.[66] The seven innkeepers listed in the neighbouring parish of Fairymount (Tibohine) in the 1749 census were probably sheebeen-owners.

Famine and Distress

Life on the land at the best of times was precarious but it deteriorated dramatically in bad times, when either crops failed or prices collapsed. Sporadic famines in the eighteenth century were usually the result of unpredictable

---

61 Neligan, op. cit., pp. 394–95
62 O'Hara Papers, Ms. 16, 943
63 Neligan, p. 361
64 Bell, op. cit., p. 29
65 *The Wild Irish Girl*, vol. 2, p. 161
66 SC Irlanda, vol. 15, f. 471rv

weather, particularly at harvest time.[67] Occasional crop failures were a constant feature of agricultural life, not only in Ireland but elsewhere in Europe.[68] The severity of these famines or near-famines often depended on the quality of the preceding harvests or whether they resulted from a succession of bad harvests.

The last two weeks of September 1701 were unusually wet. Nevertheless Kean O'Hara, then in Dublin, was informed on the last day of that month that his harvest was 'in a reasonable condition, considering the badness of the weather'. His barley was reaped and standing in stooks in the fields, as was most of his oats and the portion of wheat which had been reaped. The hay would be brought in, weather permitting. A week later all that had changed dramatically. 'There was such a storm here,' James Raghnine informed Kean, 'that it has spoilt this country forever.' All the harvest waiting in the fields was blown away. Richard Crofton was even more graphic in the description he gave Kean of this freak storm: 'I expected we should have met before now in another world, for most of us in this country was of the opinion that the last hurricane we had was ordered from the heavens to raise the dead as well as the living and convey us to another world.' He went on to describe the 'strange things that happened on the sea shores in T(ireragh) and several other places of this county'. More than twenty tons of herrings and thousands of sea birds were cast up dead more than a mile inland from the shore. Houses and fields disappeared, covered with sand 'so as not to be found', and elsewhere houses were knocked down or blown away. The storm left many facing the prospect of starvation in the winter of 1701.

Towards the end of August 1744 'there was the fairest prospect of a fine harvest'. Then on 24 August a violent storm accompanied by torrential rain so totally destroyed the harvest that 'not one acre in ten was worth reaping'. The ravages of the storm might have been borne with difficulty but heavy snow fell in January and the whole country remained covered with it until the end of March. The cattle died for want of fodder. 'There is no misery which famine can induce,' Charles O'Hara, senior, recalled, 'which did not afflict our country the following year', while Charles O'Conor of Belanagare entered in his diary, '*Ní fhacaidh Éire riamh a samhail sin do bhliadhain*' (Ireland never witnessed such a year previously).[69] Many people died. O'Hara estimated that the number of houses in the county dropped by a third from

---

67 see L. M. Cullen, 'Economic development, 1691–1750' in *A New History of Ireland*, vol. IV, pp. 145–49
68 Famines or near-famines were recorded in Ireland in 1728–9, 1741, and 1756.
69 Síle Ní Chinnéide, 'Dhá leabhar notaí le Séarlas Ó Conchubhair' in *Galvia*, vol. 1 (1954), pp. 38–9

about 6,000 in 1744 to 4,000 in 1746. Nevertheless, the recovery was rapid and in 1747 'things began to wear another face'. Joshua Cooper told Arthur Young 'that the great improvement of this part of the country commenced about the year 1748'.[70] Within a few years prosperity returned and 'people began to look cheerful again'.

Crop-failures continued to occur sporadically, including in 1755. 'This year will be long memorable for a scene of distress in Ireland,' Charles O'Hara wrote, and it was followed by 'a dreadful winter and a severe spring'. By May, according to Charles O'Conor, 'two-thirds of the inhabitants are perishing for the want of bread'. Fortunately, 1757 was 'uncommonly good', and this was followed by two more good years. The summer of 1760 was extremely wet and much of the harvest was lost and the following summer was so dry that there was no growth of hay or flax. 1765 was 'remarkably hot and dry' and the potatoes failed but the corn was 'good and plenty', and this was followed by a very fine and mild winter so that there was no want of fodder for the cattle. 1768 was wet and the corn was bad but the potatoes good and the following year was also wet and the reverse happened, plenty of corn and no potatoes. The weather turned very bad towards the end of the harvest in 1770 and though there appeared to be 'so great a plenty of the best potatoes', they could not be dug and were in danger of rotting. Straw and hay rotted, but because the following spring was 'so providentially fair and mild', there was no loss of cattle. In 1770 Charles O'Conor told a friend that there was 'at present a famine in this western province'. 1773 was 'unnaturally dry' but the rain started on 27 August and continued for a month and did great damage to the corn. Again in 1777 Charles O'Conor wrote that the potatoes and oats had failed after a severe and rainy season.[71]

Crop failures

But these crop-failures no longer caused severe famine. This was due to the diversification of the rural economy, particularly after the establishment of the linen industry. Money was now in circulation which helped cushion the harsher effects of crop-failures. This at least was the view expressed by Charles O'Hara commenting on an unusually wet season in 1760: 'The lower class of people grow more above small accidents. For instance, the wetness of this season would have created dreadful apprehensions fifteen years ago; at present, I fear little from it. Formerly tenants had nothing to trust to but the last produce of their land. The lower people now rely more upon their industry which opens an access to other markets, in case of scarcity at home.'[72]

70 op. cit., p. 76
71 Ward, Wrynn, Ward, op. cit., pp. 12–13, 236, 356
72 O'Hara Papers, Ms. 20, 397

Depression 1815

Prices collapsed dramatically in 1815 with the ending of the Napoleonic war. 'The present state of the peasantry and farmers is truly depressing,' Neligan wrote about the situation then in Tourlestrane (Kilmactigue). The price of cattle had fallen by at least a third and that of pigs was cut in half while potatoes and oats were down in similar proportions. This was corroborated by the Bishop of Clogher in his report to Rome. He reported that a hank of yarn which was sold during the war for thirteen to eighteen pence was now fetching only four or five pence. Butter and pork were down by a third and, meanwhile, rents were maintained at war levels which 'reduced great numbers to beggary'.[73] 'Peace, which at other times, and in other countries, was esteemed one of the greatest blessings, is now considered by the people of this kingdom the greatest evil that could befall them, and makes them wish for another fierce and protracted contest.'[74]

Charitable committees were set up throughout the diocese to relieve the distress of the poor and landlords. Parsons and priests sat together on these committees. One such committee in Coolaney estimated that there were 350 families in the united parishes of Coolaney (Killoran) and Collooney (Kilvarnet) totally destitute and double that number short of food. The committee raised £200 in these parishes which was used to buy meal which was sold to the poor at reduced prices. 'Tickling up the absentees a little,' who were then receiving £70,000 in rent annually from Co Sligo, was suggested to Charles O'Hara, who drafted a letter to be sent to all absentees seeking subscriptions.[75] As a result of this appeal, £2,000 pounds was raised, half of which was paid and the other half promised.[76] Some of the absentees declined to subscribe though they were liberal with their advice, such as George French in Dublin who feared encouraging laziness among the labouring poor by a gratuitous contribution. Robert Shaw, the absentee vicar of Ballisodare, made no subscription either. 'My narrow circumstances,' he wrote from Galway in January 1817, 'preclude me from doing what my heart really approves.'[77]

The Farming Year: Spring

When the weather was seasonable the farm year followed a routine pattern. 'Candlemas day, throw the candle away' was a well-known adage suggesting that the spring work began on 1 February.[78] It probably started somewhat later in that month or even at the beginning of the next.

73 SC Irlanda, vol. 22, f. 140r
74 Neligan, p. 381
75 O'Hara Papers, Ms. 20, 313 (2); Report 493, p. 3416
76 Mr and Mrs Ormsby Gore sent fifty guineas from Torkington to be spent on the poor in the parishes of Tourlestrane (Kilmactigue) and Achonry.
77 O'Hara Papers, Ms. 20, 313
78 Shaw Mason, op.cit., vol. 2, p. 458

Ploughing

Men and women, and children old enough to help, all worked in the fields and the bog. Farm implements were primitive, consisting mainly of loys, spades and shovels, and ploughs and harrows were scarce and generally light and small and all made by local blacksmiths. Most ploughing consisted in turning the sod with a loy.[79] A long-handled loy was used by men for ploughing a field or cutting turf. Because of the rotation of crops, it was rarely necessary to plough lea or fallow ground as an acre of ground was generally used to produce potatoes one year, oats the following and flax the third year.

In the rare cases where ploughs were used, they required three horses abreast, as these animals were small and not very strong. In 1776 Arthur Young found that four horses abreast were used in Co Sligo and that ploughing was done by the tail, as it was in Mayo in the neighbourhood of Castlebar and Westport: 'they harrow by the tail, the fellow who leads the horses of a plough walks backward before them the whole day long, and in order to make them advance, strikes them in the face.'[80] Young estimated that it took three days to plough an acre.

The best manure was that produced by cattle and as even the poorest cottier kept one cow, he probably had sufficient for his potato plot. This cow was housed in the cabin at night with the rest of the family and its manure had to be shovelled out every morning and thus there was a sizeable mound of manure alongside every cabin. Fertiliser was also made from a compost of what was called 'mooreen' (*múirín*) or turf mould which was spread on top of the potato-ridges and burnt. It produced good crops but it was thought that 'this practice impoverishes the land, by wasting the surface, which is the most fertile and productive part of it'.[81] In his tour of Connacht in 1791 the French Consul observed this burnt ground in several places.

Sowing the Crops

The potatoes were usually planted on the day after St Patrick's Day but that date seems to have been aspirational rather than real. In 1738 Charles O'Conor sowed his potatoes a month later, on 11 April and from 21 to 28 April

---

79 Coquebert de Montbret was so fascinated by the loy which was used in Co Sligo for planting potatoes, that he drew a rough sketch of it on the margin of his notebook. It was 18 to 20 inches long, the upper part made of wood, the lower of iron. This short-handled variety was probably used specifically for dibbling potatoes with the handle and covering them with soil with the shovel part. Women or children could have been employed at that.
80 op. cit., pp. 80–1. A description of ploughing in Tourlestrane (Kilmactigue) forty years later bears a striking similarity to that of Young: 'the man who leads these horses, standing or walking before them, with his face turned towards the horses, moving backward and dragging them after him.' Neligan, pp. 381–2. It is difficult to believe that ploughing by the tail was still practised at such a late date.
81 Neligan, p. 382

the following year, but there was then heavy snow in March. There was snow again in March in 1740 and O'Conor wrote in his Diary: '*Diardaoin na gcomaoinecha April. 3. 1740. 3 bhairille & dha bhuisel potataidh do chur aniu dhamh re Aimsir ro thirim*' ('Holy Thursday (lit. Communion's Thursday) 3 April 1740, 3 barrels and two bushels of potatoes sown today in very dry weather').[82] Oats were sown in late March or early April, followed by flax and barley. O'Conor often sowed his oats before the potatoes. This was the case in 1739, when he had sown 24 acres of oats by 28 March and even earlier the following year.[83]

Cutting Turf

Once the crops had been sown, work began in the bog. This was usually in the month of May. On Saturday 31 May 1740, Charles O'Conor entered in his Diary: '*An triomach siorraidhe uime a toisiughadh aniu ris a moin do gherradh*' ('With the continuous drought started cutting the turf today').[84] The turf was cut and spread out to dry and later 'footed' or piled up in small stacks to facilate a further drying.

By early summer the land had been ploughed, the crops sown and the turf cut and spread. As at this stage the old crop of potatoes had been exhausted the poorer classes, cottiers and spalpeens, were obliged to seek work elsewhere to support their families. Some of them found employment locally, usually road-making which was commissioned by the local landlord. 'They look on it as a part of their yearly labour,' one commentator wrote in 1739, 'and in the month of June and July fall as regularly and cheerfully to the breaking of stones and gravelling the roads, as in March to the plow and the harrow.'[85]

Road-making

Roads were considerably improved in the course of the century. 'The roads are almost universally as good as those about London,' one very critical tourist in Ireland wrote in 1775–6.[86] He did not, however, visit Connacht which he considered too wild and barbaric. John Wesley, who did, had one unfortunate experience travelling from Castlebar to Sligo in May 1778. He decided to take the new shorter road via Swinford, rather than the old road via Foxford, and his carriage got bogged down in a large pothole in the vicinity of Curry.[87] However, by the end of the century the roads were greatly improved. 'The roads and bridges of this county (Mayo) are in so very good a state that one can hardly complain of the few that are bad.'[88]

82 Ní Chinnéide, 'Dialann Í Chonchúir', in *Galvia*, iv, pp. 8, 9, 12
83 ibid, pp. 9, 12
84 Ní Chinnéide, op. cit., *Galvia*, iv, p. 13
85 William Henry, Nat. Arch., M 2533, p. 93
86 Twiss, *Tour in Ireland, 1775–6*, p. 54
87 *Journal*, vol. 6, p. 191
88 McParlan, *Statistical Survey of Mayo*, p. 93

Small cottiers and spalpeens had to migrate or emigrate. *Migrant Labourers*

> Many of the men go to England or to Leinster to get work, and the women and children, having fastened the door with a string, take their blankets on their backs and turn out to beg, until the latter end of the harvest. The men generally bring home from two to six guineas, according as they fall into work; whilst the other part of the family procure not only a sufficient quantity of potatoes to support them, but also some to sell to those who keep their houses.[89]

As most foreign travellers visited Ireland during this period they often got an exaggerated view of the state of beggary in the country. When the French consul, Coquebert de Montbret, visited Sligo in the summer of 1791 he was struck by the great numbers of beggars there. 'The habitual state of the poor in Ireland', he commented, 'is that of times of extreme scarcity among other nations.'[90] Had he come at any other season of the year, he would probably have encountered far fewer beggars. In the 1749 census of the parish of Fairymount (Tibohine) in the diocese of Elphin only two people were listed as 'beggars'.[91] Lady Morgan gave a more accurate picture of the real state of poverty in the country:

Beggars

Beggar Group
(Mr & Mrs S. C. Hall, *Ireland*)

> At certain seasons of the year, the high-roads and even the main streets of every town and village of Ireland, are infested with groups of mendicants ... These are not common beggars ... they are the necessitous families of the Irish peasants ... When the season of employment is over ... the Irish peasant quits the family for a distant province or even a distant land in search of that employment ... the mother closes the door of her desolate cabin and followed by her children and aged parent, takes to the roads to beg.[92]

These seasonal beggars were well received by those who were themselves only slightly better off.[93] 'I have seen them cheerfully received into the cabin of an

---

89   Neligan, op. cit., p. 383
90   op. cit., vol. 36, pp. 31–2
91   Census of Elphin, Nat. Arch. Ms. 2466
92   *Patriotic Sketches*, vol. 1, p. 91
93   People in Co Roscommon in 1816 were said to be 'very kind ... to the distressed and wandering poor, hardly ever refusing to such, food of whatever kind they have themselves or a night's lodgings in their homes'. Shaw Mason, op. cit., vol. 2, p. 324

equally humble, but more fortunate compatriot,' Lady Morgan wrote in 1807, 'As soon as a mendicant group appears at their door, it receives the accustomed Kead-mille-faltha (*céad míle fáilte*); the circle round the fire is enlarged; a fresh supply of potatoes brought forward; and shelter for the night, and clean straw to repose on, voluntarily offered.'[94]

Harvest

The migrants returned at harvest time either to reap their own crops or find employment at harvesting on the bigger farms. Families were once more re-united when the women and children returned home from their stint on the roads begging. On 24 July 1740 Charles O'Conor entered in his diary: '*na spailpinidh a tuilledh uile do dhiobhail oibre foghmhuir i gcoigedh laighen*' ('all the spalpeens returning for lack of harvest work in Leinster').[95] Flax was harvested towards the end of July or the beginning of August and then laid in water in a pool or a boghole for six to twelve days. When taken out it was spread out on the land for about two weeks and then laid in heaps on a hurdle fixed with posts, under which a turf fire was lit to dry it.[96]

Barley and Oats

Barley was reaped from mid-July onwards. On 14 July 1736 Charles O'Conor wrote in his Diary: '*Aniu ro thoisidh mé ar bhuaint na h-orna*' ('Today I began reaping the barley'). He began a day earlier the following year.[97] Oats, or corn as it was called in Ireland, was the main tillage crop in Co Sligo and it was cut with a reaping hook or sickle in August and bound into stooks which were left in the field to dry.[98] The harvest should be completed by St Bartholomew's Day (2 August).[99] On 19 August 1747 Edward Synge, Protestant Bishop of Elphin, wrote to his daughter Alicia in Dublin: 'All my wheat was in Stack. My Oats are all reap'd. They have begun upon my Barley. The Flax is in stack, and my hay at home; so that As to Harvest I am in a prosperous way.'[100]

An acre of oats produced four barrels at 24 stone to the barrel. Two barrels were sold to pay the rent and tithes, one barrel was kept for seed, the remaining one was made into meal for food for the family, and the oaten straw was kept for winter fodder for the cattle. Some of the oats in Tourlestrane were malted and distilled 'which, if they escape detection, will produce a profit of four to five pounds, which is a great temptation to them'.[101]

94 *Patriotic Sketches*, vol. 1, p. 98 & n
95 Ní Chinnéide, op. cit., *Galvia*, iv, p. 14
96 Young, p. 41
97 In the following two years it was early August before the barley was reaped. Ní Chinnéide, op. cit., iv, pp. 6, 7, 10, 14
98 IFC Ms 227, pp. 81–8; Wakefield, *Ireland Statistical and Political*, vol. 1, p. 386
99 Ward, Wrynn, Ward, op. cit., p. 312
100 Marie-Louise Legg, *The Synge Letters*, pp. 76–77
101 Neligan, op. cit., pp. 381, 385, 387

Hay was not generally saved, except on the larger farms. The little bit of pasture most had was about a half an acre which was barely enough to provide grazing for a single cow. This was supplemented with the tops of potato stalks and grass pulled from ditches. In winter the cow was fed straw, and if it was giving milk it was fed small potatoes.

The turf was brought home from the bog when the weather was favourable in the intervals between other pressing duties. This was generally in the month of July. On 14 July 1740 Charles O'Conor of Belanagare entered in his diary: '*deireadh na monadh sa mbaile anocht re triomach maith*' (the last of the turf at home tonight well-dried).[102] If the weather was bad the turf was not brought home until the end of August.[103] Bogs were plentiful. Arthur Young estimated that between one-sixth and one-seventh of Sligo county consisted of bog or mountain, while he gave the proportion of Mayo as one-third to a half.[104] In Tourlestrane turf 'abounds everywhere in the country, the bogs being interpersed with arable lands in every quarter'.[105] It was similar in most parishes in the diocese.

All the family were recruited to bring home the turf and everybody went to the bog at the same time, making it a great occasion for socialising. In 1813 a tourist encountered a group of barefoot teenage girls coming from the bog near Ballisodare, each carrying a basket or creel of turf on their back.[106] These baskets were made of wickerwork and had removable bottoms which were held in place by a stick, which, when removed, released the load.

When horses were used, the creels were slung across the horse's back.

Bringing Home the Turf

Woman with Turf (Mr & Mrs S. C. Hall, *Ireland*)

---

102 Ní Chinnéide, op. cit., *Galvia*, iv, p. 13. O'Conor made similar enties for 6 July 1736, 13 July 1737, 21 July 1741; see pp. 6, 7, 16
103 July was a very wet month in 1746. '21 Aug. An mhóin sa mbaile go balach re haimsir mhaith. Glóir do Dhia' (The turf completely home. Glory be to God!). op. cit., i, p. 40
104 op. cit., p. 74
105 Neligan, pp. 350–1
106 Hall, *Tour of Ireland*, vol. 2, pp. 62–3

Picking the Potatoes

Carts were not widely used as they were sledge-carts without wheels and difficult to manoeuvre over uneven terrain. 'All carriage done by horses with baskets,' Young observed in 1776 in the neighbourhood of Westport.[107] Donkeys, with or without their carts, which became such a familiar feature of the landscape in the following century, seemed virtually non-existent then.[108] The turf was stacked against the gable of the cabin and sometimes these stacks were constructed so that they were hollow on the inside and could be used to house the farm animals.

Potatoes, which were the first crop to be sown, were the last to be harvested. This was generally done in the months of September and October. 'The potatoes are often dug up when they are plentiful, towards 15 September,' the French consul wrote in 1791, ' in order to preserve them and prevent them sprouting before the next crop is available.'[109] He noted that in the neighbourhood of Collooney, one acre produced 30 barrels which were worth ten guineas then. In 1736 Charles O'Conor had his potatoes harvested by 15 October.[110] Children were kept from school to pick the potatoes which were then pitted, i.e. covered with a mound of earth, from which they were removed during the year as the family required them. Once the potatoes were dug, gathered and pitted, the farm year ended.

Slide-cart (Wood-Martin, *Sligo*)

107 op. cit., p. 84
108 Neither Young nor Neligan made any reference to donkeys. They were probably uneconomic to keep as they would compete for the scanty grazing and fodder available for the family cow.
109 op. cit., vol. 36, p. 31
110 Ní Chinnéide, op. cit., iv, p. 6

CHAPTER 4

Saol na nDaoine
Living and Leisure

For nine months of the year potatoes formed the staple diet of the poor. In 1805 it was estimated that a family, consisting of husband, wife and four children, ate 37 pounds of potatoes a day.[1] Thirty years earlier, Arthur Young gave an almost identical figure, i.e. 18 stone a week or 36 pounds a day. He estimated that such a family in the neighbourhood of Westport consumed 3 cwt a week. A half an acre produced 5 tons and 17 cwt which lasted the family 39 weeks, or almost ten months.[2] 'They have an absolute bellyful of potatoes,' he wrote of the poor in the baronies of Leyny and Corran, 'and the children eat them as plentifully as they like.'[3] Young's informant was Joshua Cooper of Markrea who told the French consul, Coquebert de Montbret, over twenty years later that when he asked a peasant how much potatoes he ate each day, he replied that a peck (i.e. 56 pounds) would last him five days. The Frenchman thought this was an exaggeration but 11 pounds of potatoes a day for a labouring man was probably not far wide of the mark.[4] They continued to be the staple diet of the people well into the next century as was clear in Tourlestrane in 1814. 'Potatoes furnish the standing dish three times a day throughout the year except in Summer, when they begin to grow scarce.'[5]

Food

Young waxed eloquent on the virtues of the Irish countryman's potato in comparison to the meagre fare of his English counterpart:

Mark the Irishman's potato bowl placed on the floor, the whole family on their hams around it, devouring a quantity almost incredible, the beggar seating himself to it with a hearty welcome, the pig taking his share as readily as the wife, the cocks, hens, turkeys, geese, the cur, the cat, and perhaps the cow – and all partaking of the same dish. No man can often have been a witness of it without being convinced of the plenty and, I will add, the cheerfulness that attends it.[6]

1 Carr, *The Stranger in Ireland,* p. 153
2 op. cit., (1892 edition), vol. 1, pp. 257-8
3 op. cit., p. 75
4 Ní Chinnéide, op. cit., vol. 36, p. 64
5 Neligan, p. 362
6 op. cit., p. 186

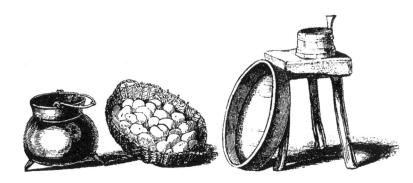

Potato pot, potato-basket, piggin, stool, bodhrán (Mr & Mrs S. C. Hall, *Ireland*)

Sometimes the potatoes were eaten with buttermilk as a beverage but, though every family had one cow and sometimes more, pasture was so poor and winter fodder so scarce that there was very little milk, particularly in winter and spring. If the cow was in calf, there was none. Only the youngest children were given fresh milk and what remained was churned and the butter sold. Those with one cow could produce a half a hundred weight of butter in the season. This was sold in Sligo in 1814 for between £2. 15s. and £3. 5s and this money contributed to paying the rent.[7] Milk called *bonny clobber* (*bainne clabair*, 'thick milk') was given to labourers in the neighbourhood of Westport.[8]

During the summer months when potatoes were in short supply, oat meal was eaten in the form of griddle cakes or made into a gruel which was called 'stirabout'. One traveller found that these oat cakes, 'baked on a griddle', were eaten in Achill in August 1752.[9] People in the baronies of Leyny and Corran preferred oat bread both to potatoes and wheat bread.[10] In the summer of 1791 the French consul observed 'great crowds of people struggling to obtain oatmeal' in the town of Sligo, which he attributed to the failure of the potato crop the previous year. It was estimated that a family of six could live on 40 pounds of oatmeal a week.[11]

Fish

Women in Tourlestrane sold their eggs to buy tobacco, 'the abominable weed', for themselves and their husbands rather than provide herrings for the family's dinner. One salted herring was enough for the whole family and in

---

7 Neligan, op. cit., p. 363
8 This was left to set for three days to allow the cream to rise. When it was skimmed, the milk that remained was 'as thick as blancmange and as sour as vinegar' and was called bonny clobber. Young, (1892 edition), vol. 1, pp. 257–8
9 *Bishop Pococke's Irish Tour*, p. 87
10 Young, p. 75
11 In Co Sligo the average price of oatmeal was less than a penny a pound in 1776 and in 1815 it cost from 10d –12d per cwt. Young, op. cit., p. 162; Neligan, p. 393

1791 they could be bought at three for a penny.[12] Apart from herrings, fish were not eaten by the ordinary people, even by those who lived on the coast. Even when potatoes were scarce in the 'hungry month' of July, a visitor to Foxford in 1779 commented that it was 'famous for abounding with Lampreys in the river, which nobody there will eat'. It was a market day there and the visitor bought four large ones for sixpence and got them packed in grass.[13] 'Fish is exceedingly plentiful, particularly oysters for 1s a cartload, and sand eels,' Young observed in Westport, 'yet they eat none', and he found a similar situation in Killala. He dined there with the Bishop of Killala and Achonry, Samuel Hutchinson, and was served three gurnet, two mackerel and one whiting. Fish was only eaten by the upper classes. In Ballisodare he found 'immense beds of oyster shells' left by inland gentlemen who used to come there 'in uncivilised times' to eat oysters in the mornings and return home 'to get drunk in the evenings'.[14]

There was also an abundance of fish in the inland rivers and lakes and a good angler with a boat on Lough Talt in Kilmactigue could take five or six dozen trout in part of a day.[15] The river Moy, which wound its way through several parishes in the diocese, was 'one of the first salmon fisheries in Ireland'.[16] Bishop Philip Philips described it in his report to Rome in 1771 as 'a great salmon fishery'.[17] Fifteen hundred salmon were being netted at the weirs in Ballina in the space of a few hours. James Neligan of Kilmactigue, himself an experienced angler, with a rod and single fly caught one hundred and sixty salmon in fourteen consecutive days, averaging more than ten a day.[18]

The salmon began their run up the rivers from the sea in February and continued until December when they spawned in shallow waters. To reach these shallow waters they had to wait for the November floods. In Tourlestrane this was the moment for the poachers to strike: 'the natives, with one accord, old and young, men, women and children, take the field against them ... and with goffs, pitchforks, reaping hooks, and long poles, they attack them in the day time, and by night take torches, made of slips of bog fir tied together, to assist them in discovering and killing the breeding fish, which is then very easily done.' There is no evidence that salmon ever

---

12 Ní Chinnéide, vol. 25, p. 11. Eggs were sold in 1814 at 3–4 for a penny, about the same price as herrings. Neligan, p. 363
13 Wilde, *Gabriel Beranger*, pp. 58–9
14 op. cit., pp. 76, 80, 83
15 Neligan, op. cit., p. 350
16 Neligan, p. 352
17 SCAR, codex 1. 4. no. 474
18 ibid, pp. 353–4

formed part of the ordinary people's diet so they were probaby sold to supplement their subsistence incomes.[19]

Meat

'It is only on such occasions as weddings and christenings, and at Easter and Christmas that they afford themselves any sort of animal food.' A goose or a chicken was generally cooked for the Christmas dinner and the same on Easter Sunday. On the eve of St Martin's Day, 11 November, a cock or a hen was killed by poor families and a sheep by the well-to-do.[20] There was a special market in Ballina, called 'St Martin's market', where fowl was sold for the feast.[21] Meat was also served on other occasions when the services of the priest were required in the home. At stations, the dinner generally consisted of 'fowl, butcher's meat with oaten bread and butter' while at baptisms and marriages 'the best fare which the country can produce is provided for the priests and the select guests'. The same was provided on Sundays when the priest was invited to dinner by 'some of the decent people'.[22] The wedding dinner 'generally consisted of mutton, salt pork, bacon and poultry, with an abundance of potatoes and common garden vegetables.'[23] While they had 'a good many fowl, and plenty of eggs' these were for sale only and chickens and ducks were sold to pay for salt, soap and candles. These items made an important contribution to the family economy.[24]

Health

In spite of the almost exclusively vegetarian diet of the ordinary people, or perhaps because of it, the people were 'in general tolerably healthy'.[25] One commentator on Co Sligo in 1739 thought the people there resembled Spaniards, 'tall and slender with fine limbs, grave countenances, long dark eyebrows and lank dark hair'. It was said of the locals who flocked to join the French in Killala in 1798 that 'the far greater part of these mountaineers were by no means deficient either in size or in person'. The O'Dowds of Bonniconlon were particularly famous for their tall stature and their gigantic bones

---

19 In the late eighteenth century salmon sold in Ballina for three-halfpence a pound. In 1815 the price was tenpence to a shilling.
20 In Coolavin, it was usually a goose. IFC, Ms. 680
21 Henry Morris, 'St Martin's Eve', *Béaloideas,* Iml. ix, uimh. 11, pp. 230–5
22 Neligan, op. cit., p. 378
23 Bell, p. 18
24 Neligan, p. 362; Young, op. cit., (1892 edition) vol. 1, p. 445. In Newport in 1752, chickens sold at a penny a piece, fat ducks for twopence and turkeys and fat geese for sixpence. *Bishop Pocockes's Irish Tour,* p. 84. By 1815 chickens in Kilmactigue fetched three to four pence, geese a shilling to 1s. 4d., and turkeys from 1s. 8d. to 2s. 2d. But 1815 was the year that prices collapsed and these items would have fetched nearly double these prices in the immediately preceding years.
25 Neligan, op. cit., p. 367

could be seen in the family burial place in Moyne Abbey where it was calculated that 'one of them exceeded seven feet in height'.²⁶

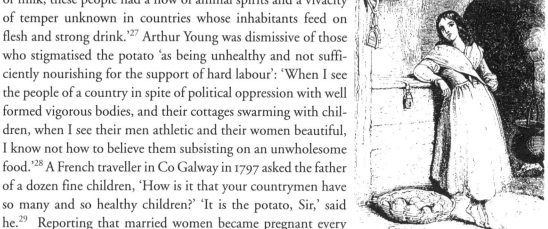

Young woman in cabin
(Mr & Mrs S. C. Hall, *Ireland*)

Others commented favourably on the health of the people: 'Living for the most part on vegetable food, and with scarcely any other beverage than water or milk, these people had a flow of animal spirits and a vivacity of temper unknown in countries whose inhabitants feed on flesh and strong drink.'²⁷ Arthur Young was dismissive of those who stigmatised the potato 'as being unhealthy and not sufficiently nourishing for the support of hard labour': 'When I see the people of a country in spite of political oppression with well formed vigorous bodies, and their cottages swarming with children, when I see their men athletic and their women beautiful, I know not how to believe them subsisting on an unwholesome food.'²⁸ A French traveller in Co Galway in 1797 asked the father of a dozen fine children, 'How is it that your countrymen have so many and so healthy children?' 'It is the potato, Sir,' said he.²⁹ Reporting that married women became pregnant every second year for twelve years, Arthur Young exclaimed, *Vive la pomme de terre!* ('Hurrah for the potato').³⁰

The potato probably also accounted for the 'wonderful teeth' of the people in Oranmore that the French consul noticed with surprise.³¹ Because of their vegetarian diet their teeth probably fared much better than those of the upper classes. Bishop Philip Philips (1776–85) was described to Rome as 'toothless' and as such unsuitable for the vacant diocese of Tuam.³² His Protestant counter-

Teeth

---

26   Henry, Nat. Arch., M 2533, p. 1; Stock, p. 18; Musgrave, *Memoirs of the different Rebellions in Ireland*. Another traveller wrote later, 'they possess in general personal beauty and vigour of frame'. He considered the peasants, male and female, in Co Roscommon, particularly handsome, 'the former are tall and fair and possess great flexibility of muscle; the men are the best leapers in Ireland'. Carr, *Tour*, pp. 247, 292
27   Bell, p. 17
28   op. cit., p. 185
29   De Latocnaye, op. cit., (1917 edition), p. 145. De Latocnaye was a French royalist officer, who fled to London at the end of 1792. He made a tour of England and Scotland, which was published in Edinburgh in 1797 as *Promenade d'un Français dans la Grande Bretagne*. In 1796–7 he undertook a similar tour of Ireland where he travelled on foot, carrying his baggage in his pockets or wrapped in his stockings and tied to the end of his sword-stick cum umbrella. In 1797 he published his notes in French, entitled *Promenade d'un Français dans l'Irlande*, which was translated in 1798 as *Rambles through Ireland*. Another edition by John Stevenson, entitled *A Frenchman's walk through Ireland, 1796-7*, appeared in 1917 and is the edition referred to here, unless otherwise stated.
30   op. cit., p. 147. Another visitor believed that the potato was 'very propitious to fecundity'. Curwen, *Observations on the State of Ireland*, p. 153
31   Ní Chinnéide, vol. 25, p. 6
32   SC Irlanda, vol. 15, f. 470v

parts suffered equally from early tooth decay. In May 1751 Bishop Edward Synge of Elphin informed his teenage daughter, Alicia, that he had just lost the last remaining tooth in his upper jaw and he was then only fifty-nine. Alicia herself was already suffering from toothaches and was threatened with having some extracted. 'I know by sad experience of what consequence it is to preserve teeth,' her father warned her, 'and without some such method taken, I fear yours will decay as your good mother's did and mine have done.' Dentistry was primitive and the cure was often worse than the ailment. Synge described to his daughter the unfortunate experience of one of his clergy, Rev William French from Frenchpark, who had a violent toothache and sent for a 'tooth operator' to pull the tooth. 'For the fellow first pulled out a sound tooth instead of the diseased one; and then in attempting to pull this out too, tore his jaw from his cheek.'[33]

Gout

Gout was another disorder which afflicted the upper classes. It took the form of swollen joints and was painful and disabling when it flared intermittently. In the eighteenth century it was believed to be caused by excessive consumption of food and drink.[34] Edward Synge suffered from it as did his brother, the Protestant Bishop of Killaloe. So did the Catholic Bishop of Achonry, Philip Philips.[35] It was a scourge from which the lower classes were spared.

Inoculation

Inoculation against smallpox was introduced in the 1770s and undoubtedly contributed to lowering the infant mortality rates. It was claimed in 1814 that it had saved the lives of thousands of children in Tourlestrane.[36] In 1797 a French tourist met 'a pleasant kind of fellow', on the road from Castlebar to Killala, who had been educated for the church but for economic reasons did not persevere. Instead, he became an inoculator and earned £30 to £40 a year. He had now been practising his trade in this area for more than thirty years and had inoculated 361 children that year, only one of whom had died. The Frenchman was impressed at how advanced the Irish were in this practice. 'On the continent I have seen not only peasants but persons in easy circumstances refuse to have their children inoculated.' England and Scotland were also trailing Ireland in the use of inoculation.[37]

Longevity

A 'dangerous malignant fever mostly of a typhus kind' which caused fatalities among the mountain dwellers was reported in Tourlestrane and attrib-

33 Marie-Louise Legg, *The Synge Letters*, pp. 282, 380–1, 384, 464, 469–70
34 In fact it was caused by a high level of uric acid in the blood, possibly from lead poisoning. Lead was used in many of the food containers of the period. Legg, op. cit., pp. 26, 72, 76–7
35 SC Irlanda, vol. 15, f. 470v
36 Neligan, p. 368
37 De Latocnaye, *Rambles through Ireland*, vol. 2, pp. 59–62

uted to the dampness of the mountain and contagion spread by the custom prevalent there of visiting the sick.[38] Lady Morgan also believed that 'the lower orders of Irish are very subject to dreadful fevers', which she thought resulted from colds caught by 'the exposed state of their damp and roofless hovels.'[39] Be that as it may, the phenomenal population growth, particularly in the latter half of the eighteenth century, suggests that many survived to a mature age. The widespread custom in the diocese of celebrating festive wakes on the occasion of deaths confirms this, as such festivities did not take place when young people died. Longevity was more common then than is popularly believed. Those of all classes for whom there are records, though admittedly few, lived to a ripe old age.[40]

'The cottages of the Irish, which are called cabins,' Arthur Young wrote in 1776, 'are the most miserable looking hovels that can well be conceived.' This poor impression was shared by most visitors to Ireland. 'Their huts are not like the houses of men,' a French traveller commented on those he saw in Co Galway in 1797, 'and yet out of them troop flocks of children, healthy and fresh as roses.'[41] Generally, they were mud huts, the walls made of mud kneaded with straw, two feet thick and six or seven feet high. Cabins varied from between 17 and 24 feet long and 13 to 15 feet wide.[42] They had neither chimneys nor windows. If there was a window, it consisted of 'a fracture in the side

Cabins (Cábáin)

Hovel near the foot of the Reek (Barrow, *Tour*)

---

38 Neligan, pp. 367–8
39 *The Wild Irish Girl*, vol. 2, p. 124n
40 Patrick Hart and his wife, 'peasants', in Kilmactigue died in their eighties. William Moore of Ballinacarrow, of the same class, was eighty-eight when he died. Both the Protestant vicar, James Neligan, and the Catholic parish priest of Kilmactigue, Dominick Kearney, were eighty-one. Other priests who lived to an advanced age were Thady O'Flaherty, PP of Kiltimagh and Patrick Knavesey, PP of Foxford. The parish priest of Charlestown (Kilbeagh), Edmund Kelly, was probably in his nineties when he died. Among the landlords, Charles O'Hara and Joshua Cooper were in their early seventies, while Charles O'Conor of Belanagare was in his eightieth year. Longevity was common elsewhere in the country such as in Co Kerry which was attested to by, among others, two priests and two medical doctors in the notarial files in Paris: 'Daniel MacCarthy of Bahught? who at the age of 77 married for the third time and had by his last wife ten children of which the last was born posthumously three months after the death of his father at 102.' AN MC et / 1 / 764
41 De Latocnaye, p. 145
42 'The walls of the poor huts are made of green or heathy sods,' one commentator described those in Mayo in 1802. McParlan, *Statistical Survey of Co Mayo*, pp. 70–1

Better sort of Connacht cabin (Barrow, *Tour*)

wall stuffed with straw'.[43] The door served to let in the light and let out the smoke. One traveller in Donegal in 1753 noticed that the cabins there had two doors, 'keeping one only open on the side that is not exposed to the wind'.[44] Cabins were sometimes excavated out of a hillock or high bank, with the roof supported on one or two sides by the hill or bank. The walls of better class cabins were made of stones and mortar while some had dry-stone walls, erected with loose stones, 'which, cunningly, were without mortar laid'.[45] Standards varied from cabin to cabin even in the same locality, like the two cabins almost side by side in Dromard, Co Sligo, 'the one wretched and ruinous, was raised with mud and thatched with sods; the other, well built and almost picturesque in its appearance, displayed all the neat comforts of an English cottage'.[46]

The roofs were usually thatched. Even as late as 1814 there were only three slated houses in the parish of Tourlestrane, two of which had been built within the previous ten years.[47] Rafters were laid across the top of the mud walls and were thatched with straw, potato stalks or heath.[48] Some roofs consisted of layers of sods of turf laid across the rafters and when the cabin was excavated out of a hillside, weeds often grew on the roof, where the family pig sometimes grazed.[49]

Furniture

Generally cabins consisted of one room, but sometimes two or even three rooms which included a kitchen and sleeping quarters.[50] Furniture was scanty and primitive. One traveller in Achill in 1752 was given a meal in a cabin there. The table was 'a long sort of stool about twenty inches high and broad and about two yards long' and the stools themselves were long and narrow. All the vessels were made of wood, most of them cut out of solid timber.

---

43 Lady Morgan, *The Wild Irish Girl*, vol. 1, p. 57
44 *Bishop Pococke's Irish Tour*, p. 63
45 Lady Morgan, *The Wild Irish Girl*, vol. 1, p. 56
46 Lady Morgan, *Patriotic Sketches*, vol. 2, p. 347. Neligan, op. cit., p. 356
48 Poor huts in Co Sligo were 'roofed with some rubbish of sticks, and thatched with heath, and straw or rushes in alternate layers.' McParlan, op. cit., pp. 70–71
49 Young, p. 187
50 A three-room cabin in Co Galway, costing five guineas in 1791, had a chimney, with the kitchen on one side of the chimney and on the other side a room for storing the potatoes and another in which all the family slept. Ní Chinnéide, op. cit., vol. 25, p. 10. A similar stone-walled, straw-thatched cabin in Co Sligo in 1802 also cost five guineas. Poorer cabins, with no chimney, cost thirty to forty shillings. McParlan, pp. 70–71

The candle consisted of several rushes twisted together, dipped in tallow and mounted on a slit stick, which was stuck into a large sod of turf as a base.[51] Cabins had an iron pot for boiling the potatoes and in Mayo and Sligo there was at least one spinning wheel with a low three-legged stool for the spinner.

There were, however, even as early as 1776, numerous better furnished cabins: 'I have been in a multitude of cabins that had much useful furniture, and some even superfluous: chairs, tables, boxes, chests of drawers, earthenware, and in short most of the articles found in a middling English cottage, but upon enquiry, I very generally found that these acquisitions were all made within the last ten years, a sure sign of a rising national prosperity.'[52]

Beds were rare and whole families slept together on the straw-covered earthen floor under a great woollen blanket in a cabin also occupied by poultry and farm animals. In Sligo 'as in all the counties of Ireland, the brute and human beings inhabit the same huts'. One traveller thought the Irish cabin resembled 'a little antideluvian ark'. The French consul, who found a night's accommodation in an 'inn' on the road from Ballina to Sligo, wrote: 'lodged with all the animals like Noah in his ark.' Some years later, another Frenchman, who shared a cabin in Co Waterford with a poor woman, half a dozen children, a pig, a dog, a cat, two hens and a duck, 'felt as if transported to the ark', and felt like Noah. Lady Morgan visited a Sligo cabin on a summer's evening before the family had gone to bed and she noticed that one of the older boys, worn out with fatigue, 'lay stretched on some straw in the corner

Four-handled madder (Wood-Martin, *Sligo*)

Three-legged armchair (Wood-Martin, *Sligo*)

Worst sort of Mayo stone cabin (Barrow, *Tour*)

51   Bishop Pocock's *Irish Tour*, p. 87
52   Young, p. 188: In 1816 the stone-walled, straw-thatched cabins of the cottiers in Glenavy, Co Antrim, were amply furnished with two chaff beds and bed clothes, three to six stools and chairs, one or two looms and spinning wheels, one or two metal pots, a small table or two, one or two boxes or chests, a small quantity of earthen or tin ware, one or two wooden bowls or dishes, a small number of wooden vessels, such as a tub, a piggin, a can, two or three noggins and a few knives and horn spoons. Shaw Mason, vol. 2, p. 246

Rush-light holder (Wood-Martin, *Sligo*)

of the cabin, the head of a calf actually reposing on his arm, and the parent cow quietly slumbering at his feet'.[53]

Arthur Young was amazed at the quantities of pigs and poultry he found everywhere in Ireland, which he attributed to the potatoes on which they were fed and the warmth of the cabins where they were housed. The thick mud-walled cabins were much warmer than English cottages with their thin mortar walls, where 'a rat hole lets in the wind'. He believed the Irishman was much better off with a cow or a pig in his cabin, than the Englishman with 'a set of tea things' in his cottage, and regretted the introduction of pig styes into Ireland, because they excluded 'the poor pigs from the warmth of their master and mistress'.[54] He could have added that the humans would also have missed the animal warmth in their cabins.

But there was a downside too to the presence of poultry and animals in the cabins. Lice thrived and spread in such an environment, though it must be said that lice were also a problem in the tenements of towns and cities all over Europe in the eighteenth century. One traveller, obliged to seek shelter in a cabin from a heavy shower, found himself surrounded by poultry. 'The cocks and hens familiarly perched on my knees to be fed. They were so tame that I suppose they would have roosted in the same position.' He observed in Donegal 'that most of the common people, especially the children, in these parts had the itch'. Later, on a sunny day between Killeshandra and Granard, he noticed 'numbers of the fair-sex sitting before their doors with their heads in each other's laps, parting with their troublesome attendants'.[55] The French traveller, who had spent a night in a cabin, left in the morning 'with some rather unpleasant companions'. When he reached Dungarvan that evening, the first thing he did 'was to go and drown in the sea the good friends of Curraghmore who had become attached to my person'.[56]

While the animals shared the cabins with humans, their treatment otherwise was not always so idyllic. Apart from ploughing with horses by the tail, visitors to Ireland were appalled by two other practices they found there. Geese were plucked alive every year, as Arthur Young observed in several places, including in the neighbourhood of Westport. 'They made a dreadful ragged figure,' he commented.[57] It was 'a most painful sight' to another English visitor almost forty years later: 'I cannot conceive that any man has any

53 McParlan, pp. 70–71; Carr, pp. 151–2; Ní Chinnéide, op. cit., vol. 35, p. 63; De Latocnaye, p. 69; *Patriotic Sketches*, vol. 2, pp. 28ff
54 op. cit., pp. 188–9
55 Twiss, *A Tour in Ireland, 1775–6*, pp. 75–6, 89, 107
56 De Latocnaye, op. cit., p. 70
57 op. cit., (1892 edition), vol. 1, pp. 214, 259

Interior of one of the better kind of Irish cottages (Barrow, *Tour*)

right to subject these poor animals to torture in the barbarous manner I have seen in every part of Ireland.'[58] He thought that the sale of feathers must form an extensive branch of trade. In 1776 the feathers of one goose fetched a halfpenny or three-farthings. Goose-feathers were used as writing quills and boys on their way to school in Killasser used to ambush a goose and pluck feathers from it, to provide themselves with them.[59] Sheep suffered a similar fate as they were not sheared, their wool being pulled or plucked by hand.

Clothes

'The common Irish are in general clothed so very indifferently, that it impresses every stranger with a strong idea of universal poverty.'[60] Many visitors commented on the near nakedness of the country people. 'The nakedness of the poor near Galway is shocking,' according to a French traveller in 1797, and this was particularly the case with children, who were 'stark naked and often play before the doors of cabins without any kind of garment'.[61] The French consul had a similar experience in Co Sligo a few years earlier. 'The children of both sexes are naked or almost so, the girls covering themselves with a piece of cloth when they emerge from the cabins', and in Foxford he noticed that 'the majority of children of up to four or five years of age were completely naked or almost so'.[62] Most visitors to Ireland came in summertime and the nakedness of the children they observed may well have been a

58 Wakefield, *Ireland, Statistical and Political*, vol. 1, p. 358
59 IFC, Ms. 227, pp. 118–9 (Killasser)
60 Young, op. cit., p. 186; see the French impressions of the poverty in Killala in 1788, chapter two, p. 66
61 De Latocnaye, (1917 edition), p. 145
62 Ní Chinnéide, op. cit., vol. 35, pp. 60, 62

summer phenomenon, as in the case of the French consul who remarked that the 'heat was extreme'. It is hard to believe that these children would be frolicking naked out-of-doors in the depths of an Irish winter. Besides, it was recorded that little homespun frieze jackets were made for children by itinerant tailors in Co Sligo about the turn of the century.[63] One explanation of the nakedness of Irish children is an interesting comment on the priorities of the poorer Irish parents: 'An Irishman and his wife are much more solicitous to feed than to clothe their children; whereas in England it is surprising to see the expense they put themselves to, to deck out children whose principal subsistence is tea.'[64]

Home-wear

Countrymen wore thickset breeches, usually made of frieze or corduroy, which reached to the knees, where it was sometimes buttoned at the sides but more often left open. Breeches had a central opening, covered by a fall-down flap which was buttoned up at the waist. The better off wore breeches made of animal skin, such as buckskin, doeskin, goatskin or lambskin. The shirt or undergarment was made of linen and often 'composed of shreds and patches'.[65]

Sunday-wear

'Early on a Sunday morning a cabin, cleaner than usual, exhibits at its door a group very different in appearance from that it sheltered the preceding day. The lower Irish, passionately fond of dress and without the means of gratifying their dominant passion, confined their wishes to the hard-earned suit which the mass-house, or dance on Sunday, or the fair of their market-town affords an opportunity of displaying'.[66]

Knee-length yarn stockings were worn on these special occasions. Men's stockings began where the breeches ended and stopped just below half-way down the shins, leaving the feet uncovered. These soleless stockings were called 'triathian' (*troithín*).[67] Like all the other clothes, they were usually made at home, though they were sold in the markets in the barony of Gallen for 1s 1d at the end of the century.[68] A Frenchman who believed in travelling light adapted his silk stockings to this Irish fashion by cutting off the soles.[69] Men wore long waistcoats made of frieze or wool, sometimes lined with flannel. Jackets or coats were long-sleeved and knee-length and, unlike waistcoats which were buttoned, were generally left open. On their heads men wore a felt hat with high narrow crown with little or no rim.[70]

63   Lady Morgan, *Patriotic Sketches*, vol. 2, p. 28
64   Young, p. 187
65   Lady Morgan, *The Wild Irish Girl*, vol. 1, pp. 68–9
66   Lady Morgan, *Patriotic Sketches*, vol. 2, p. 93
67   Lady Morgan, *The Wild Irish Girl*, vol. 1, pp. 68–9
68   McParlan, p. 88
69   De Latocnaye, (1917 edition), p. vii
70   It cost 4s 4d in 1802

But their most important item of wear was the great coat, worn all the year round, in all seasons and weathers, 'in summer for show and for cold in winter.'[71] It was also the most expensive garment, costing sixteen shillings in the barony of Gallen at the turn of the century, though it was usually manufactured at home. 'Fathers of families and settled men never can imagine a suit complete or being decently dressed without a great coat.'[72] It was a long loose coat, usually blue and made of coarse frieze or wool and though it had sleeves, it was worn cloak-wise or 'in the Spanish fashion' and 'fastened on the breast with a large wooden skewer, the sleeves hanging down on either side unoccupied'.[73]

The Great Coat

The great coat was traditional Irish menswear, dating back for centuries and was eulogised by Edmund Spenser in the sixteenth century: 'It is a fit house for an outlaw, a meet bed for a rebel, and an apt cloak for a thief ... When it raineth, it is his penthouse; when it bloweth, it is his tent; when it freezeth, it is his tabernacle. In summer, he can wear it loose, in winter he can wrap it close: at all times he can use it; never heavy, never cumbersome ... when he ... lurketh in the thick woods ... it is his bed.'[74]

Women wore a bodice with elbow-length sleeves and a wool or quilted linen petticoat or skirt which was wide flowing and reached down to the lower leg and often coloured red or green. Lady Morgan described a group of them going to Mass in Co Sligo 'dressed in white gowns'.[75] Gowns were closed on top down to the waist, with skirts that flared from the waist down, revealing the petticoat. Women and girls wore long red mantles with hoods which they seldom used and older women wore headscarves of white or coloured linen, tied beneath the chin, which were called *binnogues (beannóg)*. Young girls only 'wore their native ornament of hair, which sometimes flows over their shoulders, sometimes is tied up in tresses with a pin or bodkin'. Lady Morgan's father, Robert Owenson, who lived as a youth in the vicinity of Collooney, 'a remote skirt of the province of Connaught', remembered seeing peasant women with their heads 'encircled with folds of linen in the form of a turban.'[76]

Womenswear

Unlike men, women seem to have changed their style in summertime. Sometimes they wore muslin bonnets instead of headscarves and shed their heavy red mantles and exchanged their woollen petticoats for white or striped

71 McParlan, *Statistical Survey of Co Mayo*, p. 88
72 McParlan, *Statistical Survey of Co Sligo*, p. 72
73 Lady Morgan, *The Wild Irish Girl*, vol. 1, pp. 68–9
74 quoted in Carr, pp. 43–4
75 *Patriotic Sketches*, vol. 2, p. 95
76 *The Wild Irish Girl*, vol. 1, pp. 86–7, 138–9, 139n

Peasant girl (Mr & Mrs S. C. Hall, *Ireland*)

Barefoot

linen skirts. They wore an apron or petticoat, tied round their necks and falling over their shoulders and down their backs in the form of a cape. A visitor to Foxford on a very hot market day in July 1779 was surprised at their appearance: 'I observed all the countrywomen who came to market, having their aprons about their necks, instead of cloaks; but on being amongst them in the market, we were surprised to find that to be their only upper covering, having neither gown nor shift, which we supposed was owing to the excessive heat of the weather.'[77]

A visitor to Boyle fair in 1813 thought 'the persons of these young women reflect beauty on their dress', a beauty 'which the most artful cannot counterfeit'. The French consul thought the 'black haired and bright-eyed' women at the fair in Loughrea in 1791 wore their muslin bonnets 'rather coquettishly', an opinion shared a few years later by a compatriot: 'There are few countries in which there are more pretty brunettes, in fact, the belles of Galway are capable of instructing the French ladies in coquettry.'[78] On his visit to Connacht he commented, 'the uglier the country, the handsomer the women'.

Footwear was seldom worn: 'Shoes or stockings are scarcely ever found on the feet of children; and great numbers of men and women are without them' which 'impresses every stranger with a strong idea of universal poverty'.[79] In fact, the expression 'naked or near-naked' used by many visitors to describe the dress or lack of it of the country people may have been due to their being barefoot. Men and women sometimes got their first pair of brogues for their wedding, almost as a symbol of adulthood. They wore them very sparingly thereafter apart from Sunday Mass, weddings, fairs and other such social occasions. Lady Morgan saw groups of women 'with their rug cloaks hanging on one arm, and their shoes and stockings on the other. When they approach the chapel, they bathe their feet in the first stream, and assume those articles of luxury which are never drawn on but for shew and the public gaze of the parish.'[80] The stream served 'the double purpose of reflecting their appear-

77 Wilde, *Gabriel Beranger*, pp. 58–9. Over thirty years later, another visitor noticed women similarly dressed: 'At Boyle fair, I found many of the girls had a petticoat tied double about their neck with a ribbon, so that while there was none of it before, the petticoat flowed down the back and about the shoulders, like a lady's mantle.' Hall, *Ireland*, vol. 2, p. 52
78 Ní Chinnéide, op. cit., vol. 25, p. 3; De Latocnaye, vol. 2, pp. 22, 24
79 Young, p. 186
80 *Patriotic Sketches*, vol. 2, p. 95

ance and washing their feet'.[81] Stockings and brogues were removed again when Mass was over as most people probably found them very uncomfortable.

Brogues

The brogues of the poorer classes were quite distinct from the shoes worn by the better off. The brogue was a type of loose-fitting clog with a low back heel, into which they slipped their foot. As their stockings had no soles, they often stuffed the brogues with straw and for this reason had them made large-fitting.[82] Brogues had a square toe, leather uppers and a thick blocked heel of wood covered with leather. More perceptive visitors saw some virtue in Irish country people remaining barefoot. 'I consider it as no evil but a much more cleanly custom than the bestiality of stockings and feet that are washed no oftener than those of our own (English) poor.'[83] The French consul who admired the coquettry of the women in their bare feet at the Loughrea fair, remarked: 'I think that in time people will come to regard the custom of wearing shoes as ridiculous.'[84]

Improvements

Clothing in general improved in the second half of the eighteenth century, and more particularly at the beginning of the following, and it became rare to meet a person at a fair 'wanting shoes or stockings'. In 1816 one observer wrote of the people in Donegal: 'Their dress has improved considerably within the last fifteen years; and there are few men who have not shoes and stockings and few women who do not occasionally wear muslin gowns, with hats and bonnets.'[85] In Roscommon there was 'a considerable improvement especially observable in the females' and with the importation of cheap cottons into the country, they began to 'vie with their wealthier neighbours'.[86] In the barony of Costello 'clothing (was) very good: the men wear friezes and some a finer cloth, thickset breeches and red coating and press cloth waistcoats; the women too are neatly dressed, many of them in cottons and red cloaks'. In the neighbouring barony of Gallen, men and women appeared 'clean and decent on Sundays' and their homemade clothes consisted of 'friezes, flannels, druggets, thicksets, cottons, stuffs and baizes',[87] while in Sligo 'most of the

81 Shaw Mason, op. cit., vol. 3, pp. 25, 345
82 ibid, vol. 1, p. 49; vol. 3, pp. 72, 491
83 Young, p. 187
84 Ní Chinnéide, op. cit., vol. 25, p. 3
85 Shaw Mason, op. cit., vol. 2, p. 156
86 ibid, pp. 114, 156, 246. In Wexford, the improvement took place immediately after the 1798 rebellion and 'seems to have grown out of it'. There, the people were 'very neatly and fashionably dressed; the females in cotton gowns with short backs and long flowing skirts, black beaver hats or nice straw bonnets of their own making, white stockings and flat-heeled leather shoes; the men in cloth coats, white waistcoats and stockings, yellow pantaloons and beaver hats.'
87 ibid, p. 88

Fairs and Markets

young and the trades-people wear red and striped waistcoats of finer quality than frieze, corduroy breeches and worsted or cotton stockings'.[88]

People wore their Sunday best when they attended the fairs which were gala days on the social calendar. Fairs were held on fixed days annually in designated villages or 'towns', nine in the Sligo section of the diocese and a further six in the Mayo section. The number of fairs held in each place annually varied from one in Aclare to seven in Ballaghaderreen and Tubbercurry.[89] Larger markets were held just outside the diocesan boundaries, such as at Sligo, Castlebar, Ballina and Boyle, and the inhabitants of adjacent Achonry parishes attended.

The vast majority of fairs were held from May to December, although there were three, Banada, Bellaghy and Tubbercurry, which held fairs in January, and a further three held in February, in Ballymote, Ballaghaderreen and Carracastle. These earlier fairs may have had a social rather than an economic significance. Weddings usually took place in the early months before Lent and there is a tradition in Killasser that 'at Candlemas fair (1 February) they'd be getting the women'. The same source described the July fair as '*aonach na ngasúr*' ('the lads' fair'), where the men were 'drinking and squandering and coming home at all hours of the night'.[90]

Fairs and markets were far more than social occasions. Important business transactions were carried on, with the family economy often depending on them. Women sold butter, eggs, fowl, feathers and, of course, yarn. Yarn and unmanufactured flax, when sold, made up half the rent while half of the oats raised was also sold and provided the rest of the rent.[91] The small cottier often killed the calf after it dropped so that his wife would have milk to make butter. In 1815 such a calf sold for four to five shillings. The little tenant farmer had a foal for sale every year, for which he got eight to ten guineas, and a two- or three-year-old cow worth three to five guineas. All had pigs for sale and they sold for a guinea each. Linens were sold at weekly markets in Collooney, Ballymote, Ballina and Sligo. Purchases were also made, such as oatmeal in the summer when the potatoes ran out and, in winter, dried herrings to supplement the family diet. Sixpenny popular novels were peddled by itin-

88 McParlan, *Mayo*, pp. 90, 88; *Sligo*, p. 72
89 Sligo: Ballinacarrow (4), Ballymote (4), Ballisodare (2), Banada (2), Bellaghy (4), Bunninadden (4), Collooney (6), Templehouse and Tubbercurry (7). Mayo: Aclare (1), Ballaghaderreen (7), Caracastle (3), Foxford (4), Straide (4) and Swinford (4). McParlan, *Sligo*, pp. 26–9; *Mayo*, pp. 47–51
90 IFC, Ms. 114, pp. 365–6
91 Large quantities of oats and potatoes from the barony of Gallen were sold at the Castlebar market.

erant hawkers and used by children as schoolbooks and the egg-money paid for tobacco for the adults.

Faction fights occasionally took place at fairs, though they were also associated with patterns. 'Our county (is) quiet,' Tobias Caulfield, vicar of Ballisodare, informed Kean O'Hara in 1713, 'except some battles at Ballimote fair between the Lynians (inhabitants of Leyny) and the Corinthians (inhabitants of Corran) in which both suffered at the eyes and nose'.[92]

Faction fights

The battle was most commonly preceded by a challenge. Some fellow, whose bodily strength, whose boisterous and ferocious temper, gave him such an ascendancy over others as to be chosen their leader, would come forth and, flourishing his cudgel over his head, bid defiance to all who did not belong to his clan, parish, barony or county. A champion on the adverse side would instantly rush forward to meet him. Their followers soon joined them and the engagement became general.[93]

Faction fight
(Mr & Mrs S. C. Hall, *Ireland*)

These encounters resembled 'pitch battles, fought with cudgels by parties not only of parishes, but of counties, set in formal array against each other'.[94]

The Protestant vicar of Kilmactigue strongly disapproved of what he called the 'propensity highly injurious' of the parishioners attending fairs and markets where they had no business to transact. 'From these they seldom return without laying out some part of their small means for whiskey, which

92 O'Hara Papers, Ms. 20, 388
93 Bell, op. cit., p. 21
94 Shaw Mason, op. cit., p. 73

often produces rioting and fighting.'⁹⁵ Some faction fights were arranged well in advance. The French consul heard of a faction fight between two clans at a fair near Portumna in 1788 which had been planned a month beforehand. The contenders consisted of fifty on each side and one party had already been put to flight when the troops arrived to break up the fight.⁹⁶

Sport

Sporting activities among the lower classes were exclusively confined to Sundays and holydays which, fortunately, were fairly numerous. In summertime after Mass 'they adjourn to the fields to witness a hurling match, or some of those manly sports to which the lower Irish are so passionately addicted'. These included wrestling, jumping and weight-throwing.⁹⁷ The French consul left a fairly detailed description of how hurling, which he called 'Behare' (*báire*), was played in Galway in 1791.

> Each team is divided into three divisions, *l'arrière* or back guards the goal and seeks to stop the ball from passing through; another group is in the front to prevent the enemy's ball from coming back from that end, that is the middle, the third called the 'whip' is *sur le terrain* ... The ball is of cow's hair, very compact and covered with leather ... The sides are distinguished by the colour of their caps. It is terrifying to see the way they rush against each other to force the ball to pass under the goal.⁹⁸

He also said that hurling was only played in Munster and Connacht, usually on a dried-out swamp or marsh called a 'turlagh' (*turloch*).

Dancing

Music and dancing was always associated with these gatherings and dancing often took the form of competitions, with the 'cake dance' especially popular in Connacht.⁹⁹ The cake was usually provided by the local sheebeen and the music by a local piper. The French consul noticed outside the door of a tavern in Athenry 'a large cake decorated with a bouquet' which he was informed was a prize for the best dancer.¹⁰⁰ A visitor in Co Sligo in 1779 attended a cake dance on the shores of Lough Gill which was also attended by some of the better-off in the neighbourhood: 'The scene was pleasing – gentlemen and ladies, on horseback and on foot, mixed with the country people and formed a triple ring round the dancers, whilst a fellow standing on some bench or barrel held up a pole at the end of which the cake was hung in a clean napkin, adorned with ribbands, to be given as a prize to the best performers.'¹⁰¹

95 Neligan, p. 364
96 Ní Chinnéide, op. cit., vol. 25, pp. 3–4
97 Lady Morgan, *Patriotic Sketches,* vol. 2, p. 93
98 Ní Chinnéide, op. cit., vol. 25, p. 11
99 see Séamus Ó Duilearga, 'The Cake Dance', *Béaloideas,* uimh. 1–11, pp. 126–42
100 Ní Chinnéide, vol. 25, p. 5
101 Wilde, op. cit., p. 40

In winter the dances took place in the evening either in a sheebeen or other house where a member of the family was a musician. 'Hardly any part of a peasant's family remained at home on a Sunday evening; and in winter they would often go a distance of three or four miles, through swamps and bogs, to any place where a considerable number of people are assembled.'[102] The old sat around smoking their pipes and drinking whiskey, while the young danced the night away. Itinerant dancing masters, accompanied by a blind piper or fiddler, went from house to house teaching the children how to dance, for which they were paid sixpence a quarter. A wide range of dances were taught. 'Besides the Irish jig, which they can dance with a most luxuriant expression, minuets and country dances are taught; and I even heard of cotillions coming in.'[103]

What Arthur Young found in Munster in 1776 was mirrored in Tourlestrane almost forty years later. 'Dancing makes a considerable part of their entertainment and is considered as a necessary accomplishment amongst them; and hundreds who have never learned their alphabet, or spoken a word of English, have regularly attended the dancing schools, and, at no small expense, become adepts in that science.'[104] In the summer of 1813 a touring Protestant clergyman encountered, near Ballisodare, a party of teenage girls returning from the bog, carrying creels of turf on their back. The girls, intrigued by the umbrella the clergyman used to shield himself from the sun, stopped, laid down their creels and spontaneously performed a dance for him in their bare feet. The surprised tourist was duly impressed and 'threw about a dozen of half-pence among them to buy pins'.[105]

Singing

'The Irish peasant indeed still retains an idolatrous fondness for those strains his ear has learnt from his heart.'[106] Standards in the art of singing were fairly high and people were fond of the old songs 'which they execute with great correctness, as many of them have sweet and melodious voices, well adapted to these melancholy and plaintive strains'.[107] Songs, such as *An Chúil-fhionn (The Coolin), The Dawning of the Day, Eibhlín a Rúin (Eileen Aroon), Ceann Dubh Dílis (Sweet Dark-haired), Éamonn an Chnuic (Eamonn of the Hill)* etc, were well known and widely sung. According to Charles O' Conor of Belanagare, Handel said that he would rather have been the author

---

102 Bell, op. cit., p. 20. 'Dancing is very general among the poor people, almost universal in every cabin.' Young, p. 153
103 Young, pp. 153, 202
104 Neligan, pp. 361–2
105 Hall, op. cit., vol. 2, pp. 62–3
106 Lady Morgan, *Patriotic Sketches*, vol. 1, p. 151
107 Neligan, op. cit., p. 362

of *Eileen Aroon* than of the most exquisite of his musical compositions. It was an ancient air with seventeenth-century words. *The Coolin*, with words dating from the mid-seventeenth century, was esteemed by some to be the finest air in the whole repertoire of Irish music.[108] *Barbaro*, whose date of origin is uncertain, was particularly popular in the Mayo-Sligo border parishes. Other songs were local, such as *Condae Mhaigheo (County Mayo), Béal na hAmhnais (Ballyhaunis),* and *Mary of Meelick*.

It was not unusual for people to sing while they worked and singing while spinning gave rise to a whole new genre, the spinning-song. Other craftworkers also sang tunes in accompaniment to their work. Such a song caught the ear of Lady Morgan as she and her friends were passing a cabin in Co Sligo, late one evening: 'It was the song of an itinerant taylor; he was seated in the centre of the earthen floor, working by the light of a rush, and surrounded by a group of children, who were hanging delightedly on his song and watching with eagerness the progress of the little frieze jackets, spun by their mother, and now in the hands of the musical taylor, while their parents, released from the labours of hire, were working by the light of the moon in their little garden.'[109]

Úna Bhán

Visitors were particularly impressed by the music-loving Irish and their songs: 'The peasantry are uncommonly attached to their ancient melodies, some of which are exquisitely beautiful.'[110] Unoubtedly, *Úna Bhán*, a seventeenth-century love song which had its origins in the diocese, was the local favourite. 'I do not think there is any love song more widely spread throughout the country and more common in the mouth of the people than the poem which Tomás Láidir composed over the unfortunate and handsome girl, Una MacDermot, to whom he had given his love.'[111] Tomás Láidir was one of the Costellos of Tullaghanmore (Edmondstown) between Ballaghaderreen and Coolavin, while Una was one of the MacDermots of Moylurg. The MacDermots were not keen on the love match as they had a wealthier suitor in mind for Una who had her heart set on Tomás. But her family prevailed and she died of a broken heart and was buried on an island in Lough Key. When Tomás died he too was buried on the island 'and there grew an ash-tree out of Una's grave and another tree out of the grave of Costello, and they inclined towards one another, and they did not cease from growing until

---

108 Hardiman, *Irish Minstrelsy*, vol. 1, pp. 328–9
109 *Patriotic Sketches*, vol. 2, pp. 28ff
110 Carr, op. cit., p. 253
111 Douglas Hyde, *Love Songs of Connacht*; see also Dermot MacDermot, *MacDermot of Moylurg*, Appendix 7, pp. 514–19, and Máire McDonnell-Garvey, *Mid-Connacht*, pp. 31–4

the two tops were met and bent upon one another in the middle of the graveyard.'

The song, with its forty-four verses, is not a ballad as it was customary for the singer to recount the story before beginning his song. The song itself expresses the composer's love for Una.

> Tá an Bhothuille faoí bhrón
> Is Máigh Luirg ar fad
> Ó d'éag an Péarla, plúr na mban;
> In Oileán na Naomh
> I Loch Cé na mbád is na mbarc
> Tá sínte i gcré
> Ó an déighbhean
> Mo rún is mo shearc.
>
> The Boyle is saddened
> And all of Moylurg
> Since the Pearl of all women died;
> In Saints Island
> In Lough Key of the boats and ships
> The goodly lady, my darling and love,
> Lies in the clay.[112]

MacDermot's Castle. Lough Key, Co Roscommon (*Dublin Penny Journal*)

Music Playing

It was said of *Úna Bhán* 'that there was never yet found a piper or a fiddler to play it on the pipes or the fiddle!' But such musicians were common. In the earlier part of the century they played the harp, but in later years it 'fell into almost total disuse.'[113] It was a cumbersome instrument for itinerant musicians to carry and, with the impoverishment of the native Irish, it was not possible for most of them to keep a horse necessary for this purpose. In fact, in the older better times, itinerant harpers employed a boy with a second horse to carry their harp. In that period, both boys and girls in well-off families learned to play the harp and it was said that 'Connacht was the best part of the kingdom for Irish music and for harpers.'[114] The most common musical instrument became 'a bag-pipe on a different but superior construction to that of the Scotch Highlanders.'[115] Instrument-makers could be found in

---

112 As in Máire McDonnell-Garvey, op. cit., p. 33
113 Bell, p. 17
114 Interview of the Bard of the Magilligans by Rev Mr Sampson, 3 July 1805, quoted in Lady Morgan, *The Wild Irish Girl*, vol. 3, p. 98n
115 It was actually played by a Mr O'Farrell at a Covent Garden concert during the 1803–4 season. Bell, op. cit., p. 17 & n

Irish piper
(Mr & Mrs
S. C. Hall, *Ireland*)

'many of the smallest towns in Ireland and generally among men of the lowest professions.'[116] The fiddle does not seem to have been as common as it later became.

The frequency with which reference is made to blind musicians at this period suggests that it was not simply coincidental. The Irish then had a more enlightened attitude towards people with disabilities. *Duine dílis le Dia* ('one of God's special people') was used to describe those who were mentally retarded. Disabled children were directed towards occupations where they would not be affected by their disability, which explains why tailors and cobblers were so often lame. Blindness was a more common affliction in the eighteenth century and parents, whose child was blind, often encouraged it to become a musician, thus providing a secure and respected profession for their child. An instrument was acquired and a music teacher paid to instruct the child in the art.

'O'Carolan Country'

Turlough O'Carolan (1670–1738) was the most famous blind musician of the period. Born in Co Meath, his father moved, when Turlough was a child, to Co Rosommon where he was employed by the MacDermottroe family. Mrs MacDermottroe took a special interest in the young Turlough and when he became at eighteen totally blind, as a result of small-pox, she had him trained

116 Lady Morgan, *Patriotic Sketches*, vol. 1, p. 159

as a harper. It was a providential decision as O'Carolan was to become one of Ireland's great composers.[117]

Once he had mastered his art, which he did in record time, he took to the roads as an itinerant harper on a horse provided him by his patroness. His travels brought him to Achonry diocese, where he became a frequent and much welcomed visitor for the rest of his life. In fact, the diocese became the heart of what was later called 'O'Carolan country'. Musicians were much in demand by all classes and a harper of O'Carolan's calibre had easy entrée into the best houses. Love of music was shared by all classes in Ireland. 'The ladies of Ireland are more highly accomplished in instrumental than in vocal music; a greater musical treat can scarcely be enjoyed than to hear some of them perform their own Irish airs, which are singularly sweet, simple and affecting.'[118] Such ladies of the manor were eager to play hostess to the blind harper and in return were often immortalised by a song composed in their honour. Nancy Cooper, Kitty O'Hara, Mrs Crofton, Dolly McDonogh, Peggy Corcoran and Nancy O'Hart were just a few of the women so honoured.

Turlough O'Carolan (*Irish Lives*)

O'Carolan's compositions read like a Who's Who of Achonry diocese. Both he and his music moved easily through the religious barrier and he was entertained equally by Protestant landlords like the O'Haras of Annaghmore, the Coopers of Markrea, and the Brabazons of Swinford, and by Catholics like the O'Harts of Cloonamahon, the O'Conors of Belanagare and the MacDermots of Coolavin. *Seán Ó Háirt* was composed in honour of John O'Hart, the parish priest of Ballisodare who later became Bishop of Achonry (1735-39). Annaghmore, the home of the O'Haras, was a favourite house on O'Carolan's itinerary. Kean O'Hara (1657-1719) was fond of drink, horse-racing, music and gambling, with no particular preferences. *Cupán Uí Eaghra* expresses O'Carolan's appreciation of Kean's generous hand with the brandy bottle and is the composer's toast to Kean 'as that cup goes around'. George Brabazon was another generous host and O'Carolan's visits there are commemorated by his planxty, *Seoirse Brabson*.

While O'Carolan was usually entertained in the big house, the news of his

117 On O'Carolan, see D. O'Sullivan, *Carolan: Life, Times and Music of an Irish Harper*; J. C. McTernan, 'O'Carolan and his Sligo Patrons', in *Olde Sligoe*, pp. 118–28; J. Hardiman, *Irish Minstrelsy*; Tomás Ó Máille, *Amhráin Chearbhalláin*, (Irish Texts Society, 1916)
118 Carr, p. 253

arrival in a locality became quickly known among the lower classes. 'It is impossible to describe the joy that used to sparkle on the countenances of those rustics on the arrival of an itinerant performer of celebrity among them'.[119] His music was widely known and frequently played among them. Music was learned by ear and passed on from one musician to another in the traditional fashion and almost eighty years after O'Carolan's death, his memory as well as his music was still very much alive. In 1817, James Filan, parish priest of Curry, wrote of Bishop O'Hart: 'His praises were sung by our national bard Carolan.'[120] O'Carolan's death in 1738 inspired a lament by the Kilshalvey poet, Seán Ó Gadhra.[121]

Raiftearaí

Anthony Raftery was born on 30 March 1779 in Killedan, near Kiltimagh.[122] His father came there from Keash, Co Sligo, and was employed as a weaver by the Taaffes in Killedan House. Afflicted with smallpox as a child, Anthony was the only one of nine children to survive the disease but he became blind as a result. As a youth he enjoyed the patronage of Frank Taaffe and entertained visitors to Killedan House with his story-telling, music and poetry. He left Killedan as a young man, probably to earn his living as a wandering minstrel. The rest of his short life was spent in Co Galway. He was married to a woman called Siobhán and had two children, a boy and a girl, but Raftery separated from his family early in the marriage. He died in Craughwell on Christmas night 1835.

Over fifty poems and songs of Raftery have survived. This itself is a tribute to his extraordinary popularity since none of these was written down by Raftery. They survived in the oral tradition of the people. The themes and dedications of these poems are remarkably similar to those of O'Carolan. Many were composed in honour of women, such as Máire Ní Eidhin, Máirín Staunton, Úna Ní Chatháin, Peigí Mitchell, etc. One was composed about a priest, An tAthair Liam Ó Dushláine, parish priest of Clarinbridge. One of the best known, *Cill Liadáin*, eulogises his birthplace.

Cill Liadáin an baile a bhfásann gach ní ann,
tá sméara, sú craobh ann is meas ar gach sórt;
is dá mbeinnse i mo sheasamh ann i gceartlár mo dhaoine,
d'imeodh an aois díom is bheinn arís óg.

---

119 Bell, op. cit., p. 17
120 SC Irlanda, vol. 20, f. 127v
121 *Dánta is amhráin Sheáin Uí Ghadhra*
122 On Raftery see Ciarán Ó Coigligh, *Raiftearaí: Amhráin agus Dánta*.

Killedan is the place where everything grows,
there are blackberries, raspberry-trees and all kinds esteemed;
If I was standing in the middle of my people
Old age would vanish and I'd be once again young.

Raftery mirrors the strong religious spirituality of his time and place.

Mar is iomdha sagart, easpag is pápa
ag agairt ar Dhia, bean rialta is bráthair,
ach b'fhéidir go n-éistfí an fear ba táire
a shilfeadh le mian, ach a chroí a bheith cráite.

Though priests of hope, with nun and friar
And bishop and Pope pray prayers of fire,
God hears the sigh of the meanest spoken
who pours his cry from a heart half-broken.

He was keenly aware of the dissolute life he led, which he described in a poem he composed three years before his death.

Anthony Raftery
(Royal Irish Academy)

Nuair a bhí mé óg b'olc mo thréithe,
ba mhór mo spéis i scléip is in achrann,
b'fearr liom go mór imirt is ól,
ná maidin Domhnaigh triall chun Aifrinn.

Níorbh fhearr liom suí le cailín óg,
ná bean phósta a éileamh tamall,
do mhionnaí móra, bhí mé tabhartha,
agus drúis ná póit níor lig mé tharam.

When I was young my ways were evil,
Caught by the devil I went astray,
On sacred mornings I sought not Mass,
But I sought alas! to drink and play.

Married or single, grave or gay,
Each in her way was loved by me,
I shunned not the senses' sinful sway,
I shunned not the body's mastery.[123]

Story-telling was another favourite pastime, particularly among the older people. 'After the labours of the day they never sat looking at each other in

Story-telling

---

[123] Irish texts from Ó Coigligh, op. cit., pp. 44, 70, 74; English verse translations by Douglas Hyde, *The Religious Songs of Connacht*, vol. I, pp. 233, 243, 245

sulky silence; the aged would smoke one after another out of the same pipe, and entertain each other with stories.'[124] Often these stories were didactic, offering explanations for traditional customs, such as smoking tobacco at wakes or the origin of local holy wells or strange place-names. Many had religious overtones and some a subtle strain of anticlericalism. Money-loving priests were often the targets of these tales.

The Friars of Urlaur

One of the best known stories that has survived from the locality is *The Friars of Urlaur*.[125] It is set in the Dominican friary on the shores of Urlaur lake in the parish of Kilmovee where the devil, in the form of a big black boar, appeared in the lake. The friars resorted to prayer to rid themselves of their terrifying visitor, but the boar arrived in their midst, 'opened its mouth and cast out a litter of bonhams'. The prior tried sprinkling the monster with holy water but without success and the bishop was sent for. He informed the prior that there was 'a limb of the devil in the shape of a friar' among them but that he would smoke out the imposter. A visiting friar from the north had arrived recently and had been admitted without question. Confronted by the bishop, he turned out to be the devil in a friar's habit, whereupon he jumped into the lake where he joined his colleague. The bishop rebuked the prior because he could not tell the 'devil from a friar'. The bishop himself failed to banish the monster and when he tried, the monster informed him that he was once his pet hound, whom the bishop fed with meat that he refused to give to 'the poor people who were weak with hunger'. The monster and his companion began to screech loudly and continued without stopping so that the friars became deaf. 'And from that day to this the old saying is in the mouth of the people, "You're as deaf as a friar of Urlaur."'

Finally, the friars had reached the end of their tether and were on the point of packing up and quitting their friary when one night they had a collective dream. A woman clothed in white linen appeared to them and told them that there was only one person who could banish the devil, Donagh O'Grady, a piper from Tavraun, 'who did more good than all the priests and friars in the country'. O'Grady was sent for and was found half-drunk in a local sheebeen which he refused to leave until he had drunk another couple of noggins. When at last he reached Urlaur the prior asked what good deeds he had done in his life, to which O'Grady replied, none that he could remember. Finally, he admitted reluctantly that he once gave a tenpenny to a neighbour's child, a girl whose need was so great she threatened to sell herself for the money. She later gave up the world and became a saint and it was she

---

124 Bell, op. cit., p. 17
125 Douglas Hyde, *Legends of Saints and Sinners*, pp. 127–35

Urlaur Abbey
(Grose, *Antiquities*)

who appeared as the woman in white in the friars' dream. The piper duly played to the black boar and his companion and as he played a bolt of lightening came from the sky and struck the devil's dead. 'The piper died a happy death, and it was the opinion of the people that he went to heaven, and that it may be so with us all !'

Character of the people

Contemporary observers generally commented favourably on the qualities of the country people, and particularly their courtesy impressed strangers. 'Their native urbanity to each other is very pleasing; I have frequently seen two boors take off their hats and salute each other with great civility.'[126] A French traveller in Connemara was greeted by a group of men there who took off their hats and bowed to the ground.[127] Their expressions of gratitude were also effusive as the French consul found in the neighbourhood of Foxford. 'The Irish have a very vigorous way of expressing their gratitude. One never does them a favour in vain.'[128]

Many commented on the intelligence of the people. 'The lower Irish are remarkable for their ingenuity and docility and a quick perception. Their ingenuity had often to fill the void left by the absence of the most basic tools and implements and as one observer remarked they showed 'great fertility in expedients.'[129] 'It is curious to see with what scanty materials they will work;

126 Carr, pp. 251, 292
127 De Latocnaye, vol. 2, p. 52; see also, McParlan, *Mayo*, p. 94
128 *'Les Irlandais ont une manière fort energique d'exprimer leur gratitude et ce n'est jamais en vain qu'on les oblige.'* Ní Chinnéide, vol. 35, p. 61
129 'The innate civility and intelligence of the lower orders have frequently made me ashamed of the prejudices I had so incautiously imbibed to their disadvantage.' Curwen, op. cit., vol. 2, pp. 276, 350

they build their own cabins, and make bridles, stirrups, cruppers and ropes of every rustic purpose, from hay.'[130] All agreed that the Irish were industrious and hard working, and 'in England, an Irish labourer is always preferred'.[131]

Surprisingly, given their abject poverty and the oppressiveness of the laws imposed on them, they were a relatively happy people. 'They are infinitely more cheerful and lively than anything we commonly see in England, having nothing of that incivility of sullen silence with which so many Englishmen seem to wrap themselves up, as if retiring within their own importance.'[132] One visitor thought they were 'in gaiety of heart and genuine humour unrivalled'.[133] Another found 'a vivacity in the common people' which he attributed to their 'natural bouyancy of spirits, that makes the heaviest evils sit lightly on their hearts'.[134] Yet another commentator wrote: 'The happiness enjoyed by these simple rustics ... was such as those who live in polished societies might envy.'[135] His observation was corroborated in 1751 by the experience of Edward Synge, Protestant Bishop of Elphin. He set out on horseback before six o'clock in the morning on 15 July to ascertain the progress of his hay-mowers. There were eleven of them at work in his meadow in Elphin, Co Roscommon, and he found them 'as gay and cheerful in the midst of hard labour as the best of us, and happier far than multitudes who were at that hour sleeping on beds of down, or endeavouring to sleep. These delighted me much.' He returned later that evening at five o'clock, after a hearty dinner, and was regaled by 'more jokes from my jolly mowers'.[136] The gaiety of the girls carrying turf from a bog near Ballisodare induced the touring Protestant minister to remark: 'Had the girls had the pride of a boarding school miss or had they, instead of their sometimes scanty fare, been daily pampered with high seasoned food, they probably would not have been so happy.'[137]

---

130 Carr, op. cit., p. 247
131 Carr, op. cit., p. 247; Young, p. 185
132 Young, op. cit., p. 202
133 Carr, p. 292
134 Curwen, op. cit., vol. 2, pp. 253, 276
135 Bell, op. cit., p. 21
136 Marie-Louise Legg, ed., *The Synge Letters*, pp. 323–4
137 Hall, vol. 2, pp. 62–3

CHAPTER FIVE

Clann na nGall
'By Law Established'[1]

When the parish priest of Skibbereen was examined in 1824 by a parliamentary commission, he stated that *Sasanach* (Englishman) was the term used in the Irish language to denote a Protestant. 'It has departed from the original meaning of 'English' to 'Protestant' ... there is no Irish term for Protestant. They first knew a Protestant in the person only of an Englishman and therefore they identified it with him.'[2] James Little, the vicar of Lackan, complained that the Catholic Irish gave them 'all one common name denoting a complex idea compounded of every odious ingredient'. He believed 'that the magic sounds, *Sassanagh* & *Albanagh* (English & Scotch), like the term Aristocrate in France, were the Indian war-whoop' which roused the Killala rebels in 1798 to plunder their Protestant neighbours.[3] Little himself, who spent twenty-three years in remote Lackan, spoke no Irish though he could converse with the French officers in Latin. 'I understand not the Irish language which is the common dialect here used among the peasantry & without which no one can know the country.'[4] It was no wonder that Protestants in Ireland in the eighteenth century were regarded as foreigners by the great mass of the people. The Established Church bishops and clergy had almost invariably English surnames. At least three of the bishops were born in England, William Lloyd (1690/91–1716), Charles Cobbe (1720–26), who was the son of the governor of the Isle of Man, and Mordecai Cary (1735–51), who was born in London. In 1760 the twenty-two bishops in Ireland were equally

1 I am very much indebted to An tOllamh Pádraig de Brún, School of Celtic Sudies, Institute for Advanced Studies, who read an early draft of chapters five and six and offered much valuable advice.
2 There was no term in Irish for Catholics either and when the Irish contrasted a Protestant with a Catholic, they described the latter as *Éireannach* (Irishman). *Parliamentary Papers*, (1825) vol. 7, p. 342; see Dineen's *Foclóir Gaedhilge agus Béarla*, '*d'iompuigh sé 'na Shasanach*', 'he turned Protestant'.
3 Little, op. cit., p. 123
4 ibid, p. 73

Bishops divided between Irish and English-born, with three of the four archbisops in the latter category. Vicars, however, though Irish born, had almost exclusively English surnames, such as Sotheby, Radcliffe, Seymour etc.

Since 1622, Achonry had been united with the diocese of Killala and the cathedral and seat of the bishop was in the town of Killala. Mitres were awarded to clergymen largely as a result of government patronage. They were often younger sons of landed gentry and the church provided them with the social status that they might not have had otherwise. 'Thus, the clerical career offered a ladder by which the apt and obscure could climb, and a life-line which rescued the cadets of the genteel from sinking into social derogation.'[5] Killala and Achonry diocese seemed to have been one of the bottom rungs of the episcopal ladder. Only Clonfert occupied a still lower rung as two bishops, Mordecai Cary (1735–51) and John Law (1787–95), transferred from there to Killala. When Mordecai Cary was dying in the summer of 1751, his neigbour, Edward Synge in Elphin, only heard the news by chance. 'For he is at a great distance,' he informed his daughter, 'and I never enquire about him.' Elphin was over fifty miles from Killala.[6] For these reasons Killala tended to be a 'climbing see', a stepping-stone to better things. Out of the fourteen bishops appointed from the end of the seventeenth to early in the nineteenth century, ten of them were promoted to other dioceses.[7] One of them, Richard Robinson (1752–59) became Primate via Ferns (1759) and Kildare (1761). Another, Charles Cobbe (1720–26/7), became Archbishop of Dublin after being transferred first to Dromore (1726/7) and later to Kildare (1731).[8] Only four died in Killala and were buried in the cathedral there, and ironically two of them, Lloyd and Cary, were Englishmen.[8] This was, nevertheless, two more than their Catholic counterparts in Achonry; only John O'Hart, who died in 1739, and Philip Philips (1776–85), now Archbishop of Tuam, who died in Cloonmore and was buried in Urlaur Abbey, are buried in the diocese.

5 Toby Barnard, 'Improving Clergymen, 1660–1760' in Ford, McGuire, Milne, eds., *As by Law Established*, p. 137
6 Marie-Louise Legg, *The Synge Letters*, p. 373
7 Most of the biographical information on Church of Ireland clergy is derived from J. B. Leslie, *Biographical succession list of clergy for the dioceses of Killala and Achonry*, (typescript in the Represententative Church Body Library, Braemor Park, Dublin); see Appendix 2
8 Three were transferred to Elphin, Henry Downes (1716/7–20), who later went to Derry, Robert Howard (1726/7–29), and John Law. Of the others, Robert Clayton (1729/30–35) went to Cork and later to Clogher, William Cecil Pery (1781–84), who later became Lord Glentworth, to Limerick, William Preston (1784–7) to Ferns, John Porter (1795–7) to Clogher and Joseph Stock (1798–1810) to Waterford and Lismore.
8 The bishops interred in the cathedral in Killala were William Lloyd (1690/1–1716), Mordecai Cary who died in 1751, Samuel Hutchinson (1759–1780) and James Verschoyle (1810–34).

Apart from these four, the tenure of the others varied from two to eight years. Some, who were bishops for only two or three years, like Downes, Cobbe, Howard, Clayton, Pery, Preston and Porter, probably spent very little time, if any, in Killala. Charles Cobbe was married to Dorothea, the daughter of Sir John Levinge, speaker of the Irish House of Commons and Lord Chief Justice of Ireland. He could better further his career from a town house in Dublin while parliament was in session. Besides, Dorothea could scarcely be expected to relinquish the glittering social life in Dublin for the frugal fare of the remote little town of Killala. There were other more serious disadvantages for a bishop's family. Pregnant wives could have a miscarriage on the rough and bumpy trail west. Once arrived, there were few amenities and no medical services. One bishop complained that the area lacked not only an apothecary and a doctor but even a glazier. When Howard became Bishop of Elphin he would not allow his adolescent daughter join him in Co Roscommon because there was no doctor there.⁹ Howard, who had a reputation as an improving bishop when he moved to Elphin, was the son of a fashionable Dublin doctor, with a brother who was M.P. for Dublin and he kept a smart town-house in Dawson Street. He 'alternated between summer sojourns at Elphin, public life in Dublin with regular attendance at the House of Lords, and trips on family business into Wicklow, Carlow and England. As both bishop and landowner he behaved much as a lay peer.'¹⁰ But he did show concern for the natives of his diocese, particularly during the famine of 1729. When preparing to make his summer visitation to Killala and Achonry, he wrote to his brother: 'what indeed I dread most is the poverty and misery I shall see in the country. I have already given order to supply them with what little stock of corn I have.'¹¹ But Howard was exceptional among Protestant bishops. 'Few Irish Protestants as

Bishop John Porter *(National Library of Ireland)*

9   Toby Barnard, op. cit., p. 142; Henry Downes to Abp William Wake, 9 July 1717, Christ Church, Wake MSS, xii, ff. 180–90. Howard's successor in Elphin, Edward Synge (1740–62), refused to have his teenage daughter, Alicia, stay with him, even though there was then both a doctor and apothecary in Elphin but they were both Catholics.
10   ibid, p. 148
11   ibid

rich, intelligent or public-spirited as Howard graced the episcopal bench.'[12]

The other bishops had also town-houses in Dublin as all bishops were members of the Irish House of Lords up to 1800. Richard Robinson's house was in St Stephen's Green and Robert Clayton's house now forms part of Iveagh House. They usually came to the diocese for a few months in the summer. Richard Robinson, who was consecrated in January 1752, made his first trip to Killala in the summer of that year. He spent a night en route with Bishop Edward Synge in Elphin on 9 June and stopped there again on his way back to Dublin on 28 September.[13] Bishop Samuel Hutchinson was in residence there when Arthur Young visited him on 27–28 August 1776 and provided him with valuable information on Erris as well as a fine dinner, including among other dishes, three different kinds of fish.[14] Episcopal visitations usually consisted in the clergy coming to visit the bishop in Killala rather than vice-versa. Such was the case in 1798 when Joseph Stock was entertaining his clergy the day after Humbert's French expedition had sailed into the bay.[15] Bishop Edward Synge held his visitation in Elphin on a day in early July. 'Dinner was the most troublesome part,' he informed his daughter in 1747, 'But my company broke up early.'[16]

The bishops had usually studied in Trinity College Dublin or in Oxford or Cambridge. William Lloyd studied in Trinity, where he was awarded his M.A. in 1673. Charles Cobbe was educated at Winchester and Trinity college, Oxford, where he graduated in 1744 with a doctorate in divinity. Mordecai Cary went to Cambridge where he was awarded his doctorate in 1731. Joseph Stock entered Trinity College Dublin at the age of sixteen and he graduated from there with a doctorate in 1776. A Fellow of TCD, a fine classicist and linguist, competent Hebrew scholar and controversialist, Stock later became headmaster of Portora, the Enniskillen Royal School, before becoming Bishop of Killala and Achonry in 1798. James Verschoyle also studied in Trinity where he obtained a doctorate in law.

The bishops had extensive landholdings in both dioceses. Since the Reformation the temporalities, which consisted of lands distributed throughout the diocese, leased to rent-paying tenants, were confiscated from the Catholic Church and bestowed on the Established Church. The bishop, like other absentee landlords, employed an agent to collect these rents. In the parish of Kilmactigue he owned 640 acres in the townland of Carrowreagh, of which

12 ibid, p. 149
13 Legg, op. cit., pp. 410, 480
14 op. cit., (1927 edition), pp. 78–80
15 Bishop Stock's *Narrative 1798*, p. 5
16 Legg, op. cit., p. 51

140 were arable and the rest bog. In the townland of Kilmactigue itself he had another 268 arable acres and 340 acres of bog.[17] He owned similar amounts in other parishes of the diocese, such as Achonry where he had 1,298 arable acres and 417 waste and Ballisodare where he had 1,117 arable acres.[18] In Co Sligo these alone amounted to 6,778 acres. An early seventeenth-century register of Achonry showed that the bishop had sizeable holdings also in the Mayo parishes of the diocese, viz., Kilmovee, Killedan, Meelick and Kilconduff.[19] Add to this a similar acreage which he possessed in Killala.

Robert Howard, who transferred from Killala to Elphin in 1729, had an income there in 1731 of £1433.13s.3d.. In early June 1791 the French consul, who visited Killala, estimated the income of the bishop to be £2,500.[20] Another French visitor to Killala in 1797 commented sarcastically on the poverty of the bishop: 'This bishopric is reputed to be the poorest in Ireland, the bishop having only an income of £3,000 sterling. Poor man!'[21] The same commentator claimed that the bishop's palace was so poor that it gave rise to a proverb widely used in Connacht to describe anything of inferior quality. 'It is as bad as the palace of the Bishop of Killala.' However, he found the proverb no longer true as a 'considerable wing' had been since added to it.[22]

Not only the bishop but also the dean and archdeacon held church lands, the dean holding his in the parish of Achonry, while the archdeacon was the owner of the townland of Kilturra in the parish of Bunninadden, with 82 arable acres and 152 waste. Ironically, his tenants were the Philips of Cloonmore, where Bishop Philips (1776–1785) resided.[23] Deaneries were lucrative benefices whose holders rarely if ever were resident in the eighteenth century. The deanery of Killala was said to have been worth £500 sterling at the turn of the century, when it was occupied by the famous preacher, Walter Blake Kirwan, himself a convert from Catholicism who had studied for the priesthood.[24] Pluralism (holding several benefices) was a feature of the church at that time and that necessarily entailed absenteeism. Kirwan was at the same

Deaneries

17 Neligan, op. cit., pp. 397–8
18 Other church holdings included, Kilvarnet, 127 arable, 16 waste; Emlefad and Kilmorgan, 484 arable, 720 waste; Cloonoghill, 396 arable, 718 waste; Kilfree, 196 arable, 41 waste. O'Hara Papers, Ms. 20, 397
19 Liam Swords, Gilmartin Prize Essay, 1962, (unpublished)
20 Ní Chinnéide, op. cit., vol. 35, p. 62
21 De Latocnaye, op. cit., (1917 edition), p. 178
22 This could not have been accomplished by the then encumbent, John Porter, as the Frenchman thought, as he had only been consecrated in June 1795 and transferred to Clogher in 1797. It was the work of his predecessor, Samuel Hutchinson, as the French consul noted in 1791 that he was 'engaged in building'. Ní Chinnéide, op. cit., vol. 35, p. 62
23 O'Rorke, *Sligo*, vol. 2, pp. 195–6
24 De Latocnaye, p. 178

time the incumbent of St Nicholas Without in Dublin. Dean Richard Handcock (1753–91) was vicar of Athlone while his predecessor, Sutton Symes (1733–51), was a member of the Ferns' clergy. Such absentees employed a curate to whom they paid a small stipend.[25]

Vicarages

The parishes of Achonry diocese were grouped into nine vicarages.[26] The number of parishes in each vicarage varied from one, as in Ballisodare and Kilmactigue, to five in Templemore. The latter included Straide, Bohola, Foxford (Toomore), Killasser and Kiltimagh (Killedan). Kilmovee was attached to Ballaghaderreen (Castlemore and Kilcolman) and Charlestown (Kilbeagh) to Swinford (Kilconduff and Meelick). Ballymote (Emlefad and Kilmorgan) had Keash as well as Kilturra (part of Bunninadden), and Achonry parish included Cloonoghill. Gurteen (Killaraght and Kilfree) had also Kilshalvey (another part of Bunninadden), while Coolaney (Killoran) and Collooney (Kilvarnet) formed one vicarage.[27] Attymass and Bonniconlon belonged to the vicarage of Ardagh in the diocese of Killala.

Protestant Population

The earliest figures giving the number of Protestants in the different parishes date from 1831[28] but while the population had hugely increased in the previous sixty years, Protestants as a percentage of the population probably remained broadly similar. The total population of the diocese was then 115,650 while Protestants numbered only 5,415 or 4.68% of the population. The 1831 figures showed a wide divergence between the eastern Sligo side and the western Mayo side of the diocese. The Sligo part had a total population of 62,473, with 5,008 Protestants or 8%, while the Mayo end had a total population of 53,177, with only 409 Protestants or .76%. Ballisodare had 1,613 Protestants out of a total population of 7,562, or 21.3%, while Kilconduff, which included Kilbeagh and Meelick had only 60 out of a total population of 9,625 or .6%.[29] Next to Ballisodare came Achonry and Cloonoghill with 1,145 followed by Coolaney and Collooney (Killoran and Kilvarnet) and Ballymote (Emlefad), with just over nine hundred each. In Sligo parishes

25 James Langrishe (1792–1806) belonged to the diocese of Kilmore. James Hastings (1806–12) was rector of Drummully in the diocese of Clogher. Arthur Henry Kenney (1812–21) was from the diocese of Cork and Ross. Earlier incumbents such as William Lloyd (1684–91), Samuel Foley (1691–4) and John Ycard (1694–1733) were precenters of Killala as well as deans of Achonry. Lloyd was rector of Clondevaddock in the diocese of Raphoe. Foley later became Bishop of Down and Connor. Tobias Caulfield, who was vicar of Ballisodare in the early decades of the eighteenth century, was also archdeacon of Killala. See Appendix 4
26 Achonry, Ballisodare, Castlemore, Emlefad, Kilconduff, Killaraght, Killoran, Kilmactigue and Templemore.
27 The union of Killoran and Kilvarnet took place in 1819. O'Rorke, *Sligo*, vol. 2, p. 63
28 *Parliamentary Papers* (1835), pp. 52d–53d, 60d-62d
29 In fact there were no Protestants at all in Kilbeagh, while Meelick had only eight.

bordering Mayo, such as Gurteen (Killaraght) and Kilmactigue, there was a sharp drop in the number of Protestants, with 260 in Gurteen while Kilmactigue had about one hundred less. In 1814 there were only ten Protestant families there, amounting to about seventy persons, while there were then twelve hundred Catholic families. Two of the three Mayo vicarages had less than a hundred Protestants while the five parishes in Templemore totalled only 204 out of a total population of 23,487, with four of them ranging from eleven to seventeen in each. Kilgarvan (Bonniconlon) had eleven Protestants and Attymass thirty-six. The parish of Kilmovee had only ten, a number that could have been made up of one landlord's family and retainers.[30]

The much larger figures in the Sligo part of the diocese paints a very different picture. Not only were the large landowners in Sligo, like the O'Haras, Coopers, Percivals etc., Protestant but so were many tenant farmers and others of more modest means. Ballymote had a Protestant colony of weavers introduced into the town in the middle of the eighteenth century. There were ninety Protestant weavers there in 1776 when Arthur Young visited the town.[31] Kean O'Hara seems to have pursued a policy of leasing exclusively to large Protestant tenants.[32] Charles O'Hara M.P. brought in a number of weavers and bleachers from the north of Ireland and located them in and around Coolaney. One of the early managers of this enterprise was Albert Blest, who later became an active proselytiser in the diocese.[33]

Churches

There were eleven Protestant churches in the diocese in 1831, but some of these, such as Ballymote, dated from the early nineteenth century. Collooney's church, dedicated to St Paul, was built in 1720 and consisted of an oblong structure, with a tower at the west end.[34] It was described in 1739 as 'a neat modern church with a square steeple'.[35] The church in Killoran was built at Rathbarron in 1767–8, on an acre of ground granted in perpetuity by Charles O'Hara. It cost £921 and was intended to accommodate 450 wor-

---

30 The same could be said of Meelick with eight, Bohola with eleven or Killasser with twelve. Two Protestant families could have accounted for the sixteen in Killedan and seventeen in Straide.
31 *Tour of Ireland*, p. 72
32 Thomas Bartlett, 'The O'Haras of Annaghmore c.1600-c.1800: Survival and revival', in *Irish Economic and Social History*, vol. ix, p. 39
33 O'Rorke, *Sligo*, vol. 2, pp. 59–60
34 Trancepts were added in the nineteenth century when it was generally restored, ibid, p. 345. A meeting was held in the vestry in Collooney on 9 September 1718 'for the consideration of building a church for the union of Ballisadore, Killoran and Kilvarnet'. O'Hara Papers, Ms. 20,388. On 14 June 1720 an order in Council was issued that 'a new church be built in the market town of Collooney in quarter of land of Cashell commonly called Sweeny's Park.' J. B. Leslie typescript in Church Representative Body Library, Braemor Park, Dublin.
35 William Henry, *Co Sligo*, National Archives, Ms. 2533, p. 29

shippers.³⁶ The church in Foxford was under construction when Dr Pococke visited the town in 1752 and called on the minister, William Evelyn, who must have been responsible for building the church.³⁷ The church in Kilmactigue was in existence before 1798, when it was attacked and greatly damaged by local sympathisers of Humbert's expeditionary force. It was repaired by James Neligan shortly after he became vicar there in 1802. Churches, like the one in Kilmactigue, were very small, containing only four pews 'being suited to the number of (Protestant) inhabitants'.³⁸

Vicars In 1731 there were seven vicars resident in Achonry,³⁹ while a hundred years later there were eight as well as a further eight curates. None of the vicars were natives of the diocese except for three who were sons of vicars who had succeeded their fathers.⁴⁰ Of the others, two of them, Thomas Manningham, vicar of Kilmactigue (1760–77) and John Cromie, vicar of Templemore (1805–9), were born in England. Others were natives of Dublin, Kildare, Limerick, Down, and Monaghan. Some came from places not so far away,

Protestant church, Collooney (O'Rorke, *Ballysadare*)

36 O'Rorke, op. cit., p. 63
37 *Bishop Pococke's Irish Tour, 1752*, p. 81
38 Neligan, p. 358
39 *Arch. Hib.*, vol. III, p. 129; see Appendix 37
40 Adam Caulfield (1736–72) succeeded his father, Tobias, as vicar of Ballisodare. John Garrett (1806–55) followed his father, William (1765–1806), in Emlefad, where their joint ministries lasted ninety years. The vicar of Castlemore, Charles Seymour (1794–1811), resigned in favour of his son Joseph.

Foxford Church

such as Gideon Johnson, vicar of Castlemore (1698–1711) who was the son of a gospel preacher in Turlough, Co Mayo. James Neligan of Kilmactigue (1802–35) was born in Longford.

Vicars often came from levitical or clerical families such as William Garret of Emlefad, himself the son of a clergyman, while his son, John, had no less than three sons who became clergymen. William's predecessor in Emlefad, Charles Maturin (–1756) was the son of a clergyman in Co Down. James Neligan of Kilmactigue was the son of Michael, a clergyman in Co Longford. Two of Neligan's predecessors, Thomas Manningham and Edward Synge (1777–81) had similar backgrounds. Synge belonged to an extraordinary clerical dynasty. He was the only son of Nicholas Synge, Bishop of Killaloe (1745–71), nephew of Edward, Bishop of Elphin (1740–62) and grandson of Edward, Archbishop of Tuam (1716–41).[41] Other vicars, such as Mark Wainright in Kilmactigue (1781–97) and Joseph Verschoyle in Coolaney (Killoran) (1817–62), were younger sons of minor gentry. Joseph Borrowes, vicar of Swinford (Kilconduff) (1807–21), was born in Dublin, the son of Sir Kildare Dixon Borrowes.

---

41 The playwright, John Millington Synge (1871–1909), was a direct descendant from Edward Synge's family. On the Synge family see Marie-Louise Legg, *The Synge Letters*, pp.vii–ix, xlii–xliii. Leslie states that Edward, vicar of Kilmactigue, was the son of Edward, archdeacon of Killaloe. Charles Seymour (1794–1811), had two sons who became clergymen. The father of John O'Rourke, vicar of Templemore (1817–49), was a clergyman in Co Galway, and John's son also became a clergyman.

Most of the vicars studied in Trinity College Dublin where they obtained a B.A. after four or five years. They entered Trinity, aged between fifteen and eighteen, after completing their classical education in a local school, often conducted by a clergyman. A few, like James Sotheby of Kilconduff (1729–51), Josiah Hern of Killoran (1776?–1818), his successor, Joseph Verschoyle, Charles Maturin and William and John Garrett, went on to take an M.A. after a further three or four years study. Only one, Edward Synge, after completing his M.A. in Trinity, went on to take a doctorate in divinity in Magdalen College, Oxford. In all he spent fourteen years in university. After serving four years as vicar of Kilmactigue, he became provost of Achonry until his death in 1818.

Glebes

Some of the vicars lived with their families in glebe houses to which a farm of twenty to forty acres was attached. In 1756 Adam Caulfield of Ballisodare was granted a glebe of twenty acres and in Emlefad the glebe comprised thirty-two acres 'of the richest land'.[42] James Neligan had forty acres 'of very good land for tillage and pasture, and would let for fifty shillings an acre'. This glebe land provided sustenance for Neligan, his wife and seven children, producing an 'abundance of meat, vegetables and corn for his consumption; besides hay and pasture sufficient for his cattle.' It had been increased by twenty acres by Bishop Hutchinson (1759–1780). In 1831 there were seven glebe houses in the diocese. Only Killaraght and Templemore had none. Some were recent, such as that in Kilmactigue, which was completed in 1814 by James Neligan at a cost of £1,300.[43]

Neligan's Glebe House (McTernan, *Olde Sligoe*)

When Arthur Young visited Bishop Hutchinson in Killala in 1776, the bishop told him that he had built a house for the Protestant clergyman in the Belmullet peninsula and given him forty acres of church land.[44] He seems to have followed the same policy in Achonry. Normally the vicar paid the bishop a rent of ten pounds a year but Hutchinson waived his right to the rent of Kilmactigue, 'and acted the same generous part towards all the other clergy of the diocese, considering that they were in general poor, and badly able to support themselves and their

42 O'Rorke, op. cit., p. 172
43 He had been given a loan of £500 and a gift of £300 by the Board of First Fruits. Neligan, p. 376
44 *A Tour of Ireland*, p. 79

families, on the small incomes arising from their benefices.'[45] This assertion by Neligan is questionable since if the livings were so poor, it is difficult to understand why one of his predecessors, Thomas Manningham, would exchange his vicarage in Sussex for that of Kilmactigue with its tiny flock. Neither the time nor the Established Church was notable for its missionary zeal. Besides he could not speak Irish, if his intention was to convert the natives. On the other hand, Manningham may have been attracted by the quiet life, as he was said to be 'an excellent scholar and highly accomplished' with 'a great taste for poetry'.[46] However, it is still difficult to explain why vicars like Caulfield, Garrett and Seymour, should encourage their sons to follow in their footsteps if such livings were not lucrative.

While clergymen provided for their families with the produce of their glebe farms, their income largely derived from tithes which consisted in the payment by residents in the parish of one-tenth of the annual yeild of their farms. Such was the practice everywhere, in Catholic countries like France and Spain as well as Protestant ones like England and Germany, and everywhere people paid their tithes unwillingly. What made the custom uniquely iniquitous in Ireland was that the people were compelled to pay for the support of the clergy of another religion. As the Frenchman, De Latocnaye, observed, they were paid to the Protestant minister, who was often the only Protestant in the parish.[47] Nothing was more resented by the people than the payment of tithes.

Tithes

Vicars were only too well aware of this deep resentment and to avoid unpleasantness they often employed tithe-proctors or agents to collect the tithes, which only compounded the problem for tenants. Often an agent agreed a fixed sum which he paid the vicar and then extorted exorbitant amounts from the unfortunate tenants to maximise his profit. In 1790 the parishioners of Taunagh, just outside the diocese, petitioned Charles O'Hara, complaining of excessive tithe demands.[48] As Arthur Young commented on the proctors in Co Galway in 1776, 'they screw up the poor people to the utmost'.[49] They also applied a double standard between the rich and the poor, as Young noted in Co Leitrim, where the proctors were 'very civil to gentlemen but exceedingly cruel to the poor'.[50] Such apparently was the case in Coolaney and Collooney (Killoran and Kilvarnet) whose vicar, Josiah Hern, sent Charles

45 Neligan, op. cit., p. 374
46 He published a volume in prose and verse, partly in Latin and partly in English.
47 *Rambles through Ireland*, vol. 1, p. 92
48 O'Hara Papers (Report 493), T2812/16/19
49 *Tour of Ireland*, vol. 1, p. 275
50 ibid, p. 213

O'Hara his tithes account book for 1813 detailing the townlands and tenants who pay tithes. He noted in passing that the estate of Templehouse, the seat of the Percival family, was 'not subject to tithes' and that Nymphsfield, the O'Hara estate, had 'not paid tithes since I was Incumbent of this union'.[51] In this instance poor Catholics were obliged to pay tithes to the Protestant vicar, while rich Protestants were exempt.

When Young visited the Cooper estate in Markrea near Collooney he found that in that part of Sligo tithes were generally paid in kind.[52] There were no tithes on potatoes in Connacht and this was in marked contrast to Munster, where in addition to potatoes, 'the tenth part of the milk, eggs, chickens and vegetables may be claimed by the minister if he pleases'.[53] In Kilmactigue the vicar was entitled to tithes on corn of every kind, flax and meadow, as well as 'small dues, but these were never demanded'. His main income came from tithes on oats and flax as there was very little meadow in the parish. Oats and flax were paid by the acre at the rate of a tenth for the best crops and proportionately less for lower quality. Typically, an acre of oats produced four barrels, two of which had to be sold to pay both tithes and rent. The 'small dues' consisted of, among other things, a tithe on wool and lambs and were paid before Neligan became vicar in 1802. The number of sheep was so small and the collection of other sundry tithes so difficult, that Neligan relinquished them, 'after having on his first coming to the parish established his right to them, by citing some of the farmers to the Ecclesiastical court, and obliging them to acknowledge, and account for them. This was done for the benefit of his successors, that the church might not be a loser by neglect.'[54]

Kilmactigue was particularly hard done by in supporting the various clergy. Not only had they to pay tithes to the vicar, they also had to pay their parish priest offerings at Christmas and Easter, as well as for the other various services he provided. The priest in turn had to pay one-third of that to the bishop, as Kilmactigue was a mensal parish. Add to that the Augustinian friars at Banada, who supported themselves by levying contributions of butter and corn in the neighbourhood. Religion cost them dearly, in more senses than one.

Tobias Caulfield

It is possible, from the documentation available, to attempt a pen portrait of two vicars, one at the beginning and the other at the end of the century, the first in a populous Protestant parish and the second ministering to a tiny

50   ibid, p. 213
51   O'Hara Papers, Ms. 20,280 (30)
52   'They are let to tythe proctors who are paid, wheat 8s., barley 6s., oats 4s., flax 8s.', op. cit., p. 237
53   De Latocnaye, vol. 1, p. 92; vol. 2, p. 2
54   op. cit., pp. 376–7

flock. Tobias Caulfield, vicar of Ballisodare (1696–1735),[55] was the second son of Captain Thomas Caulfield of Dunamon, Co Roscommon and grandson of Sir William Caulfield, second Baron of Charlemont. He married Anne, the daughter of Adam O'Hara and niece of Kean O'Hara of Nymphsfield. In August 1696 Tobias wrote to Kean asking for the lady's hand:

> 'I do not value my self upon any thing more than the sincere love and affection I have for the lady, and leaving her own fortune solely to her own disposal would my self endeavour with all industry and affection to content her to the utmost of my circumstances ... My earnest desire and passion for the lady make me use all endeavours to win her ... I will undergo the most imaginable hardship to purchase content and maintenance for her.'[56]

'Leyny is dull Leyny still,' he wrote to Kean O'Hara in Dublin in 1698 but what followed in his letter showed it to be very far from dull:

> 'no novelties, but that Parson Humes and Dirk Bingham were on Monday last drowned in Loughhorn; we have had prodigious storms and violent rains; we had an account that poor Kitty Conelly was wounded by her brother desperately; but since I hear it was accidentally by struggling from her and others to get at Dan Roughnan when they were (hurt?) and she got a small scratch. The Bishop of Killala went through Collooney on Thursday last and drank your health; if you see Parson Nicholson you may assure him that Naason is the father of Mrs Lettice's child for Nolan who was the cloak came to me and acquainted me of the whole truth.'[57]

Caulfield himself was in Dublin in 1699 and was using the occasion to advance his career: 'all my friends and relations are labouring to promote me; I have been presented to the Archbishop of Dublin and the Bishop of Kilmore and both have promised to serve me the first opportunity.' He was also on the look-out for a wife for Kean: 'The lady I would recommend to you is Lady Betty Moore; a sweet young crature; admired now in town by most beaux's; her father gives her £2000'.[58]

In 1703 he had a curate who had been recommended to him by the Primate and the Bishop of Elphin but Caulfield was not happy with the arrangement. 'If their Lordships please, I'll dismiss him,' he wrote to Kean, 'for I can serve my own cure.' In 1704 Tobias was one of the clergy's proctors to Convocation, a clerical parliament with an Upper and Lower House, summoned by

---

55 O'Rorke, *Ballysadare and Kilvarnet*, pp. 112–13, 115, 118–19
56 O'Hara Papers, Ms. 20,388
57 O'Hara Paper, Ms. 20,388
58 ibid

the Crown. In 1716 he held an honorary prebend in the diocese of Raphoe. He and his parishioners petitioned in 1720 for permission to build a new church in Collooney, which was completed sometime afterwards. In 1724 he was vicar-general of Achonry and shortly afterwards became archdeacon of Killala. He died in 1735 and one of his sons, Adam, succeeded him in Ballisodare.

James Neligan

James Neligan, vicar of Kilmactigue (1802–35), was born in 1751 in Longford, the son of a clergyman. In 1769 he entered Trinity College Dublin at the age of eighteen and took his B. A. four years later. He was ordained in 1774 but there is no information on the first twelve years of his ministry. In 1786 he was a vicar in Easky, Co Sligo. It is said that he ran a classical school in Ardnaree (Ballina) towards the end of the century.[59] One of his sons, Maurice, had entered Trinity in 1792 at the age of fourteen.

He was a magistrate in Ballina when the French consul visited the town on 8 June 1791 and was invited to lunch with him.[60] He was in fact 'a very active' magistrate during the stormy events of 1798. Sir Richard Musgrave, who interviewed him when he compiled his *Memoirs of the Different Rebellions in Ireland*, described Neligan as 'a gentleman of elegant taste and extensive learning'.[61] The United Irishmen had been actively recruiting and 'used to hold meetings at the low tippling houses in Ballina', and Neligan was zealous in discovering and exposing them. His 'zealous exertions on this and other occasions became a source of many future calamities to himself and his numerous family'. When the French landed, he narrowly escaped from Ballina and took refuge with the Hillas family in Seaview, Co Sligo.

His removal to Kilmactigue in 1802 may have been occasioned by the many enemies he must have made in Ballina during the rebellion. In Kilmactigue he became very active in promoting London Hibernian Society schools and recruited and recommended teachers both there and in neighbouring Killasser. In 1808 he published *The Bible in Miniature* which consisted of 'the most useful and necessary parts of the Old and New Testaments' with commentaries. In 1816 he contributed a forty-eight page article on the parish of Kilmactigue to Shaw Mason's *Statistical Account*. In 1817 'a clergyman of the established church in Ireland' wrote *An Authentic Narrative of the Recent Conversion of Twelve Roman Catholics named Hart*, which was published by the Irish Baptist Society. As the events described took place in Kilmactigue, the

---

59   Wood-Martin, *Sligo 1691–1891*, p. 416
60   Ní Chinnéide, vol. 35, p. 61
61   op. cit., vol. 2, pp. 118, 120–21, 126–7

author was almost certainly Neligan. He died in 1835 at the age of eighty-four and was described in his obituary as 'a scholar, a poet and a gentleman'.[62]

Neligan had all the orthodox Protestant opinions of his time, believing in the primacy of the Bible: 'the Holy Scriptures are the only sure guide, both as to faith and practice'.[63] He congratulated the Irish Baptist Society for their initiative in disseminating the New Testament in Irish and was convinced that the Irish peasants, by hearing and reading the Word, would be brought to 'a sense of their errors' and 'live soberly, righteously and godly'. He was scandalised by the sports and pastimes of Catholics on Sundays and their failure to keep the strict biblical observance of the sabbath and he abhorred the 'absurd rites and usages of the Romish church', particularly their pilgrimages to holy wells and the wearing of scapulars, though he admitted it would be difficult 'to eradicate prejudice confirmed by long custom'.

John Wesley

Apart from the Established Church there was no other Protestant sect with a fixed house of worship in the diocese in the eighteenth century. By 1831 there was only one Presbyterian meeting-house in the parish of Keash (Toomour) and a Methodist meeting house, possibly situated in the same parish (Drumrat), both probably early nineteenth-century foundations. The Methodists were in communion with the Established Church and were then serviced by two itinerant dissenting ministers. John Wesley himself traversed the diocese on numerous occasions during his long missionary career in the second half of the eighteenth century. A small thin man, with black curly hair down to his shoulders, he addressed meetings frequently in Castlebar and Sligo, crossing Achonry diocese on these occasions.

In 1760, going from Sligo to Castlebar, he ran into a torrential downpour, though it was the end of June: 'I have rarely seen so heavy rain in Europe as we had in the way to Tubbercurry. I was quickly wet to my toes' end; but the day clearing, I was dry again in a few hours.'[64] Some years later a new road was laid down which shortened the distance between Sligo and Castlebar by several miles. It went via Tubbercurry, Bellaghy and Swinford whereas the old road went via Foxford. In June 1765 Wesley set out from Sligo at 5am intending to take the new road, but on second thoughts rode on from Tubbercurry to Foxford:

'At the entrance of the town I met three gentlewomen. One of them turned and cried out, "Is not that Mr Wesley?" I thought it odd but rode

---

62 *Saunders News Letter*. He was survived by his wife and seven children, to whom he bequeathed £830.
63 *An Authentic Narrative*, p. 16
64 *Journal*

on. At the other end of the town, a gentleman met me and taking hold of the bridle, said "Sir, I must beg you to turn back and dine with me at the barracks. There is a lady whom you know and who will be very glad to see you." I went back and found one whom I had wished to see more than most persons in the nation.'[65]

The person in question was a woman from Sligo, with whom Wesley spent an hour or two 'in close serious conversation'.

When he finally got to take the new road many years later, it proved to be a trying experience. It was May 1778 and this time Wesley, then seventy-five years old, was travelling in a horse-drawn carriage from Castlebar to Sligo. The road, though new, was pickled with large potholes and Wesley and his company got through the first two successfully. The third, probably somewhere in the vicinity of Curry, appeared too dangerous to attempt a crossing. Seeing their predicament, seven or eight sturdy natives came to their help: 'One of them carried me over on his shoulders; others got the horses through; and some carried the chaise. We then thought the difficulty was past.' But a half an hour later horses and carriage got completely bogged down in yet another pothole. This time Wesley decided to continue his journey on foot and, leaving the rest of the company to try and free the carriage and horses, he began to walk. It proved providential for one unfortunate countryman from the neighbourhood of Ballinacarrow.

'While I was walking a poor man overtook me, who appeared to be in deep distress. He said he owed his landlord twenty shillings rent, for which he had turned him and his family out of doors, and that he had been down with his relations to beg their help, but they could do nothing. Upon my giving him a guinea, he would kneel down in the road to pray for me, and then cried out, "Oh I shall have a house, I shall have a house over my head." So perhaps God answered that poor man's prayer by the sticking fast of the chaise in the slough.'[66]

That poor man would have enthusiastically endorsed what Daniel-Rops, the French historian, said of Wesley: 'No Catholic can speak of him without affection or remember his apostolate without admiration.'

Catholic-Protestant Relations

The relations between Catholics and Protestants varied enormously throughout the century. The beginning was a period of active persecution of Catholics while Protestants, being the minority, suffered from a siege mentality. Bishop Howard in 1729 expressed the fear 'that popery would swallow us all

---

65 ibid, vol. 5, p. 128
66 op. cit., vol. 6, p. 191

up at the last'.⁶⁷ The purpose of the penal laws was to reduce Catholics to a point where they could never again threaten the Protestant establishment. Protestants made no serious attempt to proselytise them though Howard at least retained the hope that papists might be weaned away in time 'from the barbarity of their manners and the folly of their superstition'.⁶⁸

Charles O'Hara (afterwards Lord Tyrawley) wrote to Kean from London, looking for a young Protestant boy of the O'Hara family whom he was prepared to adopt. Tyrawley was childless and would prefer to use his fortune for someone of his 'name and family than for strangers'. If there was no suitable Protestant boy, 'and any of our Roman Catholic relations who are not very tenacious of their principles will send me one of theirs to be bred a Protestant, I will take care of him. But such a one must not be more than twelve years old, lest his religion may have made too much impression on him.'⁶⁹ Kean replied early in 1695 that there was no suitable Protestant O'Hara and added: 'neither do I know any of our Roman Catholic friends of our name that have a youth that I dare venture to trouble you with, and if they had I am afraid their nature and principles are of such that they had rather have their children live miserable all their days than consent to have them bred Protestants'. Kean also assured Tyrawley that he was and always had been a Protestant, the religion in which he was bred and that 'no endeavour could or shall ever prevail with me to alter it'. In using the term 'Roman Catholics' rather than 'Papists' the O'Haras were exceptional in their time. It was a period when attitudes were polarised; 'the opposite of Catholic is heretic, and the opposite of Protestant is Papist.'⁷⁰

Catholics and Protestants rarely socialised. While staying in Elphin during the summer months, the Protestant bishop, Edward Synge, was obliged to avail of the services of the local Catholic doctor but he drew the line at allowing him to stay in his home. He recounted a revealing incident in June 1749 to his daughter Alicia: 'Monsieur le Docteur unasked returned in the evening with an intention to stay too. He told Shannon he was to lie here. But I was determined he should not, and made Cary carry him away. I suppose he is huffed at this, and am not sorry if he be. His Irish impudence deserved to be so mortified. If I had not checked it then, I had been teased with him more than I could bear. A fair riddance, if he comes no more.'⁷¹

Both religions regarded each other with mutual suspicion and hostility

67 Toby Barnard, op. cit., p. 148
68 ibid
69 O'Hara Papers, Ms. 16,942
70 Alan Acheson, *A History of the Church of Ireland 1691–1996*, p. 27
71 Legg, op. cit., p. 127

until at least the middle of the century. Their relationship began to mellow somewhat after that, though as late as 1770 Bishop Patrick Robert Kirwan (1758–76) wrote of Achonry: 'The Protestants, who are the only landlords and are powerful around here, abhor the (Catholic) ministers of the Church and detest even the lay people with particular hatred in this county of Sligo.'[72] But this attitude was to change in the last quarter of the century. It coincided with the passing of the first Catholic relief acts after the Catholic clergy agreed to take an oath of allegiance to the British crown. Nevertheless, many Protestant churchmen were alarmed and dismayed when the 1792 bill referred to 'his Majesty's Catholick subjects' rather than the more traditional 'papists'. Bishop Philip Philips (1776–85) led the Achonry priests in taking the oath in 1779 and his successor, Boetius Egan (1785–88) was actually consecrated bishop in the Protestant cathedral in Tuam, the first since the Reformation, as he exultantly informed Rome.[73] In fact, prominent local Protestants were sometimes canvassed in favour of candidates for Catholic dioceses. The support of Charles O'Hara M.P. was sought in favour of John O'Flynn for Achonry and Owen O'Conor even approached the Protestant Bishop of Elphin in favour of his brother, Dr Charles, for Achonry.[74] In the great chapel-building era in the last decade of the century and early decades of the next, Protestants vied with Catholics in making contributions. Sites were almost invariably donated by the local Protestant landlords and often they and their women-folk in all their finery attended the opening ceremonies.

There was also more socialising between Catholics and Protestants, as the French consul discovered when he visited Sligo in the summer of 1791. He was invited to dine in a Protestant home and was surprised to hear his Protestant host call on a Catholic priest, John O'Flynn, who later became Bishop of Achonry, to say grace.[75] Gestures, such as the Protestant vicar lending his tea-set for the priest's breakfast at stations, became commonplace.[76] Priests and parsons sat on the same parish committees for the relief of distress among the poor as during the severe famine of 1816–17, when Daniel O'Connor, parish priest of Coolaney (Killoran), and James Henry, parish priest of Ballisodare and Kilvarnet, served on the same committee with their Protestant counterparts, together with the Baptist, Albert Blest, and the Protestant landlords, Colonel Percival and Charles O'Hara.[77]

72 SC Irlanda, vol. 11, f. 541v
73 SC Irlanda, vol. 16, f. 29rv
74 O'Hara Papers, Ms. 20,280 (31); O'Conor Don Papers, 8.4. SH. 068
75 Ní Chinnéide, vol. 36, p. 36
76 Shaw Mason, op. cit., vol. 3, p. 243
77 O'Hara Papers, Ms. 20,313 (7)

Conversions

A number of Catholics in Ireland, of which fifteen were recorded for Achonry, converted to the Established Church during the eighteenth century.[78] There may have been many more as converts often gave a Dublin address. In the diocese Foxford had the distinction of providing the first official convert, John Gallagher, in 1719. Nationwide the majority of converts before 1731 were people of substance and five of the Achonry conversions took place within this period. Gallagher, as well as Christopher Taaffe of Ballynaglogh who converted in 1723, were described as 'gentlemen', a term used to designate a sizeable landowner.[79]

The remaining ten are evenly divided between the middle and later years of the century and the motives for these conversions are not so clear. There were three women converts listed, Mrs Ellinor Cumffe of Tullinacorra (1747), Mary McCormack of Nymphsfield (1782) and Mary O'Hara of Tullyhugh (1738). The latter was probably the wife of Henry O'Hara who also converted at the same time.[80] The conversion of Mary McCormack, whose address was the O'Hara estate of Nymphsfield, may have resulted from her marriage to a Protestant. Almost half the converts came from the more Protestant north-eastern end of the diocese, while all but two, both from Foxford, came from the Sligo section.[81]

There were a handful of others with addresses in Co Sligo but it is not known whether they resided within the boundaries of the diocese.[82] George Brabazon (1732/39) of Carrowgarry, Co Mayo, may have belonged to the family of that name who were landlords in Swinford.[83] Two converts who took the oaths in 1763 but do not appear in the convert rolls were Charles and Edmund Costello. The latter, who named his seat in Ballaghaderreen, Edmondstown or ('Ned's own town' according to a contemporary wit) after himself, was probably the father of Charles, who later claimed the right to nominate the parish priest of Ballaghaderreen (Kilcolman and Castlemore).[84]

78 Eileen O'Byrne ed., *The Convert Rolls;* see Appendix 43
79 The other three were John Higgins, Kilfree (1730), Patrick Nolan, Ballisodare (1729) and James Philips, Kilturra (1729), probably an ancestral relative of Philip Philips, the future bishop. ibid, pp. 113, 134, 213, 229, 265
80 Another O'Hara, Roger, of the parish of Achonry, converted in 1779. ibid, p. 223. Peter Dowling (1752) was from the same parish. ibid, pp. 63, 84, 173, 223
81 Patrick Nolan (1729) & Rowland Carter, Ballisodare; Francis Byrne (1750), Cloonimighane (Cloonamahon?); Neal Lawry (1782), Rathbarron; Robert Plunkett, Collooney and Bryan Murrin, Coolaney (Toolany?), Martin Joyes (1757), as well as Gallagher, Foxford, ibid, pp. 36, 143, 161, 231, 293
82 Thady McDonogh (1743) was described as 'of Co Sligo'. ibid, p. 175. Honora Conyngham (1711), Trainatriny, Co Sligo, Anne Irwin alias Brett (1731), Lisballilly, and Mathias Ward (1768), Oxfield. ibid, pp. 55, 141, 275
83 ibid, p. 20
84 ibid, p. 304; *Recollections of Skeffington Gibbon*, p. 130

Brabazon House, Swinford *(courtesy Joseph Mellet)*

Dermot O'Connor (1758) of Tuam was probably the father of Thomas who later became Bishop of Achonry (1787-1803) as it was later asserted in Rome that the bishop's father was 'a perverted Catholic who continues to live in the error he embraced'.[85]

Many, if not most of these converts conformed to the Established religion for financial and family reasons and some returned to the Catholic fold on their death-beds. John Fitzmaurice, parish priest of Ballisodare, was reputed to have made several conversions, among whom was a certain George Brabazon.[86] It is tempting to speculate that this may have been the same George Brabazon who had converted to Protestantism some forty years earlier. Fitzmaurice was also credited with the conversion of Sir Joshua Crofton whose family had been Catholic until at least the early years of the eighteenth century.

The conversions of Protestants to Catholicism, particularly among the more modest section, are more difficult to document. In 1753, the Bishop of Elphin, John Brett, himself a native of Achonry, reported to Rome that in the five years he was bishop three men and one woman in the diocese had converted to Protestantism, 'seduced by greed', while in that year ten Protestants in the town of Athlone had been converted and 'that daily many on their death-beds return to the way of salvation'.[87] Peter Blake, parish priest of Oranmore, informed Propaganda in 1783 'that in the eight years he has been

85   ibid, p. 220; SC Irlanda, vol. 16, ff. 308v–310r
86   SC Irlanda, vol. 15, ff. 471v, 478rv
87   SC Irlanda, vol. 10, ff. 422rv–425rv

in the parish he has seen no heretic die outside the bosom of our holy religion'.[88] Protestants sometimes married Catholics and subsequently converted. Some, as Albert Blest recalled of his youth, were obliged to have recourse to the Catholic priest for want of their own clergy who were absentees or non-existent, and a similar situation was found in Connemara in 1813 where many poor Protestants 'had lapsed for want of a minister of their own Church to baptize their children, to marry their daughters, and to bury their dead'. Once they had got into the habit of applying to the priest out of Christian necessity, 'the rest followed as a matter of course'.[89]

Others simply succumbed to the all-pervasive Catholic culture of their environment. Protestants of the smaller tenant class often became devotees of the holy wells or found sabbath-keeping virtually impossible, surrounded as they were by the Sunday festivities of their fun-loving Catholic neighbours. Early in the nineteenth century there were only ten Protestant families in the parish of Tourlestrane and the vicar, James Neligan, complained of losing two members of his little flock to the Catholic Church. One was a woman who, 'having being attacked by some sudden fit', sought to be cured by the priest who stipulated that she make a solemn vow to become a Catholic, 'as he could not perform the cure on any other terms'. She recovered, kept her vow and died a Catholic. A young man had a similar experience and he too became a Catholic.[90]

A new wave of conversions to Protestantism swept across the diocese early in the nineteenth century. 'Evangelism ... among Roman Catholics was attempted on a large scale for the first time since the Reformation so that from 1817 on has been called the time of the Second Reformation. Quite considerable numbers of 'conversions' took place, and it seems clear that these were very often a result of definite conviction.'[91]

'The Second Reformation'

This 'Second Reformation' was completely different from anything which had hitherto preceded it as Catholics who now converted were mainly Irish-speaking people of modest backgrounds and their conversion entailed no obvious temporal gain. In fact many of them suffered persecution from their families and neighbours, often compelled to leave their homes. The scale of conversions was also remarkable. In a period of eighteen years from 1814 to 1832 'considerably upwards of one hundred Roman Catholics were converted ... by one missionary alone'.[92] Though the documentation is almosted com-

88 SC Irlanda, vol. 15, ff. 373r, 374rv
89 Acheson, op. cit., p. 108
90 op. cit., pp. 370–71
91 Kenneth Milne, *Church of Ireland*, p. 42
92 F. Westlander, *A Memoir of William Moore*, p. 12

pletely one-sided, there seems little reason to doubt the substance of the claims made.

The conversions resulted from reading the Irish version of the scriptures which was disseminated mainly through schools by the London Hibernian Society (L.H.S.) founded in 1806, the Baptist Society (1814) and the Irish Society (1818). Local agents were appointed to supervise the schools which were grant-aided. Albert Blest from Coolaney and later Sligo, who was a dissenting evangelical Protestant, was the agent in north Connacht of the London Hibernian Society and a Mr Wilson from Sligo acted as agent for the Baptist Society. One of the earliest conversions was that of Thady Connellan, a classical schoolmaster in north Sligo, through the influence of Albert Blest whom he met in 1807. Connellan himself was instrumental in making other conversions, particularly among school-teachers, and after a brief spell as a teacher in the L.H.S. school in Coolaney, he was employed by the Irish Society to make Irish translations of the scriptures.

William Moore (1752–1839)

To assist their evangelisation, the Baptist Society adopted the practice of appointing Irish scripture readers. When two Baptist ministers, Revs Ivemey and Anderson, made a tour of Connacht in 1814, they employed Pat Feeley, a Catholic school-teacher in Tubbercurry, as a scripture reader and this marked the beginning of a new system of evangelising, with scripture readers going from house to house reading the scriptures in Irish to the people. It was said that when Feeley read the parable of Lazarus and the Rich Man, they were so moved that they asked him to read it again and again.[93]

In November 1814 William Moore, at the suggestion of Thady Connellan, was appointed a scripture reader by Mr Wilson of Sligo.[94] He was born in 1752 in Boyle, Co Roscommon, the son of a small Protestant tenant farmer and shortly afterwards his family moved to Ballymote where his father was given a farm by Lord Shelburne. A year later his father died leaving five children and the family moved again, this time to Ballinacarrow, where they were given a farm by Col Percival of Templehouse. In 1772, at the age of twenty, Moore married a girl of fourteen called Bacon, by whom he had thirteen children and with his growing family he sought and was given in 1796 a larger farm by Col Fitzgerald in Turlough, Co Mayo. When the French arrived in 1798 the little Protestant colony in Turlough felt threatened by their now triumphalist Catholic neighbours and Moore moved his family back to Ballinacarrow where he remained for the rest of his life.

His wife died in 1814 and later that year he was employed by the Baptist

93 ibid, p. 186 & n
94 ibid, pp. 10–11

Society as inspector of schools and Irish scripture reader with a salary of forty pounds per annum. For the next eighteen years he travelled throughout north Connacht reading the scriptures in Irish to all classes but particularly to the common people. Not only did he convert a sizable number of Catholics but 'he was also instrumental in leading a great number of careless and ignorant Protestants from the error of their way'.[95] He kept a journal, somewhat reminiscent of the Acts of the Apostles or the Pauline epistles, which he sent at regular intervals to the Baptist Society.[96] Moore's evangelical success derived to a large extent from the impact made on his listeners by hearing the scriptures read in their own language. 'What most gratified them,' Moore wrote in June 1816, 'was hearing the Irish.'[97] The scriptures had been translated into the spoken language of the people and not into old Irish which they could not understand. In a family he visited in the Ox Mountains, where he read the scriptures, one man exclaimed: 'What is the reason ye do not read like this man? He reads as if he was talking to us.'[98] Even in the case of those who could read and understand English, it was said that 'the Irish captivates them'.[99] An old greyheaded man in the Ox Mountains, on hearing Moore read the Bible in Irish, exclaimed in ecstasy: 'The candle is now lit, and I hope it will never be put out. We were a long time kept in darkness.'[100]

One of the first difficulties the Baptist Society encountered was to find people who could read Irish to act as scripture readers. In their Seventh Annual Report the Baptist Society stated that:

95 ibid, p. 12
96 The original journals have not survived but lengthy extracts from them for the years 1815–32 are quoted in F. Westlander, *A Memoir of William Moore*, pp. 48–221. The names of people and places are often suppressed by the author of the *Memoir* and replaced by initials as many of them were still living and in the case of converted Catholics 'to avoid the vengeance of the priests, of their flocks and, in many instances, of their own nearest relations'. ibid, p. 14. I am very much indebted to An tOllamh Pádraig de Brún for drawing my attention to this rare pamphlet.
97 ibid, p. 58
98 ibid, p. 52
99 ibid, p. 73
100 ibid, p. 55

'the committee resolved to teach the native Irish language in those provinces where it was the prevailing speech and directed all their enquiries to find out suitable agents for that undertaking. Many months, however, passed away, before they could hear of a single individual who could teach that language, or of any place where a school could be established for that purpose; fears were actually entertained that no suitable Irish scholar would be found, and that the object proposed, of teaching the aborigines of the country, must be relinquished.'[101]

Those who had learned to read English were often unable to read Irish. Shortly after Moore was appointed in 1814, he could only find three persons capable of reading the scriptures in Irish. Bartley Hart from Kilmactigue, who later became an Irish scripture reader, could read English but had to be taught by Thady Connellan to read Irish. Moore himself spent much of his time teaching others how to read Irish and he described how he was approached in Ballymote on a market day in 1819 by a young lad who had a copy of St Luke's gospel 'in the Irish character' and asked Moore to read it for him so that he might learn to read himself. Moore instructed him standing there on the street and, when they met again some time later, the lad told Moore that he had learned to read it perfectly in two months.[102] He later became a scripture reader. Writing from Foxford in 1827 Moore reported to the society that there was now 'upwards of three hundred' scripture readers in his area and that there was 'scarcely a village in which an Irish Testament may not be found'. He went on to advise the society: 'Depend on it, the only effectual plan to civilize and Christianize Ireland, is to multiply Irish Readers of the Scriptures: none but such men can get access to their rude and Popish neighbours.'[103]

'The only thing that cut priests to the quick,' Moore wrote in 1827, 'was the Scripture readers.' The opposition of the priests was the single greatest problem encountered by the Baptist Society and their scripture readers. 'The Popish bishops, priests and friars, and all the fraternity, have now taken the field and open their

The Darkness of Superstition receding before the Light of Revelation.

AN
AUTHENTIC NARRATIVE
OF THE RECENT CONVERSION OF
TWELVE ROMAN CATHOLICS,
NAMED
HART,
In the Province of CONNAUGHT,
THROUGH READING THE
IRISH TESTAMENT.

BY A CLERGYMAN
Of the Established Church in Ireland.

DEDICATED TO
THE BAPTIST IRISH SOCIETY,
For establishing Native Irish Schools, &c. &c.

LONDON:
PRINTED BY ARDING AND MERRETT, OLD BOSWELL COURT;
AND SOLD BY GALE AND FENNER, BUTTON AND SON,
PATERNOSTER ROW; DUGDALE, DUBLIN; AND
INNES, EDINBURGH.

PRICE SIXPENCE.

101 ibid, p. 37
102 ibid, pp. 89–91
103 ibid, p. 189

mouths in blasphemy against the scriptures, publicly declaring they are not the word of God.' One priest proclaimed in the chapel of Ballinacarrow in 1815, 'that there was a devil going about through the parish, and for all the people to beware of him', and another did the same in 1824, warning the people 'against wolves in sheep's clothing'. Others threatened 'any that would keep a testament in their houses or send their children to free schools', while one priest, hearing about a poor man who was reading the Irish testament, 'seized him, dragged him about and abused him dreadfully'. In 1824 Moore wrote from Ballinacarrow: 'Every fortnight or three weeks there is a conference of priests held. Whatever their secrets otherwise are, one thing is evident – they will go to the last extreme to prevent any from reading or hearing the scriptures.' He claimed that in Coolavin 'any that will hear the scriptures read are put under the ban of excommunication by the priest'. And yet after all that, Moore could write from Ballinacarrow in 1828: 'and though I speak sometimes rather harshly against the priests, suppose it cut them to the heart, they shew no bad nature to me. I have a free welcome and liberty to speak my mind.'[104]

One of the more remarkable claims made by Moore's biographer is that he converted fifteen priests, of whom presumably many, if not most, would have been priests of Achonry, where Moore chiefly exercised his ministry. There is no corroborative evidence for these conversions.[105] Bishop Patrick McNicholas (1818–53) made no reference to them in his report on the diocese to Rome in 1822. The most likely explanation is that these converts were not priests, but candidates for the priesthood. Moore, in his journals, frequently refers to such candidates as 'priests', as in 1816 when he had great expectations of a 'young priest', whose father 'had him, at the time alluded to, ready for Maynooth'. Another one who showed signs of conversion and whom Moore repeatedly called a priest, was 'a young collegian who had spent three years in Maynooth College'.[106] Three other 'priests' who held 'secret correspondence' with Moore, probably belonged to the same category.[107] Another was later employed in a college in America while yet another, this time described as a 'candidate for the priesthood', went to Trinity instead of Maynooth to finish his studies and six months later got a (Protestant) curacy in the south of Ireland. Another 'priest D–' died shortly after his conversion, having refused the services of a priest on his death-bed.[108]

104 ibid, pp. 50, 70, 116, 150, 156, 194–5, 205, 207
105 ibid, p. 12
106 He is referred to as 'Mr C–', was twenty-five years old and was employed in 1821 as a scripture reader and inspector of schools. ibid, pp. 59, 109–120
107 ibid, p. 117
108 ibid, p. 24

Bartley Hart and Family

Moore was also instrumental in the conversion of Bartley Hart of Kilmactigue, who had also been intended for the priesthood, though the chief credit for that conversion belongs to another convert, Thady Connellan. Bartley was the eldest of the five children of Patrick Hart, who occupied 'a small tract of land which, improved by their industry and frugality, afforded what was necessary for the supply of their wants.'[109] After renouncing his intention of becoming a priest, he worked for two years as a clerk in Sligo and later, with some money from his father, set up his own business as a pedlar, selling cottons and muslins etc. This occupation allowed him to indulge his passion for pilgrimages, spending nine days every year at Lough Derg and going twice a year to Balla and Croagh Patrick. 'In short, there was no place in Ireland remarkable for the performance of religious ceremonies that he did not regularly visit.'[110] At one stage he seemed to have become a religious neurotic, threatening to abandon his wife and family and devote his life to fasting and penance.

At this point, hearing that Thady Connellan who, like himself, had been educated for the priesthood, had converted to Protestantism, Bartley set out to persuade Connellan to return to the fold. He spent a month with him, during which time they read almost incessantly the New Testament in Irish and, as a result, Bartley was converted. He was then introduced to Albert Blest, an evangelical Protestant who by now had moved from Coolaney to Sligo. He spent a year with Blest learning the scriptures, became a scripture reader and also an inspector of schools in Co Leitrim for the London Hibernian Society. Eventually, persecution forced him to leave Leitrim and return to Kilmactigue. Bartley's wife, Mary, also had become a Protestant, as well as his eldest daughter, Bridget, and her husband, Bryan Brennan. Bryan's brother, Patrick, did likewise and, as he had become proficient in reading the scriptures in English and Irish, he was employed by the Irish Baptist Society. Elizabeth Hart, another daughter of Bartley, was also employed as a teacher by the Baptist Society. All these had been converted by June 1814.

Bartley's brother, Con, had been sent to Sligo by his parents to persuade Bartley to return to Catholicism. He tried for two years without success and finally Con himself was converted and 'drew down upon him the severe displeasure of the people, who loaded him with all kind of reproachful and abusive language, accompanied with violent threats.'[111] As a result, Con left

---

109 A Clergyman of the Established Church in Ireland, *An Authentic Narrative of the Recent Conversion of Twelve Roman Catholics, named Hart*, p. viii: I am indebted to An tOllamh Pádraig de Brún for drawing my attention to this pamphlet. The Harts' conversion is also recounted in *Memoir of William Moore*, pp. 15–27
110 *Authentic Narrative*, p. 12
111 ibid, p. 27

Kilmactigue and went to London, taking with him his youngest brother John, who by then had also begun reading the scriptures. When Con thought 'the rage of persecution had subsided' he returned to Kilmactigue and was employed by the Baptist Society as a scripture reader. Seven or eight men used to visit him by night 'like Nicodemus' to listen to him read the scriptures, and he reported in 1816: 'I read in their own language, and they render thanks to the Almighty, and to the Society, for publishing the word of God in the Irish.'[112]

Bartley's parents, Patrick Hart and his wife, were in their eighties when Bartley was converted. When he returned home from Leitrim, Bartley was violently attacked by his father, who tried to strike him with a loy and might have succeeded had Bartley not taken refuge behind a cow in the cabin. When finally his father had simmered down, Bartley drew his Irish Testament from his pocket and began to explain the scriptures to them. His parents' anger turned to interest and eventually to conversion. It was reported in the *Sligo Journal* by James Neligan that fourteen men and six women read their recantations in the parish church of Kilmactigue.[113] The Hart family became Calvinist dissenters, though they occasionally worshipped in the Protestant church in Kilmactigue where James Neligan was the vicar. On most Sundays they met in their father's house, where they read the scriptures and prayed and were visited there by William Moore, who gave the Lord's Supper to twelve communicants.

John, the youngest of the Hart brothers, had returned to help his elderly father on the farm 'but was obliged to fly from it, being in constant danger from the change in his religious views, and fearing every night that he should be dragged out by a party, and sworn into their rebellious combination, or lose his life.'[114] His father, Patrick Hart, died at the age of eighty-eight, refusing the services of the priest on his death-bed. The family wished him to be buried in Banada Abbey with his ancestors but the Augustinians refused to have him and his remains were brought to Kilmactigue 'where Protestants and Catholics are promiscuously buried'. A large number of Catholics, 'fearing the contamination of the ground', assembled at the graveyard to prevent the burial but eventually after the intervention of 'some respectable persons', the vicar, James Neligan, was allowed to proceed with the service.

Two others, both named Catherine Hart and distant relatives of Bartley's, were converted jointly by Albert Blest and Bartley.[115] Andrew Walsh, also

112 ibid, p. 29
113 *Memoir of William Moore*, pp. 229–30
114 Albert Blest, 26 May 1812, quoted in de Brún, *The Irish Society's Teachers*, p. 182
115 *Authentic Narrative*, pp. 37–41

from Kilmactigue, was educated for the priesthood, but abandoned the idea after an attack of scruples and instead set up a classical school in the neighbourhood of Kilmactigue, which attracted numerous scholars as he had a reputation of being a good Latin and Greek scholar. Here he came into contact with Bartley Hart and engaged in frequent controversies with him. He was also a frequent visitor of Neligan's, and attended his church where he was impressed by 'the plainness and simplicity of the service.' For a while he kept his conversion secret, but eventually it reached the ears of the parish priest who forced the parents to withdraw their children from his school. Walsh was obliged to leave Kilmactigue and his conversion was also the occasion for Bartley Hart leaving and going to live in Ballina, where he was joined by his widowed mother. But by 1819, he was back again in Kilmactigue teaching school with his daughter, Eliza, while James Neligan feared for him, 'owing to violent opposition entertained against him by the priests'.[116]

In January 1817 the anonymous author of the account of these conversions concluded his *Narrative* thus: 'Since this time, several other young men in the same neighbourhood have been led to renounce Popery, and some to relinquish their prospects of entering on the Priestly office for which they had been educated.'[117]

There were other conversions elsewhere in the diocese, very often amongst the teaching profession. James Rowley, a teacher in the parish of Killasser, is remembered locally as 'Séamas Preacher Rowley' and his sister, Máire 'preacher'.[118] John McNulty of Foxford resigned his post as Catholic schoolmaster in St Michan's, Dublin, 'wishing to abandon the Romish persuasion'.[119] Not all scripture readers became Protestants and the very first scripture reader appointed in 1814, Pat Feeley of Tubbercurry, was described in the 1824 Report as a 'Catholic'.

---

116 de Brún, *The Irish Society's Teachers*, p. 176
117 *Authentic Narrative*, p. 44
118 IFC, Ms. 227, pp. 118–9. 'Preacher' was the term used by Catholics to designate a scripture reader. *Authentic Narrative*, p. 23; *Memoir of William Moore*, pp. 27, 65
119 de Brún, op. cit., p. 240

CHAPTER SIX

'An Scoláire Bocht'

'Hedge-Schools'

Illiteracy

Many visitors and commentators in the eighteenth century commented on the lack of education among the Irish. Their assessment was superficial and closer observation would have revealed quite a different picture. In 1797 a French traveller came across many open-air schools in Co Galway. 'It is a great mistake to suppose the peasants in this country either ignorant or stupid.'[1] In some branches of culture, such as music and dancing, even otherwise hostile commentators remarked favourably on their attainment. They had a wide repertoire of songs which they sang with great precision and as to dancing, they were 'adepts in that science'.[2] There was no shortage of music players in the diocese, though Sligo may have been marginally stronger than Mayo in that field. The use of the harp seems to have waned in the second half of the century when the Irish pipes became the preferred instrument.

They were knowledgeable about nature and its workings, as the French consul observed in 1791, when he met a twelve-year old boy in Easky, Co Sligo, who could point out and name four types of seaweed used in the making of kelp. He was so impressed by his ability to name each specimen of plant life shown to him, that he exclaimed: 'What a pleasure it would be to be rich enough to seek out and educate people as clever as this remarkably intelligent child.'[3]

In the manual arts, they were equally proficient. Women and young girls could spin both cotton and wool and most of the menfolk could distil whiskey or poteen. 'Everyman understands the trade.'[4] Many had specialised skills, such as cobblers, tailors, blacksmiths, weavers, bleachers, candlemakers and a host of others, and many were expert in animal-husbandry and crop cul-

1 De Latocnaye, p. 145
2 op. cit., p. 262
3 Ní Chinnéide, vol. 35, pp. 63–4
4 op. cit., p. 305

tivation. They had to be to survive even at subsistence level. Countrymen everywhere had such skills but what made the Irish different was that they had to employ their skills in the most adverse of conditions. They had to employ nature to its maximum to extract a harvest from poor soils, having been forced on to mountainous and uncultivated land by high rents. 'In those sorts of ground, actuated as well by necessity as industry, they add every year a new quantity of arable ground to their respective farms, which are afterwards subdivided among their children, as they grow up and become married.'[5]

But nowhere were Irish country people more remarkable than in their use of language, notably in their huge repertoire of prayers, proverbs and lengthy poems and stories. Ossianic legends were widely known and frequently recounted. Lady Morgan described meeting a young man on a road in Co Sligo, on his way to a wake seven miles away, where he had been invited to recite Ossianic legends.[6] Their use of language was inventive and imaginary and their vocabulary was far richer than was usual for people of such a deprived background.

Most contemporary commentators, such as Neligan, confused education with literacy. 'The understanding of the inhabitants of this parish, though uncultivated, is acute.'[7] The vast majority, particularly of the poorer classes, were in fact illiterate, lacking what is sometimes described as 'book-learning'. Their education was almost exclusively oral. For all of the eighteenth and at least the first decade of the following century, the people of Achonry spoke only Irish and their problem in acquiring literacy was compounded by the almost total unavailability of books written in Irish. Thus, to learn to read and write, they had first to learn English. For people of their meagre resources, to acquire proficiency in reading and writing, in the way most people normally do, would have been very difficult, and to acquire it through the medium of a foreign language made it almost unattainable. That so many were illiterate is not surprising, but what *is* surprising is that there was a minority who *could* read and write.

The Irish language was almost exclusively a spoken tongue, and in situations where a written language was needed, English or another language was used instead. Not many carved tombstones have survived in Achonry for this period but those which have are all in English or Latin. The Duffy tombstone in Urlaur abbey is dated 1719 and from the symbols carved on it, particularly the anvil, it appears the family were blacksmiths by trade. Given the time, the

5   Neligan, p. 360
6   *Patriotic Sketches,* vol. 2, p. 37
7   op. cit., p. 363

isolated location of Urlaur and the relatively modest background of the family, it is almost certain that the Duffys could neither speak nor understand a word of English. Yet the language used to commemorate their dead is English. The correspondence of Catholics in this period is always in Latin, English, French or Italian. While it is understandable that Irish bishops in their letters to the Roman authorities should have used Latin – or, like Troy of Dublin, who spent many years in Rome, Italian, – many bishops, like Philip Philips of Achonry (1776–85), wrote in English to their Irish agents in Rome requiring them to translate them into Latin or Italian for transmission to Propaganda. Bishops corresponding with each other in Ireland usually used English or, occasionally, French. The letters of an Achonry priest, Terence O'Gara, sent from Paris to Dublin in the mid seventeen-thirties, are all in English sprinkled with a few gallicisms. What is more remarkable is that he employed code-words in English in case they were intercepted by the government, whereas had he written in Irish, no such code would have been necessary. Furthermore, while these letters in English often contained expressions in Latin or French, they never used Irish words or expressions. James Neligan of Kilmactigue, where 'the Irish language is universally spoken,' anglicised *Leabhar Eoin* to 'Lour Oens'. The presumption must be that people who spoke Irish fluently, and were literate in English or Latin, could neither read nor write Irish. It was said of Bartley Hart, a teacher in Kilmactigue: 'He could read English already, but, though well acquainted with the Irish language, which was that he usually spoke, he could not read it without some instruction.'[8]

There were, of course, exceptions like the antiquarian, Charles O'Conor of Belanagare, who trained a young boy, Martin Hughes, to transcribe the Irish annals for Chevalier O'Gorman.[9] The poet, Seán Ó Gadhra, wrote his poems in Irish as well as English and Latin, and some were copied by Ruaidhrí Ruadh Mac Diarmada in Collooney in 1761, but in this area Gaelic poets and scribes were exceptions to the general rule as they belonged to those few families where the skill was handed down from generation to generation. Andrew Donlevy, the author of the *Catechism*, was another exception and it is revealing that his bilingual catechism has the English and Irish texts on facing pages, thus permitting the user to learn to read the Irish through the medium of the English text. Later the Irish Society (1818) followed the same style in their Irish scriptures with an English translation in parallel pages or columns. Priests usually signed their names in English and occasionally in French or

---

8 Westlander, op. cit., p. 16
9 OCD, 8. 4. SE. 148; Ward, Wrynn, Ward, *Letters of Charles O'Conor*, p. 403

Latin, using the English, French or Latin equivalents of their Christian names while their surnames were always anglicised, suppressing the O in O-names.

For many, particularly of the lower classes, literacy was of little or no importance in their lives. It was required only in very rare circumstances and when these occurred they had recourse to the priest or the schoolmaster. A widow approached her parish priest, James Henry in Collooney, to write a letter to O'Hara in Nymphsfield, regarding her daughter's dowry. Other petitions were drawn up in formal and stilted English by the local schoolmaster cum scribe, such as the one to the wife of Charles O'Hara on behalf of the widow Preston of Ardnaglass in the the parish of Ballymote in 1819:

> Petitioner is a real object of commiseration, destitute of friends or assistance, encumbered with a helpless family and by reason of the dear summer and the death of her husband lost her wordly subsistance which was little.
>
> That Petitioner is bereft of all earthly subsistance but what is extended on her by those actuated by kindness or humanity and compassion and as an appendix to her good (sic) fortune is encumbered with her mother who is superannuated these few years past which renders her unable to provide anything towards her support.
>
> Petitioner therefore begs, entreats and beseeches your charity in honour of Almighty God and hopes your Ladyship will grant her a few sticks or principles to build a cabin for the approaching winter and for your future salvation Petitioner will most fervently pray.'[10]

While literacy may not have been *de rigueur,* numeracy on the other hand certainly was, as even the poorest classes had to calculate their rents and tithes. Their family budget was run on a knife-edge and a miscalculation could have dire consequences. Commercial transactions were frequent and important: rents were usually paid by women selling their yarn; poultry, eggs and feathers were sold to provide tobacco for men and women, and men sold their labour and at least one cow a year. The priest and the schoolmaster had to be paid and dowries saved for daughters. Basic numeracy, at least in some classes, may have been learned in the home, passed on, like their prayers, from parents to children.

Schools

Schools, though difficult to document, probably existed in every parish throughout the period and, like their masters, were often itinerant and seasonal. Figures, when available, show them to be more numerous than is generally supposed. Writing about Co Sligo in 1802, one commentator stated:

10   O'Hara Papers, Ms. 20,280 (36)

'Common schoolmasters and their schools are to be found dispersed everywhere throughout the county.' Of Co Mayo he said: 'Notwithstanding the backward situation of this county, it cannot, in point of education common to the poor of this Kingdom, be said to be inferior to other parts of it.'[11] There were no less than seven schools in the parish of Tourlestrane (Kilmactigue) early in the nineteenth century, though three of these were recent foundations. The number of schools varied throughout the century, scarce in the earlier period when persecution was rife and teachers, like priests, were specific targets of the penal laws. With a price on their heads they could only exercise their profession clandestinely since the authorities considered that 'such persons corrupt the youth of this Nation with Popish principals.'[12] But the period of active persecution was not extensive, and in 1731, in his *Report on the State of Popery*, Robert Clayton, Protestant Bishop of Killala and Achonry, listed six 'popish schools' in the diocese.[13] There were probably many more of which he was unaware since even at that date it would not have been prudent for teachers to advertise themselves or their schools.

Hedge-Schools

Primary education was provided, at least to some extent, by what were called 'hedge-schools', a name apparently conjured up by English visitors to Ireland who observed children being taught in the open-air in summertime. The term was a misnomer but, like other misnomers, it stuck and by the end of the eighteenth century it was in general use. Schools were held rarely under a hedge but beside a raised ditch. The master probably sat on the ditch where he could mount his slate or rudimentary blackboard, while the children sat on stones on the ground in a semi-circle at his feet. Given the vagaries of the Irish climate, even in summer time, continuous schooling in the open-air was not very feasible and what those visitors saw was teachers and pupils profiting from the occasional fine weather by moving outdoors. A French visitor encountered one such school in 1797:

> On the road I saw one of those schools the English take so much pleasure in ridiculing and which they call hedge-schools; the truth is that the poor peasants cannot afford to build a fine house for a school. It is generally a poor hut without a window. It is plain that the master and scholars find it unpleasant and when the weather permits, they go and sit under a hedge, where the master gives his lectures in the fresh air.[14]

---

11 J. McParlan, *Statistical Survey of Co Sligo*, p. 88. *Statistical Survey of Co Mayo*, p. 97
12 *Arch. Hib.*, vol. 6, pp. 178–9
13 *Arch. Hib.*, vol. 3, pp. 128–9
14 De Latocnaye, *Rambles through Ireland*, vol. 1, pp. 158–9

Common sort of Mayo mud cabin (Barrow, *Tour*)

Two centuries later, such visitors might have witnessed similar open-air classes in the grounds of national schools.

Another explanation of the term hedge-school was given by a contemporary writer: 'The school-houses are in general wretched huts, built of sods in highway ditches, from which circumstance they are denominated hedge-schools.' They differed little from the poorer sort of human habitation: 'They have neither door, window or chimney, a large hole in the roof serving to admit light and let out smoke, which issues from a fire in the middle of the house. A low narrow hole cut in the mud wall on the south side of the hut, affords ingress and egress of its inhabitants.'[15] Such a description probably fitted the 'miserable cabin' where Pat O'Gara taught in the parish of Kilmovee in 1824.[16]

School-houses

Other schools were probably better housed, such as that of James Durkan, senior, in 'the master's dwelling-house' in Killasser, or Pat Feeley's one, with twenty-six pupils, in his own home in the town of Tubbercurry. John Hart kept another school there 'in part of James Hart's house'. Some had more spacious surroundings, such as a barn or outhouse loaned by a wealthy farmer for that purpose. Still others used the Mass-house or chapel, as in Carracastle where Patrick Gallagher taught, and Ballymote where another Pat O'Gara taught one hundred students, including eight Protestants. Similarly, John Jourdan taught three Protestants and forty-two Catholics in Baratogher chapel in the parish of Tourlestrane (Kilmactigue). There is a tradition that Séamus 'Preacher' Rowley taught three-hundred pupils in Killasser chapel, but later became a Protestant and lost favour with both priest and people. Some had no regular schoolhouse at all, such as Thomas Leonard, who in

15 Shaw Mason, op. cit., vol. 1, pp. 598–9
16 de Brún, *The Irish Society's Teachers 1818-1827*, p. 272

1824 had sixty pupils including two Protestants in the parish of Tourlestrane (Kilmactigue).[17]

Children of both sexes began school at about five years of age and, once old enough to assist in the farm work, were taken away from school. Schools operated for about four months between spring and autumn, beginning after the potatoes were set and finishing in time to pick the potatoes. 'These schools are fully attended in summer, half empty in spring and harvest and from the cold and damp utterly deserted in winter so that children usually forget in one part of the year that learnt in the other.'[18] Some schools, however, did continue during the winter but were very poorly attended, while teachers often went from house to house where they taught in return for their dinner.[19]

The number of children who attended school is difficult to ascertain. A survey, carried out in 1799–1800 among the clergy of the Established Church, concluded that less than one third of children 'fit for school' were receiving any education at all and that most of these attended hedge schools.[20] The number of pupils in each school varied. The only official figures available are those given in the 1824 Report. The largest then was in Swinford, held in the Sessions House made available for that purpose by William Brabazon, which had on roll two-hundred and twenty-nine pupils. The smallest was also in the parish of Swinford (Kilconduff) in Tumgesh which had twenty-six pupils. Ballaghaderreen had one hundred and sixty as had Monasteraden and, with the exception of Tumgesh, these were all free schools sponsored by the London Hibernian Society.[21] In all schools, where figures are given, boys outnumber girls, with the exception of Kilmactigue which had thirty of each sex, while Foxford had forty boys and thirty girls. Ballymote was fifty-forty in favour of boys, while in Gurteen it was two to one.

Pupils

The curriculum varied according to the qualification of the teacher. In all

---

17 de Brún, pp. 134, 148, 158, 191, 207; 1824 Report; IFC, Ms. 227, pp. 118–9
18 Shaw Mason, op. cit., vol. 1, pp. 598–9
19 Hely Dutton, *Statistical Survey of Co Clare*, pp. 235–40; Carr, *Tour* (1805), pp. 250–51
20 Kenneth Milne, 'Principle or Pragmatism', in *As By Law Established*, ed. Ford, McGuire, Milne, p. 188
21 Other such schools in the diocese included in the Report were Ballymote, 154 pupils; Drumfin (Kilmorgan par.), 91; Knockdaltan (Emlefad par.), 72; Branchfield (Kilmorgan par.), 95; Castlemore, 110; Foxford, 70; Gurteen, 92; Kilmactigue, 60; Templehouse (Kilvarnet par.), 61; Carrowmacarrick (Killoran par), 60; Bo(he)rhallagh (Toomore par.), no number given; Dooragh (Kilvarnet par.), no number given; Templeconny, (Emlefad and Kilmorgan par.), no pupils, building not completed; Killasser (1) and (2), no pupils, schoolhouse not finished; Collooney, no number given; Urlaur (Kilmovee par.), no number given; Ballyfahy (Kilturra par.), no number given; Tubbercurry (1) and (2), no number given; Carracastle (chapel), no number given; Ballymote (chapel), 100; Baratogher (chapel), 45; Kilmactigue, no regular schoolhouse, 60.

Schoolbooks

hedge-schools, the three 'R's', that is reading, writing and arithmetic, were taught as well as catechism. In some instances Latin was taught, as in Andrew Walsh's school in the parish of Kilmactigue.[22] Schoolbooks were scarce, with the choice depending on what the children or their families could pick up cheaply from pedlars at fairs and markets, rather than what the teacher might have deemed more suitable. 'Readers are few in number such as those sold by pedlars and petty shopkeepers, such as histories of robbers etc and that pernicious little book "The Articles of Limerick" of which several thousand are sold every year through every part of the nation from which children imbibe a spirit of disloyalty to the government and hatred of the present royal family and the English connection.'[23] Those 'story-books or vulgar ill-written histories', which were named by various commentators, seemed innocent enough, such as *The History of Renard the Fox, The Adventures of Captain Phreny, The Adventures of Redmond O'Hanlon,* and *The History of the Irish Rogues and Rapperies.* Other types of readers were 'romances describing the manners of barbarous and superstious ages', such as *The Seven Champions of Christendom, Guy Earl of Warwick, Valentine and Orson, Don Belianis of Greece,* etc. Certainly, nobody could dare complain about the use of Chesterfield's *Rules of Politeness* in the education of Irish children.[24] But beggars can't be choosers and, as one contemporary put it, 'the poverty of the parents put it out of their power to procure the necessary books for the children.'

'Books that could have conveyed any knowledge of history were too voluminous, and consequently too dear to be purchased; books of morality were above their comprehension; and their Clergy would not permit them to read the Bible or Testament. Their reading then consisted of vile stories which, without conveying instruction to the mind, either filled it

22 Shaw Mason, op. cit., vol. 3, pp. 130, 550
23 ibid, vol. 3, pp. 626–7. One commentator described them as 'reading books such as are sold by pedlars or odd volumes of novels' and another, as 'biographies of robbers, thieves and prostitutes and seditious history of Ireland'. ibid, vol. 3, p. 166; vol. 1, pp. 598–9
24 ibid, vol. 3, pp. 291–2, 472; Robert Bell, *A Description of the Conditions and Manners of the Irish Peasantry 1780–1790,* p. 40n, 41n. Other books mentioned included, Reeves, *History of the Bible,* Chaloner's *Think well on't,* Dr England's *System of Education for Children* and Murphy's, *Catholic Education,* (3 vols.), *The History of the Seven Wise Masters and Mistresses of Rome, The Seven Wonders of the World, The History of Captain Grant, a gentleman Highwayman, The Garden of Love, The Feast of Love, The Effects of Love, The Economy of Beauty, The School of Delights, Nocturnal Revels, The Chevalier de Faublas, The Monk, The Life of Lady Lucy, The Life of Moll Flanders, Fanny Meadows, Donna Rosina, Rousseau's Eloisa, The Pleasant Art of Money Catching, The Devil and Doctor Faustus, The Feats of Astrologers, Tristam Shandy, The Arabian Nights, Pastorini's Prophecies, Parismos and Parismenos, Hero and Leander, History of Philander Hashaway, History of Renard the Fox. Parliamentary Papers* (1825), vol. 12, p. 43; see Appendix no. 221 for comprehensive list.

with extravagant romantic notions incompatible with their station in life; or gave scope and activity to the worst passions. The books that were used at these wretched schools, tended as much to prevent the peasantry of Ireland from becoming good subjects, as any of the circumstances already noticed ... '

The same writer claimed that a printer in Dublin, called Corcoran, made a large fortune by publishing halfpenny ballads about the heroes of Irish history and employing people to circulate them all over Ireland. Like the books mentioned, the ballads were not acceptable as politically correct to English observers, 'conveying sentiments the most obscene and vicious that ever tended to corrupt the human mind'.[25]

Paper, though in short supply, was used for writing on and one traveller in the mid-seventies saw a group of bare-legged boys 'sitting by the side of the road scrawling on scraps of paper placed on their knees'.[26] Quill-pens were made from goose-feathers, like those plucked by boys from Ballinacurra from 'any goose they'd meet to pull quills out of her', who then spent the first part of the morning in the chapel-school sharpening their quills. They also brought their own home-made ink with them and 'every lad brought a stone to sit on'.[27] Younger children probably used slates and chalk or soft limestone to write with.

Children paid the teacher and hence the use of the term 'pay school' used in official reports to describe them.[28] Teaching was not a lucrative profession.

Pay Schools

> Many of these poor schoolmasters do not earn sixpence per day by their continual labours, from the small allowance paid to them, and in many cases promised but not paid; so that they are often obliged to have recourse to the magistrate to recover their miserable wages of 1s 8d per quarter. They could not subsist at all in this state, but that they make a practice of going home with some of the children daily or weekly, where they get their food or bread.[29]

Many of the teachers in the pay schools were also subsidised by the bishop or priests for teaching catechism. In 1824 the parish priest of Ballymote paid Pat

---

25 Bell, op. cit., pp. 40–41
26 Twiss, *Tour in Ireland 1775–6*, p. 74
27 IFC, Ms. 227, pp. 118–19
28 In the early nineteenth century the fee was one shilling and eight pence or two shillings per quarter. In the parish of Maghera, Co Derry, where there were sixteen schools with about five hundred children, there was a charge for each subject. Spelling, 1s.7d.; reading, 2s.; writing, 4s.; arithmetic, 7s. 'These have been the terms for half a century back.' Shaw Mason, op. cit., vol. 1, pp. 598–9
29 Neligan, p. 374

Pay Schools

O'Gara, the master in the chapel-school, six pounds in addition to the 1s. 3d. per quarter paid by each of his hundred pupils. The parish priest of Swinford (Kilconduff) paid the same amount to John Ormsby, the teacher in the little pay-school in Tumgesh.[30] The parish priest of Skibbereen, who paid his schoolmaster twenty pounds a year, stated in 1824 that he raised the money in part by a tax of tenpence imposed on each of the God-parents at baptisms.[31] Something similar may have existed in Achonry. In 1760, Bishop Kirwan reported to Rome that he had divided the money received from Rome for that purpose, among the school-teachers 'adding from my own money or from collections, as much as I had pledged to them by agreement'.[32]

Free Schools

In Tourlestrane there were three free schools in 1815, two of them sponsored by the London Hibernian Society and one by the Association for Discountenancing Vice. In the latter, the teacher had a salary of fifteen pounds a year, while in the other two they were paid eight guineas which was supplemented by taking in some paying students at the usual rate of 1s. 8d. to 2s. 6d. Some believed that their salaries should be doubled, 'as the miserable salary allowed cannot enable a master even to clothe himself and family decently, without house rent or diet'.[33] With or without subsidies, the annual income of most school-teachers fell far short of that of the master in Goldsmith's *Deserted Village,* who was 'passing rich on forty pounds a year'.

Schoolmasters

The payment of teachers by students provided to some extent a sort of quality-control on that profession as their salaries depended on the number of students they could attract to their schools. People with very limited resources were hardly likely to waste money on incompetent teachers. In 1788, Mr Wood, the agent of Frances Jones, an absentee landlord, wrote to her about the poor attendance in the school on her estate in Co Sligo. He had visited it several times and never found more than eight or nine students there. When he asked the tenants why they kept their children at home, he was told 'that they could learn nothing there but to sing, for that man could neither write or teach accounts, but that while he kept an assistant that could do it they all sent their children'. Frances Jones had intended building a school-house in the centre of the estate but now had second thoughts 'as the tenants seem so unwilling and so whimsical about sending their children'.[34]

The qualification, or rather lack of it, of teachers in pay schools was a frequent target of criticism by contemporary visitors and commentators. Much

30 1824 Report
31 *Parliamentary Papers,* (1825), vol. 7, pp. 366–7
32 SOCG, vol. 792, ff. 113rv, 114r
33 Neligan, p. 374
34 O'Hara Papers, Ms. 20,291, (9) and (10)

of it was not justified since, for many of these teachers, English, which was the sole medium for teaching reading and writing, was a foreign language. 'They could barely read a common English book; and what little they knew of the English language, they spoke incorrectly. They could not therefore communicate to their scholars what they did not know themselves.' But allowing for the usual element of exaggeration in such criticisms, they were in much the same position as teachers of other foreign languages such as French. A perfect command of a language is not a prerequisite for teaching it, especially to elementary students. Other criticisms were nearer the mark, such as the well-known 'those who can, do and those who can't, teach'. 'It is evident that men who could procure a decent support in any other way, would not be disposed to undertake so laborious an occupation on so poor an allowance.' Many gave up their jobs after a brief period 'having so little at stake, they are indifferent whether they lose it or not; and are without a sufficient incitement to a laudable and diligent exertion of their talents.'[35]

Who were those teachers and how were they trained? It has been suggested that they were 'spoilt priests', i.e. those who studied for the priesthood but did not persevere. 'The common schoolmaster is generally a man intended for the priesthood; but whose morals had been too bad, or whose habitual idleness so deeply rooted, as to prevent his improving himself for that office.'[36] Some certainly studied for the priesthood. Such students would have learned Latin and possibly Greek. As the system followed throughout this period required most candidates for the priesthood to be ordained prior to going abroad to study theology, a number of scenarios were possible. A candidate could have failed the examination set by the synodal examiners as a prerequisite for ordination or, because his family's straitened circumstances could not support the cost of travel and education abroad, might have declined the priesthood. Or he may simply have lost his vocation or changed his mind. However, the sheer numbers of teachers throughout this period, with several in every parish, makes it unlikely that they were all candidates for the priesthood. In the 1731 *Report on the State of Popery*, Robert Clayton, Bishop of Killala and Achonry, stated that in Erris, Co Mayo, there was a school in every two or three villages, 'inasmuch that a Protestant Schoolmaster, were he to be had, can hardly get Bread'.[37] Many teachers probably were students who attended Latin schools, which were primarily but not solely intended for candidates for the priesthood. Some of those who attended Thady Connellan's

35 Neligan, p. 374
36 Edward Wakefield, *An Account of Ireland Statistical and Political*, vol. 2, p. 398
37 *Arch. Hib.*, vol. 3, p. 143

'seminary' in Co Sligo were destined for other professions, such as pharmacy. Those schools were probably similar to the minor seminaries which succeeded them later in the nineteenth century. While their primary purpose was to give secondary education to those wishing to study for the priesthood, they also provided for many others intending to follow lay professions, such as teaching.

Private Tuition

Better-off Catholics often kept a tutor in their homes to teach their children. Edward Synge, Archbishop of Tuam, stated in the 1731 *Report on the State of Popery* that 'many Papists keep tutors in their houses, who privately teach not only the youth of the family, but others of the neighbourhood who report to them'. Robert Clayton, Bishop of Killala and Achonry, said of some parishes in Killala that 'many private Familys keep a tutor for their children by way of servant'.[38] John Brett OP, Bishop of Elphin, reported to Rome in 1753 that 'the wealthier keep religious or scholars in their homes for the education of their children'.[39]

Wealthier Catholics paid for private tuition for their children or were helped by relatives abroad to do so, like Connor O'Rorke, who thanked his cousin in Vienna for his 'favours being an inducement to me to educate my children with a tutor at home'. Their cousins, the O'Conors of Belanagare, kept a friar in their home to teach their children. In this way Charles, the antiquarian, got his early training.

> The first who put a Latin grammar into his hands was a poor friar from the convent of Creevliagh in the county of Sligo, who could scarcely speak a word of English ... He spent some years at his father's house under the occasional tuition of this Creevliagh friar, from whom all he learned was a little Irish, which he was taught to read and write grammatically ... This was the sum of his knowledge in 1724 when he was fourteen and was put under the tuition of another clergyman, who obliged him to translate some school-books into barbarous English and Irish alternately.

He was also helped by his uncle, Thady O'Rorke, the Franciscan Bishop of Killala, who took refuge from persecution in the Belanagare home, as he told a friend in 1785: 'When we were children, our uncle O'Ruark, Bishop of Killala, gave us a preparatory prayer to our studies and pressed the following truth upon us: *Sola salus servire Deo: sunt cetera fraudes* (The only safety is in the service of God; all else is deception).' O'Conor's father, Denis, also hired a dancing master, a fencing master and an Irish master 'for the instruction

---

38 *Arch. Hib.*, vol. 3, pp. 126, 143; vol. 4, pp. 176–7
39 SC Irlanda, vol. 10, ff. 422rv–425rv

and polite education of his children'.[40] Some students of lesser means were also taught privately, like Bartley Hart from Kilmactigue: 'His father, designing him for a priest, was desirous that he should possess a superior education, and therefore employed a domestic tutor, by whom he was instructed in the branches of education which are preparatory to the Priesthood.'[41]

The Synod of Bunninadden in 1759 recommended that candidates for the priesthood should teach catechism to children 'in the houses in which they stay.'[42] Presumably they helped these children with their other subjects as well. 'Poor scholars' were given free accommodation by families living in the neighbourhood of the school.[43] In fact, they were much sought after, like those in Thady Connellan's 'seminary' as he related to Lady Morgan. 'I have,' said he, 'above twenty boys who are come from distant parts to me, who begged their way, and who are now maintained among the poor of the neighbourhood who, far from considering them a burthen, were so eager to have them that to avoid jealousy I was obliged to have lots drawn for them.'[44] While they could have helped out with the farm-work, their most obvious contribution would have been to assist in the education of the children. Older children who had acquired literacy at school probably passed on their skill to their younger brothers and sisters, the normal practice in other areas like prayers, songs, dancing and music-playing. 'Let Denis, now in the interim,' Charles O'Conor wrote in 1778 to his son, 'keep school for your children, to cultivate himself and them together.' Denis was then hoping to get a place in the Irish colleges of Salamanca or Lisbon.[45]

Charter Schools

The Society for Promoting Christian Knowledge (S.P.C.K), inaugurated in London in 1698/9, led to the creation of charity schools at first in England and later in Ireland. These were small schools, with less than twenty pupils, which were administered by Protestant landlords or vicars, maintained by voluntary subscription, with a curriculum consisting of the Protestant catechism, and the schools were dominated by the Protestant work-ethic. They did not attempt to spread Protestantism among the natives but catered mostly for poorer Protestants. Catholics were only accepted in them when no

40 de Breffny, 'Letters from Connaught to a Wild Goose,' *Irish Ancestor*, x, p. 85; Bishop Brian O'Rorke of Killala 'on account of his extraordinary genius employed a tutor at his own cost' for his godson James. Rev Charles O'Conor, *Memoirs of Charles O'Conor*, pp. 157, 158. Later Charles was sent to Dublin to attend the school of a priest, Walter Skelton, where he studied mathematics and made further progress in the dead languages. p. 162
41 *An Authentic Narrative*, p. 11
42 Moran, *Spicilegium Ossoriense*, vol. 3, pp. 272–3; Edward Rogan, *Synods and Catechesis in Ireland*, p. 55; see Appendix 48, 5
43 Bell, op. cit., p. 42
44 *Patriotic Sketches*, p. 143
45 O'Conor Don Papers, 8. 4. SE. 148; quoted in Ward, Wrynn, Ward, p. 361

Protestants were available. Three such schools were established in the diocese of Achonry in the second decade of the eighteenth century: Collooney (1712), Achonry (c.1713) and Foxford (1714). This may have been due to the fact that Archdeacon Walls of Achonry was an enthusiastic supporter of S.P.C.K.[46]

Because the 1731 *Report on the State of Popery* revealed that a network of Catholic schools continued to function in spite of the laws forbidding them, it was decided to establish an alternative system. A petition, signed by most of the Protestant bishops and a number of laymen, asking for a charter of incorporation, was presented to the king. It was granted in 1733 and the Incorporated Society in Dublin for Promoting English Protestant Schools was established. Its aim was 'that the children of the popish and other poor natives ... may be instructed in the English tongue and in the principles of true religion and loyalty in all succeeding generations'. It was given a royal grant of £1000 a year. In 1745 the Irish parliament voted it the proceeds of a tax on hawkers and pedlars, and again in 1757 grants were substantially increased and continued until the establishment of the national schools in 1832.

In his report to Rome in 1753 on the state of his diocese, Bishop Brett of Elphin stated that a charter school had been established in Sligo and twenty-three elsewhere in Ireland, with 1,409 pupils.[47] The previous year Dr Pococke saw the Sligo school in the course of construction. It had three good rooms, a kitchen and two schoolrooms and was to house sixty children. It got a grant of seven hundred pounds from the governor of the Erasmus Smith schools and Colonel Wynne gave four acres in perpetuity.[48] About fifty charter schools were eventually established throughout the country, with none in Achonry, although in 1759 Mark Skerret, Archbishop of Tuam, reported to Rome that there were many of these, which he called 'diplomatic' schools, in his province.[49] Achonry was fortunate at least in this respect. An inspection of these schools later in the century revealed all the horror of a Dickens novel, with under-nourished, overworked, scantily-clothed children, infested with lice and covered with scabs.

The Roman Reaction

The internuncio in Brussels was informed in 1739 about the charter schools and their proselytism among Catholic children.[50] Then in 1741 Michael O'Gara, on his way back to Ireland to take up his appointment as Archbishop of Tuam, stopped in Brussels where he had a meeting with the

---

46 David Hayton, 'Did Protestantism fail in eighteenth-century Ireland? Charity schools and the enterprise of religious and social reformation, c.1690–1730' in *As by Law Established*, ed. A. Ford, J. McGuire & K. Milne, pp. 168–9, 174, 185, 186
47 SC Irlanda, vol. 10, ff. 422rv–425rv
48 *Bishop Pococke's Tour of Ireland*, p. 75
49 SOCG, vol. 792, f. 120r
50 CP, vol. 88, f. 103r–108v

internuncio and three other Irish bishops. They drew up a report on the state of the church in Ireland and in a reference to the charter schools, proposed that Catholic schools, subsidised by Rome, should be set up to counteract their influence.[51] Rome was alarmed at the existence of these proselytising schools in Ireland and instructed the internuncio to send an agent to Ireland to make a first-hand report on the state of the church there. John Kent, president of the Irish College in Louvain, was sent in 1742, reported back early in 1743 and among other proposals suggested that a fund be established from which each bishop would be paid a sum annually for Catholic education in his diocese. Rome agreed to pay one thousand *scudi* (£250) a year to be divided among the four archbishops who in turn were to distribute it between the other bishops of their province.

Walter Blake (1739–58) was probably the first Bishop of Achonry to receive this grant, but the first to acknowledge the receipt of such a grant was Patrick Robert Kirwan (1758–76). In 1760 he wrote to Rome stating that the portion for his diocese was exactly eight pounds:

> One annual payment has been made to me, namely, for the one year I have been active in the episcopacy. I have appointed schoolmasters among whom I have divided the said portion adding from my own pocket or from collections, as much as I had agreed with them. Children of both sexes, who are numerous in parishes everywhere, are diligently taught the rudiments of the faith.[52]

In September 1759 the cardinals of Propaganda had held a special meeting on the subject of Catholic schools and decided that in future the usual monies for schools would not be paid unless an authentic document was produced stating:

> the location, the number of masters and pupils, whether they live in common, are supported by themselves or from common funds, whether the teachers are lay or diocesan or religious priests, by whom they were appointed and sanctioned, how many classes the students are divided into in each place, what is taught, how long students remain at school, and what is the progress of their studies.[53]

It was a tall order and showed little awareness of the real state of Catholic education in Ireland.

All four archbishops duly replied as well as the Bishop of Cloyne and Ross

51 Giblin, 'Nunziatura di Fiandra', in *Coll. Hib.*, no. 10, pp. 88–91
52 SOCG, vol. 792, ff. 113rv, 114v
53 SOCG, vol. 792, f. 61rv. This decree was communicated to the four Irish archbishops in September 1759. Lettere, vol. 194, ff. 415rv, 416r

and Kirwan of Achonry. They all agreed that the Roman subsidy was far too small to remedy the dire situation they were in. 'Since this contribution is divided into seven parts,' Mark Skerret of Tuam complained, 'each part of it is so small that little or nothing can be done with it.' The Archbishop of Cashel, who used his share to buy books and paper for the teachers, was even more specific: 'It is not sufficient for the decent support of even one teacher in each diocese.' Matthew McKenna, Bishop of Cloyne and Ross, who had been a superior of the Irish College in Paris before his appointment to Cloyne, pointed out that the laws in Ireland forbade Catholic teachers exercising their profession and non-Catholic teachers made sure that these laws were executed so that they themselves would not be deprived of students. 'It is true that in some rural and remote places some Catholic schoolmasters are tolerated, either by lenity or connivance of magistrates or by means of a certain annual tax they promise to pay to non-Catholic masters. In this way, all perhaps are tolerated, under the appearance or title of catechists or quasi parochial sacristans, and in this way they teach children reading and writing and catechism in Catholic chapels.' McKenna had twenty such teachers in his diocese and claimed it was much the same 'throughout all the districts and provinces of this Kingdom'.

All the correspondents agreed that the Irish church was facing a serious crisis. Kirwan pointed out that the shortage of Latin teachers meant that the survival of the clergy was threatened, adding: 'The ordinary people and those of slighter fortune, seeing the poverty of the priests and that perhaps they could achieve more profit for themselves by their own industry, are now tired of the effort they were once eager to make, to educate their children for the priesthood.' 'The mission must be condemned to ruin,' he wrote, 'unless it is subsidised.' He was echoed by Skerret: 'Unless God and the sacred congregation subsidises us, there will be no religion from lack of priests, because no way can be devised here of avoiding the impending calamity, since we have been almost totally deprived of wealth.' Their pleas fell on deaf ears. Rome, at the best of times notoriously reluctant to part with money, made up the very modest sum of £250 annually, by discontinuing its subsidy to the Irish Dominicans in Louvain.[54] The cardinals discussed the question again at a general meeting of Propaganda in January 1762, but no new money was forthcoming.[55] They did, however, continue to pay the existing grant until the early decades of the nineteenth century.

54 Lettere, vol. 198, ff. 274rv, 275r
55 Acta, vol. 132, ff. 19rv, 28rv, 29rv, 30rv; SOCG, vol. 792, ff. 20r, 72rv, 73rv, 113rv, 114r, 119r, 120r, 125rv, 126rv

At the turn of the century an new effort was made by Protestant societies to proselytise Irish Catholics. The Association for Discountenancing Vice and Promoting the Knowledge and Practice of the Christian Religion (APCK) was founded in 1792 by three members of the Established Church and by 1800 it was incorporated and in receipt of a parliamentary grant. From then on it became an organisation of popular educators, granting money towards the establishment of schools and the payment of teachers, and investing the local Protestant minister with the sole power to appoint and dismiss teachers, who were required to be members of the Established Church. Catholic pupils were not required to attend lessons in the Protestant catechism but were required to read the authorised version of the Bible.

Evangelical Societies: APCK

By 1819 APKC had some 8,000 children in their schools and over half of these were Catholics. One of these schools was in the parish of Kilmactigue in a 'neat house' which had been built by 1815 for one hundred pounds, partly from APKC funds and partly from funds raised by the vicar, James Neligan. The schoolmaster had a salary of £15 a year and an average number of sixty pupils, who were educated free. With only ten Protestant families in the parish, four of which had only recently arrived, a good proportion of the pupils must have been Catholic.[56]

In 1811 another educational society was founded by prominent members of the Established Church and the Society of Friends. The Society for Promoting the Education of the Poor in Ireland, (generally referred to as the Kildare Place Society (KPS)), had a government grant of £6000 by 1816. Protestant clergy and land owners were given aid to found schools where the Bible was to be read without comment and no doctrinal matters were to be raised. These schools were widely acceptable to Catholics and by 1824 there were thirty-seven schools in Mayo with 2,772 pupils, and in Sligo twenty such schools with 1,348 pupils. The Society fell somewhat out of favour after 1820, when they began to give a portion of their grants to schools associated with missionary societies, such as the London Hibernian Society and the Baptist Society.

Kildare Place Society

KPS also provided a training course for teachers in Dublin which usually lasted only a few weeks. Patrick McManus, aged nineteen, who started teaching in 1816, was recommended by Neligan to be trained by KPS for a school in Kilmactigue, as was John Hart, a brother of Bartley from Kilmactigue. In 1817 aged thirty, 'this poor fellow walked from Ballina, without purse or scrip etc. and was nearly starved since he came to Dublin'. John Mullaney, who was

56 Neligan, pp. 359, 371

recommended by John Coleman, parish priest of Swinford, as 'a very proper man', was trained by KPS in 1818, as was Timothy Carabine, a Catholic from Swinford who succeeded him, and John McNulty from Foxford. Richard Fitzmaurice, parish priest of Keash, recommended for training in 1824 Francis Soden who had been appointed by Earl Kingston to the school of Templevanny.[57]

London Hibernian Society

The London Hibernian Society for Diffusing Religious Knowledge in Ireland (LHS) was founded in 1806 with an avowedly missionary aim and soon became involved in education to further its cause. Its principal agent in the West of Ireland was Albert Blest of Coolaney, who was a dissenting Protestant layman of strongly evangelical views. By 1812 he had established one hundred and sixty schools in Sligo and its neighbouring counties.[58] Already by 1815 there were two LHS schools in the parish of Kilmactigue, with an average of sixty pupils in each, one of them recently established by the vicar, James Neligan. He was the active local agent for these schools in that part of the diocese. The teachers were Catholics and the children were taught *gratis* and supplied with suitable books. Apart from the usual subjects, pupils were taught to read the Bible and commit a portion of it to memory. LHS paid the teacher eight guineas for forty pupils, which was supplemented by other students who paid from 1s. 8d. to 2s. 6d. per quarter. Inspectors were appointed to examine the pupils and assess the teachers, reporting to Albert Blest, who could dismiss or continue the teachers.

Baptist Society

Still another evangelical society, the Baptist Society for Promoting the Gospel in Ireland by Establishing Schools for Teaching the Native Irish, became very active in education. Founded in London in 1814, ten years later it had fifty-eight schools with 3,882 pupils in Connacht, which was only one less than the number of Catholic schools in the province. According to the 1824 Report, the Branchfield school in Kilmorgan was receiving aid from the Baptist Society as was a school established in 1816 in Tubbercurry. Andrew Collins who taught at Lognahaha in Killasser parish was also grant-aided. There was also one at Lugnadeffa in the parish of Ballisodare, where Thomas Durkin, a Catholic, was the schoolmaster in 1824, and another one later at Castleloye in the parish of Achonry where a Catholic, Michael Brennan, taught.[59] There was one in Ballinacarrow in 1821, where William Moore, the famous Baptist scripture reader lived, with one hundred and four pupils.[60]

57   de Brún, pp. 85, 182, 238, 240, 256; *Parliamentary Papers* (1825), vol. 12, Appendix 223, p. 617
58   O'Hara Papers, Ms. 20,285
59   See Appendix 48
60   1824 Report; de Brún, pp. 75, 95, 135; F. Westlander, *Memoir of William Moore*, p. 40

Irish Society

In the early decades of the nineteenth century the New Testament in Irish was widely distributed throughout the west of Ireland. The 'Irish Society for promoting the Education of the Native Irish through the medium of their own language' was founded in 1818 and concentrated its efforts on the 'remotest and least instructed parts of the country where Irish prevails most.'[61] While the main aim of the Irish Society was to use Irish 'as a means for obtaining an accurate knowledge of English', they also sought 'to promote, by every means consistent with the principles and discipline of the Established Church, the scriptural instruction of the Irish-speaking natives'.

On the other hand, being primarily concerned with evangelising, the Baptist Society used their involvement in schools to propagate the scriptures. The Irish version of the New Testament was used as a text-book in their grant-aided schools and their aim was unashamedly to proselytise. A clergyman of the Established Church, who was almost certainly Neligan, wrote: 'how much more successful must the application of these means prove, when exerted in the instruction of the young and unprejudiced, whose minds are open to conviction, and their faculties well adapted to receive and retain the ingrafted Word, which is able to save their souls.'[62] The children in turn were expected to evangelise their parents. 'It is also well known that the children who are instructed in reading the Irish Testament are listened by their parents and neighbours when they return from school in the evening.' Albert Blest was even more explicit in a letter to Charles O'Hara in 1814: 'Our object in instructing pupils to read Irish is for reading the scriptures in Irish for the benefit of parents and adults in their neighbourhood, who may not understand English.'[63]

In the beginning the Catholic Church accepted these schools and sometimes even enthusiastically. A joint Catholic and Protestant group approached Charles O'Hara in 1812, seeking his patronage for a school in Sligo for the education of five-hundred children of all persuasions in reading, writing and arithmetic, explicitly excluding 'books of religious controversy'.[64] Both the London Hibernian Society and particularly the Baptist Society had another agenda which brought them into conflict with local parish priests who were unhappy with the use of the Bible in schools. In 1815 Neligan described his experience in this matter: 'Some of the Roman Catholic clergy have permitted the reading of the scriptures, when solicited to do so by the

61 see de Brún, Appendix 1, p. 329
62 *An Authentic Narrative*, p. IV
63 O'Hara Papers, Ms. 20,285
64 ibid, Ms. 20,280 (28)

Protestant clergyman; whilst others oppose the practice most strenuously, publicly denouncing wrath against the parents of such children as are permitted to attend such schools of the above description, or who would read or keep in their houses a Testament or a Bible.'[65]

The proselytising activities of the LHS and the Baptist Society swung the majority of parish priests against the whole system. Daniel O'Connor, parish priest of Coolaney (Killoran), had forbidden Catholics to attend a school whose master was a Protestant, and in June 1819 Charles O'Hara wrote to him seeking an explanation for his action.[66] O'Hara pointed out that there was no rule that the masters of such schools should be Protestants, that in fact they were often Catholics, and that it was 'a principle with the masters not to interfere with the scholars in points of religion'. 'This conduct in the R. C. clergy,' he added, 'appears too much like an hostility to the Established Church.' O'Hara was a member of parliament and warned O'Connor: 'But if you yourselves draw an invidious line and refuse an education to the poor of Ireland because proffered by Protestants, you reject conciliation and you will pardon me if I doubt the wisdom of those who govern your church; and particularly at a time when they are pressing Parliament for admission into the powers of the State and the Legislature.'

O'Connor replied that 'every Catholic pastor is invariably and conscientiously bound ... to watch over the faith and morals of his flock' and consequently, he was obliged to examine the books used by the children and the character and conduct of the masters who taught them. 'Should these books contain any doctrine considered by his church as erroneous or should the masters so employed show bad example or attempt to proselytise their pupils, the establishment of such schools never could under any circumstances meet with his approbation or concurrence.' He objected to the use in the school of the New Testament or extracts from it 'translated by the Protestant and rejected by the Catholic church'. The master, he claimed, was known on many occasions and in the presence of all the pupils 'to have bestowed the vilest epithets on the Catholic religion'. He rejected O'Hara's charge that his action had been inspired by hostility to the Established Church: 'Believe me, Sir, there is not a class of men in society more ready than the Catholic Clergy to cooperate, and that greatfully (sic) too, with their Protestant Brethern for the purposes of promoting conciliation and extending the blessings of education to the poor.'

O'Hara thanked O'Connor for his letter which had been 'carefully com-

65   Neligan, pp. 371–2
66   O'Hara Papers, Ms. 20,280 (32)

posed', expressing regret that O'Connor was to continue forbidding Catholic children attending the school while the Bible continued in use there. 'I am sorry it is the dictate of your conscience because it is a dictate inconsistant with that mutual goodwill that I hope might unite both descriptions of people in this country.' The mutual goodwill desired by O'Hara was becoming rarer, though there were some priests in the diocese, like John Coleman in Swinford, who did not share O'Connor's hostility to the system. But opinion was swinging very much in O'Connor's direction. The number of teachers converted by the Baptists, like Bartley Hart and the other members of his family in Kilmactigue, must have alarmed the priests and served to justify their opposition to these schools.

Clerical opposition to the Kildare Place Society schools, however, seems to have softened somewhat. Bishop Patrick McNicholas (1818–1853) strongly opposed the KPS schools at first but soon changed his mind and applied for 'a considerable grant'. He had been under the impression that the New Testament was a text-book which was used indiscriminately 'without note or comment, and the right of private interpretation'. Matthew Donnelan, a Catholic and one of six KPS inspectors, went to meet him at Mr Strickland's. When Donnelan explained to him that the patron had the right to make selections from the scriptures, McNicholas withdrew his opposition to the schools.[67] After 1820, in general the Catholic authorities concentrated on establishing their own pay schools, subsidised by the parish, until 1832 when the National Schools were set up.

A higher form of education was required in the eighteenth century by a certain elite of wealthier Catholics. In order to preserve what estates remained to them, they had to evade the penal law of gavelling, by which they were required to divide the estate among their sons, thus diminishing progressively their property. Younger sons were expected to seek careers abroad, in the army or in one of the professions, and those who wished to stay at home, in the church or trade. Mary O'Conor of Belanagare wrote in 1736/7 to her cousin, Count Owen O'Rorke, Stuart ambassador at the Imperial court of Vienna: 'I have two sons in Rome these eight years past that designs for the Church, and one at home a priest that studied in Paris. I've two small boys more that I am told are promising which I design for the army if I should live at the time they come (grow) up.'[68] Charles O'Conor was the eldest of this family and duly succeeded to the estate at Belanagare. For families like

Latin Schools

---

67 *Parliamentary Papers* (1825), vol. 12, p. 488
68 Brian de Breffny, 'Letters from Connaught to a Wild Goose', in *Irish Ancestor*, x (1978), p. 84

the O'Conors, and others of slightly lesser social and financial standing, a good education was crucial.

There was a number of good Latin schools in the west, like the one in Sligo in 1739, usually run by a clergyman of the Established Church.[69] They were attended by Catholics as well as Protestants, apart from those in Dublin, where Catholics were barred. Elsewhere, 'Catholics have the same facilities as Protestants in Ireland as the Irish are mixed in the schools of humanities.'[70] However, the number of Catholics who could afford such education was in decline by 1740. When Brian O'Rorke, Bishop of Killala, placed his godson, James, in the Sligo school in 1741, he informed the Count in Vienna: 'in times past there were a good many of our profession there who most commonly proved the best profitients but now there is but one more and Jemy. Our poor nation is so far reduced that few or none of them are capable of sending their children to town.' Some twenty years later, Mark Skerret, Archbishop of Tuam, made the same point: 'In these parts, there is nowhere else for teaching boys the Roman language (Latin), except in those schools kept by non-Catholics in the cities, where boys, called by the Holy Spirit to sacred orders, cannot easily support themselves.'[71] It cost eight pounds to feed and board a student in Sligo in 1741, which 'was not so dear in our time', according to Bishop O'Rorke.[72] The Count sent regular remittances from Vienna to pay the school bills. James O'Rorke was just ten years of age when he began in Sligo, while his brother, Bartley, had finished there in 1740 at the age of sixteen.

There were other schools further away. In 1717 William Percival wrote to Kean O'Hara, urging him to send his son, Charles, to John Jackson's school near Athlone 'or some other school such as the Mullingar school', where Percival's son was a student and the headmaster an English clergyman.[73] Later in the century there was one in Castlebar, conducted by Rev Henry Walker and about the same time Rev James Neligan and Rev Peter Bermingham were said to have one each in Ardnaree (Ballina), while Rev James Armstrong ran the school in Sligo.[74] The names of three Catholics who attended Armstrong's school in Sligo at the turn of the century, were recorded.[75] Mark McDonogh from Co Sligo, who may have been a Catholic as his name suggests, attended

69 William Henry, *Co Sligo,* TCD, Ms. 2533, p. 28
70 Swords, 'History of the Irish College, Paris, 1578–1800' in *Arch. Hib.* vol. xxxv, p. 69; SCAR, codex 1, vol. 2, f. 472r
71 SOCG, vol. 792, f. 120r; see Fenning, *Undoing,* p. 240
72 de Breffny, op. cit., p. 97
73 O'Hara Papers, Ms. 16,942
74 O'Hara Papers, Ms. 20,280 (9): Wood-Martin, *Sligo 1691–1891,* p. 416
75 O'Rorke, *Sligo,* vol. 2, p. 450

the Rev Henry Walker's school in Castlebar in the last decades of the eighteenth century.[76] In the parish of Fuerty in the neighbouring diocese of Elphin, there was a school in 1789 where Latin was taught by both Catholic and Protestant teachers to students of both religions. The Dominican parish priest, Daniel O'Kennedy, was obliged by Bishop French to pay an annual grant of forty-seven *scudi* from his parish income to this school.[77]

According to the Bishop of Kilfenora in 1737, 'private schools of humanities are to be found everywhere'. These were Catholic Latin schools, founded specifically for the education of students for the priesthood.[78] In 1731 there were two such schools in the diocese of Achonry. One of them, described as 'a School for Philosophy', was run by Thady O'Hara in the parish of Achonry and another was reported in Swinford (Kilconduff) with the observation, 'from whence young men have been qualify'd for Orders.'[79] The location of these two schools, one in Mayo and the other in Sligo, would have adequately provided for the needs of a small diocese. In 1731 the neighbouring archdiocese of Tuam had thirty-two 'Popish schools, many of which teach Latin, Philosophy and some Divinity'. One of them was run by the parish priest of Dunmore, Thady Glynn, 'who teaches Philosophy and Humanity in his Mass House and boards some gentlemen's children who are under his care'.[80]

At least until 1750 there was another type of Latin school, novitiates attached to friaries, such as those described by Dr Charles O'Conor as existing when his grandfather was a boy: 'A few gloomy convents where barefoot scholars were taught by poor simple friars to translate into Irish the poetry of Homer and Virgil, and the eloquence of Cicero and Demosthenes.'[81] These were established to insure a continuing supply of recruits who were taught not only the rule of the Order but other subjects such as Latin, to prepare them for philosophy and theology in one of the order's continental colleges. The two Dominican friaries of Straide and Urlaur had sizeable numbers of friars throughout this period but the novices in Straide may have been received in the mother-house in Sligo. Urlaur, however, had a long tradition as a novitiate-house having at one time been designated as the novitiate for all Connacht, because of the remoteness of its location.[82] Early in the seven-

Novitiates

---

76 O'Hara Papers, Ms. 20,280 (9)
77 O'Kennedy paid for a while and then refused to continue doing so because it was an exorbitant charge as the parish income was very poor and when the bishop threatened to expel him, he referred the matter to Rome. Fondo di Vienna, vol. 28, ff. 237rv, 238rv
78 SCAR, codex 1, vol. 2, f. 472r
89 *Arch. Hib.*, vol. 3, pp. 128–9
80 ibid, pp. 176–7
81 Rev Charles O'Conor, *Memoirs of Charles O'Conor*, p. 157
82 de Burgo, *Hibernia Dominicana*, pp. 311, 314; O'Heynes, *Irish Dominicans*, pp. 228–231, appendix, pp. 96–7

Urlaur Abbey, 1935 *(Office of Public Works)*

teenth century it had five priests and 'four or five youths', while over a century later, in 1749, no less than four novices were admitted to the habit.[83] For most of the eighteenth century the friars in Urlaur, numbering between five and eight, certainly had the manpower required to maintain a novitiate. It seems reasonable to suppose that if a Latin school was established for its own novices, other students, particularly those destined for the diocesan priesthood, would be admitted.[84]

Individual friars from these convents also established Latin schools. In 1731 Stratford Eyre reported that an Augustinian called Murphy had applied to the Protestant archbishop to use his influence with his Catholic counterpart, Bernard O'Gara, to restore Murphy to his benefice 'and to the liberty to teach school.'[85] Later, in 1759, another archbishop, Mark Skerret, reported to Rome that he paid twelve *scudi* a year to an Augustinian friar to teach Latin to a group of twenty students for the priesthood.[86] With the discontinuance of novitiates by Rome in 1750, the numbers of friars began to diminish. In 1768 the Connacht bishops (with the exception of Kirwan of Achonry) complained to Rome that 'with the religious orders so weak, the friars could no

83 SOCG, vol. 294, f. 103v; Fenning, *Irish Dominicans*, p. 249
84 Less is known about the Augustinians in Banada and Franciscans in Ballymote but the latter friary contained more than seven friars in 1731.
85 *Arch. Hib.*, vol. 3, p. 143
86 SOCG, vol. 792, f. 120r

longer conduct those little Latin schools which had previously played such an important role in preparing candidates for the diocesan and regular priesthood'.[87]

Lay Classical Schools

There were other classical schools run by laymen, such as those of Andrew Walsh in Kilmactigue and of Thady Connellan in Templeboy, on the other side of the Ox Mountains. Lady Morgan, with some members of the Crofton family, visited Connellan's school which she described as 'miserable cabin on the side of a very desolate wood'. 'The interior of Thady's cabin perfectly corresponded with its external aspect. It was divided into two apartments, which boasted no other furniture than an old deal table covered with copy-books and slates, and a few boards placed on stones which served as seats to the young students.' She also penned a portrait of the master himself:

> The next moment Thady himself appeared in all the majesty of pedagogue power: his hair, dress, and manner, were all admirable, … his low clumsy figure, clerical tonsure, rubicund face, his wrapping coat, according to the old Irish custom, fastened with a skewer, the sleeves unoccupied, and the collar of his shirt thrown open, combined with his Greek and Latin quotations, his rich brogue, and affected dignity, to render him a finished character.[88]

There were fifty students, barefoot and otherwise lightly-clad, twenty of whom came 'from distant parts', some of whom were poring over a work entitled *Seven Wise Masters of Greece,* while 'three tall fellows were endeavouring to read all at the same time out of an old tattered volume of Virgil'. Such books were scarce and Thady had only one copy of Homer. The senior class, who studied Greek, were absent that day as they had gone to cut turf 'for a poor distressed family in the neighbourhood', and they normally occupied the second apartment, which Thady called his *sanctum sanctorum* ('the holy of holies'). Thady had also five female students who were learning the humanities, philosophy, and mathematics, with the intention of becoming 'tutoresses in gentlemen's families'. The junior students paid from one to four shillings per quarter depending on their parents' means, while the senior class studying Greek did not pay for their tuition, instead assisting in teaching the others. Lady Morgan's party distributed several old books among the pupils and, as they were driving away, 'a tall well-looking young man with a satchel on his back' ran for a considerable distance alongside their carriage. He begged them to give him an old Cicero and told them that he had been studying for Apothecaries' Hall, but had lately taken up philosophy.

87 SOCG, vol. 825, f. 271–2; see Fenning, *Undoing,* p. 281
88 *Patriotic Sketches,* XVIII, pp. 138-9

Thady Connellan
(National Gallery of Ireland)

Thady gave Lady Morgan what seems a highly fanciful account of his own classical education. 'When he was a young man,' he told her, 'there were but few schools in Connaught and those few but bad.' With eight or ten other boys, 'bare-footed and bare-headed', he set off for Munster, heading for Clare where they had heard there was a famous school-master. Clare was a thinly inhabited grazing county with none of the accommodation usually given to 'poor scholars' available. 'We could not get a spot to shelter our heads in the neighbourhood of the school.' The rest of his story defies belief: 'so being a tight set of Connaught boys, able and strong, we carried off the school-master one fine night, and never stopped till we landed him on the other side of the Shannon, when a priest gave us a chapel-house, and so we got learning and hospitality to boot, and the school-master made a great fortune in time, all Connaught flocking to him.'

Apart from Thady's highly suspect tale, there is not much other evidence that Connacht students went to Munster for their classical education, though it was said that Walter Henry, who was born in the parish of Achonry about 1744, and 'finding no classical school in the neighbourhood', went to Munster to learn Latin and Greek.[89] Most commentators agreed that there was a higher standard of Latin and Greek available there. The French consul, who visited Claregalway in the summer of 1791, remarked, 'they are not (as) good classical scholars as they are in Kerry', but he did add, 'or even Mayo.'[90] Sir Jonah Barrington also coupled Mayo with Kerry in this field. 'In parts of Kerry and Mayo, however, I have met with peasants who speak Latin not badly.'[91]

Throughout the century the standard of Latin teaching appears to have declined. Bishop Brian O'Rorke of Killala complained to his cousin in Vienna in 1740 that 'the country is so reduced they are not capable of encouraging a good master.'[92] With the decline of the friaries, standards continued to fall in the second half of the century and Latin teachers were becoming scarce. 'The Latin language is acquired with great difficulty,' Bishop Kirwan reported to Rome in 1760, adding: 'apart from some priests, who cannot take on this responsibility except by leaving their parishes, those suitable for teaching (Latin) are rare among us.' A few months earlier, Mark Skerret, Archbishop of Tuam, had made the same point and Anthony Blake, Archbishop of Armagh, corroborated the view expressed by Kirwan and Skerret reporting 'that few teachers are now to be found in this Kingdom who can teach Latin.' Perhaps significantly, both the Archbishop of Cashel and the Bishop of Cloyne and Ross, who also wrote to Rome on the subject of Catholic education, made no specific mention of a crisis in Latin teaching.[93] If Munster had a surplus of such teachers, market forces suggest that some of them may have immigrated to Connacht and established schools there, but no specific instances of such schools have been found.

89 O'Rorke, *Ballysadare and Kilvarnet*, pp. 481–2
90 Ní Chinnéide, vol. 25, p. 13
91 *Personal Sketches of his own Time*, p. 83
92 de Breffny, op. cit., p. 96
93 SOCG, vol. 792, ff. 113rv, 114r, 116rv, 119r, 121rv, 122r

The 'Poor Scholar'   'Poor scholars' occupied a unique position in Irish society.

> It is no uncommon thing to see poor lads who had left their homes without shoes or stockings, or perhaps the smallest sum of money in their pockets, wandering through the country in search of scholastic instruction, and living on the bounty of those whom they had applied to for relief, which was hardly ever refused them. In this latter circumstance they were distinguished from all other mendicants, as well as in the compassionate attention they experienced from most people. They called themselves poor scholars: and that name was always sufficient passport for a temporary lodging and entertainment in the house of any peasant, whose hospitable spirit the cold hand of want had not extinguished.[94]

'The ultimate object which they had in view,' the same author added, 'was that of being admitted into the Romish Priesthood.' It is difficult to ascertain how many priests began their classical studies as 'poor scholars' though probably only a minority of them who came from less well-off families. Lady Morgan's fictional character, Father John, stated that 'poor scholars' only represented one class of priests while the other two classes were divided between the sons of merchants and farmers and the younger sons of Catholic gentry. She described an encounter between Father John and a 'poor scholar' who begged the priest in Latin for money to buy ink and paper:

> With a leathern satchel on his back, containing his portable library, he sometimes travels not only through his own province, but frequently over the greater part of the kingdom. No door is shut against the poor scholar, who, it is supposed, at a future day may be invested with the apostolic key of Heaven. The priest or school-master of every parish through which he passes, receives him for a few days into his bare-footed seminary, and teaches him bad Latin and worse English; while the most opulent of his school-fellows eagerly sieze on the young peripatetic philosopher, and provide him with maintenance and lodging.[95]

Clerical Relations   Referring to the parish of Dromore-West, Co Sligo, Robert Clayton, Bishop of Killala and Achonry, wrote in the 1731 *Report on the State of Popery* that he 'has reason to believe that some of these priests educate their relations in order to qualify them for Popish priests so that on this account schools are infinitely multiply'd upon us.'[96] In some cases in Achonry, different generations of the same family became priests. Terence O'Gara, senior, was followed by Terence O'Gara, junior, probably his nephew. Patrick McNicholas, who later

---

94   Bell, op. cit., p. 42
95   *The Wild Irish Girl*, vol. 2, pp. 131–6
96   *Arch. Hib.*, vol. 3, p. 144

became bishop had a much older cousin of the same name a parish priest in the diocese. James Henry succeeded his uncle, Walter, as parish priest of Ballisodare and Collooney. Walter taught classics in his first parish, Killasser, and later in Collooney, where he generally had about a dozen pupils, one of whom was John Coleman, later parish priest of Swinford and archdeacon of the diocese.[97]

The prevalence of similar surnames among Achonry priests in the eighteenth century suggests that many such relationships existed, and in these cases, it is quite likely that priests shared the same family home with their nephews and supervised their Latin education. Philip Philips (1776–85) lived with his nephew in Cloonmore. Thady O'Rorke, Bishop of Killala and maternal uncle of Charles O'Conor, found refuge in the O'Conor home in Belanagare for a few years and while there he supervised Charles' education. 'The Bishop obliged him to copy the most beautiful passages from the best English authors ... to commit to memory select passages from the most approved writers, ancient and modern.' He made O'Conor translate the *Miserere* psalm into Irish, which later caused the harpist Carolan to burst into tears, when Charles recited it to him.[98] O'Rorke died in Belanagare in 1734. Another Bishop of Killala, Brian O'Rorke, wrote in 1741 to his cousin, the Stuart ambassador in Vienna: 'I injoined Jemy to come to see me twice a month and that upon a Saturday that I may examine him.' The future bishop Patrick Durcan from Kilmactigue, who was born in 1790, acquired Greek and Latin 'partly at home from a maternal uncle'.[99]

The general standard of education in Ireland was higher than was generally supposed, particularly by English commentators. In 1826 the Knight of Kerry declared in the House of Commons: 'So far from being in the state of ignorance attributed to them, he was convinced that the peasantry of any district in Ireland would be found better educated than the inhabitants of any corresponding portion of the empire.'[100] Of those who had been 'poor scholars', one contemporary wrote: 'Among the Roman Catholic Clergy were many men of learning and exemplary lives, who had acquired their education in the manner just described. There were even instances of some poor scholars having been admitted into the University of Dublin, and there distinguished themselves by their progress in classical and scientific knowledge.'[101]

Standard of Education

97 O'Rorke, *Ballysadare and Kilvarnet*, p. 482
98 Rev Charles O'Conor, *Memoirs of Charles O'Conor*, pp. 161–2
99 O'Rorke, *Ballysadare and Kilvarnet*, p. 490
100 Hansard, *Parliamentary Debates*, vol. xv, cols. 18 & 19 (March 20, 1826); quoted in Michael Quane, 'Banna School, Ardfert', in *R.S.A.I. Jn.*, vol. 84, p. 162
101 Bell, op. cit., p. 42

The poet, Seán Ó Gadhra from Knockrawer in Kilshalvey parish, composed poems, not only in Irish and English, but also in Latin.[102] One Latin poem is in memory of Roderick O'Flaherty, the author of *Ogygia*, who in 1713 had addressed a poem, also in Latin, to Ó Gadhra. The latter frequently referred to and sometimes quoted from Virgil, Ovid, Horace, Homer as well as the Old and New Testaments.[103] In a lament, *Cad é an brón so*, for a priest, Ever O'Gara who was buried in 1703 in Knockmore, the family's traditional burial place, the poet described him as follows:

> *Is luath fuair bás i lár a shaégail*
> *Éimhir Ó Gadhra, bláth na cléire,*
> *Sagart sásta cráibhtheach déirceach*
> *Do scrúdadh na húghdair is Tollétus.*
> *Do thuig tú an scrioptúir go faébhrach*
> *Mar ba dhual do bhuachaill tréada.*

> Early, in the prime of his life, died
> Ever O'Gara, flower of the clergy,
> An excellent, holy, charitable priest
> who studied the authors and Tolletus.
> You had a deep understanding of the scriptures
> As befitted the shepherd of a flock.

The poet's classical education was probably the same or similar to that of his contemporary and possible kinsman, Terence O'Gara, senior, who was parish priest of Ballaghaderreen.

The standard of classical Latin achieved by Bishop Patrick Robert Kirwan (1758–76) was remarkably high and his elegantly written Latin letters impressed the Roman authorities. One of these letters, with phrases and quotations from such classical authors as Sallustius, Livius, Tacitus, Plautus and several from Cicero, also impressed a modern classical scholar in Rome:

> This most elegant letter is full of not only super-classical phrases but entire 'stock' quotations from the classical authors which the writer of the letter must have learned perfectly at some time in his career ... Every other phrase seems to be a perfect quote or replication of some very beautiful Latin phrase which the author thoroughly had absorbed in his life and mind.[104]

102 An tAthair Mac Domhnaill, ed., *Dánta is amhráin Sheáin Uí Ghadhra*
103 Nollaig Ó Muraíle, 'Aspects of Intellectual Life in Seventeenth century Galway' in G. Moran, *Galway History & Society*, pp. 192–3
104 Professor Reginald Foster, Gregorianum University, Rome.

Kirwan was also an accomplished Greek scholar.[105] Another member of the Kirwan family, Richard, entered the Jesuit novitiate, where it was found his Latin was so good that he was immediately appointed professor of humanities.[106]

Some of those who received their classical training in Achonry followed academic careers later in their lives. Patrick McNicholas became president of the lay college in Maynooth in 1815, a post he occupied until becoming Bishop of Achonry in 1818. He entered Maynooth in 1795 at the age of twenty-five. He must have acquired his classics in Achonry because he matriculated in theology. In 1806 McNicholas was appointed junior lecturer and the following year professor of Latin and Greek. He was said to 'have received his early education, for the most part, in his native parish'.[107] James Filan, who like McNicholas came from Killasser, entered Maynooth in 1799 and was also professor of Latin and Greek in the lay college for three years, which supposes the existence of a good classical school in the vicinity of Killasser towards the end of the century. Filan left Maynooth to set up a school in Sligo for boarders and day boys in 1807, with a curriculum including Latin, Greek, French and English as well as history, geography, mathematics and book-keeping. Dancing was an optional extra.[108] Yet a third Achonry priest, James Henry, later parish priest of Ballisodare and Collooney, was said to have taught Latin and Greek in Maynooth for three years and to have attended an 'excellent classical

Kirwan's Latin Letter
(Propaganda Fide, Rome)

---

105 SCAR, codex 1. 4. no. 426
106 Charles Chenevix Trench, *Grace's Card*, pp. 95–6
107 Healy, *Centenary History of Maynooth*, pp. 549–550, 733
108 *Sligo Journal*, 15 May 1807; quoted in O'Rorke, *Sligo*, vol. 2, p. 139n

school' which had been established in Tubberscanavin towards the end of the century.[109]

All Achonry priests who studied philosophy and theology in one of the colleges of the University of Paris, had to do so through the medium of Latin. A number of them went on to take higher degrees, and they were required to defend their theses orally in a lengthy Latin exposition. Andrew Donlevy, the author of the bilingual catechism, became prefect of the community of clerics and scholars in Collège des Lombards in Paris in 1722, presided over it for twenty-four years and was regarded as the founding-father of that institution. As he was thirty-eight years old in 1718, when he registered in the faculty of law in the University of Paris, the presumption must be that all his classical education must have been acquired at home.

Corpo Santo (Irish Dominican College in Lisbon) 1776 From a painting by John Coates

109 O'Rorke, *Ballysadare and Kilvarnet*, pp. 484–5, 488

CHAPTER SEVEN

'Des Messes et des Arguments'

Educated Abroad

Priests, for the most part, were recruited from the more comfortable classes. The cottier class had not the financial or educational resources to train or maintain a member of their family in the priesthood. The church, like the rest of society, was an aristocratic institution and it was church policy to recruit its second order from the ranks of the middle if not the upper classes. In a *Mémoire* from Paris to Rome about 1750, it was recommended that bishops be forbidden to seek candidates for the priesthood from the poorer classes *('dans la plus vile populace')* whose status, education, morals, etc., were always suspect.[1]

An analysis of the family names of the priests for the period shows that many of them belonged to the former Gaelic or Anglo-Norman ruling clans who had managed to salvage sizeable landholdings from the various confiscations. There were no less than eight O'Haras among the very incomplete list of priests which exists from 1683 to 1818. One of them, Dr Charles O'Hara, was described in 1704 by Hugh MacDermot, then apostolic vicar of the diocese, as a man 'with the most illustrious name in all of Co Sligo'.[2] The others included MacDermots, McDonoghs, O'Garas, Costellos, Jordans, O'Connors, O'Flynns, O'Kellys, Philips, Bretts and others only a little less illustrious.

Philip Philips, then a parish priest in the diocese, was recommended to Rome in 1758 as 'a noble of an illustrious family with powerful connections *('con gran parentado')*. James Dalton was entered as a student in the Irish College, Salamanca, as of 'noble parents'. That college itself enjoyed the title of 'college of the noble Irish'. In 1731, the Franciscans in Ballymote were described as 'related to the best popish families in the barony', and these included among others one Brett and two McDonoghs.[3] One of the Bretts was then the land agent of the absentee Lord Taaffe who had an extensive estate in Ballymote. At the turn of the century Lady Morgan's fictional character,

---

1 CP, vol. 110 ff. 153rv–156r. I am indebted to Dr Hugh Fenning OP for reading an early draft of chapters seven and eight and making many useful suggestions.
2 O'Hara Papers, Ms 20,384 (iv); see Appendices 5–28
3 CP, vol. 133, ff. 167rv, 168rv; *Arch. Hib.*, vol. 4, p. 58; vol. 3, pp. 128–129

Father John, divided priests into two classes, 'the sons of tradesmen and farmers, and the younger sons of Catholic gentry', but by then the social background of priests had deteriorated somewhat.[4]

Some, at least, of the prestige enjoyed by these priests may have been that accorded to their families for centuries. The well-established tradition in France and elsewhere of designating one son for the succession, one for the army and another for the church, was followed to some extent also in Ireland. The difference in Ireland was that the first son inherited no political influence, and soldiers, like Colonel Oliver O'Gara and General Dalton, served abroad. The priest, however, was at home and often in his family home and, to some extent, he inherited the mantle of influence of the ancestral family chief. Thomas Costello belonged to a family which had given its name to the barony of Costello in the Mayo section of the diocese, while the head of the family of Roger MacDermot, parish priest of Gurteen, enjoyed the imposing title of 'Prince of Coolavin'. It was no surprise that Thomas Costello became parish priest of Ballaghaderreen (Castlemore and Kilcolman), as his family claimed to have the right to nominate to that parish *(ius patronatus)*.

Not all the priests of the diocese could show such illustrious connections but they all came from comfortable backgrounds. Many of them became parish priests where their family held modest estates, like Philip Philips in Bunninadden, John O'Hart in Ballisodare and Roger MacDermot in Gurteen (Kilfree). Earlier in the century Terence O'Gara was parish priest of Ballaghaderreen, where he resided not far from the former castle of the O'Gara's in Coolavin. In neighbouring Elphin diocese, Charles O'Conor became parish priest of Castlerea, which was in the gift of his own family.

Irish College, Rome

Only the names of four students of the diocese who were ordained abroad have survived and they must have belonged to families of some means, as the maintenance of a student abroad was expensive. 'The expense is certainly not trifling,' Charles O'Conor wrote while studying in Rome, 'and they must be parents of a tolerable condition who send their children here.' Thomas Costello was about seventeen when he entered the Ludovisian College in Via degli Ibernesi in Rome in September 1762. He immediately took the usual oath to obey the rules, return to the Irish mission after ordination and not to ask for the *viaticum*, i.e. expenses for the return journey to Ireland.[5] There were only nine students in this college and places were eagerly sought after and difficult to obtain. Charles O'Conor of Belanagare had to exercise his considerable influence with the Irish bishops to have his grand-nephews,

4   *The Wild Irish Girl*, vol. 2, p. 136
5   AICR, Jesuit Records, Lib. 12, ff. 261r, 264r; see *Arch. Hib.*, vol. 27, p. 72

Charles and Matthew, accepted there. One of Costello's fellow-students was Valentine Bodkin who later became the Roman agent of the western bishops and ended his life as Warden of Galway. Another near-contemporary in the college was John Butler, who resigned as Bishop of Cork when he succeeded to the title of Lord Dunboyne. The college was then run by Italian Jesuits. After seven years, Costello was ordained in the Lateran Basilica and went on to take a doctorate in the Gregorianum, the Jesuit university, before returning to Ireland, probably about 1772.[6]

The College of Propaganda Fide in Rome provided four places for Irish students, one from each province and they were greatly sought after. Though they were supposed to be rotated among the dioceses of each province, no Achonry student gained a place there. They seem to have been monopolised by the two larger dioceses, Tuam and Elphin. Brian O'Rorke, Bishop of Killala, invoked in 1740 the aid of his cousin, the Stuart ambassador in Vienna, to secure a place for his nephew from the diocese of Elphin. 'I sent my nephew abroad last month to the Propaganda Fide to fill a vacancy that was for Connaught. I am confident I secured the place for him ere he begun his journey, but if he should meet with any opposition (as there were many candidates), I request your interest in his favour.'[7] Later in the century Boetius Egan (1785–8) secured a place there for his nephew and namesake from the archdiocese of Tuam. Those educated there had to take an oath to write every year to Propaganda describing their ministry and as a result Rome was kept informed on the grassroots situation in different parts of the country.

Street sign, Rome

There were two other Irish colleges in Rome, St Isidore's for Franciscans and San Clemente for Dominicans. Franciscan novices from Ballymote were sent to St Anthony's in Louvain to study philosophy and to St Isidore's, or their college in Prague, for theology. Between 1756 and 1783 Prague sent no less than one hundred and fifteen trained missionaries to Ireland. Their Dominican counterparts from Urlaur and Straide were sent either to San Clemente in Rome, Corpo Santo in Lisbon or Holy Cross in Louvain. Bishop Dominick O'Daly OP made his studies in Rome while Terence McDonnell of Urlaur was stationed in Lisbon in 1755. The Augustinians from Banada were trained at San Matteo in Rome or one of the other Italian or Spanish convents of their order.

Other Colleges

6   Vicariato Archivio Storico, *Liber Ordinationis,* vol. 38
7   *Irish Ancestor,* vol. 10, p. 96

The continental colleges

Two Achonry students went to the Irish College in Salamanca. John Joyce studied philosophy in Santiago before entering the college in Salamanca in May 1733. He took the triple oath to keep the rules, become ordained and

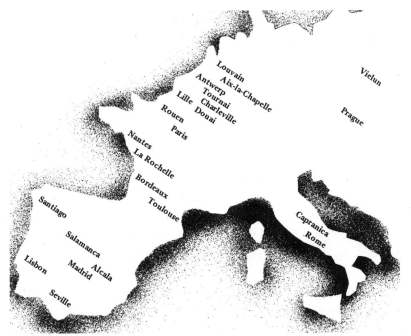

Salamanca

returned to Ireland. He was ordained in Salamanca probaby in 1736,[8] and may have worked in Achonry diocese for about five years as Bishop Blake gave him a testimonial in 1742 declaring him fit for employment by any other bishop. He went to Galway, where he eventually became warden. Later he was recommended by the Archbishop of Tuam and the Bishop of Kilmacduagh to succeed Philips as Bishop of Achonry, and they described him then as the former vicar-general and present archdeacon of Achonry.[9] James Dalton was listed by Patrick Curtis, the rector of the college, as one of the students in April 1789. He returned to Achonry in September 1797. Two other students there at the same time were Thomas and William Costello, nephews of Thomas, former parish priest of Ballaghaderreen but students for Elphin diocese.[10] William was later recommended as coadjutor to Bishop John O'Flynn (1809–1818), who was also his uncle.

Dominick Kelly OP, who later became parish priest of Kilmovee, was ordained at Toledo in 1761 and probably studied at a Spanish house of his

8   *Arch. Hib.*, vol. 4, pp. 6, 28–9
9   SOCG, vol. 844, ff. 273rv, 274v; ACTA (1776), vol. 146, ff. 93v-95r
10 *Arch. Hib.*, vol. 4, pp. 56, 58; vol. 6, p. 13

order.¹¹ Michael O'Gara had been rector of the Irish College, Alcalà, for twelve years before becoming Archbishop of Tuam. Terence O'Gara moved there from Paris in 1740 and with the O'Gara connection, it would be surprising if some other students from Achonry did not study in Alcalà. Other students from the diocese went to Bordeaux and Douay, which accepted only students and not priests. Bishop Kirwan (1758–76) declared to Rome that he had sent students to both Bordeaux and Douay among other colleges.¹² Boetius Egan, who later became bishop of the diocese, was educated in Bordeaux. There may have been Achonry students in other colleges such as St Patrick's in Lisbon or the Irish Pastoral College in Louvain but their names have not been recorded. There were almost certainly Achonry priests in Nantes which was the largest Irish College after Paris and accepted priest-students.

Ordinations

By far the greatest number of Achonry priests were ordained at home at the age of twenty-four or twenty-five, as required by canon law, and then went abroad to study, mostly in Paris. Candidates for the priesthood had to submit to an examination by synodal examiners consisting of senior priests with degrees in theology. Such candidates were expected to be competent in Latin, familiar with the catechism, and proficient in the use of the *Roman Ritual*. The latter provided detailed instructions on how to say Mass and perform the other sacraments. The examination was conducted orally and mostly in Latin.

John O'Hart and seven other priests complained to Rome in 1734 about the cavalier attitude adopted by Bishop Dominick O'Daly (1725–35) to the examination. One particular case was cited where a candidate was asked in Latin his name: 'the question might just as well have been put in Hebrew, as the candidate was not able to answer'. In spite of the vehement protests of the examiner, the bishop went ahead with his ordination.¹³ Another whose suitability was called into question by John O'Hart, when he succeeded O'Daly as bishop, was James Gallagher. Gallagher, who had been taken on as O'Hart's curate in Ballisodare after he became bishop in 1735, then applied to Rome for the parish and was duly sent a bull conferring the parish on him. It must be said that the question of his suitability only came up when O'Hart attempted to have the bull revoked.¹⁴ Apart from these two cases, there is no evidence to suggest that the results of these examinations were not strictly adhered to in choosing candidates for ordination.

11 *Arch. Hib.*, vol. 1 (1912), p. 71
12 SC Irlanda, vol. 11, f. 541v
13 ASV, Nunz. di Fiandra, vol. 130, ff. 10r, 11rv
14 ACTA, vol. 109, ff. 277–78; vol. 139, ff. 317–20

All seven orders, minor and major, were conferred by the bishop over the course of three successive days, usually Friday, Saturday and Sunday. Rome had granted this concession to Ireland due to the peculiar difficulties the church was experiencing there. Elsewhere in the church, the major and minor orders were conferred over a period of a few years. The four minor orders were tonsure, porter, lector and acolyte, and the three major orders, sub-diaconate, diaconate and priesthood. The four minor orders were conferred on the first day, sub-diaconate on the following and diaconate and priesthood on the Sunday.

In the early part of the century, when bishops were persecuted and ordinations illegal, they took place in great secrecy wherever the bishop was hiding (*'in loco refugii'*). Of the parish priests registered in 1704, eleven were ordained by Teige Keoghy, Bishop of Clonfert, at Clonfert or at Creggin, near Portumna, Co Galway. A further three were ordained by his successor, Bishop Donnellan, at Kilconnell or Clonfert. Four others were ordained by the Archbishop of Tuam, James Lynch, three of them at Cloonbare, Co Galway and one at Cong, Co Mayo and another two were ordained at Oranmore, Co Galway by Andrew Lynch, Bishop of Kilmacduagh. The parish priest of Kilmactigue, William Kennedy, had to go all the way to Dublin to be ordained by Patrick Plunkett, Bishop of Meath, who resided there.

After 1707, when Achonry had its own bishop, the priests were normally ordained within the diocese at a place chosen usually to suit the convenience of the bishop. Bishop Philips (1776–85) ordained Francis Donlevy in Kilturra, near Philips' home in Cloonmore. O'Daly ordained Dominick Kearney, later parish priest of Tourlestrane (Kilmactigue), somewhere in the barony of Gallen, and Kirwan appears to have performed all his ordinations in Kiltimagh where he certainly did so in 1765, 1769, and 1771. This may account for the twenty-one guineas he left in his will to the parish priest of Kiltimagh, Thady O'Flaherty, to discharge a debt he owed there.[15] Kirwan performed at least one ordination, that of Anthony McNamara, at his home in Bunnitubber, Co Galway. Significantly, both O'Daly and Kirwan lived in Co Galway and they chose the extreme western edge of the diocese closest to that county for ordinations.

The newly-ordained was given an ordination certificate which consisted of a postcard-size piece of parchment where the bishop certified in Latin that he had ordained the young man on a certain date after he had been examined. In the earlier period the location was given as *'in loco refugii'* (in his refuge). It was signed and sealed by the bishop and secretary or other diocesan func-

---

15 *Arch. Hib.*, vol. 1, p. 225

tionary. This was not only a licence for the holder to practise as a priest, but more importantly, his passport to an Irish College on the continent. In fact, it was virtually the only legal document he possessed there and it is not surprising that, among the few that survive, two are in the notarial archives in Paris, and one of these was signed by Teige Keoghy at Creggin, Co Galway.[16]

It seems unlikely that the bishop was paid for his services although some gratuity would normally be offered. Dominick O'Daly was accused in 1734 of demanding payment on these occasions: 'He promotes as many candidates to sacred orders as present themselves provided each of them can offer him a sum of money to the value of 60 French pounds' (£15 sterling). The accusation added: 'He ordains more for his small diocese than would be necessary for the whole province of Tuam.'[17] There were then in the Paris college no less than five Achonry priests, all ordained by O'Daly.

A statement made by one priest, Peter McCook (McHugh), and forwarded to Rome, alleged that he was informed by the dean two days before ordination that it was absolutely necessary for him to have £4 for the bishop plus a large sum to compensate the examiners for their trouble. The dean told McHugh's father: 'If you were giving your son in marriage you would have to bestow £5 on him and yet you refuse to donate the same sum to the prelate who is to confer sacred orders on him.' McHugh had to borrow the money from non-Catholic neighbours. Rome immediately wrote to the Archbishop of Tuam to enquire into the allegations and he found them to be substantially correct, though O'Daly continued to deny the charge. After his death in 1735, Rome, considering that 'it would be quite easy for a Bishop of Achonry to take such gratuities, because of the wretched state of the diocese', suggested that it should be united to Killala.[18] O'Daly's tarnished reputation lingered on in the diocese. In 1817 the Achonry clergy, in a review of their previous bishops, summed up O'Daly in one terse line: *'nil de mortuis nisi bonum'* (speak no ill of the dead).[19]

Ordinations probably took place in the autumn with September the most usual month, as appears in the 1704 registration. For candidates who had long distances to travel in the earlier period, and the non-resident bishops who had similar distances to travel later, September was often the last month when weather conditions were still dependable. By then bishops had com-

---

16 Swords, 'Calendar of Irish material in the files of Jean Fromont', in *Coll. Hib.*, nos. 34 & 35, (1992–3), pp. 99, 104
17 ASV, Nunz. di Fiandra, vol. 130, f. 9r
18 ASV, Nunz. di Fiandra, vol. 130, f. 9r; vol. 131, f. 72rv; see Giblin, *Coll. Hib.*, no. 9, pp. 46–7
19 SC Irlanda, vol. 20, f. 127v

pleted their visitations and were well rested before setting out on their travels again. For the candidates and their families, much of the harvest would have been completed by September. However, other months were possible. At least four had to travel to Creggin, Co Galway in December and another to Oranmore in February. But all these months had one advantage since they allowed the newly-ordained sufficient time to earn money from Mass stipends to acquire a wardrobe and pay for his voyage. He may also have found temporary employment as an assistant to an elderly or invalid parish priest and benefited from a share of the Christmas and Easter offerings.

Charles O'Conor wrote from the Irish College Rome in 1786 advising on the wardrobe of his younger brother, Matthew, who was about to join him. 'Let my brother bring suits of clothes to make himself genteel in appearance at the cardinal's palace, and remember that what you call a genteel appearance in Dublin is but a common one in Rome, where there is almost as much luxury amongst the laity as there was in the days of Juvenal.' He suggested that his clothes be light and 'of a lively colour', that he bring a broad-rimmed round hat with silver or gold band and tassel. He could buy sky-coloured silk stockings in Italy when he arrived as they were half the price there:

> Let him bring only 2 pair of thread stockings for sea, 3 of speckled fine worsted and 2 of black do. He should have four fine shirts clean for this city and 8 ordinary which he shall use on his voyage. Some pen-knives, razors and 2 strops, £20 sterling at least for his deposition, 5 or 6 guineas for his journey from Naples or Leghorn and 5 for pocket money in the college.

Going abroad Something of the nature of what was called elsewhere in Ireland 'the priest's wedding' probably took place after the newly-ordained priest returned home. A party was given by his family to which all the neighbours and relations were invited, who showered the priest with gifts, preferably money, while the family entertained them with the best of food and drink.[20] The newly-ordained priest made the rounds among his relatives and neighbours 'raising contributions on the pious charity of his poor compatriots: each contributes some necessary article of dress, and assists to fill a little purse, until completely equipped; and for the first time in his life, covered from head to foot, the divine embryo sets out for some sea-port, where he embarks for the colleges of Douay or St Omers.'[21]

20 Some such custom would have got over an earlier prohibition of the Tuam synod against priests soliciting money on the occasion of their first Masses.
21 *The Wild Irish Girl*, vol. 2, pp. 134–5

Sailing ships, Dublin Bay (*Jean Rocque, 1757*)

Whether all the priests went abroad for their education after their ordination is difficult to ascertain. In some dioceses they were obliged to go within six months under penalty of suspension, suggesting that pressure had to be brought to bear on some of them to do so. In 1670, a provincial synod in Armagh ordered priests, ordained within the previous six years, to go abroad or be deprived of their parishes. In Achonry there is only one certain case, James Gallagher, who did not do so but his refusal was linked to the fact that Rome had provided him with the parish of Ballisodare which he feared losing by his departure. He was already a few years ordained in 1739 when ordered by John O'Hart to go to Paris but pleaded to be allowed to wait until the following May, but by then O'Hart was dead. His successor, Walter Blake (1739–58), deprived Gallagher of Ballisodare but he appears to have remained at home. Thirty years later he was still disputing the case with Patrick Robert Kirwan, who had him examined again by his synodal examiners.

There may have been other cases too, because when Kirwan took over in 1758 he claimed he was forced to take on 'ignoramuses who would simply say Mass and carry out the necessary duties', while he prepared candidates to send abroad.[22] In 1818, when Patrick McNicholas became bishop, he found fifteen priests, ordained four or more years, who had never studied theology, and his neighbour in Killala found two-thirds of his priests in a similar state,

22 SC Irlanda, vol. II, f. 541v

Travel

but this was due to the exceptional circumstances of the French Revolution and the closure of the Irish colleges in France, Belgium and Italy.[23]

For some, like Thomas Costello, summer was the preferred time for travelling. Long-distance travel was rarely undertaken in winter. Though Sligo was a fairly prosperous port by 1765, with boats trading with several continental countries like France and even Italy, it was not a port of departure for any of the priests because traffic there was probably too irregular. Galway was a busier port and it was there that Dominick O'Daly embarked for Brest, with four other novices in June 1698.[24] For most, Dublin was the usual port of embarkation as there was a regular supply of boats there bound for several continental destinations.

The journey from Achonry to Dublin took, on average, two days. There was a coach service from Kinnegad to Dublin later in the century, but most of the journey had to be made on horse-back and the priest was probably accompanied by a member of his family who could bring the horse home. Once arrived in Dublin, he had to wait for a suitable boat, which in turn had to wait for suitable winds, and this could take days and even weeks. Delays were costly and ate into his limited resources. The fare had to be negotiated with the captain and even Catholic captains showed little sentiment in setting their prices. They were more accommodating in the earlier period of active persecution. The nuncio in Brussels informed Rome in 1709 that Ambrose MacDermot, the newly-consecrated Bishop of Elphin, was 'hoping to find a vessel with a Catholic captain, who in other times had helped the holy missionaries in the journey they had to make to that kingdom.'[25] Travelling directly to Italy by sea was much cheaper than going overland, which was estimated in 1783 at £40 sterling while a direct sea crossing from Ireland to Italy cost from £10 to £15.[26]

Most ships then were cargo vessels and passengers had to sleep rough on deck with whatever bedding they could provide themselves with. Many were Italian vessels but there were Irish captains who plied this route as well.[27] Nearly all travellers suffered severe bouts of sea-sickness like Charles O'Conor and a friend. 'We were not long at sea when both O'Caroll, who was our

23 SC Irlanda, vol. 23, f. 611v
24 Fenning, *Irish Dominicans*, p. 22
25 CP, vol. 34A, f. 6371r
26 SC Irlanda, vol. 11, f. 123rv; vol. 15, ff. 377rv, 378rv; Fenning, *Coll. Hib.*, no. 11 (1968), pp. 90–110. The Marseilles-Leghorn crossing in a hundred-ton three-masted boat, took six and a half sailing days and cost five *scudi*. Michael Nall, who travelled direct from Leghorn to Ireland, was asked for 60 *scudi* (£15) by three English captains, but was willing to pay only 40 (£10).
27 SC Irlanda, vol. 8, ff. 71r, 72r, 73r; Lettere, vol. 10, ff. 559rv, 560r

companion on the voyage, and I fell sea-sick. In this condition we remained for 8 days during which time we could not bear even the smell of flesh meat, nor stand up out of our seats.'[28] O'Conor made the crossing direct from Dublin to Leghorn, leaving Ireland on 1 July 1779. When he eventually arrived in Rome, he wrote a lengthy account of his voyage to his mother at Belanagare. Once the sea sickness had passed and he had recovered his appetite, the supply of fresh meat had run out. Live fowl were kept on board for this eventuality but these were destined for other stomachs. By now after twelve days' voyage they had reached the Bay of Biscay, where they spied a privateer belonging to Guernsey with 18 guns and 92 men bearing down on them:

> They boarded us and gave us bad treatment which we expected from such an uncivilized set of people whose voices were hoarse through excessive intemperance. They plundered as much as they could, and drank near half our liquors, and not content with this they took away the greater part of our fowl. They also took away a penknife from me for which I am now greatly distressed; they at length departed and let us pass.

The following morning they were chased and boarded by an American privateer with 26 guns. They did not let them continue 'without drinking what remained of our liquors and taking away all our fowl except an old cock of the captain's which they did not think worth carrying off'. Soon after they were boarded by another American frigate of 24 guns and 142 men in search of fowl but, finding that the old cock was all feathers, they left it. As soon as they had gone, the captain ordered the cock to be killed and cooked for the table. By now they were close to Lisbon where they encountered alternately a strong gale and a thick mist. Eventually they passed through the Straits of Gibraltar, sailed up the Mediterranean and arrived at Leghorn. 'Here we met with a disappointment, the last and most grievous; for when we were just prepared to go on shore we were surprised with the diasagreeable and unexpected news of a quarantine in which we were all enrolled for 15 days.'

By contrast, the journey to Paris, taken by most of the Achonry priests, was comparatively easy. They crossed to England, travelled overland to Dover where they crossed the Channel and from there by coach to Paris. One priest who made the journey, Charles O'Donnell from Derry, kept a diary in 1777 which showed that he took exactly eighteen days, leaving Strabane on 8 July and arriving in Paris on 26 July.

The Irish College in Paris had been acquired in 1677 and continued to be known by its original Italian name, *Collège des Lombards*. It was situated in

The Irish College, Paris

---

28 *The Seven Hills*, vol. 3, no. 2, p. 240

Chapel of Collège des Lombards

rue des Carmes on the Mont-Ste Geneviève in the heart of the Latin Quarter where all the other colleges of the University of Paris were located. At the top of the street was Collège de Montaigu, which had housed a sizeable Irish community in the previous century, while Collège de St Barbe was a little lower down, and the Irish College itself was back-to-back with Collège des Trente-Trois, where the famous Abbé Edgeworth had been a student. The Sorbonne was a short walk away, between rue St Jacques and boulevard St Michel. There were no lectures in Collège des Lombards and the Irish priests went out to some of the other colleges, studying philosophy for two years at Collège des Grassins, just around the corner in rue des Amandiers, and three years of theology in the Sorbonne or Collège de Navarre on rue Mont Ste Geneviève. Michael Moore, a Dublin priest, was principal of the latter college for a number of years and also *rector magnificus* of the University of Paris. The final year was spent preparing for the mission and this was done sometimes at the seminary of St Nicolas du Chardonnet.

The community of priests in Collège des Lombards usually numbered about a hundred and, though no student registers have survived, there are in what sporadic lists exist almost always some Achonry names. Both Charles O'Hara and Bernard Morvornagh are mentioned among the community in 1692, and John O'Hart and James Tymon were in Collège des Lombards in 1711, as was Edmund Kelly in 1721. There were at least five of them there in 1734, all ordained by Dominick O'Daly. A 'Philips' was listed in 1746, who could well have been Philip Philips, as he was ordained in 1741. Those probably only represent a tiny fraction of the total number of Achonry priests who studied in the Irish College.[29]

Community of Priests

The community of priests were governed by four superiors, called provisors, who were drawn from the four provinces and elected every three years by the priest-students of their province. One of them was made principal and the others were prefect of studies, chaplain and bursar. No Achonry priest was elected to any of these posts but Walter Blake, who later became bishop, briefly held the post of bursar in 1734.

29 see Appendix 29

The priests paid for their keep, amounting to about £100 a year, with their Mass stipends. One of the senior priests among them was appointed sacristan and his job was to collect stipends, while some Irish priests working on the French mission also collected Mass stipends for the priests-students. Irish soldiers, and others who died in France, often left money to the college for Masses to be said for the repose of their souls. There was no scarcity of these offerings until the decade before the French Revolution, when there was a steep decline. A French wit satirised the Irish priests as:

Les pauvres Hibernois qui viennent à Paris,
vivre des Messes et des arguments.
(The poor Irish who come to Paris,
to live on Masses and arguments.)

For about twelve pence a day, the priests were provided with food, linen, candles and wood while they themselves had to provide their own basic furniture such as table, chair and bed, and of course books. One priest, who had to return home because of illness, left a catalogue of his books amounting to over fifty volumes, including the works of the Fathers, such as Augustine and Athanasias, the *Summa* of St Thomas, works on canon and civil law, Cicero and the Latin poets and a French-Latin dictionary. There were other works devoted to 'controversies' which formed an important part of their theology studies, training them to deal with the arguments of Protestants and others to various Catholic teachings.[30]

As the Irish College only housed a percentage of the Irish priests in Paris, particularly in the early period, many of them found accommodation in some of the other colleges. In 1733, Abbé de Vaubrun informed Cardinal Imperiali that there were more than three-hundred Irish priests in the diocese of Paris.[31] John Duffy and Edmund Jordan were in Collège de Navarre in 1721. Some other names appear in the university registration lists, such as Thomas Moore, Patrick Henican, Michael Daly and John Fitzmaurice.[32]

There was also in Collège des Lombards a community of students who were either fee-paying or burse-holders. They usually started about the age of fifteen and followed a six-year course in humanities, consisting mainly of Latin and Greek, in Collège des Grassins or Sorbonne-Plessis. They then started philosophy there or elsewhere and after a further six years completed their theology. No records have survived listing the students of this community either, but it would be surprising if there were no Achonry students

Community of Students

30 Swords, *Coll. Hib.*, nos. 34 & 35, p. 80
31 SCAR, codex 2, vol. 2, f. 411rv
32 Brockliss and Ferté, op.cit., nos. 1015, 1022

there, given that Andrew Donlevy was in charge of it for twenty-four years. There were three who later became bishops of Achonry, Thomas O'Connor, Charles Lynagh and John O'Flynn, and who studied at Collège des Irlandais, where the student community was housed from 1769.

The great dispute

Much of the increasing tension between the two communities resulted from their differing financial resourcing, but it also derived from a reforming party *(zelanti)* in the Irish church in Ireland as well as in France, who believed it was high time that Ireland conformed to the mainstream church system of clerical education. They believed that only students should be accepted in the college and that the Irish practice of ordaining priests prior to their education should be discontinued. In Paris this reform was spearheaded by Andrew Donlevy, after he became head of the student community in 1722, and he enjoyed the support of Abbé de Vaubrun, a wealthy ecclesiastic who was a major-superior of the college. He was also supported by his patron, Cardinal de Fleury, Archbishop of Paris. Within the college, he was enthusiastically backed by two of the other superiors, John Burke of Cashel and Walter Daton of Ossory. Their campaign had already built up a big head of steam by the time a sizeable contingent of Achonry priest-students had arrived in the college, probably in 1733. One of them, Dominick Kearney, had been ordain-ed in 1732 and another, Terence O'Gara, soon became the spokesperson of the community of priests in the college.[33]

Collège des Irlandais, Paris (watercolour 1986)

The row between the reformers and the priest-students came to a head with the election in February 1734 when the incumbents were ousted and replaced by four new superiors, including Walter Blake. However, Burke and Daton succeeded in having the election overturned on a technicality and the former superiors were brought back in the interim. Terence O'Gara and the other Achonry priests were among the 114 signatories to a petition sent to

---

33 Their names, with those of Patrick Knavesey and Patrick and Luke Beirne, appeared on all the petitions sent by the Paris priests to Rome. There may even have been two other Achonry priests, Edmund Kelly and James McDonogh, in Paris. SCAR, codex 2, ff. 412rv, 464, 465, 466, 467, 497, 498

Rome in protest.[34] The majority of the Irish bishops, who favoured the existing system of sending pre-ordained priests to the college, appointed Daly, the absentee Bishop of Kilfenora, then residing in Tournai, to act as their agent in Paris and insure no change in the existing system. The Connacht priests in Paris wrote to their bishops who pledged their support in a letter in July 1736 signed by John O'Hart of Achonry among others. The Archbishop of Tuam stated that the student community had only provided three or four priests for his province in the last twenty-six years. It was even worse in the northern province, where the Bishop of Derry declared that he knew of no priest from the student community in his own diocese or in the five or six neighbouring ones for the previous forty years.

Terence O'Gara wrote in February 1736 to Dr Linegar, Archbishop of

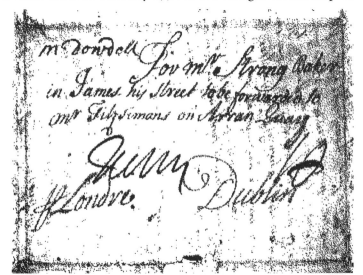

O'Gara's letter to Dr Fitzsimons, addressed to Mr Strong, baker, James's Street, Dublin *(Dublin Diocesan Archives)*

Dublin, informing him that a decision had already been taken by the royal commission set up to solve the dispute, and this was now sent to Versailles to be signed by the king in his council. 'This news pierced the hearts of the poor Irish priests, but determined them rather to seek for refuge in the utmost parts of Europe, than live under the jurisdiction of three unhappy countrymen (Donlevy, Burke and Daton), who have sacrificed the honour and reputation of their afflicted church and superiors.' O'Gara also informed Linegar that they had sent a petition, signed by a hundred priests, to Cardinal Imperiali, warning him of the great loss to the Irish mission if he approved 'Donlevy's system', i.e. of maintaining only students in Paris.

34 SCAR, codex 2, vol. 2, ff. 466–7

Later that year the Bishop of Kilfenora commissioned O'Gara to inform the Irish bishops about the situation of the college. Cardinal Imperiali had just written to Cardinal de Fleury asking him to side with the priests and, as a result, the publication of the new decree was suspended. Kilfenora had already made a formal protest againts the decision of the commission which proposed removing priests from the college. O'Gara wrote another letter to Ireland, this time to Patrick Fitzsimons, the vicar-general (and later archbishop) in Dublin. He listed the four articles of the draft decree, the first of which stated that in future no Irish priest was to be admitted to the college or even those returning from Spain allowed to stay there, 'under pain of being fettered among publick malefactors'.

The Bishop of Kilfenora had written to ask that Donlevy be recalled home by John O'Hart, as well as Burke and Daton by their bishops, and was expecting a reply by every post. But by now the crisis was on the point of being resolved, with the interventions of Imperiali and Corsini proving decisive. The status quo remained, with priest students continuing to study at the Irish College for the rest of the century. The king issued a decree abolishing elections and from now on the superiors were appointed by the Archbishop of Paris for an unlimited term. So ended what was one of the great disputes in the Irish church in that century. It is ironic that Achonry, one of the most insignificant dioceses in that church, should have played such a large role in the conflict. It was provoked by bishops like O'Daly, with his practice of 'multiplying sacred beings unnecessarily', as one of his confrères put it. Two of the leading antagonists, Donlevy and O'Gara, were Achonry priests and Walter Blake, who was briefly caught in the crossfire, was a future bishop of the diocese.

Terence O'Gara's criticism of Donlevy seemed particularly harsh. O'Gara had been expelled from the Irish College and was acting as a curate in a French parish. His parish priest was a brother of David Flynn, who was chaplain at the Stuart chateau of St Gemain-en-laye. O'Gara recounted an encounter, which took place in the sacristy of the parish church there, between Flynn and Donlevy. Donlevy boasted that that he 'clipped the prelates of Ireland's wings, and that he would soon make manifest in Rome and France that bishops were as useless to the mission of Ireland as their priests *à la hate* are to the church of France.' Flynn retorted that Donlevy 'deserved to be dragged between wild horses' and that 'his end would be to become a Calvinist minister'.

Donlevy's Catechism

Donlevy, however, remained as head of the student community. Whatever esteem he had lost in the Irish church from his role in the dispute, he quickly regained with publication of his *Catechism* in 1742. *An Teagasg Críosduidhe do*

Donlevy's *Catechism* (First edition, 1742)

réir Ceasda agus Freagartha was the last such book printed on the continent in Irish characters. It was approved in April 1741 by Michael O'Gara on his way from Alcalà to Ireland, where he had succeeded his brother as Archbishop of Tuam. Its publication had been made possible by a wealthy Frenchman, Philippes Joseph Perrotin, who donated 3,000 *livres* to the college to establish a school of Irish there and 'to print from time to time catechisms and other little works of piety in Irish, which will be given free to the students and ecclesiastics who return to Ireland, for distribution among those who instruct the young'. The catechism ran into several editions and was still in use up to the present century.

The first edition also included an essay on *The Elements of the Irish Language*. 'Not only the several provinces of Ireland have a different way of pronouncing, but also the very counties, and even some baronies in the same counties, do differ in the pronunciation.' As Donlevy left Ireland early in the century and never returned, the language of the catechism was the language spoken in Achonry at that time. 'The Irish language is said to be spoken best in Sligo,' according to the French consul who attended a Mass in Sligo in 1791 where the congregation prayed out loud in Irish, and to him at least it sounded *'plus doux dans leur bouche'* (sweeter in their mouths).[35] Donlevy described Irish as a 'language of neither court, nor city, nor bar nor business', and praised it as 'one of the smoothest in Europe, no way abounding in monosyllables, nor clogged with rugged consonants, which make a harsh sound, that grates upon the ear'. He believed that 'Irishmen without Irish is an incongruity and a great bull'.

Donlevy died in Paris in December 1746 at the age of sixty-six. In his will he declared that he owned nothing, 'not even the bed on which I lie', appropriate words from the author of a catechism. Everything he owned belonged to the community of students in Collège de Lombards which he had done so much to establish and foster. He was buried in the vaults of the college chapel which is today L'Eglise St Ephraim des Syriens.

University

While all priests followed their courses in recognised colleges of the University of Paris, only a fraction of them went on to take university degrees. The names of ten Achonry priests survive in the university registers. Others may have taken degrees elsewhere, like Thomas Costello, who took his doctorate at the Gregorianum in Rome. Bordeaux had its own university as had Nantes, both of which had Irish colleges, while Salamanca had a famous university as had Alcalá in Spain and Louvain in Flanders, where other Irish colleges were located. In 1734 there were in the diocese five priests with university degrees, a sizeable percentage for a diocese with only some twenty parishes and not many more priests. Of these, four had doctorates and only two of them, John O'Hart and John Duffy, had registered in Paris. Where the other three studied is unknown.[36]

For priests who had already spent six years in Paris and were then in their early thirties, taking degrees was a long and expensive undertaking. An M.A. was normally taken by priests who wished to pursue a degree after they had completed their ordinary theology course. These degrees were in the higher

35 Ní Chinnéide, op. cit., vol. 36, p. 32
36 William McDonogh and James Howley had doctorates in canon and civil law and M. Dowell is decribed as an M.A. and a doctor. ASV, Nunz. di Fiandra, vol. 130, ff. 10r, 11rv; vol. 131, f. 107rv

faculties of theology, law and medicine, with law the faculty most favoured by Achonry priests. Here, the baccalaureate could be taken after two years of study, the licence and doctorate at the end of the third. Theology was a much longer affair, taking eight or nine years. John O'Hart would have got his baccalaureate normally after three years while the licence and doctorate could be taken after a further five or six years. John Fitzmaurice, who got his M.A. in 1758, took his licentiate six years later, but Walter Blake, who got his M.A. in 1720, had to wait another eight years before taking his licentiate and doctorate.[37] Charles O'Hara was only twenty-two when he was ordained in 1684, thirty-three when he registered in the law faculty in 1695, and thirty-seven when he took his doctorate there. Andrew Donlevy seems to have been a late-starter. He was already thirty-eight when he registered in the same faculty in 1718 and forty when he took his licentiate in 1720.[38] Bernard Morvornagh, if he was twenty-five when ordained, would have been thirty-six when he took his doctorate in 1696.[39]

Theses for those degrees were not written but defended orally in Latin, each degree awarded after a series of oral examinations and public debates. The theology debates were particularly harrowing, lasting at least five hours. While O'Hart and Blake had probably private resources to fund their further studies, others had not. John Duffy was described as a 'priest and pauper' when he registered in the law faculty in 1727 and, by claiming poverty, the fees were waived. He had been a student in Collège de Navarre in 1721, registered in the law faculty in 1727, took his doctorate in 1731 and three years later he was a canon and parish priest of Ballaghaderreen (Kilcolman and Castlemore). By 1739, he was the dean and vicar-general and was proposed as a candidate to succeed John O'Hart as bishop. His modest background may have told against him as Rome chose the more aristocratic Walter Blake.[40]

James Lyons from Sligo has left the most detailed account of his journey from Rome to Ireland. He set out in May 1763, taking seven days to reach Leghorn from Rome. There he boarded a 100-ton, three-masted sailing boat bound for Marseilles but was forced to put in at St Tropez for a day and a night because of bad weather. After six and a half days at sea, during which Lyons suffered from sea-sickness, he reached Marseilles where he spent four days with an old family friend, Fr Hart OP, who had lived in the city for twenty years. From there he went overland, stopping at first at Avignon

Homeward Bound

---

37 Brockliss & Ferté, op.cit., no. 1114
38 Brockliss & Ferté, op.cit., no. 1114; no. 1018
39 Brockliss & Ferté, op.cit., no. 1023; no. 1016
40 Duffy was still dean in September 1760. AN MC et / XVII / 614; Brockliss & Ferté, op. cit., 1296; ASV, Nunz. di Fiandra, vol. 131, f. 107rv; SCAR, codex 4, f. 466

which he reached in two days. He was still sick and was obliged to remain in Avignon for nineteen days to recuperate. From Avignon he went to Lyons where he took a canal barge drawn by four horses and with over 300 people aboard. At Chalons he took the stage-coach to Paris and on 15 July he left that city for Dublin which he hoped to reach in sixteen days.[41]

The length of the sea-voyage from Italy varied depending not only on the weather and the prevailing winds but on the length of the quarantine imposed. In May 1763 Michael Nall accompanied James Lyons from Rome to Leghorn. There they parted, with Nall choosing to travel all the way by boat. He reached Dublin on 1 November, the journey taking 110 days, of which 43 were spent in quarantine in Carlingford. On average, the whole journey took between three and four months though at least one priest arrived in Ireland six months after he left Rome.[42] Some travelled from Italy to Lisbon, Marseilles or Bordeaux, and from there to Dublin. One priest took fifty-nine days to reach Lisbon from Genoa while Ignatius Daly from Athenry took thirty-six days in 1755 to make the crossing from Lisbon to Dublin.[43] Much time was spent on shore, waiting for a boat. Luke O'Reilly had to spend eighteen days in Lisbon before he found a boat ready to sail for Cork.

The Sorbonne

41 Fenning, *Coll. Hib.*, no. 11 (1968), pp. 90–110
42 SC Irlanda, vol. 9, ff. 215r, 216r
43 SC Irlanda, vol. 10, ff. 503rv; vol. 11, f. 211rv

Even shorter distances could turn out to be lengthy voyages. Ambrose MacDermot, Bishop-elect of Elphin, set out for Ireland from Amsterdam on 30 July 1809, a journey normally lasting a week or two. He spent thirty-four days tossed about in the North Atlantic by a succession of violent storms, before landing in Cork on 2 September.

Not all Achonry priests returned home after they had completed their studies. Bernard Morvornagh became chaplain to the regiment of Dauphins Dragoons. In 1718, he made his will in Paris, establishing a burse there for his relatives in Kilmovee and shortly afterwards he set out for home and died in Co Mayo in January 1719.[44] Michael Daly, who was listed as Achonry diocese in the university register, took a baccalaureate in theology and stayed on in Paris as assistant priest in the parish of St Paul. In 1785 he founded two burses in Collège des Lombards for priests of Elphin diocese, which throws some doubt on his diocese of origin.[45]

Coming home

Many of them did return. James Tymon, who was a student in Collège des Lombards in 1711, got his baccalaureate in law in 1815 and by 1731 was parish priest of Keash.[46] Edmund Jordan who was a student in Collége de Navarre in 1721, later became a parish priest of Kiltimagh.[47] Patrick Henican, who took his licentiate in theology in 1738, returned home to become parish priest of Ballisodare, dean and vicar-general.[48] Other Paris students who returned included Terence O'Gara, Patrick Knavesey and Dominick Kearney.[49]

Those who stayed on in France could often plead that there was no place for them at home. In 1782, Matthew White of Armagh had to stay in his mother's house in Dunleer when he returned from Rome and he expected to be there for some time as 'there are in this country more priests than there is need for'.[50] Earlier in the century, a Limerick priest returned also from Rome to find that there was no vacancy for him, and he failed to find employment

---

44   AN MC et / XVII / 534, 538, 542, 550, 561, 595 ,614; see Swords, *Coll. Hib.* nos. 34–5, pp. 98, 100, 102, 106, 110; nos. 36–7, pp. 94, 104
45   Brockliss & Ferté, no. 1015; Swords, *Arch.Hib.*, vol. 35 (1980), nos. 388, 595. Thady Jordan and Thomas Moore, who registered in the law faculty in 1713 and 1718 respectively, make no subsequent appearance in documents in France or elsewhere. As neither of them completed any degree, they may well have died in Paris. Brockliss & Ferté, nos. 1021, 1022. The same may have happened to Edmund Costello, who was in Collége des Lombards in 1721 where he attested to Morvornagh's death. AN MC et / XVII / 614
46   Swords, *The Irish-French Connection*, p. 66; Brockliss & Ferté, op. cit., no. 1024; *Arch. Hib.*, vol. 3, p. 129
47   AN MC et/XVII/614; Nunz. di Fiandra, vol. 131, f. 107rv; SCAR, codex 4, f. 466
48   Brockliss & Ferté, no. 1020; Burke, pp. 437–8
49   SCAR, codex 1. 4, no. 411; codex 4, f. 466r; SC Irlanda, vol. 16, f. 208r; *Arch. Hib.*, vol. XIX, p. 263
50   SC Irlanda, vol. 9, ff. 219rv, 220rv; vol. 15, f. 398rv

in Clonmel or Waterford either.[51] It was similar in the western province, as James Lyons discovered when he travelled down from Dublin to meet his bishop only to find there was no place available. Charles O'Conor of Belanagare wrote to the Archbishop of Dublin seeking an appointment there for Francis Xavier Blake, who belonged to the diocese of Tuam, 'where no provision can be made for him.'[52]

If such was the situation in large dioceses, the problem must have been acute in Achonry. The number of priests in parishes was determined not by the religious needs of the people but by their ability to support them. Between 1780 and 1810 the population had doubled. 'Is there one priest more now in these parishes so doubled and quadrupled,' Dr Charles O'Conor wrote in 1810, 'than there were thirty years ago?'[53] Curates were rare, except when the parish priest was incapacitated. By 1816 there were only six in the diocese of Achonry. The prospects of newly-trained priests were not helped either in a small diocese by the longevity of some priests, like Dominick Kearney, Patrick Knavesey and Edmund Kelly, who lived well into their eighties.

Irish Franciscan College of St Anthony, Louvain

51 SC Irlanda, vol. 9, f. 112rv
52 Ward, Wrynn, Ward, pp. 432–3
53 *Letter of Columbanus,* 1st letter, pp. 20–21

CHAPTER EIGHT

Saggart Aroon
The People's Priest

Priests, particularly from Rome or Lisbon, must have suffered something of a climatic shock, returning to what some called 'this western Siberia'. A Limerick priest complained to Rome in 1731 that he suffered some debilitating fevers, 'partly because it was too cold in the countryside in the winter and partly because he had not the clothes to support the great cold of this country'. James Lyons of Elphin, who arrived in Dublin in the middle of August 1763, decided to spend the winter in Dublin, 'as the Irish cold was beginning to trouble him', and he felt that Connacht in the winter would be more than he could take. Peter Blake from Oranmore, who arrived in September 1772, suffered bad health and could not start work until the following spring. Another priest from Rome decided not to assume any pastoral work 'until his health was completely restored'.[1]

Culture-shock

The loss of the Irish language was another problem faced by the returned priests, particularly by those, like Thomas Costello or James Lyons, who left Ireland in their middle or late teens. 'Much occupied in learning the Irish language,' Lyons wrote to Rome in 1765, 'and almost despair of ever learning it to perfection.' This was less of a problem for the priests returning from Paris, partly because they had gone there in their mid-twenties and partly because they had an Irish school there. Thomas Bray, who later became Archbishop of Cashel, asked for permission to spend a year in the Irish College in Paris to study English and Irish which he had almost completely forgotten.[2]

The cultural shock returning priests experienced can only be guessed at. Thomas Costello had arrived in renaissance Rome at about the age of seventeen and spent nine years there living in the Irish College in via degli Ibernesi, overlooking the Roman Forum. From his window he could see the Colliseum

Mass-rocks

1   SC Irlanda, vol. 9, ff. 215r, 216r; vol. 12, ff. 44rv, 45r; f. 380r; Fenning, *Coll. Hib.*, no. 11, pp. 90–110
2   SC Irlanda, vol. 12, f. 35rv

Altar and stones, Toomour (Wood-Martin, *Sligo*)

and other impressive remains of imperial Rome. He defended his doctorate in the lavishly ornate Jesuit church, San Ignazio, as big as a football stadium. When he returned to his native parish of Ballaghaderreeen (Kilcolman and Castlemore) in 1771, he had to celebrate Mass in a thatched Mass-house little bigger than an ordinary dwelling house. His predecessors had to make do with a stone altar in the open-air or the slightly more elaborate 'four altars' in his native townland of Cregane.

The association of altars and holy wells suggests that the latter may have been the site of many Mass-rocks. In the absence of any fixed places of worship, these were the obvious 'holy grounds' where people could congregate for Mass. There was an altar at St Attracta's well at Clogher, Ballaghaderreen. The Mass-rock in Knocknaganny, Callow, was only a few yards from a well and white thornbush.[3] As people regularly gathered at wells, the authorities would not necessarily suspect the presence of a Mass-saying priest there.

There were other Mass-rocks not associated with wells such as the altar at Toomour (Keash) or Masshill in Kilmactigue. In a fort in Cloonfinnish, Killasser, a timber structure between two ash trees was known locally as *Geata na hAltóra*.[4] Hill-top locations, such as Masshill and the 'four altars' in Cregane, meant that any approaching posse could be seen well in advance to assure the priest's escape. The 'four altars', inserted in four alcoves facing the four points of the compass, protected the priest from the prevailing winds and the driving rain. In fact, given the climate of the west of Ireland, Mass-rocks were not a practicable location for Mass except in summertime.

Open-air Masses continued longer in the north of Ireland than elsewhere in the country and longer in Co Sligo than elsewhere in Connacht. A traveller witnessed one such Mass near Dunfanahy, Co Donegal in the summer of 1752. In an amphitheatre formed by the mountains, with several hundred people present, a priest celebrated Mass under a rock on an altar made of loose stones. 'In all this country for sixty miles west and south as far as Connaught, they celebrate in the open air, in the fields or on the mountains.'[5] Twenty-five years later, James Crawley was still celebrating Mass under a tree a few miles outside Armagh, though he had a chapel in the town.[6]

3   It was about three feet high and flat on top measuring three feet square. IFC, Ms. 227, pp. 109–110
4   It was in a deep hollow between the two clay ramparts of the fort. IFC, Ms. 114, p. 395
5   *Bishop Pococke's Irish Tour*, p. 60
6   SC Irlanda, vol. 13, f. 110rv

Terence O'Gara, Sr

Terence O'Gara, senior, parish priest of Ballaghaderreen early in the eighteenth century, may well have said Mass at the 'four altars'. Fear of persecution was aggravated by another problem, as he was almost completely blind. Presumably, to say Mass he used a reader and repeated the words after him, which obviously lengthened the Mass and encreased the danger of being apprehended. He was already sixty-five years old when Bishop Hugh Mac Dermot wrote in 1715 to the internuncio in Brussels asking permission for O'Gara to say the Mass of the Blessed Virgin Mary or the Mass of the Dead instead of the ordinary Mass of the day. He probably knew these two Masses by heart. MacDermot underlined the urgency of his request pointing out that 'no other priest would have the courage to celebrate Mass in the said parish because of the known severity of the government', and that 'the Catholics of the parish greatly desire to attend his Mass, because of the great veneration they have for his person'.

The request was duly referred to the Sacred Congregation of the Council and of Rites in Rome, where it was apparently shelved. Six years later Mac Dermot tried again, this time sending his request with a Dominican friar travelling to Rome to attend the general chapter of his order. His name was Dominick O'Daly from Athenry who, by an odd turn of events, was to succeed MacDermot as Bishop of Achonry. MacDermot emphasised the danger of O'Gara 'being molested by the heretics' because of the length of time he took to say Mass. The secretary of Propaganda passed on the request to the secretary of the Council and of Rites. The wheels of bureacracy grind slowly. Finally, in October 1721, six years and two months after the original request, the required permission was given to O'Gara. By now seventy-one, he may even

'Four Altars'
(*Photograph, Patrick Glynn*)

have been dead, worn out as much by Rome's procrastination as by Protestant persecution.[7]

Mass-rock in Masshill, Tourlestrane *(Photograph, Jack Ruane)*

Mass-houses

By the time O'Gara died, persecution was easing somewhat and Mass-houses were becoming more common. Ballymote (Emlefad) had one by 1725 and by 1731 there were thirteen in the diocese. The distribution of them is revealing with all, but the one in Ballymote, located in Mayo in the baronies of Costello and Gallen, where Viscount Dillon, a Catholic, was the principal landowner. Many of the substantial tenants were also Catholics, and Protestant tenants were rare. The *Report of the State of Popery* of 1731 makes an interesting observation about Meelick which had a Mass-house but also 'most gentlemen's houses serve as such'. Charlestown (Kilbeagh, which then included Carracastle), in the heartland of Dillon country, had in fact two Mass-houses. Only two parishes, Bonniconlon and Attymass, which were then served by one priest, had none. This may have been due to their proximity to Ballina, where the Protestant Lord Tyrawley was the most powerful landowner.[8]

The only Mass-house in the Sligo section was in Ballymote (Emlefad) where the Catholic Lord Taaffe had large holdings. For the rest, from Tourlestrane (Kilmactigue) to Ballisodare, there were none. This was strongly Protestant country where attitudes became more virulent the closer it approached Sligo town, which had a reputation for bigotry right through the

7   Acta, vol. 85, ff. 504v–505r, vol. 91, ff. 298v–299r; SOCG, vol. 601, ff. 203–4, vol. 630, ff. 260–261; Lettere, vol. III, ff. 334v, 335r; SC Irlanda, vol. 8, f. 77r
8   *Arch. Hib.*, vol. 3, pp. 128–9

century. The Catholic dean did not reside in his parish of Achonry, where Catholics 'seldom have service two Sundays successively in the same place'. Mass in Coolaney (Killoran) was said in private houses, as it was also in Keash (Drumrat and Toomour) and Bunninadden (Kilturra).

Mass-houses were small, mud-walled, thatched, clay-floored buildings, only distinguishable by their size from ordinary dwellings. There were usually fifty feet long by fifteen feet wide and some Protestant landlords gave their grudging consent to them, provided they had false chimneys to disguise their real purpose. 'The Mass-house was of the same order of architecture as the generality of Irish cabins; with no other visible mark to ascertain its sacred designation than a stone cross, roughly hewn, over its entrance.'[9] There was generally no internal decoration, but a flat slabstone raised on supports served as an altar at one end of the building. Their sole purpose was to shelter the priest and the more vulnerable section of his congregation during Sunday Mass. Their name describes their function. No other church service was performed in them except Mass on Sundays and feastdays, but they were used sometimes on weekdays as a school-house.

Their Irish name, *teach an phobail*, probably describes their origin and ownership as they were built by the people, using local labour, skills and materials. Their location was determined by the convenience of the greatest number of the parishioners and the approval of the local landowner. Often the sites were in hollows or in obscure spots to avoid offending the authorities. As the population continued to grow, they were extended by adding annexes, making them L-shaped or T-shaped. They continued in existence until the end of the century, when they were gradually replaced by chapels.

Later visitors were impressed by their poverty and simplicity. Lady Morgan had to make her way through a crowd of devotees, gathered round outside a 'simple tabernacle'. People were 'prostrated on the earth, praying over their beads with as much fervour as though they were offering up their orisons in the golden-roofed temple of Solyman.'[10] In the summer of 1791, the French consul was equally impressed when he attended Sunday Mass in a Mass-house in Partry, Co Mayo. On the altar there was a single rush candle and a pewter chalice. 'This simplicity,' he wrote, 'far from diminishing devotion, seemed to me to add to it.'[11]

Many visitors commented on how well people were dressed at Sunday Mass. Women, in particular, who dressed shabbily during the week, were a

Sunday Mass

9   Lady Morgan, *The Wild Irish Girl*, vol. 2, p. 155
10 *The Wild Irish Girl*, vol. 2, p. 155
11 *Carnets de voyage*, microfilm, NLI., pos. 119

sight to behold as they made their way in groups to the Mass-house, walking bare-foot, carrying their brogues draped over one arm and their beads over the other. A short distance from the Mass-house, they washed their feet in a stream and put on their brogues and stockings. A prayer said when entering the Mass-house has survived in Killasser:

> Ó mo Dhia, táim ag iarradh mo dhéirce. Dá ligfeá isteach mé go teach na féile nach n-iarrfad biadh no éadach, ach glóir na Flaithis agus a ghlór d'éisteacht.
> (O my God, I am asking this one request. If you let me into your feast-house, I will not ask for food or clothes, but the glory of heaven and to hear the voice of God.)

Inside, the congregation was segregated, men standing or kneeling on one side and women on the other, a custom also followed in Protestant churches. With such limited accommodation, large numbers of men remained outside, their natural gallantry yeilding precedence to womenfolk and the elderly. Later, when chapels became more spacious, irate parish priests tried and largely failed to break this tradition. The Mass offered by the priest in Latin was usually drowned out by the active and loud participation of the people, reciting in Irish suitable prayers at different parts of the Mass, such as the Gloria, Gospel, Creed, Consecration, Our Father and Communion. The French consul was left under the impression that the Mass he attended in Sligo was actually conducted in Irish, 'and judging by the loud manner in which they express their devotion, certain passages in the service rouse the emotions of those present'.[12] The priest preached in Irish, often after Mass, as happened at Partry where he preached on St Jarlath, patron of the archdiocese. At the end of Mass, he distributed among the people a bucket of holy water, with which they sprinkled their homes weekly. Such a custom may have derived from the earlier Sunday Masses held at holy wells.

Mass Attendance

It is now almost impossible to estimate the parish attendance at Sunday Mass but it was probably not in excess of fifty per cent and may have been considerably lower. In 1851, when figures first became available, the average Sunday Mass attendance in the diocese of Achonry was about thirty per cent. There was then a striking variation in attendances in different parishes, with fifty-one per cent in Kilmovee while Ballisodare, Coolaney and Collooney had less than twenty per cent.[13] The young generally did not begin attending until they had reached their mid teens and it was said that in the west of Ireland teenage girls began going to Mass when their parents wished to advertise

12 Ní Chinnéide, vol. 36, p. 32.
13 In 1831 there were 30 chapels in the diocese. *Parliamentary Papers*, vol. 35 (1835), pp. 60d–63d

that they were in the market for proposals.[14] There was also a wide seasonal variation between winter and summer, with the highest attendance probably at the great feasts of Christmas and Easter. In 1822, when the diocese could boast of twenty-three parish chapels, Bishop McNicholas reported to Rome that many of the poorer people rarely came to Mass in winter because they lacked clothes and they recited prayers at home while Mass was being celebrated.[15]

Towards the end of the century chapels began to replace the Mass-houses. From about 1790, with the new prevailing climate of tolerance, chapel-building all over Ireland epitomised the new Catholic assertiveness. Prominent locations were chosen for chapels, replacing Mass-houses with their underground character. Boetius Egan adorned his chapel in Castlebar with an Italian-style campanile, borrowed from his student days in Rome. Protestants like Lord Lucan, who donated an organ for the Castlebar chapel, contributed generously and they and their ladyfolk attended the gala openings in all their finery. The earliest and most elaborate chapels were first erected in the large county-towns like Waterford and Drogheda, both of which were still under construction in 1794.[16] Rural parishes erected theirs in the following twenty years, though in Achonry between 1787–92 seven new chapels were built.[17] Two chapels dating from this period, Ballisodare and Keash, are still in use as parish churches. By 1822, Achonry had twenty-three parish chapels, five of them built after 1817.[18]

Chapels

Keash Chapel, aerial view

14 Shaw Mason, op. cit., vol. 2, p. 460
15 SC Irlanda, vol. 23, f. 613v
16 *O'Connor's Journal through the Kingdom of Ireland,* c. 1794, TCD., Ms. 2568. Much of the information on chapels in this section is based on this Ms.
17 Fondo di Vienna, vol. 28, f. 37v
18 SC Irlanda, vol. 23, f. 611r

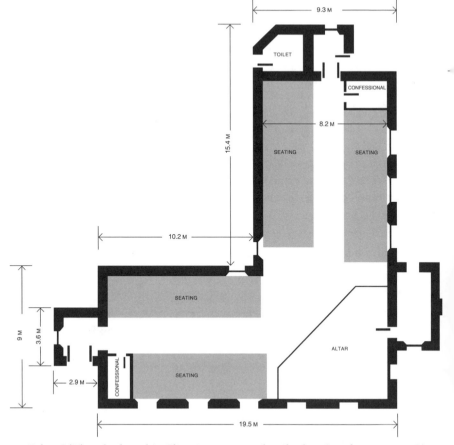

Plan of St Kevin's church, Keash *(courtesy Fr James Finan)*

John O'Flynn's chapel in Sligo in 1791 was decribed as *'une bonne grange'* (a fine barn), though a few years earlier Charles O'Conor considered it 'one of the best at present in this kingdom'.[19] These 'barn-chapels' were much larger than the Mass-houses they replaced in order to accommodate a population which increased enormously in the last three decades of the century. They were usually eighty to ninety feet long by thirty to forty feet wide, although Waterford was 112 feet long and almost as broad, and Wexford was 130 feet long. Rural chapels, of course, were proportionately smaller.

Another feature which helped to cater for the increased population, was the erection of galleries inside the chapels, normally two, as in Drogheda, running along each side of an oblong chapel. Elsewhere they were more elaborate, making the chapel more like an opera-house than a place of worship. Mullingar had six galleries, in two layers, one over the other. They were gradated, with the front portion four feet lower than the rear, allowing all a view

19 Ní Chinnéide, vol. 36, p. 36; O'Conor Don Papers, 8.4 SH 150

of the altar. Access to the galleries was by a stairs inside the chapel, though in some, like Newry, they could be entered by a stairs outside the chapel. T-shaped chapels usually had galleries also in the two wings. Galleries sometimes introduced an element of snobbery into the Sunday worship, as in Armagh where they were often reserved for the 'genteeler class' who could look down on their poorer neighbours huddled below.

The altar was raised with six to eight steps leading up to it. Ornamentation was introduced. Carlow had a large glass chandelier hanging in front of the altar and three other chandeliers elsewhere in the chapel. St Peter holding an open book was represented on one side of the altar and Christ's *Descent from the Cross* on the other. Mullingar had also a painting of the latter. The quality of the vestments was also improved and tin chalices were replaced with silver ones. 'In the beginning, I found among the parish priests,' McNicholas informed Rome in 1822, 'many tin chalices. Now they are all silver.'[20] Organs were installed and choirs formed. In 1794 Graiguenamanagh had a confraternity of sixty young women, dressed in white, and as many young men 'who sing in concert canticles of praise to the almighty'. It was claimed then that Carlow had 'the finest Catholic choir in the kingdom', consisting of twenty young women, thirty young men, students and boys and also twelve clergymen', obviously due to the recently-founded seminary there.[21] Places like Carlow were trail-blazers but were probably emulated elsewhere later.

Before chapels were established, the Blessed Sacrament was reserved in priests' homes or lodgings. This was convenient for the priest called out to attend the dying at all hours of the day and night, winter as well as summer. Priests lived either in their family homes or had lodgings with some comfortable farmer. Philip Philips lived with his family in Cloonmore when parish priest of Bunninadden, while Thomas Costello, parish priest of Ballaghaderreen (Kilcolman and Castlemore), lived at Cregane where the Costellos had their home. One of his successors in 1796, Michael Farrell, was staying with Walter Plunkett who leased from Lord Dillon a farm in Castlemore of almost four hundred acres.[22] Priests also changed their lodgings frequently. 'There are people in each parish, farmers and gentlemen, with whom the priests lodge for part of the year. From all this, it can be understood that the mode of living for priests in Ireland is that of the mendicant monk in the most strict sense.'[23]

Priests' Lodgings

---

20 SC Irlanda, vol. 23, f. 611r
21 TCD, Ms. 2568
22 Fondo di Vienna, vol. 28, f. 256rv
23 Ní Chinnéide, vol. 25, p. 14

Some priests may well have been tenant-farmers themselves. Anthony McNamara, the parish priest of Curry, applied for a farm in 1784 and promised to build a house there. Mr Wood, the agent of the absentee landlord, Frances Jones, who thought MacNamara would make 'a reputable good tenant', wrote informing her of 'the priest of Lyney's' offer. Miss Jones, however, would prefer a Protestant tenant but if none made an equally good offer she would 'like Mr McNamara better than any one else of his persuasion – as priests are generally deemed good tenants'.[24]

While the priest brought considerable prestige to the family with whom he lodged, he cost them very little as 'his domestic expenses cannot be extravagant'.[25] During the week he dined with whatever parishioners required his services, and on Sundays he was invited to dinner by 'some of the decent people'. Wherever he went, he was always treated to the best on offer. It probably cost the family with whom he lodged more to feed his horse, though priests were often given gifts of oats and hay for that purpose. The houses where priests lodged became the hub of the parish, with a constant stream of callers seeking the services of the priest.

Pastoral Life

A priest's work-load was daunting, particularly from late autumn to the following Easter. The stations began in October and lasted up to Christmas, which itself was a busy season with numerous feastdays and Masses. This was immediately followed by the wedding season, culminating in Shrove Tuesday, when he often performed weddings from sunrise to sunset. In Lent the second round of stations began and continued up to Easter. Holy Week and Easter week were crammed with ceremonies with the entire population receiving Holy Communion. This was also the time for whatever marriages still remained. To all of this must be added christenings and funerals. In the last decades of the century and the early ones of the next, christenings increased dramatically with the population growth. In 1814, there were 230 baptisms in the parish of Tourlestrane (Kilmactigue) as well as fifty-two marriages and sixty deaths. The latter entailed two separate visits from the priest, first to anoint the dying and later to bury the dead. 'In this routine his time passes and indeed in this parish a very laborious time it is, from the numbers necessary to be attended to, the distance he has to ride, and the bad roads through the interior and mountainous parts.'[26] Neligan himself had only one marriage, two baptisms and one burial among his little Protestant flock of some ten families.

24 A year later Miss Jones wrote to her agent, inquiring 'if Mr McNamara has got his lands.' O'Hara Papers, Ms. 20, 291(3) & (5)
25 Neligan, p. 378
26 Neligan, p. 378

Priests were 'almost every day on horseback'. James Lyons, now a curate in Sligo, informed Rome in 1765: 'Not a day passes but I am on horseback and I am now as accustomed to my boots as I formerly was to my shoes and stockings.' He had two Masses on Sundays, in Mass-houses fifteen miles apart and all this on an empty stomach.[27] Dr Charles O'Conor, one-time parish priest of Castlerea, described parish ministry graphically: 'Men who start up from their uneasy repose, in the pelting storm and darkness of a winter's night, and undertake a dangerous journey of eight or ten miles, traversing dreary mountains, or wading through rivers and marshes, to administer the comforts of Christianity to the distressed.'[28]

Priests sometimes died after having been thrown by a horse, and the riderless horse returning home often first alerted neighbours to such accidents. James Gallagher, as ill-fated in death as he was in life, met such an end. Early in February 1776, when 'about eight o'clock, a most violent storm arose, accompanied with a heavy rain, which continued with very little intermission until twelve', Gallagher, riding from one village to another, was thrown by his horse near Banada, where he was found smothered the next morning.[29] The time and season suggests that he might have been returning from a wedding.

Summertime brought some relief and the priest's workload eased somewhat. But deaths and christenings have no seasons. Priests' services were always urgent, as popular belief imposed on him awesome responsibility with no less than eternal salvation often depending on the promptness of his response to a call. Summer brought other demands on his time with the bishop's visitation. In theory, the priest had to prepare the children for confirmation every third year. From May to September, priests were required to attend monthly conferences. For this purpose the diocese was divided into four regions, where the conferences were presided over by senior priests, designated Vicars Forane. Here cases of conscience were discussed and, with the maze of canonical and moral complexities existing at the time, these discussions could prove helpful to the priest. There was also a large social dimension to these clerical get-togethers. Summer also brought with it fairs and patterns and inevitably faction-fights, and priests were often called upon to arbitrate the ensuing disputes. Tenants in arrears with their rents also had recourse to their priest to intervene with the landlord on their behalf.

Parishes

Throughout the century, the parish structure varied. In 1704, Kiltimagh and Bohola were united, as were Bonninconlon and Attymass. The latter two

27 Fenning, *Coll. Hib.*, no. 11, pp. 90–110
28 Dr Charles O'Conor, *Letter of Columbanus*, p. 34
29 *Arch. Hib.*, vol. XVIII, p. 178

were still served by one priest in 1731. Foxford (Toomore) was divided between Killasser and Straide but had its own priest in 1731. Meelick was a parish in its own right, at least until 1776, when Henry O'Neal was the parish priest. It also had a certain status, as John Roddy moved there from Swinford (Kilconduff) where he was parish priest in 1684. Killaraght and Kilfree (now Gurteen) were separate parishes and so were Kilmorgan and Emlefad (now Ballymote) at least until 1758. Carracastle and Curry were not then constituted parishes. Curry was established by Bishop Boetius Egan in 1786, with Anthony McNamara as its first parish priest. Mullinabreena was established at the same time, when John Duffy was appointed.[30] Kilcolman and Castlemore (now Ballaghaderreen) were separate parishes in 1684 and almost a hundred years later there were still two parish priests there, John Duffy who was resident in Ballaghaderreen, and Thomas Costello in Cregane.[31]

Levitical Families

Parishes often passed down through the same family, like Achonry through the O'Haras. The O'Hara Reogh branch formerly occupied Meemlough castle in this parish and this family provided a continuous stream of its parish priests for over one hundred and thirty years. Phelim was dean and parish priest there in 1684, while twenty years later Dr Charles was in the same parish. In 1758 Moriarty was listed as parish priest of St Cuthberts (which may have been Curry), then part of Achonry parish. Dominic O'Hara was parish priest of Achonry and resident in Cloonacool in the early 1780s and he was still alive in 1816. The O'Hara pattern may have been followed by the other families such as the McDonoghs, but the information is too scanty to be conclusive. James McDonogh was parish priest of Bunninadden (Kilturra) in 1684 and Teige was there twenty years later. Anthony was parish priest of Bunninadden (Kilshalvey) in 1758.[32] The ministry of the two O'Garas, Terence senior and junior, spanned more than eighty years between 1684 and 1760.

Friars

Though the monasteries had been suppressed and confiscated in the sixteenth century, friars continued to lodge in their vicinity and became the shock-troops of the counter-reformation. The only bishop appointed to Achonry in the seventeenth century was a Franciscan friar, Louis Dillon, who died before reaching the diocese. Before him, the diocese was run by a Dominican friar who was prior of Sligo. Friars continued to minister in the diocese right through the eighteenth century and the early decades of the following.

Augustinians

The Augustinians' friary at Banada was founded early in the fifteenth

---

30 SC Irlanda, vol. 16, ff. 149rv, 150rv
31 *Arch. Hib.*, vol. 1, pp. 70–71; see Appendix 18
32 There was another James McDonogh in the diocese in 1738 and he was still alive thirty years later, but his parish is unknown.

century by the O'Haras and dedicated to Corpus Christi. Its greatest claim to fame is that it was the first house of the observant movement in Ireland. It was confiscated about 1613. Very few names of friars there in the eighteenth century have survived. The prior in 1742 was John O'Hara and William Hurly was prior in the 1780s. In the beginning of the next century, there were still three friars there, Matthew Leonard, John Smyth and James Conmy.[33]

Court Abbey, in Achonry parish, was founded in the middle of the fifteenth century on land granted by the O'Haras. It was a Third Order foundation having both Franciscan brothers and sisters. It was confiscated in 1588, having then a thatched church, a dormitory and two other thatched houses with eighty acres of land. The three friars named in Achonry parish in the 1731 Report may have been attached to Court Abbey but there is no later record of friars there. Ballymote was also a Third Order, like Court, and was founded and confiscated about the same time. In 1731 there were at least six friars with the guardian. A complete list of the guardians of Ballymote from 1797 to 1826 has survived.[34]

Banada Abbey (Wood-Martin, *Sligo*)

The Dominicans were located in the Mayo section of the diocese. Straide was founded in the middle of the thirteenth century by the Anglo-Norman Jordan family who had their castle nearby at Ballylahan. Like its motherhouse, Sligo, it was dedicated to the Holy Cross. It was confiscated in 1578. Copious lists of friars at Straide exist for the eighteenth century.[35] In 1702 there were five there and thirty years later there were ten and two absentees. By 1767, the number was down to four and by the early nineteenth century there were three. The last prior, Edward Clarke, died in 1840 and his nephew,

Dominicans: Straide

---

33 See Appendix 41; *Arch. Hib.*, vol. 1, p. 71; SOCG, vol. 918, f. 172rv; SC Irlanda, vol. 23, f. 613r
34 Cathaldus Giblin, *Liber Lovaniensis*; A. Faulkner, *Liber Dublinensis*; see Appendix 39
35 Fenning, *Irish Dominicans*, pp. 31, 91, 197, 259, 355, 495, 625

Urlaur

Patrick Albert Lyons, said his first Mass there in 1834 when the friary was suppressed by the order.³⁶

Urlaur was dedicated to St Thomas and founded in the middle of the fifteenth century by the Costello family. Prior to suppression, it had been a novitiate for Connacht because of its remoteness and, probably as a result, it was not confiscated until early in the seventeenth century.³⁷ It subsequently came into the possession of Viscount Dillon, a Catholic, and novices continued to be received there. In 1703 there were five friars there including two Costellos. Thirty years later that figure had risen to eight (including two other Costellos) and some absentees. Its remoteness probably caused its

Sculpted tomb, Straide *(Office of Public Works)*

36 Fenning, *Coll. Hib.*, no. 33, p. 203
37 Burke, *Hibernia Dominicana*, pp. 311, 314; O'Heynes, *Irish Dominicans*, pp. 228–231

omission from the 1731 *Report on the State of Popery.* Four novices were admitted in 1749. In 1756 there were six friars and, ten years later, seven. Luke Leyden was prior in 1816 with at least one friar, James McNicholas. Leyden remained in office until his death in 1833.[38] The last Dominican friar in Achonry, Patrick Sharkey, died there in 1846. Thus ended over four hundred years of uninterrupted presence of Dominican friars in Urlaur. Besides the friars based in the diocese, there were Achonry men in Sligo friary.

The friars were mendicants who maintained themselves by begging, and people were accustomed for centuries to support them with alms, as they had ancient questing rights in these districts. Parish priests may have resented them as a drain on very limited resources but grudgingly accorded them their ancient rights. In any case, some friars became parish priests, often where their friaries were located. Such was the case of Andrew Duffy, who was prior of Urlaur and parish priest of Kilmovee in 1758. In the same year friar Peter Philips from Urlaur was the parish priest of Ballymote (Emlefad). Anthony McDonogh, parish priest of Bunninadden (Kilshalvey) and Terence McGuan, parish priest of Gurteen (Killaraght), were Franciscans from Ballymote.[39] Earlier in the century, Anthony Henegan, who replaced Maurice Frain as parish priest of Swinford (Kilconduff), was a Dominican from Straide.[40]

Friaries

At first the friars may have lived with their own families like the Franciscans in Ballymote, where the 1731 Report stated that 'these Fryars live dispersed'. Normally, they lived together in a stone-walled thatched cabin, similar to but larger than the common dwelling-house. In 1733, the Urlaur friary, though it housed ten friars, was described as 'poor'. 'In country districts all the convents, with few exceptions, rented one or two fields where they built a stone house, roofed with thatch, and a chapel.'[41] Urlaur could have used as a chapel one of the vaulted rooms in the ruins, which are still roofed. The Franciscans in Claregalway had converted their chapel into a Mass-house which was in use in 1752.[42]

The friars instruct the peasantry by means of catechetical teaching and sermons. Hither to their respective convents the members often return, but for the greater part of the year only three or four remain at home. The others are absent helping the parish priests, acting as chaplains to the

38 Fenning, *Irish Dominicans*, pp. 32, 197, 249, 259; *Coll. Hib.*, no. 8, pp. 94–5, no. 29, pp. 116, 127; see Appendix 38
39 SCAR, codex 4, f. 468r
40 Burke, op.cit., p. 431
41 T. Burke, *Hibernia Dominicana*, p. 716, quoted in Fenning, *Undoing*, pp. 84–5
42 *Bishop Pococke's Irish Tour*, p. 103

wealthier members of the laity, or leading a fairly hard life among the peasantry, collecting barley or oats, to support the house, to pay the annual rent of the building, and to provide the rough clothing of the community.[43]

One Dominican, Edmund Fitzgerald, acted as chaplain to Charles O'Conor of Belanagare for a time. O'Conor, at the age of eight, was first introduced to Latin by a Franciscan from Creevelea. Early in the nineteenth century a poor woman in Kilmactigue brought her daughter to be cured by a friar 'who was hearing confessions in the neighbourhood'.[44]

Friaries acted as recruiting-grounds to insure the continuation of the order. Urlaur had a long tradition as a novitiate. One friar acted as master of novices, teaching them Latin and instructing them in the rule of the order. The novitiate lasted a year, after which they were professed and then sent abroad to be educated in one of the order's Irish colleges on the continent where they were then ordained. In practice, it seems that most of them, like diocesan priests, may have been ordained after their novitiate in Ireland before going abroad. Pre-ordaining candidates so that they could subsidise their studies abroad may have been an Irish solution to an Irish problem, but it spawned other problems. By the third decade of the century there were too many priests chasing too few souls or, more importantly, two few shillings, sparking an unholy rivalry between diocesan priests and friars over the division of the people's offerings.

Reformers in Ireland and on the continent complained to Rome about the crisis created in the Irish church by the increasing number of Irish priests. Some reformers tried to have the bishops stopped from ordaining, at least for a number of years. The bishops favoured another solution to the problem, the closing of novitiates. Rome pondered the problem for ten years.

Finally, a decision was taken at a special meeting of cardinals in Rome in 1750 when fourteen decrees were issued. 'The religious superiors are forbidden henceforth to give the religious habit to anyone in Ireland.' From now on novices could only be professed in their houses abroad where neither they nor their colleges had the resources to keep them. What two hundred years of persecution had failed to achieve, Rome, at the prompting of Irish bishops, achieved by a stroke of the pen. It was the 'undoing of the friars of Ireland'. To his credit Mark Skerret, Archbishop of Tuam, issued a statement deploring 'that steps should have been taken in Rome against religious to whom the mission owes so much.'[45] Friars in his province were almost as numerous as

43 Burke, op. cit., p. 716
44 Neligan, p. 370
45 Full statement quoted in Fenning, *The Undoing of the Friars of Ireland*, p. 214

in the three other provinces put together.

Decline

The 1750 decree marked the beginning of the decline of the friars. Straide had seven friars in 1746 and was down to four twenty years later. Of these, one was almost eighty, another sixty-one, and the two others in their fifties. Urlaur fared a little better mainly because it professed four novices just a year before the boom was lowered. It had six in 1756 and seven in 1767 when Walter Morley, who was then prior, returned from Drogheda where he had been chaplain to nuns. Of the seven, he was the second youngest at forty-nine while four others were in their sixtieth year and Thomas Lally, who was 'formerly an outstanding preacher', was seventy-one. The youngest at forty-four was Michael Jordan who was parish priest of Kilmovee. The decline continued so that by the beginning of the next century there were only two friars in Urlaur and one in Straide. The Augustinians in Banada had three friars in 1822.

Priests' Dues

Ireland was unique among the Catholic countries of Europe in that its priests were entirely funded by the offerings of the people. In countries such as France, Italy and Spain, many of the priests had remunerative benefices, some of which were even honorary. The church was a large landowner and received considerable income from rents. Irish priests in France, like Peter Flood who was a professor in Paris, had an honorary benefice from which he received a tidy annual income. Before the Reformation the Catholic Church in Ireland was also a large landowner but these temporalities were confiscated and became the property of the Established Church. The lands attached to the monasteries were granted to laymen, for the most part Protestants. Tithes, which existed in all countries, i.e. a tax for the support of the clergy, were attributed to the Protestant ministers thus making Irish Catholics unique in having to pay also for a religion other than that of the majority population.

At Christmas and Easter, people paid the parish priest voluntary offerings from a penny to a shilling according to their means. They also paid fees for

Court Abbey (Wood-Martin, *Sligo*)

the sacraments which in 1814 amounted to two shillings and sixpence for baptism, two shillings and twopence for confession for a married couple, (sixpence for servants and young people), one pound two shillings and ninepence for marriage, (plus five shillings to the bishop for dispensing from the banns), and eight shillings for anointing the dying. They also paid two shillings and sixpence for a letter of freedom for those marrying outside the parish. Stipends for Masses for the dead and those said in private houses varied according to people's ability to pay.[46]

Clerical Incomes

With two hundred and thirty baptisms, fifty-two marriages and sixty deaths in Tourlestrane in 1814, the parish priest earned two hundred and forty pounds, excluding Mass-stipends. Oddly enough, most of that, one hundred and thirty pounds, came from confessions. His total annual income was estimated at three hundred pounds which in many parishes was equal to that of the Protestant minister and, in some, far greater. Every penny of it was hard-earned, after long hours in the saddle in all kinds of weather. 'The priest cannot have a shilling of his dues,' Dr Charles O'Conor, one-time parish priest of Castlerea wrote, 'without personal attendance throughout the whole course of the year.'[47]

Tourlestrane was a mensal parish since 1789, which meant that the parish priest had to pay a hundred pounds annually to the bishop.[48] It was also unusual in that it had to support three friars in Banada who went from house to house, especially at harvest time collecting oats and barley and whatever else the people could give them. But there is little evidence that either they or the parish priests were mercenary in their commitment to their ministry. While there was no Whiteboy agitation in Achonry as in Munster in the latter part of the century, the diocese was to originate another version of it, the Threshers, early in the next. Both these movements were organised by the people to force a reduction not only in tithes but also in the fees charged by priests. Given that the priests came from and continued to live with their families who, though now somewhat reduced, were once local chiefs, they would have retained a certain disdain for money that characterised their class. This was true particularly in the early period when those who came forward for ordination were certainly not drawn by the lure of riches. Later, there is a notice-

---

46 Neligan, p. 379. These fees were proportionately lower at the beginning and middle of the previous century. The French consul, de Montbret, gave the following figures in Claregalway in 1791: baptism, 1s 9½d, marriage, 2s 6d, last anointing, 2s 6d, house Mass, 2s 6d. Ní Chinnéide, vol. 25, p. 13. In 1776 Arthur Young found in Limerick that baptism cost 1s 6d, and confessions, 2s 2d. op.cit., vol. 1, p. 456
47 *Letter of Columbanus*, p. 23
48 SOCG, vol. 884, f. 209rv

able change in the class priests were recruited from and the phenomenon of the money-grasping priest, more common in later times, occasionally made an appearance.

Popular stories which survive, explaining how priests became covetous, may date from this period. One of the best known in the diocese recounts a journey by the sea in Gallilee undertaken by Jesus in the company of St Peter. On their way, they passed a poor beggarman who appealed to them for alms. Peter was amazed when Jesus passed by, ignoring the beggarman. Some time later they returned the same way and found the beggarman dead by the side of the road. Peter rebuked Jesus for his earlier neglect. Jesus told him to go and search in the dead man's pockets and when he did so he found them full of gold and silver coins. Peter was told to throw the coins into the sea:

'That none may fish them up again,
For money is often the curse of men.'

He separated the gold from the silver, which he threw into the sea, while he pocketed the gold. Jesus, aware of the deceit, rebuked Peter:

'Ah, Peter, Peter,' said Our Lord,
'You should have obeyed me at my word.
For a greedy man you are I see,
And a greedy man you will ever be;
A covetous man you are of gain,
And a covetous man you will remain.'

So that's the reason, as I've been told,
All clergy are since so fond of gold.[49]

Clerical Dress

Priests performed many services, particularly for the very poor, at no charge and it would be surprising if the latter were not often the beneficiaries of the priest's charity. 'His hand is the private channel of pity and benevolence through which relief passes to indigence, comfort to affliction, and consolation to shame.'[50]

'Ours is a civilized country, where ecclesiastics must be tidy and well-groomed,' was the rather surprising comment of James Lyons when he arrived in Dublin from Rome in August 1763. He and a companion 'were both ashamed to step out of doors, until our friends had clothes made for us'.[51] Priests wore no distinctive clothes nor friars habits, for obvious reasons, during the period of active persecution. Later they dressed in the style of minor

49 Douglas Hyde, *Saints and Sinners*, pp. 22–5. Hyde heard the story in Irish in Co Galway and turned it into rhyme.
50 Dr Charles O'Conor, op. cit., p. 34
51 Fenning, *Coll. Hib.*, no. 11, pp. 90–110

gentlemen or comfortable farmers. They wore wide-bottomed leather breeches, usually made of goat-skin, reaching to and tied just below the knee, and knee-length yarn stockings and riding-boots. Once out of the saddle they exchanged boots for shoes with silver buckles. Over a linen shirt, waistcoats were worn which split into two tails at the rear, reaching down to the knees and over these again jackets or coats similarly cut. Out-of-doors large frieze greatcoats were worn, tied under the neck with bodkins in the manner of cloaks. Round the top of their collarless shirts, priests wore white linen neckerchiefs, the fore-runner of the Roman collar. Heads, if not already bald, were closely cropped to facilitate tight-fitting wigs which reached down to cover the nape of the neck. On horseback, priests carried their wigs in leather wig-bags for protection from the rain and wore high-crowned top-hats with drooping rims.

Clerical Vices

Clerical vices were no different from those of the laity. Drunkenness is the one most frequently referred to by bishops in their communications with Rome. In 1770 Bishop Kirwan referred to a Franciscan called Sweeny whom he 'sent packing from the diocese and from the care of souls, because he was given to excessive drinking ... and showed no hope of mending his ways.'[52] 'It would have been good for the Irish mission,' James Crawley of Armagh wrote fifteen years later, 'if St Francis had entirely forbidden his friars the use of wine and spirits.'[53] But Franciscans had no monopoly on this particular vice. Bishop McNicholas excommunicated an Augustinian in Banada and also suspended a parish priest and his curate for excessive drinking. Another parish priest, who by drunkenness and bad morals 'inflicted grave wounds on religion', went (or was sent) to America, an early example of Ireland exporting its problems.[54] As there were then approximately thirty-six priests in the diocese, this represented a little more than ten per cent with this problem. The laity were probably more tolerant than bishops of such lapses among their priests.

Nor did they regard horse-racing as 'scandalising the faithful' as the scholarly McNicholas did. Such prowess probably enhanced a priest's reputation among them. With the amount of time most priests spent in the saddle, they must have been excellent horsemen and the only Catholics who could compete with fox-hunting landlords. It would have been a great source of pride to parishioners when their priest took on and beat the son of the big house or other local Protestant squireen.

52   SC Irlanda, vol. 11, f. 541r
53   SC Irlanda, vol. 16, f. 77rv
54   SC Irlanda, vol. 23, f. 612rv

No records have come to light of sexual misdemeanours among the priests of Achonry, though some exist for a few other dioceses. In 1776 four canons reported to Rome that John Fitzmaurice kept for two years in his house a 'suspect' woman who was under the canonical age. Priests' housekeepers were required to be of a mature age *(super adulta)*. The report may have been an attempt on the part of the four canons to damage the prospects of Fitzmaurice who was elected vicar-capitular following Bishop Kirwan's death and chosen by nineteen priests of the diocese to succeed him. The charge was not seriously considered in Rome nor widely believed in the diocese, nor in Killala, where three years later the dean and the *'sanior pars'* (sounder portion) of the chapter put Fitzmaurice forward as a candidate for their bishop.[55]

One vice shared equally between bishops and priests was their liberal use of villification in disputes. Their pens were often dipped in venom and libellous comments were not unusual. Terence O'Gara's remarks about Andrew Donlevy were only matched by similar ones made by Donlevy's colleague, John Burke, about O'Gara and his fellow-priests. Bishops could be scathing about bishops too. Kirwan described Philips as an 'enemy who sowed cockle among the seeds' which Kirwan had sown in the diocese.[56] Matthew McKenna, later Bishop of Cloyne, said that Kirwan had nothing to recommend him for high office 'except his ambition for it'.[57] Patrick Grady, parish priest of Ballymote, in his pamphlet 'circulated the most base and scurrilous libel against his own bishop', who was then John O'Flynn.[58] Not only did he accuse O'Flynn of many abuses, he did not spare his mother either, alleging that the bishop was 'the son of a woman well-known to have led an infamous life'.[59] Small wonder that a French minister, Hely d'Oisel, should exclaim in 1820 that he knew 'of no class of people in the world more prone to calumny and more self-opinionated, than Irish priests.'[60]

Earlier in the century the Bishop of Killaloe described Irish priests as living: 'Saggart Aroon'

> in such wild and miserable countries, where none hardly remains but the common people who can't speak a word but Irish, who feed for the most part upon oaten bread and potatoes, lying on straw in their poor thatched huts and cottages ... who can afford them but the aforesaid miserable entertainment and beds, whom they must visit in night as well as in day

---

55   SOCG, vol. 844, ff. 267r, 269r; vol. 852, f. 155r; Acta, vol. 149, f. 218rv; SC Irlanda, vol. 15, f. 478rv
56   SC Irlanda, vol. 11, f. 542r
57   SCAR, codex 4, f?.
58   SC Irlanda, vol. 20, f. 205v
59   op.cit. p. 50
60   quoted in Swords, *The Green Cockade*, p. 209

time, through hills, mountains, rivers, etc., most commonly on foot from one extremity of their walk to another, distant perhaps seven or eight miles. All this our own honest and laborious workmen can do, having been inured to hardships of all kinds ... Such are the labourers we want.[61]

Describing the period 1780–90, an Englishman wrote:

> But there were no persons for whom the people entertained more respect and veneration than their priests. They considered them as the most virtuous, the most learned and religious of all men. In their private disputes they would often appeal to, and abide by, the decision of their priests who, in many remote parts of Ireland, had all the authority, without any of the responsibility of Civil Magistrates. From these men the common people received all their religious, moral and political instruction; and placed implicit faith in every thing they said, however absurd or monstrous.[62]

Lady Morgan 'discovered the manners of a gentleman, the conversation of a scholar, and the sentiments of a philanthropist, united in the character of an Irish priest.'[63] Though her fictional Father John is highly romanticised, her sentiments were re-echoed by the nineteenth century historian, Lecky, who described that generation of priests as having 'the manners and feelings of cultivated gentlemen and a high sense of clerical decorum'.

Perhaps the greatest compliment paid to priests came from a most unlikely source. Thomas O'Beirne, Protestant Bishop of Ossory (himself a converted priest), exhorted his clergy in 1796 to emulate their Catholic counterparts and thus secure 'the respect, the love, the attachment and the confidence of' their flocks:

> Their clergy are indefatigable. Their labours are unremitting. They live in a constant familiar intercourse with all who are subject to their pastoral inspection. They visit them from house to house. Their only care, their sole employment, is to attend to the administration of their sacraments, and to their multiplied observances and rites. They watch and surround the beds of the sick.[64]

By the end of the century the 'saggart aroon' was already becoming a folk-memory, frequently replaced by another breed, often more respected than loved.

61 Moran, *Spicilegium Ossoriense*, vol. 3, pp. 163–4
62 Bell, p. 23
63 *The Wild Irish Girl*, vol. 1, pp. 174–7
64 quoted in Acheson, *A History of The Church of Ireland 1691–1996*, p. 107

CHAPTER NINE

Pobal Dé

The Cradle to the Grave

Christenings were occasions for elaborate and expensive celebrations. As James Neligan described it, friends and neighbours were invited, nobody was turned away and beggars and itinerants found their way there too, like moths round a lamp. Food and drink were provided in abundance. It was one of the rare ocasions when flesh-meat, geese or chickens, were eaten by the poorer classes. The better-off enjoyed the choicer cuts of beef, pork and mutton with a select group of neighbours of the 'more decent sort' presided over by the priest. There was no shortage of locally-distilled whiskey. A piper was engaged and the young people danced the day and much of the night away, watched by their elders smoking their short-stemmed clay pipes and drinking whiskey.[1]

Christenings

Infants were usually baptised on the day they were born. Infant mortality was high. Many children died when one or two days old from what was then called 'jaw-fall'. To prevent this, the infant at birth was forced to swallow poteen and the mid-wife suspended the baby by the upper jaw with her forefinger.[2] The catechism taught that 'without baptism ... nobody can be saved' and the existence of separate burial grounds for unbaptised children, such as at Killvanloon in the parish of Ballaghaderreen (Castlemore), graphically illustrates the general acceptance of that teaching. Priests were regularly encouraged to train the people, especially women, how to baptise when the child's life was in danger, though Donlevy's *Catechism* states that 'it is not permitted to a woman to baptise in the presence of a man'. When several children were baptised together, priority was given to the males. People had a positive view of the value of the sacrament: '*Sacraméid a ghlanas sinn agus a osclaíos doras chlann dhá Dhia agus dhá Eaglais fhéin go bráth go deo*' ("The sacrament that cleanses us and opens the family door to God and his church forever).[3] A

---

1 op. cit., p. 379. Much of the information in this chapter is derived from that article, pp. 340–399.
2 Shaw Mason, op. cit. vol. 2, p. 157
3 IFC, Ms. 194, p. 160. I am deeply indebted to Réamonn Ó Muirí and An tOllamh Pádraig de Brún who read an early draft of chapters nine and ten and particularly for correcting the numerous Irish texts in them.

French traveller, who was present at a baptism in 1797 in Co Antrim, noticed that the child was given a mixture of melted butter, bread and sugar from an egg-shell to stop it crying, whereas he had seen the same effect achieved in Scotland with a spoonful of whiskey.[4] In many parishes of Achonry, where home distillation was widespread, the Scottish practice may well have been the norm. Baptisms were administered in the home and, with the rapid growth in the population at the end of the eighteenth century, added enormously to the work-load of the priest. In Kilmactigue parish, consisting of twelve hundred families in 1814, there were 230 baptisms. The baptismal fee that year was two shillings and sixpence. The fee had risen from about one shilling at the beginning of the century to one shilling and sixpence in 1752 in the Tuam province.

Churching

Women were usually blessed after childbirth in a brief ceremony called 'churching'. 'No woman thinks of taking any concern in her household affairs until she has been churched after child-birth.'[5] In a time when fixed places of worship were few or non-existent, such blessings must have taken place in the home. The synod of Bunninadden decreed in 1759 that priests would be liable to suspension if they 'churched' the mother of a child born outside wedlock before she repented publicly. This severity was to act 'as an example to others'.[6] Such children took their mother's name.

Families of all classes tended to be large. Charles O'Conor of Belanagare, informing a friend in 1762 that the wife of his cousin and publishing agent, Michael Reilly, had just given birth to her tenth child, added 'in all likelihood (she) will contribute several more.'[7] Rev James Neligan, who was married three times, fathered twenty-four children in all.[8] Children were not regarded as a burden, particularly by the poor, but as an insurance against old age. *'Ná raibh slíocht ná lorg ort'* ('may you leave neither clan nor trace after you'), is an Irish curse that survived from Killasser parish.[9] New babies were greeted with joy, even though they meant extra mouths to feed, which for most simply in-

---

4   De Latocnaye, vol. 2, p. 116
5   Shaw Mason, op.cit. vol. 3, p. 349
6   Moran, *Spicilegium Ossoriense,* vol 3, pp. 272–3
7   Ward, Wrynn, Ward, p. 136: original, OCD, 8.3. HS 023
8   Information supplied by his great-great-grandson, David Neligan, European Commission, Brussels.
9   IFC, Ms. 321, p. 417

volved more potatoes. But there was a downside too – the loss of earnings of the mother from spinning which was the main contribution to the rent, due to the time she had to spend nursing and caring for the baby. Even nights were threatening. In cabins where whole families shared the same bedding, Donlevy's *Catechism* cautioned mothers not to sleep with their babies for twelve months, lest they be accidentally smothered.

Confirmation, or the more descriptive *Dul faoi láimh Easbaig* ('going under the bishop's hand'), was irregularly administered and then mostly to adults. Some may never have received this sacrament. With no bishop at all in Achonry from 1603 until Hugh MacDermot was nominated in 1707, and most of his successors like him non-resident, this was inevitable. Up to the early nineteenth century only two natives of Achonry were appointed bishops, John O'Hart and Philip Philips, and their combined ministries hardly exceeded a dozen years. O'Hart was old and ailing for the three-and-half years he was bishop. His predecessor Dominick O'Daly was a Dominican who resided normally at his friary in Athenry where he had previously been prior. Bishops Patrick Robert Kirwan, Boetius Egan and Thomas O'Connor were all natives of Co Galway where they continued to live. Charles Lynagh had been parish priest of Westport when he was appointed and remained living in his house there. Only Bishop Walter Blake, who lived in the family home in Ballinafad, Co Mayo, some ten miles from the western edge of the diocese and more than fifty from its most easterly parish, was within striking distance of most parishes.

Confirmation

In theory, bishops were required to complete a visitation of their diocese every three years and it was during the visitation of each parish that confirmation took place. Ideally, the bishop should have spent a night or two in each parish and it would have taken a minimum of about six weeks to two months to cover the twenty or so parishes. The lack of suitable accommodation posed a real problem for the visiting bishop. 'In a large part of the diocese there are neither inns nor Catholic dwelling houses where I could lodge,' Kirwan informed the nuncio in Brussels in 1770. 'The inhabitants there are for the most part very poor people and their little hovels and bedding would excite horror.'[10] Kirwan's health was fragile and he suffered from a weak chest. Like MacDermot, O'Hart and Philips, he was not a young man when he was appointed. Philip Philips, who transferred from Killala to Achonry in 1776, was described a few years later as 'a septuagenarian, toothless and goutish.'[11] Patrick McNicholas, the first native resident bishop in the next century, was

10 SC Irlanda, vol. 11, f. 541v
11 SC Irlanda, vol. 15, f. 470v

appointed in 1817. He reported to Rome that he had found there had been no Confirmation in some parishes for more than twenty years.[12] His immediate predecessor, John O'Flynn, who came to live in Gurteen (Kilfree), suffered a stroke and lost the use of his right arm. In any event, as the sacrament was not essential for the salvation of the recipient, it could be and often was put on the long finger, depending on the health of the bishop and the vagaries of the weather.

When Confirmation took place there was usually a carnival atmosphere, with hundreds and sometimes thousands of men and women, young and old, assembled in the open air on a summer's day to receive the sacrament. Though it normally took place in June or July at the height of the working season, people downed tools willingly and flocked to the appointed place. The bishop, with whom for most of them it would be their first and last encounter, wearing his mitre and cope and carrying his crozier, moved among them imposing hands on each kneeling figure and anointing their foreheads. He was like a king receiving the submission of his subjects. He preached to them at length in Irish, sometimes before, sometimes after administering the sacrament. As Confirmation was particularly recommended for those who suffered persecution, that would have been an obvious theme for the bishop to choose.

Stations

While people had a general awareness of sin, there were none of the exaggerated guilt feelings which were to oppress Catholics in later centuries. People were expected to confess once or at most twice a year, usually just before Easter, as they were bound to receive Communion then. This became known as their 'Easter duty'. With a thousand and more families to confess in many parishes it was neither easy nor convenient for them to approach the priest at his lodgings or residence. A system of confessional 'stations' was devised to meet the problem. Twice yearly, before and during Advent leading up to Christmas and similarly during Lent up to Easter, these stations were held. The times chosen were liturgically and seasonally suitable. Thus they began in mid-October when harvesting had been completed and re-started in late February, before the spring sowing began. The priest, who had to make these journeys daily on horseback, often had to cope with wintry conditions.

When the time of the stations arrived, the priest announced on Sunday from the altar in the Mass-house or chapel the townland or village in which the station would be held on each day of the following week. The name of the family in whose house the station would take place was also mentioned.

---

12   SC Irlanda, vol. 23, ff. 611r-614rv

The Station
(Carleton, *Traits and Stories*)

These 'station houses', as they came to be called, required a certain minimum of amenities. It is evident that the mud cabins of the majority cottier population were excluded. Only the houses of the middling to wealthy farmers or graziers would suit. These were stone-walled thatched buildings, usually with three chambers and modestly furnished with tables and chairs and cupboards. On these occasions they would be spotlessly cleaned inside and outside, and no expense would be spared to meet the expectation of the priest and the critical gaze of the neighbours.

At first light, the priest, wearing his great black frieze coat, cloakwise in the Spanish style, and broad-rimmed felt hat and knee-length riding boots, mounted his horse and set out for the appointed place, probably accompanied by his horse-boy carrying the Mass-kit on his *gearrán*. Country roads were non-existent. He followed boreens and sheep-tracks, waded through shallow streams and skirted round bogs. Once arrived, the table was prepared for Mass. The Mass-kit contained most of what was required – a chalice and paten often made of tin or pewter, wooden cross, old thumb-stained Latin missal, a few linen cloths of uncertain colour and, of course, bread and wine. The family provided the rush candle and a mug of water. The priest also brought a portable altar-stone, containing the relics of some obscure and distant saint, which was placed on the centre of the table. The vestments –

Roman chasuble, alb, stole and maniple – were old, well-worn and much degraded by frequent drenchings. The horse-boy acted as Mass server, making the Latin responses. The room was crowded with the family and friends, standing or kneeling round the table, which was propped against the wall. Most stood outside the house, catching an odd glimpse of the priest's back through the open door or window. Mass was said at a brisk pace. There was probably no sermon and Communion was not distributed. The priest had been fasting since midnight.

Once the Mass was finished the table was cleared and laid again for the priest's breakfast, which probably excited even greater interest among the onlookers. It was described in Tourlestrane as 'a good breakfast of tea, eggs, bread and butter, together with a bottle of whiskey'. The tea rather than the whiskey would have caused some excitement. It was a rarity in rural Ireland and did not become common until the growth of towns with the enterprise of little shopkeepers in the early decades of the next century. In 1786 Charles O'Conor had to purchase his tea in Dublin.[13] Tea sets, particularly the kettle and teapot, had to be borrowed from wealthier neighbours for the occasion. In one instance they were provided by the local Protestant minister in a charming and practical ecumenical gesture.[14] The same set may well have preceded the priest from house to house on his circuit.

Confessions Somewhere between ten and eleven o'clock the main business of the day began. Confessions were heard in one of the adjoining rooms in the house or sometimes in a barn or outhouse specially cleared out and readied for that purpose. A fire was set and a stool or chair was placed beside it for the priest. Penitents queued up in a line outside awaiting their turn. After asking the 'ghostly father's' blessing and reciting the Confiteor as far as the *'mea culpa'*, each recounted his or her sins of thought, word, deed or omission. Then the penitent finished the Confiteor and the priest imposed a penance which was usually the obligation to recite some well-known prayers. Occasionally for grave offences, penitents might be obliged to make a pilgrimage or perform the stations at a holy well.

Certain sins were reserved and could only be absolved by the bishop. The Synod of Tuam in 1817 appended a list of reserved sins to the statutes. Besides the usual ones of apostasy, murder, incest, sodomy, bestiality, etc., they included deliberately striking a father or mother and neglect of one's Easter duty. As the bishop was rather an elusive figure, reserved sins could pose enormous problems for the unfortunate sinner. 'The priests have consider-

13 Ward, Wrynn, Ward, op. cit., p. 479
14 Shaw Mason, op. cit., vol. 3, p. 243

able difficulties,' Kirwan reported to Rome in 1772, 'in dealing with cases of conscience where ignorance is the main cause of grave sin and unlawful liaisons.' He cited the unusual case of a man who had a child by his sister after a single act of intercourse. They confessed their sin immediately but the mother failed to have the child baptised. Furthermore, for ten years the father had practised bestiality, which fact he had concealed, though he had gone to confessions twice a year for thirty years. The mother also indulged in 'unclean practices' for seven years and she also received the same sacrament twice a year. Kirwan pleaded with Rome that priests be given the powers to deal with such cases as the diocese was in 'missionary territory and the people were sorely oppressed and deprived of normal civilized living'.[15]

It was likely that first Confessions were made on the occasion of the station. The candidates were usually in their middle to late teens. One possible reason for deferral of this sacrament, at least by the poorer classes, was the fee charged on each occasion. For young people and servants it was sixpence in 1814, a labourer's daily wage, while married couples paid two shillings and twopence. These fees might even have served as an additional deterrent to those tempted to sin grieviously. However, in 1817, they were discontinued for women and young people in the Tuam province.

Confessions continued until three or four in the afternoon. This was followed by dinner. It was a substantial meal 'consisting of fowl, butcher's meat with oaten bread and butter' to which many of the 'decent neighbours' were invited. Often the sun had gone down when the priest and his horse-boy made their return journey home.

The neighbours waited on for the usual festivities which accompanied such house gatherings. In spite of the expense entailed, the indications are that people vied with each other to host the station. Having the station confirmed the social status of the host family, and others on the fringes of respectability sought to enter that elite circle. More importantly, with their deep religious sense, people regarded it as a privilege to have the Mass in their homes and believed that many blessings would flow on their families.

Weddings

Towards the end of the eighteenth century the growth in population began to accelerate rapidly. One of the chief causes was early marriages, particularly among the lower classes. Girls married from between fifteen and twenty years old while the boys were twenty and upwards.[16] 'In the West a girl's first appearance at Mass is well understood to be an intimation that her

15 SC Irlanda, vol. II, f. 669
16 Neligan, p. 360. 'The common Irish marry very young.' John Carr, *The Stranger in Ireland*, p. 281

parents wish to receive proposals for her.'[17] Early marriages encountered few obstacles. A mud cabin could be erected with a little help in two days at the most. A potato patch could be acquired by ploughing further up the mountain or reclaiming bogland. Even the lowest dowry of ten pounds would provide the new couple with a cow and perhaps a few fowl, and with that and the bride's spinning wheel they were assured of a subsistence little changed from what they had both just left behind. Whole families, including grown-up daughters, shared the same sleeping accommodation. The description given by the Bishop of Cloyne in 1766 to the nuncio in Brussels of the sleeping arrangements of the poor in his diocese applied equally to Achonry. 'Their extreme poverty obliges them to have their children of both sexes sleep all together pele-mele or promiscuously with their fathers and mothers on the same heap of straw in a common bed.' This 'is the unfortunate source of all their sins of impurity'. Girls in particular ran the risk of having their marriage prospects seriously compromised, an added incentive for parents to get their daughters marrried early.

Match-making Most weddings took place between Christmas and Lent, with the greatest number celebrated on Shrove Tuesday and the days leading up to it. They were forbidden during Advent and Lent, and only rich farmers could afford dispensations. This was the only extended leisure period in an agricultural economy. Time was needed for the match-making which sometimes involved protracted negotiations. Friends of the young people, or go-betweens, entered into negotiations 'which is done by sitting up the whole night, talking over the terms, drinking whiskey and smoking tobacco'.[18] The terms to be agreed consisted of what each party was prepared to contribute.

Dowries A girl's dowry in the early nineteenth century in Kilmactigue varied between ten and fifty pounds. There were a few instances where the dowry amounted to a hundred pounds but these obviously involved wealthier Catholics seeking to consolidate or improve their sizeable holdings. Such families with large numbers of daughters to be provided for could sometimes be impoverished as a result. 'I provided husbands for both my eldest daughters,' Connor O'Rorke informed his cousin in Vienna in 1738, 'and in portioning both I had the misfortune that both deceased and no restitution of any part of what I gave them.' To provide their dowries O'Rorke had 'stript himself the years before of live stock'. Had O'Rorke's eldest daughters lived 'they would be a prop to the young ones in his drooping days'. He had in fact seven daughters and:

17 Shaw Mason, op. cit., vol. 2, p. 460
18 Neligan, p. 361

he always supported a long family and that with more decency than those that had ten times his income but now that his rent is better than doubled and himself growing somewhat stiff, I fear he will have enough to do having five daugters still to provide for, very good girls and well bred, each of them exceeding one another in parts and behaviour.[19]

The poorer classes with daughters growing up had to put money aside well in advance. Sometimes they deposited it with their Protestant landlord for safe keeping. In 1813 James Tighe petitioned O'Hara of Annaghmore on behalf of his recently married daughter 'in hopes your Honour will pay me the money I have left in your Honour's care for her'. O'Hara instructed his steward to pay the twenty-one guineas in question. A few years later James Henry, parish priest of Collooney, wrote to the same landlord on behalf of a young girl called McCarrick of Rathbarron. Her young man had broken off the match because of her failure to produce the dowry. Her widowed mother 'of narrow means' told Henry that 'it would be an eligible match for her, that it is approved by all her friends and that no obstacle intervenes except the young man's having the certainty of the money her father left for her use'. It had been deposited some years previously with O'Hara and the receipt was now in the hands of her uncle who refused to deliver it. Henry asked O'Hara to 'have the goodness to point out to her how she is to act'.[20] While women always required a dowry, paid in cash or sometimes in cattle, men were expected to provide the cabin and potato patch or small holding, with a cow or perhaps a few cattle. A farmer with one or more sons to marry gave each of them a division of his holding for which they were expected to pay a proportion of the rent.

Marriages among all classes were arranged. The higher up the scale the parties were, the more arrangement was required. The poorer classes had little to offer and little to lose. In such cases it would seem that there might have been some element of romance. It was claimed that in most instances in Kilmactigue marriages were arranged 'without any regard to love, affection or any of the finer feelings', and that it frequently happened 'that the bride is dragged to the Hymeneal altar, bathed in tears, and compelled to take a companion for life, who is chosen by her parents from prudential motives'. However, where love was a factor in the marriage, elopement was common, 'notwithstanding the absence of all difficulties which might stand in the way

---

19 de Breffny, 'Letters from Connaught to a Wild Goose', pp. 85, 98
20 O'Hara Papers, Ms. 20, 280 (25) & (29)

of the union of the lovers'.²¹ Arthur Young declared, 'It is scarcely credible how many young women have even of late years been ravished and carried off'.²² This was regarded as the only means to insure for their marriages the aura of romance. It also insured the wrath of the church which declared the violent abduction of a woman for the purpose of contracting marriage with her a reserved sin.

Dispensations

People lived in a closed society and had to search for marriage partners usually within the bounds of the parish and sometimes within their own village. With the constant subdivision of holdings among sons, it was inevitable that a large percentage of families became related to each other to some degree. These relationships often constituted an impediment to marriage according to the church's teaching. Even the children of great-grandparents were prohibited from marrying each other. These prohibitions also extended to certain marriage relationships – to in-laws, and to what was termed 'spiritual kindred', for example, a god-parent was not permitted to marry a god-child. Marriages within certain of these prohibited degrees could only take place with a prior dispensation from Rome. In practice, bishops sought and were given the power to dispense in a fixed number of cases over a set period of time. In 1735 Rome granted such power to Bishop John O'Hart to dispense cousins and similar in-law relations for five cases only. Normally this power extended for three years as in the case of Bishop Walter Blake in 1754 and 1757 and Bishop Patrick Robert Kirwan in 1763 and 1766.²³ The civil law, in this case administered by the Protestant minister, was more accommodating. It recognised marriage contracted within these degrees as valid and some Catholics had no qualms about approaching the Protestant minister to marry them. Bishops, such as Boetius Egan, were quick to point out this disturbing practice to Rome.²⁴

Marriage Banns

The general church law also required that the banns be published, that is that the prospective marriage be announced on three consecutive Sundays so that anybody who knew of some grave reason why the marriage should not take place could come forward. Given the circumstances of the times, such a practice was virtually impossible. Bishops gave a general dispensation, though the law remained on the statute books. A fee was imposed on all couples for this dispensation which in time became known as the 'bishop's dues'. It amounted to five shillings in 1817. The bishop was expected to use this

21 Neligan, p. 159
22 op. cit. vol 2, p. 154
23 Lettere, vol. 142, f. 176rv; vol. 184, f. 107v; vol. 191, f. 160v; vol. 203, f. 2v; vol 209, f. 45r
24 Fondo di Vienna, vol. 28, ff. 324rv–327r

money and the fees for the other marriage dispensations, for charitable purposes, such as to help the poor or later towards the building of chapels. Some bishops were accused of pocketing the money. In 1751 Walter Blake with the other Connacht bishops in a reply to Rome vehemently rejected the allegation.[25] Patrick Grady, parish priest of Ballymote, published in 1814 a similar accusation against Bishop John O'Flynn. Grady's evident hostility towards the bishop makes him a highly suspect witness.[26]

The wedding ceremony took place in the home of the bride, usually in the afternoon or early evening. The bride, occasionally overcome by shyness, had sometimes to be coaxed from her hiding place when the priest arrived.

'Bringing home the Bride'
(Mr & Mrs S. C. Hall, *Ireland*)

She was dressed in her Sunday best which was described in Co Sligo at the end of the century as consisting of 'red cloak, stripped linen or cotton gown, cotton stockings, cambric cap and green or red petticoat'.[27] The young women among the guests would have been similarly dressed. The bride was attended by a bridesmaid and bridesman. The priest wore an alb or surplice and a stole. The ceremony normally took place without Mass. The marriage register was not signed.[28] For much of the early part of the century, such a book would have been regarded as incriminating evidence if found in the

25 CP, vol. 110, ff. 119rv, 120v
26 *The Radical anti-Veto*, pp. 11–12
27 McParlan, *Statistical Survey of Co Sligo*, p. 72
28 'The registers of baptisms, marriages and burials … are almost totally unknown in Ireland', Carr, p 525

possession of the priest and later, despite frequent exhortations from bishops on visitation, marriage or baptismal registers were rarely kept until well into the next century. In a world where everybody knew everybody else and baptisms and marriages were very public occasions, the parties' freedom to marry could easily be established without recourse to records. Strangers were only permitted to marry after they had lived for two years in the parish and had performed their Easter duty once there.

After the wedding the usual custom of 'throwing the stocking' was observed, which one commentator remarked was 'too well-known to need a description'.[29] It was probably the ancestor of the modern throwing of the garter. Whichever girl caught the stocking was regarded as next to be married.

Dinner, which 'generally consisted of mutton, salt pork, bacon and poultry, with an abundance of potatoes and common garden vegetables', followed. Relations of the parties frequently contributed some of the dishes for the wedding dinner.[30] Sometimes the door was taken down and placed on benches to serve as the dinner table. Only the head of the table, where the priest sat, was covered with a cloth. The other guests were seated according to property, rank and age. The father and mother of the bride did not partake in the meal, preferring instead to wait on the other guests. The meat was usually cut into pieces about the 'size of brickbats' and placed on the table in large wooden platters, from which the guests helped themselves with their hands. The few knives and forks which could be borrowed for the occasion were reserved for the priest and 'the select party whom he chose to honour with his conversation'.

After dinner the entertainment began with singing, dancing and drinking. Whiskey was supplied in abundance, which was estimated in Kilmactigue at ten gallons or more, 'the price of which would purchase a middling cow'. Next to the priest, the musician was the most sought-after guest. Generally he played the pipes and might have been brought from twenty or thirty miles away, though in Sligo, with its strong musical tradition, there was no shortage of musicians. All were accomplished dancers, having been trained in the art from childhood. 'As long as the reverend pastor holds the chair, he keeps them to regularity and good order.' He usually retired about eight or nine o'clock.

The door was put back on its hinges and the festivities began in earnest. As the night progressed, all semblance of order disappeared. 'Perhaps three

29 Shaw Mason, op. cit. vol. 1, p. 593
30 Robert Bell, *A description of the customs and manners of the Irish peasantry, 1780–1790*, pp. 18–19; the present description is largely based on the foregoing and Neligan's 'Parish of Kilmactigue', pp. 360–362.

musicians may be found playing to as many sets of dancers, a dozen men and women singing as many different songs, and other groups employed in altercation and quarrelling.' The festivities often continued for two or three days and nights. A week passed and sometimes a fortnight before the bridegroom brought his new bride home. Like all married women, she continued to be called by her maiden name. Weddings were expensive affairs costing as much as half the dowry of the bride. 'Such however is the custom of the country and such the pride and spirit of the people, that they would lay out their last shilling to furnish the feast, rather than be thought singular or churlish.' Marriage was a very popular institution in Ireland and bachelors and spinsters were virtually non-existent. In England it was not usual for the servants of the manor to marry while their Irish counterparts usually did.

It must have been a very hectic period for the priest. In 1814 in Kilmactigue there were fifty-three marriages and, if most of these took place during this season, they would have averaged almost one a day. His fee then was one pound two shillings and nine pence. The average fees in Clare at the time varied between one and five guineas.[31] The fee varied according to people's ability to pay. Recalling the old times in Killasser, one old lady remarked, 'If they hadn't the price of their dinner, they'd get married. An' maybe the priest would have to marry them for nothin'.'[32]

The Sick and Dying

The other great service rendered by the priest in the homes of the people was the pastoral care of the sick and dying. In normal times sickness was confined to the very young and the old and dying. 'The sick bed was usually a wad of straw laid on the floor near the fire or sometimes on a bedstead.'[33] Winter or summer the fire was kept up, filling the cabin with smoke for the patient's comfort. The smoke was deemed therapeutic. Visiting the sick was a well-observed custom. Neighbours called and spent long periods chatting with the sick person and of course smoking tobacco. The bed-clothes were rarely if ever changed.

Doctors, where they existed, only plied their dubious trade for the benefit of the upper classes. The poor preferred their own traditional cures. They had great faith in the healing power of the priest. He was frequently called on to 'perform an office'. In our own century, in the diocese of Raphoe, a packet of salt was brought to the priest to be blessed and it was applied to the ailment

---

31 Shaw Mason, op. cit., vol. 2, p. 460
32 IFC, Ms. 114, p. 366
33 The description of sickness here is largely based on Neligan, pp. 367–8

of the sick person.[34] 'They also bring the priest to perform the same ceremony for a cow, a horse or a pig, if any of these valuable domestics should be suddenly taken ill.'[35] Even some Protestants had recourse to the priest in times of illness, and he duly obliged, provided usually that they converted to Catholicism. The Reverend Mr Neligan complained that he had lost two of his tiny flock in Kilmactigue as a result. People also applied to the priest for what they called *Leabhar Eoin*. This consisted of the first verse of St John's gospel, written on a piece of paper, sewn into a piece of cloth, blessed by the priest and worn round the neck of the sick person. This practice was widespread throughout the country. Children near Slane were observed by a French traveller in 1797 wearing little woollen bags tied round their necks and when he enquired why, he was told it was the gospel. 'In some countries the priests strive to make the people superstitious; in others the people endeavour to make the priests so.'[36]

Special prayers were said to ward off sickness and disease. Death was often associated with night and sleep and night prayers reflected that association.

Ceithre choirnéal ar mo leaba,
Ceithre aingle ortha sgartha,
Má fhaghaim bás go dtí an mhaidin,
Gur i bhFlaithis Dé bhéas mo leaba.

Four corners on my bed,
Four angels placed on each of them,
If I die before morning,
May my bed be in God's heaven.

Another example also comes from Killasser:

Luighim ar an leaba seo
Mar a shínfear mé san uaigh.
Diúltaím an t-ainspiorad,
Glacaim leis an Spiorad Naomh.

I lie on this bed,
As I will be stretched in the grave
I reject the devil,
I embrace the Holy Spirit.[37]

---

34 I am indebted to Seán MacEntee for this information. As the term 'office' was used to describe the priest's daily obligation to recite the breviary, in this instance he may have recited a portion of it over the sick person.
35 Neligan, p. 369
36 De Latocnaye, vol. 2, p. 29
37 IFC, Ms 127, p. 582

Other prayers invoked Christ's suffering on the Cross for the sick person:
>   Créatúr lag mé faoi ualach trom
>   Méad mo pheaca is aithreach liom,
>   Ag bun na croiche screadaim suas
>   'Do thrua, a Dhia, claon anuas.

> Under a great weight, a weak creature am I,
> I repent the size of my sin,
> At the foot of the Cross, upwards I cry,
> O God in pity bend down to me.[38]

The following prayer was well-known in Mayo and Sligo:
>   Guím péin a Chríost,
>   A Chríost dhílis dheas,
>   Galra ar bith atá amuigh,
>   Nár leigí Dia é 'steach.

> I pray thee, O Christ,
> Dear kind Christ,
> Any disease that roams abroad,
> May God keep out of the house.[39]

Wake
(Mr & Mrs S. C. Hall, *Ireland*)

38 ibid
39 ibid, Ms. 227, p. 73

Last Anointing

People were very familiar with death. Several times in the course of their lives they watched it in all its stages as it carried off family members. They recognised the death rattle and knew the signs of impending death. At this point the priest was summoned. Too soon and the patient would be alarmed, too late and he would be lost. *Ola Deireannach* (the Last Anointing) was widely regarded as a passsport to paradise. A saying in Killasser described it:

Bás, ola agus aithrí
Agus leaba Chríostaí i bhFlaithis Dé

Death with oil and repentance
and a Christian bed in God's heaven.[40]

Such a belief placed an enormous responsibility on the priest. Day or night he was expected to come when he was called. The consequences of his failure to do so were awesome. One priest who ignored such a call was Michael Farrell, parish priest of Ballaghaderreen, for which he was reported to Rome. The sick call had come from no less a personage than Myles MacDermot, the Prince of Coolavin. Farrell refused to come because he had received the message from a servant of Bryan Donbroy with whom he had some quarrel. Fortunately for MacDermot, another priest was found in the neighbourhood who came and remained with him for two days until he died.[41]

The priest administered this sacrament by anointing with oil the eyes, ears, nose, mouth and hands and feet of the dying person. These five senses

Irish Wake (Wood-Martin, *Traces of Elder Faiths*)

40   ibid, Ms. 127, p. 581
41   Fondo di Vienna, vol. 28, ff. 256rv, 257v

were considered to be the chief agents of sin. It was widely believed that the devil launched his greatest assaults when his victim was weakest in the hour of death. Like the other sacraments, it was performed in Latin. His last blessing was in Irish: *Go raibh Dia leat, mar a bhí tú le do chomharsain* (May God may be with you, as you were with your neighbours).[42] If the person was capable of receiving Communion, it was given. This was called *Viaticum*, food for the journey to the next world.

Immediately the person had died, the bed of straw was carried out and set alight on a piece of high ground, 'whilst the air resounds with the doleful cries of the survivors'. The French consul found this custom in Co Roscommon in 1791.[43] The idea was to notify the neighbouring villages of the death and invite them to the approaching wake and funeral. Not to attend such was regarded as an unforgiveable offence. All work was suspended in the village until after the burial.

Wakes

At night the body, with the face exposed and the rest covered with a white sheet, placed upon some boards or an unhinged door supported by some stools, is waked, when all the relatives, friends and neighbours assemble together, candles and candlesticks borrowed from the neighbourhood are stuck around the deceased, and according to the circumstances of the family, the company is regaled with whiskey, ale, cake, pipes and tobacco.[44]

In more prosperous homes a second wake-room was opened. Here the next-of-kin and the old people sat with the corpse, smoking pipes and drinking whiskey and passing the night telling stories. Smoking the pipe itself formed part of the ritual. When offered the pipe the recipient said a prayer:

Nár ba liachtaí gráinne gainimh ar an tráigh,
Ná ribe féir a' fás,
Ná braon drúchta ar a bharr
Seacht lán déag de bheannachtaí Dé agus na hEaglaise
Ar an té a bhronn an píopa sin orm.

May the grains of sand on the seashore,
The blades of grass a'growing,
The drops of dew on the earth,
Be no more numerous than the seventeen full blessings of God and the church
Upon the person who bestowed this pipe on me.

42 IFC, Ms. 114, p. 33
43 Neligan, p. 368; Ní Chinnéide, vol. 25, p. 11; Carr, pp. 257–8
44 John Carr, *The Stranger in Ireland*, pp. 257–8

The custom was to take a few draws from the pipe and say this prayer for the deceased:

> *Go raibh beannachtaí dílse Dé agus na hEaglaise leis an anam a fhágfaidh an corp a raibh an tabac sin os a chionn agus le gach anam bocht go hiomlán.*
> May the sweet blessings of God and the Church be with the soul which must leave the body over which that tobacco sat, and copiously with every other poor soul.

The significance of tobacco at wakes was locally explained by fanciful tales relating to Christ's death. One such recounted how the Roman soldiers were smoking their pipes after completing the crucifixion. One of them, seeing Our Lady weeping uncontrollably at the foot of the cross, offered her his pipe to smoke to console her.[45]

The 'Irish Cry'

Women arriving for the wake began their lament within twenty yards of the house. The 'Irish cry' or 'howl' excited considerable interest among foreign visitors. One Frenchman rendered it phoneticaly as 'hu lu lu' or 'pille-lu' or 'lu lu lu' and compared it to the *ululatus* of the Romans. He speculated that it might have been an imitation of the *De Profundis* which priests chanted at burials.[46] Commentators varied regarding its musical quality. It was described in Athlone as a 'savage howl of discordant sounds'.[47] John Wesley, who first heard it in 1750, when he preached at a Protestant burial in Rathcormack, called it 'a dismal inarticulate yell'.[48] Arthur Young heard it in Castlebar in 1776 where it was performed 'in a most horrid manner'.[49] Yet another observed that it was 'not destitute of modulation'.[50] It also varied in quality from the south to the north where it was 'arranged with more melancholy sweetness than in any other part of Ireland'. Here it consisted of six notes, the first four of which were chanted in a low and solemn tone, the concluding two more loud and rapid.[51] Achonry probably occupied the middle band where it was described as 'the air resounding with the melodious voices of a large assemblage of females'.[52] There also seems to have been a regional variation in the duration and frequency of

Bean caointe (Mr & Mrs S.C. Hall, *Ireland*)

---

45 IFC, Ms. 277, p. 90; Ms. 114, pp. 359–60
46 De Latocnaye, vol. 1, p. 155
47 Shaw Mason, op. cit., vol. 3, p. 77
48 Wesley's *Journal*, vol. 3, p. 47
49 op. cit., vol. 1, p. 249
50 Bell, op. cit., p. 19
51 Shaw Mason, vol. 2, p. 510
52 Neligan, p. 367

Musical notation of the keen
(Mr & Mrs S.C. Hall, *Ireland*)

the cry. An English commentator stated that it took place every hour or half-hour and lasted five or six minutes, while all conversation and amusement ceased and everybody joined in. A different version comes from Killasser where there were relays of *mná caointe* (keening women). They performed continuously outside the house and replaced each other at intervals. This is similar to the wake witnessed by a Frenchman in Killarney. Here the keening was done by four women for about a quarter of an hour, after which they were replaced by four others, and the former refreshed themselves outside with a large glass of whiskey.[53] There is no evidence that they were hired or paid but they were given *togha is rogha bídh is dighe* (the best of food and drink). This crying by women had been forbidden by the Synod of Tuam as early as 1631 and repeated again in 1660. The people, however, remained attached to their keening women and 'it was said that their cries were better than the best prayers and that God would sooner listen to them'.[54] Surprisingly, the rosary, though widely popular, does not appear to have been said on these occasions.

The young people engaged in amusements and games, something which never failed to astonish foreigners. They were for the most part mimes, well-known by all the company and expertly performed. Generally, they fell into two categories, kissing or courting games and beating or punishment games. The object of the former was to provide the opportunity to kiss with the company's approval some chosen girl, while the aim of the latter was to settle some grudge. *Ag déanamh an bhríste* ('making breeches') was a popular kissing game. Boys and girls, mixed together, sat in a circle. Each had a straw and a piece of cloth and pretended they were sewing a pair of breeches. While they sewed, they sang:

Wake Games

Déanfaimid an bríste	We are making the breeches
Agus déanfaimid é,	And we are making it
Agus beidh sé déanta	And it will be made
Ag éirighe an lae.	At the start of day.
Soro lae agus soro lae.	*Soro lae agus soro lae.*

53 De Latocnaye, vol. 1, p. 182
54 IFC, Ms. 194, pp. 121–2

One man was appointed to act as judge. The person found unsatisfactory at the mime was obliged to go around and kiss everybody in the circle and, if some person was not kissed properly, they were compelled to go around again and again until the judge was satisfied. The term, *briste tórraimh* (wake-breeches), was used in everyday language to describe something useless. *Jack Dowdle* was a similar game involving one girl. She sat on a stool in the middle of the floor and all the boys were put outside the door. One boy bent down and the others leap-frogged over him. Whoever did not do it right had to come in and kiss the girl. The judge then asked the girl if she was satisfied with the kiss and if she answered no, it had to be repeated over and over again until she was satisfied.

Na naoi dtincéirí spóirteamhla ('the nine jolly tinkers') was a beating game. Punishments were more severe in other games, such as *The Spy*, where the victim was thrown on the manure heap.[55]

To speculate on the significance of these wake-games would be in the words of one writer 'unbearably pretentious', though he himself did not altogether succeed in avoiding the temptation.[56] Suffice it to say that young people behaved on these occasions as young people always behave in mixed company. Though they may now appear incongruous to modern eyes, these activities had been legitimised by centuries of use. Their purpose was to perpetuate the memory of the deceased. The more memorable the wake, the longer the name of the deceased survived in the folk-memory. At worst, they were, as Charles O'Conor described them, 'ludicrous farces' and at least in Achonry there is no evidence of any of the more obscene performances occasionally referred to elsewhere. They were of course frowned on by the church but, in spite of the warning of the western bishops in 1660 against this custom of 'excessive drinking, revels, dances, games and similar corrupt practices', they continued to thrive well into the second half of the nineteenth century and even into the early twentieth century in Donegal.

---

55 Other wake games played in the districts of Killasser and Kilmovee were *Thart an bhróg* ('passing the shoe') *Babhta bróg, Cor-éisg, Luigíní, Ag díol an choirce* ('selling the oats'), *Cráin finiche agus a hál bainbh* ('wild sow and her litter of bonhams'), *Ceann cabáiste* ('head of cabbage'), *Lurabog, Cleas an tailliúra* ('the tailor's trick'), *An Gabhar* ('the goat'), *Ordogaí suas* ('thumbs-up'), *Ag cur thart an fháinne* ('putting round the ring'), *An Coileach* ('the cock'), The ould *cailleach*, Slappin', Marryin', Chasing the rat, Hiding the spoons, The black cap, *Pigin agus muc,* Scutching the lamp, Thatching the stack, Spinning the tin; see IFC, Ms. 193, pp. 714–720, 811–14; Ms. 227, pp. 244–6; Ms. 114, pp. 363, 436; Ms. 194, pp. 121, 122, 267–70; Ms. 277, p. 103; see also Seán Ó Súilleabháin, *Irish Wake Amusements,* and Seán Connolly, *Priests and People in pre-Famine Ireland.*
56 Connolly, op. cit., p. 151

Funerals

The wake usually continued for two nights. Certain days were preferred for burials, especially Fridays, following Christ's example. *Bás Aoine, adhlacadh an tSathairn, is guidhe an Domhnaigh* (Death on Friday, burial on Saturday, prayer on Sunday).[57] Monday burials were avoided because it was believed that a burial on that day would bring about the immediate death of somebody else in the neighbourhood.[58] The corpse was placed in an open deal box or coffin and covered with a white cloth. It was carried by four men to the cemetery. A French traveller encountered in 1797 a funeral procession near Slane. It was led by a child carrrying a white rod with cut paper on it, followed by the keening women.[59] Lady Morgan described the funeral of a young person which was led by a number of young people of both sexes, each couple holding each other by a white handkerchief, and these were followed by the keeners.[60] The crowd, often consisting of hundreds, followed the

Funeral procession of a farmer (Barrow, *Tour*)

remains. Failure to attend a funeral was regarded as an unforgiveable offence by the bereaved family. Even a stranger who encountered a funeral by chance was expected to accompany it for some distance.

Some commentators referred to the cairns or heaps of stones constructed on the roadside where the funeral stopped briefly, perhaps to change the

Cairns

---

57 IFC, Ms. 127, p. 581
58 Ní Chinnéide, op. cit., vol. 25, p. 11
59 De Latocnaye, (1917 ed.), p. 274
60 *The Wild Irish Girl*, pp. 41–60

bearers. The French traveller, who observed these cairns in Connemara, stated that the remark, 'I would not throw a stone on your tomb' was a gross insult.[61] A visitor to Erris in 1752 noticed these cairns raised 'to the memory of the dead, mostly in the shape of sugar loaves, which are kept up as long as their friends remain.' Some were even built with mortar and had inscriptions on them. He found larger ones about twenty feet high in the vicinity of Ballinrobe which he was told were raised to the memory of those slain in a battle on that spot.[62] An nineteenth century visitor said they were 'beautifully and expressively called clogh-breegh or stones of sorrow'.[63]

The women began their cry about a hundred yards from the cemetery or in some instances, as at Urlaur, when the ruins of the monastery first came into view. The priest met the funeral at the entrance to the cemetery and led it three times round the graveyard while he and all the congregation recited the *De Profundis*.[64] After the grave was opened, it was covered by the spade and shovel in the form of a cross, to keep out evil spirits.[65] After the interment, an ozier rod 'twisted into the form of a cross' was planted at the head of the grave and, if it later took root, it was regarded as a happy omen.[66]

Cemeteries

The most popular cemeteries were those located in the ruins of monasteries or ancient churches. They were used by Catholics and Protestants alike. Those who were separated in life were united in death. The O'Haras of Annaghmore were buried with their Catholic ancestors in Court Abbey. The upper classes had their family tombs, as the O'Conors of Belanagare had at Ballintubber Abbey or the Philips of Cloonmore at Urlaur Abbey. Bishop Thomas O'Connor was buried with his parents in the family tomb in the churchyard in Tuam. Only the two native bishops, O'Hart and Philips, were buried in the diocese.

Visitors remarked the mounds of human bones and skulls they found in monastic ruins, usually near the altar. A visitor to Court Abbey early in 1818 found 'melancholy memorials of mortality, the recesses in the walls being entirely filled with human skulls; the whole presenting a scene of desolation

---

61 De Latocnaye, (1917 ed.), p. 154
62 *Bishop Pococke's Irish Tour*, p. 101
63 Carr, pp. 256–7
64 De Latocnaye, on the other hand, stated that it was not said in Ireland, like in other Catholic countries.
65 This custom derived from a County Sligo legend relating to St Patrick, his servant-boy and the fairies.
66 De Latocnaye, op.cit., vol. 1, pp. 183–4; vol. 2, pp. 29, 232; William Henry, *Survey of Co Sligo*, National Archives, Ms. 2533

perfectly in unison with the wildness of the surrounding country'.⁶⁷ These were skulls that were disinterred, once the flesh was consumed, to make room for others. A French traveller found 'more than one skull still covered with hair' in Muckross Abbey. 'This crowding does not trouble the peasantry; they are content that the dead of a year or two should give way to those of today.'⁶⁸

Tobacco pipes in churchyard in the West of Ireland (Wood-Martin, *Traces of Elder Faiths*)

Those who could afford it placed a horizontal stone over their deceased, perhaps as much to prevent the remains being disturbed as to preserve their memory. Strangely, in a locality where Irish alone was spoken, all the inscriptions which have survived are in English or Latin. There is a Latin inscription on the grave of the parish priest of Ballisodare, James O'Connell, who died in April 1710 and was buried at the eastern gable of the old church there. Latin was also used for lay people, such as Oliver O'Hara of Meemlough who was buried in Court Abbey and Thady McMulrunisin who was buried in the graveyard of Ballisodare Abbey in 1753. A simply carved chalice and paten indicated the gravestone of a priest, while the hammer, anvil and nails on the Duffy stone in Urlaur suggest that they were blacksmiths.

Wakes and funerals were expensive. The burial of a wife in Tourlestrane (Kilmactigue) could often amount to half her dowry. Not to have a decent funeral was unthinkable and those who could not afford it sometimes petitioned their Protestant landlord for help. Charles O'Hara received such a petition in 1794:

> The Humble Petition of Owen Collery sheweth petitioner has no earthly substance to enable him to bury his wife and hopes you will deign to allow him some assistance to help to see her Interred as the Lord knows petitioner's weakness at present is such that he can do nothing …

The rich also found burials financially crippling and the same Charles O'Hara a few years later mentioned in his will that he wished to be buried privately as 'expensive burials are of very pernicious consequences in the West of Ireland'. Almost eighty years previously, his father Kean had laid out £100

---

67 *The Scientific Tourist by an Irish Gentleman*
68 De Latocnaye, (1917 ed.), pp. 101–2; Henry, op. cit., p. 23; Twiss, *A Tour of Ireland 1775–6*, p. 131

for his funeral, and a further £50 for repairing the tomb at Court Abbey.[69] Bishop Kirwan, who died in 1776, had expressed a wish to be buried with his parents and left twenty guineas for the funeral expenses. Thomas O'Connor, who also wished to be buried with his parents in the family tomb in Tuam churchyard, ordered the sale of all his horses, cows and sheep, furniture, hay, corn, potatoes and working utensils of every kind, to pay his debts and for his funeral which he wished to be decent and frugal. His successor, Charles Lynagh, who died in 1808, had requested to be buried in Aughagour, near Westport, in such a manner as his executors think 'most decent and befitting'.[70] Eight shillings was the priest's fee in 1814 for attendance on a person dying. In that year there were sixty-one deaths in Kilmactigue. Mass offerings were in proportion to people's ability to pay them.

Funeral ceremonies for the rich were somewhat more elaborate. A requiem or funeral Mass may have been said in the house in the presence of the corpse. This was hardly feasible in the case of cottiers and labourers. They usually made a small offering to the priest to say a private Mass for the deceased. Among 'the genteel and opulent families' the custom of holding a 'Month's Mind' was firmly established. This was often attended by several priests and continued for a number of days to mark the month following the death. Masses were said in the forenoon, followed by a banquet in the afternoon, which were spent 'in conviviality and innocent recreation'.[71] Bishop Kirwan complained in 1770 to the nuncio in Brussels that Philip Philips, then Bishop of Killala, though residing in Cloomore, presided at a Month's Mind for his paternal uncle, on the feastdays of Holy Thursday/Good Friday.[72]

---

69 O'Hara Papers, Ms. 20,280 (6); O'Hara Papers Report 493, pp. 3530, 3534
70 *Arch. Hib.*, vol. 1, pp. 225, 227, 229, 230
71 Neligan, p. 366
72 SC Irlanda, vol. 11, f. 541rv

CHAPTER TEN

'B'fhéidir le Dia'

Prayers and Patterns

The working year was liberally punctuated with the numerous feastdays of *Feastdays* the church's calendar. The number and dates of these were established for the western province in 1631 and continued through most of the following century. Besides the great Christian feasts of Christmas and Easter, there were other feastdays dedicated to Christ and Our Lady, and to a wide variety of saints.[1] These were termed 'holydays of obligation', i.e. the people were bound to attend Mass and abstain from work as on Sundays. There were a few other devotional feastdays to be observed without that obligation.[2] Excluding all Sundays, feastdays amounted to an additional thirty-six holidays from work. There were also the great traditional pagan festivals which continued to be observed on the four quarter-days of the year. The first and the last of these had been christianised, *Imbolg* into *Lá Fhéile Brighde* (1 February) and *Lá Samhna* (1 November) into All Saints. *Lá Bealtaine* (May Day) and *Lá Lughnasa* (1 August) remained stubbornly secular but enormously popular.

Some feastdays were steeped in tradition and had become encrusted over *St Brigid's Day* time with a rich growth of local customs. Such was the case with *Lá Fhéile Brighde*, St Brigid's Day. Brigid's Crosses were made and hung under the roof

1 Circumcision (1 Jan), Epiphany (6 Jan), St Brigid (1 Feb), Purification (2 Feb), St Matthias (14 May), St Patrick (17 Mar), Annunciation (25 Mar), Easter Sunday and Monday, St Mark (25 April), Ss Philip and James (3 May), Finding of the Holy Cross, Ascension, Whit Sunday and Monday, Corpus Christi (6 June), Birth of St John the Baptist (23 June), Ss Peter and Paul (29 June), St Thomas (3 July), St James the Apostle (25 July), St Laurence (10 Aug), Assumption (15 Aug), St Bartholomew (24 Aug), Birth of the Blessed Virgin Mary, St Matthew the Evangelist (21 Sept), St Michael the Archangel (29 Sept), Ss Simon and Jude (8 Oct), St Luke (18 Oct), All Saints (1 Nov), St Martin (11 Nov), St Andrew (30 Nov), Immaculate Conception (8 Dec), St Stephen (26 Dec), St John the Evangelist (27 Dec), Holy Innocents (28 Dec) and the patron saint of the local church.
2 These were Visitation (31 June), Exaltation of the Cross (14 Sept), All Souls (2 Nov), St Catherine, Ash Wednesday and Good Friday. Each feastday extended from midnight of the previous day to midnight of the feastday.

to protect the family. The styles differed in different parts of the country. In Co Sligo the cross was made by interlacing a number of strands of reeds or rushes in a crisscross pattern and tying each of the four sets of the projecting end to form a cross. An elaborate ritual was followed. When the evening meal had been prepared, a girl from the family went outside the house. She knocked three times repeating, 'Go down on your knees, do homage and let Blessed Brigid enter.' She came in and placed the rushes on the table. Grace was said, supper eaten and thanksgiving made. Then the crosses were made, sprinkled with holy water and hung from the roof or over the door. The old crosses were usually left when the new ones were put up.

The saint and her cross were frequently invoked to protect the house and family, as is illustrated by this prayer from Kilmovee on raking the fire:

Coiglim a' teine seo mar choigleann Críosta cách.
Brighid i mullach an tighe
Máire ina lár
Cumhdach an tighe seo agus ár ndaoine go lá.
I rake this fire as Christ rakes every human being.
May Brigid in the house-top,
And Mary at its centre,
Be the protectors of our house and household until morning.

Other night prayers, which have survived from Killasser and Kilmovee, invoke *Brighid agus a brat*. The *brat* was a piece of linen or cloth left outside the house on the eve of the feast. It was believed that the saint travelled the country during the night and touched the cloth, endowing it with healing powers. It was particularly effective against headaches, toothaches, ear aches and sore throats, when wrapped around the painful area. Migratory workers from Mayo wore it when going to England or Scotland.

The young people made *brídeoigíní*, which were little dolls with heads roughly carved from a turnip or large potato, into which a short stick or stump was inserted and wrapped with straw to form a body. Boys and girls went begging from house to house with their *brídeoga* and reciting at each door:

St Brigid's Cross from Co Sligo

Féil' Bríghde bricín
Bain a' chluas de'n toirtín,
Agus tabhair a sháith do'n dailtín.

Brigid's feast a little fish,
Take an ear of the potato-cake,
And give the foster-child its fill.[3]

3   IFC, Ms. 321, pp. 496, 507 (Killasser); Ms. 903, p. 165 (Attymass); Ms. 248, p. 375

The potato-cakes referred to here may well have been the same as the *bairín na gcapall* or 'horse's cakes' which the French consul found eaten in Co Galway on that day.⁴

Patterns were held where holy wells were dedicated to the saint, like Toberbride in the parish of Ballisodare and another in the parish of Keash (Drumrat). Some may have travelled further afield to the more famous Bride's Well in the diocese of Elphin. At least one parish (possibly Ballisodare) in the diocese claimed Brigid as its patron. The following day, known locally as Candlemas, was also a feastday. Young men went to Candlemas fairs to search for a bride.

Brídeog (Ó Catháin, *The Festival of Brigit*)

On St Patrick's Day the shamrock was worn and 'drowned at night in a flowing bowl'. When the day was over the sprig of shamrock was placed in a bowl of whiskey-punch. Once the whiskey was consumed, the drowned shamrock was picked out and thrown over the left shoulder.⁵ There was a lively belief in the power of St Patrick to grant favours and answer prayers.

St Patrick's Day

A Phádraig atá i bPárthas Mhic Dé gan locht
Tabhair sláinte le do ghrásta don té a bhíos bocht.
Tháinig mé i do láthairse is mé lag gan lúth,
Tabhair áras dom i bPárthas, an áit a bhfeicfidh mé thú.

O Patrick who is in Paradise of God's blameless son,
Give health with your grace to one who is poor,
I came into your presence powerless and weak.
Give me a dwelling in Paradise where I will see you.⁶

St Patrick's Day brought a welcome break from the rigours of Lent. Meat never formed part of the regular diet of the poorer classes. During Lent every body abstained from eggs, milk, butter and other milk foods, as they also did on Fridays throughout the year. A French traveller remarked that 'they

Lent

4 Ní Chinnéide, vol. 25, p. 11
5 Shaw Mason, vol. 3, p. 347; see also on this and other feastdays, Caoimhín Ó Danachair, *The Year in Ireland.*
6 IFC, Ms. 195, p. 167

observe Lent and fast-days with a degree of regularity that terrifies a man who wishes to fast in the Scotch fashion only'.[7] Wealthier Catholics found it even more punishing. 'I am growing old,' Charles O'Conor complained in 1761 to a friend, 'I suffered in the last Lent and I fear for my constitution in this.'[8] The universal custom in the country of making pancakes on Shrove Tuesday possibly derived from the necessity of using up all the surplus eggs and milk before Lent began. Priests officiated at marriages 'from sunrise till midnight' on Shrove Tuesday. Small pieces of pancakes were rolled up in stockings which were placed under the pillows of those who had to defer their weddings until Easter Monday.[9] Strangely, the Lenten fast did not extend to alcohol which was consumed in the same generous measure as in other seasons.

On Ash Wednesday one member of the family brought turf ashes to Mass to be blessed for the others. The 'black' fast, i.e. no food at all, was observed on that day and again on Good Friday. People carried sprigs of palm on Palm Sunday. They were bound to make their 'Easter duty', i.e. to receive Holy Communion, between then and the first Sunday after Easter. Good Friday was observed as a day of mourning. Girls and married women let their hair down over their shoulders as they did at burials. Such was the explanation in Killasser of the expression about women on these occasions 'tearing their hair'.[10] They also made pilgrimages to monastic sites dedicated to the Holy Cross, such as the Dominican friary at Straide. This was a daughter-house of Sligo Abbey, similarly dedicated, where such a pilgrimage was observed on Good Friday 1739. They came in crowds at daybreak and went round it in a long circuit on their bare knees over sharp stones. They were 'sorely wounded' and often, to support themselves, used a thigh bone taken from the mound of bones in front of the altar, as a crutch.[11]

Masshouses and chapels were packed on Easter Sunday, with the largest part of the congregation gathered outside. Eggs, which had accumulated in every home during Lent, were eaten. Such is the humble origin of the modern Easter Egg. The poorer classes cooked a goose for dinner. The better-off dined on beef, lamb or kid. Easter Monday was devoted to festivity and was a favourite day for fairs and markets, as indeed was Whit Monday.

Lady Days

The Lady Days were observed 'with the most scrupulous attention'.[12] These were the feasts of Our Lady, the Annunciation on 25 March and the As-

---

7   De Latocnaye, vol. 1, p. 54
8   Ward, Wrynn, Ward, p. 98
9   Shaw Mason, op. cit., vol. 2, p. 458
10 IFC, Ms. 227, p. 178
11 William Henry, op. cit., Ms. 2533, p. 23
12 Neligan, p. 364

sumption on 15 August. The latter was the greater feast and was also a favourite day for patterns. Our Lady occupied a dominant position in popular devotion and loomed large in people's prayers. This one was said in Kilmovee:

> *A Mhaighdean ghlórmhar, mhodhamhail, bheannaithe*
> *Is tú mo stór, is tú mo thaisce*
> *Is tú réalt an eolais romham ins gach bealach,*
> *I ngleann na ndeor go mba tú mo chara.*

> Glorious, gracious, blessed Virgin,
> You are my wealth and treasure,
> My guiding star on every journey,
> May you be my friend in this valley of tears.

At the Last Judgement her intercession was believed to be decisive. Christ will say to her then: *'Ó a mháthair, tabhair amharc do shúile leat'* (O Mother, take with you all you can see).[13]

While some feasts, like that of Peter and Paul, enjoyed no special celebration, others such as St Martin's had a ritual out of all proportion to his status in the calendar of saints. St Martin's Eve fell on 10 November when every family ritually killed an animal, the prosperous a sheep and the less well-off a goose, cock or other fowl. About a week before the feast, the bird or animal was segregated from the rest and specially fed in preparation for the sacrifice. Ballina had a special St Martin's market where live fowl were sold for those who did not keep them. The killing was a formal affair done by the head of the house and then the blood, in a gesture reminiscent of the biblical Passover, was sprinkled in the four corners of the house. Sometimes it was daubed on the door-posts or sprinkled over the threshold. This was supposed to preserve the house against all forms of misfortune during the following year. In some places a cloth was dipped in the blood and was kept as a cure for aches and pains in people or animals. The blood was never used for making puddings as was done at other times when fowl were killed. The bird or beast was cooked and eaten by the assembled family.

St Martin's Eve

Feathers from a sacrificial goose were made into quills for the children to help them improve their writing skills. If a cow was sick on this feastday, a few drops of its blood were let in honour of the saint and, reputedly, it was never sold or slaughtered afterwards. All this blood-letting was based on the notion that the saint had been martyred or killed. St Martin of Tours in fact died in his bed of natural causes and was the first non-martyr to be canonised. No work involving a wheel, such as spinning or milling, was permitted

13 IFC, Ms. 277, p. 197; Ms. 321, pp. 496–7. The Kilmovee version has *sgór* and *gaisce* (hero and champion) instead of *stór* and *taisce*.

Ballisodare river and mills (O'Rorke, *Ballysadare*)

on that day as it was widely and wrongly believed, particularly in Co Sligo, that the saint was a miller who was killed by a millstone. When the meal and flour mills were first started at Ballisodare, the workers refused to work on St Martin's Day. The Protestant owners insisted and according to local tradition the mills were burned to the ground that night.[14]

Secular Feasts

The two secular festivals, *Lá Bealtaine* (May Day) and *Lá Lughnasa* (1 August) had their own crop of traditions and customs which were meticulously observed. A May bush was planted in front of every door and decorated with primroses and wild crocuses which were also strewn over the floors. Open-air gatherings took place where young people held wrestling and dancing competitions. *Lughnasa* was a first-fruits or harvest festival. Fruits like bilberries began to ripen and harvests turn to gold. It became centred on the last Sunday in July called, among many other names, Garland Sunday. *Lughnasa* rites were especially associated with hill-tops and water. It became christianised in the west as Reek Sunday when pilgrims climbed Croagh Patrick. Bohola held its pattern on that Sunday at Lough Keeran, a bog lake. They swam their horses in the lake to preserve them from harm during the year. They also threw lumps of butter (*clad ime*) into the lake in the hope that their cow would give greater yeilds. However, after the crowds had left, poor people dived in to retrieve the butter.[15]

Between *Bealtaine* and *Lughnasa* came St John's Eve or Midsummer Night (23 June), which was a mixture of the sacred and the secular. Bonfires were lit

14 Henry Morris, 'St Martin's Eve', *Béaloideas,* Iml ix , Uimh. II, (Nodhlag 1939), pp. 230–235; see also Wood-Martin, *Traces of the Elder Faiths,* vol. 1, p.305; IFC, Ms. 680, pp. 86–90 (Monasteredan), pp. 100–115 (Ballymote), pp. 116–119 (Curry), pp. 124–8 (Tubbercurry)
15 Ordinance Survey Letters for County Mayo, II, pp. 142–3; Ó Danachair, op. cit., pp. 174–5

on top of the highest hills all over the country and people danced round the fires. Halloween had thoroughly christianised the older festival of *Samhain* when the spirits of the dead walked and visited their old earthly homes. It was observed in Co Longford 'with the usual necromantic ceremonies' but regrettably that observer did not elaborate. There was a special supper in the Swinford area which consisted mainly of cally, i.e. potatoes mashed with milk and butter. Nuts and apples were eaten and all the usual Halloween tricks were played.[16]

The custom known as 'the waits', practised in places as far apart as Longford and Clare, may also have been found in Mayo and Sligo. For some weeks before Christmas several musicians, generally pipers, serenaded the inhabitants of a village at midnight or in the early hours of the morning. They stopped outside each house and called out the hour of the morning and whether it was cold, wet, frosty or fine. They came back during the Christmas holidays, played a tune and collected at each door the expected remuneration. On Christmas Night a large candle was lit and allowed to burn out. Should it sputter out without reason, it was a bad omen foretelling the death of the head of the family. There was a special supper, consisting mainly of boxty and oatmeal potato-cakes.

Christmas

The Nativity scene could have been reproduced in any young cottier's cabin with a new-born baby, where the family shared their single room with the cow and other farm animals. A prayer found in Aclare and Killasser has extraordinary resonances of the German *Stille Nacht* (Silent Night):

Oíche chiúin bhán, Muire agus Iósaf ar fán,
Stábla is tuighe mar fothain don Rí,
Agus é go fíorbhocht ar mhainséar 'na luí.
Ó cuirim-se fáilte ort, a Íosa thláth,
Agus ár dTiarna go deo gráim go bráth.

Silent white night, Mary and Joseph astray,
A stable and thatch to shelter the King,
And he really poor, lying in a manger,
O I welcome you, weak Jesus,
And Our Lord forever, I love forever.

A goose was eaten on Christmas Day, followed by singing, dancing and storytelling. Children in Co Longford, and perhaps elsewhere, made and painted circular crosses and were given Christmas gifts. In some parts of the country

---

16 Shaw Mason, op. cit., vol. 2, pp. 249, 460; vol. 3, p. 348; IFC, Ms. 114, p. 367

bull-baiting was common on St Stephen's Day as were mummers and wrenboys. On Twelfth Night (Epiphany) twelve candles were lit in honour of the twelve Apostles.[17]

Efforts were made to have the number of feastdays reduced. To abstain from work and attend Mass on so many days was an intolerable burden for many. Protestants believed that a reduction in the number of feastdays would make Catholics 'more sober, industrious and useful to their country'. One journalist, allowing a shilling for each person, computed the loss of labour at almost half a million pounds in 1756. He was commenting on the announcement from the altar by Dublin priests that 18 or 19 feastdays were henceforth to be abolished. They were also abolished in Armagh at the same time.[18] It must have taken longer for this concession to reach the west of Ireland. In 1773 Bishop Kirwan wrote to Cardinal Castelli seeking a reduction which was duly granted. About the same time Bishop Philips asked to have the Mass obligation on feastdays transferred to the following Sunday.[19]

Holy Wells

The people continued to celebrate enthusiastically the patron saints of their parishes. These celebrations or 'patterns' took place usually, though not always, at a holy well. Holy wells were numerous in the diocese. Almost every parish had at least one and some had several. Attymass and Bonninconlon had three, Tourlestrane (Kilmactigue) had four. Eight were dedicated to St Attracta, patroness of the diocese. St Patrick had seven and St Brigid four. Feichín, Kieran, Cuimhne and Barbara, a companion of Attracta, had one each. Kingstone Well in the parish of Keash was probably dedicated to Christ, as its pattern was celebrated on Easter Sunday. *Tobar na Naomh* in Gurteen (Kilfree) was dedicated to Our Lady, with patterns on great and little Lady Days. Surprisingly, there is none dedicated to St Nathy, patron saint of the diocese. Some of these wells probably fell into disuse from natural causes. Supernatural causes were sometimes alleged. Others were deemed to have lost their potency by some form of desecration. St Molaise's Well in Templeboy dried up after Frank Mason, a local Protestant, washed his hands in it.[20] Another, called Toberoddy, in the parish of Kilmactigue, is said to have lost its efficacy in 1755. A local landlord used an inscribed flagstone from the well to build his new house. The house fell down and the flagstone was found in its original position but the people believed the well had lost its power.[21]

17 Shaw Mason, op. cit., vol. 2, p. 460; vol. 3, p. 348; IFC, Ms. 194, pp. 24, 163
18 *Pues Occurences*, 17 April 1756; *Faulkner's Dublin Journal*, 4 & 11 May 1756, quoted in *Arch. Hib.*, vol. XVI, pp. 89–90
19 SC Irlanda, vol. 12, f. 27r; Lettere, vol. 222, f. 226rv
20 O'Donovan, *Sligo Letters*, p. 310
21 Ms. RIA referred to in Wood-Martin, op. cit., p. 358

PRAYERS AND PATTERNS 273

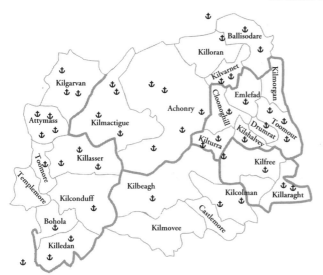

List of Holy Wells in Achonry Diocese.*

Achonry: Toberaribba, Tobercurry, Toberaraght, Tobercully.
Attymass: Tobbaracloon, Tobbar Patrick (Corrower), Atty's Well or Tobar Attracta, St Feichín's Well (Mullahowney).
Ballaghaderreen: St Attracta's Well, Clogher.
Ballisodare: Tullaghan (dedicated to St Patrick), Tobar Bhrighde, Toberloonagh.
Ballymote: Holywell.
Bohola: Lough Keeran.
Bonniconlon: Tobar Feichín, Tobar Bréunnal, Tobberberreen.
Bunninadden: Toberneerin (Cloonoghill), Tobar Phádraig, Tobereraght (Kilturra).
Charlestown: Tobar Athracht (Tample).
Collooney: Tobarbride, Tobarscanavan.
Coolaney: Tullaghan (dedicated to St Patrick).
Curry: Tobar Aibhistín (Ballyglass).
Foxford: Tobar Bhríde (near Teampall Maol graveyard in Coolaga).
Gurteen: Tobar na Naomh, Tobar na mBráthair (Kilfree), Tobar Athracht, Toberpatrick.
Keash: Tobar Chloiche Rígh (Kingstone Well), Tobernacarta, Tobernamalla, Toberliubhan,
Killasser: Tobar a Clun, St. Patrick's Well (Shrone Cam), St Attracta's Well (Callow).
Kiltimagh: Tobar Cuimhne (Lisnamaneeagh), St Patrick's Well (Carrowndangan).
Swinford: Tobar Bhrighde (Kilbride).
Tourlestrane: Tubber Keeraun (near chapel in Kilmactigue), Tubber Arraght,

*   List compiled from Wood-Martin, *History of Sligo,* pp. 355–6; O'Donovan, *Sligo Letters,* pp. 144–6, 149, 229, 233–4,235, 344–5, 375, 422, 425; *Mayo Letters,* vol. 1, pp. 108–10, 129; vol. 2, p. 360, 375, 378, 386, 387; Kilgannon, *Sligo and its surroundings,* pp. 257, 268, 284; Bernard O'Hara ed., *Killasser A History,* and from information supplied by Peter Sobolewski, Fr Martin Jennings, Tom Hennigan, Michael Murphy, Paddy Brady, James Flanagan, Tom McGettrick, Fr Tom Colleary, Sean Reynolds N T, Fr Tommy Mulligan, Sean Owens, Fr Christy McLaughlin, Seamus O'Donnell, Vincent Coleman, Martin McNulty RIP, Padraig Gavin N T, Fr Paddy Kilcoyne, Fr Joe Spelman, Liam Gillard, Fr Tommy Towey.

The 'stations' performed at the wells shared a large number of features. Pilgrims circled the well a number of times on their bare knees. This was done usually seven times, though Dr Charles O'Conor states that any uneven number such as three or nine, would suffice. They followed the sun in an east–west direction. Women tucked up their petticoats so that their knees would be exposed to the sharp stones and they were often well bloodied when they had finished their rounds. A set number of prayers was said invoking the saint, or sometimes they told their beads. Hands and feet and particularly any injured or ailing part of the body were washed. A cup or bowl was provided at the well, from which they drank. Once the station was completed, a piece of cloth torn from one of their garments was tied to the tree which usually overshadowed the well. Different explanations have been given for this custom. One commentator in 1739 stated that each pilgrim took a rag already on the tree and replaced it with one of their own. This was worn round wherever they wished to be cured. The rag had gained the curative powers that the tree had absorbed from the well.[23] Fifty years later a French traveller watched them hanging rags at a well in Iar-Chonnacht 'and for nothing in the world would they allow these to be removed'.[23] Dr Charles O'Conor gives a further detail, that they spat on the rag before it was tied to the tree. He asked Owen Hester, one of the O'Conor tenants who used to make the pilgrimage to Killaraght, what it meant. He replied that their ancestors always did it, that it was a preservative against *Geasa-Draíocht*, the sorceries of the Druids, that their cattle were preserved by it from infectious disorders and that the *daoine maithe* (fairies) were kept in good humour by it.[24] Whatever the reason for it, the custom was followed everywhere and is documented for Tyrone, Derry, Fermanagh, Roscommon, and Galway as well as Killaraght in Co Sligo.

St Attracta's Well, Clogher (Wood-Martin, *Sligo*)

Different curative powers were attributed to different wells. The one at Slane in Co Meath was considered effective in making women prolific, 'a virtue they do not by any means want in this country.'[25] The well at Cortoon

---

22 William Henry, op. cit., Ms. 2533
23 De Latocnaye, p. 154; see also Carr, p. 255 who describes these rags as 'memorials of their having performed their penitential exercises'.
24 Charles O'Conor, *Letter of Columbanus*, 3rd Letter, p. 83
25 De Latocnaye, p. 276

in Bohola parish was associated with curing diseases in cattle, as was Tubber Keeran in Kilmactigue. St Attracta's Well in the same parish was reputed to cure certain diseases such as epilepsy. St John's Well at Killery on the south side of Lough Gill was reputed to be especially powerful. Early in the century its reputation became tarnished after a certain Laurence Jackson visited it with a sprained leg, fell down a precipice and broke his neck.

Not only the country people but their social superiors and even Protestants made these pilgrimages. Not everyone was gullible enough to believe in the cures. When a French traveller asked an honest soul at a well in Co Galway what the well was good for, the Frenchman was rewarded with a fine specimen of Irish wit. 'Ah Sir,' said he, 'it is good for everything: it enables the blind to walk, the lame to speak and the deaf to see.' Some came to wells for the company rather than devotion. When asked why he came, one countryman answered 'to see the women', and there was a lot of them to see.[26]

Wells were frequented privately by individuals throughout the year. Lady Morgan, who visited St Patrick's Well in Dromard, described in her novel, *The Wild Irish Girl,* an old woman doing the station all alone. Near the waterfall in Ballisodare a Frenchman saw a holy well 'where the good people were saying their prayers'.[27] But the high point came each year with the pattern. Pattern is a corruption of the word 'patron' and the devotion was celebrated on the feast of the patron. Early in the seventeenth century, parish priests in the western province were urged to investigate the names of the patrons of their churches. In a petition to Rome in 1759 seven of the Achonry parish priests designated their parishes by giving the patron's name.[28] These included St Attracta (Killaraght), St Morgan (Kilmorgan), St Movidus (Kilmovee), and St Mary (Emlefad). The other three, St Patrick, St Brigid and St Cuthbert, are more difficult to locate. St Patrick's may well be Killasser as it held its pattern on St Patrick's Day. The patron of Ballisodare was probably St Brigid as it held its pattern on 1 February. The parish where St Cuthbert was the patron remains a mystery.[29]

Eight parishes had wells dedicated to St Attracta. Her feastday was 11 August when patterns were held in Gurteen (Killaraght), Charlestown (Kilbeagh), and Kilcolman (4 miles from Ballaghaderreen), and probably also in Bunninadden (Kilturra), Achonry, Attymass, Killasser and Tourlestrane (Kilmactigue). There were two patterns in the one week in the area around

Patterns

---

26 De Latocnaye, pp. 110, 136
27 De Latocnaye, p. 180
28 SCAR, codex 4, f. 466rv
29 It may have been Tubbercurry (or Curry) as the Irish name *Cothraí* may have been translated as 'Cuthbert'.

Gurteen. St Attracta's at Killaraght was followed a few days later on 15 August at *Tobar na Naomh* in Kilfree. Not all patterns were held at wells. Kilmovee held theirs on St Dominic's Day (8 August) in the Dominican friary at Urlaur, while Ballymote had theirs on the feast of St Mary of Portiuncula (1 August) in the Franciscan monastery. Bohola held its pattern at Lough Keeran on Garland Sunday.[30]

St Patrick's Well, Tullaghan
(Photograph, Fr P Kilcoyne)

Patterns began by the people performing the stations. Earlier in the century the priest probably celebrated Mass. This is suggested by the number of wells that have 'altars' associated with them. There were no fixed places of worship then and it is reasonable to suppose that priests and people would have resorted to what was the only 'holy' ground in the parish. Later with their growing respectability, priests disassociated themselves from the patterns before finally becoming downright hostile to them.

Once the pilgrims had completed their prayers and penances, the entertainment began and often lasted well into the night. Large numbers attended these patterns, often running into several thousand. There were 5,000 people at Balla in 1802. Here, and at some other wells, fairs were held in conjunction with the pattern. Some travelled ten or twenty miles, like the O'Conor tenants to Killaraght. Many from the Mayo end of the diocese came to *Tobar Muire* in Balla on 8 September. Such large crowds inevitably drew 'all sorts of

30 O'Donovan, *Mayo Letters*, vol. ii, pp. 142–3; Ó Danachair, op. cit., pp. 174–5

hawkers, mountebanks, conjurors and itinerant musicians'.[31] Tents and booths were erected for the sale of whiskey and beer and the evening and much of the night was spent in dancing and drinking. Sometimes as a result of the whiskey, and the presence of 'foreign' contigents from other parishes or baronies, challenges were issued and faction fights resulted. 'At these assemblies many droll things are said, many engagements of friendship are made, and many heads are broken as the power of whiskey develops itself: but revenge rises not with the morning.'[32] A man was killed at one such fight at the pattern at St Attracta's Well in Kilturra about 1776. It happened quite close to the priest's (perhaps Bishop Philip's) residence and as a result the pattern was banned forever.[33]

It was such disorderly behaviour that provoked the hostility of the church. But like other quasi-religious practices, such as wakes, certain customs were steeped in tradition and immune to anathemas. In 1660 the Synod of Tuam had forbidden 'dancing, flute-playing, musical bands, riotous revels and other abuses at wells and other holy places'. In 1704 the government, in an 'act to prevent the further growth of popery', banned 'the riotous and unlawful assembly together of many thousands of papists to the said wells'. It imposed a fine of ten shillings on each one who attended and twenty shillings on the sellers of alcohol and a public flogging in default of payment. But all to no avail. In spite of the best efforts of the Catholic Church and the Protestant government, patterns not only survived but increased in popularity throughout the century. Only with the relaxation of the penal laws and the ensuing construction of chapels in most parishes at the turn of the century were the patterns finally threatened with extinction. In transferring the focus of religion from the well to the chapel, the priests betrayed no sentiment and brooked no opposition.

The fate of the famous well at Balla is illustrative of others. Boetius Egan, nephew and namesake of the former Bishop of Achonry, returned to Ireland with a doctorate from Propaganda College in Rome and with a bright future at the disposal of his uncle, now Archbishop of Tuam. He was quickly made parish priest of Castlebar and vicar general of the archdiocese. He built an imposing chapel in Castlebar with an Italian-styled campanila. On the death of his uncle

Balla Holy Well

---

31 Bell, p. 21
32 Carr, p. 255
33 Wood-Martin, op. cit., p. 371; Bell, op. cit., p. 21; Shaw Mason, op. cit., vol. 1, pp. 328, 494, vol. 2, pp. 146, 181, 194, 325, vol. 3, pp. 72–4, 626; De Latocnaye, op. cit., vol. 1, pp. 189–90, 239, vol. 2, pp. 29, 67, 238; Lady Morgan, *Patriotic Sketches*, vol. 2, pp. 20–24; *The Wild Irish Girl*, vol. 2, pp. 213–16; William Henry, op. cit., pp. 95–6, 350–1

he had high hopes of succeeding him. Instead Edward Dillon was chosen and this was resented by Egan. The feeling was mutual. Dillon promoted the parish priest of Balla as president of the deanery much to the chagrin of Egan.

In a fit of pique Egan rode out to Balla on 8 September 1802 to slay the dragon of superstition.[34] A huge pattern was being held there in honour of the birth of the Blessed Virgin. At the well the parish clerk, 'wearing a hood on his head', was carrying a large crucifix, which he offered to the pilgrims who had completed the station to kiss, together with his blessing. He had a box at his feet into which they had to put two copper coins. Otherwise they were not permitted to kiss the cross or receive the blessing. Harshly rebuking the 'villain', Egan made an 'energetic and impassionate appeal to the people', for which, according to himself, he 'was loudly applauded by the bystanders'.

Tobar Cuimhne

Informed of the incident, Archbishop Dillon, who detested patterns only slightly less than he detested Egan, reacted swiftly. He condemned Egan's 'apostolical exploits' and suspended him, his vicar general, from all priestly functions. In a letter to Egan the archbishop wondered how his 'great zeal against the abuses at Balla did not manifest itself during the late archbishop's administration'. Much as he was distressed by the 'scandalous outrages' taking place at patterns, Dillon, unlike Egan, would never have attempted 'to curse, interrupt or insult 5,000 persons who on bleeding knees were calling to heaven for mercy'. Egan's once promising career went into decline. He was transferred from Castlebar to the less prosperous parish of Dunmore.

The patterns at Balla and elsewhere were also doomed. Egan typified a new breed of priest that was to become more common, now that Maynooth was moving into full production. More prone to arrogance, they were quick to forget the earlier days of persecution. A people's religion, centred on the home and the holy well, was giving way to a priest's religion centred on the chapel. Less than forty years later, O'Donovan's researchers found that people in many parishes no longer remembered even the date of the pattern.

Prayers

The people of the diocese were described as 'exuding piety' (*pietatem spirant*).[35] They had prayers and blessings for all occasions, from getting up in

---

34   SC Irlanda, vol. 18, ff. 131r–134v, 161r–162v
35   SC Irlanda, vol. 23, f. 611v

Pattern Day
(Barrow, *Tour*)

the morning to raking the fire at night. A morning offering from Killasser, runs as follows:

Ó Aingil Dé, cumhdach mo láimhe deise,
Go gcumhdaí tú mé, go dtreoraí tú mé,
In uair mo bháis is lá mo breithiúnais
Bí a' pléidáil ar mo shon.

O Angel of God, protection of my right hand,
Guard me, guide me in the hour of my death,
And in the day of Judgement plead my cause.[36]

Grace was said before and after meals:

Beannuigh mé a Dhia,
Beannaigh mo bhia is mo dheoch,
Bail na gcúig arán a roinn Dia ar an gcúig mhíle fear.
Rath ó Dhia a rinne an roinn
Go dtige agam le mo chuid is mo chomhroinn.

36 IFC, Ms. 321, p. 496

> Bless me God,
> Bless my food and drink
> The blessing of the five loaves God shared out to the five thousand men.
> May I have God's blessing for my food and sharing
> That he shared with others.[37]

Dr Pococke heard this grace recited by a few countrymen in Donegal in 1752. He wrote it out phonetically and translated it thus: 'God blessed the five loaves and two fish and divided them among the five thousand; may the blessing of the Great King, who made this distribution, descend on us and our provision.'[38]

Only the first line of this night prayer still continues in use:

> *Go mbeirimid beo ar an am seo arís,*
> *Fé shaoghal agus fé shláinte*
> *I ngrádh Dé agus i ngrádh na gcomharsan*
> *Lus an peacadh is lugha agus an grásta is mó.*

> May we be still alive at this time again,
> Full of life and health,
> In God's love and in the neighbour's love
> Fruit of the smallest sin and the greatest grace.[39]

They were imbued with a deep awareness of God's help and grace. *Is foigse cabhair Dé ná an doras* (God's help is nearer than the door). Another little verse describes it more poetically:

> *Imtheóchaidh an fuiseóg is áilne ar craobh,*
> *Imtheóchaidh a chuid saothar go deo 'na dhiaidh.*
> *Acht grásta Dé ní imtheóchaidh sé*
> *Fhad is a bhfhuil muinighin againn i Mac Dé.*

> The sweetest lark on the branch will go,
> Soon after forever will go his song
> But the grace of God will never go
> As long as we trust in God's Son.[40]

People were very attached to the rosary. They called it *An Paidrín Páirteach* (the shared prayer). They never recited it without first making an offering prayer, such as the following:

37 ibid, Ms. 127, p. 582
38 op. cit., p. 64
39 IFC, Ms. 114, p. 360
40 ibid, Ms. 194, p. 271

Ofrálaimid suas an Paidrín Páirteach seo
In éiric bás agus páis do chroise
In éiric cúig dóláis na Maighdine
In éiric ár bpeacaí marbhtha
— ar maidin is tráthnóna
Le Dia mór an tAthair uilechumhtachtach
A choinneóchaidh slán as aicid sinn
Is ó dhíobháil na bhFlaitheas.

We offer up this Family Rosary
In reparation for the passion and death of your Cross
In reparation for the Five Sorrows of the Virgin
In reparation for our mortal sins
— in the morning and in the evening
To great God, the all-powerful Father
Who will keep us safe from disease
and the loss of Heaven.[41]

Contemporary writers are almost unanimous in describing the people as superstitious. One person's religion is sometimes another person's superstition. Special numbers such as seven were believed to have special power. *Ofrálaim seacht bPaidreacha agus seacht Abhé Máire in onóir don Mhaighdean ghlórmhar* (I offer seven Our Fathers and seven Hail Marys in honour of the glorious Virgin). Not only did pilgrims make their rounds at the holy wells from east to west, following the course of the sun, they also carried corpses round the graveyards in the same way. They even passed around a shared drink at a wedding or a wake in the same manner. To do otherwise was regarded as unlucky. Some practices, such as sprinkling their homes weekly with holy water, though regarded by some writers as superstitious, were sanctioned by their church. Others, such as throwing butter into Lough Keeran in Bohola or Lough Conn, or belief in the 'evil eye', were not easily reconciled with their religion. When a touring Protestant clergyman asked a young girl near Woodford, Co Galway, why she wore the gospel (*Leabhar Eoin*) round her neck, she replied 'to keep away our canny neighbours' (witches etc). Lady Morgan described an old man asking the priest to visit his sick child who had been looked at by somebody with the 'evil eye'. He explained to the priest that he had not put the *Leabhar Eoin* (St John's gospel) around the neck of this child, as he had done with his other children.[42] But this custom, widely practised in

Superstitions

---

41 ibid, Ms. 194, p. 263
42 Hall, vol. 1, pp. 324–5; *The Wild Irish Girl*, vol. 2, pp. 139–40. Wood-Martin claimed it was a cure for epilepsy, op. cit., p. 275

Achonry diocese and elsewhere, had the blessing of the priests and was not dissimilar to the practice of wearing scapulars in the universal church.

Belief in fairies was very prevalent. Certain mounds, called generally 'fairy forts', with their thorn bushes, were believed to be their dwelling places. Even with land at a premium, no one would dare to disturb these mounds.

> Is any man so daring
> As dig them up in spite
> He shall find their sharpest thorn
> In his bed at night.

Yet, it seems clear that this belief, which visitors classed as superstition, was little more than an imaginative local transformation of the church's teaching on devils. When questioned earlier in this century about what people believed the fairies were, an old woman in Killasser said they were the 'fallen angels'. It is significant that they, like devils, were beings only capable of inflicting harm. Consequently, they were treated with great deference. As Owen Hestor, O'Conor's tenant, put it, it was important to 'humour them'. This deference even extended to the name they gave them, *daoine maithe* (good people).

Hospitality

Of all the virtues, hospitality was the most highly-rated and the most widely practised among all classes of people. Visitors to the country were unanimous in their praise of this custom which they found everywhere they went. 'Their hospitality to all comers, be their own poverty ever so pinching, has too much merit to be forgotten.'[43] The Frenchman, who spent eight or nine months travelling round Ireland in 1797, only stayed at inns six times, which 'will give a better idea of this hospitality than could be done by many a laboured phrase'. With typical French adventurousness, he often spent a night in the poorest of mud cabins. On one occasion he was welcomed by an old woman covered with rags who offered him the few potatoes she had got by begging. She spread a mat on a chest, which was the only piece of furniture in the cabin, and invited him to sleep there. He did, surrounded by half a dozen almost naked children sleeping on a little straw, with a pig, a dog, a cat, two chickens and a duck. The next day, he had great difficulty in getting her to accept a shilling.[44] Seven years earlier his compatriot, the French consul, said of Co Sligo: 'Nowhere is hospitality more prevalent than in this part of the country'.[45] Early in the next century the Protestant minister in Athlone wrote, 'It is hardly credible to those who have not witnessed it to what extent instinctive hospitality reaches.'[46]

43 Young, vol. 2, pp. 146–7
44 De Latocnaye, vol. 1, pp. x, 114
45 Ní Chinnéide, vol. 35, p. 61
46 Shaw Mason, op. cit., vol. 1, p. 123, vol. 3, p. 104

Hospitality was by no means confined to the poorer classes. It was encumbent also on the rich. Wandering beggars entered the kitchens of country gentlemen 'with as much ease and freedom as if they were part of the family'. Bishop Philips complained to Rome that it would cost about fifty pounds a year to set up house in Killala, instead of remaining in the family home at Cloonmore. 'Especially in this land of hospitality,' he wrote, 'where it is expected by all ranks of people that they will be entertained in a manner suitable to their dignity.'[47]

Next to hospitality came courtesy: 'they display natural urbanity in rags and penury.'[48] A visitor to Co Mayo was rescued by a parcel of men on their way to an illicit still to make poteen. They pulled out his horse which had got stuck in the mud 'and with that charming suavity of kindness, which so conspicuously identifies the Connaught peasant', accompanied him upwards of a mile to safety.[49] Lady Morgan and her riding party lost their way in the Ox Mountains. They asked directions from a countryman who was returning from work to his cabin in the mountains. He insisted on leading them for almost two miles which he had to retrace to return home. She also remarked on the 'courtesy which invariably distinguishes the manners of the peasantry'. She visited a mud cabin, accompanied by a countryman called Murtagh. 'May God and the Virgin Mary pour a blessing on this house,' Murtagh said as they entered. When she left she was followed for several paces by the whole family, who parted with her as they had received her, with blessings. 'Their courtesy upon all occasions seems to be interwoven with their religion, and not to be pious in their forms of etiquette, is not to be polite.'[50] A French traveller also experienced this courtesy in Connemara. Some men who met him took off their hats and bowed to the ground. One of them accompanied him for a mile with his hat under his arm, refusing to put it back on again.[51]

Courtesy

Irish women generally enjoyed a well-deserved reputation for purity, 'although it might be supposed, from a whole family of different sexes being crowded together in one room, that much indecency and consequent sensual depravity must occur'.[52] An English traveller, who met a priest in 1813 on the road from Westport to Ballinrobe, was told that 'the number of children born out of wedlock was small' and that 'with respect to married women, infidelity was scarcely ever heard of'. He believed that 'in no place does greater decorum

Modesty

47 SCAR, codex 1. 4., no. 474
48 Carr, p. 292
49 McParlan, *Statistical Survey of Co Mayo*, p. 94
50 *Patriotic Sketches*, pp. 4, 90; *The Wild Irish Girl*, vol. 1, pp. 82, 85, 88–9
51 De Latocnaye, vol. 2, p. 52
52 Carr, pp. 265–6

or respect to the delicate feelings of the sex prevail than in Ireland. Even among the lower orders any offence to modesty, or insult to female delicacy, is resented not by one, but by all'.[53] The touring Protestant clergyman who met the dancing girls coming from the bog in Ballisodare in 1813 had another close encounter with Irish females. He found accommodation in the home of a fairly prosperous farmer in Co Galway recommended to him by a priest. The room he shared with the rest of the family had three beds, one occupied by the farmer and his wife and another by two grown-up daughters. When he got up in the morning he found the two girls had already risen and their bed was occupied by 'a beautiful girl' about 17 or 18 years old who had been out at a wake earlier in the night. She woke up while the clergyman was shaving, sat up in the bed and chatted to the visitor 'and such is the innocence and simplicity among the people in this part of the country, that she felt no shame, nor seemed to think there was either impropriety or danger in being in bed in the same room with a man she had never seen'.[54] In 1739 an observer at a pattern in Co Fermanagh wrote, 'the people, having said some prayers, strip off their clothes and then stark naked, young and old, impotent and healthy, plunge into the fountains in crowds where men and women of all ages, without the least rag of covering, bathe and wash one another at noon day in the presence of a thousand spectators, not discovering the least appearance of shame'.[55]

Swearing

In a report to Rome in 1771 Bishop Philips singled out the 'abominable vice of cursing and swearing' as all too common, adding that 'those who do not speak English curse and swear in that language'.[56] Over thirty years later Lady Morgan also remarked on their penchant for swearing, 'No intercourse passes between them where confidence is required, in which oaths are not called in to confirm the transaction.' The local people swore 'by my father who is no more' or 'by my mother who is in the grave' or 'by my hand' or 'by the blessed stick he holds in his hand'. The people were very much given to litigation or, as Lady Morgan so kindly put it, had 'the nicest sense of right and justice of any people in the world'.[57] Most disputes were over land boundaries and straying cows resulting from the system of rundale they followed. In most cases these disputes were settled by calling in locally recognised arbitrators called 'brehoons' (*breitheamh*). Compromise was achieved after a lot of whiskey had been consumed by the brehons, friends and witnesses.[58]

53 Curwen, vol. 2, pp. 334–5
54 Hall, vol. 1, pp. 321–4
55 William Henry, op. cit., pp. 95–6
56 SCAR, codex 1. 4., no. 474
57 *The Wild Irish Girl*, vol. 2, p. 110
58 Neligan, pp. 364–5

At the beginning of the next century, Bishop McNicholas listed drunkenness as the most prevalent vice among them.[59] Other observers agreed. This is hardly surprising given that there were very few townlands in parishes like Killasser or Kilmactigue where one or more families did not distil their own poteen. Christenings, weddings, wakes, as well as fairs and patterns, were all occasions where drinking was one of the main activities. James Lyons, who was a curate in Sligo in 1765, said they were the best Catholics in the world 'if oaths and drunkenness were not their second nature and essence'.[60] 'Those were drinking days,' Dickens said of that century, 'and most men drank hard'. Yet a French visitor could comment, 'They drink much less in Dublin and in every part of Ireland than I had imagined.'[61]

Drunkenness

Arthur Young, virtually alone, accused the Irish country people, and especially those of Achonry diocese, of being addicted to stealing. 'The common people are so amazingly addicted to thieving everything they can lay their hands on, that they will unshoe the horses in the field in the barony of

Stealing

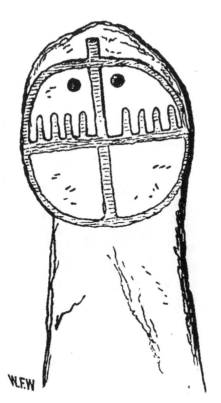

Ancient Cross at St Attracta's Well, Kilturra (Wood-Martin, *Sligo*)

---

59 SC Irlanda, vol. 23, f. 613v
60 Fenning, *Coll. Hib.*, no. 11 (1968), pp. 90–110
61 De Latocnaye, vol. 1, p. 56

Lyney.'⁶² The poor people in this barony did not own horses and why they should steal horseshoes defies comprehension. As Young travelled the country from one gentleman's seat to another, his informants were almost exclusively Protestant landlords. In this case his informant was probably Joshua Cooper of Markrea. Time did little to mellow Cooper's opinions. In 1791 he described Collooney to the French consul as 'nothing but a nest of robbers that he would dearly like to wipe out'. The Frenchman reflected that he had already largely succeeded, as Collooney recalled for him Goldsmith's *Deserted Village*.⁶³ Young claimed that children were trained in the art of hoking potatoes, i.e. removing them from the bottom of the ridges, replacing the soil and leaving the stalk untouched.⁶⁴ Another visitor to Sligo in September 1813 contradicted this claim. 'It is the general custom to bank potatoes in the fields; and great as was the scarcity last year, very few losses indeed were sustained in consequence of the mounds being broken into.'⁶⁵ The Protestant vicar of Kilmactigue was probably close to the truth when he described the people there as 'generally hospitable, complaisant and honest'.

Irish College, Prague

62 op. cit., vol. 1, p. 238
63 Ní Chinnéide, vol. 35, p. 64
64 Young, p. 190
66 J.C. Curwen, *Observations on the State of Ireland*, vol. 2, p. 285

CHAPTER ELEVEN

Na hEaspaig 1707–1808
Occasional Visitors

When Rome appointed Hugh MacDermot bishop in April 1707, he was the first Bishop of Achonry for more than a century. The previous bishop was Eugene O'Hart who died in 1603. In the interim the diocese had been governed by apostolic vicars, the third and last of whom was MacDermot himself. He was a priest of the diocese of Elphin who had been ordained in 1675 at Cloonsellagh by his own bishop, Dominick Burke. He was then twenty-three years old. By 1676 he was in the Irish community in Paris, where he had gained a scholarship.[1] In 1678 he registered in the law faculty of the university of Paris.[2] Sometime later he moved to Bologna in Italy and continued his studies at the famous law school there. From there in 1683 he petitioned Propaganda for the post of apostolic vicar of Achonry.[3] The incumbent, Maurice Durcan, had died in May of that year. By this time he was a doctor of theology and of civil and canon law, 'having at different times publicly defended *con gran applauso* ('to great applause') theological and legal theses'. In June Cardinal Buoncompagno of Bologna wrote to Propaganda recommending Mac Dermot, who was 'very well-acquainted with Holy Scripture and the Fathers and had recently taken a doctorate in civil and canon law'.[4] In August Phelim O'Hara, dean and vicar general of Achonry, sent a recommendation in favour of MacDermot to the internuncio in Brussels signed by three canons, eleven priests and fourteen lay nobles.[5] The lay nobles included no less than six Taaffes, as well as two Bretts, two McDonoghs and two O'Harts, Charles and Teige. The remaining two were William Dalton and Donnell O'Hara.

Propaganda had already held a special meeting in July to discuss the vacancy. They were under the impression that, besides MacDermot, there was another candidate in the field who was seeking to become the bishop of the diocese. This was Maurice Donnelan, the dean of Clonfert. The cardinals erroneously understood that he had been recommended by the 'clergy of

1   Patrick Boyle, *Irish College, Paris*. This was probably Collège de Montaigu, where the main Irish community was located, as Collège des Lombards did not become operational until the following year. I am indebted to Dr Hugh Fenning OP for reading an early draft of chapters eleven and twelve.
2   Brockliss & Ferté, op. cit., no. 1072
3   CP, vol. 30, f. 197r
4   CP, vol. 30, f. 223r
5   CP, vol. 30, f. 242rv; see Appendices 5 and 42

Achonry and the nobles of Ireland'. He had in fact been proposed for Killala and a copyist had mistakenly read *Achadensis* (Achonry) for *Alladensis* (Killala).[6] The nuncio also informed Propaganda that Charles Tiernan of Ardagh had been solicited by his friends to seek the post but he declined, convinced that MacDermot 'would achieve great good in the service of God' there. It was a favour MacDermot was later to return, by recommending Tiernan for the same post in Ardagh. The December meeting duly appointed MacDermot apostolic vicar of Achonry.[7]

Hugh MacDermot, Apostolic Vicar (1683–1707)

Apostolic vicars had the power to govern the diocese, appoint priests to parishes and make decisions concerning the day-to-day running of the diocese. In addition Rome provided them with powers normally reserved for bishops, such as to grant dispensations particularly in marriage cases. Advised from Ireland, Rome accepted that two bishops in each province would be sufficient. 'In my humble opinion,' Oliver Plunkett had written to Rome ten years earlier, 'a metropolitan (archbishop) with one suffragan (bishop) would be enough in each province.'[8] The population of Ireland was then probably less than a million. Appointing bishops in Ireland was a sensitive political issue, and particularly in dioceses like Achonry which had none for almost a century. The cardinals alluded to this at their July meeting: 'To create a bishop of that diocese (Achonry) would appear to the English a major innovation, since it has been governed by apostolic vicars.' They added significantly, 'All the more so as in other cases the internuncio and the bishops have warned that new bishops should not be created but to re-establish them in the vacant dioceses after a short time so as not to annihilate the order.'[9] Apostolic vicars were continued in England until the end of the eighteenth century.

Once back in Ireland, MacDermot immediately sought to have his post changed to that of bishop. In September 1684 Phelim O'Hara sent a petition, signed by the clergy, to that effect.[10] O'Hara's petition was signed by himself and 'the dignitaries and the rest of the priests of Achonry', which only amounted to eleven priests. This could not be the total number of priests, because at least three, Terence O'Gara, Maurice Frain and Bernard Brennan whose signatures did not appear, were still alive and would be for a long time yet. There were no priests mentioned for a number of parishes, particularly in the Mayo section of the diocese, where only Swinford (Kilconduff) and Kilmovee are mentioned, while O'Gara was in Castlemore and Frain in Kilcol-

6   Fortunately for the diocese, no decision was taken at this meeting. By the time they met again in December, the nuncio in Brussels had forwarded the genuine recommendation from Achonry.
7   CP, vol. 30, ff. 208v, 209v
8   SOCG, vol. 447, ff. 311rv–312r; quoted in John Hanly, *Letters of Oliver Plunkett*, pp. 393, 394
9   CP, vol. 30, ff. 117v, 118r
10 SC Irlanda, vol. 5, f. 289r; see Appendix 6

man. The solitary three canons were Walter Henry of Kilmovee, Thady Higgins of Ballymote (Emlefad), and John Tougher of Bonniconlon (Kilgarvan) and Attymass. Two months earlier MacDermot himself had written to Cardinal Colonna, stating that 'he had already set up the chapter'. He had experienced some opposition from Anthony Henigan, who may have been the Dominican of that name from Straide who later replaced Frain in Swinford (Kilconduff). MacDermot had written a few days previously complaining about him and now dashed off this note to explain that Henigan had now submitted and MacDermot was now 'in peaceful possession' of the diocese and would 'begin shortly to preach in every parish of the diocese'.

The campaign to have him made bishop continued. In December 1685, Phelim O'Hara wrote again to the nuncio in Brussels about the matter. O'Hara pointed out that the province was fairly extensive and that he would 'prefer nothing more than that a man of such great virtue and other good qualities should preside over this diocese'. There may have been other candidates seeking that post because six months later James Lynch, Archbishop of Tuam, and Bishop Dominick Burke of Elphin, wrote to the Pope suggesting 'that when it seemed expedient to your holiness, to give new bishops to the vacant sees in this province, he would deign to look upon the merits of doctor Hugh MacDermot, apostolic vicar of Achonry, in preference to other aspirants for that dignity.'[11]

Sculpted Bishop from Straide Abbey *(Office of Public Works)*

Communication with Rome was interrupted by the Williamite war in Ireland. In May 1693 the nuncio in Brussels wrote to Propaganda 'that he had lost all contact with the prelates (in Ireland) because of the incidents of the war in that kingdom'. He had written to MacDermot using an Irish resident in Louvain as intermissary. He was relaying instructions from Propaganda regarding 'disorders caused by the apostolic vicar of Achonry, MacDermot, in the diocese of Elphin'. Elphin was now vacant and it appears that complaints were made to Rome that MacDermot was interfering in the affairs of that diocese. An undated memo in Propaganda complained that MacDermot 'never went to his residence and that he stayed in the diocese of Elphin with abuse of his authority'. The internuncio in Brussels was instructed 'to reprimand him and order him to refrain from exercising jurisdiction outside his vicariate to which he should betake himself'.[12] The nuncio also revealed that

11 SC Irlanda, vol. 5, f. 322r
12 SOCG, vol. 553, f. 394v. This memo is crossed out.

James Lynch, Archbishop of Tuam, had left Ireland and was now living in the abbey of St Amande near Louvain. By now MacDermot was the only prelate left in Connacht apart from the aged Bishop of Clonfert.

In 1697 the government published an act banishing all the bishops from Ireland. The act also included all those, like MacDermot, who exercised jurisdiction in the church. However, MacDermot and others like him evaded the law by masquerading as simple parish priests. Another act followed in 1704 'to prevent the further growth of popery'. By this act all parish priests were obliged to register and MacDermot registered, not for a parish in Achonry, but for the parish of Ardcarne (Cootehall) in Elphin. He was then fifty-two years old and residing in Knocknacarew. His sureties were provided, not by members of his own powerful family, but by Fergus Naughtin of Athlone and Christopher Kirwan of Raheverin. In those unsettled times the MacDermots may have preferred to keep a low profile.

MacDermot, together with the apostolic vicar of Ardagh, wrote to Rome in 1703 seeking powers to grant marriage dispensations. They pointed out that 'scandals arise from Catholics having recourse to heretical ministers as the heretical bishops have published that they have such powers'. In fact, Protestant ministers were simply applying civil law, which was much less restrictive with regard to marriage impediments. Rome advised the apostolic vicars to apply directly to the nuncio in Brussels, who could grant such powers.[13] In that year too, John Nugent, an influential Augustinian friar in Rome, wrote recommending that MacDermot be made Bishop of Achonry.[14]

By now the Irish Church was facing a serious crisis. In the autumn of 1706 Carbry O'Kelly, vicar general of Elphin, and Bernard O'Donogher, apostolic vicar of Ardagh, wrote to Edmund Burke, a Dominican in Louvain, pointing out that they urgently required a bishop before the following Easter. The Bishop of Clonfert was now three months dead. Of only two others still in the country, Patrick Donnelly of Dromore was in prison and the aged Archbishop of Cashel lived a hundred miles away from their dioceses. At Easter there would be no bishop to consecrate the oils. These oils were required not only for the sacraments of confirmation and ordination, but more importantly, for daily use by the priests in anointing the dying. Burke passed on their appeals to the nuncio in Brussels who duly forwarded it to Rome. A special meeting of the cardinals was held in February 1707 to deal with the crisis in the Irish Church. Three new bishops were appointed, all in Connacht, which the cardinals deemed 'the most Catholic and the safest part of Ireland'. A Franciscan, Thady O'Rorke, an uncle of Charles O'Conor of Bela-

13 SC Irlanda, vol. 6, ff. 185r, 534r; see also vol. 7, f. 314r
14 CP, vol. 32, ff. 164r, 167rv

nagare, was appointed Bishop of Killala. Ambrose MacDermot, a Dominican, was appointed to Elphin and Ambrose Maddin to Kilmacduagh.[15]

On the last day of April 1707 Hugh MacDermot became Bishop of Achonry. He was the first diocesan priest to fill that post for several centuries. The other three bishops did not reach their dioceses until much later. Ambrose MacDermot arrived back in Elphin in October 1709. Unlike priests, bishops were illegal in the country. Hugh MacDermot and the Bishop of Elphin sent a joint letter to Rome in August 1710, seeking permission to consecrate the oils on Holy Thursday with only one priest present instead of the usual five. They also asked permission to ordain priests on Sunday and two feastdays occurring the following week 'because of the danger'.[16] In a preface to their letter, they gave a surprisingly mild account of their condition:

Hugh MacDermot, Bishop (1707–1725)

> Here (in Connacht) we are living quietly and although we cannot publicly exercise our functions as formerly, the people however lack no necessary services and, praise be to God, the fervent devotion of the people increases daily more and more. The zeal of all (with the exception of a worldly few) is doubled by oppression. We cannot but acknowledge gratefully that the authorities who govern show us much moderation and seem rather sympathetic to our condition: this is now our position.[17]

The living conditions of Ambrose MacDermot, however, seemed particularly harsh. He had been living in comparative luxury in Rome where he taught philosophy and theology for twenty years and was prior of San Sisto for four.[18] Now he was reduced to living in a hut on a hillside, perhaps in the Curlew mountains overlooking his native Boyle. Without a serving boy to look after him, he had to pay a man a penny to fetch him water from half a mile away. He could get milk easily enough but not the light beer of which he was so fond. In spite of that and of the fact that 'he was too old to walk and too poor to buy a horse', he had already visited and consoled the people of his own and other dioceses.[19]

Thady O'Rorke, the Franciscan Bishop of Killala, was also constantly on the move. He was seen in 1712 'travelling on the road in the barony of Corran'.[20] He had then taken refuge in the home of Denis O'Conor of Belanagare and was probably visiting his diocese.

Hugh MacDermot was the registered priest in Ardcarne (Cootehall) where he could legally live and operate as a priest. That changed when a new act in

15   CP, vol. 32, ff. 219–220
16   SOCG, vol. 573, ff. 588r, 589r, 590r, 591r
17   SOCG, vol. 573, f. 590r
18   SOCG, vol. 559, ff. 237r, 238r
19   Fenning, 'Ambrose MacDermott OP, Bishop of Elphin 1707–1717', *Archivium Fratrum Praedicatorm*, xl, pp. 267–8
20   Burke, op. cit., p. 435

1709 required registered priests to take an oath denying the Stuart pretender's right to the throne. The vast majority of priests refused and went into hiding. Some agrarian disturbances occurred in 1711 involving the houghing of cattle for which priests were thought to be responsible. Seven parish priests in Elphin, including Hugh MacDermot, voluntarily surrendered themselves to the authorities on 4 March 1711 and were lodged in Roscommon jail, but they were released for want of evidence at the end of the month.[21] Magistrates were given powers to compel any papist to reveal on oath when and where he last attended Mass and what priest had celebrated it. Some witnesses were questioned in 1712 under oath in Sligo and while some of them confessed to have seen both Bishop MacDermot of Elphin and Bishop O'Rorke of Killala, no one mentioned Hugh MacDermot.[22]

Priests continued to be on the run and pursued by the authorities for a number of years. The Dominican, Thomas MacDermot, was arrested and imprisoned when he arrived in Ireland in the summer of 1714. Later he was banished and went to Spain. From there he wrote to Cardinal Imperiali in Rome, informing him that there was great persecution in Ireland and that 'registered priests cannot carry out their functions without being arrested'.[23] It was at this time that Hugh MacDermot made his first request to Rome on behalf of Terence O'Gara, the blind parish priest of Castlemore. His visits to Achonry were becoming less and less frequent 'on account of persecution', as he informed Rome. In 1716 he wrote to the nuncio in Brussels requesting that John O'Hart, who had recently returned from France, be appointed dean and vicar general to oversee the diocese in his absence.[24] The nuncio passed on his request to Rome with a note stating that, while the appointment of a dean was a matter for Rome, MacDermot could appoint his own vicar general.[25]

By now MacDermot was in his late sixties and, between old age and active persecution, probably no longer took an active part in the running of the diocese. He could continue to communicate with it through his vicar general, John O'Hart. One of his last recorded acts was to renew in 1721 his request to Rome on behalf of Terence O'Gara. His messenger this time was a Dominican travelling to Rome to attend a general chapter there.[26] By an odd coincidence, the messenger, Dominick O'Daly of Athenry, was to return to Ireland as MacDermot's successor. MacDermot died sometime before September 1725 when O'Daly was nominated to replace him. He was then seventy-three years old. He had governed the diocese for forty-two years, twenty-four as

21 see chapter one
22 Burke, op. cit., p. 435
23 Acta, vol. 85 (1715)
24 SOCG, vol. 606, ff. 425r, 427v
25 Acta, vol. 86, f. 366
26 Acta, vol. 92, ff. 298v, 299rv; SOCG, vol. 614, ff. 230r, 231v

apostolic vicar, and eighteen as bishop. And all this during a period of intense persecution.

John O'Hart, parish priest of Ballisodare, would seemed to have been the obvious successor to MacDermot. He had almost ten years' experience of running the diocese as vicar general and a degree in theology from the University of Paris. He would also have been the choice of the priests of the diocese. Another contender would have been Dr Charles O'Hara who was elected vicar capitular of the diocese when MacDermot died.[27] But his age was probably against him. He was sixty-three then. In the event neither of them were considered because there was another in the right place at the right time.

Dominick O'Daly was in Rome attending the general chapter of his order. He was the son of Dermot O'Daly of Killimor (near Oranmore) in Co Galway. In 1697 he received the habit as a Dominican in their convent in Athenry. Following the Banishment Act of 1698, he set sail from Galway in June of that year with three other novices for Brest in France. They were placed in the general novitiate of the Dominicans in St Germain-en-laye where they made their profession. From there he was sent to San Sisto, their Irish house in Rome, where he continued his studies. He also studied at the Minerva. When he had completed his studies in 1713 he applied to Propaganda for money to enable him return to Ireland. A year later he was elected prior of Athenry, a post he held for three years. He attended the provincial chapter of the Dominicans in Dublin in 1720 and was nominated as their delegate to a general chapter in Rome, where he went in 1721 at his own expense. It was on this occasion that he was chosen by MacDermot to convey O'Gara's request to Propaganda. While there, Achonry became vacant and O'Daly, with the nomination of the Stuart king, was appointed its bishop on 20 September 1725.[28]

Dominick O'Daly (1725–1735)

Eighteenth-century Pectoral Cross *(St Nathy's, Ballaghaderreen)*

---

27 Acta, vol. 95, ff. 533v; SOCG, vol. 649, ff. 558–9
28 Fenning, 'The Athenry House-Chronicle 1666–1779', *Coll. Hib.*, vol. 11, pp. 39, 44, 45; *Irish Dominicans*, pp. 22, 89–90, 112, 595; Acta, vol. 91, ff. 298v, 299rv; SOCG, vol. 630, f. 260r; Stuart Papers, vol. 861, nos. 50, 51

Consecration

He travelled home to Ireland via Brussels in Belgium (or Flanders as it was then called). There on the last day of November, feast of St Andrew the Apostle, he was consecrated bishop by the nuncio assisted by the Bishops of Antwerp and Tricolense. The ceremony was conducted 'with the minimum of pomp and in profound silence'.[29] He was still in Brussels two weeks later when he wrote to the Pope requesting the usual powers granted to bishops. The nuncio had already written on his behalf asking for power 'to absolve in all cases and to dispense in other cases', pointing out, 'that because of persecution by the heretics it was not possible to send to Rome (from Ireland) for them'.[30] Presumably, O'Daly was still waiting in Brussels for a reply because the nuncio wrote again on 14 December saying that O'Daly 'was thinking of departing shortly to his residence'.[31]

The nuncio was unaware that the residence he alluded to was not in Achonry but in Athenry and there it remained for the next nine years. This was to become a major bone of contention between O'Daly and the priests of the diocese. 'He resides about fifty miles away from it,' they later complained, 'and enters it only once a year on the pretension of visiting it.'[32]

Vicar-general

The day-to-day running of the diocese was left to a vicar general appointed by the bishop. It is not certain who O'Daly appointed to carry out this function. It may have been Charles (Thady) O'Hara, who in 1731 was the parish priest of Achonry and Cloonoghill and also ran a school of philosophy. The *Report on the State of Popery* of that year describes him as the 'titular dean'. Dr

Athenry Abbey *(from an eighteenth-century drawing by Bigari)*

29 SC Irlanda, vol. 8, ff. 245rv, 246rv, 248rv
30 SOCG, vol. 650, f. 143r
31 SOCG, vol. 650, f. 48r
32 ASV, Nunz. di Fiandra, vol. 130, f. 12r; see Giblin, *Coll. Hib.*, no. 9, p. 37

Charles had been elected vicar capitular before O'Daly's appointment and had all the qualifications to run a school of philosophy. In 1731 he would have been sixty-nine. Incidentally, the report makes no mention of O'Daly, suggesting that the Protestant bishop who compiled the report was unaware of his existence.

Normally, the oils were blessed by the bishop on the Thursday before Easter Sunday when the bishop celebrated what was called the Mass of the Chrism, in the presence of the assembled priests of the diocese. Afterwards they dispersed to their parishes, each with a container of oil which they needed for the following year to anoint the dying. On this occasion each parish priest made a contribution to the bishop, known as the 'cathedratics', which constituted the main source of the bishop's income. For most of the century it amounted to one pound sterling per parish priest. Thus, Achonry with about twenty parishes was estimated to be worth about twenty pounds.[33] Some Achonry priests wrote to Rome in 1734 via the nuncio in Paris alleging that O'Daly was attempting to 'extort from the poor priests more money than they can possibly give him'. There were eight signatories to the letter including John O'Hart, Dominick Kearney, and Terence O'Gara.[34]

Cathedratics

They also made more serious accusations against O'Daly. He ordained unsuitable candidates provided they paid him 'a sum of money to the value of sixty French pounds' (i.e. twenty pounds sterling), and he 'gives the care of souls to the unworthy and uneducated rather than to the good and learned'. O'Hart and the others requested that the Pope depute the Archbishop of Tuam and the Bishop of Killala to submit these unsuitable parish priests 'to a rigorous examination and deprive them of their parishes unless they find they are fit to instruct the people'. They concluded their letter with a plea: 'Let the parishes be filled by those members of the clergy who went abroad to study and who have returned well-equipped for such work.'

Accusations

Rome forwarded the letter to the nuncio in Brussels who immediately wrote to the Archbishop of Tuam asking him to investigate the allegations. The nuncio informed Rome that, if the allegations proved to be true, he would 'protest to the Bishop of Achonry about his irregular way of acting, so that the bishop will rectify his mode of conduct in the future'. Bernard O'Gara, Archbishop of Tuam, found the allegations to be substantially true and

---

33 In another small diocese, Ardagh, priests were paying the bishop twenty shillings each in 1739. *Arch. Hib.*, vol. 16, p. 60. In his report to Rome on the Irish church John Kent put the priest's contribution at 'about six *scudi*' (a pound was worth four *scudi*). SC Irlanda, vol. 17, ff. 2r–17v. Achonry was valued in 1758 at 'scarcely twenty pounds sterling'. CP, vol. 133, ff. 167rv, 168rv. It changed very little in later years. At the end of 1778 Bishop Philips valued it at twenty-four guineas. SC Irlanda, vol. 13, ff. 464rv, 465rv

34 Nunz. di Fiandra, vol. 130, ff. 10r, 11rv; see Giblin, *Coll. Hib.*, no. 9, pp. 35–37; see Appendix 9

the nuncio reprimanded O'Daly. O'Daly denied the charge.[35] These allegations were widely known, if not always completely believed, not only in Ireland but also in France. John Burke in Paris wrote in December 1733 to Sir Tobias Burke in Rome warning him that 'Mr Daly, a Dominican friar, Bishop of Achonry, alone, if not stopped, will ordain enough for the whole kingdom'.[36] Burke, who was making a case for the exclusion of ordained priests from the Irish College in Paris, probably exaggerated.

O'Daly died 'of a cold' on 6 January 1735 in Castlebar without ever clearing his name.[37] In spite of everything, the nuncio in Brussels continued to reserve judgement. 'He was always suspicious of accusations such as these surreptitiously forwarded to the Holy See,' he wrote in January, 'when the accusers can so easily and so freely write to the nunciature at Brussels or refer such matters to their respective archbishops in Ireland.' On hearing of O'Daly's death, he wrote in February to inform Rome explaining, 'it would be quite easy for a Bishop of Achonry to be tempted to take such gratuities (for ordinations) because of the wretched state of the diocese although Daly might never have succumbed to the temptation'.[38]

John O'Hart, 1735–9

O'Daly had left a legacy of bitterness in the diocese. Fifteen Achonry priests requested Rome on 27 January 1735 to appoint John O'Hart as his successor 'so that the faithful of the diocese be no longer harassed by ravening wolves in the guise of men'.[39] Other candidates were being proposed and one of them was a Dominican, Colman O'Shaughnessy, who was recommended by the Bishop of Meath, himself a Dominican. The Archbishop of Armagh had suggested that Achonry be united to Killala which was 'at present being governed so admirably by Thady O'Rorke'. He thought that 'one bishop could easily take care of both sees'. He also put forward an alternative proposal. He suggested that Gallagher, Bishop of Raphoe, might be made administrator of Achonry. Persecution had flared up in Raphoe which was overrun by Scottish Presbyterians. Gallagher was living 'in misery and wanders about like a fugitive at the greatest risk to himself'. While Armagh admitted that Raphoe was a good distance from Achonry, he thought that Gallagher, with 'his extraordinary zeal and youthful vigour', could take care of both dioceses satisfactorily. The Achonry priests were not prepared to accept an outsider and strongly intimated to Rome that, should one be appointed, 'it would probably lead to serious disturbances, a persecution of the clergy and the ruin of ecclesiastical discipline in the diocese'. In February three of the provincial bishops, O'Gara

---

35 Nunz. di Fiandra, vol. 131, f. 72rv; see Giblin, op. cit., pp. 46–7
36 quoted in Fenning, *Undoing*, p. 114
37 Fenning, 'The Athenry House-Chronicle', *Coll. Hib.*, no. 11, p. 52; Stuart Papers, vol. 178, no. 63
38 Nunz. di Fiandra, vol. 131, f. 72rv; see Giblin, op. cit., pp. 46–7
39 Nunz. di Fiandra, vol. 131, f. 107rv

of Tuam, O'Rorke of Killala and Patrick French, Bishop of Elphin, gave their support to O'Hart.

He also had warm support from an unusual source which, however, carried little weight in Rome. The blind harper O'Carolan, who was a frequent visitor to his home, composed a planxty in his honour:

O'Carolan

Dá mbéinn san Róimh ar bh'ait liom
Is biodh mo roghain ionghlactha
Is cinnte go ndéanfainn easbog mór dhiot féin.
If I were in Rome, as I would like,
And my choice were acceptable
I would certainly make yourself a great bishop.

Charles O'Conor, whom Carolan also visited, said that this song 'has often excited sentiments of the most fervent piety'. O'Carolan painted a sympathetic portrait of the then parish priest of Ballisodare:

Bhéara mé anois an chuairt so gan bhréig
Mar bhfuil an sagart geanamhail d'uaislibh árd Gaodhal,
Fear breágh ioghmhar tapuidhe,
Fear a riaradh gastruidhe,
Ar Sheághan Ó hAirt go ceart a labhraim-se féin;
Fear don aicme scapadh fíon go réidh,
Is d'ólfadh go fras le mac'r cheoil is a léighin.⁴⁰

Hereby, I will make this visit now
To where the lovable priest of high Gaelic ancestry,
A fine, sensitive, quick-witted man,
A man of great hospitality,
I'm speaking, of course, of John O'Hart,
The kind of man who is generous with wine
And drinks well with musicians and the learned.

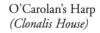

Charles O'Conor believed that O'Carolan composed another song about O'Hart which has not survived. 'It is a loss to the public that this truly virtuous dignitary had been so insensible to all emotions of self-love as to have the first of O'Carolan's compositions for him entirely suppressed.'⁴¹ O'Hart had been elected vicar capitular by the priests and governed the diocese while Rome deliberated. A decision was made on the last day of September and John O'Hart was nominated. He was the first priest of the diocese to become its bishop since the death of another O'Hart, Eugene, in 1603. In 1707 he had been a student in Paris and living in Collège de Navarre. Four years later he took his baccalaureate in the university there.⁴² Early in 1714 he was living in

O'Carolan's Harp (Clonalis House)

---

40 Donal O'Sullivan, *Carolan*, vol. 1, p. 33
41 Walker, *Historical Memoirs of the Irish Bards*, p. 316
42 Brockliss & Ferté, op. cit., no. 1019

the parochial house in the parish of Marle in the diocese of Meaux, where he may have been the parish priest.[43] He was reported in June of that year to be back in Ireland, living at an unknown address.[44] His exact age in 1735 is difficult to establish. If he had gone to Paris as a young student, he would have been in his mid-fifties now. On the other hand, if he arrived there as an ordained priest, he would be in his early sixties when he became bishop. Be that as it may, he was not in good health and appointed James Gallagher as a curate to look after his parish of Ballisodare which he retained for his support.

The Priest of Collooney

The O'Hart family estate was in Cloonamahon near Collooney and the bishop lived there with his brother, Charles. It was said that Charles lost the estate to a Protestant 'discoverer' called Laurence Bettridge and the bishop was given a residence in Annaghbeg by the Protestant Charles O'Hara, a gesture not at all in character.[45] This was later to inspire William Butler Yeat's poem, *The Priest of Collooney:*

Good Father John O'Hart
In penal days rode out:
To a shoneen in his freelands
With his snipe and his trout.

In trust took he John's lands
– shoneens were all his race –
And he gave them as dowers to his daughters,
And they married beyond their place.

But Father John went up
And Father John went down;
And he wore small holes in his shoes
And he wore large holes in his gown.

While in France, O'Hart had an investment which yielded an annual dividend of seventy-five pounds. After his return to Ireland he disposed of this investment to Lady Jane MacDermot, the widow of Chevalier Terence Mac Dermot who had died in St Germain-en-laye. The transaction was legalised in 1716 by a solicitor in Boyle.[46] O'Hart was scarcely reduced to wearing 'holes in his shoes'!

The Gallagher Affair

James Gallagher, the curate in Ballisodare, in an unusual move applied directly to Rome to have the parish conferred on him. By making John O'Hart bishop, Rome had now the right to dispose of his parish. Rome sent

---

43 AN, MC et/XVII/553/ 4,62; see Swords, *Coll. Hib.*, nos. 34, 35, p. 106
44 Burke, op. cit., p. 436
45 O'Rorke, *Ballysadare & Kilvarnet*, pp. 198–200, 206; no sources are given for this assertion.
46 AN MC et/XVII/618

Gallagher at the end of May 1737 a bull appointing him parish priest and he was duly installed by Peter Conry, vicar general of Elphin. O'Hart ordered Gallagher to submit himself for examination in his presence in September. To 'his great surprise' he found him completely unsuitable and tore up the bull in the presence of the examiner. Afterwards the vicar general ordered Gallagher to take himself to Paris or other university to be educated for the care of souls, and to insure that he went, he suspended him '*a sacris*' until he left the country. But as the season was already advanced, he lifted the censure, allowing him to wait until the following May before departing. In the meantime Gallagher procured another bull from Rome. On 20 May he presented the bull to the bishop, to whom it was addressed. The bishop summoned the chapter to decide the matter. Gallagher was summoned to appear before the chapter but failed to turn up. Having considered the matter, with 'the respect due to papal bulls', the chapter decided that Gallagher should submit himself again for examination and, if found satisfactory, the bull would be executed. Four examiners were nominated and a time and place decided for the examination. Gallagher turned up with the bull and asked for a month to prepare himself for the examination, which he was given. On this occasion he was examined before 'a numerous gathering of ecclesiastics' and found 'completely incapable'. His suspension was judged legitimate and was to remain until he went to a university to study.

Irish Romanesque doorway inserted in the south side-wall of Ballisodare church (Wakeman, *RHAAI Jn*)

Gallagher approached the bishop and asked him to lift the suspension. The bishop told him to return in a few days. Three days later Gallagher said Mass and administered the sacraments while still under suspension. Earlier he incurred another suspension by assisting at two marriages without the publication of the banns. This practice was forbidden in the diocese, under penalty of an *ipso facto* suspension. On a Sunday in December 1738 he struck Knavesy, the curate appointed to replace him, 'in front of the altar and in the presence of the people', and 'had the temerity to don the sacred vestments and celebrate Mass'. At this point O'Hart wrote to the nuncio in Brussels, requesting him to have the case examined by the Archbishop of Tuam or some other archbishop.[47]

Gallagher was not without friends in the diocese. Four priests, James and Francis McDonogh, Denis Gormley, and Eugene Sweeney wrote to Rome in October 1738 claiming that Gallagher 'had administered well the parish of Ballisodare for the past three years, living always with the odour of a good reputation'. Their testimonial was validated by Edmund Henigan, vicar general of Killala. Rome also received a testimonial in favour of Gallagher signed by ten parishioners.[48] They claimed that he administered the parish so well that he 'was revered and esteemed by all, both rich and poor'. They also denied that he had ever participated in a clandestine marriage.

The parish had been conferred on Gallagher by a Roman congregation, called the Datary. The latter wrote on 3 June 1739 to the secretary of Propaganda, instructing him to order O'Hart to remove all obstacles to Gallagher's appointment. Meanwhile, Gallagher, who had been compelled to leave the parish because of opposition from parishioners, which he claimed had been fomented by O'Hart, had had himself examined and passed as suitable by the synodal examiners of Raphoe and by the vicar general of Elphin. One of the Raphoe synodal examiners was Bonaventure O'Gallagher, guardian of the Franciscan friary of Donegal.[49]

By this time O'Hart was dead. He died about 7 May 1739 after only three and a half years as bishop.[50]

The birds of Knocknarea
And the world round Knocknashee
Came keening in that day.[51]

In a notice on his death the *Dublin Daily Post* of 5 June 1739 wrote that he 'was beloved by those of his acquaintance'.[52] Time did little to diminish his reputation. It was said in 1817 that 'his memory is still revered in Achonry for his piety, learning and hospitality'.[53]

Walter Blake (1739–1758)

The diocese was divided in their choice of a successor to O'Hart. The clergy of Elphin, who put forward Peter Conry, parish priest of Roscommon,

---

47 O'Hart sent the foregoing account to John Brett OP, penitentiary in St Mary Major's in Rome, who translated it from English into Italian and in April 1739 presented it to Propaganda.
48 Two of them were also called James Gallagher, while three others had the unusual name of Ponn: see Appendix 42
49 SOCG, vol. 699, ff. 347rv, 348rv, 349rv; vol. 823, ff. 219rv, 220r
50 de Breffny, 'Letters from Connaught to a Wild Goose', in *Irish Ancestor*, p. 90. He is said to be buried at Annaghbeg. O'Rorke, *Sligo*, vol. 2, p. 109
51 W.B. Yeats, *The Priest of Collooney*
52 *Arch. Hib.*, vol. xvi, p. 59
53 SC Irlanda, vol. 20, f. 127v

as a candidate, claimed that there was in Achonry 'great controversy and contention among the clergy and people in promoting a successor' to O'Hart.[54] Eleven Elphin parish priests signed the recommendation as well as Edmund Fallon, the Irish provincial of the Augustinian Hermits. Conry must have been the first candidate in the field as their recommendation was dated 21 May 1739, the very month in which O'Hart had died.

Only five Achonry canons signed the petition in favour of John Duffy, parish priest of Ballaghaderreen (Kilcolman and Castlemore) and dean and vicar general of the diocese.[55] They claimed to be the '*sanior pars*' ('sounder section') of the chapter and that the election was vitiated by 'suggestions and

O'Gara's Castle (Grose, *Antiquities*)

threats of lay-people which caused great discord, with the result that the majority of the chapter favoured nobody'. Duffy was supported outside the diocese by three abbots, one from Dublin as well as the Abbots of Cong and Annaghdown.[56] Duffy had been appointed vicar general by O'Hart three years earlier and was now confirmed in this office by the chapter. He had also been commissioned by the nuncio in Brussels to adjudicate cases in dispute in Galway and Dunmore.

It emerged later that there was another candidate. Less than a year later when Michael O'Gara, superior of the Irish College in Alcalà, was recommended for Tuam by the clergy of the archdiocese, they stated that 'many men of standing recommended him for Achonry which fell vacant recently'.[57] These 'men of standing' may have been the laymen who tried to influence the election by the Achonry chapter. The O'Gara name would have had strong resonances among them.

Rome decided in August in favour of another Tuam priest, Walter Blake of Ballinafad in Co Mayo.[58] He had been nominated by James III.[59] Blake was the son – possibly the eldest – of Maurice Blake and Anastase Darcy of

54 SC Irlanda, vol. 9, f. 623r
55 see Appendix 12
56 The recommendation was authenticated by Patrick Fitzsimons, vicar-general of Dublin. Nunz. di Fiandra, vol. 135, f. 194v
57 Nunz. di Fiandra, vol. 135A, f. 76r; see Giblin, *Coll. Hib.*, no. 10, pp. 72–138
58 SC Irlanda, vol. 9, f. 292r
59 Stuart Papers, vol. 217, no. 68

Gorteen, Co Mayo, and had two brothers, Mark and John, and three sisters, Mary, Anastase and Margaret. His brother Mark succeeded to the sizeable family estate in Ballinafad.[60] Walter was then in his mid-fifties. A later undated memo in Propaganda on the suitability of candidates for Armagh, stated that Blake of Achonry was 'the best but from the province of Connaught, which is the most detested by Ulstermen'.[61]

Non-Residency

At least in his early years, Blake could fairly easily have carried out his annual summer visitation. His family home in Ballinafad was about ten miles from the western edge of the diocese. More serious cases of non-resident bishops were troubling Rome at this period. Worst of all were those, like Waterford and Kilfenora, who lived abroad. In 1735, The nuncio in Brussels wrote to Rome claiming that a non-resident bishop 'sets a bad headline for others' and that 'there are even stronger reasons why Irish bishops should personally attend to the spiritual direction of their flocks and be present to help these poor Catholics who live under a Protestant government, surrounded by so many enemies of their religion'.[62]

Laurence Richardson, Bishop of Kilmore, wrote to Rome in 1750 to justify his living in Dublin. He named ten other dioceses, excluding his own, where bishops were non-resident. He omitted Walter Blake which meant that there were then at least twelve dioceses whose bishops lived elsewhere. Richardson argued that the penal laws made it impossible for him to live in Kilmore as 'there are not three Catholic houses in which a bishop could be received *commodé aut debité*'. The situation was similar in Achonry.[63] Walter Blake could have made his summer visitation of some of the Mayo parishes in the diocese, returning to his home in Ballinafad each evening.

Rome issued a number of decrees in an attempt to reform the Irish church and these were sent to the four Irish archbishops in January 1751. The first decree stated, 'The archbishops are to reside in their dioceses and see to it that their suffragans do likewise.'[64] Blake attended a meeting of the western bishops in July which drew up a reply to Rome.[65] The western bishops dealt with three specific items. Concerning residency, they stated that it was strictly observed by all, with very few exceptions, 'whose homes are so near their dioceses that they can reach the centre of them in the space of an hour'.

Another of the Roman decrees stated that 'no bishop is to exact first fruits from the pastors he appoints'. The western bishops protested vehemently

60 *Arch. Hib.*, vol. 1, pp. 194–6
61 CP, vol. 133, f. 173r
62 Nunz. di Fiandra, vol. 131, ff. 294r–296r
63 Richardson made his visitation every year in the months of May, June, July and September. CP, vol. 110, ff. 176rv, 177rv
64 see Fenning, *Undoing*, pp. 206–207 for translation of full text.
65 He had already signed in February, with nine other bishops, a letter rejecting the complaints made in Rome against them.

that they never received money before or after making appointments and never demanded the first year's income. With regard to 'payment for the dispensation of the banns of marriage', they replied that 'whatever they imposed by way of fine for the dispensation of the marriage banns, which was granted rarely and only for serious reasons, was applied for the use and sustenance of the poor'. Bination, i.e. priests saying two Masses on the same day, was regarded as an abuse because Rome was aware that such occasions could be used for doubling the collections. But in many rural parishes priests had to say Mass in two different locations to facilitate their widely-dispersed congregations. The bishops assured Rome that every care was taken to insure that the Roman norms were observed.

Relatio Status of Killala by Philip Philips, 1771 (San Clemente, Rome)

No reference was made by the bishops to another decree which ordered that 'the bishops are to send every two years to the nuncio in Brussels reports on their dioceses'. As far as Achonry was concerned, this decree fell on very deaf ears indeed. Not only did Blake not comply with it, but neither did any of his successors. Not until the next century was any detailed account of the diocese sent to Rome.[66] A native of Achonry, John Brett, Bishop of Elphin, compiled a report on that diocese in 1753 and, though a much larger diocese, the situation pertaining there was broadly similar to Achonry during Blake's period.[67] The population was decreasing as landlords were converting their lands from tillage to pasture. Protestants were one in thirty in rural areas. Many Protestants lived in the towns, of which there were five in his diocese, but even here Catholics outnumbered them by three to one. Two of these, Sligo and Athlone, were sizeable towns. Achonry then had no towns at all,

Relatio Status

66 This omission not only deprived Rome of valuable information, but also deprived Achonry of invaluable historical documentation. For that, it must rely on what can be gleaned from such reports on neighbouring dioceses.
67 SC Irlanda, vol. 10, ff. 422r–425v

only a number of villages where fairs were held. All magistrates, military people, the legal profession and other officials, as well as the landlords and the wealthier merchants, were Protestants. Small traders, tenants, tradesmen and householders were Catholics.

There were then forty-five parishes in Elphin. Most of them were served by a parish priest alone. There were, however, seventeen curates. Achonry had only about twenty parishes, and none of them comparable to Sligo, Athlone or Roscommon. Curates were very rare and then only where parish priests were too old or sick to function. Such parish priests hired their own curates from 'priests in good standing' in the diocese. In Achonry apparently there was no shortage of priests. Blake released John Joyce in 1742 from serving in the diocese and gave him a testimonial as fit for employment by any bishop.[68] Joyce went to Galway where he later became warden. Elphin had five friaries, four Dominican and one Franciscan. Achonry had a similar number. Each friary in Elphin had five or six friars. While one or other of them remained at home, the others dispersed throughout the diocese, acting as curates where needed or chaplains in the homes of richer Catholics, or engaging in preaching and questing. Richer Catholics also employed them as tutors for their children.[69]

Brett raised a problem which was equally prevalent in Achonry, viz. the observation of feastdays. With the exception of Sundays and a few others, they were poorly observed. 'Nor can the people be compelled to observe them since they are poor and many of them subject to Protestant landlords who oblige them to work, whether they want to or not.' Brett asked for a relaxation of the rules, particularly during the sowing months of February and March, with the exception of the feasts of Purification (2 February) and of Annunciation (25 March). He requested the same for the harvest months of July, August, September and October.

Synod of Balla

The western bishops held a synod in Balla in September 1752. The choice of Balla may have been due to it being the home parish of Blake who was then in his seventies. His family home at Ballinafad could also have provided suitable hospitality for the bishops. This synod ordered the reprinting of the earlier seventeenth-century statutes and regulated the fees due to priests for their various services.

Blake's Will

Though he governed the diocese for almost twenty years, very few records survive of his activities there. He appointed Patrick Henican his vicar general and gave him the parish of Ballisodare, which was not disputed by James Gallagher on this occasion. Like Blake, Henican had also taken his licentiate in

---

68 SCAR, codex 1, vol. 4, f. 695
69 As Brett was himself a Dominican his information on the friaries is particularly important.

the university of Paris.⁷⁰ After Henican's death, which took place about 1751, Blake appointed Philip Philips as his vicar general. Given Blake's age then, the daily running of the diocese was probably largely in Philips' hands. Blake made his will at the end of April 1758.⁷¹ He left ten pounds to Philip Philips 'to be disposed of him as I directed'. His legacy amounted in all to three hundred and sixty pounds. The bulk of it – three hundred pounds – was left to his 'beloved niece Catto Blake of Clooneen'. He left ten pounds to his sister, Anstace Lynch, to his nieces, Anstace and Bridget Blake of Clooneen, and his nephew, Mark Blake of Knockmore, and five pounds each to his cousins, Judy Blake and Mary French. He left his books to his nephew, John Blake of Dublin, 'to be disposed of as I directed'. Later that year he died.

Patrick Robert Kirwan was appointed Bishop of Achonry in August 1758. He was in his late fifties. Like his predecessor, Blake, he was to govern the diocese for nineteen years. He also lived outside the diocese but, while Blake was only fifteen miles distant, Kirwan lived over fifty miles away. Patrick Robert was the son of James Kirwan of Bunnitubber, a wealthy landowner in east Co Galway. He grew up in an area where landlords were usually Catholic rather than Protestant. Peter Blake, describing his parish of Oranmore in 1776, said there were only three or four Protestants in it, while there were about six thousand Catholics, some of whom were 'lords of large estates' (*signori di grandi eredità*).⁷²

Patrick Robert Kirwan (1758-1776)

Kirwan was educated in France but exactly where is not known nor whether he went there as a young student or an ordained priest. Nicholas Browne from Athenry, who spent all his life in Paris, described Kirwan at the end of February 1749 as a 'doctor of Sorbonne' but his name does not occur in the register of graduates there. A month later Browne informed the agent in Rome that he 'wrote to Nants (*sic*) by the last post to have the gentleman's (i.e. Kirwan's) pedigree'.⁷³ This suggests that he was educated at the Irish College in Nantes and at that city's university. He returned to the diocese of Tuam early in the seventeen-thirties and was later appointed vicar general under both Bernard and Michael O'Gara.

In his first visitation of Achonry diocese in June 1759 Kirwan held a diocesan synod at Bunninadden.⁷⁴ It was the only recorded synod ever held in the diocese. Eleven statutes were enacted. All priests, including friars, were to teach the catechism before or after Mass on Sundays and feastdays. They

Synod of Bunninadden

---

70 Brockliss & Ferté, op. cit., no. 1020
71 *Arch. Hib.*, vol. 1–2, pp. 223–4
72 They were Blake's relatives and landlords of almost all the parish. SC Irlanda, vol. 12, ff. 453rv, 454rv
73 SCAR, codex 1, vol. 4, ff. 430, 431
74 Moran, *Spicilegium Ossoriense*, vol. 3, pp. 272–3; the original was in the archives of the Irish College, Rome.

were to do it personally or employ someone else to do it under pain of suspension and irrespective of whether they celebrated Mass in parish chapels or private houses. Kirwan attached great importance to education and to the training of candidates for the priesthood. Such candidates were also to teach catechism in the parishes in which they lived, not only on Sundays and feast-days, but also on one weekday chosen by the parish priest. The candidates themselves were required to have character references from their parish priests at least a year before they presented themselves for examination, and they were to show these to the bishop in the course of his visitation.

When he first arrived in Achonry Kirwan found that 'priests with experience were unfit because of age and there were none at all suitable to replace them.'

> Therefore, I was forced without any choice to make do indiscriminately for the time being with ignoramuses and drunkards who would simply celebrate Mass and carry out the necessary duties. I quickly took upon myself the task of preparing candidates whom I enticed in every way to attend schools for orders and for the pursuit of liberal studies abroad ... and should his Eminence the Prefect have any doubt about the truth of this report, at least as regards the money given and spent on new young priests ... I earnestly request him to question the superiors of the colleges in Paris, Douay, Bordeaux and Nantes, who have had a verbatim account from the alumni of my diocese and have written to me accordingly.

Immediately the newly-trained priests arrived home from the continent, Kirwan 'revoked the faculty of hearing confessions of (those who were) ignorant and given to drunkenness and loose morals, with the result that as there was no longer any need to employ them, the scandal given by them would come to an end.'[75]

Two decrees of the synod dealt with such priests. Priests who were found guilty of fornication or adultery would be suspended *ipso facto* from their parishes. Those who were charged with consorting with 'suspect' women would be suspended from exercising their priesthood and without any hope of restoration if they continued their association with such women after a third warning. Kirwan made no complaints to Rome about specific priests on this score. Priests who indulged in alcohol to the point where they were 'out of their minds' would be suspended and remain so at the discretion of the bishop. Each priest was to say Mass at least three times a week unless necessarily impeded, and parish priests should not assist at funerals outside their parishes to make money.

The Bunninadden synod also encouraged schoolmasters to teach catechism both in schools and in the houses where they stayed. Rome became

75 SC Irlanda, vol. II, f. 541rv

alarmed at the growth of charter schools in Ireland and voted an annual grant to the Irish bishops to help them counteract the influence of these proselytising schools.[76] Kirwan received eight pounds in his first year from this fund, and he used it with money of his own to employ schoolmasters. The results, apparently, were spectacular:

> they avidly drank in and became wonderfully well-versed in (the catechism), with the youth of both sexes flocking in throngs on weekdays as well as feastdays and Sundays to obtain that spiritual knowledge, and in the course of a visitation, they recited from memory in my presence the entire contents from start to finish, to the astonishment of everybody.[77]

Only one statute dealt with the laity and in particular with the 'churching' of mothers of babies born outside wedlock. The enactment of this statute suggests that the birth of babies outside wedlock was a relatively common occurence. Yet visitors to the country often state the reverse. One visitor early in the next century wrote that there are very few 'spurious children' in Ireland and he attributed it to the very early marriages and 'the inviolate sanctity with which the marriage contract is kept'.[78] Kirwan himself later reported to Rome one case of incest from which a child was born.

The 'Gallagher affair', which had lain dormant during the Blake administration, was once again reactivated. Philip Philips was vicar general of the diocese up to 1759. Philips had been the choice of the Achonry clergy to succeed Blake. Perhaps, due to his rejection on this occasion, relationships between the two men soon deteriorated. Kirwan replaced him as vicar general with Charles Brett.[79]

The Gallagher Affair

Charles Brett died in 1768 and Kirwan used the opportunity to appoint a new parish priest of Ballisodare and vicar general. He invited a Tuam priest, John Fitzmaurice, to fill both posts. Gallagher, however, decided to re-assert his claims to the parish simply by taking possession of it. Opposition to him within the parish had since disappeared and he was egged on by a number of priests who resented Kirwan's high-handedness in intruding a foreigner into these two plum posts. Kirwan threatened to excommunicate Gallagher and the parishioners who supported him.

Gallagher appealed to Rome in 1768 seeking support for his original bull of appointment to Ballisodare.[80] Kirwan excommunicated him and the

76 see chapter six
77 SC Irlanda, vol. 11, ff. 541v, 542r
78 Carr, op. cit., pp. 281, 485
79 O'Rorke, *Ballysadare & Kilvarnet*, p. 480, describes Charles as 'brother or cousin' of Bishop Brett of Elphin.
80 He claimed that Fitzmaurice had been expelled from Tuam because he had recourse to the secular authorities against his archbishop and that Kirwan, instead of bringing in a 'foreigner', had suitable priests 'in Paris and elsewhere who had completed their studies' and whom he could appoint to Ballisodare.

Ballisodare Village
(Dublin Saturday Magazine)

parishioners who supported him and ordered neighbouring parish priests to announce the excommunication from the altar on three consecutive Sundays. On 1 October Rome wrote to the Archbishop of Tuam asking him to adjudicate the case. The archbishop summoned Gallagher to appear before him. Gallagher produced a certificate attesting to his suitability from McDonogh (now deceased), a vicar forane of Achonry who had examined him in the chapter in the presence of the bishop. He also presented a statement from two priests, Dominick Kearney, parish priest of Tourlestrane (Kilmactigue) and Daniel Mullarkey, parish priest of Ballaghaderreen (Kilcolman), who were present at the examination. In a letter to Rome they claimed that the vicar general, Dr Charles Brett, asked Gallagher to look after the parish while he was sick. Brett died shortly afterwards and the parishioners 'with one voice' asked Gallagher to stay.

When asked by the archbishop why he had not had recourse to Walter Blake after O'Hart's death to be re-instated in Ballisodare, Gallagher replied that it would have been useless because of the strength of the faction against him in the parish. Asked why he had now intruded himself into the parish without first consulting Kirwan, Gallagher replied that he did not regard his action as an intrusion as he had already been appointed there by the Holy See and that now he was recalled by the parishioners who had earlier opposed him. The archbishop recommended Kirwan to come to an amicable agreement with Gallagher 'for the good and peace of his diocese' and make some provision for him 'in his old age'. Kirwan replied that he would leave the case to the judgement of Propaganda.[81] On 16 October a petition signed by eighty parishioners in favour of Gallagher was sent to Rome.[82] Surprisingly, among the signatures were those of Ann O'Hart, a sister of the former bishop and seven of his nephews, John, Charles and William Brett, John and Bernard Verdon, and Michael and Laurence O'Hara.

Kirwan wrote to Rome in October stating that Fitzmaurice was loved and cherished by all the parishioners (with the exception of eight or ten) 'for his zeal, knowledge and gentleness of manner, with which he captivated not only Catholics but Protestants as well'. Gallagher on the other hand was hated 'for his ferocity, ignorance, lack of zeal and disobedience to his bishop'. Regarding the bull, Kirwan declared that it was now old and 'invalidated by time'. Only three priests were still alive from that period and they remembered nothing about it. None of those who had examined Gallagher on that occasion had survived. Kirwan wrote again in November alleging that Gallagher's ignorance made him unfit to be a parish priest and that he had celebrated and administered the sacraments while excommunicated. Gallagher had the audacity to appeal to the Holy See, which caused amazement to Protestants, seeing the quarrel of 'an ignorant, arrogant priest, given to secular trafficking' against a superior in whose conduct no one has ever found the slightest reproach. Kirwan sent his letters to the nuncio in Brussels to be transmitted to Rome. He took the unusual step on each occasion of writing a separate letter to the nuncio himself. It was a policy which paid off handsomely. He succeeded in making an ally of the nuncio in this dispute. The latter transmitted Kirwan's letters to Rome with a covering letter of his own arguing in favour of Kirwan whom he described as 'one of the most worthy bishops in Ireland, for his zeal, learning and probity'.

The case was discussed at a general meeting of the cardinals of Propaganda on 23 January 1769. It was found that Gallagher's right was not based on sound law. However, the cardinals recommended that Kirwan should take care to provide in some way for Gallagher's needs. They communicated their decision to Kirwan on 28 January. He had Gallagher examined once more on 1 May and the result proved Gallagher's 'crass ignorance'. Notwithstanding, Kirwan offered him one of the best curacies in the diocese. Gallagher refused, demanding to be made parish priest. Far from being in need according to Kirwan, Gallagher had an income of £30 sterling annually which derived from 'some properties' he held in the diocese as well as other non-negligible rents in the province of Leinster. 'He had a lot of ability in trafficking and business of every kind.' In fact only two parish priests in the diocese equalled him in 'the amount of goods and money which he possesses'. The case was

81 Lettere, vol. 212, ff. 378v, 379r, 381v, 382r, 388rv, 407rv
82 see Appendix 42

raised again at the general meeting of the cardinals on 22 August. Their decision on this occasion was to leave Gallagher's fate to the discretion of Kirwan.[83] Gallagher may have become a curate to Dominick Kearney in Tourlestrane (Kilmactigue) where he died about six years later.[84]

A Clerical Conspiracy

Kirwan claimed that the 'Gallagher affair' was a conspiracy orchestrated against him both inside and outside the diocese. Its spokesman in Rome was no less than the bishops' agent there, the Dominican Charles O'Kelly. Kirwan believed that O'Kelly was retaliating against complaints Kirwan made about him to the Prefect of Propaganda. 'I most earnestly entreat,' Kirwan wrote in 1770, 'that he (O'Kelly) be instructed to keep his distance from my affairs and from my subordinates.' He accused another Dominican, Edmund Fitzgerald, 'a strolling monk who comes every year to the diocese', of 'stirring up the crowds in that misfortunate disturbance caused by the priest Gallagher'.[85] In 1764 Charles O'Kelly launched a campaign to have the 1750 decree against novitiates mitigated. He canvassed support among the Irish bishops. The Connacht bishops signed a petition in 1766 in favour of the admission of novices. Kirwan alone withheld his signature. Two years later they sent another petition to Rome, outlining the important role the friars played in the Irish mission. If the prohibition against novitiates was not lifted the friars would soon disappear to the great loss of the Irish church. Once again Kirwan was the only one who refused to sign.[86] Why he was opposed to the friars is not clear. It may have been due to his experience of them in Achonry. He did mention a Franciscan called Sweeney whom he expelled from the diocese in 1768 for being addicted to drink. If the Dominicans were involved in the 'Gallagher affair', it may have been retaliation for his unwillingness to support their petition.

Within the diocese the ring-leader of the conspiracy against him, according to Kirwan, was Philip Philips. The rivalry between the two men dated from the selection of Kirwan for Achonry. The Achonry clergy then had unaninmously opted for Philips. In 1760 Killala became vacant and the Achonry clergy put forward Philips as a candidate. Kirwan objected to Philips as unsuitable but he was duly selected. However, Philips while Bishop of Killala continued to live in his family home in Cloonmore in his native diocese. It was a situation which was bound to lead to trouble. Kirwan was

---

83 SOCG, vol. 823, ff. 207r–218r, 222r–224v, 225r–228r, 230rv, 231rv, 232r, 234r, 235rv, 236r, 238r–239v, 240rv; vol. 825, ff. 64rv, 65r–66v; Acta, vol. 139, ff. 57r–66v, 317r–319v; SC Irlanda, vol. 11, ff. 485r, 541rv, 542r; Lettere, vol. 214, ff. 69v, 70rv, 268rv, 269r
84 *Arch. Hib.*, vol. xviii, p. 178
85 Two other Dominicans were named by Kirwan in his complaints to Rome. One was Martin French from Athenry who later became provincial of the order. The other was Thomas Burke, Bishop of Ossory, and author of *Hibernia Dominicana*.
86 see Fenning, *Undoing*, pp. 274–5, 281–2

absent for most of the year, living in Co Galway, while the only resident bishop in the diocese was Philips. 'He zealously encourages the priests in their conspiracy,' Kirwan complained, describing Philips as the 'enemy who sowed cockle among the seeds'. Specifically, Kirwan alleged that Philips and his family never offered him 'humane hospitality for one or two nights, when in dire straits, in the course of his visitation.'[87]

Philips categorically denied the charge. Writing to Charles O'Kelly in Rome, he insisted that he and his family had repeatedly offered hospitality to Kirwan who had consistently declined it. 'I never met him anywhere contiguous to my uncle's or brother's house, as I had none, but I would at their instance, as well as from my own inclination, press him to come with me to their houses but he always declined coming.' Six or seven times in different years Philips went to different places up to nine miles away to meet Kirwan 'in a fraternal manner'. He used 'to sit with him and his clergy whilst on business and frequently dined with him'. His brother went twice in person to pay his respects to Kirwan and show him the way to his house but he did not come then or ever since. 'From this conduct I judged he did not chose a close connection with me or mine.' From then on he ceased 'to dance attendance on him', but he remained adamant that he was not responsible for the rift between them. Rome had written to Mark Skerret, Archbishop of Tuam, to patch up the unseemly quarrel between the two bishops. 'I challenge the Doctor,' Philips asserted to Charles O'Kelly, 'to point out one single instance of my acting an unfriendly part by him or ever denying him fraternal love in any shape.' But he and O'Kelly were implicated in the 'Gallagher affair' as one sentence of his letter made clear. 'Gallagher assured me upon oath, he never shewed any of your letters to Dr Kirwan, but one.' Philips was also on close terms with another co-conspirator, Edmund Fitzgerald, whom he frequently mentioned in the same letter.[88]

By the late 1760s Kirwan had almost reached breaking-point. He begged the nuncio to prevail on Cardinal Castelli to transfer him to the first vacant diocese or procure him 'a benefice in Belgium or somewhere else'.

> My health is fragile, my poverty extreme, the district wild and mountainous; the revolt of the clergy, the proclivity of the bishops to favour them somewhat, as appears from the recent destructive tumult, will advance my case before his Eminence the Prefect to whom I beg that this letter be transmitted, with your Eminence's commendation.[89]

His health had deteriorated to the point where he had to employ in October 1768 an 'ignorant school-teacher' to whom he dictated his elegant Latin letters. He described his ailment then as a 'weak chest'. There was also some

87 SC Irlanda, vol. 11, ff. 541r–542v
88 SCAR, codex 1, 4, no. 474; SC Irlanda, vol. 11, f. 605rv
89 SC Irlanda, vol. 11, f. 542r

deterioration in the fortunes of his family. 'A relative from whom I had hitherto received hospitality has found his own situation greatly deteriorating and has become unable to provide this service any longer.' His last recorded ordination was that of Patrick McNicholas, later parish priest of Bonniconlon (Kilgarvan) in Kiltimagh in 1771.[90] In March 1773 he wrote to Rome seeking a reduction in the number of feastdays, which was duly accorded to him two months later.[91]

Administrator of Clonfert

Rome consulted Kirwan in 1774 about the appointment of a coadjutor to the Bishop of Clonfert. Peter Donnellan was well into his eighties and according to Kirwan, 'out of his mind with old age and the dizzy confusion of his episcopal ministry'. Donnellan was already a doctor of the Sorbonne when Kirwan was a little boy and a priest before he was born. His brother Andrew, also an octogenarian, was dean and vicar general and strongly suspected by Peter of scheming to become his coadjutor.[92] Peter himself wished to have a Dominican, Martin French, as his coadjutor. Kirwan left Rome in no doubt about the unsuitability of French and he made no secret of his own wish to escape from Achonry: 'My enemies hope to so wound me secretly that there is no hope that I will ever migrate from the uncultivated and wild see of Achonry but will waste away miserably there.'[93]

At the general meeting of Propaganda on 10 April 1775 Kirwan was nominated administrator of Clonfert.[94] He was asked as a matter of urgency to draw up a list of suitable candidates for bishop with particular attention to former students of the Irish pontifical colleges of Rome or Douay. Martin French was deemed by Rome as unsuitable for such an appointment.[95] The other bishops in the province, including Philips, were strongly in favour of French. The appointment of Kirwan as administrator was also a great disappointment to them. 'Clonfert had been fobbed off to a septuagenarian administrator who could scarcely ride five miles a day,' Mark Skerret of Tuam complained to Rome.[96] Thomas Burke OP of Ossory was equally critical. 'Yet they name Dr Kirwan administrator, the remotest of all the bishops in the province and the most unfit as very sickly and infirm, hardly able to mind his own diocese.'[97] But the septuagenarian Kirwan was ecstatic. 'May God reward you most generously for such remarkable patronage,' he wrote to thank the nuncio in Brussels. He seemed to gain a new lease of life: 'I therefore set

---

90 *Arch. Hib.*, vol. 1, p. 70
91 SC Irlanda, vol. 12, f. 27r; Lettere, vol. 222, f. 226rv
92 SC Irlanda, vol. 12, f. 203v
93 SOCG, vol. 841, f. 276r
94 Acta, vol. 145, ff. 43–49; SOCG, vol. 841, ff. 257–322, 452–455
95 Lettere, vol. 226, ff. 137rv, 138rv
96 SC Irlanda, vol. 12, ff. 187, 192
97 DDA, 29/4

out immediately for that diocese where I was joyfully received by the bishop, clergy and people, being already quite well-known to some individuals on account of the help I had given, for the most part successfully, in the disputes and quarrels that threatened to overwhelm them.'[98]

Kirwan's Will

But this renewed burst of activity was illusory. His age and his health were against him. It was to be his one and only summer in Clonfert. On 13 February 1776 he made his will. Less than two months later he was dead. He left five debentures in the national funds in Dublin to the value of about £500, to be distributed at £50 each to nine nephews and nieces, the sons and daughters of his brother John. To his sister Julia French he left an annuity of ten pounds. He had a further sum of 'sixty-five guineas, forty-four shilling pieces and two moydores' which were lodged with his kinsman, Augustine Kirwan. The latter, one of his executors, later became warden of Galway. Out of this sum, he stipulated that twenty pounds were to be spent on his funeral expenses and twenty-one guineas to be paid to Thady O'Flaherty, parish priest of Kiltimagh (Killedan), in discharge of a debt. He also gave O'Flaherty a gift of ten pounds.[99] The debt he owed O'Flaherty was possibly incurred during the ordinations held in Kiltimagh. Kirwan held ordinations there on at least three occasions, in 1765, 1769 and 1771.[100] Before his death he may have effected some measure of reconciliation with his adversaries in the diocese, as he wrote to explain to the nuncio in Brussels in July 1775: 'On your salutary advice I shall make every effort to continue my forbearance amidst the disturbances provoked against me in my own diocese; for I warmly indulge the very leaders of the conspiracy and devote myself to them and this clearly wins me their goodwill and respect.'[101] He was buried with his parents as he requested.

Philip Philips (1776–1785)

Propaganda wrote to Philip Philips on 22 June 1776 informing him of his transfer from Killala to Achonry.[102] The letter was addressed to Cloonmore, Philip's family home. From now on correspondence between Rome and the Irish bishops tended to be direct rather than through the medium of the internuncio in Brussels. Gone are the days when bishops used the address *'in loco refugii'* (in the place of refuge), a measure of the changing climate in Ireland towards Catholics. Philips had been Bishop of Killala for almost sixteen years. He had been ordained a priest in 1742 and must have been by now sixty years of age. He appointed Thomas Costello, parish priest of Ballaghaderreen (Kilcolman and Castlemore), as his vicar general. Costello was then in his mid-thirties and working in the diocese for about five years.[103]

98 SC Irlanda, vol. 12, f. 203r
99 *Arch. Hib.*, vol. 1, pp. 224–6
100 ibid, pp. 70–71
101 SC Irlanda, vol. 12, f. 203v
102 Lettere, vol. 228, ff. 311v, 312r
103 Philips wrote to Rome in March 1777 recommending Costello as a suitable candidate for bishop. SC Irlanda, vol. 12, f. 358r; Lettere, vol. 230, ff. 257v, 258r

Reports had been reaching Rome of certain abuses being practised by Irish bishops. A letter was dispatched in December 1777 to the four archbishops warning them against ordaining priests 'with too great facility'.[104] This was followed six months later by another letter detailing the abuses. Some bishops who did not personally reside in their dioceses only came there to collect their dues which caused bitterness among the priests. It was also alleged that in some places the appointment of parish priests was deferred for years. A curate was appointed instead so that the bishop could receive the income of the vacant parish. New parish priests were obliged to agree, in word and in writing, to increase by a half or double the annual subscription of one guinea which they made the bishop. Money demanded in return for marriage dispensations was expressly forbidden. The archbishops were asked to bring these matters to the attention of the bishops in their respective provinces.[105]

Tuam Meeting

Philips joined the other bishops of the western province in a special meeting in Tuam to draw up a reply to these charges.[106] Only one bishop in the province, Alexander Irwin, Philips' successor in Killala, was non-resident. Killala had an even worse record of non-resident bishops than Achonry. Irwin was a priest of the diocese of Elphin and the bishops claimed that he could reach his diocese 'in a fairly short time'. He did not reside there because of the poverty of the diocese which could not afford to maintain him there. His predecessor, Philips, had written to Rome to justify his non-residency. 'How could I pretend to keep house there for about £50 a year!' he exclaimed.[107] For Rome's information the Tuam meeting listed the incomes of the various bishops in the province. Tuam and Elphin amounted to forty-five guineas annually, Achonry, Killala and Clonfert, twenty-four guineas and Kilmacduagh and Kilfenora together, nineteen. 'We are compelled for the greater part of the year to live with some rich friends.'

They rejected the charge that they ever deferred appointing parish priests so that they could appropriate some of the revenues. They also denied that they demanded an increased annual contribution from new parish priests.[108] They admitted that they received some money for marriage dispensations but insisted that they demanded nothing at all from the poor. From the rich and noble they accepted what they spontaneously offered for the relief of the poor. Their purpose was to restrain people from seeking dispensations and so that they might have something in hand to meet the needs of the poor.

104 Lettere, vol. 230, ff. 64v, 66rv
105 Lettere, vol. 232, ff. 385r–392r
106 SC Irlanda, vol. 13, ff. 464rv, 465rv
107 SCAR, codex 1. 4. no. 474
108 Bishop Kirwan a few years earlier claimed that the opposition he experienced from the other bishops was linked to his criticism of the practice of some of them of demanding remuneration for ordinations and appointments to parishes. SOCG, vol. 825, f. 66r

Dunmore Affair

Rome asked Philips in 1783 to intervene in a financial settlement between priests in the parish of Dunmore in Tuam diocese. Nicholas Lovelake had resigned his parish because of old age in favour of Thomas Fallon. It was agreed that Lovelake would continue while he lived to receive half the annual income. Archbishop Mark Skerret computed the parish income at forty pounds sterling. Lovelake contested this, claiming the value was higher and appealed to Rome. Rome asked Philips to investigate the real income. He conducted the investigation in the parish chapel in Dunmore, assisted by his vicar general, Thomas Costello, in the presence of Boetius Egan, Canon Jordan and four other priests. It was found that the parish was worth sixty-two pounds sterling. As a result Rome decided that Lovelake should be paid a pension of thirty pounds sterling.[109]

The Oath of Allegiance

Philip's period in Achonry coincided with the beginning of the government's relaxation of the penal laws. A bill was introduced in 1774 to enable Catholics to swear the oath of allegiance. This was to become 'the cornerstone of their future emancipation'.[110] About 1782 Bishop Philips led thirteen parish priests and two priors in taking the oath. The date and the place is uncertain.[111] It may have taken place in Castlebar as the priests concerned were mostly from the western end of the diocese. It is not certain whether or where the others took the oath. Sligo would have been the most likely venue. With the exception of the parish priest of Kilmactigue, Dominick Kearney, who was seventy-six, the priests were strikingly young. They ranged in age from Francis Donlevy, parish priest of Bunninadden (Killshalvey), who was twenty-nine to Thady O'Flaherty of Kiltimagh (Killedan) and Patrick O'Connor of Swinford (Kilconduff), who were both fifty.

Philips to Tuam

The same could not be said about the bishops of the province. Philips himself in his mid-sixties was among the youngest. Tuam, Elphin and Clonfert were all elderly. Already by 1780 Rome was looking for a coadjutor for Mark Skerret in Tuam. Troy of Ossory proposed Philips for the post then. His other candidate was Thomas Costello. Troy lamented the fact that most of the diocesan clergy were 'French'. They loved new doctrines and defended the four Gallican principles emphasising their independence of Rome. Troy's informant on western affairs was Fallon of Elphin who recommended Philips as 'conspicuous for his prudence, gentleness and suavity'. O'Reilly of Armagh also proposed Philips and Costello and Peter Blake, parish priest of Oranmore. Significantly, the latter two were Roman graduates.[112] Rome wrote in

---

109 SC Irlanda, vol. 15, ff. 405r, 406v; Lettere, vol. 242, ff. 533v, 534rv, 535r; 828rv, 829v; 842rv, 843r

110 see Thomas Bartlett, *The Fall and Rise of the Irish Nation*, pp. 77–81

111 It was probably after 22 July 1782 when Lewis Williams who took the oath was appointed guardian of Ballymote. *Arch. Hib.*, vol. 1, pp. 70–71; also Appendix 18

112 ASV, Fondo Missioni, no. 117

May 1783 to Skerret proposing these names. Philips was the favourite but it was felt that his age might present a problem. Skerret wanted his vicar general, Thomas Kirwan, whom Rome regarded as unsuitable. In the appointment of coadjutors Rome always sought the agreement of the incumbent. Another letter followed in March 1785 underlining the urgency of making a speedy appointment as it understood there were abuses in the archdiocese regarding ordinations and appointments to parishes. Skerret died in August of that year and the Tuam canons proposed Philips to succeed him. The four Irish religious superiors also supported Philips. In spite of Valentine Bodkin's warning that Philips was then 'a toothless, goutish septuagenarian', Rome was in no doubt and on 1 October a letter was dispatched to inform Philips of his appointment to Tuam. Significantly, Cardinal Antonnelli wrote on the same day to Troy of Ossory informing him of their decision and thanking him for his clear report on Philips and Boetius Egan. On the following day a letter was sent informing Boetius Egan of his appointment to Achonry.[113] Philips wrote in November requesting the parish of Tuam as his mensal. He left the family home in Cloonmore and took up residency in Tuam.[114]

Boetius Egan (22 Nov 1785– 3 Dec 1787)

It appears that the Achonry clergy had no say in Egan's appointment. Later opinion is divided on the question. Dr Charles O'Conor, who consulted Egan's original correspondence, claimed that his appointment was influenced by O'Conor's grandfather (Charles of Belanagare), his cousin Charles O'Kelly OP in Rome and 'assisted by the good wishes of many of the diocesan clergy'.[115] It was not how it was later remembered in the diocese. James Filan, recalling in 1817 Egan's election, declared that the Achonry clergy were 'convinced by experience of the futility of postulating in favour of any favourite of their own, they seemed to regard with cold indifference those appointments which vitally concerned their dearest interests. There was no clerical postulation – they tamely bent their necks to the yoke.'[116]

Mensal Parish

Egan's first act on appointment to Achonry was to petition Rome to grant him the parish of Achonry as his mensal. He claimed that it had been granted to his predecessor, Philips.[117] When Rome promoted a parish priest to be a bishop it reserved the right to appoint to his parish and had to be consulted when a replacement was appointed there. It was quite protective of its rights in this matter. Rome wrote twice, in April and December 1787, to the four Irish archbishops complaining that some bishops were resigning such parishes in favour of family and relations. It wished this practice to be eliminated and

113 SC Irlanda, vol. 15, f. 470v; ASV, Fondo Missioni, no. 117; Lettere, vol. 246, ff. 675rv, 676r, 678rv, 679v, 674rv, 680v, 681r, 706rv, 707r
114 Udienze, vol. 23, ff. 413r, 414r
115 *Letter of Columbanus*, 3rd Letter, pp. 15–16
116 'Address to the Clergy of Achonry', Banada, 24 July, 1817, SC Irlanda, vol. 20, f. 234r
117 Udienze, vol. 23, ff. 405r, 406r, 408v

Bishop
Boetius Egan
(St Jarlath's, Tuam)

instructed the archbishops to send a complete list of the mensal parishes in each province.[118] Egan's reference to Philips' possession of Achonry parish was the first mention of an Achonry bishop having a mensal parish. Such parishes were usually run by a curate or administrator so that a substantial part of their revenues was reserved for the use of the bishop to meet his living costs.[119] Achonry bishops had always justified their non-residency on the fact that the diocese could not afford to maintain them. But Egan had no intention of quitting his family home at Dunbleany, near Tuam, and, in fact, he informed Rome that his postal address for the future would be Tuam.[120] In such circumstances there was little justification for such mensal parishes. Rome, however, granted his request.

Egan was consecrated by Philips in Tuam and made his first visitation of the diocese in the summer of 1786. In May Thomas Costello had been made

118 Lettere, vol. 250, ff. 222v, 223rv, 793v, 794rv
119 If Philips held the parish of Achonry, as Egan now claimed, it gives the lie to the statement of the western bishops in 1778 that Achonry was worth only twenty-four guineas. SC Irlanda, vol. 13, ff. 464rv, 465rv

St Mary's Cathedral, Tuam *(Restoration and History)*

coadjutor to the ancient Andrew Donnellan, Bishop of Clonfert. While Rome consistently rebuked Irish bishops for non-residency in their dioceses, it was itself one of the main contributary causes of the problem. Having appointed the non-resident Egan to Achonry, six months later the Achonry priest, Costello, with a home in Cregane, Ballaghaderreen, was appointed to Clonfert. In fairness to Costello, he packed his bags and set out for Loughrea where he encountered at first some fearsome local opposition. Ballaghaderreen (Kilcolman and Castlemore) was now vacant and Egan asked Rome for that parish in exchange for Achonry.[121] In granting his request Rome asked for a report on the situation in Achonry parish, including 'in what diocese the same parish is situated'.[122] It also requested that the parish priest there should be appointed by concursus, i.e. choosing the best candidate by examination. Should the circumstances not permit a concursus, Egan was asked to forward the names and qualities of the priests he wished to appoint to the vacant parish.

In his reply at the end of November 1786 Egan said that there were 'three quasi parochial churches in the parish of Achonry with their own certain and distinct boundaries and revenues'.[123] Anthony McNamara served the parish of Curry. His abode was given as Achonry when he took the oath of allegiance about 1782. John Duffy served Mullinabreena parish. He must have moved from Ballaghaderreen where he gave his address and was described as 'vicar of Castlemore and Kilcolman' when he took the oath. Francis Donlevy, whose address had been given as Killevil, was the parish priest of Tubbercurry (Cloonacool). Regarding appointments by concursus, Egan stated that the matter had been discussed by the western bishops at their meeting in April and they had decided that because of local circumstances it was not feasible.

In September after his first visitation, Egan had given Rome an account of the diocese. The priests 'with a few exceptions' were exemplary. The exceptions had drink problems. Rome praised Egan's zeal and solicitude in trying to wean them by threats and exhortations from this 'detestable vice'. He was urged to exercise patience and forbearance lest he provoke their anger and apostasy, 'the worst of all evils'. Rome was pleased that the people were properly instructed in the precepts of the faith and 'that many youths had been withdrawn from non-Catholic schools'.[124]

120 SC Irlanda, vol. 16, ff. 149rv, 150rv
121 SC Irlanda, vol. 16, f. 101rv
122 Lettere, vol. 248, ff. 582rv, 583r
123 SC Irlanda, vol. 16, ff. 149rv, 150rv
124 Lettere, vol. 248, ff. 691v, 692rv

Fallon of Elphin died early in December 1786 at the age of seventy-seven and Egan was mooted as a possible successor. He was suggested by both Troy of Ossory and O'Reilly of Armagh. Count O'Kelly, the ambassador in Mainz, and Cardinal de Bernis, were also active on his behalf. His nephew and namesake, then a student of the Propaganda College in Rome, argued that in Achonry 'he was constrained to reside more than fifty miles from his diocese' whereas if transferred to Elphin he could reside in the midde of that diocese in a house owned by his family. Valentine Bodkin, Egan's agent in Rome, put forward the same case, explaining that his brother owned 'an excellent house' in the diocese.[125] Rome decided in favour of Edmund French, parish priest of St Peter's, Athlone, though the Elphin chapter had shown a preference for John O'Flynn, parish priest of Sligo. Shortly afterwards Egan's attention focused elsewhere.

Philip Philips died in September 1787. He had just held a provincial synod in Tuam which lasted five days from 28 August, and he sent an account of it to Rome on 16 September.[126] Soon after he became ill and was taken home to Cloonmore where he died.[127] He is said to have been buried in Urlaur Abbey which was the Philips family burial place.[128] One of his last joint acts together with Egan and Costello prior to the synod was to recommend Laurence Nihil of Kilfenora to replace John Butler in Cork. Butler had resigned Cork in December 1786 when he inherited the title of Lord Dunboyne and married a distant cousin in the hope of propagating the family line. It was an ironic consequence of Rome's predilection for promoting to the hierarchy those of aristocratic birth.

Urlaur Abbey (Grose, *Antiquities*)

The Tuam canons favoured Egan as their archbishop though they also expressed support for their dean and vicar general, Thomas O'Connor. Egan was also recommended by Troy of Ossory and the four Irish religious superiors. Rome was quick to reach a decision. Within barely three months of Philips' death Egan was appointed Archbishop of Tuam and on the same day, 3 December 1787, Thomas O'Connor was nominated Bishop of Achonry.[129]

125 SC Irlanda, vol. 16, f. 307rv; SOCG, vol. 875, ff. 10rv, 31rv, 32r, 33rv, 42rv
126 SC Irlanda, vol. 16, ff. 320rv–325rv
127 *Arch. Hib.*, vol. xix, p. 258
128 Burke, *Archbishops of Tuam*, p. 199
129 SOCG, vol. 877, ff. 507r, 509rv, 510rv, 519rv, 522, 523rv, 525; Acta, vol. 157, ff. 2v, 520v, 521rv

Thomas O'Connor (3 Dec 1787– 18 Feb 1803)

Rome wrote to O'Connor on 22 December 1787 to inform him of his appointment to Achonry.[130] Achonry priests later complained, 'O'Connor had been already appointed their bishop clearly without the slightest reference to their wishes.' Egan had written to Mark Rush, then vicar capitular, saying that 'it was quite needless (for them) to postulate in favour of any candidate for the mitre'.[131] This was nothing less than a statement of fact as the letters of appointment of both Egan and O'Connor were dated the same day. O'Connor was consecrated in April 1788 in St Nicholas' chapel outside the walls in Dublin by Thomas Troy, now archbishop there. Troy was assisted by James Caulfield of Ferns and Edmund French of Elphin and there were two other bishops present, Kildare and Leighlin and Ossory, in the large congregation.[132] The Irish church had finally emerged from the underground.

Thomas was the son of Dermot O'Connor of Woodquay, Beagh and Silane, Co Galway, and Mabel, the second daughter of Edmund O'Flynn of Torlagh, Co Roscommon.[133] He was then only in his early thirties. His portrait, which must have been painted shortly afterwards, represents him as a very young man. His rise had been nothing short of meteoric. Elected vicar capitular on the death of Mark Skerret, he served his successor as dean and vicar general of the archdiocese. In fact, his first letter to Rome as Bishop of Achonry requested permission to retain the deanship of Tuam. Rome wondered 'why one now placed in the sublime dignity should solicit the retention of the deanery of Tuam'. They pointed out to him that 'those who attained superior grades in the church should not be seen to be attached to inferior ones'.[134] But his request boded ill for his future commitment to Achonry. His record as the non-resident parish priest of Ballinrobe did nothing to allay suspicions on that score. His two predecessors had been promoted to Tuam and O'Connor, who had already been recommended for that post by the Tuam canons, could be forgiven such an ambition. He continued to live at Woodquay and take a close interest in the ecclesiastical affairs of Tuam.

Relatio Status 1792

In compliance with Rome's demand that bishops submit a report on the state of their diocese (*relatio status*) at least once every five years, O'Connor sent his in August 1792. It took the unusual form of an attestation signed by fourteen canons.[135] Presumably, O'Connor had collected their signatures during his visitation of the diocese that summer. It is a single page document, very short on detail. The canons certify a number of aspects of O'Connor's administration of the diocese. He had seven new chapels built and subsidised

130 Lettere, vol. 250, ff. 790v, 791r
131 James Filan, 'Address to the Clergy of Achonry', 1817, SC Irlanda, vol. 20, f. 234r
132 DDA, *Regestrum*, 1, p. 51; see *Repertorium Novum*, vol. 1, no. 2, p. 493
133 *Arch. Hib.*, vol. 1, p. 227
134 Lettere, vol. 251, ff. 108rv, 109r
135 Fondo di Vienna, vol. 28, f. 37v; see Appendix 20

the repair of the others in the diocese. This was a great period of chapel building all over Ireland. The new chapels referred to here are not specified. The present churches of Keash and Ballisodare date from a slightly later period of his tenure of office. Confirmation was administered throughout the greater part of the diocese. O'Connor was lenient in inflicting penalties 'unless compelled by the gravity of the matter' and was generous to the poor 'placing some of them to be instructed in the mechanical arts'. The rest of the report reveals little about the practical nature of his activities. He was assiduous in preaching and conspicuous for his zeal and piety. Compared to his non-resident predecessors, 'no one came to us as often or remained as long'. Such an attestation signed by inferiors at the request of their superior scarcely inspires confidence!

Rome commented on the brevity of O'Connor's report in a letter which itself was lengthier.[136] They would have preferred had he informed them of the number of parish churches and oratories and if there were sodalities, hospitals or other pious institutions in his diocese. Other information they required included the number of priests and Catholics, the doctrine and morals of the clergy, the educational standard of parish priests, whether they kept baptismal and marriage registers and how they administered these sacraments, whether they preached to the people and instructed the young in the rudiments of the faith, whether there were Catholic schools. Were there theological conferences where priests discussed the ritual and cases of conscience? What were the abuses among the people, what depraved customs existed? The secretary of Propaganda conveyed the displeasure of the cardinals at the inadequacy of O'Connor's report. O'Connor was clearly rapped on the knuckles.

In the letter to O'Connor, Rome referred to 'these calamitous times'. It was a reference to the French Revolution then in full spate. O'Connor's old *alma mater*, *Collége des Irlandais*, was caught at the eye of the storm in the French capital. The closure of the Irish colleges in France, and particularly the two in Paris, was potentially a fatal blow to the Irish church. It cut off their supply line. O'Connor subscribed to a letter with the other western bishops on the subject to Rome. They raised the possibility of founding a seminary in Ireland.[137] Rome doubled the number of places available for Irish students in their Propaganda College from four to eight which made no appreciable difference. Those who could afford it, like William Costello, went to the Irish College in Salamanca to complete their education.

'Calamitous Times'

O'Connor applied in 1788 to Rome to be granted the parish of Ballaghaderreen (Kilcolman and Castlemore) as a mensal, stating that he could

The Costello Affair

---

136 Lettere, vol. 264, ff. 221rv, 222rv
137 Lettere, vol. 262, ff. 646v, 647rv, 648v

not maintain himself on the income of the diocese alone.[138] There was a problem as the patronage of that parish was in dispute between two Protestant magnates, Viscount Dillon and Charles Costello. Dillon's claim was probably based on his family having been granted Urlaur Abbey, with the advowson of a number of parishes including Kilcolman and Castlemore. Costello's claim rested on the fact that his family founded the friary at Urlaur. In fact he claimed the right of presenting to all the parishes in the barony of Costello.[139] O'Connor wrote again in July 1789 asking this time for Tourlestrane (Kilmactigue) instead.[140] It was now vacant due to the death of Dominick Kearney, reported in a newspaper on 4 December 1788 where the journalist claimed that 'for sixty years and upwards (Kearney) was parish priest of Kilmactigue.'[141] This was something of an exaggeration as he had been ordained by O'Daly in 1732. Rome consulted Egan, emphasising that it did not wish to create new mensal parishes 'unless for urgent and grave reasons.' O'Connor's request was supported by Egan and he was duly given Kilmactigue.[142]

Appointing the parish priest of Ballaghaderreen (Kilcolman and Castlemore) still remained the prerogative of Rome. O'Connor requested the Holy Father in August 1792 to confer the parish on Michael Farrell, 'a suitable subject for such a ministry'. His suitability consisted in his determination to take on the might of the local Protestant landlord, Charles Costello. O'Connor chose Farrell, according to Costello, because he knew he was 'very obnoxious' to Costello.[143] Rome agreed to Farrell's appointment and the tension between the Protestant landlord and parish priest continued to mount. Farrell became something of a David in his clash against this local Goliath and was greatly admired by his fellow priests.

Towards the end of O'Connor's reign, the row with Charles Costello over his pretended patronage (*ius patronatus*) of the parish of Ballaghaderreen (Kilcolman and Castlemore) flared up again.[144] In fact it had been simmering all the time, with Michael Farrell goading the tenants into open revolt against their landlord. Now Costello appealed to the 'court of Rome'. Rome referred the case in 1797 to Archbishop O'Reilly of Armagh. O'Reilly made the journey 'of almost 250 Italian miles' to Achonry to question the two litigants, O'Connor and Costello. It was the first visit of a primate to Achonry since

138 Udienze, vol. 26, ff. 179r, 180r, 181r
139 SOCG, vol. 911, ff. 445rv, 446r
140 SOCG, vol. 884, f. 209rv
141 *Arch. Hib.*, vol. xix, p. 263
142 Lettere, vol. 255, f. 472rv; SOCG, vol. 884, f. 208rv
143 SOCG, vol. 911, ff. 445rv, 446r
144 SOCG, vol. 911, ff. 432rv, 433v, 437r, 438v, 439rv, 440rv, 441r, 442v, 445rv, 446r, 447rv, 448rv, 451rv, 453rv, 455rv

Bishop Thomas O'Connor
(St Nathy's, Ballaghaderreen)

Oliver Plunkett met Maurice Durcan there in the previous century. A trial was instituted in Ballaghaderreen. O'Reilly found that Costello could produce no evidence that he or any of his ancestors had ever exercised their pretended right. The predecessors of Bishop O'Connor had freely conferred the parishes in question. Thomas Costello, now Bishop of Clonfert and related to Charles, told O'Reilly that he had not been presented to the parish of Kilcolman by his family but had been appointed there by Bishop Kirwan. Another parish priest stated under oath that he had been offered one of these parishes by Bishop Philips 'without the intervention of the Costello family'.

This was most likely John Duffy, who was parish priest in Castlemore in the seventeen-eighties. Several parish priests declared under oath that they had never heard of this pretended right until Charles Costello first laid claim to it. Archbishop O'Reilly compiled and dispatched to Rome his report in which he found against Costello.

Dr Charles O'Conor, parish priest of Castlerea, was appointed by the bishop to act as a legal expert for the diocese at the trial. Ironically O'Conor himself had been given Castlerea by his family who claimed to have its patronage. The Achonry chapter rewarded him with an honorary canonry 'for his uniform and zealous support of our interests, for the legal knowledge and convincing arguments he so judiciously employed in support of the episcopal rights of the diocese at the late memorable trial in Ballaghaderreen.'[145]

Tuam Succession

Boetius Egan died in his home in Dunbleany on 1 July 1798 and was buried in the family vault in Clontern.[146] O'Connor took a keen interest in the subsequent election held in the Tuam chapter and wrote an account of it to Dr Charles O'Conor. The chapter were evenly split on their choice of a vicar capitular and Dr Bellew of Killala called the bishops of the province together at Moylough to decide the matter. O'Connor dined there with Dr Bellew and John Joyce, the warden of Galway. 'The clergy of this diocese (Dr Egan's three nephews excepted) and many others I am told are not idle for the Bishop of Achonry.' The warden and clergy of Galway wrote to Pius VI recommending Thomas O'Connor for Tuam. Their petition was signed by the Dominicans, Franciscans and Augustinians of Galway as well as six Augustinians of Ballyhaunis, one of whom was called Terence O'Gara. It was also signed by a number of parish priests including those of Shrule, Spiddal, Aran and Tuam as well as some curates.[147]

Owen O'Conor wrote to his brother Charles suggesting the possibility of Thomas being promoted to Tuam and Charles replacing him in Achonry.[148] Charles must have suggested to Thomas that he use his influence with the Achonry chapter in his favour. 'The chapter of Achonry are a hearty pious set of men,' Thomas assured him. 'They have given you, your family and connections a proof of their good wishes. It would be indelicate of me to recommend any person at this moment.' Instead he suggested that Charles' father and brother Owen should 'wait on Doctors O'Reilly and Troy' then in Dublin. All their efforts came to nought when Rome eventually decided in favour of Edward Dillon, Bishop of Kilmacduagh and Kilfenora. According to O'Connor he had the support of Lord Dillon and the government.

Charles Costello had refused to accept the verdict of Archbishop O'Reilly

145 OCD. 8. 4. SH. 058
146 *Arch. Hib.*, vol. xxvii, p. 305
147 SC Irlanda, vol. 17, f. 520rv; see Fenning, *Coll. Hib.*, Nos. 36 and 37, pp. 189–91
148 OCD, 8. 4. SH. 058, 068; see Dunleavy & Dunleavy, op. cit., pp. 43, 45

Dr Charles O'Conor
(Clonalis House)

and had appealed his case to the late Archbishop Boetius Egan, but the latter's death in 1798 had retarded a decision. He now appealed directly to Rome. 'I have during the late confusion of the times for some years kept quiet, still keeping my claim alive,' he informed Cardinal Gerdil in May 1802. He was scathing about Bishop O'Connor. 'I shant now say more of him than wishing he was a more learned and better prelate.' He was now prepared to send documentation of his claim to Rome or submit it to the Archbishop of Tuam or

O'Connor's Will

any other bishop chosen by Rome. He claimed he was acting for the welfare of the parishes which 'are suffering much during this controversy'.

John Joyce wrote in July 1802 a lengthy account to Rome of a dispute with Archbishop Dillon and he cited Thomas O'Connor as a witness in his defence against the 'false accusations' made against him.[149] It is the last recorded mention of O'Connor in Rome. O'Connor became ill in November 1802 and made his will.[150] He died on 12 or 18 February 1803 and was buried as he had wished with his parents in the O'Connor burial enclosure in Tuam churchyard. He was only forty-eight years old. He was survived by two sisters, Anne Melville and Bell Donellan, and a number of nephews and nieces. His lands in Beagh, Trinebane, Silane, Woodquay and Pulnemal were divided between his two sisters on condition 'that they must absolutely take the name O'Connor'. O'Connor himself had occupied the family seat at Silane amounting to about one hundred acres. The other lands were let out to tenants. He also owned a plot in Tuam, known as the Old Pool Plott, which he left to a niece 'with all its appertinancies'. His horses, cows, sheep, hay, corn, potatoes and all his furniture and utensils were to be auctioned to pay his funeral expenses and five pounds sterling for each of his nephews and nieces to buy mourning outfits. Unusually, he named the Protestant Archbishop Beresford of Tuam as one of three executors.

Charles Lynagh (13 May 1803–1808)

Charles Lynagh's appointment to Achonry came within less than three months of O'Connor's death. He was the third Tuam priest in succession to be chosen. He had been listed third among the candidates proposed by the priests of Achonry 'merely because he stood the best chance of succeeding'. He was, however, the choice of the four archbishops who were assuming a more dominant role in the appointments of bishops. He was the favourite of his own archbishop, Edward Dillon, or his 'new creature', as the disgraced and disgruntled priest Boetius Egan described him. Dillon indeed was loud in his praise to Cardinal Borgia: 'Besides the experience, knowledge and cultured manners, what recommends him principally is the ease with which he explains the truths of religion in the Irish language which is almost the only one used by the people of this diocese.'[151] He was credited with a doctorate in civil and canon law which he must have acquired in the university of Paris as, like his predecessor, he was a former student in *Collège de Irlandais*. He became parish priest of Westport where he had recently built a new chapel and was vicar general of the archdiocese. He asked and was granted Kilmactigue as his mensal parish though, seemingly, he continued to live in his house in Westport.

149 SC Irlanda, vol. 18, ff. 33r–42v
150 *Arch. Hib.*, vol. i, pp. 227–9
151 SC Irlanda, vol. 18, f. 90r

O'Connor's death in February 1803 brought a new urgency to the Costello case, especially when Costello learned that Achonry's preferred candidate to succeed him was none other than Michael Farrell. In fact the Costello-Farrell controversy had dominated the selection process. Costello dashed off another letter to Rome urging a decision before the new bishop was appointed, adding that he sincerely hoped 'for the good of the diocese neither of the two expectants may succeed to it'. These were Farrell and Dr Charles O'Conor, the first and second choices of the Achonry clergy. He went on to recommend John O'Flynn whom the Achonry clergy specifically wished to be excluded as he was related to Costello.

The Costello affair again

In July Rome referred the controversy to Richard O'Reilly, Archbishop of Armagh. Apparently O'Reilly's original report in August 1797 never arrived or was subsequently lost in Rome.[152] By now Charles Lynagh had been appointed bishop and Costello's worst fears were not to be realised. Costello had heard of O'Reilly's unfavourable report to Rome and wrote twice in May 1804 from Edmondstown to Luke Concanen OP, the bishops' agent and his go-between with Propaganda in that city. 'I trust your court after my long patience will decree for me, and not put me to the disagreeable necessity of ascertaining my right in another manner.' This threat set alarm bells ringing and when he repeated it just over a week later he claimed that 'the incontrovertible proofs of my right of presentation are in the proper office in Dublin'. In July Concanen passed on Costello's two letters, which he had translated into Italian, to the secretary of Propaganda. 'The threat to have recourse to the civil power and non-Catholic government,' Concanen warned, 'can only be prejudicial to the bishop and religion.' He suggested that the case should be referred to the next annual meeting of the western bishops. The matter was discussed at the December general meeting of Propaganda where they followed the line set out in O'Reilly's report.[153] Their unfavourable decision was communicated to Costello in the following March.[154] He did not carry out his threat to have recourse to the civil power. However, he did eventually have some consolation. When Lynagh died in 1808, he was succeeded by none other than John O'Flynn, who proceeded to clip the wings of Farrell by imposing a curate on him with wide powers.

Lynagh made his will on 25 April 1808.[155] From this it emerged that he owned 'houses, offices and plot on the east side of the chapel of Westport' and also a park in the parish of Oughval, Co Mayo. These he divided between his nephews and nieces, children of his deceased sister, Winifred O'

Lynagh's Will

---

152 Lettere, vol. 285, ff. 388rv, 389rv
153 Acta, vol. 171, ff. 120rv, 121v
154 Lettere, vol. 289, ff. 69v, 70rv
155 *Arch. Hib.*, vol. i, pp. 230–32

Malley, and Maryanne Lynagh, the daughter of Jane Cusack and his deceased brother, James. He was also administrator of the landed property of James and as such he had granted leases to several poor people. If Maryanne or her mother broke these leases, she would be written off with the proverbial shilling. He divided his library between three Tuam priests, the parish priest of Turlow and his curate and the parish priest of Burrishoole. He left nothing to Achonry. He died shortly afterwards and was buried in Aughagour.

Meemlough Castle (Grose, *Antiquities*)

CHAPTER TWELVE

Cara sa Chúirt

'All this for Achonry!'

After Kilfenora and Kilmacduagh, Achonry was one of the smallest and poorest dioceses not only in the province but in the whole country. It was described in an internal memo in Rome as *'piccola e piutosta povera'* (small and rather poor).[1] The bishop's annual income 'scarcely yeilds twenty pounds sterling'.[2] The *Dublin Daily Post* in 1739 said of Ardagh, which was vacant and had a similar income then, that 'there are said to be as many candidates for it already as for the Archbishoprick of Toledo'.[3] What was true of Ardagh then, was true of Achonry for all of that period. Competition was keen and canvassing unremitting. In *A Man for all Seasons*, Thomas More, commenting on the perjury of Richie Rich, remarked, 'And all this for Wales!'

Postulations

Within eight days of the death of a bishop, the chapter met to elect a vicar capitular, i.e. one of the priests to rule the diocese until a successor was chosen. The chapter consisted of parish priests who were also canons. There were twelve canons in the diocese. On that occasion, or soon afterwards, they chose a candidate whom they proposed to Rome to be their new bishop. Rome was not bound to follow their advice. In fact, in Achonry it rarely did. Only once, in the case of John O'Hart, did Rome nominate the diocese's choice. He had already been passed over and had now only about three years to live. Sometimes parish priests were split on their choice of candidate and each side canvassed for support. Their petitions, called 'postulations', were signed by the individual priests and forwarded to Rome.

Lay people also played a role, though this was more common in the previous century. Fourteen lay people signed with the priests a petition in favour of Hugh MacDermot in 1683.[4] These were usually members of the leading Catholic families. Later in the century Protestant nobles occasionally also wrote to Rome on behalf of some candidate. Lord Louth wrote in 1787 on behalf of Thomas O'Connor for Achonry as he had done two years previously when Tuam was vacant.[5] Charles O'Hara of Nymphsfield was canvassed on

---

1   SOCG, vol. 844, ff. 270rv, 271rv, 272r; SC Irlanda, vol. 19, ff. 18rv, 19rv. A complete list of Bishops of Achonry during the period is given in Appendix 1.
2   CP, vol. 133, ff. 167rv, 168rv
3   *Arch. Hib.*, vol. 16, p. 60
4   CP, vol. 30, f. 242rv; see Appendix 42
5   SOCG, vol. 897, f. 516r

Lay postulation of Hugh MacDermot 1683 (Propaganda Fide, Rome)

behalf of John O'Flynn. 'Dr Flinn has long appeared to me,' he wrote, 'to be most respected amongst the R.C. clergy of this county ... I do not know anyone else amongst the candidates I could more wish to succeed.'[6]

The other bishops in the province also made recommendations. Archbishop James Lynch of Tuam recommended MacDermot in 1686. Towards the end of the century these recommendations by other bishops, and particularly by the archbishops of Armagh and Dublin, became more numerous and more influential. The Archbishop of Armagh recommended Boetius Egan in 1779.[7] Thomas Troy, Archbishop of Dublin, was a virtual king-maker and, according to Patrick Grady, parish priest of Ballymote, could 'thrust any sort of head he pleases into an Irish mitre'. Troy's voice proved decisive with Rome in the appointments of Egan, O'Connor, O'Flynn, Lynagh and McNicholas.[8]

Up to about 1770 contact was made with Rome through the internuncio in Brussels. He relayed the petitions to the congregation of Propaganda in Rome. These were then discussed at a weekly meeting between the prefect and the secretary of the congregation. As it sometimes happened, as in the case of Spinelli, nuncios in Brussels subsequently became prefects of Propaganda or, as in the case of Mgr and later Cardinal Borgia, secretaries did. They became expert on matters relating to the Irish church. Once a month a general meeting was held of the whole congregation, consisting of about nine cardinals. Normally, this meeting dealt with matters relating to other missionary countries as well. Thus it would not be unusual for the cardinals to make decisions relating to matters in Bosnia, Mesopotamia, Egypt, North America, Africa and India, as well as to make an appointment to an Irish diocese. These decisions were then submitted to the Pope for his approval. Occasionally, a special general meeting was called to deal solely with the Irish church. One such was held in the middle of the century to deal with the question of schools.

6   O'Hara Papers, Ms. 20, 280 (31)
7   SC Irlanda, vol. 4, f. 322r; CP, vol. 133, ff. 167rv, 168rv; SOCG, vol. 852, f. 285r
8   SC Irlanda, vol. 15, ff. 488rv, 491rv; vol. 18, f. 81rv; vol. 21, f. 62rv

For the monthly meeting, a memorandum was prepared, summarising all the relevant information *(ponenza)*, on which their decision would be based. The merits of each candidate were listed. These usually consisted of good morals, academic qualifications, pastoral experience and family background. In practice the latter was paramount. It was required for all the appointees to Achonry during the century. It was decisive in the case of some like Philips and O'Connor. Neither of them had university degrees in theology or law, as had MacDermot, O'Hart, Blake, Kirwan and Egan. But Philips belonged to an 'illustrious family with powerful connections *('con gran parentado')*, while O'Connor was even better endowed in this matter. This consideration weighed heavily with the cardinals. Preoccupation with social status was not unique to Ireland. It was the same elsewhere in the Catholic world, such as in France. But it was more important in Ireland, and nowhere more so than in Achonry which could only afford bishops who could support themselves. An additional advantage, frequently alluded to by the cardinals, was that such men were often related by blood to powerful local Protestant lords who could provide them, their priests, and their people with a certain measure of protection from over-zealous magistrates. Such was the case with the Butlers of Cashel and, to a lesser extent, the Costellos of Castlemore. Even as late as 1816, Bishop George Plunkett of Elphin, in his recommendation of William Costello as coadjutor of Achonry, wrote: 'In manners, appearance and address as well as by descent and birth he is a gentleman ... and these considerations must of course give peculiar weight to his pastoral exertions.'[9] The

Postulation by the clergy of Philip Philips 1758 *(San Clemente, Rome)*

9   SOCG, vol. 918, ff. 170rv, 190rv

French Revolution was to change all this, but old habits die slowly and the preoccupation with aristocracy lingered on in the church. The first commoner to be appointed in Achonry was Patrick McNicholas in 1817. He had been recommended by Archbishop Oliver Kelly of Tuam who later confessed to Rome that he was not aware at the time of McNicholas' plebeian background.

'Taking time by the forelock'

A disquieting feature in the selection of bishops was the ambition so often evident among the candidates. 'They intrigue for it,' Charles O'Conor wrote to a friend in 1769, 'they find it through the medium of intrigue and they enjoy it!' In what he called 'the scramble for the loaves and fishes', O'Conor complained that 'the place of merit is given up to intrigue (and) to favouritism'. But he was not above reproach in this matter himself. He used his cousin, Charles O'Kelly, to have Patrick Fitzsimons promoted to Dublin, as he did later for Carpenter. He acted as mentor for Boetius Egan in his bid for Achonry. In the previous century candidates like Hugh MacDermot wrote personally to Rome on their own behalf. Oliver Plunkett, then a professor in the Propaganda College, asked for no less than the primacy before he returned to Ireland.

Some candidates were already in the field and active even before the vacancy occurred. Nicholas Browne wrote from Paris in 1749 to the agent in Rome on behalf of Patrick Robert Kirwan. He enclosed a letter from Lady Blake recommending Kirwan for the first vacancy. It appeared to be Kilmacduagh where the bishop was 'drooping and on his last legs'. Kirwan was not the only one making an early move. 'The number of the candidates is great,' Browne wrote, and 'it is necessary to prevent (warn) timely those who can be of service to him.' Browne followed this with another letter a week later. There was now a better prospect on offer, Tuam itself, where Archbishop Michael O'Gara was 'attacked by the gout in the stomach and despaired of by the physicians'. He warned the agent not to mention O'Gara in his application to Propaganda on behalf of Kirwan, lest he should recover and hear about Kirwan's premature move. 'It may indispose him against our friend's interest.' The agent was asked to solicit the Cardinal of York on behalf of Kirwan. 'If Mr O'Gara goes off the stage, it is doubtless that his See will be put in for by numberless postulations of different factions.'[10] O'Gara did die shortly afterwards but despite his best efforts Kirwan failed to replace him. He had to wait almost ten years for the much lesser prize of Achonry.

Kirwan was no exception in this matter. Boetius Egan was just as quickly off the mark in his bid to succeed Kirwan in Achonry, even though the latter was not yet dead. Egan's two brothers wrote to Charles O'Conor of Belanagare on 15 March 1776 informing him that though 'Doctor Kirwan's disorder

10   SCAR, codex 1, vol. 4, 431, 432

turned to a dropcy, he may linger a little time'.[11] In fact Kirwan died six days later on 21 March. The Egans had already written to O'Conor a week earlier informing him how far Egan's campaign had advanced. John Egan had by then called on Archbishop Mark Skerret of Tuam to get his signature in favour of Boetius. They had also written to get Bishop Cheevers of Ardagh to sign. 'We know it will give you pleasure to find your friend has met with all the success that can be hoped in this climate.' O'Conor himself would not have been in the least scandalised by the indecent haste of Egan's campaign. He had already written to Boetius advising him that 'time should be taken by the forelock'. Boetius quoted this elegant phrase back to him when he wrote on 30 March. Egan was disappointed that when Skerret signed the petition he mentioned that Egan had asked him to do so. 'Yet it's not criminal,' he told O'Conor quoting St Paul in his own defence, '*qui Episcopatum desiderat bonum opus desiderat*' (he who desires a bishopric desires a good thing). His nephew had already been dispatched to Philip Philips, then Bishop of Killala, to get his support. Philips assured the nephew that in his next letter to Charles O'Kelly 'he would make mention of me in the most interesting manner'. Philips in fact proposed his own transfer from Killala to Achonry. Charles O'Kelly passed on Philip's request to Propaganda and in due course he was appointed. In spite of having 'taken time by the forelock', Egan had to wait for his prize for another nine years.

Letter of Boetius Egan *(Royal Irish Academy)*

Canvassing was by no means confined to Ireland. In 1683 Cardinal Buoncompagno of Bologna recommended Hugh MacDermot to be apostolic vicar of Achonry. MacDermot had taken his doctorate in law at the famous university in that city.[12] However, for those in search of a mitre the first port of call had to be the Stuart court in exile. In the early part of the century they were installed in the chateau of St Germain-en-laye but later moved to Rome where they occupied a *palazzo* in Piazza dei Dodici Apostoli. Though James II

Stuart Nomination

---

11 RIA Stowe Ms. B 12
12 CP, vol. 30, f. 223r

Papal tiara in Ballymote Friary (Photograph, Tom McGettrick)

had lost his crown after the treaty of Limerick, he continued to cling to the trappings of royalty which included the right to nominate Irish bishops. This Rome accorded to him and to his successors, as to other kings in Catholic countries. Realpolitik asserted itself in 1697 in France when Louis xiv recognised William as King of England but Rome and the Irish bishops continued to recognise the Stuart claims. Old loyalties continued to be fostered, particularly by Irish soldiers, many of whom served in the regiment of the Duke of Berwick, the natural son of James ii. Their sentiments were shared by many Irish priests in France, many of them their brothers and some of whom served as chaplains to the Irish regiments.

The old pretender carried out his responsibility conscientiously. Thanking His Holiness 'for granting him the full and free exercise of his right of nomination as he granted to other crowned heads', he assured him that he took on this responsibility 'not by inclination but out of a sense of duty'. He also assured Cardinal Imperiali, the cardinal-protector of Ireland, that 'to discharge his conscience, he took all possible measures to be well-informed about the sound doctrine, good morals, prudence, ability and all the other qualities required in those he nominated, giving preference always to the most worthy'. He had already ordered that 'it be constantly communicated to Ireland that postulations and authentic recommendations be forwarded to him'.[13] It was for this reason that Nicholas Browne secured for Kirwan in 1749 a recommendation 'to be brought to the attention of his majesty', signed by three of the superiors and the prefect of the community of the Irish College in Paris.[14] The superiors of the Irish college in Paris were key intermediaries in the process.[15] The 1749 recommendation was not Kirwan's first attempt to secure a mitre. Ten years earlier he had been put forward to succeed Bernard O'Gara in Tuam. George Waters, an Irish banker in Paris, wrote to Edgar, the Stuart secretary: 'I have heard two worthy honest men speak much in favour of Mr Kirwan in whose favour a postulation has been sent recommending him to the vacant archbishopric of Tuam.' Edgar replied

13 n.d. CP, vol. 34B (1713–14), f. 157r
14 SCAR, codex 1, vol. 4, 433
15 Andrew Donlevy wrote in 1726 to Dan O'Brien warning against a candidate for Cork: 'Tis not, Sir, that I fear the King, who has but the good and satisfaction of his people in view, will have any regard for this postulation.' Stuart Papers, vol. 96, no. 67

that there were several competitors and that 'his majesty will give his nomination to the person he thinks most deserving and who he judges most conducive to the good of the Mission.'[16] That person on this occasion was Michael O'Gara. Besides his impressive academic and moral qualifications, Kirwan had impeccable Jacobite credentials. His paternal uncle, John, had been governor of Galway city and played a leading role in the Jacobite war in Ireland, something underlined in the recommendation signed by the canons, clergy and knights of Tuam. It was also signed by Walter Blake of Achonry and his secretary, Patrick Henican, together with the bishops of Clonfert, Kilmacduagh and Killala.[17]

A constant trickle of soldiers and priests like Andrew Donlevy, made their way to St Germain-en-laye on various errands, seeking mostly either commissions in the army or benefices in the church. Many of them, like Chevalier Terence MacDermot and Colonel Oliver O'Gara, took up residency there. A Tuam priest, David Flynn, was chaplain in the chateau and performed many of the Irish baptisms in the neighbourhood. He also played a role in Stuart nominations. In 1750 he wrote to Edgar complimenting him on 'having made the proper use of their recommendation in favour of Doctor Kirwan'.[18] Philips was the last Achonry bishop so nominated. The last of the Stuarts became a priest and later Cardinal Duke of York.

The large and influential Irish network of priests and soldiers and other *émigrés* on the continent were also active, sometimes on behalf of family members. One of the most influential was Owen O'Rorke, Stuart ambassador at the imperial court in Vienna from 1727 until his death there in 1742. His relatives in Ireland kept him informed of vacancies in dioceses there and proposed suitable candidates, usually from their own family.[19] Hugh O'Donnell, a descendant of the Earls of Tyrconnell and a relative of O'Rorke's, proposed a Franciscan friar, O'Donnell, to fill the vacancy in Achonry caused by the death of John O'Hart in May 1739. 'I beg you'll use your most efficacious means with our Master to have this worthy man preferred to the said See of Achonry.' The friar had 'become somewhat unweildy, being 64 years of age' but his family at least thought 'that he should be promoted to some little government becoming his old age and great abilities'. The ambassador in Vienna was not successful on this occasion. However, he did succeed in having a cousin, Brian O'Rorke, appointed Bishop of Killala that same year. 'Doctor O'Rorke had an account from Rome that his match was made with the

Irish Network

---

16 Stuart Papers, vol. 223, no. 24; vol. 224, no. 28
17 SCAR, codex 1. 4. no. 426
18 Stuart Papers, vol. 310, no. 137
19 de Breffny, 'Letters from Connaught to a Wild Goose', in *Irish Ancestor*, x, pp. 90–91, 94; the writers employ a code referring to the Stuart Pretender as 'our Master' or 'head landlord', a diocese as a 'farm' and a vacant diocese as a 'widow'.

Widow Killala,' Hugh O'Donnell informed the ambassador in May 1739. Later the bishop himself acknowledged the ambassador's contribution. 'I had the honour of writing to you in September last after I got peaceable possession of the farm of Killala, giving you thanks for the great trouble you have taken and the industry you have used with the head landlord in procuring said farm.' The bishop added that 'Mr Blake would (have) obtained, were it not for your good interest with the landlord.' Walter Blake was nominated to Achonry by James Edward in 1739.[20]

Appointment of Philips, 1776

Irish officers in European armies were thought to have a substantial clout in these appointments. Count Dalton, a general in the imperial service and a member of the council of state of their imperial majesties, secured the support of the Empress of Austria in 1776 in favour of his brother, Thomas, for promotion to Achonry. Thomas was a Dominican and at that time chaplain to a convent in Dublin. There appears to have been a Dalton connection with the diocese. 'General Dalton has sent for two of Mrs Dalton's sons,' Bishop Philips wrote to Charles O'Kelly in 1771.[21] Be that as it may, the general left no stone unturned in advancing his brother, the friar. The Empress instructed her grand chancellor, Prince Kaunitz, to convey her wishes to Rome. He wrote to the Secretary of State, Cardinal Allessandro Albani, who 'on the express orders of her imperial majesty' passed on the request to Propaganda. Another soldier, General Plunkett, who was governor of Antwerp and related to Dalton, also weighed in.[22] With such august supporters, it is difficult to imagine how Dalton could have lost in his bid for Achonry. He had failed on a previous attempt for Kerry. In fact, his name was put forward for no less than eight Irish dioceses without success.

This time there were other important players on the field. When sending on Dalton's impressive dossier, the nuncio in Brussels included another one for Edmund O'Ryan. The latter was chaplain to the bodyguards of his most Catholic majesty in Madrid and he had the support of the Infanta of Spain. Another candidate appeared literally out of nowhere. Cardinal de Bernis, the French ambassador to the Holy See, asked the secretary of Propaganda, Mgr Borgia, to propose to the Pope one Mark Parlan, the royal professor of theology at the university of Caen. He had the backing of the Bishop of Bayeux and Cardinal de Rochechouart.[23]

It would appear that Boetius Egan was pursuing a lost cause but he also had some aces to play. His uncle, Chevalier Egan, after long service as a captain in Berwick's regiment in France, passed into the Spanish service with Berwick's son, Duc de Lyria. A cousin of Boetius, Don Demetrio MacEgan,

20 Stuart Papers, vol. 217, no. 68
21 SCAR, codex 1, vol. 4, 474
22 SOCG, vol. 844, f. 276rv
23 SC Irlanda, vol. 12, ff. 399rv, 400r

was a colonel in the Spanish service and at that time governor of the vast province of Peru. His brother, also a colonel, was chief engineer in the service of Naples. As one correspondent to the nuncio in Brussels put it: 'The house of Bourbon is indebted for the services of the distinguished family' of Egan.[24]

By now, the courts of Vienna, Paris and Madrid, not to mention the Chancellor of Austria and the Prime Minister of France, with the nuncios in Paris, Brussels and Vienna, and Cardinals de Bernis and de Rochchechouart, the Archbishop of Bordeaux, and the Bishop of Bayeux, were all involved. And all this for Achonry! As Ignazio Busca, the nuncio in Brussels, explained to Mr FitzHerbert, the English ambassador there in 1782, 'the ambitious clergy of Ireland plot in the oddest ways to obtain bishoprics and, to the great scandal of religion and the wonderment of good-thinking people, do not hesitate to make use of all the courts of Europe to obtain their ends.'[25] To its credit, Rome was not unduly impressed by all this name-dropping. Its short-list included six candidates in all. In addition to Dalton, Egan and O'Ryan, there was also the dean of Elphin, Alexander Irwin, and John Joyce, the warden of Galway. Irwin had the support of his own bishop. John Joyce, a native of the diocese, was recommended by Tuam and Kilmacduagh. He seemed to have retained at least a titular connection with the diocese. Kilmacduagh described him as former vicar general of Achonry and Tuam said that he was its archdeacon.[26]

The choice of the Achonry priests, John Fitzmaurice, parish priest of Ballisodare, was not included on this final list. Eighteen priests of the diocese had signed a petition in his favour.[27] It was dated 3 May 1776 and too late for presentation, as was mentioned in a note a few years later.[28] The same probably happened to the recommendation of another Dominican, Edmund Fitzgerald, by Killala and Dublin, which was dated even later in May.[29] They had ignored O'Conor's golden rule to 'take time by the forelock'. Mark Parlan's candidacy was dated three days after the result was announced. Rome made its decision on 10 June, apparently based solely on pastoral reasons. The cardinals were worried by the non-residency of certain bishops in Ireland and, particularly, in Achonry. They decided to transfer Philips back to his native diocese and appointed Irwin to replace him in Killala.[30]

But all these efforts on behalf of Egan were not lost. They were put on file until the next suitable vacancy occurred. Meanwhile, his friends continued

Egan's Appointment, 1785

24 SC Irlanda, vol. 15, ff. 51rv, 55rv, 56r
25 ASV, Nunz. di Fiandra, vol. 135, ff. 30r–32v; see Giblin, *Coll. Hib.*, 11, pp. 70–72
26 SOCG, vol. 844, f. 273rv
27 ibid, f. 267r
28 SOCG, vol. 852, f. 155r
29 ibid, vol. 844, f. 268r
30 Acta, vol. 146, ff. 93v–95r

their campaign. O'Conor wrote to Archbishop Carpenter in 1781, thanking him for his recommendation of Egan. 'He is a worthy man, and will undoubtedly answer your description of him in whatever station of dignity he is placed.'[31] Count O'Kelly, French ambassador to the Elector of Mainz, took a personal interest in seeing 'Egan's elevation to that order he is so worthy to occupy'. He wrote to the nuncio in Paris later that year to add his recommendation to that of Comte de Vergennes. The latter was then French primeminister. O'Kelly suggested that de Vergennes should urge Cardinal de Bernis, French ambassador to the Holy See, to use his influence with the cardinals of Propaganda to promote Egan to the first vacant diocese or coadjutorship in Munster or Connacht.[32] Egan was recommended in 1784 as coadjutor to Andrew Donnellan, the elderly Bishop of Clonfert, by the French Prime Minister, the Archbishop of Bordeaux and three of the Irish archbishops.[33] Meanwhile, Philips was being suggested as coadjutor to the ailing Mark Skerret of Tuam.[34] Skerret died in 1785 and the Tuam canons asked for Philips as his successor. He was also recommended by Troy and the four Irish religious superiors.[35] Philips packed his bags once more, this time for Tuam. Egan's hour had finally come and Achonry was his prize. On 2 October 1785 he was informed of his appointment, one day after Philips was sent a similar notification.[36]

Irish Agents

There were in Rome other key figures in the making of bishops – priests living in one or other of the Irish colleges in that city, who represented the Irish bishops at the Vatican. For much of the eighteenth century this role was played by a Dominican living either at the Minerva or at their own college of San Clemente. Charles O'Kelly from Roscommon occupied this post for a considerable period and two of his successors, Luke Concanen and John Connolly, later became bishops themselves, succeeding each other in New York. O'Kelly was a cousin of Charles O'Conor of Belanagare which explains why the latter was courted by prospective candidates like Boetius Egan.[37]

Valentine Bodkin

For some reason the western bishops appointed Valentine Bodkin, a diocesan priest from Galway, as their own agent in Rome. Boetius Egan referred to him in 1786 as *agens meus in Curia* (my agent in the Vatican). Bodkin had been a student in the Irish College in Rome, having registered there just two years ahead of Thomas Costello. He was a colourful character and

31 Ward, Wrynn, Ward, op. cit., p. 401
32 SC Irlanda, vol. 15, ff. 51rv, 55rv, 56r
33 SC Irlanda, vol. 15, ff. 259r, 260rv, 261rv
34 ibid, f. 482r
35 ibid, vol. 16, ff. 94rv, 96r; ASV, Fondo Missioni, 117
36 Lettere, vol. 246, (1785), ff. 674rv, 678rv, 679rv
37 O'Conor was even requested in 1786 to write to O'Kelly in favour of Troy's translation from Ossory to Dublin but he had already written in favour of another. Ward, Wrynn, Ward, op. cit., p. 479

his comments on the various candidates were refreshingly frank, if somewhat partisan. His first opportunity to exercise his peculiar talent came in 1786 when Elphin became vacant. Egan's old mentors, Count O'Kelly of Mainz and Cardinal de Bernis, were back in action once more on his behalf. They recommended him for Elphin, as did the Archbishop of Armagh and Troy of Ossory. Bodkin made the same suggestion in a letter to Cardinal Antonelli.[38] The ageing Philips died in September 1787 and the focus switched to the bigger prize. Egan was chosen by the Tuam canons as a candidate together with Thomas O'Connor.[39] Bodkin of course championed Egan for the post.

However, in a lengthy submission to Cardinal Antonelli, he was scathing in his remarks on O'Connor.[40] He claimed he knew him personally and fairly well from a tender age. They had even exchanged letters. Bodkin had passed through Paris in December 1780 when O'Connor was beginning his second year of theology in the Irish college there. He described him as a person of 'mediocre talent which his very brief course of studies could do nothing to supplement'. O'Connor's letters bear this out, as do his colleagues who studied with him in Paris. 'It seemed to me,' Bodkin reflected, 'that he started too soon seeking a mitre.'

Old Irish College, Rome
(Photograph, Liam Swords)

> This priest O'Connor was not five years on the mission and scarcely disembarked, when he began to hunt for a bishopric, cajoling and persuading laity and Protestants to recommend him to bishops and those who can and do persuade your Eminence and the sacred congregation, in order to be promoted and become a bishop. He is parish priest of Ballinrobe and has never resided in his parish according to canon law but lives and resides in Tuam, twenty-five miles away from his own parish under the pretext of being required there and not in his own parish.

Bodkin next turned his attention to O'Connor's father.

> He is the son of a Protestant and not one (born) as such, but of a perverted Catholic, who continues to live in the error he embraced. His father was a pleasure-seeking spendthrift who, having squandered a fine fortune, con-

---

38 SOCG, vol. 875, ff. 10rv, 23, 31rv, 32r, 33rv, 42rv; SC Irlanda, vol. 16, f. 307rv
39 SOCG, vol. 877, ff. 507r, 509rv, 510rv
40 SC Irlanda, vol. 16, ff. 308v, 309rv, 310r

sisting of lands, defrauded certain of his closest friends of thirty-six thousand *scudi* which they lent him in good faith on good security when he assured them that he had not already mortgaged his properties. This parent is now in hiding to avoid arrest and spending the rest of his days in prison.

O'Connor enjoyed the patronage of Lord Louth, a Protestant whom Bodkin accused of having 'contributed more than anybody else to the perversion' of O'Connor's father. More recently, he 'caused the perversion' of two of Bodkin's nephews which probably accounts for the bitterness of Bodkin's attack. 'Such therefore is Mylord who recommends a subject for a Catholic bishopric. A layman, a Protestant of such a type that he is rather an atheist, a deist and a missionary of Lucifer, than a friend of ours and our holy faith.'

Irish College, Paris

This was a devastating indictment of O'Connor and at first sight scarcely seems credible. Obviously, Bodkin's outburst was provoked by the defection of his two nephews. However, it does contain some truths and these are verifiable. O'Connor followed the ordinary course of studies in Paris. He certainly never graduated in the university there. More seriously and more surprisingly, his father, Dermot, did in fact conform to the Established Church in 1758.[41] The allegations that Dermot was a spendthrift, a debtor and a swindler on the run from the law seem, to say the least, gross exaggerations. In any case, Thomas was still in possession of a not inconsiderable amount of property at the time of his death, though it may have been only a portion of the original family estate. Lord Louth's two letters to Charles O'Kelly in favour of Thomas O'Connor are documented elsewhere. His role in the change of religion of Thomas' father, or others, is not verifiable now but it was scarcely in Bodkin's interest to admit in Rome the defection of two members of his own family. Thomas' non-residency in his parish of Ballinrobe was not that unusual, at least among Tuam priests. The parish priest of Dunmore had lived for fifteen years in the house of a gentleman miles away, while he paid a friar twenty

41 *The Convert Rolls*, p. 220

pounds a year to run his parish. Besides, O'Connor's non-residency as a parish priest tallies with his subsequent history as a bishop.

Bodkin himself had just returned to Rome fresh from a stint as parish priest in Galway city. Galway was the centre of a network of old wealthy Catholic families, like the Blakes, Kirwans, Frenchs, O'Dalys etc., and indeed Bodkins also. They had a virtual monopoly over episcopal appointments in the western province. The information he gave Antonelli would have been current parlour-talk among these families. It was rare for Rome to get such information from the horse's mouth. Bodkin was also Roman-trained and familiar with its ways. His memorandum was actually written in Italian. He was to end his career in the quasi-episcopal position of warden of Galway. But Roman bureaucracy was not accustomed to such bluntness. They were more discreet in their observations, more measured in their language, and much shorter in their submissions. Above all, they had a built-in suspicion of outspokenness and were also well used to Irish calumnies.

Others, however, extolled the virtues of O'Connor and they were people of considerably higher standing then in the church than Bodkin. When Elphin became vacant Troy, now Archbishop of Dublin, recommended both John O'Flynn and O'Connor to fill the vacancy.[42] O'Connor had been made dean of the archdiocese almost immediately after his arrival home from Paris. When Mark Skerret died in 1784, the Tuam canons elected him vicar capitular, as they did again three years later when Philips died.[43] Edmund French, who had become Bishop of Elphin, stated that O'Connor carried out this function with such distinction that 'the chapter had a public document drawn up as a testimonial to him'. French, who had been his fellow-student in Paris, said of him: 'For piety, zeal, nobilty of birth, and favour among the great, he has no equal. He renounced a large patrimony to serve the church.' French also mentioned that he had been recommended by Lord Louth, 'his kinsman and very worthy friend'. Charles O'Kelly, the chief representative of the bishops in Rome, who was in a position to refute Bodkin's allegations, recommended O'Connor 'as a subject of illustrious birth, exemplary life and endowed with rare talents and an outstanding preacher'.[44]

Thomas Costello's rise was only slightly less meteoric than O'Connor's. Soon after his return to the diocese from Rome he was made vicar general by Bishop Philips who also recommended him for a bishopric.[45] When Killala became vacant he was not only sought by the Killala canons but also recommended by the bishops of Kilmacduagh and Elphin, as well as Philips.[46]

Thomas Costello's appointment to Clonfert, 1786

42 SC Irlanda, vol. 16, ff. 228rv, 235rv
43 ibid, f. 96r
44 Acta, vol. 157, ff. 520rv, 521r
45 SC Irlanda, vol. 12, f. 358r
46 SOCG, vol. 852, ff. 153r, 154r

Archbishop Troy
(National Library of Ireland)

However, it was given to Dominick Bellew from Drogheda directly by the Pope himself. Andrew Donnellan of Clonfert was very old and badly in need of a coadjutor. Costello was suggested for the post.

Like O'Connor, he was the subject of some strong criticism from Bodkin.[47] Bodkin had been a fellow-student of Costello's in via degli Ibernesi, just two years his junior. His animosity towards Costello may have dated from then. Bodkin thought him 'very incapable of governing a diocese' and stated that it was 'well-known and notorious in all the diocese that he never bothered, even though vicar general, to defend or argue any of the cases of conscience or polemics at the customary conferences held in the diocese'. He also added 'that during the space of so many years, he never opened his mouth to instruct the young or the flock committed to his care'. Bodkin grudgingly admitted that he was not unlearned 'but that he was not a subject of high merit or elevated talent or worthy to be promoted to a vacant diocese in opposition to so many others of greater merit who abound in the province,

47 SC Irlanda, vol. 15, f. 471rv

more distinguished by birth, by pastoral zeal and rarity of talent'. His criticism followed a familiar pattern. 'Furthermore, Costello is the son of a man who keeps a country inn and sells beer on the public street.' He acknowledged that Costello came from a good family but that it 'had been much degraded by the profession of his father.' He explained the warm recommendations Costello received from both Philips and Fallon of Elphin as due to the fact that he was related to them on his mother's side, and especially to Fallon. Intermarriage between wealthy Catholic families was normal and if a certain nepotism resulted, it was not dissimilar to practices elsewhere in the Catholic world and in Rome itself.

While Bodkin was devastating in his criticism of the two cases just cited, he was not sparing in his praises of others. He described Bishop Kirwan (1758–76) as a 'prelate of such outstanding merit ... that he would have adorned any diocese in Europe by his impeccable manners, his great zeal and his knowledge of theology, canon law and indeed literature'. Bodkin may have found it easier to extol the virtues of the dead, but he was also generous in his praise of the living. Although he described Philips as a 'a toothless, goutish septuagenarian', unsuitable for Tuam because of his age, he did concede that he was 'of distinguished birth, pious and exemplary'. Of course, he extolled Boetius Egan, then Bishop of Achonry, whose agent he was.[48]

John Fitzmaurice

It would appear that Bodkin was a man much given to hyperbole. He waxed eloquently and at length on the merits of John Fitzmaurice whom he strongly recommended for Tuam in 1787. He also provided interesting biographical information on Fitzmaurice. After taking his doctorate at the Sorbonne, he taught in the Irish College where he was prefect of studies for seven years. Sixteen years ago (i.e. c. 1761), he returned home against the advice of his friends and 'the inclination of the Archbishop of Sens who wished to have him with him and offered to provide him with a good benefice'. However, he was called back by Bishop Kirwan to reside in Achonry 'where there was a scarcity of good men'. He went there with the permission of the Archbishop of Tuam, to whose diocese he belonged, and became vicar general for about ten years under Kirwan. When Kirwan died Fitzmaurice was elected vicar capitular and unanimously chosen by the chapter and entire clergy to be their next bishop. (In fact, there were four dissenting voices, including Costello's.) Their postulation arrived in Rome too late. Philips was chosen and picked his relative, Costello, as his vicar general.

Fitzmaurice became a simple vicar forane, i.e. he presided over one of four regional conferences of priests held monthly during the summer.

He was the most learned in all the diocese, more pious, prudent and zealous and more capable of teaching than anyone in the said diocese, and of

---

48 SC Irlanda, vol. 15, ff. 471v, 478rv

occupying any chair whatsoever in dogmatic or scholastic theology. This is an indubitable and incontrovertible fact. No man is as foreign to ambition as is Fitzmaurice and as much as he is learned, he is humble and meek and far removed from Parisian or Florentine intrigue.

Fitzmaurice was then fifty-two years old and indefatigable as a confessor, preacher and teacher. He was responsible for converting many Protestants. Bodkin even cited names, e.g. John George Brabazon, who was related to Lord Lucan and Sir Joshua Crofton. The latter were favourably disposed to Catholics and recently gave some parish priests 'for a bagatelle' small parcels of land to build parochial chapels and presbyteries with gardens attached.[49]

Neither Bodkin's lengthy diatribes or fulsome praises made any impact on the Roman authorities. Costello was appointed in 1786 coadjutor in Clonfert with the right of succession.[50] The fate of Tuam dragged on until the end of the following year. Rome's decision in December 1787 was a virtual replay of the musical chairs type they made some ten years previously. Egan was transferred to Tuam and replaced by O'Connor in Achonry.[51]

Lynagh's Appointment, 1803

When O'Connor died in 1803, the stage was set for a new contest for Achonry. By now a new system for the election of bishops was in operation. Proposed initially by the Irish bishops, Rome at first was reluctant to adopt it. Under this system the clergy of the diocese and the bishops would choose three candidates (known in Latin as a *terna*) to present to the Pope. He would then appoint one of the three. As early as 1782 Ignazio Busca, the nuncio in Brussels, submitted a memorandum on the proposed change to Mr FitzHerbert, the English ambassador there, asking him to intervene with the king to prevent any change from the old system where the clergy recommended only one candidate. 'The new system would give rise to intrigues, factions and manouvres of the lowest type.'[52] His forecast was to prove prophetic, at least in the case of Achonry. Despite Roman misgivings, the system was in fact adopted.

On 24 February 1803, within a week of O'Connor's death, the Achonry canons met, elected the dean, Mark Rush, as vicar capitular and chose three candidates to fill the vacancy, Michael Farrell, Dr Charles O'Conor and

---

49 Bodkin also stated that Fitzmaurice was a distant relative of Baron Blaise Lynch MP. Bodkin claimed that he was present among others at Kirwan's death-bed in county Galway. 'In that awesome moment,' after receiving the last sacraments of the church, Kirwan declared, 'that he knew of no better man, no one more learned, more zealous or more worthy of promotion than his vicar general, Fitzmaurice and that he was sorry to be so close to death only because he could no longer recommend him to the sacred congregation.' ibid, f. 478rv
50 Acta, vol. 156, ff. 149r–151r; SOCG, vol. 873, ff. 9rv, 10rv; Lettere, vol. 249, ff. 52rv, 71r, 478v, 479r
51 Acta, vol. 157, ff. 520v, 521rv; Lettere, vol. 250, ff. 791rv, 792r
52 ASV, Nunz. di Fiandra, vol. 135, ff. 30r–32v; see Giblin, *Coll. Hib.*, 11, pp. 70–72

Castlemore (Grose, *Antiquities*)

Charles Lynagh, parish priest of Westport.[53] Only Farrell was an Achonry priest. He was then archdeacon of the diocese and parish priest of Ballaghaderreen (Kilcolman and Castlemore). He had been appointed there by the late bishop, much to the displeasure of the local landlord, Charles Costello, who claimed the right of patronage to this parish. Farrell's robust opposition to Costello had made him, in the eyes of the clergy, something of a white knight. 'In addition to his other fine qualities outlined in the recommendation,' John Connolly OP informed Cardinal Borgia, 'he is cherished by the whole diocese for the firmness with which he has always opposed the Protestant, Charles Costello.'[54]

The meeting of the chapter was overshadowed by Charles Costello and his claims. The canons took the almost unprecedented step of demanding that Rome exclude two candidates from the race. 'We refuse and will refuse the Bishop of Clonfert, Thomas Costello, who always supported in writing and in deed the pretended right of patronage of his cousin, Charles.' With equal vehemence they rejected also John O'Flynn, parish priest of Sligo and dean and vicar general of Elphin, who was also a cousin of Charles. O'Flynn was strongly recommended by Bishop Edmund French and had also the support of Dublin and Armagh as well as the bishops of Meath and Cork.[55] He had been a favourite also of French's predecessor, Fallon, who sought him as coadjutor and successor, and was recommended in 1786 for Elphin by the canons and clergy there. The following year he was in the running for Tuam after Philip's death.[56] O'Flynn's name had circulated for some time in Roman corridors.

The Achonry canons had proposed two other candidates but it is clear that this was done merely to comply with the regulations. Dr Charles O'Conor

53 SC Irlanda, vol. 18, ff. 104rv, 105rv
54 ibid, f. 96rv
55 ibid, f. 108v
56 SC Irlanda, vol. 16, f. 129r; SOCG, vol. 875, ff. 10rv, 18v, 19r, 21v, 22r, 24rv; Acta, vol. 157, ff. 1v, 2rv, 520v, 521rv

Dr Charles
O'Conor
(Clonalis House)

was proposed in second place. He was the grandson of the famous Charles O'Conor of Belanagare and parish priest of Castlerea. An honorary canon of Achonry, he was then a rising star with impeccable credentials and it appeared he would not have long to wait for promotion. He had kept up a lively correspondence with Propaganda, keeping them informed of political developments in Ireland as well as keeping his own name to the fore. He regarded himself as sort of papal ambassador. However, it was only a matter of time before he came in conflict with his bishop who, among other things, resented the O'Conor patronage of Castlerea. O'Conor later claimed that his dispute with the bishop originated from O'Conor turning away the bishop's brother from the altar because he got another man involved as a second in a duel.[57]

O'Conor soon tired of his rural retreat. He left it in the charge of his curate, with a new chapel uncompleted and considerable debts, and secured a place for himself as chaplain to the Marchionness of Buckingham and went to live in Stowe. The Marquis of Buckingham became Lord Lieutenant of Ireland in 1782. His wife, Mary Nugent, had secretly become a Catholic when she was fourteen. When they returned to England they became involved in helping French *émigrés* and some French priests stayed in their home at Stowe. They had an impressive library which was greatly enhanced with O'Conor's arrival with his grandfather's manuscripts. O'Conor spent his time here translating the manuscripts in order to write a history of Ireland. He went out occasionally to do research at the Bodlean Library in Oxford or the British Museum. He wrote in 1800 to his cousin, Charles MacDermot of Coolavin, that he had no intention of returning but two years later had second thoughts. He told MacDermot that he once thought it 'a grand affair to live amongst the great' but that he was now 'cured'. MacDermot had no sympathy for him and had lacerated him for being 'Buckinghamised and desecrating grandfather's memory'.[58] The vacancy in Achonry in 1803 considerably whetted his interest in returning. He gave MacDermot specific instructions for drawing up a petition on his behalf for Achonry.[59]

Troy had written to Rome on 26 February commenting on the candidates. He described O'Conor as 'a canon of the cathedral of Achonry and a man of letters'.[60] O'Conor's own bishop, French, wrote to Luke Concanen, urging him to communicate to Propaganda his total opposition to O'Conor's nomination.[61] Concanen duly passed on the information to Mgr Coppola,

57 Dunleavy & Dunleavy, op. cit., p. 103
58 ibid, pp. 78,102, 103
59 ibid, p. 103
60 SC Irlanda, vol. 18, f. 81rv
61 ibid, f. 108r

the secretary of Propaganda. Rome had written to John Douglas, the apostolic vicar in London, for an account of O'Conor's activities there. He replied that he was at Stowe where 'his presence is valuable'.[62]

Achonry's first choice, Michael Farrell, received no backing elsewhere and the race by now was between O'Conor and Charles Lynagh. Charles Lynagh was parish priest of Westport where he built a new chapel in 1797. He was also vicar general of the diocese. He had been a student in Collége des Irlandais in Paris where he received the diaconate in 1771. The following year he was in the seminary of St Nicolas-du-Chardonnet where Irish students spent their final year. He must have stayed on in Paris for some years as the four archbishops described him as a 'doctor of canon and civil law'.[63] Lynagh was now supported by the four archbishops and was preferred to O'Conor by the other bishops of the province.[64] Once more ignoring the wishes of the Achonry clergy, Rome appointed Lynagh who did nothing to smooth their ruffled feathers. In his first address to his clergy he 'assured them it was by no means to them he felt indebted for his appointment'.[65]

Eighteenth-century Pectoral Cross (St Nathy's, Ballaghaderreen)

One other candidate made a late appearance on the horizon. Thomas Costello, parish priest of Glinsk in Elphin and nephew and namesake of the Bishop of Clonfert, was recommended by Bartholomew Crotty, rector of St Patrick's College in Lisbon. The recommendation was also signed by a Portuguese nobleman, two Killala priests called Kelly, and Bernard MacDermot of Elphin.[66] Costello had studied in the university of Salamanca where he had taken a doctorate in theology and later spent three years in Lisbon before returning home. However, by the time his candidature arrived in Rome, the contest had already been decided. The Portuguese nuncio and Prince Augusto Federico made another attempt later that year on behalf of Costello, this time for Waterford. Costello was then described as 'an intimate friend of General Humbert, one of the principal revolutionaries of Ireland', which was scarcely likely to improve his prospects in Rome.[67]

The man Rome chose to succeed Lynagh in 1809 was none other than John O'Flynn, whom the Achonry canons had vigorously rejected in 1803.[68]

O'Flynn's appointment, 1809

62 ibid, ff. 94rv, 95rv
63 Udienze, vol. 41, f. 256rv
64 Udienze, vol. 41, ff. 254rv, 255rv
65 SC Irlanda, vol. 20, f. 234r
66 SOCG, vol. 910, f. 523r
67 SOCG, vol. 910, ff. 511r, 512rv, 523r; Acta, vol. 170, ff. 426rv, 427r
68 The other candidates on this occasion are not known as the relevant volumes are missing from the Roman archives. When the Napoleonic army occupied Rome, they seized the papal archives and transported it elsewhere. Some of these documents were subsequently returned from Vienna and are since known as Fondo di Vienna but the volumes relevant to O'Flynn's appointment remain missing.

O'Flynn had finally made it. It was twenty-three years since he was first recommended to Rome, on that occasion for his own diocese of Elphin. He had been a contemporary of Lynagh's in Collége des Irlandais in Paris and attended the university where he received an MA in 1772. At that time he was in minor orders.[69] After his return home he became parish priest of St John's in Sligo and later dean and vicar general of the diocese. He was highly regarded in Sligo, particularly among Protestants, even though that town had a reputation for bigotry. Five years earlier, when he had been proposed by the Elphin canons as coadjutor for his elderly bishop, Charles O'Conor of Belanagare wrote: 'He is certainly a learned gentleman whose zeal and knowledge are recommended in a town of Presbyterians, whose virulence is so far abated as to permit Mr Flyn erect a chapel in that town, one of the best at present in this kingdom.'[70]

Dr Charles O'Conor may well have been a candidate again on this occasion. Immersed in his library in Stowe in the summer of 1808, O'Conor, now in his forty-sixth year, reviewed his life. He decided he would seek no further advancement. But six months later, he was becoming nostalgic for home. Not surprisingly, his nostalgia coincided with the new contest for Achonry. Later that year he wrote to his brother Owen to ask whether the Catholic gentry and clergy and some of the chief Protestants might be canvassed to send a postulation in his favour to Troy of Dublin and O'Reilly of Armagh. His old enemy, Edmund French, congratulated Luke Concanen in Rome on O'Flynn's appointment. 'The appointment of Dr Flynn to Achonry entitles you to no small share of the merit', and 'by that act, you have, I may say, rescued that portion of Christ's flock from the jaws of a wolf'.[71] But O'Conor had not thrown in the towel yet. When French himself died, O'Conor wrote several times about his possible nomination for Elphin.[72] By now his published works, 'crammed with every type of convicton against the Apostolic See', put his promotion out of the question. Daniel Murray, coadjutor Archbishop of Dublin, informed Rome: 'This is the judgement of all the bishops of Ireland, that the Catholic religion would suffer the maximum damage if he were raised to the episcopal order.'[73]

---

69 Brockliss & Ferté, op. cit., no. 1142; Patrick Boyle, *The Irish College in Paris*, p. 200
70 Ward, Wrynn & Ward, op. cit.
71 SC Irlanda, vol. 18, f. 514r
72 ODC. 9.1. SH. 150; 9.1. HL. 017; 9.1. HS. 027; 9. 1. SE. 182; see Donleavy & Dunleavy, op. cit. pp. 78, 79
73 SC Irlanda, vol. 18, f. 575v

CHAPTER THIRTEEN

Deireadh Ré
The Last Straw

John O'Flynn, parish priest of St John's, was consecrated on 12 November 1809 in the chapel he himself had built in Sligo.¹ His selection must have been greeted with foreboding by many of the Achonry clergy who had expressly demanded his exclusion six years earlier. Michael Farrell, archdeacon of the diocese, who had spearheaded the opposition in Ballaghaderreen to his cousin, Charles Costello, had more reason than others to be worried by O'Flynn's appointment. His worst fears were soon realised. O'Flynn removed his curate and imposed a new one with the power of dispensing from marriage banns. Farrell was thus deprived of the marriage dues 'as well as every other emolument he (the curate) can lay hold of'. He sought redress from Rome. 'After being twenty-seven years on the mission and twenty-two years parish priest,' he complained, 'I should now, only for the assistance of friends, see myself reduced to want the common necessities of life.'²

Bishop John O'Flynn (1809–17)

At least one other priest in the diocese, Patrick Grady, parish priest of Ballymote (Emlefad and Kilmorgan), made no pretence about his opposition to O'Flynn. In his pamphlet, *The Radical Anti-Veto*, published in Dublin in 1814, he strongly criticised O'Flynn. Grady's comments were later described as 'the most base and scurrilous libel'.³ He accused the bishop of appropriating the money paid for the dispensation of marriage banns which he 'metamorphosed into bishop's dues'. Other dispensation money, hitherto applied to charitable purposes, such as to build and repair chapels and to support the poor, was now used to support 'the poor Bishop'.⁴ Grady alleged that the bishop was so deeply in debt that he had to 'reside at the mearing of the county, the better to avoid meeting with the Sheriff', (O'Flynn had taken up residence in Kilfree), and that he was 'the grandson of a woman notoriously and memorably infamous'. He had ordained an unsuitable candidate because he owed his father the price of a horse and had no other alternative but to ordain him whether the candidate was 'a Bossuet or a broom-stick'.⁵

Patrick Grady

1 *Connaught Journal,* 13 November 1809, quoted in O'Rorke, *Sligo,* vol. 2, p. 111n
2 SC Irlanda, vol. 19, ff. 116rv, 117rv; see OCD, 9. 1. LS 205
3 SC Irlanda, vol. 20, f. 205v
4 *The Radical Anti-Veto,* pp. 11–12
5 op. cit., pp. 50–51

The Radical Anti-Veto (Russell Library, Maynooth)

FIRST NUMBER.

THE

Radical Anti-Veto,

IN WHICH IT IS PROVED TO A DEMONSTRATION,
THAT THE MISMANAGEMENT OF CATHOLIC BISHOPS,
IN THE MATTER OF THE

VETO,

ESPECIALLY OF THE MOST REV. DR. TROY,

Has proved a Serious and Positive Obstacle to the

EMANCIPATION OF CATHOLICS.

DR. MILNER'S AGENCY UNDER THE IRISH PRELATES;

As also his and the Catholics of England's Case are relatively considered.

IT IS PROVED, THAT NEITHER
PREFECT QUARANTOTTI, THE POPE, OR THE CHURCH,
ARE COMPETENT TO GRANT A VETO TO AN ACATHOLIC GOVERNMENT;

IT IS ALSO PROVED, THAT A

VETO

Ought not to be Granted to any Lay Power.

SOME APPROPRIATE OBSERVATIONS

ARE MADE ON

Catholic Aggregate Meetings and the Catholic Board.

By the Reverend PATRICK GRADY,
P. P. of Emlifad and Kilmorgan, in the Diocese of ACHONRY.

Dublin:

PRINTED FOR THE AUTHOR.

1814.

Price 3s. 4d.

Grady was an intelligent but unbalanced individual and his subsequent career suggests that he was an irreformable 'stormy petrel'. The reason for his vitriolic attack on the bishop is not difficult to fathom. Shortly after taking office, probably in 1811, O'Flynn suspended him. Grady alleged that his suspension was due to his repeated opposition to O'Flynn's appointment. He also claimed that he could only carry out his duties at the risk of his life because he was persecuted by a landlord in his parish whose sexual morals he had condemned.[6]

Soon after O'Flynn became bishop he suffered a stroke which paralysed his right arm. He was then nearly seventy. In the beginning of 1816 he decided to look for a coadjutor. His choice of candidate fell on none other than his own nephew, William Costello. O'Flynn's attempt at nepotism may have been blatant but it certainly was not the only example of it. Boetius Egan was very fulsome in his praise of his nephew and namesake, the parish priest of Castlebar, in his letters to Rome but he was prudent enough to include others, like Charles Lynagh, in his praise. Nepotism was by no means confined to Ireland. It had a long tradition on the continent and particularly in Rome itself. Cardinal Borgia, with whom the Irish dealt, both as secretary and later prefect of Propaganda, was a descendant of a family which was notorious for that and other abuses. It must be remembered that society was very much family-centred and the church very often mirrored that society. The incidence of this abuse in Ireland was aggravated by the peculiar circumstances there. Bishops were recruited from a very narrow band within society, the Catholic gentry. Not surprisingly, these families were very often interrelated through marriage. So it was with the O'Flynns and the Costellos. O'Flynn was also related to the Fallons, and Philips allegedly to the Costellos. More importantly, some families, like the O'Conors of Belanagare, were also related to Charles O'Kelly in Rome, who played such a crucial role in the selection process. The situation among the more powerful Galway families was similar. Families like the Blakes and the Kirwans were all connected in some way or other.

The Coadjutor Campaign

Costello was parish priest of Tibohine just across the diocesan border in Elphin. He was a native of Achonry but switched his allegiance to the neighbouring diocese probably because his uncle was dean and vicar general there. He had been a student in Collège des Irlandais in Paris when an incident during the French Revolution almost drastically shattered his prospects, episcopal and otherwise. He was on an outing with the other Irish students to the Champs de Mars where the revolutionaries had erected an imposing 'altar to

6 SC Irlanda, vol. 20, ff. 179rv, 180rv

Pamphlet on Champs-de-Mars incident, 1790 (Archives Nationales, Paris)

> **RÉCIT VÉRITABLE**
> DE CE QUI S'EST PASSÉ
> AU CHAMP-DE-MARS.
>
> CITOYENS,
>
> IL est infiniment intéressant pour l'ordre public, et pour votre tranquillité, que vous connoissiez les véritables circonstances de l'évènement qui s'est passé au Champ-de-Mars lundi, six du mois. Les jeunes étudians du collège des Irlandois, ainsi que ceux de bien d'autres collèges de l'université, sont dans l'usage d'aller jouer au Champ-de-Mars le jour de congé de chaque semaine : ils y ont été lundi dernier, jour de Saint-Nicolas, la fête des écoliers. Quelques-uns d'entre eux se détachèrent des autres pour aller s'asseoir sur les marches de l'autel de la patrie. Un jeune homme qui le voyoit pour

the fatherland' to commemorate the fall of the Bastille of the previous year. The Irish students engaged in some horse-play in the vicinity of the altar. French onlookers became enraged at what seemed to them a deliberate act of desecration. A fight ensued. Completely outnumberd, the Irish boys took to their heels. Six of them, including Costello, were caught. They were about to be lynched or, as the French termed it 'lanternised', from their practice of using lamp-posts for that purpose. Fortunately for them, General Lafayette was passing by at the head of a detachment of the national guards. He took the Irish students into custody and marched them across Paris to Hôtel de

Ville. They were tried and imprisoned but released after a brief period and soon afterwards made their escape from France.[7] Costello was in Salamanca in 1796. Following the closure of the Irish Colleges in Paris, he had gone with his brother Thomas to finish his studies at the Irish College there.[8] On his return to Ireland, he served for two years as a curate to his uncle, John O'Flynn, in Sligo.

Early in 1816 O'Flynn circulated a letter to all the priests of the diocese seeking their signatures in favour of Costello. The dean and the vicar general and ten parish priests with three priors signed, claiming they 'were actuated solely by the dictates of our own judgement and feeling'.[9] However, six canons refused to sign as well as Patrick McNicholas, then president of the lay college in Maynooth, and wrote to Rome on 8 March objecting to Costello's appointment.[10] The others included McNicholas' uncle and namesake, James Henry, and James Dalton. Two others, Dominick Philips and John McNulty, were either hedging their bets or had succumbed to episcopal pressure as they also signed the bishop's petition in favour of Costello. Three days later O'Flynn wrote to Dr Troy seeking his 'powerful assistance' in forwarding and recommending his petition for Costello to Rome. O'Flynn believed that it was not absolutely necessary to consult the other bishops in the province.[11] But it was, and so he communicated with the others by post. George Plunkett of Elphin responded enthusiastically. Others, like Peter Waldron of Killala, refused to commit themselves. Fortunately, an ideal occasion presented itself. On 5 May the bishops gathered in Loughrea to attend the consecration of Thomas Coen as coadjutor to Bishop Costello in Clonfert. Plunkett suggested that they hold a synod there to settle the Achonry business. Costello of Clonfert, also an uncle of William's, and O'Flynn cajoled the others into supporting their nephew. Five bishops signed as well as the warden of Galway. Archbishop Oliver Kelly of Tuam withheld his signature. One at least of the signatories, Peter Waldron of Killala, was reluctant to give his support. He refused at first, caught between having 'peace with his very dear colleagues and peace with his conscience'. Eventually, fearing that O'Flynn would have a relapse, he agreed to sign the joint recommendation.

The question of a coadjutor for Achonry was discussed at the general meeting of Propaganda on 13 May. It was decided to postpone a decision and

---

7 For a full account of the incident see Swords, *The Green Cockade*, pp. 31–34
8 *Arch. Hib.*, vol. 4, p. 58
9 SOCG, vol. 917, f. 271rv; see Appendix 23 (C)
10 SOCG, vol. 918, f. 171rv; see Appendix 23 (A)
11 SOCG, vol. 918, ff. 189rv, 172rv, 173rv

to write to Tuam and Killala for further information.[12] Rome wrote on 1 June to Oliver Kelly and Peter Waldron seeking their opinion on the suitability of Costello.[13] Kelly replied that he could in no way recommend him. Waldron replied in French explaining at length the circumstances surrounding his signature. His conscience had been troubling him ever since. He had grave misgivings about the manner in which the votes of the Achonry priests had been obtained, believing that they had been influenced by fear or some other human consideration rather than the good of the church. 'Those who were opposed seemed to me at least as worthy of belief and trust as all the others.'[14]

New Roman Regulations

The question was shelved until the following year when it was discussed again at the general meeting of Propaganda on 19 May 1817. The whole business prompted Rome to draw up a new set of regulations for the appointment of bishops.[15] Within at most ten days of the death of the bishop, all the parish priests were to assemble. One 'of the more worthy' among them was to be appointed president and two others to count the votes. Each parish priest was to choose by secret ballot at least three candidates either from his own or another diocese. When the count was completed, the president announced the names of the three who had gained the most votes. The votes were then burnt. The result was sent to the archbishop of the province. He in turn communicated it to the other bishops in the province. They replied, giving their opinions within twenty days. The archbishop communicated theirs and his own opinion in a sealed envelop to the president. He then sent this to Rome together with an authentic act of the election.

The following procedure was to be followed in the election of a coadjutor. The bishop was to assemble all the parish priests of his diocese and inform them whom he wished as his coadjutor. He then left the meeting. A secret ballot was held as above. After burning the votes, the president communicated the result to the bishop. If the clergy were found to disagree with the bishop, he could then propose others until he got the priests' agreement. He then communicated this to Rome, together with a testimonial from the president. The advantages of the new system were that it excluded bishops imposing their relatives or favourites, prevented dissensions among the priests and united them with their bishop, and gave both priests and bishops a say in the election. Moreover, it conformed to the ancient practice of the church, which was 'still operating in the East'. Most importantly, it left Rome the final choice as it was no longer confined to one candidate as before.

12   Acta, vol. 180, ff. 9rv, 10rv
13   Lettere, vol. 297, ff. 123v, 124r
14   SOCG, vol. 918, f. 273rv
15   Acta, vol. 180, ff. 10v, 11rv, 12r

The new system would also have benign political consequences in Ireland: 'The English government and all Protestants in general hold that the pope has great influence and exercises a certain authority over the kingdoms of Great Britain, because he nominates at will all the bishops, something which they say could cause damage to the state. Therefore, since the time of Henry VIII and Elizabeth, to counteract this influence, the penal laws were established against Catholics who were considered as foreigners, namely, dependent on a foreign power, and unfit for any responsibility; and these laws were regarded as just and necessary for the security of the state. Now since it is not the pope, but actual nationals, who elect their bishops (which they call domestic nomination), it may cancel the prejudice of the government and public opinion, that the pope, by choosing bishops at his pleasure, exercises authority and has a certain influence over the nation. By removing the principal cause which gave rise to the penal laws, Catholics will be able more easily to obtain emancipation and be admitted on an equal basis to others, to their full civil rights.'

Rome also realised that these new regulations would lessen the government's demand for a veto in the selection of bishops in return for emancipation. By giving parish priests the central role in that selection, rather than the bishops, it lessened the possibility of the government secretly interfering to ensure somebody 'acceptable to the court'. Priests were too numerous and too diverse to be thus influenced. Also, they could be required to take an oath not to elect anyone suspect to the government.[16]

The Four Banada Resolutions

If the selection of a coadjutor for O'Flynn had no other outcome than these new regulations, it would have been worthwhile. Not only did it reduce the role of bishops in the process, but it widened the constituency to include all the parish priests and not only the canons as hitherto. It produced another exciting spin-off in Achonry. To further the cause of his nephew, O'Flynn had called a synod of the priests. At last they had been given a platform to express their feelings. They expressed publicly their gratitude to O'Flynn for 'condescending' to consult them, 'setting a precedent which must reflect honour upon the prelate, while it restores diocesan clergy their ancient, but we are sorry to add, of late neglected privileges'. With no decision still from Rome, the priests continued to flex their muscles. Another synod was held on 20 June 1817 and four resolutions were passed and signed by the bishop and priests.[17] They were surprisingly radical:

16   Acta, vol. 180, ff. 10v, 11rv, 12r
17   SC Irlanda, vol. 20, f. 234r; see Appendix 24 (A)

Resolved: That it is an inalienable right of Diocesan Clergy to be at least consulted with regard to the nomination of their Bishops and Coadjutor-Bishops.

Resolved: That any Bishop whosoever, (his Holiness of course excepted), who would take upon himself to nominate a Bishop for any diocese, without previously having consulted the clergy of such diocese, thereby commits an unwarrantable and canonical aggression upon the dearest rights and privileges of the Diocesan Clergy and consequently, that it becomes their imperative duty to exclaim against such an innovation.

Resolved: That we have strong grounds to apprehend that the presumed power of nominating a bishop without the consent of the Diocesan Clergy, which has been lately practised, with regard to our own, by nominating a Coadjutor-Bishop or a Bishop for the See of Achonry, without consulting either our own prelate (Right Rev Dr Flyn) in the first case or the clergy of the diocese in either case.

Resolved: That should such an event take place, we do hereby solemnly protest against it; and we pledge ourselves collectively and individually to use all canonical means within our reach, to counteract such an appointment, by laying our remonstrate, in humble but firm language at the feet of his Holiness.

There were twenty-one signatures in all, including the bishop's and that of James Filan, the vicar general. The others were made up of six canons, six parish priests and six curates. Predictably missing were those of the archdeacon, Michael Farrell, and of course, Patrick Grady. Missing also were the original four recusants, the two McNicholas's, Henry and Dalton. The priests of the diocese were now divided into at least three discernible camps, which boded ill for the future. That the bishop should have lent his support to such radical resolutions may have more to do with his state of health than his democratic leanings. He died less than four weeks later on 15 July 1817. The scene was set for an unprecedented succession race.

James Filan

The priests met in Banada on 21 July and elected James Filan vicar capitular to govern the diocese in the interim. He was also proposed as one of three candidates to succeed O'Flynn. Filan was born in Killasser in 1775. He matriculated in the class of humanity in Maynooth in 1799 when he was twenty-four, and spent five years in the college.[18] For three years he taught Latin and Greek in the lay college in Maynooth. He left to set up a school in Sligo which he advertised in the *Sligo Journal* on 15 May 1807.[19] The school was in-

18 Healy, *Centenary History of Maynooth*, p. 735
19 quoted in O'Rorke, *Sligo*, vol. 2, p. 139n

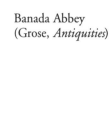
Banada Abbey
(Grose, *Antiquities*)

tended 'to fit out boys for business or for entrance into the colleges of Maynooth or Dublin'. O'Flynn was then parish priest of St John's, Sligo, and soon after his appointment to Achonry in 1809 he recalled Filan to his diocese where he appointed him parish priest of Curry, administrator of Kilmactigue and vicar general of the diocese.[20]

At a meeting in Banada on 24 July Filan delivered an address to the clergy of Achonry which was later published in the newspapers, and a copy was immediately forwarded to Rome by Dr Troy.[21] Filan began his address with a quotation from Montesquieu's *L'Esprit des Loix*. '*La servitude commence toujours par le sommeil.*' It is probably best translated by a another better-known adage: 'The price of liberty is eternal vigilance.' His message to his fellow-priests in Achonry was to be vigilant lest yet another outsider be thrust upon them as bishop. He recalled the four resolutions they had passed recently and cited some examples from early church history to prove that bishops were appointed 'with the consent of all the clergy'. Troy, in his covering letter to Rome, stated that Filan 'tried to establish that chapters had a *de jure* right to elect bishops' which Troy considered 'erroneous'. Filan was not attacking the Roman prerogatives – the second resolution expressly excepted the Pope –

Address to the Clergy of Achonry

20 ibid
21 SC Irlanda, vol. 20, ff. 234r, 235r

but 'Irish Catholic Prelates, or rather a few of them, who have lately assumed a power (of) appointing their compeers, which has few or no precedents in antiquity'. He probably had Dr Troy himself in mind, and more particularly in the case of Achonry, the Archbishop of Tuam.

In his address, Filan listed the last nine bishops of Achonry, beginning with Dominick O'Daly, and 'almost uniformly selected from the diocese of Tuam'. They were chosen always 'not only without the least reference to the feelings of the subordinate clergy, but, in some instances, in direct opposition to their most decided wishes'. His highly rhetorical conclusion was aimed at rousing the Achonry clergy to elect one of their own this time.

> Alas! despised, though not despicable Achonry, how hard is thy fate! What is there in thy soil or climate to entail Boeotic ignorance and perpetual degradation upon thy children? And what is there in the soil and climate of Tuam to entitle her children exclusively to hold absolute and perpetual sway over thee? Shall the sun of science never illumine the minds of thy subordinate clergy? Have virtue and talents bade them an eternal farewell? Or should any of them be possessed of these united qualifications, shall they remain forever the proscribed victims of an assumed power, which can find few or no precedents in ancient or modern times?

Whether or not Filan's stirring words 'illumined the minds of the subordinate clergy', his rhetoric on this occasion could only have improved his own prospects.

Patrick McNicholas

The first of the three candidates proposed was Patrick McNicholas, president of the lay college in Maynooth. He too was a native of Killasser where he was born in 1780. He came from a modest background though probably not 'of the meanest extraction' as claimed by those who opposed his appointment.[22] Some doubt exists as to when exactly he entered Maynooth. There is a Patrick McNicholas listed among the very first students there in 1795 but his age is given as twenty-five whereas the present candidate of that name would only have been fifteen then.[23] There was another Patrick McNicholas in Achonry who was now a canon and closely related to the candidate but he could not have been the student who entered Maynooth in 1795 as he was ordained in 1771. It would appear that Patrick McNicholas, the candidate, began his studies there in 1799 or shortly afterwards when he was about twenty. His subsequent career is better documented. He was appointed junior lecturer by the trustees on 27 June 1806 and the following year professor of humanity. In 1808 he was described in the Parliamentary Papers as 'second professor of Greek and Latin'. He moved to the chair of logic, metaphysics and ethics in November 1812, and he resigned it in January 1815 when he became president of the lay college.

The third candidate was Roger MacDermot, a member of the ancient Coolavin family and then parish priest of Gurteen (Kilfree). The petition was signed by ten canons, seven parish priests, eight curates, the Dominican priors of Straide and Urlaur as well as two other friars, a Dominican and a Franciscan.[24]

The Dalton Campaign

Two canons, Patrick Grady and James Dalton, refused to sign and stormed out of the meeting in protest. James Dalton was in the Irish College in Salamanca in April 1789 where he was described as 'of noble parents and nineteen years of age' and beginning philosophy. He left Salamanca in September 1797.[25] Less than three years later he was a parish priest and canon in the diocese.[26] Dalton now toured the diocese with Grady canvassing support for himself as a candidate. Grady and Michael Farrell had sent a letter on 22 July to Propaganda objecting to the three candidates proposed at Banada.[27] Apart from McNicholas' 'ignoble birth', he had no pastoral experience having

---

22 SOCG, vol. 918, ff. 100rv, 103rv
23 Furthermore, the 1795 entrant matriculated in theology and only spent three years in the college and was described in 1808 as being 'in the ministry'. Healy, op. cit., p. 733. None of this fits the candidate who would have been only eighteen when he completed theology and well short of the canonical age for ordination. Besides he was still working in the college in 1808. 24 See Appendix 24 (B)
25 Arch. Hib., vol. 4, p. 58, vol. 6, p. 13
26 SC Irlanda, vol. 18, ff. 104v, 105r
27 SOCG, vol. 918, ff. 100rv, 103rv

spent twenty years in Maynooth. If elected, he would continue his salaried position there and commit the diocese to the care of a vicar general. Filan was also dismissed as a man of lowly birth. The promotion of the inferior classes to the episcopal dignity would, because of the number of Protestants in the region, bring religion into disrepute. Filan was 'swollen with pride and ambition, disposed to promote dissensions in the diocese rather than to settle them'. Grady's vitriolic pen is much in evidence in this letter. Filan was said to have admitted publicly in a diocesan synod that a watch he had lost was found in a brothel. Roger MacDermot was deemed intellectually unqualified to be a bishop.

The Grady-Dalton tour of the diocese did rally some support for Dalton. However, the methods they used to win that support were roundly condemned by McNicholas.

> During the course of their canvass, it is well ascertained that they held out the most corrupt and profligate inducements by promising to some preferment and to others an extension of the parishes they already held. I can assure you that not only religion but common decorum would be shocked at the other means resorted to by those two gentlemen.[28]

Be that as it may, a total of fifteen priests signed a postulation in favour of Dalton in Ballaghaderreen on 30 July.[29] Ballaghaderreen was probably chosen as the venue for their meeting because of the deteriorating health of the archdeacon, Michael Farrell, whose name tops the list of the signatories. The others included four canons and two other parish priests as well as four curates and the priors of Straide and Urlaur and the prior and ex-prior of Banada. Eight of these signatories had already signed the original postulation at Banada nine days earlier. Now they supported Dalton whom they stated was from a noble family and held a bachelor's degree in theology. The document was authenticated by Grady as public notary, an office which he claimed had been conferred on him by Bishop Lynagh.

Dalton and Grady had approached the Archishop of Tuam, claiming that the election of Filan as vicar capitular was open to question. Nine canons, including McNicholas' cousin and James Henry of Collooney, signed an affidavit stating that Filan had been duly elected by the chapter on 21 July, receiving the great majority of the votes. A letter, dated 26 August and signed by Filan and twenty-three other priests, attacked Dalton's character as unsuitable for the episcopacy.[30] He had been publicly accused more than once by the deceased

28 SC Irlanda, vol. 20, ff. 205rv, 206rv
29 SOCG, vol. 918, ff. 66rv, 71v; see Appendix 24 (c)
30 SOCG, vol. 918, ff. 68rv, 69rv; see Appendix 24 (d)

bishop of showing no pity for the poor or peace or charity towards his neighbour. He was involved in brawls and quarrels with his curates. As to the nobility of his family, 'no vestiges of his estates exist anywhere'. It appears from this that Dalton's support had largely eroded. Four parish priests, a curate and the prior of Urlaur, who had signed his postulation, now publicly retracted.

Grady had been deposed from his parish by O'Flynn six years before and was not appointed to another parish. Notwithstanding, a few days previously he had intruded himself into the parish of Ballaghaderreen (Kilcolman and Castlemore), asserting that Michael Farrell on his death-bed had resigned it in his favour. O'Flynn would never have approved of such a resignation nor did the vicar capitular. The priests requested the Pope not to accept this resignation 'without previously examining the life and morals' of Grady.

When Dalton got wind of this protest against him, he wrote on 14 September, from Greyfort near Ballina, to Cardinal Litta, the prefect of Propaganda. 'As neither I nor any other clergyman here, who does not belong to the faction in favour of the Revd Mr McNicholas, got notice of attending at the very curious meeting where this protest was signed, I am totally ignorant of the objections advanced against me. But I am certain they must be both futile and totally groundless.'[31] He referred the cardinal to 'the candid and conscientious opinion' of the Archbishop of Tuam and Bishop of Killala, who were well acquainted with him. His confidence in the Archbishop of Tuam was misplaced. 'As to the Rev Mr Dalton, although application has been made to me in his behalf,' Dr Kelly later wrote to Rome, 'I would not venture to recommend him.'[32]

The 'Forgery'

While the Achonry priests showed a fairly united front in their opposition to Dalton, it was very much otherwise with regard to the main contenders, McNicholas and Filan. Once Dalton was disposed of, the way was cleared for the main contest. It was 'discovered' that McNicholas had made a postulation exclusively in his own favour, to which he had affixed the names of all the clergy in the diocese. The 'discovery' was made by none other than his principal rival, Filan. George Plunkett, Bishop of Elphin, believed that there was 'some truth in the charge'. He did not 'consider the document altogether suppositious but some things have been suppressed which should have been inserted'.

The forgery had come to light when it was discovered that the original postulation, presented to the provincial bishops for their endorsement, contained no reference to Filan having been chosen as dean by the deceased bishop

31 SOCG, vol. 918, f. 85r
32 ibid, f. 87rv

who had died before he could ask Rome to confirm it. Filan wrote to the bishops asking them not to sign the postulation unless it contained that reference. George Plunkett had received Filan's letter when he was approached by Canon McNicholas, cousin of the candidate, to sign a postulation without that reference. Plunkett refused at first but yielded when he was given 'the most positive assurance that what the vicar capitular requested would be inserted'. Later he learned that the canon 'did not make good his word'.

Filan called a general meeting of the clergy on 19 September to expose the alleged forgery. A new postulation was drawn up, recommending the same three candidates but stating explicitly this time that 'any one of them would be worthy of such an honour'.[33] Rome was told about the forgery and asked that McNicholas should not be promoted 'without a prior examination of his motive for acting in this manner'. This postulation was signed by twenty-three priests, which included eight canons, eight other parish priests, five curates, the prior of Urlaur and the guardian of Ballymote. The only surprising signature is that of James Henry, a strong supporter of McNicholas. The pendulum was swinging back very much in Filan's favour. 'The Revd Mr Mc Nicholas' party was at starting the most numerous,' Plunkett observed, 'but a very considerable falling off occurred of late.'

Factions and Parties

Plunkett urged Francis O'Finan, his newly-appointed agent in Rome, on 20 October to communicate, 'without one moment's delay', to the Cardinal Prefect of Propaganda 'the following sketch of the present state of the vacant See of Achonry which exhibits a most afflicting picture of confusion, distraction and disorder'.[34]

> The priests are divided and subdivided into petty clans, factions and parties, inveterately hostile and irreconcilably inimical to each other. Four candidates, all natives of the diocese, have started for the vacant See and each of them commands a corps of active and zealous partizans ... There is therefore no end to protests, remonstrances and complaints and I fear a recurrence of these evils which have already digraced this province when contending parties were seen in the sanctuary lacerating the sacred robes and dragging each other from the altar ... Scandalous abuses, unheard of excesses, crept into that diocese owing to the long protracted illness of the late bishop ... We live in turbulent and troubled times. Opinions very injurious to the hierarchy are publicly avowed. Bishops begin to be considered as mere ciphers in this country. Parishes have been forcibly taken possession of and kept in despite of the bishop in the very diocese of Achonry.

33 ibid, ff. 77rv, 82v; another copy, ff. 79rv, 80rv, appears to be the original and includes the signature of Roger MacDermot, making a total of forty-four.
34 ibid, ff. 91rv, 92rv; see also Italian translation, ff. 88rv, 89rv, 90rv, 93rv

Plunkett was now wavering in his support of McNicholas, wondering whether he would be 'equal to the task of reconciling jarring interests and putting down faction and party and restoring peace and good order to the diocese of Achonry too long shamefully torn and distracted'.

Three days later, Archbishop Oliver Kelly also wrote to Rome.[35] He too was wavering. 'Since my recommendation of the Revd Mr McNicholas,' he informed the secretary of Propaganda, 'a report has reached me concerning his parentage and family, which would perhaps strongly militate against him were he appointed to that See.' However, he rejected the other two candidates, claiming that the names of Filan and MacDermot were only inserted

Archbishop Oliver Kelly

---

35   ibid, f. 87rv; Italian translation, ff. 86rv, 97rv

in the original postulation '*pro consuetudine*' (i.e. as a matter of form). 'I do not hesitate to declare that Mesrs Filan and MacDermot are extremely unworthy of being promoted to the episcopal dignity and I confidently hope his Holiness will never be induced to promote them.' Whatever gains Filan was making among the priests of the diocese were more than off-set by the almost total lack of support for him among the bishops. Kelly was now moving towards a resolution of the problem which would realise Achonry's worst nightmare, the appointment of an outsider as bishop. He put forward the names of two Tuam priests, Malachy O'Kelly of Westport and Pat Nolan, 'in the event that Mr McNicholas be not appointed'. Likewise, Plunkett of Elphin proposed the parish priest of Boyle for the post.

McNicholas' Letter

McNicholas, though he remained throughout the campaign in seclusion in Maynooth, was not inactive on his own behalf. He corresponded with the Dominican, Dr Gibbons, at the Minerva in Rome whom he kept informed of developments. He informed him on 25 October of the probable defection of Plunkett to support his own candidate, the parish priest of Boyle.[36] McNicholas accepted the loss of Plunkett's support with equanimity. 'I think the solitary signature of one bishop will have no great weight against the postulation of the diocese, subscribed by the metropolitan and his suffragans and also by the primate and Dr Troy.' His remoteness from the diocese was more than compensated by his proximity to Troy in Dublin, whom McNicholas described as 'an admirable old man'. Troy remained unwavering in his support of McNicholas. He wrote to Cardinal Litta at Propaganda: 'I hope the scandalous troubles in the diocese of Achonry will end soon with the appointment of a suitable bishop, in the person of the Revd Mr McNicholas, recommended by the archbishop and provincial bishops and by Armagh and myself. He is also recommended by the majority of the chapter and the diocesan clergy.'[37]

In his letter to Gibbons, McNicholas seemed unaware of any wavering on the part of the Archbishop of Tuam but he was taking no chances on that score. 'My avocations have rendered it highly inconvenient to myself to wait on Dr Kelly but I went to a confidential friend of mine in the country who will execute the commission with equal zeal.' The friend in question was possibly James Henry, whom McNicholas described as 'one of the more active and zealous in the cause'. It is said that James Henry taught Latin and Greek in the lay college of Maynooth for three years after McNicholas was appointed its president. The same source claimed that Henry had been a class-fellow of

36 SC Irlanda, vol. 20, ff. 205rv, 206rv
37 SOCG, vol. 918, ff. 108rv, 113v

Oliver Kelly's in Salamanca and that their friendship continued after their return home.[38] Henry is not recorded as a student of Salamanca. Whatever earlier doubts he may have had, Henry was now spearheading the McNicholas campaign in the diocese.

While McNicholas had the support of the influential Dominican in Rome, Dr Gibbons, Filan had the backing of equally-influential Franciscans. Anthony Garrahan, the Franciscan provincial, wrote in December to the guardian of St Isidore's to exert his 'powerful influence' to have Filan appointed bishop, which 'would be at once a triumph to our order, to the cause of truth and religion'.[39] He gave a detailed account of a general meeting of the chapter and clergy of Achonry called by Filan on 15 December. At this meeting yet another postulation was drawn up.[40] It stated that it was known by the signatories that O'Flynn had chosen Filan as dean 'a few days before his death'. In the original postulation of 21 July it was left to the free choice of his Holiness to nominate any one of the three candidates proposed and that the names of Filan and MacDermot were not inserted '*pro consuetudine*' (i.e. to complete the formalities), as McNicholas claimed in his 'forged' postulation. McNicholas had employed the services of James Henry and Canon McNicholas to procure 'his secret and fraudulent postulation' and, consequently, the signatories now wished McNicholas to be excluded.

St Isidore's College, Rome

Should his Holiness wish to refer the whole business to any archbishop or bishop acquainted with the facts, the Bishops of Elphin and Clonfert were to be preferred. They asked that it should not be referred to Oliver Kelly, Archbishop of Tuam because they feared – and not without reason – that Kelly,

---

38 O'Rorke, *Ballysadare and Kilvarnet*, pp. 485, 488
39 SOCG, vol. 918, ff. 105rv, 106rv; Italian translation, ff. 104rv, 107rv
40 ibid, ff. 78rv, 81rv

like his predecessors, might wish to promote one of his own priests as their bishop. 'For over a hundred years,' they informed the Pope, 'almost all Achonry bishops were born in the archdiocese of Tuam and scarcely any of them had a residence in our diocese.' Not only did the clergy of the diocese not ask for them but they were even imposed on them against their wishes.

> Our lately deceased bishop, the most illustrious and reverend John O'Flynn, together with his clergy, publicly declared last summer that this manner of nominating Achonry bishops, always from an outside church, was contrary to the canons, so that in future no cleric born in Tuam should be accepted as Bishop of Achonry, especially if it was against the wishes of our clergy, unless he was expressly sent by Your Holiness.

This postulation had seventeen signatures, including six canons and four other parish priests, five curates and the priors of Urlaur and Banada.[41]

The Counter-Postulation

A counter-postulation was drawn up by the McNicholas faction on 4 January 1818 and addressed to Cardinal Litta at Propaganda. It had thirteen signatories.[42] There were two other canons, besides Henry and McNicholas. One of them was John Durkan, who had entered Maynooth on the same day as James Filan in 1799.[43] They reiterated their contention that the original postulation on 21 July included the names of Filan and McDermot only to complete the formalities of providing three names and that the intention then of all the clergy, with very few exceptions, was to recommend McNicholas. 'So great was the unanimity that everyone congratulated us on the peaceful outcome of the election, having avoided the contentions which usually give rise in this area to serious scandal.' Once included as a candidate, Filan, 'left nothing undone to alienate the clergy' from McNicholas. He abused his position as vicar apostolic to win support for his candidacy. He gave the faculty of hearing confessions to priests newly-ordained without experience or theology and expanded parishes by uniting to them portions of vacant parishes. For confirmation of their statement, they referred Rome to Oliver Kelly or any of the Connacht bishops, except George Plunkett of Elphin who had put forward his own candidate, James Branly, parish priest of Boyle. If Filan had offered such blandishments to win support, he was not remarkably successful. Two of the seven parish priests who signed this postulation had been recently

41 see Appendix 24 (E)
42 ibid, ff. 76rv, 83rv; see Appendix 25
43 The other, Francis Boland, had apparently become a canon, since September when he signed the petition which accused McNicholas of forgery. Since then, James McHugh, another signatory, had become a parish priest. He was one of three parish priests who signed this postulation. The others consisted of four curates and two Dominicans, Edmund Clarke and James McNicholas, who may have been related to the candidate.

promoted and yet switched their allegiance to McNicholas. Another recently appointed parish priest, Robert Hepburne, did vote for Filan.

At the beginning of 1818, both parties enjoyed almost equal support in the diocese, with Filan marginally ahead. He was supported by seventeen priests as against fourteen for McNicholas. The canons were more evenly divided, six to five in favour of Filan, while the other parish priests were four to three and curates, five to four in his favour. The friars were evenly divided, two Dominicans for McNicholas, and one Dominican and one Augustinian for Filan. Support for Dalton was now whittled down to a handful. The archdeacon, Michael Farrell, had died, probably in the late summer or early autumn of 1817. Apart from Grady, he could only count on the support of one or two curates.

The McNicholas party canvassed among the laity for support. It was the first such intervention by that body in the election of a bishop since the seventeenth century. There were thirty signatures from the diocese to a petition sent to Cardinal Litta to be transmitted to Pius VII.[44] It was also signed by fourteen citizens of Sligo town, including a doctor, an attorney at law and five merchants. Of the Achonry signatories, almost half of them came from from Swinford, although John Coleman, the parish priest there, was a firm supporter of Filan. Equally surprising is that there were only three signatories from Collooney, even though their parish priest, James Henry, was almost certainly the moving force behind the petition. It was authenticated by him

The Lay Postulation

Collooney waterfall (O'Rorke, *Ballysadare*)

44 SC Irlanda, vol. 20, ff. 56rv, 57rv; see Appendix 42, 10 Feb 1818

in Collooney on 10 February. Besides, its criticism of Filan re-echoes closely in sentiment and language that of the McNicholas-party postulation of 4 January:

> Revd James Filan, as soon as his name was inserted as a candidate (which was done as a matter of form) attempted to subvert the union and harmony which subsisted among the clergy; he left nothing undone to alienate their affections for the Revd Mr McNicholas; he impressed on their minds that nothing was more certain than his appointment to the diocese; he conferred favours on some and to others he made large promises; in a word, he left nothing unattempted to answer his ambitious projects and vanity to which we are of the opinion he would sacrifice even religion itself.

Much of this petition is nothing less than a character-assassination of Filan.

> Tho' we would reluctantly and unwillingly impeach the conduct of any ecclesiastic, yet the present occasion obliges us to declare that the Revd James Filan is not a man of good fame and that he is considered not only by us but by the public at large as an ambitious, giddy and petulant character and that his appointment to this diocese would eventually prove highly detrimental to our holy religion.

But McNicholas' real power-base lay elsewhere. Thomas Troy wrote again on 9 January urging Rome to appoint McNicholas and describing Filan in his letter as '*capo brigante*' (i.e. chief trouble-maker) among the Achonry clergy.[45] Oliver Kelly of Tuam, whose support had previously wavered, was now firmly committed to McNicholas. On 13 January he also wrote to Cardinal Litta recommending McNicholas, 'as does Dublin and Armagh'.[46]

McNicholas' appointment

The cardinals of Propaganda met in general congregation on 23 February. There were eight present, including Litta and Quarantotti and Napoleon's uncle, Cardinal Fesch. The appointment to Achonry was on the agenda. A '*ponenza*', consisting of a summary in Italian of all the relevant documents, running to several foolscap pages, had been prepared by the secretary.[47] It included all six postulations from the various parties in Achonry, as well as the letters from Farrell and Grady and from Dalton, from the Franciscan provincial, from the Bishops of Elphin and Killala, from the Archbishop of Tuam and two from Troy of Dublin.

The cardinals found themselves caught between a rock and a hard place.

---

45 SOCG, vol. 918, ff. 126rv, 130r
46 SC Irlanda, vol. 21, f. 62rv
47 Acta, vol. 181, ff. 42v, 43rv, 44rv, 45rv; SOCG, vol. 918, ff. 35v, 36rv, 37rv, 38rv

They debated whether they should make a nomination or suspend the election. The latter course could only lead to increased dissensions in the diocese. In similar circumstances, where parties were bitterly divided over their choice of candidate, Rome usually chose an outsider. Three such candidates had been proposed, two by Oliver Kelly of Tuam and one by George Plunkett of Elphin. But the final paragraph of the '*ponenza*' underlined the strong opposition of all factions in Achonry to the appointment of yet another outsider. In the end they opted for McNicholas whom they recommended to the Pope.[48] The Pope approved their choice on 7 March and his brief was issued ten days later.[49] The only document which the cardinals had not seen before making their choice was the postulation from the laity. Two months later it was forwarded from Paris, probably by Dr Gibbons, with a covering note expressing the hope that 'it will be an auxiliary proof of the choice you have made for the diocese of Achonry, in the person of Doctor McNicholas'.[50] Appropriately enough, McNicholas was consecrated in Maynooth college chapel on 17 May and by Thomas Troy, Archbishop of Dublin.[51]

Epilogue: The Filan Affair

Dissensions continued to wrack the diocese for a number of years. It probably did not help that the new bishop took up his residence in Collooney, the parish of his chief supporter, James Henry. Relations with his chief rival, Filan, continued to deteriorate. Writing from Collooney on 20 May 1821, McNicholas reported to Rome:

> There is in this diocese a certain parish priest by the name of James Filan who last month bitterly attacked the popes, which was published in the newspapers, declaring that in the twelfth century they had usurped the rights of the chapter and clergy in this region and have retained them up to the present.[52]

McNicholas renewed his attack on Filan when he submitted his first report to Rome on the state of his diocese in January 1822.[53] Filan 'was using all sorts of machinations to foment dissent among the clergy and seduce them from the common good of religion'. He hoped, in a few days, to forward the offensive article Filan had published but wondered whether he should leave it in the original language or translate it into Latin. In May of that year Filan was again reported to Rome, this time on a more serious charge.[54] McNicholas

---

48 Udienze, vol. 56, f. 140r
49 Lettere, vol. 299, f. 128v; *Hierarchia Catholica*, vol. vii, p. 57
50 SC Irlanda, vol. 20, ff. 56rv, 57rv
51 DDA, *Regestum* 1, p. 40 quoted in *Reportorium Novum*, vol. 1, no. 2, p. 495
52 SC Irlanda, vol. 23, ff. 354rv, 355rv. Apparently, Filan was continuing to adhere to the tenor of his Address to the Clergy of Achonry, published in July 1817.
53 ibid, f. 613v

had suspended him for allegedly striking two priests and threatening a third. In spite of his suspension, Filan continued to celebrate Mass and carry out all the other parochial functions. McNicholas wrote to Propaganda because he 'did not know how he can reduce the transgressor to duty and remove from this diocese such a great scandal'. Propaganda referred the case to the cardinal secretary of state as 'it seems ecclesiastical arms are not sufficient to break the audacity and incorrigibility of the obstinate offender'.[55] Rome seemed more concerned by Filan's published article than his alleged violence against the priests and requested that not just a summary but a copy of the entire work be sent on as soon as possible. Its reply to McNicholas spoke of the 'unbridled audacity and arrogance of Filan who dared, in a published work, to impudently deny the right of the Supreme Pontifs in the election of bishops ... In this case, he deserved indeed the severest penalties and I fear lest his teaching and example in the future cause great scandal to Ireland.'[56]

Filan himself wrote in October to Propaganda denying the charge of violence and asking that the case be referred to the Archbishop of Tuam, which was duly done.[57] The row suddenly petered out and early in 1823 McNicholas reported to Rome that Filan had repented.[58] He sought faculties to absolve him and transfer him to another parish because he had given 'sure and constant signs of reform' and withdrew the work published against papal preogatives.[59] Before granting the faculties, Rome insisted that Filan make a public retraction and that an authentic copy of this retraction be sent to Rome 'lest he resume his previous opinions'.[60] James Filan died in 1830 at the age of fifty-five. His tombstone in Drumahillan graveyard describes him as 'matchless in talent, unrivalled in erudition, parent to the orphan, and a helper to the distressed and a solace to the afflicted.'[61]

The two other candidates, James Dalton and Roger MacDermot, also continued in opposition to McNicholas for a number of years. When McNicholas took over the diocese he found there fifteen priests, ordained for four years and more, who had received no theological training. He set up a seminary for them 'in a secluded place' and imposed a modest tax on the

---

54 ibid, ff. 661rv, 662v
55 ibid, f. 667rv
56 Lettere, vol. 303, ff. 493v, 494r
57 SC Irlanda, vol. 23, ff. 709rv
58 ibid, vol. 24, ff. 11rv, 12v
59 Udienze, vol. 61, f. 153v
60 Lettere, vol. 304, ff. 138v, 139r
61 O'Rorke, *Sligo*, vol. 2, p. 140

parish priests to offset the costs of the seminary. Most priests paid 'cheerfully' except four who included Dalton and MacDermot, a well as Filan.[62]

Patrick Grady continued his aberrational ways under the new bishop. Though still under suspension, he had seized possession of the parish of Ballaghaderreen (Castlemore & Kilcolman) in 1817 claiming that Michael Farrell had resigned it in his favour before he died. He wrote to Rome asking for that parish or the other mensal parish of Tourlestrane (Kilmactigue) which had become vacant by the death of Bishop O'Flynn. Surprisingly, his request was supported by the Archbishop Oliver Kelly in a covering note on 16 September 1817: 'I am of the opinion that if the prayer of this petitioner is granted it will tend much to restore peace and tranquillity to the diocese and relieve the future bishop from trouble … and by appointing the Revd Mr Grady to the parish of Kilmactigue, it would be a sort of compensation for the privations he has endured for some years back.'[63]

The Grady Case

Rome expressed amazement at Kelly's recommendation of a suspended priest who had never been absolved and continued to administer the sacraments in the parish he had usurped.[64] Kelly defended his action, claiming that he treated Grady as 'a distressed and afflicted brother in Christ who, I hope, feels deep contrition for his past aberrations'.[65] Grady's case was discussed at the general meeting of the cardinals in February 1818 where McNicholas had been elected bishop and it was decided there to refer the matter to the new bishop. McNicholas, however, sought and was granted both Tourlestrane (Kilmactigue) and Ballaghaderreen (Castlemore & Kilcolman) as mensal parishes.[66]

Apparently, after promising to amend his ways and the lifting of his suspension, Grady was moved to Kiltimagh in 1818. Scarcely a year after Grady's appointment parishioners were complaining to the bishop about Grady's fondness of money and his harsh and bitter manner. The bishop admonished him frequently to improve his ways and maintain peace with his parishioners. Finally, things came to a head in 1826.

On a certain Sunday, while Mass was being celebrated, he (Grady) fell on his bare knees in front of the altar and bearing his bald head (to cause greater terror), and having first invoked the power of the Blessed Virgin, he cursed the unfortunate people unless they paid within a few days a certain sum of money to which he was in no way entitled.[67]

62 SC Irlanda, vol. 23, f. 611v
63 SC Irlanda, vol. 20, ff. 179rv–80rv
64 Lettere, vol. 298, f. 619rv
65 SC Irlanda, vol. 21, f. 63r
66 Udienze, vol. 55, f. 607v; Lettere, vol. 299, ff. 445v, 446rv
67 SC Irlanda, vol. 24, f. 685r

The incident had been reported to McNicholas by three priests who were present on that Sunday. When the bishop arrived in Kiltimagh on the following Sunday to examine the matter, Grady locked the doors of the chapel against him and those who were coming to Mass. The bishop then publicly suspended him, deprived him of the parish and appointed James McNicholas in his place.

Grady had also published in the newspapers 'atrocious calumnies' against the bishop, claiming that he had sold indulgences, abolished the chapter and promoted unworthy people. He had the three priest-witnesses summoned before the civil magistrates 'where he was frustrated in his attempt to have them severely penalized'. Finally, after ten months trying by every means to discredit the bishop, Grady took his case to Rome on 2 May 1826.[68] His lengthy Latin letter was vintage Grady, full of wild accusations against McNicholas, reminiscent of those he had published against O'Flynn in his *Radical Anti-Veto* in 1814. He gave his own version of the incident in Kiltimagh. He had built there an 'elegant' chapel 'at his own expense'.[69] Once the chapel was completed, McNicholas threatened to impose a curate on Grady unless he resigned. Grady refused. When the bishop arrived with three priests 'and a huge mob of peasants from elsewhere', he refused to open the chapel door. The door was broken down and the bishop went in and publicly declared Grady suspended and deprived of the parish. Grady's letter was sent from Kiltimagh but he asked that the reply be addressed to him in Boyle, where apparently he planned to take refuge.

Rome sent a copy of Grady's letter to Archbishop Kelly who totally rejected Grady's accusations against McNicholas. His earlier benign opinion of Grady had changed totally. 'For more than seventeen years Patrick Grady is very well known to me and to the whole province for the dissent and trouble he has caused in the diocese of Achonry.'[70] Rome fully approved of McNicholas' action and Grady's fate was sealed.[71] He was now in his seventies. He was last heard of in Rabbitt Hall, near Roadstown, Co Sligo in 1831, from where he wrote to Charles King O'Hara, suggesting a new road should be built from Coolaney to Ballaghaderreen which would reduce the distance to fourteen miles.[72]

---

68   SC Irlanda, vol. 24, ff. 595r–97rv
69   Elsewhere, he stated that it cost £400. NLI, O'Hara Papers Report 493, p. 3440
70   ibid, f. 605r
71   Lettere, vol. 307, f. 538rv, f. 685r
72   NLI, O'Hara Papers Report, 493, p. 3440

The career of James Henry, parish priest of Ballisodare and Collooney (Kilvarnet) and former leader of the McNicholas party, followed an altogether different course. The bishop established his residence in Henry's parish at Collooney and remained there for thirteen years. Henry was appointed apostolic notary, vicar general and later, in 1827, dean of the diocese. He resigned the deanship when he became paralysed in 1832.[73] He died in July 1833.[74]

The appointment of McNicholas as bishop in 1818 marked the beginning of a new age for the Achonry church. He was the first Maynooth-trained priest to become bishop of the diocese. No continentally-trained priest was subsequently appointed. He was the first commoner. Class was never again a prerequisite in the selection of a bishop. The egalitarianism of the French Revolution had finally reached Achonry diocese and, more importantly, Rome itself. Though not the first resident bishop – his predecessor had established his residence in Kilfree – when McNicholas moved to Ballaghaderreen in 1831, it became the home of all future bishops and site of the cathedral built by his successor.

Towards a New Age

His reign, extending over thirty-four years, was to be the longest in the history of the diocese since Eugene O'Hart in the sixteenth century. During

Ballinacarrow chapel (O'Rorke, *Ballysadare*)

---

73 Lettere, vol. 302, ff. 348v, 349r; Udienze, vol. 67, f. 957rv
74 O'Rorke, *Ballysadare and Kilvarnet*, p. 489

that time he witnessed many far-reaching changes, including Catholic Emancipation in 1829 and the establishment of National Schools in 1832, which greatly affected the lives of the people. He saw the population of the diocese increase dramatically, reach its peak and then be decimated by the disaster of the Great Famine of 1845–47. The network of roads throughout the diocese improved and expanded considerably. Small towns, like Swinford, Ballaghaderreen, Tubbercurry and Ballymote began to prosper and grow, as did others, only slightly less in size, such as Foxford, Charlestown and Kiltimagh. Their development was promoted by the siting of the new chapels there as well as the priests' residences. A new Catholic middle class, consisting mostly of shopkeepers and professionals, was replacing the remnants of the old Catholic gentry and strong tenant-farmers, in their influence over church affairs. Clerical discipline was progressively imposed, with the bishop exercising tighter control over parish priests, and they in turn over their curates. The latter increased rapidly to meet the pastoral needs of an exploding population.

But there was a downside too. The growth of towns contributed to the spread of the English language, as did the National Schools. The gradual loss of Irish entailed the loss of the remarkable native spirituality it had nurtured and preserved. It was eventually replaced by imported foreign devotions which characterised a religion that was centred on the chapel, the priest and the town. While the stations continued to survive, gone forever were the holy wells and their patterns, the home-based sacraments and all the celebrations that surrounded them.

Ní fheicfimid a leithéid arís.

'A Swineford Car' (Barrow, *Tour*)

Appendices

Bishops

APPENDIX 1: Catholic Bishops of Achonry[1]   *Catholic Bishops*

Hugh MacDermot, apostolic vicar, 1685-1707
    Bishop, 13 April 1707 – pre-Sept 1725
Dominick O'Daly OP, 20 Sept 1725 – 6 Jan 1735
John O'Hart, 30 Sept 1735 – c. 7 May 1739
Walter Blake, 13 Aug 1739 – May 1758
Patrick Robert Kirwan, 21 Aug 1758 – pre-July 1776
Philip Philips, 1 July 1776 – 22 Nov 1785
Boetius Egan, 22 Nov 1785 – 4 Jan 1788
Thomas O'Connor, 4 Jan 1788 – Feb 1803
Charles Lynagh, 13 May 1803 – pre-June 1809
John O'Flynn, 13 June 1809 – pre-Mar 1818
Patrick McNicholas, 17 Mar 1818 – 1852

APPENDIX 2: Protestant Bishops of the United Dioceses of Killala and Achonry.[2]   *Protestant Bishops*

William Lloyd, 23 Aug 1690/91– 11 Dec 1716
Henry Downes, 1716/17 – 1720
Charles Cobbe, 14 Aug 1720 – 1726/27
Robert Howard, 19 Mar 1726/27 – 1729
Robert Clayton, 1729/30 – 1735
Mordecai Cary, 19 Mar 1735/36 – 2 Oct 1751
Richard Robinson, 19 Jan 1752 – 1759
Samuel Hutchinson, 22 April 1759 – 27 Oct 1780
William Cecil Pery, 18 Feb 1781 – 1784
William Preston, 1784 – 1787
John Law, 1787 – 1795
John Porter, 7 June 1795 – 1797
Joseph Stock, 18 Jan 1798 – 1810
James Verschoyle, 6 May 1810 – 13 April 1834

---

1 List compiled from *Hierarchia Catholica*, vols V, p. 67, VI, p. 63, VII, p. 57. Exact dates of death not always known.
2 J.B. Leslie, *Biographical Succession List of the Clergy of Achonry*, typescript in the Representative Church Body Library, Braemor Park, Dublin

Deans

Catholic Deans   APPENDIX 3: Catholic Deans / VGs

Phelim O'Hara, 20 Aug 1683, 4 Sept 1684[1]
John O'Hart, 5 Oct 1716 [2]
John Duffy, 6 June 1739 [3]
Patrick Henican, 9 Mar 1743 /44[4]
1751-58, Philip Philips, VG [5]
John Duffy, 10 May 1758, 16 Sept 1760 [6]
16 Sept 1760, Charles Brett, VG[7]
22 June 1769, John Ruane, VG[8]
26 April 1776, John Joyce described as former VG of Achonry [9]
24 Feb 1803, Mark Rush[10]
20 June 1817, James Filan, VG[11]

Protestant Deans   APPENDIX 4: Protestant Deans of Achonry [12]

William Lloyd, 1684 – 1691
Samuel Foley, 1691 – 1694
John Ycard, 1694 / 5 – 1733
Sutton Symes, 1733 – 1751
Richard Handcock, 1753 – 25 July 1791
James Langrishe, 1792 – 1806
James Hastings, 1806 – 1812
Arthur Henry Kenney, 1812 – 1821

1 CP, vol. 30, f. 242r: SC Irlanda, vol. 5, f. 289r
2 Acta, vol. 86, ff. 366r-367r.
3 ASV, Nunz. di Fiandra, vol. 135
4 Burke, *Irish Priests,* p. 437
5 SCAR, codex 1.4. f. 467r
6 SCAR, codex 4, ff. 466r, 469r
7 SCAR, codex 1. 4. f. 469r
8 SOCG vol. 825, f. 65r
9 SC Irlanda vol. 12, f. 122r
10 SC Irlanda, vol. 18, ff. 104v, 105r
11 SC Irlanda, vol. 20, f. 122r
12 J.B Leslie, op. cit.

Priests

APPENDIX 5: List of Priests 1683[1]

Phelimeas O Hara, vicarius generalis Achad. et decanus Acadensis,
Johanes Thogher, canonicus Eccliae Cathedralis Achadensis,
Thadeus Higginus, canonicus Eccliae Cathedr. Accadensis,
Galterus Costelloe, canonicus Eccliae Cathedr. Accadensis,
Jacobus O Connell, parochus de Ballisadara in Diocesi Achadensi,
Johanes Mc Donogh, parochus de Killtora,
Thadaeus Brynane, parochus de Clunoghil,
Terentius Gara, parochus de Castelmore,
Maurittius Frayne, parochus de Kilcolman,
Bernardus Brynane, parochus de Killmacteig,
Milerus McDonogh, parochus de Drumratt,
Petrus Nelly, parochus de Killmoraghan,
Thadeus Higginus, parochus de Killfry,
Rich. Cluan, parochus de Killoran,
Pattritius Henry? parochus de Killvarnad.

APPENDIX 6: List of Priests 1684[2]

John McDonogh, parochus, Kilturra:
James O'Connell, parochus, Ballysodare:
Richard Cluane, parochus, Killoran & Kilvarnet:
Thady Brynane, parochus, Clunoghil:
John Mortagh, parochus, Kilmactigue:
John Roddy, parochus, Kilconduff:
Phelim O'Hara, dean, Achonry:
Thady Higgins, praebendarius, Monlagh:
Walter Costello, praebendarius, Kilmovee:
John Tougher, praebendarius, Dughern:
John Donough, parochus, Kill Carva (?):
Miler Donough, parochus, Drumrat

---

1   Postulation of Hugh MacDermot for Apostolic Vicar of Achonry, 20 Aug 1683, CP, vol. 30, f. 242rv
2   Postulation of Hugh MacDermot for Bishop of Achonry, 4 Sept 1684, SC Irlanda, vol. 5, f. 289r: see *Coll. Hib.*, nos. 27-28, pp. 105-6

List of Priests 1704   APPENDIX 7: List of Priests 1704[3]

"A LIST of the Names of the Popish Parish Priests as they are Registered at a General Quarter Sessions of the Peace held in and for the said County of *Mayo*, on the Eleventh day of *July*, 1704, and were since Return'd up to the *Council-Office* in *Dublin*, pursuant to a Clause in the late Act of Parliment, Intituled, "*An Act for Registring the Popish Clergy.*"

Com. Mayo.

Popish Priests' Names.	Places of Abode.	Age.	Parishes of which they pretend to be Popish Priests.	Time of their receiving Popish Orders	Places where they received Orders.	From whom they received them.	Sureties Names that entered into recognizance for such Priests according to the said Act.
James O'Hara.	of Knocknatanvally.	55	Templemore, Twomore.	1670	at Cloonbare.	Dr. Lynch, pretended Archbp. of Tuam.	Andrew Brown, of Breagwey, Gent. 50*l.* Theohald Burk, of Urlure, Gent. 50*l.*
John Durkein.	of Taucannanagh.	58	Killedan and Boghola.	1671	at Cloonbare.	from the said pretended Archbp. of Tuam.	Neal O'Neal, of Carrowrory, Gent. 50*l.* Roger O'Donnell, of Shyane, Gent. 50*l.*
John Roddy.	of Belahagh.	55	Meelick.	1677	at Oranmore.	from Dr. Andrew Lynch, pretended Bp. of Kilfinory.	Thomas Brown, of Kiltecolla, Gent. 50*l.* Myles Bourk, of Belahagh, Gent. 50*l.*
John Thogher.	of Munichenolan.	49	Killegarvan & Atrymass.	1679	at Portumney.	from Teige Keoghy, pretended Bp. of Clonfert.	Mark Lynch, of Garachloon, Gent. 50*l.* Terence mac Donnel, of Ellagh, Gent. 50*l.*
Jonin Ruane.	of Carrownedin.	56	Killasser Parish, half Parish of Toomore.	1682	at Killmolass.	from Teige Keoghy, Bp. of Clonfert.	Mark Lynch, of Garachloon, Gent. 50*l.* John Fad Galagher, of Cordrissagh, Gent. 50*l.*
Morrish Frayne.	of Lisserightis.	54	Killconduffe.	1674	at Cloonbare.	Dr. Lynch, pretended Archbp. of Tuam.	Neal O'Neal, of Corrowrory, Gent. 50*l.* Charles Jordan, of Roslevin, Gent. 50*l.*
Walter Costello.	of Sunvolhane.	54	Kilmovey.	1672	at Cloonkelagh.	Dr. Keogh, pretended Bp. of Clonfert.	Garret Daniel, of Clagnagh, Gent. 50*l.* Manus O'Donnel, of Roseturke, Gent. 50*l.*
Dominick Berne.	Carroriwagh.	45	No Parish.	1683	Portumna.	Teige Keogh, Bishop of Clonfert.	Valentine Brown, Kinturk. John Brown, Neale.

"A LIST of the Names of the Popish Parish Priests as they are Registered at a General Sessions of the Peace held for the said County, at *Sligoe*, the Eleventh day of *July*, 1704, and were since Return'd up to the *Council-Office* in *Dublin*, pursuant to a Clause in the late Act of Parliment, Intituled, "*An Act for Registring the Popish Clergy.*"

Com. Sligoe.

3   1704 Registration Act: see *Irish Catholic Directory*, 1838; William J. Walsh, *Irish Ecclesiastical Record*, (April-Sept) 1876.

APPENDICES 379

Name	Townland	Acres	Parish	Date	Place	From	Witnesses
Cha. Hara.	Tullyhugh.	42	Aconry.	Sept.14 1684	at Cregin, Co. of Gallway.	from Teige Keohy, Tit'. Bp. of Clonfert.	Thomas Corcoran; and Patrick Duany, Merchants, Sligoe.
James Connell.	Annaghbegg.	56	Ballisadare.	Sept.14 1670	Cong, County Mayo.	James Lynch, Tit'. Archbp. of Tuam.	James Crean, Sligoe, Merchant; and James Dolan, Collony, Merchant.
John Murtagh.	Poonengane.	45	Aconry.	Sept.6 1683	Cregin, Com. Gallway.	Teige Keohy, Tit'. Bp. of Clonfert.	Bryan O'Harra, of Milleagh; and Dudly Costello, of Cully.
James Howly.	Kill mac Teige.	46	Kill mac Teige.	Dec. 1682	Cregin, Com. Gallway.	Teige Keohy, Tit'. Bp. of Clonfert.	Naughten O'Donell, of Carne; and John Gallagher, Shesugarra.
Patrick Kenry.	Leytrim.	50	Aconry.	Dec. 1697	Cregoh, Com. Gallway.	Teige Keohy, Tit'. Bp. of Clonfert.	James Rahmine, of Ederieme; and John Gallagher, of Shessogaruff.
Rich. Cloane.	Karricloonine.	50	Killoran.	Dec. 1678	Cregin, Com. Gallway.	Teige Keohy, Tit'. Bp. of Clonfert.	Francis King, Junior; and Thomas Jones, of Rathmore.
Will. Kenedy.	Gurtoh Mone.	60	Kill mac Teige.	1666	City Dublin.	Patrick Plunket, Tit'. Bp. of Andrew Lynch,	Thomas Jones, of Rathmore. Dennis mac Alaster, Collracell.
Bryan Brenane.	Lislea.	60	Kill mac Teige.	Feb. 1677	Oranmore, County Gallway.	Tit'. Bp. of Killfonora.	Bartholomew Hart, of Banady. Dennis mac Alaster, Collracell.
William macDonaugh.	Tialooher.	28	Killvarnett.	Sept. 1670	Clonfert	Donnelan, Tit'. Bp. of Clonfert.	Morgan mac Donnagh, of Roscrib. Charles Phillips, of Oghane.
Peter Nelly.	Ballybrenan.	73	Emlaghffad.	Dec. 1678	Clonfert	Teige Keohy, Tit'. Bp. of Clonfert.	John Brett, of Dorrowne; and Roger Horohy, Balimote.
Teige Davy.	Coolany.	33	Killasalvy.	March 1697	Killconell.	Donnelan, Tit'. Bp. of Clonfert.	George Enerist, of Balimole. Bryan mac Donagh, Carrowhobid.
Teague macDonagh.	Knockrany.	52	Killtorruffe.	Sept. 1678	Clonfert	Teige Keohy, Tit'. Bp. of Clonfert.	Miles Phillips, of Ballindune. Morgan macDonnagh, of Rossgreb.
Edmonde Conane.	Dunmigan.	31	Kilmorhan.	Sept. 1697	Killconell.	Donnelan, Tit'. Bp. of Clonfert.	Miles Phillips, of Ballindune. Morgan macDonnagh, of Rossgreb.
James Mullruniffin.	Temple a Vany.	60	Jewhmoure.	Sept. 1671	Cloonbar, Co. Gallway.	James Lynch, Tit'. Archbp. of Tuam.	Owen Mullruniffin, Templeavany. Morgan macDonnagh, of Rossgreb.
Teige Brenane.	Ballinrea.	53	Cloonoghill.	Nov. 1672	Cregin, Co. Gallway.	Teige Keohy, Tit'. Bp. of Clonfert.	Thomas Corcoran, and Patrick Duany, of Sligoe.
John macDonnagh.	Tavnagh.	50	Drumratt.	Sept. 1679	Cregin, Co. Gallway.	Teige Keohy, Tit'. Bp. of Clonfert.	Morgan macDonnagh, of Rossgreb, Miles Phillips, of Ballindune.
John Marran.	Ardgalen.	41	Killaraht.	June 1693	Cregin, Co. Gallway.	James Wheelan, Tit'. Bp. of Ossory.	Charles Phillips, of Ogham, Miles Phillips, of Ballindune.
David Henery.	Killreenane.	50	Killfree.	Sept. 1697	Cregin, Co. Gallway.	Teige Keohy, Tit'. Bp. of Clonfert.	Dr. Francis mac Lea, of Killteenane; and Phelem Gara, of the same.
Terence Garra.	Cloonciher	54	Killcolman.	Feb.11 1677	Orranmore, Co. of Gallway.	Andrew Lynch, Tit'. Bp. of Gallway.	James Garra, of Lunncloo, in the half Barony of Colavin. Francis Garra, of Lishocunian, of the same.
Thady Higgin.	Ballybrenane	65	Emlaghffad.	1667	Dublin	Patrick Plunket, Tit'. Bp. of Ardagh.	John Maley, of Sligoe; and Stephen Crean, of the same.

State of Popery 1731 APPENDIX 8: Report on the state of popery 1731

Parishes	Priests	Mass Houses	Popish Schools	Observations
Achonry	Thady O'Hara Pat Brenan	0	A School for Philosophy by Thady O'Hara	The Titular Dean of Achonry does not reside in the Parish. Seldom have Service two Sundays successively in the same place
Cloonoghil				These three Fryars officiate as assistants to O'Hara in the Parish of Cloonoghil
Ballysodara Kiloran Kilvarnet	none settled	0	0	These Parishes mostly Inhabited by British Debentures. The Priests here have a Custom of Alternative Services so that one Priest does not serve above two years successively in one place
Tumore	1	1		
Straid	1	1		Fryars meet sometimes at this Abby, tho I cannot learn that they have Residences near it
Kilasser.	1	1		
Melick .	1	1		The Mass Houses in these Parishes have been Rebuilt & placed in a more convenient place within these few years
Bochola.	1	1		
Kiledan	1	1		
Kilconduff	1	1	1	From whence young men have been qualify'd for Orders
Kilbeagh	2	2		
Emlafada	Thady Davey	1 built about 6 yrs. ago	1	These Fryars live dispersed but are related to the best Popish Familys in the Barony
Kilmurragh Drumrat Tumower	Jas. Tymon his assistants are Nich. O Hara, John Henery & Edwd. Mulrunifine		1	Mass frequently said in private houses. This Country swarms with a new set of priests who live dispersed so that the poor groan under their burthen.
Kilturragh	Edmd. Mulrunifine			Resident Clergy of the Established Church 7
Kilcolman	1	1	1	Popish Priests beside vagrant Priests & Fryars 26
Castlemore	1	1		
Kilmovee	1	1		Friars 13
Attamas Kilgarvey	1	0	1	
Kilaraght Kilfry Kilashalvy	1 1 1	0	0	
Kilmacteig	1	0	0	ROBT. KILLALA & ACHONRY

NOTE.–In the Diocese of Achonry according to the Return there were no "Nunnerys" and no "Fryarys" except "one reputed Fryary in a bog" in the parish of Kilcolman. There were no "Private Chapels," but in the returns for the parish of Kiloran it is noted that "most private houses serve as such," and in the returns for the parish of Melick it is stated "that most gentlemens houses serve as such." There were no "Fryars" except in Achonry, Cloonoghil and Emlafada. In Achonry parish the names of the Fryars were "O'Hara, Raughnin, McTeere"; in Cloonoghil, Ant McDonagh, Mick McDonagh, Mich. Harte"; and in Emlafada, "Fra Cormack, Guardian, Fra Brett, Fra Cunane, Fra King, Hugh McDonagh, Mich. McDonagh, Fra Davey, etc.'

4   Arch. Hib., vol. 3 (1914), pp. 128-9

APPENDIX 9: List of Priests 1734[5]

John O'Hart, B.Th.
M. Dowell, MA & Dr
P Burne
L. Beirne
Thomas Jordan
Dominick Kearney
Peter McHugo
Terence O'Gara

APPENDIX 10: List of Priests 1734/5[6]

William McDonnagh, archdeacon, D.U.I.P.
John Duffy, Dr. Paris, PP, Castlemore and Kilcolman
James O'Hara
James Howley, D.U.I.P.
Henry Jordan, canon, Killedan
Edmund Kelly
Thady Davey
David Henry
Michael Costello
Eugene Sweeney
Thomas Bourke
Edmund Mulrunifin
Patrick Brennan, apostolic notary.

APPENDIX 11: List of Priests 1738[7]

James MacDonnough,
Francis MacDonnogh,
Denis Gormley,
Eugeny Proceny? (Sweeny)
also mentioned 'Knavesi '(Patrick Knavesy?)

---

5 Accusations made against Bishop Dominick O'Daly by a number of priests, ASV, Nunz. di Fiandra, vol. 130, ff. 10r, 11v
6 Postulation by Achonry chapter of John O'Hart, 27 Jan 1734/5, ASV Nunz. di Fiandra, vol. 131 f. 107rv
7 Priests who testified in favour of James Gallagher against Bishop John O'Hart, 29 Oct 1738, SOCG, vol. 699, f. 352r

List of Priests 1739   APPENDIX 12: List of Priests 1739[8]

Owen Sweeney, canon
John Ruane, canon
Thomas Bourke, canon
Patrick Beirne, canon
Patrick Brennan, canon & apostolic protonotary:

List of Priests 1758   APPENDIX 13: List of Priests 1758[9]

John Duffy, dean & VG
James McDonogh, canon
Eugene Sweeney, canon
Dominick Kearney, canon
John Hart, canon
Charles Brett, canon
Terence O'Gara, canon & apostolic notary
John Ruane, canon
Henry Jordan, canon
Patrick Knavesey, PP Foxford
Dominick Finn, PP Kilfree
Terence McGuan, PP St Attracta (Killaraght?)
Moriartus O'Hara, PP St Cuthbert's (Tubbercurry ?)
Edmund Kelly, PP Kilbeagh
Peter McHugo, PP St Morgan's (Kilmorgan?)
fr. Andrew Duffy, PP St Movidy's (Kilmovee?)
fr. Peter Philips, PP St Mary's of Emlefad
fr. Anthony McDonogh, PP Kilshalvey
Patrick McHary, PP Achonry
James O'Donnell, PP Killcuon (Kilconduff?)
Denis Gormley, PP St Patrick's (?)
David Kearney, PP St Brigid's (?)

8   Five Achonry canons postulate John Duffy, dean, canon & VG for bishop, ASV Nunz. di Fiandra, vol. 135, f. 194r: see *Coll. Hib.*, no. 10, p. 76
9   9 Achonry canons & 13 clergy postulate Philip Philips for Achonry, 10 & 26 May 1758, SCAR, codex 4, f. 466rv

APPENDIX 14: List of Priests 1760[10]

John Duffy, dean
Charles Brett, VG & secretary
James MacDonogh, canon
Dominic Kearney, canon
John O'Hart, canon
Edmund O'Kelly, canon
Francis O'Hurley, canon
John Ruane, canon
Eugene Sweeney, canon
Terence O'Gara, canon

APPENDIX 15: List of Priests 1768[11]

Dominick Kearney, VF & PP Kilmactigue
Daniel Mullarkey, PP St Colman's & B.V.M. (Kilcolman?)
Charles Brett, VG & PP Ballisodare
James MacDonogh

APPENDIX 16: List of Priests 1769[12]

John Ruane, VG & synodal examiner
Edmund Kelly, PP & canon
Anthony McNamara, scribe & curate of Achonry

---

10   10 Achonry canons postulate Philip Philips for Killala, 16 Sept 1760, SCAR, codex 4, f. 469r
11   Attestation in favour of James Gallagher mentioned four priests, 3 Oct 1768, SOCG, vol. 823, f. 240rv
12   Letter of Bishop Kirwan to Propaganda re James Gallagher mentioned three priests, 22 Aug 1769, SOCG, vol. 825, f. 65r

List of Priests 1776   APPENDIX 17:   (A) List of Priests 1776[13]

Anthony McDonogh, PP Killoran
Eugene Banaghan, PP Kilfree
Anthony McNamara, PP of part of parish of Achonry
Laurence O'Connor, PP Monte Rixoso (?)
Patrick O'Connor, PP of Kilturra & Cloonoghill
John Duffy, PP Kilshalvey
Dominick O'Hara, PP Cloonacool
John Duffy, PP Drumrat & Toomour
— Joyce? (signature illegible) canon & prebendary of Kinaffe
Patrick Knavesey, canon & prebendary of Killoran
Thady O'Flaherty, canon & prebendary of Killedan
Anthony Ruane, canon & prebendary of Kilmactigue
James McManus, canon & prebendary of Attymass
Michael O'Brien, PP — (illegible, Mequest?, possibly Attymass)
John Durcan, PP Kilgarvan
Francis Kearney, PP Kilconduff
Henry O'Neal, PP Meelick
Edward Hust (Hurst?), PP Ballelahon

List of Priests 1776   APPENDIX 17:   (B) List of Priests 1776[14]

Dominick Kearney, canon
Edmund Kelly, canon
Mark Rush, canon
Thomas Costello, canon & protonotary apostolic

---

13 18 Achonry priests postulate John Fitzmaurice, vic. cap. for bishop, 3 May 1776, SOCG, vol. 844, f. 269r
14 4 priests postulate against John Fitzmaurice, 14 May 1776, SOCG, vol. 844, f. 267r

APPENDIX 18: List of Priests n.d. (1779-83)[15]

Names	Abodes	Ages	Parishes	Times and Places of receiving Popish Orders
Philip Phillips	Cloonmore	64	Titular Bishop of Achonry	Ordained in 1742, consecrated in 1761, at Dublin
Patrick McNicholas	Killgarvin	37	Vicar of Kilgarvey	Ordained at Killtemagh 1771
Patrick O'Connor	Swineford	50	Vicar of Killconduff	Ordained in 1760
John Duffy	Ballaghadereen	41	Vicar of Castlemore and Killcolman	Ordained in 1765
Thady Flaherty	Bushey Park	50	Vicar of Killedan	Ordained in 1760
Henry O'Neal	Barley Hill	36	Vicar of Bucholla	Ordained in 1769
Dominic O'Hara	Cloonacool	40	Vicar of Achonry	Ordained at Killtemagh in 1769
Dominic Kearny	Killmactige	76	Vicar of Killmactige	Ordained at Gallen in 1732
Anthony McNamara	Achonry	49	...	Ordained at Bunnitubber in 1760
Dominic Kelly**	Kilmovee	49	Vicar of Kilmovee	Ordained in 1761 at Toledo
Thomas Costello	Cregane	38	Vicar of Killcolman and Castlemore	Ordained at Rome, 1769
Mark Rush*	Ballinalack	39	Vicar of Cloonoghill	Ordained at Killtimagh in 1765
Francis Dunlevy	Killevil	29	Vicar of Killshalvey	Ordained at Killtorrow in 1779
Andrew Dunlevy	Ballimote	32	Vicar of Emlafadd and Killmorgan	Ordained at Killtemagh
William Hurly	Banada	35	Prior of Banada	Ordained in 1774
Lewis Williams	Ballimote	...	Superior of Ballimote	

15 Bishop Philips & 13 Achonry priests took the Oath of Allegiance, *Arch. Hib.*, vol. 1 (1912), pp. 70-71
* Mark Rush d. 1 April 1817 (O'Rorke, *Sligo*, p. 197) b. 1740, 39 in 1779
** Probably a Dominican attached to Sligo Convent. Hugh Fenning.

List of Priests 1786   APPENDIX 19: (A) List of Priests n.d. (1786)[16]

Dominick Kearney, archdeacon & PP
Mark Rush, canon & PP, Cloonoghill
Andrew Donlevy, canon & PP, Kilmovee
Eugene Banaghan, canon & PP
Edmund Kelly, canon & PP
Francis Quinan, canon & PP
Thady O'Flaherty, canon & PP
Walter Henry, canon & PP
Patrick Knavesey, PP & canon of Killoran
Patrick O'Connor, canon of Meemlagh

List of Priests 1786   APPENDIX 19: (B) List of Priests 1786[17]

Thomas Costello
Antonius MacNamara, PP Corry
Joannes Duffy, PP Mullynabrena
Franciscus Dunlevey, Cloonacola

List of Priests 1792   APPENDIX 20: List of Priests 1792[18]

Mark Rush, archdeacon & VG
Eugene Banaghan, canon of Kilturra
Anthony McNamara, canon of Killoran
Walter Henry, canon of Kilmorgan
Andrew Donlevy, canon of Kilmovee
John O'Flynn, canon of Kilshalvey
Patrick Grady, canon of Kilfree
Michael Farrell, canon of Dohorn
John Fitzmaurice, canon of Kilvarnet & VF
Patrick O'Connor, canon of Meemlagh
Thady O'Flaherty, canon of Killedan & VF
Patrick McNicholas, canon of Kinaffe
Michael O'Brien, canon of Emlefad
Edmund Kelly, canon of Kilmactigue

---

16   Achonry chapter (10 canons) postulated Thomas Costello for bishop, SC Irlanda, vol. 16, f. 208r
17   Letter of Bishop Egan to Propaganda which mentioned four priests, 28 Nov 1786, SC Irlanda, vol. 16, ff. 149rv, 150rv
18   14 canons attested the quinquennial report to Rome of Bishop Thomas O'Connor, 26 Sept 1792, Fondo di Vienna, vol. 28, f. 37v

APPENDIX 21: List of Priests 1797[19]

Mark Rush, archdeacon
Thady O'Flaherty, canon
Robert Dillon, canon
Michael O'Brien, canon
Michael Farrell, canon
John O'Flynn, canon
Patrick Grady, canon
Owen Banaghan, canon
Walter Henry, canon
Daniel O'Connor, canon
Patrick O'Connor, canon
Edmund Kelly, canon
Patrick McNicholas, canon

APPENDIX 22: List of Priests 1803[20]

Mark Rush, dean & vic. cap.
Michael O'Brien, PP & canon
Patrick Grady, PP & canon
Robert Dillon, PP & canon
Daniel O'Connor, PP & canon
Patrick O'Connor, PP & canon
James Dalton, PP & canon
Dominick Philips, PP & canon
Walter Henry, PP & canon
John O'Flynn, PP & canon
Thady O'Flaherty, PP & canon
Andrew Carilan (Conlan?), PP & canon

---

19 Petition signed by 13 canons to Bishop Thomas O'Connor asking him to make Dr Charles O'Conor, an Elphin priest, a canon of Achonry diocese, 10 Dec 1797. OCD, 8. 4. SH 058
20 12 canons postulate Michael Farrell for bishop, 24 Feb 1803. SC Irlanda, vol. 18, ff. 104v, 105r

List of Priests 1816 APPENDIX 23: (A) List of Priests 1816[21]

Michael Farrell, archidiaconus & parochus Acchadensis
Jacobus Henry, canonicus & parochus
Jacobus Dalton S.T.B., canonicus & parochus
Patricius McNicholas, canonicus & parochus
Joannes McNulty, canonicus & parochus
Joannes Durkan, canonicus & parochus
Dominicus Philips, canonicus & parochus
Patritius McNicholas, philosophiae professor

List of Priests 1816 APPENDIX 23: (B) List of Priests 1816[22]

Ja(me)s. Filan, VG and canon
Mark Rush, dean
Roger McDermot, canon & PP
Rich(ar)d Fitzmaurice, canon & PP
Andreas Conilan, canon & PP
Dominick Philips, canon & PP
Daniel O'Connor, canon & PP
Francis Boland, canon & PP
John McNulty, PP
John Coleman, canon & PP
Dominick O'Hara, PP
John O'Flynn, canon & PP
Ja(me)s. Feighney, PP
Rob(er)t Hepburne
Ja(me)s. Gallagher
Barth(o)l(ome)w Kearns
Mich(ae)l Filan, coadjutor
Edm(un)d Clarke, prior of Straide
Luke Leyden, prior of Urlaur
James McNicholas, f(ria)r, Urlaur
Patto Sweeny, coadjutor
Matthew Leonard, prior of Banada
Edm(un)d Kelly, prior of Ballymote
John Doddy
Michael Donoghue, coadjutor

21 7 Achonry canons and Patrick McNicholas to Cardinal Litta postulating against William Costello, 8 Mar 1816. SOCG, vol. 918, f. 171rv
22 Copy of letter of Bishop O'Flynn to secular & regular clergy of Achonry asking for their signed support of William Costello addressed to Bishop Troy, Dublin, Kilfree, 11 Mar 1816. SOCG, vol. 918 (1818), f. 172rv

APPENDIX 23: (C) List of Priests n.d. (1816)[23]

List of Priests 1816

Mark Rush, dean
James Filan, canon & VG
Roger Dermot PP
John O'Flynn, canon
Mich(ae)l Fitmaurice PP
Dominick O'Hara, canon
John McNulty PP
Patrick Sweeny PP
Robert Hepburne
John Doddy, canon
Edmond Kelly, guard(ia)n
James McHugh
Mich(ae)l Donoghue
Daniel O'Connor, PP
Dominick Phillips, PP
John Coleman, PP
Andrew Conilon, PP
Michael Filan
Edm(und) Clarke, prior Straid(e)
Fra(ncis) Boland, PP
James Feighny, PP
Luke Leydin, prior of Orlar

Templehouse
(Photograph, Jack Ruane)

23 Achonry clergy postulated William Costello for coadjutor in Achonry, n.d. (1816), SOCG, vol. 917 (1817), f. 271rv: Italian translation: f. 269rv

List of Priests 1817   APPENDIX 24: (A) List of Priests 1817[24]

Bishop John O'Flynn
James Filan, canon & VG
R. McDermot, canon & PP
R. Fitzmaurice, canon & PP
John Coleman, canon & PP
J. Durkan, canon & PP
A. Conlan, canon & PP
F. Boland, PP
J. Doddy, PP
D. O'Hara, PP
J. O'Flynn, canon & PP
J. Feyghna, PP
D. Philips, PP
D O'Connor, PP
P. Sweeney, PP
M. Filan, CC
R. Hepburne, CC
J. McHugh, CC
L. Leyden, CC
W. McHugh, CC
M. Fitzmaurice, CC

List of Priests 1817   APPENDIX 24: (B) List of Priests 1817[25]

Andreas Conilin, can. & parochus
Dominicus Philips, can. & parochus
Joannes Durkan, can. & parochus
Jacobus Feighney, parochus
Joannes Coleman, can. & parochus
Joannes Doddy, parochus
Patricius McNicholas, can. & parochus
Dominicus O'Hara, parochus
Franciscus Boland, can. & parochus
Joannes McNulty, parochus
Ricardus Fitzmaurice, can. & parochus
Patricius Sweeney, parochus
Daniel O Connor, can. & parochus
Michael Filan, parochus
Jacobus Henry, can. & parochus
Michael Fitzmaurice, parochus
Joannes O'Flynn, can. & parochus
Jacobus McHugh, vicarius

24 Bishop O'Flynn and 20 priests signed protest, 20 June 1817. SC Irlanda, vol. 20, f. 122r
25 Achonry clergy to Cardinal Litta postulating Patrick McNicholas for bishop, 24 July 1817. SOCG, vol. 917 (1817), ff. 65rv, 72v

Robertus Hepburne, vicarius
Fr Edmundus Clarke, prior ordinis Predicatorum
Andreas Hannan, vicarius
Fr Lucas Lydon, prior ordinis Predicatorum
Jacobus Gallagher, vicarius
Fr Jacobus McNicholas, ordinis Predicatorum
Thomas McNicholas, vicarius
Fr Franciscus Fitsimmons, ordinis Sancti Francisci
Michael Donoghue, vicarius
Patricius Hegan (Kegan?), vicarius
Petrus Cooke, vicarius

APPENDIX 24: (C) List of Priests 1817[26]

Mich(ae)l Farrell, archid(iaconu)s Accaden(si)s
Dominicus Philips, parochus & can(onicu)s
Patritius Grady, par(ochu)s & can(onicu)s
Edwardus Roddy, coadj(uto)r
Joannes Smyth, conventus Banadensis ex-Prior
Edmundus Clarke, Prior conventus Stradensis
Jacobus Feighney, parochus
Lucas Lydon, prior et coadj(utor) – prior conventus Orlarensis
Andreas Conilon, can(onicu)s & parochus
Franciscus Burke, A:M vic(arius) de Killedan
Gulielmus? McHugh, coadj(utor) pastor
Matthaeus Leonard, Prior conventualis Banadensis
Joannes McNulty, parochus
John Doddy, can(onicus) & parochus
Jacobus McHugh, coadj(utor)

APPENDIX 24: (D) List of Priests 1817[27]

Michaele Farrell, hujusce Dioesceos Archidiaconus
R. McDermot, can(onicus) et p(arochus)
Richardus Fitzmaurice, can(onicus) et p(arochus)
Patricius McNicholas, can(onicus) et p(arochus)
Joannes O'Flynn, can(onicus) & par(ochus)
Jacobus Henry, can(onicus) et p(arochus)
Joannes Durkan, can(onicus) & par(ochus)
Dominicus Philips, can(onicus) et par(ochus)
Joannes Coleman, can(icus) et par(ochus)
Daniel O'Connor, can(onicus) et par(ochus)
Jacobus Filan, can(onicus) et VG
Joannes McNulty, par(ochus)

---

26   15 Achonry clergy to Cardinal Litta postulating James Dalton for bishop, Ballaghaderreen, 30 July 1817. SOCG, vol. 918 (1818), ff. 66rv, 71v
27   Achonry Clergy to Felice Argenti, 26 Aug 1817. SOCG, vol. 918 (1818), ff. 68rv, 69rv

Richardus Fitzmaurice, c(anonicus) et p(arochus)
Jacobus Feighny, p(arochus)
R. McDermot, can(onicus) et p(arochus)
Michael Fitzmaurice, p(arochus)
Dominicus Philips, can(onicus) et p(arochus)
Joannes Doddy, p(arochus)
Jacobus Henry, can(onicus) et p(arochus)
Dominicus O'Hara, p(arochus)
Joannes Coleman, can(onicus) et p(arochus)
Patricius Sweeny, p(arochus)
Patricius McNicholas, can(onicus) et p(arochus)
Michael Filan, p(arochus)
Joannes Flynn, can(onicus) et p(arochus)
Robertus Hepburne, vic(arius)
Daniel O'Connor, can(onicus) et p(arochus)
Jacobus McHugh, vic(arius)
Joannes Durcan, can(onicus) et p(arochus)
Michael Donoghue, vic(arius)
Franciscan Boland, p(arochus)
Petrus Cooke, vic(arius)
Fr Jacobus Leyden, Or(dinis) Pred(icatorum) Prior
Fr Franciscus Fitzimons, O(rdinis) S(ancti) Fr(ancisci)

List of Priests 1817   APPENDIX 24: (E) List of Priests 1817[28]

Daniel O'Connor, p(arochus). & can(onicus)
Joannes Flyn(n), p(arochus) & can(onicus)
Joannes Coleman, p(arochus) & can(onicus)
And(reas) Conilan, p(arochus) & can(oni)us
Dominicus Philips, p(arochus) & can(onicu)s
Richardus Fitzmaurice, p(arochus) & can(onicus)
Joannes Doddy, p(arochus)
Michael Filan, p(arochus)
Jacobus Feighney, p(arochus)
Robertus Hepburne, p(arochus)
Mich. Fitzmaurice, vic(arius)
Lucas Leyden, Prior de Orlar, O.S.D.
Matthaeus Leonard, P(rio)r conventus Corporis Christi, Banada
Patricius Keegan, vic(arius)
Joannes McHugh,
Fr Franciscus Egan, vic(arius) (?)
Edwardus Roddy, vic(arius)

28 Achonry clergy to Cardinal Litta postulating against McNicholas & in favour of Filan, 15 Dec 1817. SOCG, vol. 918 (1818), ff. 78rv, 81rv

APPENDIX 25: List of Priests 1818[29]

Jacobus Henry, canonicus & parochus
Jacobus McHugh, parochus
Franciscanus Boland, can(onicus) & parochus
Joannes McNulty, parochus
Dominicus O'Hara, parochus
Patricius McNicholas, can(onicus) & parochus
Joannes Durkan, can(onic)us & parochus
Petrus Cooke, vic(arius)
Michael O'Flynn, vic(arius)
Mathaeus H(e)aly, vic(arius
Edmundus Clarke, O(rdinis) Praed(icatorum)
Michael Donoghu(e), vic(arius)
Jacobus McNicholas, Ord(inis) Praed(icatorum)

APPENDIX 26: List of Priests 1792–1818[30]

Philip Philips, mentioned in Will of Bishop Walter Blake, 28 April 1758.[31]
Thady O'Flaherty, parish priest of Killedan, 13 Feb. 1776.[32]
Anthony McNamara, Bunacrannagh, 1792[33]
Rev John Fitzmaurice, Collooney, 1794
Andrew Donlevy, Ballymote, 1795
Owen Banaghan, Drumratt, 1801
Rev James Feighny, Kilmovee, 1818

29 Some Achonry clergy to Cardinal Litta postulating McNicholas, 4 Jan 1818, SOCG, vol. 918 (1818), ff. 76rv, 83rv
30 Index to Administration Bonds, National Archives, Dublin. These are usually for people who died intestate and legal recourse had to be taken for the administration of their property and the date given is usually within a year or two of the date of death.
31 *Arch. Hib.*, vol. 1, p. 223
32 Will of Bishop Patrick Robert Kirwan, *Arch. Hib.*, vol. 1, p. 225.
33 Possibly Anthony McNamara who was parish priest of Curry in 1786 and last mentioned in Sept 1792.

List of Priests 1710–1833

APPENDIX 27: List of Priests 1710–1833 [34]

James O'Connell, parish priest of Ballisodare, died April 1710.[35]
Thady O'Flaherty, parish priest of Kiltimagh (Killedan), built and dedicated chapel to the Blessed Virgin 1779.[36]
Owen Banaghan, parish priest of Keash?, died 3 April, 1800, aged 68 years.[37]
Walter Henry, parish priest of Ballisodare and Kilvarnet, died 3 July 1805, aged 60 years.[38]
Patrick Henry, 9 Sept 1806.[39]
Richard Fitzmaurice, parish priest of Keash for 33 years, died 7 April 1831.[40]
James Henry, parish priest of Ballisodare and Kilvarnet, died July 1833.[41]

List of Priests

APPENDIX 28: List of Priests[42]

29 Mar 1731, James O'Hara.[43]
John O'Hart, Bishop of Achonry, died May 1739.[44]
1770, John Cooke.[45]
28 May 1772, died the Rev Mr O Rorke of Ballymote, Co Sligo.[46]
Mr Vernon, 'a Romish clergyman' died at Ballymote, 1775.[47]
James Gallagher, 'a Romish clergyman', going from one village to another near Banada, was found smothered after a violent storm, Feb 1776.[48]
Philip Duffy, died at Ballymote, 1782.[49]
Dominick Kearney, 'who for 60 years and upwards was parish priest of Kilmactigue' died, 1788.[50]
Andrew Donlevy, died at Ballymote, aged c. 44 years, 1794.[51]

---

34 From gravestone inscriptions.
35 Tombstone outside the eastern gable of the old church in Ballisodare.
36 Commemorative plaque in old Killedan churchyard. Probably also his tomb.
37 Tombstone in Knockbrack graveyard, Keash: see O'Rorke, *Sligo*, vol. 2, p. 215n
38 Inscription on vault in Collooney graveyard (?); see O'Rorke, *Ballysadare and Kilvarnet*, p. 489
39 Inscription in Kilturra graveyard; see O'Rorke, *Sligo*, vol. 2, p. 196n. Identity uncertain.
40 Tombstone in Knockbrack graveyard, Keash; see O'Rorke, *Sligo*, vol. 2, p. 216n. See also inscription on chalice, 1802.
41 Inscription on vault in Collooney graveyard (?): see O'Rorke, *Ballysadare and Kilvarnet*, p. 489
42 From newspapers: J. Brady, *Catholics and Catholicism in the 18th-century Press*
43 *Dublin Intelligence*, *Arch Hib.*, vol. XVI, pp. 51–2
44 *Dublin Daily Post*, 5 June 1739, quoted in *Arch. Hib.*, XVI, p. 59
45 McDonagh, *Ballymote & the parish of Emlaghfad*, p. 202
46 *Arch. Hib.*, vol. XVII
47 27 Mar 1775, *Arch. Hib.*, vol. XVII
48 13 Feb 1776, *Arch. Hib.*, vol. XVIII, p. 178
49 *Freeman's Journal*, quoted in McDonagh, op. cit., p. 202
50 4 Dec 1778, *Arch. Hib.*, vol. XIX, p. 263
51 *Walker's Hibernian Magazine*, 1794; McDonagh, op. cit., pp. 122, 202

Students

APPENDIX 29: List of Priest-Students in Paris 1676–1772[1]

Hugh (Mac)Dermot, (Tuam) gained a scholarship to Irish College Paris in 1676.[2] In October 1678, MacDermot, a priest, registered in the faculty of law in the university of Paris.[3]
Bernard Morvornagh, ordained 21 December 1685, registered in the faculty of Law, Paris, Oct 1687, M.A., 8 July 1690, 5 Dec 1692, student in Collège de Montaigu, 14 Aug 1694, B.U.I.P., 8 Mar 1695 L.U.I.P., member of the German Nation, 7 April 1696, D.U.I.P.[4]
Charles O'Hara registered in the faculty of Law, Paris in October 1695, 30 June 1698 B.C.L., 3 April 1699, L.C.L., 31 Dec 1699, D.C.L.[5]
John O'Hart, M.A. Paris, 2 Aug 1707, 1711, B.Th. Paris, sustained *tentativa*, and was resident in Collège des Lombards.[6]
James Tymon, 17 Feb 1711, resident in Collège des Lombards.[7] In October 1713 Tymon registered in the faculty of Law, Paris, 9 Aug 1715, B.U.I.P.[8]
Thadaeus Jordan (no diocese recorded) registered in the faculty of Law, Nov 1713.[9]
Thomas Moore, M.A. Paris, 22 Oct 1715, registered in the faculty of Law, Paris, Oct 1718.[10]
Andrew Donlevy registered in the faculty of Law, in the University of Paris in Oct 1718, 1 Sept 1719, baccalaureate in Law, 15 Mar 1720, licentiate in Law.[11] 10 June 1722, appointed prefect of the community of clerics and scholars in Collège des Lombards by the Archbishop of Paris.[12] 1741, published Catechism. 7 Dec 1746, died age 66 and was buried in Collège des Lombards.[13]
Walter Blake, M.A. Paris, 2 Sept 1720, on the roll of Paris licensiands and resident in Collège de Navarre, 1726, L.Th., 1728, elected Connacht provisor of Collège des Lombards, 1734.[14]

---

1 No student registers have survived for the Irish colleges in Paris. The following list of Achonry priests and bishops have been extracted from the university registers and various other sources and probably represents only a fraction of the Achonry priests who studied in Paris.
2 Possibly, Hugh MacDermot who later became apostolic vicar and Bishop of Achonry. Boyle, *History of the Irish College Paris*, p. 199
3 Brockliss & Ferté, op. cit., no. 1072; cf also no. 1132. AN, MM 1061 p. 19
4 AN, MC et / XVII / ; Brockliss & Ferté, op. cit., no. 1023
5 Brockliss & Ferté, op. cit., no. 1018
6 Brockliss & Ferté, op. cit., no. 1019; Swords, *The Irish-French Connection*, p. 67
7 Swords, *The Irish-French Connection*, p. 66
8 Brockliss & Ferté, op. cit., no. 1024
9 Brockliss & Ferté, op. cit., no. 1021
10 Brockliss & Ferté, op. cit., no. 1022
11 Brockliss & Ferté, no. 1016
12 AN, MC et / XVII / 627
13 Boyle, *Irish College Paris*, p. 227
14 Brockliss & Ferté, op. cit., no. 1114; cf BN Ms. L. 9157 f. 79rv, Ms. FR. 22823, p. 177, Ms. L. .15440, p. 177; Swords, 'History of the Irish College, Paris, 1578-1800' in *Arch. Hib.*, XXXV (1980), p. 69

Edmund Jordan was a student in Collège de Navarre, Paris, 1721.[15]
John Duffy was a student in Collège de Navarre, 23 Feb 1721.[16] In Jan 1727 he registered in the faculty of law, Paris where he was describd as a 'priest & pauper'. 25 April 1727, B.U.I.P., 22 April 1728, L.U.I.P., 27 Aug 1731, D.U.I.P.[17]
Edmund Costello, priest of the diocese of Achonry, was a student in Collège des Lombards, 23 Sept 1721.[18]
Terence O'Gara was a student in Collège des Lombards c. 1734-37.[19]
Luke Beirne was a student in Collège des Lombards c. 1734-37.[20] L. O'Beirne signed a letter to Rome accusing Bishop Dominick O'Daly of certain irregularities, 8 Jan 1734.[21]
Patrick Beirne was a student in Collège de Lombards c. 1734-37.[22] P. Burne signed a letter to Rome accusing Bishop Dominic O'Daly of certain irregularities.[23]
Edmund Kelly, was a student in Collège des Lombards, Paris c. 1734-37. (Possibly the same as priest of that name in Achonry.)[24]
James McDonogh was a student in Collège des Lombards, Paris c. 1734-37. (Possibly the priest of the same name in Achonry.)[25]
Patrick Henican, M.A. Paris, 1 Sept 1729, S.T.L., 1738.[26]
Dominick Kearney was a student in Collège des Lombards, Paris c. 1734-7 and signed protests.[27]
Patrick Knavesey was a student in Collège des Lombards c. 1734-37.[28]
Michael Daly was a student in Collège des Lombards in 1737.[29] 29 Nov 1738, M.A. Paris, B.Th. in the faculty of Paris, former procurator of the German Nation.[30] 9 Mar 1785, he founded two burses for priests of Elphin in Collège des Lombards.[31]
'Philips' listed as a student of Collège des Lombards, 27 June 1746. (Possibly Philip Philips who later became Bishop of Achonry.)[32]
John Fitzmaurice, M.A. Paris, 7 Jan 1758. 1764, priest, L.Th. Paris.[33]

15 AN MC et / XVII / 614
16 AN MC et / XVII / 614
17 Brockliss & Ferté, op. cit., no. 1296; AN MM 1077 p. 429, MM 1123, pp. 660, 691, 806
18 AN MC et / XVII / 614
19 SCAR codex 2, ff. 412rv, 464-5, 466-7, 497-8; DDA 12v8
20 SCAR codex 2, ff. 412rv, 464-5, 466-7, 497-8
21 ASV, Nunz. di Fiandra, vol. 130, ff. 10r, 11rv
22 SCAR, codex 2, ff. 412rv, 464-5, 466-7, 497-8
23 ASV, Nunz. di Fiandra, vol. 130, ff. 10r, 11rv
24 SCAR, codex 2, ff. 412rv, 464-5, 497-8
25 SCAR, codex 2, ff. 464-5, 497-8
26 Brockliss & Ferté, op. cit., no. 1020
27 SCAR, codex 2, ff. 412rv
28 SCAR, codex 2, ff. 412rv, 497-8
29 SCAR, codex 2, ff. 464-5, 497-8
30 Brockliss & Ferté, op. cit., no. 1015
31 Swords, 'History of the Irish College, Paris, 1578-1800' in *Arch. Hib.*, vol. XXXV (1980), nos. 388, 595
32 AN v7 331
33 Brockliss & Ferté

Charles Lynagh was a subdeacon in the Irish College, Paris in 1770 and a deacon on 21 Sept 1771. In 1772 he was a member of the community of clerics in the Irish College.[34]

John Baptist O'Flynn, M.O (?). Paris, May 1771 was an acolyte in Collège des Irlandais, 1772, M.A. Paris, 17 Oct 1772.[35]

Thomas O'Connor was a student in Collège des Irlandais c. 1777–1783. He began his second year of theology there in Sept 1780.[36]

William Costello was a student in Collège des Irlandais on 6 Dec 1790.[37]

APPENDIX 30: List of Students in the Irish College, Salamanca

John Joyce came from Santiago to begin theology in the Irish College, Salamanca in 1733. 18 May 1733, he took the triple oath to observe the rules, to take Orders and to return to the mission in Ireland. 29 July 1734 he was examined in first year theology and on 29 July 1735 in second year theology.[38] 1736 (?), ordained in Salamanca and given an attestation by the rector.[39]

James Dalton 1789-97.[40]

William Costello named in a list of Salamancan students in 1796.[41]

APPENDIX 31: List of Students in the Irish College, Alcalà

Terence O'Gara signed an postulation in favour of Michael O'Gara, rector of the college, for Archbishop of Tuam on 18 June 1740. It appears that he came to Alcalà from Collège des Lombards, Paris, to complete his studies.[42]

Elsewhere in Spain, Dominick Kelly was ordained at Toledo in 1761.[43]

APPENDIX 32: List of Students in the Irish College, Rome

Thomas Costello took the oaths to obey the rules and to return to the mission in Ireland on 18 Sept 1762.[44] He received tonsure on 29 August, porter and lector on 30 Aug, exorcist and acolyte on 8 Sept, subdiaconate on 19 Sept and diaconate on 30 Nov 1767.[45] He was ordained in Rome in 1769.[46]

---

34   Boyle, 'Some Irish Ecclesiastics at the Seminary of St Nicolas du Chardonnet, Paris', in *IER* 11 (1910) pp. 490-1; *The Irish College in Paris*, p. 200
35   Boyle, *Irish College Paris*, p. 200; Brockliss & Ferté, op. cit., no. 1142; cf MN Ms L. 9161 f. 69v
36   SC Irlanda, vol. 16 ff. 308v, 309rv, 310r
37   AN F 7 4624; see Swords, *The Green Cockade*, pp. 33-35
38   *Arch. Hib.*, vol. 4, pp. 28-9
39   SCAR, codex 1, f. 695
40   *Arch. Hib.*, vol. 4, pp. 56, 58; vol. 6, p. 13
41   *Arch. Hib.*, vol. 4, p. 58
42   SCAR, codex 4, f. 466r
43   *Arch. Hib.*, vol. 1, p. 70, Kelly was probably a Dominican. Hugh Fenning.
44   AICR, Jesuit Records, Lib. XII, ff. 261r, 264r
45   Vicariato Archivio Storico, Rome, *Liber Ordinationis*, vol. 38
46   *Arch. Hib.*, vol. 1, p. 71

List of Students in Maynooth 1795–1818

APPENDIX 33: List of Students in Maynooth 1795–1818[47]

6 Aug 1795, Patrick McNicholas matriculated in theology, aged 25 years and spent three years in the college. He was ordained 26 May 1804.

5 Aug 1799, James Filan matriculated in humanities, aged 23 years and spent five years in the college. He was ordained on 26 May 1804.

5 Aug 1799, John Durkan matriculated in humanities, aged 24 years and spent five years in the college.

14 Feb 1800, Darby Coleman matriculated and was ordained 24 May 1806.

24 May 1804, Mark Gunning, son of Roderick and Brigid Henry, was promoted to first tonsure.[48]

17 Nov 1804, Patrick Henry matriculated and was ordained on 11 June 1808.

19 Nov 1804, John McNulty matriculated and was ordained S 1807.

7 June 1805, Francis Boland, son of Bartholomew and Catherine Gethings, was admitted to first tonsure; matriculated 29 Sept 1804 and was ordained 27 May 1809.[49]

27 Nov 1805, Patrick Sweeney matriculated and was ordained on 17 June 1810.

9 Sept 1806, James Doyle matriculated and died in 1810.

1 Sept 1808, John O'Flynn matriculated and was ordained 31 May 1814.

18 Sept 1809, John Doddy matriculated and was ordained 13 June 1813?

27 Sept 1809, Bernard Donlevy matriculated.

4 Sept 1811, Michael Filan matriculated and was ordained on 20 May 1815.

23 Oct 1812, Patrick Durcan matriculated and was ordained 27 May 1820.

18 Dec 1812, James McNicholas matriculated and was ordained 5 June 1819.

17 June 1813, Michael Donoghue (extern) was ordained.

1813, James Flynn (John O'Flynn?) ordained S.

21 April 1814, Patrick O'Gorman matriculated and died in 1817.

19 Nov 1814, Patrick McDonnell matriculated and was ordained 5 June 1819.

20 May 1815, Thomas McNicholas (extern) ordained.

31 Aug 1815, John Givlahan matriculated and was ordained 1 Aug 1821.

16 Sept 1815, James O'Hara matriculated and was ordained 27 May 1820.

1816, Edmund Fitzmaurice died.

1816, Michael Fitzsimons died.

29 Aug 1817, Richard Fitzmaurice matriculated and was ordained on 12 June 1824.

29 Aug 1817, Bryan (Bernard O') Kane matriculated in theology.

Other names: Carroll 1808, Coleman 1800, Crosbie 1815, Devine 1806.

---

47 Healy, *Centenary History of Maynooth College,* Appendix xv, pp. 733, 735; Patrick J. Hamell, *Maynooth Students and Ordinations*
48 *Arch. Hib,.* vol. XLIII, pp. 25-30
49 *Arch. Hib,.* vol. XLIII, pp. 25-30

Parish Priests

APPENDIX 34: Succession of Parish Priests

Succession of Parish Priests

Achonry[1]

20 Aug 1683, Phelim O'Hara, dean & VG.[2]
4 Sept 1684, Phelim O'Hara, dean of Achonry.[3]
1704, Charles O'Hara resided at Tullyhugh, John Murtagh at Poonengane, and Patrick Kenry (Henry?) at Leytrim.[4]
1731, Thady O'Hara (Probably Charles O'Hara), Pat Brennan.[5]
9 Mar 1743–4, Murtagh (O')Hara, parish priest, Patrick Keregan, vicar.[6]
26 May 1758, Patrick McHary, parish priest.[7]
22 June 1769, Anthony McNamara, scribe & parochial vicar of Achonry.[8]
3 May 1776, Anthony McNamara, 'parish priest of part of the parish of Achonry' (Curry).[9]
28 Nov 1786, Anthony McNamara (Curry), John (Owen?) Duffy (Mullinabreena) and Francis Donlevy (Cloonacool).[10]
1814, Owen Duffy died and was buried in Achonry graveyard.[11]
1814–34, Dominick O'Hara.[12]

Attymass

20 Aug 1683, John Thogher, canon, (parish not given).[13]
4 Sept 1684, John Tougher, canon of Dohorn.[14]
1704, John Thogher (Tougher) was parish priest of Attymass and Bonniconlon (Kilgarvan) and resided at Munichenolan.[15]
1731, Attymass was coupled with Bonniconlon (Kilgarvan), with one priest and no Mass-house.[16]
1769, Thomas Durkan, parish priest of Attymas, died

---

1 Achonry was a mensal parish until at least 1787. Udienze vol. 23, f. 405r, 406r, 408v. Achonry was the largest parish in Co Sligo. In 1881 it was greater in acreage and population than the four other parishes combined in the barony of Leyny. It was divided into three districts, Mullinabreena, Cloonacool and Curry, with a priest in each district. O'Rorke, *Sligo*, vol. 2, p. 117
2 CP, vol. 30 (1682-1709), f. 242rv
3 SC Irlanda, vol. 5, f. 289r
4 1704 Registration Act
5 Observations: 'The Titular Dean of Achonry does not reside in the Parish'. *Arch. Hib.*, vol. 3, pp. 128-9
6 Burke, op. cit., p. 439
7 SCAR, codex 4, f. 466
8 SOCG, vol. 825, f. 65r
9 SOCG, vol. 844, f. 269r
10 SC Irlanda, vol. 16, ff. 149rv, 150v
11 O'Rorke, *Sligo*, vol. 2, p. 123
12 ibid
13 CP, vol. 30 (1682-1709), f. 242rv
14 SC Irlanda, vol. 5, f. 289r
15 Registration Act
16 *Arch. Hib.*, vol. 3, p. 129

Succession of Parish Priests

3 May 1776, Michael O'Brien was parish priest.[17]
24 Feb 1803, latest documented mention of Michael O'Brien, as a canon, with parish not given. Also mentioned on 26 Sept 1792 and 10 Dec 1797.[18]

Ballaghaderreen (Castlemore & Kilcolman)

20 Aug 1683, Terence O'Gara was parish priest of Castlemore. Maurice Frain was parish priest of Kilcolman.[19]
1704, Terence O'Gara, resident at Clooncither, aged 54 years, registered as parish priest of Kilcolman.[20]
3 Oct 1721, Terence O'Gara, *'paroco della chiesa di S. Columbano nel Castello di Castrello'*.[21]
1731, one priest and one Mass-house in Kilcolman and one priest and one Masshouse in Castlemore.[22]
27 Jan 1734–5, John Duffy, parish priest of the churches of Castlemore and Kilcolman.[23]
16 Sept 1760, last documented reference to John Duffy, who was then dean.[24]
3 Oct 1768, Daniel Mullarkey, *'rector ecclesiarum S. Colmani et B.M.V. Majoris'*.[25]
n.d. (29 Nov 1779), Thomas Costello was parish priest of Kilcolman & Castlemore.[26]
c. 1780, John Duffy, resident in Ballaghaderreen, was described as 'Vicar of Castlemore and Kilcolman' and Thomas Costello, resident in Cregane, as 'Vicar of Kilcolman and Castlemore'.[27]
29 May 1786, Thomas Costello became Coadjutor Bishop of Clonfert.[28]
16 Sept 1786, Bishop Egan requested Castlemore & Kilcolman, vacant by the promotion of Thomas Costello to Clonfert, as a mensal parish.[29]
13 April 1788, Bishop O'Connor asked for Kilcolman & Castlemore as mensal, now vacant & reserved to Holy See as Bishop Egan was transferred to Tuam.[30]
28 July 1789, Bishop O'Connor asked Rome for Kilmactigue as mensal instead of Kilcolman & Castlemore.[31]

---

17   Name of the parish is difficult to decipher. James McManus is described as canon and prebend of Attymass in the same document. SOCG, vol. 844, f. 269r
18   SC Irlanda, vol. 18, ff. 104v 105r; Fondo di Vienna, vol. 28, f. 37v: OCD. 8. 4. SH. 058
19   CP, vol. 30 (1682-1709), f. 242rv
20   1704 Registration Act
21   Acta, vol. 91 (1721), ff. 298v–299v
22   *Arch. Hib.*, vol. 3, p. 129
23   ASV Nunz di Fiandra, vol. 131, f. 107rv
24   SCAR, codex 4, f. 469r
25   SOCG, vol. 823, f. 240rv; Acta vol. 139, ff. 317r–320v
26   SOCG, vol. 852, ff. 153r, 154r
27   *Arch. Hib.*, vol. 1, pp. 70–1
28   Acta, vol. 156, ff. 149r–151r; SOCG, vol. 873, ff 9rv, 10rv
29   SC Irlanda, vol. 16, f. 101rv
30   Udienze, vol. 26, ff. 179r, 180r, 181r
31   SOCG, vol. 884, f. 209rv

26 Aug 1792, Bishop O'Connor requested the Holy Father to confer the united parishes of Kilcolman & Castlemore on Michael Farrell.[32]
24 Feb 1803, Michael Farrell, archdeacon and PP of Castlemore & Kilcolman.[33]
1817, Michael Farrell died.
1817, Patrick Grady siezed possession of the parish of Ballaghaderreen.[34]
26 July 1818, Bishop McNicholas requested and was granted Kilcolman & Castlemore, together with Kilmactigue as mensal parishes because of the poverty of the episcopacy.[35]
1820-23, Patrick Durcan, administrator of Ballaghaderreen.[36]

Succession of Parish Priests

Ballisodare

20 Aug 1683, James O'Connell, PP of Ballisodare.[37]
4 Sept 1684, James O'Connell, PP of Ballisodare.[38]
1704, James O'Connell, resident at Annaghbeg, aged 56 years, registered as PP of Ballisodare.[39]
April 1710, James O'Connell died.[40]
1710, Teige Davey replaced James O'Connell.[41]
29 Oct 1712, Teige Davey (Dawney) reported to have celebrated Mass at Carrickbanagher in the parish Ballisodare.[42]
18 June 1714, Teige Davy, PP of Ballisodare.[43]
18 June 1714, John O'Hart, abode unknown, reported to have returned from abroad.[44]
1731, Ballisodare coupled with Killoran & Kilvarnet, with no priest settled and no Mass-house, no school.[45]
pre-Oct 1735, John O'Hart, PP of Ballisodare.[46]
30 Sept 1735, John O'Hart became Bishop of Achonry. He appointed James Gallagher curate of Ballisodare, retaining the income for his own support.

32   Udienze, vol. 30, f. 435rv
33   SC Irlanda, vol. 18, f. 104rv
34   SC Irlanda, vol. 20, ff 179rv–180rv
35   Udienze, vol. 55, f. 607v; *Lettere,* vol. 299, ff. 445v, 446rv
36   O'Rorke, *Sligo,* vol. 2, p. 112
37   CP, vol. 30 (1682-1709), f. 242rv
38   SC Irlanda, vol. 5, f. 289r
39   1704 Registration Act
40   Tombstone outside Eastern gable of old Ballisodare church: O'Rorke, *Ballysodare & Kilvarnet,* pp. 474–5
41   Burke, op. cit., p. 436
42   Burke, op. cit., p. 434
43   Burke, op. cit., p. 436
44   Burke, op. cit., p. 436
45   Observation: 'The Priests here have a custom of alternative Services so that one Priest does not serve above two years successively in one place'. *Arch. Hib.,* vol. 3, p. 128
46   SC Irlanda, vol. 20, f. 127v

Succession of Parish Priests

1737, James Gallagher appointed PP of Ballisodare by Papal Bull. John O'Hart disputed the Bull and suspended Gallagher.[47]

29 Oct 1738, 'Knavesi, Patrick Knavesey? ('Knavesi'), appointed curate of Ballisodare by O'Hart.[48]

May 1739, Bishop O'Hart died and was succeeded by Walter Blake.

c. 1740, Patrick Henican appointed VG and PP of Ballisodare.

9 Mar 1743–4, Patrick Henican, dean, VG and PP of Ballisodare.[49]

c. 1758–68, Charles Brett, VG & PP of Ballisodare.[50]

Mar 1768, Charles Brett died.[51]

1768, John Fitzmaurice appointed PP of Ballisodare by Bishop Patrick Robert Kirwan.[52]

1768–c. 1794, John Fitzmaurice, PP of Ballisodare. He was the first to reside at Collooney and died c. 1794.[53]

1794–3 July 1805, Walter Henry, PP of Ballisodare & Kilvarnet.[54]

1805–July 1832, James Henry, PP of Ballisodare & Kilvarnet.[55]

Ballymote (Emlefad & Kilmorgan)

20 Aug 1683, Peter Nelly was PP of Kilmorgan.[56]

1704, Peter Nelly, resident at Ballybrenan, aged 73 years, registered as PP of Emlefad, and Thady Higgins, also resident at Ballybrenan, aged 65 years, also registered as PP of Emlefad. Edmund Conane, resident at Dunmigan, aged 31 years, registered as PP of Killmorhan (Kilmorgan?).[57]

1714, Thady Higgins was dead and Peter Kelly (Nelly?) replaced him.[58]

1731, Thady Davey was PP of Emlefad with a Mass-house built about six years ago.[59]

27 Jan 1734–5, Thady Davey was described as 'prebendary'.[60]

26 May 1758, Peter Philips was PP 'of the church of St Mary of Emlefad'. Peter McHugh was described as PP of 'St Morgan's' (Kilmorgan?)[61]

1770, John Cooke.[62]

---

47 Acta, vol. 109 (1739), ff. 277r–8v; Gen. Congr. 25 May 1739, no. 25
48 SOCG, vol. 699, f. 355v
49 Burke, op. cit., pp. 437–8
50 SOCG, vol. 823, f. 240rv
51 O'Rorke, *Ballysadare & Kilvarnet*, p. 480
52 SOCG, vol. 823, ff. 222rv, 223rv, 243v, 244r
53 Index to Administration Bonds, National Archives, Dublin; see O'Rorke, *Ballysadare & Kilvarnet*, p. 481
54 O'Rorke, *Ballysadare & Kilvarnet*, pp. 482, 489
55 O'Rorke, *Ballysadare & Kilvarnet*, pp. 486, 489
56 CP, vol. 30 (1682–1709), f. 242rv
57 1704 Registration Act
58 Burke, op. cit., p. 436
59 *Arch. Hib.,* vol. 3, p. 128
60 Nunz di Fiandra, vol. 131, f. 107rv
61 SCAR, codex 4, f. 466
62 McDonagh, *Ballymote & the parish of Emlaghfad*, p. 202

Succession of Parish Priests

28 May 1772, died the Rev Mr O'Rorke of Ballymote, Co Sligo.[63]
27 May 1775, died at Ballymote, Mr Vernon, a Romish clergyman.[64]
1782, Philip Duffy died at Ballymote.[65]
c. 1780, Andrew Donlevy, resident in Ballymote, aged 32, PP of Emlefad & Kilmorgan.[66]
1794, Andrew Donlevy died at Ballymote.[67]
1811–1817, Patrick Grady, PP of Emlefad & Kilmorgan.[68]
16 Sept 1817, Patrick Grady, PP of Emlefad & Kilmorgan suspended and requested change to Kilmactigue.[69]
–1823, Francis Boland.[70]
1823–1832, Patrick Durcan was PP of Ballymote.[71]

Bohola

1704, John Durkan, resident at Taucannanagh, aged 58 years, registered as PP of Killedan and Bohola.[72]
4 April 1715, Dominick Berne had replaced John Durkan, who had taken the oath of abjuration, as PP of Killedan and Bohola.[73]
1831, there was one priest and one Mass-house in Bohola.[74]
c. 1780, Henry O'Neal, resident at Barley Hill, aged 36 years, was PP of Bohola.[75]

Bonniconlon (Kilgarvan)

23 Aug 1683, John Thogher (no parish given) was a canon of Achonry.[76]
4 Sept 1684, John Togher was canon of Dohorn. John (Mc)Donogh, was PP of Kill Carva (Kilgarvan?).[77]
1704, John Thogher registered as PP of Bonniconlon (Kilgarvan) and Attymass.[78]

---

63 *Arch. Hib.*, vol. XVII
64 *Arch. Hib.*, vol. XVII
65 *Freeman's Journal, Arch. Hib.* vol. XVII
66 *Arch. Hib.*, vol. 1, p. 71
67 Index to Administration Bonds, National Archives, Dublin; *Walkers Hibernian Magazine,* 1794, McDonagh, op.cit., pp. 122, 202
68 SC Irlanda, vol. 20, f. 180rv
69 SC Irlanda, vol. 20, ff. 179rv–180rv
70 O'Rorke, *Sligo,* vol. 2, p. 185, calls him 'Patrick'.
71 O'Rorke, *Sligo,* vol. 2, p. 112
72 1704 Registration Act
73 Burke, op. cit., p. 431
74 *Arch. Hib.*, vol. 3, p. 128
75 *Arch. Hib.*, vol. 1, p. 70
76 CP, vol. 30 (1682–1709) f. 242rv
77 SC Irlanda, vol. 5, f. 289r
78 See Attymass: 1704 Registration Act

Succession of Parish Priests

1731, Bonniconlon was still united with Attymass with one priest and no Mass-house.[79]
3 May 1776, John Durcan was PP of Bonniconlon.[80]
c. 1780, Patrick McNicholas, resident at Kilgarvan, aged 37 years, was PP of Bonniconlon.[81]
c. 1780–1819, Patrick McNicholas was still alive on 4 Jan 1819 and probably still PP of Bonniconlon.[82]

Bunninadden (Kilshalvey, Kilturra and Cloonoghill)

20 Aug 1683, John McDonogh, PP of Kilturra.[83]
4 Sept 1684, John McDonogh, PP of Kilturra.[84]
1704, Teige McDonogh, resident at Knockrany, aged 52 years, registered as PP of Kilturra. Teige Davy, resident at Coolaney, aged 33 years, registered as PP of Kilshalvey.[85]
1731, Edmund Mulrunifin was PP of Kilturra. Kilshalvey was coupled with Killaraght and Kilfree, with one priest each, and no Mass-houses. Cloonoghill was served by Thady (Charles?) O'Hara, PP of Achonry, who was assisted by three friars, Anthony McDonogh, Michael McDonogh and Michael Hart.[86]
27 Jan 1734, Edmund Mulrunifin was still alive.[87]
26 May 1758, Anthony McDonogh was PP of Kilshalvey.[88]
3 May 1776, Patrick O'Connor was PP of Kilturra and Cloonoghill and John Duffy, PP of Kilshalvey.[89]
c. 1780, Mark Rush, resident at Ballinalack, aged 39 years, was PP of Cloonoghill and Francis Donlevy, resident at Killevil, aged 29 years, was PP of Kilshalvey.[90]
c. 1780–1 April 1817, Mark Rush was PP of Bunninadden. He died on 1 April 1817 and was buried in Kilturra.[91]
20 June 1817–1822, John Doddy.[92]

---

79 *Arch. Hib.*, vol. 3, p. 129
80 SOCG, vol. 844, f. 267r
81 *Arch. Hib.*, vol. 1, p. 70
82 SOCG, vol. 918, ff. 76rv–83rv
83 CP, vol. 30 (1682–1709) f. 242rv
84 SC Irlanda, vol. 5, f. 289r
85 1704 Registration Act
86 *Arch. Hib.*, vol. 3, pp. 128–9
87 ASV Nunz. di Fiandra, vol. 131, f. 107rv
88 SCAR, codex 4, f. 466
89 SOCG, vol. 844, f. 269r: c. 1780, Patrick O'Connor was PP of Swinford.
90 *Arch. Hib.*, vol. 1, p. 71: 28 Nov 1786, Francis Donlevy was PP of Tubbercurry, SC Irlanda, vol. 16, ff. 149rv, 150rv
91 O'Rorke, *Sligo*, vol. 2, p. 197
92 SC Irlanda, vol. 20, f. 122r; O'Rorke, *Sligo*, vol. 2, p. 198 states that Doddy succeeded John Coleman but this is unlikely as Coleman was already PP of Swinford. Doddy was suspended by 9 Jan? 1822. SC Irlanda, vol. 23, f. 612r

Carracastle[93]

Charlestown (Kilbeagh)

1704, no priest registered for the parish of Kilbeagh.
1731, there were two priests and two Mass-houses in the parish.[94]
10 May 1758, Edmund Kelly was PP of Kilbeagh.[95]
1758–10 Dec 1797, Edmund Kelly was still alive on 10 Dec 1797 when he signed a petition to Bishop Thomas O'Connor.[96]
24 July 1817–7 Jan 1828, Michael Filan was parish priest of Charlestown.[97]

Collooney (Kilvarnet)[98]

20 Aug 1683, Patrick Henry? was PP of Collooney (Kilvarnet).[99]
4 Sept 1684, Richard Cluane was PP of Coolaney (Killoran) and Collooney (Kilvarnet).[100]
1704, William McDonogh, resident at Tialooher, aged 28 years, registered as PP of Collooney (Kilvarnet).[101]
1731, Collooney was coupled with Ballisodare and Coolaney (Killoran) and there were no priests settled there and no Mass-houses.[102]
27 Jan 1734, William McDonogh was still alive, aged c. 58 years and archdeacon of the diocese.[103]
9 Mar 1743–4, Peter Cluane was PP of Collooney (Kilvarnet) and there was also a friar, John Henry, in the parish.[104]
1768, John Fitzmaurice appointed PP of Ballisodare by Bishop Patrick Robert Kirwan.[105]
1768–c. 1794, John Fitzmaurice, PP of Ballisodare. He was the first to reside at Collooney, which was then apparently united to Ballisodare. Fitzmaurice died c. 1794.[106]

Succession of Parish Priests

93 Carracastle did not become an independent parish until the nineteenth century. For succession of priests serving Carracastle see Charlestown (Kilbeagh).
94 *Arch. Hib.*, vol. 3, p. 128
95 SCAR, codex 4, f. 466rv
96 OCD, 8. 4. SH. 058
97 SOCG, vol. 917, ff. 65rv–72v; O'Rorke, *Sligo*, vol. 2, p. 137
98 See Ballisodare
99 CP, vol. 30 (1682–1709), f. 242rv
100 SC Irlanda, vol 5, f. 289r
101 1704 Registration Act
102 Observation: 'The Priests here have a custom of Alternative Services so that one Priest does not serve above two years successively in one place.' *Arch. Hib.*, vol. 3, p. 128
103 ASV Nunz. di Fiandra, vol. 131, f. 107rv
104 Burke, op. cit., p. 438; see also p. 437; Peter Cluane and John Henry were both Dominican friars from Holy Cross Friary, Sligo.
105 SOCG, vol. 823, ff. 222rv, 223rv, 243v, 244r
106 Index to Administration Bonds, National Archives, Dublin; see O'Rorke, *Ballysadare & Kilvarnet*, p. 481

Succession of   1794–3 July 1805, Walter Henry, PP of Ballisodare & Kilvarnet.[107]
Parish Priests   1805–July 1833, James Henry, PP of Ballisodare & Kilvarnet.[108]

Coolaney (Killoran)

20 Aug 1683, Richard Cluane, PP of Coolaney (Killoran).[109]
4 Sept 1684, Richard Cluane, PP of Coolaney (Killoran) and Collooney (Kilvarnet).[110]
1704, Richard Cluane, resident at Carrickclooneen, aged 50 years, registered as PP of Coolaney (Killoran).[111]
1731, Killoran coupled with Ballisodare and Collooney (Kilvarnet), with no priest settled and no Mass-house.[112]
9 Mar 1743–4, Henry Prendergast, prior of Knockmore Carmelites was PP of Coolaney (Killoran).[113]
10 May 1758, Terence O'Gara II?[114]
3 May 1776, Anthony McDonogh, PP of Coolaney (Killoran).[115]
10 Dec 1797, 3 Feb 1803, Robert Dillon.[116]

Curry[117]

28 Nov 1786, Anthony McNamara became the first PP of Curry.[118]
26 Sept 1792, Anthony McNamara described as a canon.[129]
-1830, James Filan.[120]

---

107 O'Rorke, *Ballysadare & Kilvarnet*, pp. 482, 489
108 O'Rorke, *Ballysadare & Kilvarnet*, pp. 486, 489
109 CP, vol. 30 (1682-1709), f. 242rv
110 SC Irlanda, vol. 5, f. 289r
111 1704 Registration Act
112 Observation: 'The Priests here have a Custom of Alternative Services so that one Priest does not serve above two years successively in one place.' *Arch. Hib.*, vol. 3, p. 128
113 Burke, op. cit., p. 438
114 O'Rorke, *Sligo*, vol. 2, p. 62; O'Rorke mentions a Father O'Gara in the latter half of the eighteenth century. The only priest of that name then was Terence O'Gara II.
115 SOCG, vol. 844, f. 269r
116 OCD, 8. 4. SH. 058; SC Irlanda, vol. 18, ff. 104v, 105r Robert Dillon is described in these two documents as a canon and PP but no parish is given. O'Rorke, *Sligo*, vol. 2, p. 62 states that McDonogh succeeded Dillon in 1790 but it was more probably the reverse.
117 See Achonry. Curry did not become an independent parish until late in the eighteenth century. Prior to that it formed part of Achonry parish.
118 SC Irlanda, vol. 16, f. 149rv, 150rv
119 Fondo di Vienna, vol. 28, f. 37v
120 O'Rorke, *Sligo*, vol. 2, p. 137, states that Filan was McNamara's successor. This is not likely as Mc Namara appears to have died c. 1792, Index to Administration Bonds, and Filan did not return to the diocese until c. 1809.

Foxford (Toomore)

Succession of Parish Priests

1704, Foxford was divided, half of it attached to Straide (Templemore) and the other half attached to Killasser. James O'Hara, resident in Knocknatanvally, aged 55 years, registered as the PP of the Straide (Templemore) part and Jonin Ruane, resident in Carrowneddin, aged 56 years, registered as PP of Killasser and the half parish of Foxford (Toomore).[121]
1731, Foxford had one priest and one Mass-house.[122]
27 Jan 1734, James O'Hara signed a postulation for John O'Hart as bishop.[123]
10 & 26 May 1758, Patrick Knavesey was PP of Foxford.[124]
3 May 1776, Patrick Knavesey described as a canon.[125]
1786, last documented signature of Patrick Knavesey, canon and PP.[126]
1798, Fr Brown(e) was said to be the PP of Foxford and active in the Rebellion of that year.[127]

Gurteen (Kilfree and Killaraght)[128]

20 Aug 1683, Thady Higgins was PP of Kilfree.[129]
1704, David Henry, resident at Kilteenane, aged 50 years, registered as PP of Kilfree and John Marran, resident at Ardgalen, aged 41, registered as PP of Killaraght.[130]
1731, Kilfree was coupled with Killaraght and Kilshalvey, with one priest in each parish and no Mass-houses.[131]
27 Jan 1734, last documented signature of David Henry.[132]
26 May 1758, Dominick Finn was PP of Kilfree and Terence McGuan was PP of 'the church of St Attracta' (Killaraght?)[133]

---

121 1704 Registration Act
122 *Arch. Hib.*, vol. 3, p. 128
123 ASV Nunz. di Fiandra, vol 131, f. 107rv
124 SCAR, codex 4, f. 466rv. Knavesey returned to Ireland c. 1740 and may have become PP of Foxford shortly after that.
125 SOCG, vol. 844, f. 269r
126 SC Irlanda, vol. 16, f. 208r
127 Hayes, *Last Invasion of Ireland,* p. 197. Hayes described Brown(e) as an uncle of Admiral Browne. Brown(e)'s name does not occur in any other of the lists of priests of the period. O'Rorke, *Ballysadare and Kilvarnet*, pp. 485–6, states that Fr Brown was parish priest of Swinford and uncle of John Brown, parish priest of Bunninadden, later in the nineteenth century.
128 Kilfree and Killaraght were independent parishes until well into the eighteenth century.
129 CP, vol. 30 (1682-1709), f. 242rv
130 1704 Registration Act. Henry's age is difficult to reconcile with his date of ordination, 1697, as he would have been then 43 years old.
131 *Arch. Hib.*, vol. 3, p. 129
132 ASV Nunz. di Fiandra, vol. 131, f. 107rv
133 SCAR, codex 4, f. 466. Terence McGuan was a Franciscan friar and guardian of Ballymote 1759, 1760, 1763, 1765. Giblin, *Liber Lovaniense.*

Succession of Parish Priests

3 May 1776, Owen (Eugene) Banaghan was PP of Kilfree.[134]

1786, Owen Banaghan described as canon and PP. Francis Quinan (Cunnane?) also described as canon and PP.[135]

26 Sept 1792, Owen Banaghan signed report as a canon.[136]

10 Dec 1797, Owen Banaghan signed a petition to Bishop Thomas O'Connor.[137]

3 April 1800, Owen Banaghan died and is buried in Knockbrack in the parish of Keash.[138]

1804, Frank Cunnane resided here.[139]

11 Mar 1816, Roger McDermot was PP of Kilfree.[140]

Keash (Drumrat)

20 Aug 1683, Miler McDonogh was PP of Keash (Drumrat).[141]

4 Sept 1684, Miler McDonogh was PP of Keash (Drumrat).[142]

1704, John McDonogh, resident at Tavnagh, aged 50 years, registered as PP of Keash (Drumrat) and James Mulrunifin, resident at Templevanny, aged 60 years, registered as PP of Toomour.[143]

1731, James Tymon was PP and his assistants were Nicholas O'Hara, John Henry and Edward Mulrunifin.[144]

29 Oct 1738–3 Oct 1768, James McDonogh.[145]

3 May 1776, John Duffy was PP of Keash (Drumrat and Toomour).[146]

–1800, Owen Banaghan may have transferred from Gurteen to Keash as he is buried in Knockbrack cemetery.[147]

1796–7 April 1831, Richard Fitzmaurice was PP of Keash.[148]

---

134 SOCG, vol. 844, f. 269r
135 Cunnane may have been PP of Killaraght. SC Irlanda, vol. 16, f. 208r
136 Fondo di Vienna, vol. 28, f. 37v
137 OCD, 8. 4. SH. 058
138 O'Rorke, *Sligo*, vol. 2, p. 215n; Index to Administration Bonds
139 O'Rorke, *Sligo*, vol. 2, p. 379
140 SOCG, vol. 918 (1818), f. 172rv
141 CP, vol. 30 (1682–1709), f. 242rv
142 SC Irlanda, vol. 5, f. 289r
143 Given his age John McDonogh may be the same person as the previously mentioned Miler. 1704 Registration Act
144 Drumrat coupled with Kilmurragh and Toomour. Observation: 'Mass frequently said in the private Houses.' *Arch. Hib.*, vol. 3, p. 129
145 SOCG, vol. 699, f. 352r; SCAR, codex 4, f. 466rv; SOCG, vol. 823, f. 240rv. O'Rorke, *Sligo*, vol. 2, p. 215, states that James McDonogh was PP of Keash
146 SOCG, vol. 844, f. 269r
147 O'Rorke, *Sligo*, vol. 2, p. 215n gives the inscription on his grave
148 O'Rorke, *Sligo*, vol. 2, p. 216n gives the inscription on his tombstone in Knockbrack which states that Fitzmaurice was 35 years PP of Keash.

Succession of Parish Priests

Killasser

1704, Jonin Ruane, resident in Carrownedin, aged 56, registered as PP of Killasser and the half parish of Foxford (Toomore).[149]

1731, there was one priest and one Mass-house in the parish.[150]

c. 1760–1768, John Fitzmaurice, a Tuam priest, was brought into the diocese by Bishop Patrick Robert Kirwan and was said to have been appointed PP of Killasser.[151]

–1794, Walter Henry was PP of Killasser until he transferred to Collooney.[152]

1794?–3 Oct 1815, Michael O'Brien. Tombstone in Killasser cemetry.*

Kilmovee

4 Sept 1684, Walter Costello was PP and prebendary of Kilmovee.[153]

1704, Walter Costello, resident at Sunvolhane, aged 54 years, registered as PP of Kilmovee.[154]

1731, there was one priest and one Mass-house in the parish.[155]

26 May 1758, Andrew Duffy OP, PP of Kilmovee ('parochus ecclesiae St Movidy').[156]

2 Sept 1767, Michael Jordan OP, PP.[157]

c. 1780, Dominic Kelly OP, resident at Kilmovee, aged 49, was PP of Kilmovee.[158]

11 Mar 1816–3 Dec 1817, James Feighny was PP of Kilmovee.[159]

1818, James Feighny died.[160]

Kiltimagh (Killedan)

1704, John Durkan, resident at Taucannanagh, aged 58 years, registered as PP of Killedan and Bohola.[161]

4 April 1715, Dominick Berne (Bera) 'John Durkan who took the Oath of Abjuration turned out of his parish'.[162]

1731, there was one priest and one Mass-house in the parish.[163]

---

* I am indebted to Fr Patrick Holleran for this information.
149 1704 Registration Act
150 *Arch. Hib.*, vol. 3, p. 128
151 O'Rorke, *Ballysadare and Kilvarnet*, p. 480
152 O'Rorke, op. cit., p. 482
153 SC Irlanda, vol. 5, f. 289r
154 1704 Registration Act
155 *Arch. Hib.*, vol. 3, p. 129
156 SCAR, codex 4, f. 466
157 AGOP XIII, 157; see Fenning, *Coll. Hib.*, no. 8, pp. 94–5. Jordan was a friar attached to Urlaur.
158 *Arch. Hib.*, vol. 1, p. 71
159 SOCG, vol. 917, ff. 65rv–72v, vol. 918, ff. 78rv–81rv, 172rv, 269rv; SC Irlanda, vol. 20, f. 122r
160 Index to Administration Bonds
161 1704 Registration Act
162 Burke, op. cit., p. 431; Dominic Berne, resident at Carroriwagh, aged 42, registered for no parish in 1704. See Registration Act
163 *Arch. Hib.*, vol. 3, p. 128

Succession of Parish Priests

27 Jan 1734–5, Henry Jordan was canon and theologian of Killedan.[164]
10 & 26 May 1758, Henry Jordan was a canon.[165]
3 May 1776, Thady O'Flaherty was canon and prebendary.[166]
1779, Thady O'Flaherty was PP of Kiltimagh (Killedan).[167]
c. 1780, Thady (O') Flaherty, resident at Bushey Park, aged 50 years was PP of Kiltimagh (Killedan).[168]
1786, Thady O'Flaherty was PP and canon of Killedan.[169]
26 Sept 1792, Thady O'Flaherty, canon of Killedan and VF.[170]
24 Feb 1803, Thady O'Flaherty was PP and canon.[171]
c. 1818–1826, Patrick Grady was PP of Kiltimagh.[172]

Straide (Templemore)

1704, James O'Hara, resident at Knocknatanvally, aged 55 years, registered as PP of Straide (Templemore) and Foxford (Toomore).[173]
1731, there was one priest and one Mass-house in the parish of Straide.[174]
27 Jan 1734, James O'Hara signed a postulation for John O'Hart as bishop.[175]
3 May 1776, Edward Hu(r)st was PP of Ballylahan (Ballelahon).[176] He died c. 1792.

Swinford (Kilconduff and Meelick)

4 Sept 1684, John Roddy PP of Kilconduff.[177]
1704, Maurice Frain, who had transferred from Ballaghaderreen (Kilcolman) and was now resident at Lisserightis and aged 54 years, registered as PP of Swinford (Kilconduff). John Roddy, resident at Belahagh, aged 55 years, now registered as the PP of Meelick.[178]
1715, John Roddy, PP of Meelick was dead. Maurice Frain, PP of Swinford (Kilconduff) was also dead and Anthony Henigan had replaced him.[179]

---

164 ASV Nunz. di Fiandra, vol. 131, f. 107rv
165 SCAR, codex 4, f. 466rv
166 SOCG, vol. 844, f. 269r
167 Chapel in old Killedan churchyard built and dedicated to B.V.M. by Thady O'Flaherty parish priest of Killedan (commemorative plaque)
168 *Arch. Hib.*, vol. 1, p. 70
169 SC Irlanda, vol. 16, f. 208r
170 Fondo di Vienna, vol. 28, f. 37v
171 SC Irlanda, vol. 18, ff. 104v, 105r
172 SC Irlanda, vol. 24, ff. 595r, 596r, 597rv, 602rv, 603rv, 605rv, 606rv, 685rv, 686rv
173 1704 Registration Act
174 *Arch. Hib,.* vol. 3, p. 128
175 ASV Nunz. di Fiandra, vol. 131, f. 107rv
176 SOCG, vol. 844, f. 269r
177 SC Irlanda, vol 5, f. 289r
178 1704 Registration Act
179 Burke, op. cit., p. 431. Anthony Henigan was probably a Dominican friar who was a member of the Straide community on 16 Sept 1702. Fenning, *Irish Dominicans*, p. 31

Succession of Parish Priests

1731, there was one priest and one Mass-house in the parish of Kilconduff and one priest and one Mass-house in Meelick.[180]

26 May 1758, James O'Donnell was PP of Killcuon? (Kilconduff?).[181]

3 May 1776, Francis Kearney was PP of Kilconduff.[182]

c. 1780, Patrick O'Connor, resident in Swinford, aged 50 years, was PP of Kilconduff.[183]

24 Feb 1803, last documented signature of Patrick O'Connor, PP and canon. He was then aged about 73 years.[184]

–1805, James Henry.[185]

30 Dec 1817, John Coleman was PP of Swinford (Kilconduff and Meelick).[186]

Tourlestrane (Kilmactigue)

20 Aug 1683, Bernard (Brian)Brennan was PP of Kilmactigue.[187]

4 Sept 1684, John Murtagh was PP of Kilmactigue.[188]

1704, William Kennedy, resident at Gurtogh Mone, aged 60 years, registered as PP of Kilmactigue, James Howley, resident at Kilmactigue, aged 46 years, also registered as PP of Kilmactigue, as did Brian Brennan, who was resident at Lislea and aged 60 years.[189]

1731, there was one priest and no Mass-house.[190]

27 Jan 1734, James Howley was still alive and aged about 76 years.[191]

c. 1734–1788, Dominick Kearney was PP of Kilmactigue.[192]

---

180 Observation (on Meelick): 'The Mass Houses in these Parishes have been Rebuilt & placed in a more convenient place within these few years.' *Arch. Hib.*, vol. 3, p. 128
181 SCAR, codex 4, f. 466
182 SOCG, vol. 844, f. 269r
183 *Arch. Hib.*, vol. 1, p. 70. Patrick O'Connor was PP of Bunninadden on 3 May 1776, SOCG, vol. 844, f. 269r
184 SC Irlanda, vol. 18, ff. 104v, 105r; see also SC Irlanda, vol. 16, f. 208r (1786), Fondo di Vienna, vol. 28, f. 37v, OCD, 8. 4. SH. 058
185 O'Rorke, *Ballysadare and Kilvarnet*, pp. 485-6, states that James Henry was assistant to Fr Brown, PP of Swinford and succeeded him and remained until 1805. Brown, whom O'Rorke states was an uncle of Fr John Brown of Bunninadden, is an elusive figure. He does not appear on any of the contemporary lists of priests. A Fr Brown was said to have been PP of Foxford in 1798, Hayes, *Last Invasion of Ireland*, p. 197
186 KPS, 838 / 218, de Brún, *The Irish Society's Teachers*, p. 257. 14 May 1822, Robert Hepburne was the curate. SC Irlanda, vol. 23, ff. 661rv, 662v
187 CP, vol. 30 (1682-1709), f. 242rv
188 SC Irlanda, vol 5, f. 289r
189 Brian Brennan was probably the same as Bernard Brennan in 1683. John Murtagh had moved to Achonry. 1704 Registration Act
190 *Arch. Hib.*, vol. 3, p. 129
191 ASV Nunz. di Fiandra, vol. 131, f. 107rv
192 Kearney's signature first appeared in January 1734, ASV Nunz. di Fiandra, vol. 30, ff. 10r, 11rv. He was in Collège des Lombards, Paris c. 1734-7, though he may have been appointed PP of Kilmactigue before he went to Paris to study, as he was ordained in 1732. SCAR, codex 2, vol. 2, ff. 412rv, 466, 467

Succession of Parish Priests

10 May 1758, Dominic Kearney was a canon.[193]

3 Oct 1768, Dominick Kearney described himself as 'Vicar Forane and Rector of the church of Kilmactigue'.[194]

c. 1780, Dominick Kearney was resident at Kilmactigue and aged 73 years.[195]

4 Dec 1788, it was reported that 'the Rev Mr Carney, who for 60 years and upwards was PP of Kilmactigue' had died.[196]

28 July 1789, Bishop Thomas O'Connor asked Rome for Kilmactigue, now vacant by death of Dominick Kearney, as a mensal parish instead of Kilcolman and Castlemore.[197]

9 Sept 1804, Bishop Charles Lynagh asked for Kilmactigue as a mensal parish, now vacant by the death of his predecessor Bishop O'Connor.[198]

c. 1813, there was a change in administrators.[199]

16 Sept 1817, Patrick Grady, PP of Emlefad and Kilmorgan (suspended), asked Rome for the parish of Kilmactigue, vacant by the death of Bishop John O'Flynn.[200]

26 July 1818, Bishop Patrick McNicholas asked Rome and was granted Kilmactigue as a mensal parish in addition to Ballaghaderreen (Castlemore and Kilcolman).[201]

Tubbercurry (Cloonacool)[202]

3 May 1776, Dominick O'Hara was PP of Cloonacool.[203]

c. 1780, Dominick O'Hara, resident at Cloonacool and aged 40 years was described as 'Vicar of Achonry'.[204]

28 Nov 1786, Francis Donlevy was PP of Cloonacool.[205]

1806–1815, Patrick Henry was PP of Tubbercurry.[206]

1815–1830, John McNulty was PP of Tubbercurry

---

193 SCAR, codex 4, ff. 466rv, 469r
194 SOCG, vol. 823, f. 240rv; *Acta* vol. 139, ff. 317r–320v
195 *Arch. Hib.*, vol. 1, p. 78
196 *Arch. Hib.*, vol. XIX, p. 263
197 SOCG, vol. 884, ff. 208rv, 209rv; Acta, vol. 159, f. 432rv
198 Udienze, vol. 42, ff. 584r, 587v
199 Neligan, op. cit., p. 367
200 SC Irlanda, vol. 20, ff. 179rv–80rv
201 Udienze, vol. 56, f. 607v
202 See Achonry. Tubbercurry did not become an independent parish until late in the eighteenth century.
203 SOCG, vol. 844, f. 269r
204 *Arch. Hib.*, vol. 1, p. 70
205 SC Irlanda, vol. 16, ff. 149rv, 150rv
206 O'Rorke, *Sligo*, vol. 2, p. 133. O'Rorke states that Henry is buried in Kilcummin graveyard.

APPENDIX 35: List of Parish Priests with no identifiable parishes

Parish Priests with no identifiable parishes

27 Jan 1734, James O'Hara,[207] Michael Costello,[208] Eugene Sweeney (canon),[209] Thomas Burke (canon),[210] M. Dowell,[211] Patrick Beirne (canon),[212] L(uke) Beirne.[213]

29 Oct 1738, James McDonogh (canon),[214] Francis McDonogh,[215] Denis Gormley, parish priest of the 'church of St Patrick'.[216]

6 June 1739, John Ruane (canon and VG).[217]

10, 26 May 1758, Murtagh O'Hara, PP of the 'church of St Cuthbert,'[218] John O'Hart (canon),[219] David Kearney, PP of the 'church of St Brigid'.[220]

16 Sept 1760, Francis Hurley (canon).[221]

3 May 1776, Laurence O'Connor, PP of 'Monte Rixoso,'[222] Anthony Ruane, canon and prebendary of Kilmactigue,[223] James McManus, canon and prebendary of Attymass.[224]

n.d. (1786), Francis Quinan, canon and PP (possibly Francis Cunnane, Gurteen).[225]

26 Sept 1792, John O'Flynn, canon of Kilshalvey.[226]

24 Feb 1803, James Dalton, PP and canon,[227] Dominick Philips, PP and canon,[228] Andrew Conlon, PP and canon.[229]

---

207 ASV Nunz. di Fiandra, vol. 131, f. 107rv
208 ASV Nunz. di Fiandra, vol. 131, f. 107rv
209 ASV Nunz. di Fiandra, vol. 131, f. 107rv; (29 Oct 1738), SOCG, vol. 699, f. 352r; ASV Nunz. di Fiandra, vol. 135, f. 194r; (10, 26 May 1758 & 16 Sept 1760), SCAR, codex 4, ff. 466rv, 469r
210 ASV Nunz. di Fiandra, vol. 131, f. 107rv; (5 June 1739), ibid. vol. 135, f. 194r
211 ASV Nunz. di Fiandra, vol. 130, ff. 10r, 11rv
212 ASV Nunz. di Fiandra, vol. 130, ff. 10r, 11rv; (5 June 1739), ibid. vol. 135, f. 194r
213 ASV Nunz. di Fiandra, vol. 130, ff. 10r, 11rv
214 SOCG, vol. 699, f. 352r; (10, 26 May 1758, 16 Sept 1760) SCAR, codex 4, ff. 466rv, 469r; SOCG, vol. 823, f. 240rv
215 SOCG, vol. 699, f. 352r
216 SOCG, vol. 699, f. 352r; (10, 26 May 1758), SCAR, codex 4, f. 466rv
217 ASV Nunz. di Fiandra, vol. 135, f. 194r; (10, 26 May 1758, 16 Sept 1760), SCAR codex 4, ff. 466rv, 469r; (22 June 1769), SOCG, vol. 825, f. 65r
218 SCAR, codex 4, f. 466rv
219 SCAR, codex 4, f. 466rv; (16 Sept 1760), ibid. f. 469r
220 SCAR, codex 4, f. 466rv
221 SCAR, codex 4, f. 469r
222 SOCG, vol. 844, f. 269r
223 SOCG, vol. 844, f. 269r
224 SOCG, vol. 844, f. 269r
225 SC Irlanda, vol. 16, ff. 149rv, 150v
226 Fondo di Vienna, vol. 28, f. 37v; (10 Dec 1797), OCD, 8. 4. SH. 058; (24 Feb 1803), SC Irlanda, vol. 18, ff. 104v, 105r; (11 Mar 1816), SOCG, vol. 917, f. 271rv; vol. 918, f. 172rv; (20 June 1817), SC Irlanda, vol. 20, f. 122r; (24 July 1817), SOCG, vol. 917, ff. 65rv–72v; (26 Aug 1817), SOCG, vol. 918, ff. 68rv, 69rv; (15 Dec 1817), SOCG, vol. 918, ff. 78rv–81rv.
227 SC Irlanda, vol. 18, ff. 104v, 105r; (30 July 1817), SOCG, vol. 918, ff. 66rv–71v, f. 85r (Greyfort, near Ballina); (25 Oct 1817), SC Irlanda, vol. 20, ff. 205rv, 206rv
228 SC Irlanda, vol. 18, ff. 104v, 105r; (8 Mar 1816–15 Dec 1817), SOCG, vol. 917, f. 271rv, vol. 918, ff. 66rv–71v, 78rv–81rv, 171rv, 172rv
229 SC Irlanda, vol. 18, ff. 104v, 105r; (20 June 1817), vol. 20, f. 122r; (11 Mar 1816–15 Dec 1817), vol. 917, f. 269rv; vol. 918, ff. 66rv–71v, 78rv–81rv, 172rv

Parish Priests with no identifiable parishes

n.d. (1816), Michael Fitzmaurice, PP[230], Patrick Sweeney, PP.[231]
8 Mar 1816, John Durkan, PP and canon.[232]
15 Dec 1817, Robert Hepburne, PP.[233]
4 Jan 1819, James McHugh, PP.[234]

Urlaur Chalice 1722 (St John's Seminary, Camarillo, California)

230 SOCG, vol. 917, f. 271rv; (26 Aug 1817), SOCG, vol. 918, ff. 68rv, 69rv
231 SOCG, vol. 917, f. 269rv. Sweeney was a curate on 11 Mar 1816, SOCG, vol. 918, f. 172rv; he was a PP by 20 June 1817, SC Irlanda, vol. 20, f. 122r; (24 July 1817), SOCG, vol. 917, ff. 65rv–72v; (24 Aug 1817), SOCG, vol. 918, ff. 68rv, 69rv. Sweeney had emigrated to America by 9 Jan 1822, SC Irlanda, vol. 23, f. 612r
232 SOCG, vol. 918 f. 171rv; (20 June 1817), SC Irlanda, vol. 20, f. 122r; SOCG, vol. 917, ff. 65rv–72v; (26 Aug–15 Dec 1817), SOCG, vol. 918, ff. 68rv, 69rv, 76rv–83rv
233 SOCG, vol. 918, ff. 78rv–81rv. Hepburne was still a curate on 26 Aug 1817, SOCG, vol. 918, ff. 68rv, 69rv
234 SOCG, vol. 918, ff. 76rv–83rv. James McHugh was PP of Tubbercurry (Cloonacool) 1830–59, O'Rorke, *Sligo*, vol. 2, p. 133

Curates

APPENDIX 36: List of Curates[1]

1737?, James Gallagher in Ballisodare.
29 Oct 1738, Patrick Knavesey, curate in Ballisodare.[2]
22 June 1769, Anthony McNamara, curate in Achonry.[3]
11 Mar 1816, Robert Hepburne, James Gallagher, Bartholomew Kearns, Michael Filan, Patrick Sweeney, John Doddy, Michael Donoghue.[4]
14 May 1822, Robert Hepburne was a curate in Swinford to John Coleman.[5]
n.d. (1816), Robert Hepburne, James McHugh, Michael Donoghue, Michael Filan.[6]
20 June 1817, Robert Hepburne, Michael Filan, James McHugh, L. Leyden, W. McHugh, Michael Fitzmaurice.[7]
24 July 1817, Robert Hepburne, Andrew Hannon, James Gallagher, Thomas McNicholas, Michael Donoghue, Patrick Hegan ?, Peter Cooke, James McHugh.[8]
30 July 1817, Edward Roddy, Luke Leydon OP, Francis Burke, curate Kiltimagh, William? McHugh, John McHugh.[9]
26 Aug 1817, Robert Hepburne, James McHugh, Michael Donoghue, Peter Cooke.[10]
15 Dec 1817, Michael Fitzmaurice, Patrick Keegan, John McHugh, Francis Egan, Edward Roddy.[11]
4 Jan 1819, Peter Cooke, Michael O'Flynn, Matthew Healy, Michael O'Donoghue.[12]

1 Curates did not become common until early in the nineteenth century.
2 ASV Nunz. di Fiandra, vol. 699, f. 352r
3 SOCG, vol. 825, f. 65r
4 SOCG, vol. 918, f. 172rv
5 SC Irlanda, vol. 23, ff. 661rv, 662v
6 SOCG, vol. 917, f. 271rv
7 SC Irlanda, vol. 20, f. 122r
8 SOCG, vol. 917, ff. 65rv–72v
9 SOCG, vol. 918, ff. 66rv–71v
10 SOCG, vol. 918, ff. 68rv, 69rv
11 SOCG, vol. 918, ff. 78rv, 81rv
12 SOCG, vol. 918, ff. 76rv, 83rv

Vicars

List of Protestant Rectors and Vicars

APPENDIX 37: List of Protestant Rectors and Vicars[1]

Achonry[2]
See List of Protestant Deans, Appendix 4

Ballaghaderreen (Castlemore)[3]

5 June 1686, James Echlin.
2 Aug 1698, Gideon Johnson.
7 Feb 1711, Edward Furey.
5 Aug 1724, Thomas Vesey.
29 June 1743–Feb 1768, Oliver Carter.
1768, (?)
24 Oct 1789, George Paley.
1794–1811, Charles Seymour.
23 Oct 1811–7 Sept 1850, Joseph Seymour.

Ballisodare

? –1695, Robert Whitelaw.
1695–1736, Tobias Caulfield.
1736–1772, Adam Caulfield.
1772–1817, Robert Shaw.
1817–1820, Joseph Verschoyle.
1821, William Handcock.

Ballymote (Emlefad)[4]

1746, John Walls nominated George Weir as his curate.[5]
? –1756, Charles Maturin.
1765–1806, William Garrett.
1806–1855, John Garrett.

Coolaney (Killoran)[6]

c. 1770–1818, Josiah Hern.
1818–1862, Joseph Verschoyle, Sr.

1   J.B. Leslie, *Biographical Succession List of the Clergy of Achonry* (1938), typescript in Representative Church Body Library, Braemor Park, Dublin. The parishes of Achonry were grouped into nine vicarages.
2   Included the parishes of Achonry and Cloonoghill.
3   Included the parishes of Kilcolman and Kilmovee.
4   Included the parishes of Kilmorgan, Keash and Kilturra.
5   O'Rorke, *Sligo*, vol. 2, p. 185
6   Included also the parish of Collooney (Kilvarnet).

List of Anglican Rectors and Vicars

Gurteen (Killaraght)[7]

c. 1684–1695, Thomas Langdall.
23 Aug 1695–1729, Thomas Bethell.
1735–1782, Zachary Langton.
1782–1796, Robert Lloyd.
1796–June 1820, Veitch Simpson.
1820–1836, James Elwood.

Kilmactigue

1693–1721, Henry Crofton.
4 Dec 1721–1760, Robert Faussett.[8]
26 Jan 1760–?, James Hutchisson was rector and vicar of Kilmactigue.[9]
24 April 1770, Thomas Manningham was rector of Kilmactigue and vicar of Kilbeagh (Charlestown).[10]
13 Dec 1777–1781, Edward Synge was rector of Kilmactigue.[11]
22 June 1781–1797, Mark Wainwright was rector and vicar of Kilmactigue.[12]
1797–1802, Robert Shiell (Thomas Weldridge?).[13]
4 June 1802–1 June 1835, James Neligan was rector of Kilmactigue.[14]

Straide (Templemore)[15]

1682, Patrick Read.
1711, John Price.
1729, James Sotheby.
1751?, Thomas Manningham.
1752, William Evelyn.
1782, J. Hazlett.
1805–1809, John Cromie.
1809–1816, J. Gorges.
1817–25 June 1849, John O'Rorke.

---

7 Included also the parishes of Kilfree and Kilshalvey.
8 Neligan, op. cit., pp. 390–91
9 Neligan, op. cit., p. 391
10 Neligan, op. cit., p. 391
11 ibid
12 ibid
13 Neligan, op. cit., p. 391, states that he replaced Robert Shiell and makes no mention of Weldridge.
14 ibid
15 Included also the parishes of Bohola, Foxford (Toomore), Killasser, and Kiltimagh (Killedan).

List of Anglican Rectors and Vicars

Swinford (Kilconduff)[16]

20 June 1682, Patrick Read.
1711–1729, John Price.
28 July 1729–Nov 1751, James Sotheby.
1751–c. 1805, (?).
c. 1805–1807, Thomas Radcliffe.
1807–1821, Joseph Borrowes.
1821–1827, E. Davis.

Kilbarron Protestant church *(Photograph, Jack Ruane)*

16 Included also the parishes of Meelick and Charlestown (Kilbeagh).

Friars

APPENDIX 38: List of Dominican Friars[1]

Holy Cross, Straide

16 Sept 1702, James Cullen (of Burrishoole) prior, Anthony Henegan, James McNicholas, Raymond Henegan, Cormac Corcoran.[2]
15 July 1721, Dominick Ruane, Preacher General, Straide.[3]
1731, 'Fryars meet sometimes at this Abby, tho I cannot learn that they have residences near it.'[4]
1734–5, Dominick Ruane, preacher general, James McNicholas, Thomas Roche, Matthew Higgins, Thady Touhy, James Nunne (Noone), Dominick McNicholas, James Manni(o)n, Anthony Burke, Peter Laughnan. Absent: Anthony Ruane, Dominick Gavan.[5]
Oct 1739, Thomas Roche and James Noone.[6]
30 Dec 1741, Thomas Roche and James Noone.[7]
1745, Thomas Healy was transfiliated from Burrishoole to Straide.[8]
1746, Straide had seven friars.[9]
SEPT 1756, Thady Touhy, prior, aged 60, professed 30 years; Matthew Higgins, sub-prior, aged 55, professed 30 years; Thomas Roche, aged 67, professed 40 years; James Mannin, aged 66, professed 39 years; Anthony de Burgo, aged 55 years, professed 24 years; Thomas McNicholas, aged 42 years, professed 19 years; John Blake, aged 37, professed 18 years.*De Burgo, *Hib. Dom.*, p. 254
2 Sept 1767, John Blake, prior, aged 49 years and professed 32 years; Thomas McNicholas, subprior, aged 53 years and professed 35 years; Thomas MacHale, aged 61 years and professed 35 years; Thomas Roche, aged 79 years and professed 56 years.[10]
1767, Thomas Roche.[11]
c. 1780, John Blake.[12]
1799–1800, William McNicholas, prior, Patrick Bartley, master of theology.[13]
1816, Albert Clarke.[14]
11 Mar 1816–4 Jan 1819, Edward Clarke, prior of Straide.[15]
17 June 1817, Edward Clarke, prior, aged 60 years, professed 30 years and has been on the mission for 20 years, John Horan, Peter McNicholas.[16]

1 Fenning, *Irish Dominicans* unless otherwise stated.
2 p. 31
3 p. 91
4 *Arch. Hib.*, vol. 3, p. 128
5 p. 197
6 p. 175
7 p. 180
8 p. 205
9 p. 259
10 AGOP, XIII, 157: see Fenning, *Coll. Hib.*, no. 8, p. 95
11 p. 355
12 p. 495. Blake was a first cousin of Walter Blake, Bishop of Achonry, *Arch. Hib.*, vol. 1, p. 196
13 SC Irlanda, vol. 17, ff. 616r–618rv
14 p. 625
15 SOCG, vol. 917, ff. 65rv, 72v, 271rv; vol. 918, ff. 66rv, 71v, 76rv, 83rv, 172rv
16 CP, vol. 152 (1819), ff. 85r, 86r

List of Dominican Friars

8 May 1819, Edward Clarke.[17]
1824, Patrick Dominick Kelly was clothed at Esker for the convent of Straide.
1829, Kelly was a curate at Castlebar subject to Edward Clarke OP Straide.[18]
31 Jan 1830, Patrick Albert Lyons, who was a nephew of Edward Clarke, was clothed for convent of Straide at Corpo Santo, Lisbon and returned to Ireland in Feb 1834.

St Thomas, Urlaur

18 Aug 1703, Peter Costello, prior, Richard MacMorrisroe, Edmund MacMorrisroe, John McDaniel, Raymond Costello.[19]
1706, Edmond MacMorrissy, Miler MacMorrissy, Miler MacPhilip, John MacDonnell, Pierce Costello, Redmond Costello.[20]
1734–5, Anthonium MacDonnell, prior, Hugh Morelly, Laurence O'Heynes, John Costello, Richard Jordan, Andrew Costello, Peter Philips, Denis Daze (Deasy?) and some absentees.[21]
1749, four were admitted to the habit.[22]
1755, Terence MacDonnell OP of Urlaur, Co Mayo, was stationed at Lisbon, age 30, but was only 5 years professed.[23]
1756, Walter Morilly of Urlaur, who was chaplain to the nuns of Drogheda, was sent back to Urlaur where there were six friars.[24]
1756, Andrew Duffy, aged 65, was prior of Urlaur.[25]
10 May 1758, fr Andreas Duffy was parish priest of Kilmovee.[26]
2 Sept 1767, Walter Morilly, prior, aged 49 years and professed for 27 years; Martin O'Heynes, subprior, aged 59 years and professed for 29 years; Michael Jordan, PP, aged 44 years and professed for 17 years; Walter Morris, aged 59 years and professed for 21 years; Dominick Jordan aged 59 years and professed for 16 years; Thomas Lally, aged 71 years and professed for 41 years; James McDonnell, aged 59 years and professed for 36 years.[27]
1799–1800, Dominick Kelly, prior.[28]
15 June 1782, Dominick McDonogh, a promising student from Urlaur at S. Marco, Florence in 1775. He as assigned to SS. Sixtus and Clement, Rome on 24 Feb 1803.[29]
11 Mar 1816–4 Jan 1819, Luke Leydon, prior, James McNicholas.[30]

17 CP, vol. 152, f. 228
18 Fenning, *Coll. Hib.*, no. 33, p. 202
19 p. 32
20 O'Heyne, *Irish Dominicans*, pp. 229-31
21 p. 197
22 p. 249
23 *Hib. Dom.*, p. 429; *Arch. Hib.*, vol. xxv, p. 96
24 pp. 257, 259, 263
25 *Hibernia Dominicana*, p. 314. Census of Elphin 1749 listed a friar, A. Duffy, in the neighbouring parish of Tibohine (Fairymount), Nat. Arch. M. 2466
26 SCAR, codex I. 4. f. 468v
27 AGOP, XIII, 157: see Fenning, *Coll. Hib.*, no. 8, pp. 94-5
28 SC Irlanda, vol. 17, ff. 616r, 618rv
29 p. 624
30 SOCG, vol. 917, ff. 65rv, 72v, 271rv; vol. 918, ff. 66rv–71v, 76rv, 83rv, 78rv, 81rv, 172rv; SC Irlanda, vol. 20, f. 122r

1832, Luke Leydon, prior of Urlaur and the only friar there, aged 69 years.[31]
3 Dec 1833, Leydon was apparently dead.[32]
1846 Patrick Sharkey OP died. He was ordained in Salamanca and brought to Urlaur by Bishop McNicholas. He lived in the house of Peggy Williams of Williamstown. He put the following inscriptions on the pillars of Peggy Williams' cottage: *Magna aliena parva, parva propria magna – rure tibi dum, vixeris aliis vivis in urbe.*[33]

Holy Cross, Sligo (Dominican friars with Achonry connections)

1703, Thomas Haran.[34]
1703, Gregory Nelly, a Dominican friar in Sligo, may have had Achonry connections as the Kilshalvey poet, Seán Ó Gadhra, wrote a lament for him.[35]
9 Mar 1743–4, Peter Cluane, a Dominican from Sligo was PP of Collooney (Kilvarnet) and John Henry, also from Sligo was a friar in the same parish.[36]
19 Oct 1770, Edmund Fitzgerald, prior of Sligo (1757–1760), came every year to Achonry diocese.[37]

APPENDIX 39: List of Franciscan Guardians and Friars

Ballymote[38]

1687–9, Anthony McDonnell, guardian.
24 Aug 1690, Anthony McDonogh, guardian.
18 Feb 1693, Francis Farry, guardian.
28 July 1697, Daniel Kelly, guardian.
26 July 1699, Bernard O'Lorcan, guardian.
17 Oct 1700, Terence O'Hart.
9 June 1702, Peter Donnellan, guardian.
13 Nov 1703, Anthony O'Cullane, guardian.
9 June 1705, Anthony McDonogh, guardian.
13 Nov 1706, Michael McDonogh, guardian.
12 May 1708, John Hanley, guardian.
12 Oct 1709, John Hanley, guardian.
7 June 1711, Michael McDonogh, guardian.
13 Oct 1714, Luke Brennan, guardian.
10 May 1716, Michael McDonogh, guardian.
16 Oct 1717, John O'Kelly, guardian.
30 May 1719, John O'Gara, guardian.
3 Sept 1720, Anthony Kelly, guardian.

31 *Coll. Hib.*, vol. 29 (1987), pp. 116, 127
32 TA, Letters
33 Conversation in 1965 with George, 87 year old son of Nicholas Sharkey, brother of Patrick, OP.
34 Haran Chalice, Ballaghaderreen
35 'Marbhna an tSagart Riaghalta foghlumtha Grioghoir Maigniallus', *Dánta is Amhráin Sheáin Uí Ghadhra*, pp. 468; Fenning, p. 32
36 Burke, op.cit., pp .437–8; on Cluane see Fenning, pp. 37, 146, 197, 593; on Henry, p. 197
37 SC Irlanda, vol. 11, ff. 541r–542v; on Fitzgerald see Fenning, pp. 309–13
38 Cathaldus Giblin, *Liber Lovaniensis;* A. Faulkner, *Liber Dublinensis.*

List of Franciscan Guardians and Friars

22 July 1724, Anthony Kelly was dead and Michael McDonogh was guardian.
16 Aug 1727, Francis Brett, guardian.
17 Nov 1729, Francis Brett, guardian.
1731, Francis McCormick, guardian, Francis Brett, Francis Cunane, Francis King, Hugh McDonogh, Michael McDonogh, Francis Duffy.[39]
5 Sept 1733, Francis Cunane, guardian.
5 Mar 1735, Hugh McDonogh, guardian.
6 Sept 1736, John O'Gara was dead, and Hugh McDonogh was guardian.
6 Mar 1738, Francis Brett, guardian.
24 July 1739, Francis Brett, guardian.
25 May 1741, Francis Cunane, guardian.
16 Aug 1742, Francis Cunane, guardian. Anthony Kelly died since last chapter.
9 Mar 1743–4, Michael Cunane, guardian, Francis McDonogh, Anthony McDonogh, Francis Davey. Henry Brett was a friar in the parish of Kilmorgan (Ballymote).[40]
16 April 1744, Francis Brett, guardian. Michael McDonogh died since last chapter.
12 Aug 1745, Francis Brett, guardian.
12 Feb 1747, Francis Cunane, guardian.
22 Aug 1748, Francis Cunane, guardian.
16 Feb 1751, Anthony McDonogh, guardian.
26 Aug 1751, Anthony McDonogh, guardian.
26 Feb 1753, James O'Hara, guardian.
26 Aug 1754, James O'Hara, guardian.
24 Sept 1755, Anthony McDonogh, guardian.
29 Aug 1757, Anthony McDonogh, guardian.
10, 26 May 1758, Anthony McDonogh was PP of Bunninadden (Kilshalvey) and Terence McGuan was PP of Gurteen (Killaraght? – St Attracta's).[41]
19 Feb 1759, Terence McGuan, guardian.
18 Aug 1760, Terence McGuan, guardian. Anthony McDonogh died since last chapter.
19 Oct 1761, James Naughton, guardian.
22 Aug 1763, Terence McGuan, guardian.
17 April 1765, Terence McGuan, guardian.
12 Nov 1767, John Cuffe, guardian.
8 Oct 1770, Anthony French, guardian. Richard Martin died at Charlestown, Co Roscommon? Oct 1770.
19 Oct 1770, fr. – Sweeney OFM.[42]
31 Aug 1772, Eugene Hanley, guardian; Anthony French was elected provincial.
13 Nov 1773, Anthony Martin, guardian.

39 'These Fryars live dispersed but are related to the best Popish Familys in the Barony', *Arch. Hib.*, vol. 3, p. 129
40 Burke, op. cit., p. 438, 439. Michael Cunane is probably the same person as Francis, which may have been his religious name. 29 Oct 1738, Francis McDonogh testified in favour of James Gallagher, SOCG, vol. 699, f. 352r
41 SCAR, codex 4 f. 466rv
42 SC Irlanda, vol. 11, ff. 541r–542v. Bishop Patrick Robert Kirwan banished Sweeney from the diocese in 1768 but he had returned by 1770.

1 July 1776, Luke Farrell, guardian. James Naughton died since last chapter.
30 April 1778, Thomas Corry, guardian. Eugene Hanley died since last chapter.
19 July 1779, James Bennett, guardian.
29 May 1781, James Bennett, guardian.
22 July 1782, Lewis (Louis) Williams, guardian.[43]
12 May 1784, James Bennett, ex-diffinitor.
25 July 1785, Ludovicus Williams, guardian
9 May 1787, Francis Garvey, guardian.
14 July 1788, Anthony Kelly, guardian.
18 May 1790, John Cummins, guardian. James Bennett died 7 Mar 1790.
11 July 1791, Anthony Kelly, guardian.
23 July 1793, Anthony Kelly, guardian.
14 July 1794, Anthony Kelly, guardian.
6 June 1796, Daniel Magloin, guardian. Francis Garvey died since last chapter.
22 Sept 1800, Francis McHugh, guardian. Daniel McGloin died since last chapter.
13 July 1801, Anthony Kelly, guardian. Francis McHugh died since last chapter.
13 July 1803, Laurence Dolan, guardian. John Cuffe died since last chapter.
16 July 1804, Francis Ferguson, guardian.
14 July 1806, Anthony Kelly, guardian.
12 July 1815, Anthony Lyons, guardian.
11 Mar 1816, Edmund O'Kelly, guardian.[44]
24 July 1817, Francis Fitzsimons OFM.[45]
14 July 1819, Hugh O'Donnell, guardian. Anthony Kelly died since the last chapter.
1822, John Magrath, guardian.
1824, Anthony Cuniffe, guardian.
1825, Anthony Green, guardian
13 July 1826, Anthony Green, guardian.

Court

1731, O'Hara, Raughnin and McTeere.[46]
9 Mar 1743–4, fr McCoye.[47]

APPENDIX 40: Names of Carmelites in Knockmore.

1731, Anthony McDonogh, Michael McDonogh and Michael Hart. These friars assisted Thady (Charles?) O'Hara, the PP of Achonry, in the parish of Cloonoghill, which was then attached to Achonry.[48]
9 Mar 1743–4, Henry Prendergast, prior and parish priest of Coolaney (Killoran), (Michael?) Hart, James Nangle.[49]

43 See also *Arch. Hib.*, vol. 1, p. 71
44 SOCG, vol. 917, f. 271rv; vol. 918, f. 172rv
45 SOCG, vol. 917, ff. 65rv, 72v; vol. 918, ff. 68rv, 69rv
46 *Arch. Hib.*, vol. 3, p. 129
47 Burke, op. cit., p. 439
48 The 1731 Report on the State of Popery, situates this friary in the parish of Bunninadden (Cloonoghill) which borders Gurteen (Kilfree and Killaraght) where Knockmore was situated. *Arch. Hib.*, vol. 3, pp. 128–9
49 Burke, op. cit., p. 438

Names of Augustinians in Corpus Christi, Banada

APPENDIX 41: Names of Augustinians in Corpus Christi, Banada.

9 Mar 1743–4, John O'Hara, prior.[50]
c. 1780, William Hurly, aged 35 years, was prior.[51]
1782, there were two friars in Banada.[52]
11 Mar 1816–15 Dec 1817, Matthew Leonard was prior and John Smyth was ex-prior.[53]
9 Jan 1822, Matthew Leonard, John Smyth and James Conmy.[54]

Lay People

Names of Lay People

APPENDIX 42: Names of Lay People

20 Aug 1683, fourteen lay people who signed a petition to Rome in favour of Hugh MacDermot:[55] William Taaffe, baron, Frank Taaffe, Christopher Taaffe, Geo(orge) Taaffe, Michael Taaffe, Tho(mas) Taaffe, Jo(hn) Brett, Charles O'Hart, Teige O'Hart, Donnell O'Hara, Luk(e) Taaffe, John Brett, junior, John McDonogh, Pat(rick)? McDonogh.

30 Dec 1738, persons who signed a petition to Rome in favour of James Gallagher:[56] Patrick Sweeney, Daniel Lunchard, Michael O'Donnell, Martin Haran, Terence Ponn, Thady O'Hara, Daniel Ponn, James Gallagher, James Gallagher, Laurence Ponn.

16 Oct 1768, parishioners of Ballisodare who signed a petition to Rome in favour of James Gallagher:[57] John Brett, Wm Brett, James Conilan, James Haran, – Gallagher, Manus Gallagher, Ann O'Hart, sister of Bishop John O'Hart, Wm Kelly, senior, James Kelly, James Kelly, junior, William Kelly, junior, Michael Kelly, Martin Kelly, John Kelly, Matthew Kelly, Daniel Kelly, Terence O'Donnelly, Michael O'Hara, Martin O'Dogherty, Michael Henry, Thady McDonogh, – McDonogh, Charles O'Flanagan?, James Trenna?, Thomas Dwyer, James Dwyer, Thomas McDonogh, Tully Gallagher, Thomas Fallon, Daniel O'Connor, Ambrose O'Connor, Owen O'Connor, John Scanlan, Dominick ?, Geraghty, Nathaniel O'Donnell, Patrick Connell, – Connell, Stephen Fitzpatrick, Robert Madden, Thomas Leeson, Thomas Henry, Pat Kielly, Patrick Tonry?, Peter Killahuley, Andy Connolly, Martin Connolly, John Dunn, Luke Dunn, Pat Walsh, Peter Davey, John Verdon, Bernard Verdon, Patrick O'Connor, Owen O'Connor, Thomas Nicholson, John Gallagher, Peter Gallagher, senior, Tully Gallagher, Peter Gallagher, junior, Roger O'Donnell, Oliver Sweeney, Michael O'Donnell, Pat McNulty, Denis McCoy?, Thady Higgins, Luke Mc Donogh, Maurice Conry, Peter Conry, John Conry, Patt: Conry, senior, Pat Conry, junior. Thady Banaghan, Owen Banaghan, Charles Banaghan, Coll McDonnell, Francis? Hills, Francis McDonnell.

Banada Chalice 1641 *(St Augustine's, Ballyboden, Dublin)*

50 Burke, op. cit., p. 438
51 *Arch. Hib.*, vol. 1, p. 71
52 *Arch. Hib.*, vol. 30, p. 19
53 SOCG, vol. 918, ff. 66rv, 71v, 78rv, 81rv, 172rv
54 SC Irlanda, vol. 23, f. 613r
55 CP, vol. 30 (1682–1707), f. 242rv
56 SOCG, vol. 699, ff. 352v, 353r
57 SOCG, vol. 823, ff. 242rv, 243v, 244r

10 Feb 1818, Lay people in the diocese who signed a petition to Rome in favour of Patrick McNicholas:[1] Daniel O'Connor, Roadstown, Ballymote; Denis O'Connor, Sullygrove; Charles O' Connor, Mantua; John Rice, Achonry; Thomas Rice, Cloonamahon; James McHugh, Newgrove, Collooney; Michael McHugh, Carra; Arthur Nicholson, Glann; Thomas Corcoran, Glann; Coll Deane, Swinford; Michael Cuniffe, Swinford; James Jourdan, Swinford; Andrew Kelly, Camphill; Edward Howley, Ellagh, Ballina; Patrick Mullan, Foxford; Pat Kelly, Longfield, Swinford; Hugh Deane, Ashbrook, Edward Deane, Ashbrook; Francis Taaffe, Killedan, Patrick Sweeney, Swinford; Owen Sweeney, Swinford; Michael Sweeney, Swinford; Anthony Kelly, Swinford; Richard Costello, Swinford; Michael Costello, Swinford; John McLaughlin, Swinford; Pat McLaughlin, Ballylahan; Peter Prendergast, Gorteen?; Myles Jordan, Rathslevin; Henry Jordan, Rathslevin. Inhabitants of Sligo town who signed the same petition: Bart Coyne M.D., – Wallis, Martin Madden, merchant, Sligo, Charles McDonogh, Atty, Sligo, J. O'Beirne, merchant, Sligo, Matthew Walsh, junior, Seafield, Michael Kelly, merchant, Sligo, James Feeny, merchant, Sligo, Matthew Walsh, Seafield, Sligo, Michael Gaffny, merchant, Sligo, Patrick McDonogh of Sligo, William Henry, Sligo, Thomas Madden, Sligo, John McDonogh, Attorney at Law, 12 North East St, Dublin.

Names of Lay People

APPENDIX 43: List of Converts to the Established Church [2]

List of Converts to the Established Church

Brabazon, George, gent., Carrogarry, Co Mayo. Conformity 24 Sept 1732/22 May 1739.
Byrne, Francis, Cloonmighane (Cloonoghill?) diocese of Achonry. Conformity 17 Dec 1749.
Carter, Rowland, gent., Ballisodare, Co Sligo. Enrolled 4 May 1781/2 Feb 1784.
Costello, Charles, 9 Mar 1763.
Costello, Edmund, Esq., 9 Feb 1763.[3]
Cumffe (Cuniffe?), Mrs Eleanor, Tullanacorra (Swinford?), diocese of Achonry. Conformity 10, 20 May 1747.
Dowling, Peter, Achonry parish. Conformity 9 Aug 1752.
Gallagher, John, gent., Foxford parish, diocese of Achonry. Conformity 26 May 1719.
Higgins, John, Kilfree, Co Sligo. Conformity 29 July 1730.
Irvin (or Irwin) alias Brett, Anne, Lisballilly (Lisbaleely, Kilfree?), Co Sligo. Conformity 27 June 17?.
Joyes, Martin, Foxford, Co Mayo. Conformity 10 Apr 1757.
Lawry, Neal, Rathbarin (Rathbarron?, Coolaney), Co Sligo. Enrolled 5 Dec 1782.
McCormick, Mary, Nymphsfield (Collooney?). Co Sligo. Enrolled 5 Dec 1782
Nolan, Patrick, Ballysadarragh (Ballisodare?), diocese of Achonry. Enrolled 13 Dec 1729.
O'Connor, Dermot, Esq., Tuam. Conformity 3 Aug 1758.[4]
O'Hara, Henry, Tullyhugh (Achonry), diocese of Achonry. Conformity 16 Apr 1738.
O'Hara, Mrs Mary, Tullyhugh (Achonry), diocese of Achonry. Conformity 16 Apr 1738.

1   *SC Irlanda* vol. 20, ff 56rv, 57rv
2   ed. Eileen O'Byrne, *The Convert Rolls*
3   May have been the father of Charles Costello of Edmondstown.
4   Probably the father of Bishop Thomas O'Connor.

O'Hara, Roger, Achonry parish. Enrolled 15 June 1779.
Philips, James, Killtomagh (Kilturra?, Kiltimagh?), diocese of Achonry. Conformity 7 Sept 1729.
Plunkett, Robert, Collooney, Co Sligo. Enrolled 11 May 1780.
Taaffe, Christopher, gent., Ballynaglogh, diocese of Achonry. Conformity 1 Aug 1723.
Murrin, Bryan, Toolaney (Coolaney?), Co Sligo. Enrolled 27 Nov 1790.

Ulster Families who settled in Foxford in 1796

APPENDIX 44: List of Ulster Families who settled in Foxford in 1796[1]

22 Dec 1796, M. McConville, weaver, Armagh, with family of four; Edward Whitelock, farmer, Armagh, with family of two; Neil Ryan, weaver, Armagh, with family of seven; Thomas Cunningham, weaver, Armagh, with family of two; Pat McCann, weaver, Armagh, with family of two; James Fox, weaver, Armagh, with family of six; William Smith, weaver, Derry, with family of three; M. McConville, weaver, with family of three; Philip McConville, weaver, Down, with family of six; Charles McConville, weaver, Down, with family of three; M. Devlin, weaver, Armagh, with family of seven; Charles McCann, weaver, Armagh, with family of three; Daniel McGinear, Antrim; Pat Branigan, weaver, Armagh, with a family of six; John Branigan, weaver, Armagh, with a family of seven; Francis McNeas, weaver, Armagh, with family of three; Henry McNeas, weaver, Armagh, with family of three; Pat McNeas, weaver, Armagh, with family of five; John McNeas, weaver, Armagh, with family of one.

People in the Diocese engaged in the 1798 Rebellion

APPENDIX 45: Names of Persons in the Diocese engaged in the 1798 Rebellion[2]

James O'Dowd, Bonniconlon, Thomas Farrell, Coolcarney, Pat O'Hara, Tubbercurry, Dudley Scanlan, Ballybrennan, Michael Scanlan, Quarryfield, Martin and Michael Rogers, – Scanlan, Loondorroch, Pat Kearns, John and Brian Whoody, Bunninadden, Tim Killoran, Killanty?, Matthew Doyle, Curry, – Scanlan, Ballinacarrow, James Killalea, Carrowanru, Brian Scanlan, Patrick and Michael Davey, Cloonaur?, James, Patrick and Michael Davey, John Finan, son of Laurence Finan, Aghnaglas, Denis O'Hara, Achonry, Anthony Curley, innkeeper, Swinford, William Brabazon, Swinford (natural son of Sir Anthony Brabazon), Seamas Duv Horkan, Swinford, Patrick Brennan, blacksmith, Swinford, three women from Swinford called Larkin, Ryan and Brennan.

List of Suffering Loyalists who claimed compensation in 1798

APPENDIX 46: List of Suffering Loyalists who claimed compensation in 1798[3]

John McDonogh, Collooney, Mary Farrell, Collooney, Michael Haran, Glan, Robert Kivleghan, Collooney, John Thompson, Killoran, Patrick Phibbs, Leitrim, Robert McKim, Collooney, John Low, Collooney, Thomas Church, Coolaney, James Simpson, Tullaghan, Elizabeth Ormsby, Coolaney, James Connelly, Collooney, Henry Meredith, Tubbercurry, Edward Simpson, Ballisodare, John Connelly, Collooney, William Hopps, Collooney, Winifred Dogherty, Collooney, Thomas McCarrick, Coolaney.

1 Rebellion Papers, 620 / 26 / 145
2 Compiled from Rebellion Papers, 620 / 40 / 58, O'Hara Papers, Ms. 20, 303 and Hayes, *Last Invasion*, pp. 274–5
3 Extracted from O'Rorke, *Sligo*, vol. 2, Appendix 1, pp. 593–9

APPENDIX 47: List of those in Sligo and Mayo charged as Threshers in 1806[1]

28 Oct 1806, in custody in Mayo: Francis McDonnell, James McDonnell, James Bodkin, Michael Bodkin, Richard Maitland.
10 Sept 1806, committed by John Ormsby Esq.: Thomas Reap, Michael Reap, Patrick McEnrea, Patrick Hubert, William Gillespie, Thomas Mahedy, Patrick Hagerty, James O'Boyle, Charles Doosey, Peter O'Boyle, James Merrick, Edmund Loughane, Thady Lorin.
14 Sept 1806, Thomas Durkin, Mary Gallagher.
20 Sept 1806: John Golden.
17 Oct 1806, committed by Denis Browne: James Coleman, Richard Murphy, James Maune. Andrew Higgins, John P(r)endergast.
1 Oct 1806, committed by James Burke Esq.: Bartholomew Cowley.
17 Sept 1806, in custody in Sligo: Daniel Devorny, James Corcoran, Walter Henry, William Creary, Thomas Kilmartin, Patrick Cogan.
13 Oct 1806, committed by Mr Costello: Thomas Collery.
John Killraine.

Schools

APPENDIX 48: Schools and Teachers[1]

Achonry: 13 Aug 1822, Patrick Golden, applied for appointment as a schoolmaster in Achonry parish. 1829, M. Brennan, Catholic, taught in Castleloye under the Baptist Society.
Ballaghaderreen: 1824, there were two LHS schools, one at Ballaghaderreen, with 160 boys and 60 girls another at Castlemore with 110 boys and another LHS school with 100 boys and 60 girls. John Casey, Catholic, taught a pay school in a thatched barn in Monasteredan, unconnected with any society, with 100 boys and 60 girls.
Ballisodare: 13 Jan 1821, Thomas Durkan, Catholic, appointed to teach school in Ballisodare. 1824, Durkan taught a pay school at Lugnadeffa in Ballisodare in connection with the Baptist Society, with 8 Protestant and 10 Catholic pupils
Ballymote: 1824, Ballymote LHS school had 99 boys and 40 girls. Another LHS school in Knockdaltan townland in the same parish had 48 boys and 24 girls. There were no pupils in a third LHS one in Templeconny as the building was not yet completed in 1824. In its sister parish of Kilmorgan, there was an LHS one in Drumfin townland with 56 boys and 35 girls and a school aided by the Baptist Society in Branchfield with 50 boys and 45 girls. A Catholic pay school was held in the chapel in Ballymote with 100 pupils including 8 Protestants. Pat O'Gara, Catholic, was the teacher and was paid £6 p.a. by the parish priest and the pupils paid 1s 3d per quarter.
Bunninadden: 1824, Patrick Davey, Catholic, taught school at Ballyfahy in the parish of Kilturra, unconnected with any society.

Those in Sligo and Mayo charged as Threshers in 1806

Schools and Teachers

1   PRO (London) HO 100 / 136 36303
APPENDIX 48
1   Pádraig de Brún, *The Irish Society's Teachers* (due for publication). I am indebted to Dr de Brún for allowing me to consult the proofs. 1824 Report.

Schools and Teachers

Carracastle: 1824, Patrick Gallagher, Catholic, taught a pay school, unconnected with any society, in the chapel in Carracastle in the parish of Kilbeagh (Charlestown). The Scriptures were read in the Douay version.

Collooney: 1824 a Catholic, James O'Burne, taught in Dooragh in Kilvarnet and there was a girl's school in Templehouse in the same parish with 61 on roll. 1824, John Bree, Catholic taught a pay school in the the chapel of Collooney, unconnected with any society, Scriptures read in Authorised version and there were 5-10 Protestant and 54-60 Catholic pupils.

Coolaney: 1824, in Killoran parish there was a school in Carrowmacarrick townland with 43 boys and 17 girls.

Foxford: 1824, John Barden, a Protestant, was the master of Foxford school with 40 boys and 30 girls. James Swift, Catholic, taught a free school, under LHS, assisted by Col. William Jackson, who provided the schoolhouse, in Boherhallagh in the parish of Toomore. There were 2 to 3 Protestants and 28 to 49 Catholic pupils and the Scriptures were read in the Authorised version.

Gurteen: 1824, there was an LHS school in Gurteen with 62 boys and 30 girls.

Killasser: 30 October 1819, Andrew Brown, James Rowley and – Jourdan taught in schools in the parish of Killasser under Rev James Neligan. 1824, Andrew Collins, Catholic, taught a school supported by the Baptist Society and Col. William Jackson at Lognahaha in Killasser. He later succeeded Timothy Carabine in Swinford. 1824, James Durkan, senior, Catholic, taught school in master's dwelling-house, at Bouleboy, supported by the Irish Society and received £3 p.a. from Col. William Jackson and James Durkan, junior, Catholic, taught an LHS school, at Cartron with 4 to 5 Protestants and 50 to 53 Catholics. Rent of schoolhouse paid by Col. Jackson. Edward Hart, Protestant, taught a school in connection with the Baptist Society and KPS at Croghan in the townland of Lehardan, materials for schoolhouse supplied by Col. Jackson. The Scriptures were read in the Authorised version and there were 5 Protestant and 60 Catholic pupils.

Kilmovee: 1824, Andrew Duffy, a Catholic, was the teacher in Urlaur in Kilmovee parish with 80 boys and 60 girls. Scriptures read in the Authorised version. Patrick O'Gara taught a pay school in 'a miserable cabin', unconnected with any society, at Rodestown (Cloonrow tld Urlaur?), in the parish of Kilmovee.

Swinford: 1800, John Mullaney, Catholic, commenced teaching. 30 Dec 1817, Rev James? Coleman, PP of Swinford and Meelick, recommended Mullaney for KPS training. 16 Feb 1818, KPS informed Coleman that regulations totally precluded the use of catechisms during school hours. Jan 1819, the school was closed by Bishop Mc Nicholas. 29 Mar 1821, the school had been re-established as an LHS school under Sir William Brabazon a few months previously, 'opposition of the RC clergy having abated' and the best boy and girl in each of six classes every four months were to be given a new jacket or frock or gown. 1824, John and daughter, Sarah Mullaney were teaching a free school, with 10 Protestants and 110 to 130 Catholic pupils, in the market-house, given by Sir William Brabazon, supported by LHS and KPS. (1824 Report stated that there were 134 boys and 95 girls). The Scriptures were read in the Authorised version. John Mullany was followed by Timothy Carabine who commenced teaching in 1822 and he was succeeded by Andrew Collins. In 1824 there was a Catholic pay school in Tumgesh, with 26 pupils. The teacher, John Ormsby, Catholic, was paid a gratuity and the Douay Bible was read.

Tourlestrane: c. 1814 there was a school aided by the Association for Discountenancing Vice who paid the teacher £15 p.a. and built 'a neat house' which cost upwards of £100. There were two other LHS schools. All three schools had an average of 60 pupils, who pay from 1s 8d to 2s 6d per quarter. Two of the teachers were Catholics and the third was a Protestant of whom James Kelly was one. There were also four Catholic hedge schools with Catholic teachers and the tuition was 1s 8d per quarter.[2] 16 May 1819, Bartley Hart and his daughter Eliza had a school for teaching Irish in the parish of Kilmactigue, with 30 pupils. 27 Mar 1820, P. Brennan and Eliza Hart taught a school with 40 to 60 pupils. 1824, John Jourdan, Catholic, taught a school, unconnected with any society, in Baratogher chapel, with 3 Protestant and 42 Catholic pupils. In 1824 Thomas Leonard, Catholic, with no regular schoolhouse, taught in the parish of Kilmactigue.

Tubbercurry: 23 May 1818, Rev James Neligan wrote that a house 40 feet long at a rent of £6 p.a. had been procured for a school in Tubbercurry, where Patrick McManus was to be the teacher. 6 Oct 1821, Pat Feeley, Catholic, had 26 pupils. 1824, he taught a pay school in his own dwelling-house in Tubbercurry, with 4 Protestant and 31 Catholic pupils, unconnected with any society and the Scriptures were read in the Authorised version. In 1824 John Hart, Protestant, taught a pay school, 'kept in part of James Hart's house, unconnected with any society and the Scriptures were not read.

Synod

APPENDIX 49: Synod of Bunninadden 1759[1]

27 June 1759, *Decreta seu statuta Dioecesana facta in Congressu Capitali et Cleri Acchadensis, nec non Deputatorum in loco vulgo dicto Bunadiaden, Praesidente IImo ac Rmo Domino Patricio-Roberto Kirwan Episcopo Acchadensi, Die 27 Junii, 1759.*

1° Statuitur quod Decreta a Praedecessoribus condita in robore et fermitate permaneant.
2° Ut omnia statuta provincialia, quorum quisque transumptum habeat, bis in anno hiemali videlicet Colluctione menstrua, Eademque Desinente, sub vernum puta et autumnale tempus legant vel eorum Lectioni intersint, in suis respectivis Conventibus.
3° Ut quilibet Confessarius casus reservatos vel in Breviario, vel in Directorio ob oculos habeat.
4° Decernitur quod omnes sacerdotes tam saeculares quam Regulares missas in hac Dioecesi celebrantes tenentur singulis Diebus Dominicis, festivisque ante vel post missam exhortari vel catechizare, vel per se vel per alium sum poena suspensionis non solum in Capellis parochialibus, verum etiam in Domibus privatis, nisi rationabilis causa excuset. interea sedulo moneant populum de obedientia ac

---

2   Neligan, op. cit. pp. 371–5
APPENDIX 49
1   Archives of the Irish College, Rome; published in Moran, *Spicilegium Ossoriense*, vol. 3, pp. 272–3

Synod of Bunninadden 1759

Reverentia Debita Praepositis ac praesertim Episcopis, quos spernere et ipsum spernere, ut Christus affirmat.

5° Decernitur quod omnes sacramentum ordinis in statu saeculari suscipere volentes, annum ad minus antequam ad Examen admittantur proprios parochos de sua vocatione certiores facere tenentur, ut eorum vitae ac moribus invigilant, Eorumque singuli Ordinario se in decursu visitationis sistent cum testimonio Sui Parochi de ejusmodi intimatione facto: Insuper Candidati in parochiis in quibus resident singulis diebus Dominicis et festivis, nec non una alterave Die feriali a Parocho Designanda anno currente et plebiscitum christianis moribus nec non necessariis capitibus informent, Catechismo utantur super nostro concinnato et juris publici facto in usum Dioecesis nostrae. Ubi vero Ludimagistrum agunt, huic suo operi navent operam assiduam tam in schola quam in aedibus in quibus pernoctari contigerit, quorum diligentiam promovere pro suo munere sataget parochus. Item singulis mensibus penata sua deponent et ad sacram synaxim accedent de consilio Confessarii, cujus fideliter peracti testimonium adducent sui pastoris, secus a sacris ordinibus se noverint arcendos.

6° Siquis Sacerdos in futurum (quod absit) fornicationem vel adulterium perpetret, ipso facto ab officio et beneficio suspenditur: Insuper siquis sacerdos de suspectae mulieris consortio postulatos, tertio admonitus de ulteriore cum ea convictus, ab exercitio ordinis sui sine spe redintegrationis suspensus maneat.

7° Cum Crapula ebrietasque in Clerico foedam characteri suo maculam inurat, fomites ignitas lubricitati administret, decernitur ut qui prejudicioso huic vitio usque ad alienationem mentis indulserit vel qui viles cauponas omnium fere malorum officinas studio ingressus fuerit in propria parochia ad arbitrium Ordinarii suspensus remaneat.

8° Statuitur ut pium purificandi mulieres ritum honestis tantum debitum, nullus in posterum cuipiam ex illegitimo consortio postulanti sub poena suspensionis impertiri praesumat, nisi publice plectatur supplicio, ut opprobrio ac dedecore affecta, justas sceleris sui poenas luat, aliis sit exemplum ad similia praecavenda.

9° Decernitur ut excipiendis confessionibus tempore Nativitatis Jesu Christi et in Paschate quilibet Parochus Confessarium adhibeat suum ad sui levamen, ne vel effuso poenitentium numero fatescat, vel tanto munere cursim et desertorie defungi cogatur, vel denique ne timor et infelix verecundia ostium conscientiae claudat obturetque usque adeo ut iis abrepti peccata pastori suo aperire saepe saepius nolint.

10° Statuitur ut saltem ter in hebdomada quilibet sacerdos sacrum faciat seclusa necessitate.

11° Statuitur ne quis parochus aut parochi vices gerens extra parochiam ad exequias turpis lucri gratia se ingerat.

Mass-rocks

APPENDIX 50: List of Mass-rocks[1]

Attymass: Trassy Hill (in former Grayfort estate), Log an Aifrinn (Carracastle), Mass-rock (Kilgrellia near present chapel).
Ballaghaderreen: Four Altars (Tullaghan), Atteentaggart (site uncertain).
Ballymote: Mass-rock (Carrigans), Mass-rock (Ballybrennan, status doubtful).
Bohola: Mass-rock (Carragolda).
Bonniconlon: Mass-rocks said to have been in the townlands of Glenree and Ellaghmore.
Bunninadden: Mass Pass (Cloonameehan).
Foxford: Corr an Fhaire (hill overlooking Foxford).
Killasser: Mass-rocks in Creggane, Knockaganny (Callow), Cartron, Graffey (cross near the site), Loobnamack Rock (in River Moy between Tumgesh and Loobnamack), Geata na hAltóra (Cloonfinish).
Swinford: Páirc na hÍobartha (Carnacross / Ballivoher).
Tubbercurry: Mass-rock (Masshill).

Townlands

APPENDIX 51: Baronies, Parishes, Townlands[1]

LEYNY: This barony in Co Sligo comprised the parishes of Achonry (which consisted of the modern parishes of Curry, Mullinabreena and Tubbercurry), part of Ballisodare, Collooney, Coolaney and Tourlestrane.
Achonry: Achonry, Ballincurry, Ballinvally, Ballyara or Falduff, Ballyglass, Bellahy, Belra, Bunnacrannagh, Carnyara, Carraun, Carrowcarragh, Carrowclare, Carrowkeel, Carrowmore, Carrowmurray, Carrownacreevy, Carrownaleck, Carrownaworan, Carrownedin, Carrowntawa, Carrowntober, Carrowreagh (*Cooper*), Carrowreagh (*Knox*), Carrowreilly, Carrowwilkin, Cashel North, Cashel South, Castleloye, Chaffpool, Cloonacool, Cloonaraher, Cloonarara, Cloonbaniff, Clooncunny, Cloondrihara, Clooningan, Cloonlaughil, Coolrawer, Corsallagh, Cully, Cunghill, Curraghbonaun, Curry, Derreens, Doomore, Drumbaun, Gortnadrass, Kilcummin, Knocknashee Common, Laughil, Lavagh, Leitrim North, Leitrim South, Lissaneagh, Magheranore, Montiagh, Moylough, Muckelty, Mullaghanarry, Mullanabreena, Mullaun, Oghambaun, Powellsborough, Pullagh, Rathmagurry, Rathscanlan, Rinbaun, Sandyhill, Sessuecommon, Sessuegarry,

---

1   List compiled from Wood-Martin, *History of Sligo,* pp. 355–6; O'Donovan, *Sligo Letters,* pp. 144–6, 149, 229, 233–4,235, 344–5, 375, 422, 425; *Mayo Letters,* vol. 1, pp. 108–10, 129; vol. 2, p. 360, 375, 378, 386, 387; Kilgannon, *Sligo and its surroundings,* pp. 257, 268, 284; Bernard O'Hara ed., *Killasser A History,* and from information supplied by Peter Sobolewski, Fr Martin Jennings, Tom Hennigan, Michael Murphy, Paddy Brady, James Flanagan, Tom McGettrick, Fr Tom Colleary, Sean Reynolds N T, Fr Tommy Mulligan, Sean Owens, Fr Christy McLaughlin, Seamus O'Donnell, Vincent Coleman, Martin McNulty RIP, Padraig Gavin N T, Fr Paddy Kilcoyne, Fr Joe Spelman, Liam Gillard, Fr Tommy Towey.

APPENDIX 51
1   From Townland Index, Landed Estate Court Rentals, Nat. Arch., Dublin.

Baronies, Parishes, Townlands

Sessuegilroy, Streamstown, Tawnavoultry, Tobbercurry, Toberscardan, Tullycusheen Beg, Tullycusheen More, Tullyhugh, Tullyvellia.

Ballisodare: (Part of the parish in Leyny barony): Abbeytown, Ardcotton, Billa, Bleachgreen, Carricknagat, Cooney, Corhawnagh, Crockscullion, Glen, Halfquarter, Kilboglashy, Kilnamanagh, Kinnagrelly, Knockmuldoney, Knoxspark, Largan, Larkhill, Lisduff, Lugawarry, Lugnadeffa, Lugnamackan, Mullanashee, Rinn, Stonehall, or Carrownageeragh, Streamstown, Tullaghan, Ballysadare Town. (Part in Tirerrill barony): Annaghmore, Ardcurley, Ballynaboll, Ballysadare, Belladrihid, Carrickbanagher, Carrigeensallagh,, Cloonacurra, Cloonamahon, Cloonmacduff, Collooney, Coolteen, Glennagoolagh, Knockbeg East, Knockbeg West, Knockmullin, Lisruntagh, Lissaneena, Markrea Demesne, Mullaghnabreena, Rathrippin, Spotfield, Toberbride, Union.

Collooney (Kilvarnet): Annagh Beg, Annagh More, Ardcree, Ballymurray, Ballynacarrow North, Ballynacarrow South, Carrowntawy, Claragh (*Irish*), Claragh (*Scotch*), Falnasoogaun or Ropefield, Fetherneen, Finlough, Glebe, Kilvarnet North, Kilvarnet South, Ranaghan Beg, Ranaghan More, Rathbaun, Rathgran, Rathnarrow (*Brett*), Rathnarrow (*O'Hara*), Rockfinlough, Templehouse Demesne.

Coolaney (Killoran):Ballinvally, Cabragh, Cappagh, Carha, Carrowclooneen, Carrowgavneen, Carrownabanny, Carrownacarick, Carrownacleigha, Carrownagleragh, Carownaskeagh, Carrownateewaun, Carrowleam, Carroloughan, Coolaney, Creevaun, Deenodes, Gortakeeraun, halfquarter or Curraghaniron, Killoran North, Killoran South, Knockadoo, Knockatotaun, Lissalough, Moymlough, Rathbarran, Rathmactiernan, Rathmore, Rathosey, Seevness, Shancough, Coolaney Town.

Ballymote Chalice 1685 *(St Mary's Cathedral, Sligo)*

Tourlestrane (Kilmactigue): Annagh, Banada, Belclare, Carns, Carraun, Carrigeenagowna, Carrownagappul, Carrownlobaun, Carrowreagh, Castlerock or Castlecarragh, Claddagh, Cloonbarry, Cloonca, Cloongoonagh, Cloonydiveen, Coolrecuill, Corray, –, Culdaly, Curraghboy, Dawroa, Drimina, Drummartin, Eskragh, Glennawoo, Gortermone, Gortsrahain?, Killure, Kilmactigue, Kincullew, Knockshoney, Knockbrack, Knocknasliggaun, Largan, Letterbrone, Lislea, Meenagleeragh, Meenaglogh, Meenamado, Oughaval, Ounagh, Rue, Tawnaneillen, Tobberroddy, Tourlestraun, Tullaghaglass, Tullanaglug, Tullymoy, Aclare Town.

CORRAN: This barony in Co Sligo comprised the parishes of Ballymote (Emlefad and Kilmorgan), Bunninadden (Kilshalvey, Kilturra and Cloonoghill), and Keash (Drumrat and Toomour).

Ballymote (Emlefad): Ardconnell, Ardnaglass, Ardree, Ballybrennan, Ballymote, Camross, Carrigans Lower, Carrigans Upper, , Carrigeenmore, Carrowcauly or Earlsfield, Carrocushely, Carrowkeel, Carrownanty, Carrownree, Cartron (*Percival*), Cartron (*Phibbs*), Cloonagun, Cloonamanagh, Cloonkeevy, Clooneen, Cluid, Corhober, Derroon, Emlagh, Emlaghfad, Emlaghgissan, Emlaghnaghtan, Keenaghan, Kilbrattan, Knockadalteen, Lecarrow, Lissananny Beg, Lissananny More, Maghera, Portinch, Rathdoony Beg.

(Kilmorgan): Ardrea, Branchfield, Cappagh, Cloonagashel, Clooneen, Cloonlurg, Deerpark, Doo Beg, Doo More, Doonmeegin, Doorly, Drumcormick, Drumfin,

Kilcreevin, Kilcreevin (*Phibbs*), Kilmorgan, Knockmoynagh, Knocknagroagh, Lackagh, Lisdoogan, Lugacaha, Newpark, Tiraree, Turlaghygraun.
Bunninadden: (Kilturra): Ballyfahy, Bellanalack, Doobeg, Everlaun, Kilturra, Knockalass, Knockgrania, Knockrawer, Ogham, Rathbaun North, Rathbaun South.
(Kilshalvey): Ardkeeran, Ardminnan, Ardraheen Beg, Ardraheen More, Attiville, Baghloonagh, Ballintrofaun, Balloghnahan or Harristown, Ballynacarriga, Ballynakillew, Carrigeen, Cloonaraher, Clooncunny, Cloonena, Coagh, Derrynagraug, Drumanaraher, Drumdiveen, Drumrolla, Emlagh, Greyfield, Kildarganmore, Killavil, Killined, Kilnaharry, Kilshalvey, Kiltycreen, Knockahurka, Knockalass, Knockanimma, Knockrawer, Liskeagh, Phaleesh, Rinn, Riverstown, Spurtown (*Duke*), Spurtown Lower, Tawnagh, Tawnaghmore, Tunnagh.
(Cloonoghill): Aughris, Ballinvally East, Ballinvally West, , Ballinvally or Roadstown, Ballynaraw North, Ballynaraw South, Brackloonagh, Carrowloughlin, Carrowreagh, Cartronroe, Church Hill, Cloonacleigha, Cloonagahaun, Cloonahinshin, Cloonameehan North, Cloonameehan South, Clooncose, Cloondorragha, Deechomade, Drinaun, Drinaun Bog, Drumfarnoght, Drumraine, Farranmaurice, Flowerhill, Killandy, Knockalough, Knocknakillew or Woodhill, Lecarrow, Lislea, Lismagore, Meelick Park, Moyrush, Quarryfield, Rinnarogue, Shancarrigeen or Old Rock, *one island in Templehouse Lough*.
Keash: (Toomour): Ardsallagh, Ballinvoher, Battlefield, Bellanascarrow East, Bellanascarrow West, Brougher, Carnaweelan, Carrickhawna, Carrowcrory, Carrowmaclenany, Carrownacreevy, Carrowreagh, Cletty, Cloonagh, Corradoo, Cross, Dernaskeagh, Derrygolagh, Drumnagranshy, Fallougher, Feenaghmore, Graniamore, Graniaroe, Greenan, Greyfield, Kingsfort, Knocklough, Knocknacroy, Knocknawhisoge, Knockoconor, Levally, Lurgan, Meenmore, Mullaghoor, Murhy, Roscrib East, Roscrib West, Templevanny, Tonaponra, Toomour, Treanmore, Tully.
(Drumrat): Abbeyville or Ardlaherty, Bearlough, Bearvaish, Bingranagh, Bunnamuck, Carrickrathmullin, Cloonacaltry, Cloonbannan, Cloonshanbally, Daghloonagh, Drumaneel, Finisklin, Kilsallagh, Kiltyteige, Knockanaher, Knockatelly, Knockbrack, Knockgrania, Knocknagore, Lisconwy, Listrush, Roosky Beg, Roosky More, Sniggeen, Sralea, Tawnalion.

COOLAVIN: This half-barony comprised the parishes of Gurteen (Kilfree and Killaraght) and part of Kilcolman (part of Ballaghaderreen).
Ballaghaderreen (Kilcolman): Annaghbeg or Monasterredan, Clogher, Falleens, Monasteredan, Shroove, Tawnymucklagh. *Islands in Lough Gara; Crow island and two others.*
Gurteen (Kilfree): Annaghmore, Calteraun, Carrowntemple, Chacefield, Cloonanure, Clooneagh, Cloonlaheen, Cloonsillagh, Cloontycarn, Cuilmore, Cuilprughlish, Doon, Gorteen, Gortygara, Greyfield, Kilfree, Kilstraghlan or Ragwood, Knocknahoo, Knocknashammer, Knocknaskeagh, Lisbaleely, Mahanagh, Mountirvine, Moydough, Moygara, Mullaghroe, Mweelroe, Rathmadder, Seefin, Sragh, Gurteen Town, *Eagle Island in Lough Gara*.
(Killaraght): Annagh, Ardgallin, Ardlona, Ardmoyle, Ardsoreen, Carrownaun, Carrownurlaur, Cashel, Clooncunny, Cloonloogh, Cuppanagh, Derryoghran, Derrybeg, Emlagh, Killaraght, Lisgullaun, Lismerraun, Lisserlough, Lomecloon,

Baronies, Parishes, Townlands

Baronies, Parishes, Townlands

Rathtermon, Rathtinaun, Reask, Ross, Stonepark, Tawran. *Islands in Lough Gara; Derrinatallan, Derrymore, Inch, Inch Beg, Inch More and three others.*

COSTELLO: This barony in Co Mayo comprised the parishes of Ballaghaderreen (Castlemore and part of Kilcolman), Charlestown and Kilmovee.
Ballaghaderreen (Castlemore): Ardkill Ballymaging or Castlemore, Barnaboy, Bogtaduff, Bohalas, Cashelard, Cashelcolaun, Cloonavullaun, Crunaun, Doogarry, Drumnalassan, Friarshill, Glebe, Ishlaun, Kilkeeran, Killadangan, Kilvanloon, Knockanaconny, Lung, Pollboy, Toomanagh.
(Part of Kilcolman): Attiantaggart, Ballaghaderreen, Ballyoughter, Bokagh, Boleysillagh, Brogher, Cloonlumney, Cloonmeen, Coolaghtane, Coollena, Creggan, Cross North, Cross South, Derrynacross, Derrynagur, Doogary Drumacoo, Fallsolus, Frasnadeffa, Hanksford, Islandmore, Kilcolman, Largan, Magheraboy, Tonregee, Toobracken, Tullaghan More, or Edmondstown, Tullaghanrock.
Charlestown (Kilbeagh): Ballintadder, Ballyglass East, Ballyglass West, Barnacahoge, Barnalyra, Barroe, Botinny, Bracklagh, Brackloonagh North, Brackloonagh South, Bulcaun, Calveagh Lower, Calveagh Upper, Cappulcorragh, Carn, Carrowntober, Cartron, Cashel, Cashelduff, Cloonalison, Cloonaweema,Clooncous, Cloonfane, Cloonlarhan, Cloonlyon, Cloonmeen East, Cloonmeen West, Cloonmore, Corragooly, Cragagh, Cranmore, Currinah, Derrydorneen, Derrykinlough, Derrynabrock, Derrynanaff, Fauleens, Glastrasna, Glenmullynaha East, Glenmullynaha West, Gortanure, Gowel, Gowlaun, Kilgarriff, Kilgarriff West, Killeen, Lavy Beg, Lavy More, Lecarrow, Lissymulgee, Lowpark, Lurga Lower, Lurga Upper, Mullenmadogue, Park, Puntabeg, Ranaranny, Roosky, Sonnagh, Speck, Shrah Lower, Shrah Upper, Stripe, Tawnyinah Lower, Tawnyinah Middle, Tawnyinah Upper, Temple, Tomboholla, Tonnagh, Tonroe, Treanacally or Hagfield, Trouthill or Knockbrack, Charlestown or Newtown-Dillon Town.
Kilmovee: Aghadiffin, Ballinrumpa, Ballyglass, Barcull, Carrowbeg, Carrownlacka, Cashellahenny, Clooncarha, Cloonfaulus, Cloonfeaghra, Cloonierin, Cloonamna, Corgarriff, Cuilliagh, Derragh, Derrynaleck, Glentavraun, Gowlaun, Kilcashel, Kilkelly, Killaclare, Kilmore, Kilmovee, Knockbrack, Leveelick, Magheraboy, Raherolus, Ranagissaun, Rusheens East, Rusheens West, Shanmerbaun, Shammerdoo, Skeheen, Sonvolaun, Shraheens, Tavraun, Tullyganny, Uggool, Urlaur.

GALLEN: This barony in Co Mayo comprised the civil parises of Attymass, Bohola, Bonniconlon (Kilgarvan), Foxford (Toomore), Killasser, Kiltimagh (Killedan), Straide (Templemore), Swinford (Kilconduff and Meelick).
Attymass: Ardrass, Ballycong, Ballymore, Boyhollagh, Bunnafinglas, Carrick, Carrowdoogan, Carrowkeribly, Cartron, Corradrishy, Corrower, Derrynabaunshy, Derryvicneill, Drumscoba, Glendaduff, Kildermot, Kilgellia, Mullaghawny, Roosky, Treanlaur, Treanoughter.
Bohola: Altbaun, Ardacarha, Ballinlag, Barleyhill, Bohamore, Bohola, Carroward, Carrocastle, Carrowgowan, Carrowkeel, Carrowmore, Carrowntleva, Gortnasillagh, Lisgormin, Lismiraun, Lissaniska, Listrisnan, Rathrowan, Rathslevin, Shanaghy, Shraheens, Tawnaghaknaff, Toocannagh, Tooromin, Treanfohanaun.
Bonniconlon (Kilgarvan): Bunnyconnellan East, Bunnyconnellan West, Carha,

Haran Chalice 1703 *(St Nathy's, Ballaghaderreen)*

Carrowcastle, Carrowconeen, Carrowcrom, Carrowleagh, Carrownlabaun, Carrowreagh, Cloonta, Craggera, Drumsheen, Ellagh Beg, Ellagh More, Graffy, Kilgarvan, Lissardmore, Rathreedaun.

Foxford (Toomore): Aghaward, Ballinillaun, Belgarrow, Bohershallagh, Cabragh, Cashel, Cloonmung, Creggagh, Cregnafyla, Foxford, Kilmore, Leckee, Moorbrook, Rinnananny, Shanwar, Toomore.

Killasser: Askillaun, Attimachugh, Attinaskollia, Bellanacurra, Blackpatch, Boleyboy, Callow, Carrow Beg, Carroweeny, Carrowliam Beg, Carrowliam More, Carrow More, Carrowmoremoy, Carrownageeragh, Carrowneden, Cartron, Cartronmacmanus, Cloonainra, Cloongleevragh, Cloonfinish, Cloontubbrid, Coolcashla, Coollagagh, Corlee, Cornageeha, Creggaballagh, Creggaun, Cuildoo, Cuillonaghtan, Cullin, Darhanagh, Doonmaynor, Doonty, Dromada (*Duke*), Dromada (*Gore*), Dromada (*Joyce*), Drumagh, Drumalooaun, Graffy, Killeen, Knockfadda, Knockmanagh, Knockmullin, Knocknaskeagh, Knocks, Larganmore, Lislaughna, Lismoran, Listernan, Loobnamuck, Magheraboy, Prebaun, Rubble, Tiraninny, Toorard, Treanrevagh, Tulleague, Tumgesh.

Kiltimagh (Killedan): Annagh Hill, Attavally, Ballinamore, Ballooclerhy, Ballynamona, Brownespark, Camderrynabinnia, Canbrack, Carrick, Carrownageeragh, Carrowndangan, Carrownteeaun, Carrowreagh, Cartron, Cloondoolough, Cloonkedagh, Cordorragh, Corrahoor, Craggagh, Cuilgar, Cuillalea, Cuiltrasna, Derrykinlough, Derryvohy, Devleash, Garryroe, Gortgarve, Gowelboy, Killedan, Kiltamagh, Knocknaskeagh, Largan, Lisduff, Lisnamaneeagh, Oxford, Pollronahan Beg, Pollronahan More, Shavally, Treankeel, Treanagleragh, Woods, Kiltimagh Town.

Straide (Templemore): Aghalusky, Ardcloon, Ashbrook, Ballylahan, Carrowgallda, Carrownaraha, Cloonconlan, Clooncoura, Cloongee, Derreenyanimna, Gorteen, Gurraunard, Knockafall, Knockagarraun, Knocknakillew, Knocksaxon, Knockshanbally, Lakill, Longfield, Oughtagh, Pollagh, Rathrushel, Redhill, Straide, Tawnagh More, Tawnagh Beg, Ummoon. *Two islands in Lough Cullin.*

Swinford (Kilconduff): Ardlee, Ballindrehid, Ballydrum, Ballyglass, Brackloon, Cara, Carrowbeg, Carrowcanada, Carrownaculla, Castlebarnagh, Castlecrunnoge, Castleroyan, Cloonacannana, Cloonaghboy, Cloonfinnaun, Cloongullaun, Cloonlara, Cloonlumney, Cornaveagh, Cuillaun, Cuilmore, Cuiltybo, Curryaun, Derryronan, Drumshinnagh, Esker, Faheens, Johnsfort, Kilbride, Kinaff, Knockbrack, Knockranny, Lagcurragh, Liscottle, Lissanumera, Newpark, Rathscanlan, Swineford, Tawnaglass, Tawnawullagh, Tonroe, Treanlaur, Tullanacorra, Tullynahoe, Woods.

(Meelick): Ardhoom, Ballintemple, Ballinvoher, Ballymiles, Bothaul, Carrowbaun, Carrownacross, Carrowreagh, Castlesheenaghan, Cloonagalloon, Clooneen, Clooninshin, Cloonygowan, Collagh, Esker, Killeen, Knockavilla, Laghtmacdurkan, Lecarrow, Lisbaun, Lisbrogan, Lisduff, Lisdurraun, Lisheenabrone,Lislackagh, Meelick, Oldcastle, Pollnagawna, Pollsharvoge, Rabaun, Rinbrack, Tullyroe.

Baronies, Parishes, Townlands

Bibliography

ARCHIVES

London   *England*
Public Record Office
HO 100/136 36303

Oxford
Oxfordshire County Record Office
The Dillon Papers, DIL. XII/B/7

Windsor
Windsor Palace
The Stuart Papers, vols. 96, 178, 217, 223, 224, 310 (on microfilm in the Library of the University of London)

Paris   *France*
Archives Nationales, FM. 2 18, MC et/I/764, MC et/XVII/164, MC et/XVII/534, 538, 542, 550, 553, 561, 595, 614, 618, MC et/XLVII/564
Archives of the Irish College, Paris
Archives de Paris

Versailles
Archives de Versailles

Belfast   *Ireland*
Public Record Office Northern Ireland
O'Hara Papers, T. 2812/4/16/19/25/26/29/31/40, T. 3725/26

Castlerea
Clonalis House
O'Conor Don Papers, 8. 3. HS. 023, 8. 4. SE. 148, 8. 4. SH. 058, 068, 150, 9. 1. H. 26, 9. 1. SH. 150, 9. 1. HL. 017, 9. 1. HS. 027, 9. 1. SE. 182, 9. 1. LS. 205

Dublin
Dublin Diocesan Archives
Irish College Paris Papers, 29/4
Registrum, 1

National Archives
Rebellion Papers, 620/26/82, 620/26/145, 620/40/58, 620/46/74, 620/46/83, 620/47/28, 620/52/123,125, 620/56/200
State of the Country Papers, 1015/21
Henry, William, 'Hints towards a natural and topographical history of the counties of Sligo, Donegal, Fermanagh and Lough Erne', (1739), Ms. 2533
Index to Administration Bonds, Townland Index, Landed Estate Court Rentals, Census of Elphin, 1749, Ms. 2466

National Library
de Montbret, Coquebert, *Carnets de voyage,* (microfilm, pos. 119)
MacDermot Papers
O'Hara Papers, Mss. 16,942, 16,943, 20,280, 20,282, 20,283, 20,285, 20,291, 20,313, 20,303, 20,338, 20,384, 20,388, 20,397
O'Hara Papers Report, 493

Royal Irish Academy
Stowe M. B 12

Trinity College
O'Connor's Journal through the Kingdom of Ireland, c. 5 May 1794, Ms. 2568
Stock, Joseph, *Killala Diary,* Ms. 1690

University College
Irish Folklore Commission, Ms. 114, Ms. 117, Ms 127, Ms. 193, Ms. 194, Ms. 195, Ms. 227, Ms. 248, Ms. 277, Ms. 321, Ms. 680, Ms. 903

Italy Rome
Irish College Archives
Jesuit Records, Lib. 12
Synod of Bunninadden

Propaganda Fide
Acta, vols. 85, 86, 91, 92, 95, 109, 132, 139, 145, 146, 149, 156, 157, 170, 171, 180, 181
Congregazioni Particolari, vols. 30, 32, 34A, 34B, 88, 110, 133, 152
Fondo di Vienna, vols. 28
Lettere, vols. 111, 142, 184, 191, 194, 198, 203, 209, 212, 214, 222, 226, 228, 230, 232, 242, 246, 248, 249, 250, 251, 255, 262, 264, 285, 289, 297, 299, 302, 303
Scritture riferite nei Congressi, Irlanda, vols. 4, 5, 6, 7, 8, 9, 10, 11, 12, 13, 15, 16, 17, 18, 19, 20, 21, 22, 23, 24
Scritture originali riferite nelle Congregazioni Generali, vols. 294, 447, 553, 559, 573, 601, 606, 614, 630, 649, 650, 699, 792, 823, 825, 841, 844, 852, 873, 875, 877, 884, 897, 910, 911, 917, 918
Udienze, vols. 23, 26, 30, 41, 42, 55, 56, 61, 67

San Clemente Archives
Codex 1. 4. nos. 426, 474, codex 2, vol. 2, codex 4

Vatican Archives
Fondo Missioni, no. 117
Nunciatura di Fiandra, vols. 130, 131, 135, 135A, 573

Vicariato Archivio Storico
Liber Ordinationis, vol. 38

PRINTED MATERIAL

Acheson, Alan, *A History of the Church of Ireland 1691–1996* (1997)
Barnard, Toby, 'Improving Clergymen, 1660–1760', A. Ford, J.McGuire, K. Milne (eds), *As by Law Established* (1995)
Barrington, Jonah, *Personal Sketches of his own Time*
Barrow, John, *A Tour round Ireland* (1835)
Bartlett, Thomas, 'The O'Haras of Annaghmore c.1600-c.1800: Survival and Revival', *Irish Economic and Social History*, vol. IX (1982), pp. 34–52
— *The Fall and Rise of the Irish Nation; The Catholic Question 1690-1830* (1992)
—(ed.) with Hayton, D.H, *Penal Era and Golden Age: Essays in Irish History, 1690–1800* (1979)
Bell, Robert, *A Description of the Conditions and Manners of the Irish Peasantry such as they were between the years 1780 and 1790* (1804)
Boyle, Patrick, *The Irish College in Paris, 1578–1901* (1901)
—'Some Irish Ecclesiastics at the Seminary of St Nicolas du Chardonnet, Paris', *Irish Ecclesiastical Record*, vol. II (1910)
Brady, John (ed.), *Catholics and Catholicism in the Eighteenth-century Press,* (1965)
Brockliss, L. W. B. and Ferté, P., 'Irish clerics in France in the seventeenth and eighteenth centuries: a statistical survey', *Proceedings of the Royal Irish Academy,* vol. 87, pp. 527–72
—*A Prosopography of Irish Clerics who studied in France in the 17th and 18th centuries, in particular at the universities of Paris and Toulouse,* (unpublished typescript in the Royal Irish Academy)
Burke, Ulick, *Archbishops of Tuam*
Burke, W. P. (ed.), *Irish Priests in the Penal Times 1660–1760* (1914)
Byrne, Miles, *Memoirs of Miles Byrne,* 2 vols. (1863)
Carleton, William, *Traits and Stories of the Irish Peasantry,* (1830)
Carr, John, *The Stranger in Ireland or a Tour in the Southern and Western Parts of that Country in the year 1805* (1806)
Census of Elphin, Ms. 2466, National Archives, Dublin
Clergyman of the Established Church, A, *An Authentic Narrative of the Recent Conversion of Twelve Roman Catholics named Hart*
Coleman OP, Ambrose, 'The General Exile of 1698', *Irish Ecclesiastical Record,* vol.v, 4th series (Jan-June 1899), pp.19–21

Conlan OFM, Patrick, 'The Franciscans in Ballymote', *Corran Herald*, no. 21 (1991)
Connell, K.H, *The Population of Ireland, 1750–1845* (1950)
Connolly, Seán, *Priests and People in pre-Famine Ireland* (1981)
Corish, P. J., *The Catholic Community in the Seventeenth and Eighteenth Centuries* (1981)
Costello, Nuala (ed.) *'Journal de l'expédition d'Irlande suivi de notes sur le Général Humbert qui la ommandé'*, *Analecta Hibernica*, no. 11 (1941), pp. 7–55
—'Little's Diary of the French Landing in 1798', *Analecta Hibernica*, no. 11 (1941), pp.59-168
Cullen, Louis M., 'Catholic Social Classes under the Penal Laws', Power and Whelan (eds.), *Endurance and Emergence*
—'Catholics under the Penal Laws', *Eighteenth Century Ireland*, vol. 1, pp. 23-36
—'Economic development, 1691–1750', *A New History of Ireland*, vol. IV, pp.123–58
—'Economic development, 1750–1800', *A New History of Ireland*, vol.IV, pp. 159–95
Curwen, J. C., *Observations on the State of Ireland*, 2 vols (1818)
de Breffny, Brian, 'Ambrose O'Higgins', *Irish Ancestor*, vol. II (1970), pp.81–9
—'Letters from Connaught to a Wild Goose', *Irish Ancestor*, vol. x (1978), pp.81–98
de Brún, Pádraig, *The Irish Society's Teachers 1818-1827* (forthcoming publication)
de Burgo, Thomas, *Hibernia Dominicana* (1762)
De Latocnaye, *Promenade d'un Français dans l'Irlande* (1797), translated as *Rambles through Ireland* (1798)
Desbrière, Edouard, *Projets et Tentatives de Débarquement aux Iles Britanniques*, 3 vols. (1898–1901)
Dineen, P. S., *Foclóir Gaedhilge agus Béarla* (1927)
Donlevy, Andrew, *An Teagasg Críosduidhe do réir Ceasda agus Freagartha* (1742)
Dowling, P. J., *The Hedge Schools of Ireland* (1935)
Duffy, P. J., *Killaville and its People* (1985)
Dunleavy, G. W. and Janet, (eds.) *The O'Conor Papers: a descriptive catalog and surname register of the materials at Clonalis House*
Dutton, Hely, *Statistical Survey of Co Clare* (1808)
Farry, M., *Killoran and Coolaney: a local history* (1985)
Faulkner, A., *Liber Dublinensis*
Fenning OP, Hugh, *The Irish Dominican Province, 1698–1797* (1990)
— *The Undoing of the Friars Minor in Ireland* (1972)
— 'Ambrose MacDermott OP, Bishop of Elphin 1707–17', *Archivium Fratrum Praedicatorum*, vol. XL (1970), pp. 231–75
—'The Athenry House-Chronicle, 1666–1779', *Collectanea Hibernica*, no. 11 (1968), pp. 36–52
—'Journey of James Lyons from Rome to Sligo, 1763–5' *Collectanea Hibernica*, no. 11 (1968), pp. 90–110
—'Two Diocesan Reports: Elphin (1753), by John Brett OP, and Killaloe (1972)' *Archivium Hibernicum*, vol. 30 (1972), pp. 21–8
—'Letters from Galway', *Collectanea Hibernica*, nos. 36 & 37 (1994–5), pp.174–95
Finn, J., *Gurteen, Co Sligo: Its history, traditions and antiquities* (1981)
Ffolliott, R. (ed.), 'Index to Killala and Achonry Administration Bonds, 1782-1856', *Irish Ancestor*, vol. 7 (1) (1975)

Fortescue Ms., Irish Manuscript Commission, vol viii, pp. 463-7, 475, 479, 480
Gibbon, Skeffington, *Recollections of Skeffington Gibbon from 1796 to 1829*
Giblin, Cathaldus, 'Catalogue of material of Irish interest in the collection Nunziatura di Fiandra, Vatican archives', *Collectanea Hibernica*, vols. I, III, IV, V, IX, X, XI, XII, XIII
— *Liber Lovaniensis*
Gilbert, J. T. (ed.), *Documents relating to Ireland, 1795–1804* (1893)
Grady, Patrick, *The Radical Anti-Veto* (1814)
Grose, Francis, *Antiquities of Ireland, 1791-5,* vols. 1 & 2
Hall, Rev James, *Tour through Ireland,* 2 vols. (1813)
Hall, Mr and Mrs S.C., *Ireland: Its scenery, character, etc.,* (1841)
Hamell, Patrick J., *Maynooth Students and Ordinations*
Hanly, John, *The Letters of Oliver Plunkett*
Hayes, Richard, *Biographical Dictionary of Irishmen in France* (1949)
—*The Last Invasion of Ireland* (1937)
—'A Limerick Medal of 1798', *North Munster Antiquarian Journal*, vol. 1, no. 2 (1944), pp. 77–8
Hansard, *Parliamentary Debates,* vol. XV
Hardiman, J., *Irish Minstrelsy*
Hayton, David, 'Did Protestantism fail in early eighteenth-century Ireland? Charity schools and the enterprise of religious and social reformation, c.1690–1730', *As by Law Established*, pp. 166–86
Healy, John, *Maynooth College Centenary History* (1895)
Hewson, George James, 'Siver Medal struck by the Corporation of Limerick in connection with the Engagement at Collooney 5 Sept 1798', *Royal Historical and Archaeological Association of Ireland Journal*, ser. 4, vol. 3, pt. 1 (1874), pp. 241–3
Hierarchia Catholica, vol. V, p. 67; vol. VI, p. 63; vol. VII, p. 57
Hogan, Patrick, 'The Migration of Ulster Catholics to Connaught, 1795–96', *Seanchas Ard Mhacha*, vol. 9, no. 2 (1979), pp. 286–301
Hyde, Douglas, *Love Songs of Connacht*
— *The Religious Songs of Connacht*
— *Legends of Saints and Sinners*
Irish Catholic Directory (1838) pp. III–241
Jennings, Martin, 'Ballymote Franciscan Abbey: Guardians 1697–1826', *Corran Herald,* no. 20 (1991)
Jobit, Jean Louis, 'Journal de l'Expédition d'Irlande suivi de notes sur le Général Humbert sui l'a commandé', Nuala Costello (ed.), *Analecta Hibernica,* no. 11 (1941), pp. 7–55
Jones, J., *The Irish Rebellion*
Kelly, James, 'Interdenominational Relations and Religious Toleration in late Eighteenth-Century Ireland', *Eighteenth-Century Ireland,* vol. III (1988), pp. 39–60
Keogh, Dáire, *'The French Disease': The Catholic Church and Radicalism in Ireland 1790-1800* (1993)

Kilgannon, T, *Sligo and its Surroundings: A descriptive and pictorial guide to the history, antiquities, scenery and places of interest in and around Sligo* (1926)

Lecky, W. E., *A History of Ireland in the 18th century*, 5 vols. (1913)

Legg, Marie-Louise (ed.), *The Synge Letters: Bishop Edward Synge to His Daughter Alicia, Roscommon to Dublin 1746–1752* (1996)

Leslie, J. B., *Biographical Succession List of the Clergy of Achonry and Killala*, (typescript in the Representative Church Body Library, Braemor road, Dublin.)

List of Persons to whom Premiums for sowing flax-seed in the year 1796 have been adjudged by the Trustees of the Linen Board (1796)

Little, James, 'Little's Diary of the French Landing in 1798', Nuala Costello (ed.), *Analecta Hibernica*, no. 11 (1941), pp. 59–168

Logan, Patrick, *The Holy Wells of Ireland* (1980)

MacDermot, Dermot, *MacDermot of Moylurg*

MacDomhnaill, An tAthair (ed.), *Dánta is Amhráin Sheáin Uí Ghadhra*

MacDonagh, J. C., *History of Ballymote and the Parish of Emlaghfad* (1936)

— 'Counsellor Terence MacDonagh', *Studies*, XXXVI (1947), pp. 307–17; XXXVII (1948), pp. 65–74

McDonnell-Garvey, Máire, *Mid-Connacht* (1995)

McDowell, R. B., 'Colonial nationalism and the winning of parliamentary independence, 1760–82', *A New History of Ireland*, vol. IV, pp. 196–235

McGuinn, J., *Curry* (1984)

McParlan, J., *Statistical survey of County Sligo, with observations on the means of improvement in the year, 1801, for the consideration and under the direction of the Dublin Society* (1802)

— *Statistical survey of County Mayo* (1802)

McTernan, John C., *Olde Sligoe* (1995)

— *Worthies of Sligo* (1994)

— *Sligo: Sources of Local History* (1994)

Mason, W. S., *A Statistical Account or Parochial Survey of Ireland*, 4 vols (1814–19)

Maxwell, Constantia (ed.), *A Tour in Ireland by Arthur Young*, 1 vol. (1925)

Maxwell, W, *Wild Sports of the West* (1832)

Millet, Benignus, 'Catalogue of Irish Material in 14 volumes of *Scritture originali riferite nelle congregazioni generali* in Propaganda archives', *Collectanea Hibernica*, nos. X-XII (1967–9)

Milne, Kenneth, *Church of Ireland*

— 'Principle or Pragmatism', *As by Law Established*, pp. 187–94

M. O'R. 'The Rev Charles O'Conor D.D. (Columbanus)', *The Seven Hills Magazine*, vol. 3, no. 2 (September 1908), pp. 229–274

Moran, P. F. (ed.), *Spicilegium Ossoriense*, 3 vols (1874–84)

Morgan, Lady (Sydney Owenson), *Patriotic Sketches of Ireland written in Connaught*, vols. I–II (1807)

— *The Wild Irish Girl* (1846)

Morris, Henry, 'St Martin's Eve', *Béaloideas*, iml. IX, uimh. II, pp. 230–5

Murphy, Ignatius, *The Diocese of Killaloe in the Eighteenth Century*, (1991)

Musgrave, Richard, *Memoirs of the Different Rebellions in Ireland* (1801)

Neligan, James, 'Parish of Kilmactige', in W. S. Mason, *A Statistical Account or*

Parochial Survey of Ireland, vol. 2, pp. 349–98

Ní Chinnéide, Síle, 'Dialann Í Chonchúir', *Galvia*, vol. IV (1957), pp. 4–17

— 'A Frenchman's tour of Connacht in 1791', *Galway Archaological Society Journal*, vol. XXV (1952–3), pp. 1–14; vol. XXXV, pp. 52–66; XXXVI (1977–8), pp. 30–42

— 'Dhá leabhar nótaí le Séarlas Ó Conchubhair', *Galvia*, vol. 1 (1954), pp. 32–41

O'Byrne, Eileen (ed.), *The Convert Rolls* (1981)

Ó Coigligh, Ciarán, *Raiftearaí: Amhráin agus Dánta*

O'Conor, Rev Charles, *Memoirs of the life and writings of the late Charles O'Conor of Belanagare* (1796)

— *Letter of Columbanus*

Ó Danachair, Caoimhín, *The Year in Ireland*

O'Donovan, John, (see Ordinance Survey), *Letters relating to the Antiquities of Co Mayo* (Ordnance Survey Letters, vols. II & II)

— *Sligo Letters* (1926)

O'Dowd, Mary, *Power, politics and land: Early Modern Sligo 1568-1688* (1991)

— 'Land Inheritance in early modern County Sligo', *Irish Economic and Social History*, vol. X (1983), pp. 5–18

Ó Duigeannáin, Mícheál, 'Three seventeenth-century Connacht documents', *Galway Historical and Archaeological Journal*, XVII (1936), pp. 154–61

Ó Duilearga, Séamus, 'The Cake Dance', *Béaloideas*, uimh. I–II, pp. 126–42

Ó Fiaich, Tomás, 'The Registration of the Clergy in 1704', *Seanchas Ard Mhacha*, vol. VI (1971), pp. 46–96

O'Hara, Bernard (ed.), *Killasser: A History* (1981)

— (ed.), *Mayo: Aspects of its Heritage* (1982)

O'Heyne OP, John, *The Irish Dominicans of the Seventeenth Century* (ed. A. Coleman 1902)

Ó Laoghaire, Diarmuid, *Ár bPaidreacha Dúchais* (1975)

Ó Máille, Tomás, *Amhráin Chearbhalláin*, Irish Texts Society vol. XVII (1916)

Ó Muraíle, Nollaig, 'Aspects of Intellectual Life in Seventeenth Century Galway', *Galway History & Society* (1996), pp. 149–210

— 'Toirialach Ó Cearúlláin', *Léachtaí Cholm Cille iv: Litríocht an 18ú hAois* (1975)

Ordnance Survey, *Letters containing information relative to the antiquities of County Sligo during the progress of the Ordnance Survey, 1836*, (1928)

— *Name Books of County Sligo. Compiled by John O'Donovan during the progress of the Ordnance Survey in 1836*

— *Miscellaneous items relative to the Parishes of Emlaghfad and Kilmactigue, collected in the course of the Ordnance Survey, 1836; to which is appended stastistics on Killoran and Kilvarnet, dated 1796*

O'Rorke, Terence, *History, antiquities and present state of the Parishes of Ballysadare and Kilvarnet in the County of Sligo with notices of the O'Haras, the Coopers, the Percivals and other local families*

— *The History of Sligo: Town and County*, 2 vols.

Ó Súilleabháinn, Seán, *Irish Wake Amusements* (1967)

O'Sullivan, D., *Carolan: Life, Times and Music of an Irish Harper* (1958)

Parliamentary Papers (1825) vols. 7 & 12

Parliamentary Papers (1835) vol. 35
Pococke, *Bishop Pococke's tour in Ireland in 1752*, G.T. Stokes (ed.) (1891)
Power, T. P., and Whelan, Kevin (eds.), *Endurance and Emergence: Catholics in Ireland in the Eighteenth Century* (1990)
Quane, Michael, 'Banna School, Ardfert,' *Royal Society of Antiquaries of Ireland Journal*, vol. 84, pp. 156–72
— 'Aspects of Education in Ireland, 1695–1795', *Journal of the Cork Historical and Archaeological Society*, vol. LXXIII (1968), pp. 120–36
Quinn, J. F., *History of Mayo* (1993)
Reportorium Novum, vol. 1, no. 2
Rogan, Edward, *Synods and Catechesis in Ireland*
Simms, J. G., 'County Sligo in the eighteenth century', *Royal Society of Antiquaries of Ireland Journal*, vol. 91 (1961), pp. 153–62
— 'Sligo in the Jacobite War, 1688–91', *Irish Sword*, vol. 7 (1965–66), pp. 124–35
— 'The Irish on the Continent, 1691–1800', *A New History of Ireland*, vol. IV, pp. 629–56
— 'Mayo Landowners in the Seventeenth Century', *Journal of the Royal Society of Antiquiries of Ireland*, vol. 95 (1965)
— 'The Bishops' banishment act of 1697', *Irish Historical Studies*, vol. XVII (1970), pp. 185–99
Smythe-Wood, P., 'Index to Killala and Achonry Wills, 1698–1837', *Irish Genealogist*, vol. 3 (XII) (1967)
Stephenson, Robert, *Reports and Observations 1760–61* (1762)
Stevenson, John (ed.), *A Frenchman's walk through Ireland, 1796–7* (1917)
Stock, Joseph, *Narrative of what passed at Killala in the County of Mayo and the Parts adjacent during the Summer of 1798* (1800)
— *Killala Diary*, Ms. 1690, TCD
Story, G., *Impartial history of the affairs of Ireland*
Swords, Liam, *The Green Cockade: The Irish in the French Revolution 1789–1815* (1989)
— (ed.) *The Irish-French Connection* (1978)
— *Soldiers, Scholars, Priests* (1985)
— 'Notes towards an edition of Registrum Episcopatus Achadensis assumptum ... tempore Eugenii O Hart' (Gilmartin Prize Essay, 1962, unpublished)
— 'History of the Irish College, Paris, 1578–1800', *Archivium Hibernicum*, vol. XXXV (1980), pp. 3–233
— 'Irish material in the files of Jean Fromont, notary, 1701–30, in the Archives Nationales, Paris', *Collectanea Hibernia*, nos. 34 & 35 (1992–3), pp. 77–115; nos. 36 & 37 (1994–5), pp. 85–139
The Scientific Tourist by an Irish Gentleman
Trench, Charles Chenevix, *Grace's Card: Irish Catholic Landlords 1690–1800* (1997)
Twiss, Richard, *A Tour in Ireland in 1775*
Vane, C., *Memoirs and Correspondence of Viscount Castlereagh*, 12 vols. (1848–53)
Wakefield, Edward, *An Account of Ireland Statistical and Political*
Walker, Joseph C., *Historical Memoirs of the Irish Bards* (1786)

Wall, Maureen, *Catholic Ireland in the 18th Century: Collected essays of Maureen Wall* (1989)
Walsh, Micheline, 'Irish Soldiers and the Irish College in Paris 1706–1791', in Swords, *The Irish–French Connection*, pp. 63–87
Walsh, William J., 'Registry of Irish Parish Priests Anno 1704', *Irish Ecclesiastical Record*, (April-September 1876)
Ward, Robert E., Wrynn, John F., and Ward, Catherine Coogan (eds.), *Letters of Charles O'Conor of Belanagare. A Catholic Voice in Eighteenth-Century Ireland* (1988)
Wesley, John, *The Journals of John Wesley*, (1902)
Westlander. F., *A Memoir of William Moore* (1843)
Whelan, Kevin, 'The Catholic Community in Eighteenth-Century County Wexford', *Endurance and Emergence*, pp. 129–70
— 'The Catholic Parish, the Catholic Chapel and Village Development in Ireland', *Irish Geography*, vol. XVI (1983), pp. 1–15
Wilde, W. R. W., *Memoir of Gabriel Beranger and his labours in the cause of Irish art and antiquities from 1760 to 1780* (1880)
Wood-Martin, W. G., *History of Sligo, County and Town*, vol. 1: *From earliest ages to close of reign of Queen Elizabeth*, vol. 2: *From accession of James I to the Revolution of 1688*, vol. 3: *From close of Revolution of 1688 to the present time.* (1882-92)
— *Traces of the Elder Faiths of Ireland: A Handbook of Pre-Christian Traditions*, 2 vols. (1902)
Yeats, W. B., *The Priest of Collooney*
Young, Arthur, *A tour in Ireland: with general observations on the present state of the kingdom: made in the years 1776, 1777, and 1778, and brought down to the end of 1779.* 2 vols. (1780)

Straide Abbey (*Dublin Penny Journal*)

Index

Abbreviations: APP/S = *Appendices*; n = *reference to footnote*; fr = *Friar*

Achill Island 63, 110, 116
Achonry parish 16, 17, 34, 44, 46, 46n, 47, 51, 52n, 94n, 141, 142, 155n, 178, 182, 187, 191, 223, 231, 273, 275, 294, 317, 318, APPS 6, 7, 8, 13, 16, 17, 18, 34, 36, 37, 40, 42, 43, 48
Aclare 85, 124, 124n, 271
Adragool 74
Aghamore 18n
Aldworth, Mary 23
Altamont, Lord 56, 84
Anderson, John 76
Anderson, Rev 158
Annagh 18n
Annaghbeg 298, APPS 7, 34
Annaghdown 301
Annaghmore 18, 85, 86, 131, 249, 262
Aran 324
Ardagh diocese 288, 290, 329, 333
Ardagh parish 74
Ardcarne see Cootehall 34, 290
Ardgallen APPS 7, 34
Ardnaglass 168
Ardnaree 150, 186
Armstrong, James 186
Armstrong, John 95
Athenry 30, 126, 293, 294
Attymass 16, 18, 34, 44, 51, 66, 142, 143, 222, 229, 266n, 272, 273, 275, 289, APPS 7, 8, 17, 34, 50, 51
Aughagour 264, 328
Aughrim, Battle of 22, 26
Backs 74
Bacon, Miss 158
Baken, Mary 41
Balla 76, 162, 276, 277, 278, 304
Ballaghaderreen *(Castlemore and Kilcolman)* 17, 18, 34, 36, 42, 43n, 44, 52, 69, 85, 88, 88N, 89n, 96, 97, 99, 124, 124n, 128, 142, 155, 171, 194, 198, 200, 215, 220, 221, 230, 241, 256, 273, 275, 301, 308, 313, 318, 321, 322, 323, 324, 345, 349, 361, 371, 372, 373, 374, APPS 18, 24N, 34, 37, 48, 50, 51
Ballavary *(Kildacommogue)* 18n
Ballina 17, 56, 57, 59, 60, 64, 67, 68, 69, 72, 73, 74, 75, 95, 111, 112, 112n, 117, 124, 150, 164, 181, 186, 222, 269, 361, APP 42
Ballinacarrow 115n, 124n, 158, 161, 182, APP 45
Ballinacurra 173
Ballinafad 243, 301, 302, 304
Ballinalack APPS 18, 34
Ballinamuck 68, 70, 71, 76
Ballinasloe 55, 91
Ballindoon 36n, APP 7
Ballinrea APP 7
Ballinrobe 69, 262, 283, 320, 339, 340
Ballintra 68
Ballintubber Abbey 262
Ballisodare 16, 17, 21, 22, 23, 29, 34, 36, 38, 39, 43n, 44, 45, 51, 52n, 70, 79, 80, 84, 94n, 102 107, 111, 124n, 125, 127, 131, 136, 141, 142, 143n, 144n, 146, 149, 150, 154, 155n, 156, 182, 193, 195, 198, 201, 205, 217, 222, 224, 225, 263, 267, 270, 273, 275, 284, 293, 297, 298, 299, 304, 307, 308, 321, 337, 373, APPS 7, 8, 15, 27, 34, 36, 37, 43, 46, 48, 51
Ballybofey 20
Ballybrennan APPS 7, 34, 50
Ballyfahy 171n, APP 48
Ballyhaunis 48, 128
Ballylahan 231, APPS 17, 34, 42
Ballymote *(Emlefad and Kilmorgan)* 17, 18, 19, 23, 24, 34, 36, 36N, 37, 38, 43, 43n, 46n, 48, 50, 56, 76, 80, 82, 84, 84n, 93, 94, 95, 124, 125, 142, 158, 160, 168, 170, 171, 173, 188n, 222, 230, 233, 239, 251, 270n, 273, 276, 315n, 330, 334, 349, 362, 374, APPS 7, 18, 26, 28, 34, 37, 42, 48, 50, 51, 289
Ballymote castle 19–20

Ballymote Friary 29, 43, 45, 45n, 51, 197, 199, 231, APPS 23, 39
Ballynaglogh 48, 155
Ballynakill 74
Ballysokeary 74
Banada 36n, 49, 59, 75, 124, 124n, 148, 229, 355, 356, 359
Banada Abbey 29, 43, 45, 51, 163, 188n, 199, 230, 231, 235, 236, 238, 357, 360, 366, APPS 18, 23, 24, 28, 41
Banaghan, Charles APP 42
Banaghan, Eugene (Owen) APPS 17, 19, 20, 21, 26, 27, 34
Banaghan, Owen APP 42
Banaghan, Thady APP 42
Baratogher 170, 171n, APP 48
Barden, John APP 48
Barley Hill APPS 18, 34
Barnacuaige 57
Barnageeha 68, 76
Barrington, Sir Jonah 191
Barry, Edward 52
Bartley OP, Patrick APP 38
Beakan 18n
Beatly 75
Beirne, Luke 210n, APPS 9, 29, 35
Beirne, Patrick 210n, APPS 9, 12, 29, 35
Belahagh APPS 7, 34
Belanagare 193, 207
Bellaghy 19, 59, 69, 76n, 124, 124n, 151
Belleek 21
Bellew, Bishop Dominick 74, 77, 324, 342
Bellew, Matthew 74
Belmullet 146
Beltra 18, 19, 77
Bennett OFM, James APP 39
Beresford, Archbishop 326
Bermingham, Peter 186
Berne, Dominick 38, APPS 7, 34
Bethel, Thomas APP 37
Bettridge, Laurence 298
Bingham, Dirk 149
Blake, Anastase 302
Blake, Anstace 305
Blake, Archbishop Anthony 191
Blake, Bridget 305
Blake, Catto 305
Blake, Francis Xavier 218
Blake, John 302, 305
Blake OP, John APP 38

Blake, Judy 305
Blake, Lady 332
Blake, Margaret 302
Blake, Mark 302, 305
Blake, Mary 302
Blake, Maurice 301
Blake, Peter 156, 219, 305, 315
Blake, Bishop Walter 45, 46, 179, 200, 205, 208, 210, 212, 215, 243, 250, 251, 300–5, 307, 308, 331, 335, 336, APPS 1, 26, 29
Blest, Albert 143, 154, 157, 158, 162, 163, 182, 183
Bodkin, James APP 47
Bodkin, Col John 22
Bodkin, Michael APP 47
Bodkin, Valentine 199, 316, 319, 338–44
Boherhallagh 171n, APP 49
Bohola 16, 18, 34, 38, 43, 142, 143n, 229, 270, 273, 275, 276, 281, APPS 7, 8, 18, 34, 50, 51
Boland, Bartholomew APP 33
Boland, Francis 366n, APPS 23, 24, 25, 33, 34
Bonniconlon 17, 18, 34, 36n, 37, 44, 47, 56, 66, 80n, 112, 142, 143, 222, 229, 272, 273, 289, 312, APPS 34, 45, 50, 51
Borrowes, Joseph 145, APP 37
Bouleboy APP 48
Boyle 21, 59, 84, 96, 122, 122n, 124, 129, 158, 291, 298, 366, 372
Boyne, Battle of 21, 24
Brabazon, Sir Anthony 76n, APP 45
Brabazon family 86, 131, 156
Brabazon, George 48, 131, 155, 156, APP 43
Brabazon, John George 344
Brabazon, William 76n, 171, APP 45, 48
Brady family 57
Branchfield 171n, 182
Branigan family 57
Branigan, John APP 44
Branigan, Pat APP 44
Branly, James 366
Braxton, Edward 36
Bray, Archbishop Thomas 219
Breaffy 36n, APP 7
Bree, John APP 48
Brennan, Miss 76n
Brennan, Bernard 288, APPS 5, 34
Brennan, Bryan 162, APP 7
Brennan, M APP 48
Brennan, Michael 182

Brennan, Miss APP 45
Brennan, Patrick 76n, 162, APPS 8, 10, 12, 34, 45
Brennan, Teige, 35, APPS 5, 6, 7
Brett, Charles 307, 308, 309, APPS 3, 13, 14, 15, 34
Brett family 197, 287
Brett OFM, Francis APPS 8, 39
Brett OFM, Henry 46n, APP 39
Brett, John 309, APPS 7, 42
Brett, Bishop John 156, 176, 178, 300n, 303, 304
Brett, William 309, APP 42
Bridgeman, James 95
Brown, Andrew 36n, APPS 7, 48
Brown, John APP 7
Brown, Thomas APP 7
Brown, Valentine APP 7
Brown(e), Fr 74, 74n, APP 34
Browne, Denis 56, 57, 57n, APP 47
Browne family 47
Browne, Nicholas 305, 332, 334
Buckingham, Marquis of 78, 79
Bunacrannagh APP 26
Bunninadden *(Cloonoghill, Kilturra and Kilshalvey)* 18, 34, 35, 36, 43, 44, 48, 51n, 52, 80, 88, 94n, 124n, 141, 142, 177, 198, 223, 227, 230, 233, 242, 273, 275, 305, 306, 315, APPS 34, 39, 45, 48, 50, 51
Bunnitubber 202, 305, APP 18
Burke OP, Anthony APP 38
Burke, Bishop Dominick 287, 289
Burke, Edmund 91, 290
Burke, Francis APPS 24, 36
Burke, James APP 47
Burke, John 210, 211, 212, 239, 296
Burke, Michael 68
Burke, Myles APP 7
Burke, Theobald 36n, APP 7
Burke, Thomas APPS 10, 12, 35
Burke OP, Bishop Thomas 312
Burke, Sir Tobias 296
Burke, William 39
Burrishoole 328, APP 38
Bushy Park APPS 18, 34
Butler, Bishop John (Lord Dunboyne) 199, 319
Byrne, Francis APP 43
Callow 220
Cannon, Peter 89n
Carabine, Timothy 182, APP 48

Carbury barony 17
Carhampton, Earl of 58
Carlingford 216
Carlingford, Earl of 18, 24, 86
Carmichael, Lady Mary 87
Carmichael, Archbishop William 87
Carne APP 7
Carpendale, Thomas 62
Carpenter, Archbishop 332, 338
Carracastle 85, 124, 124n, 170, 171n, 230, APPS 34, 48, 50
Carrick 68
Carrickclooneen APP 7, 34
Carrigbanagher 39, 76, APP 34
Carrignagat 70
Carroll, Charles 89n
Carroll, Patrick 89n
Carroll, Rev APP 33
Carroriwagh APP 7
Carrowgarry 155
Carrowhobit APP 7
Carrowmacarrick 171n, APP 48
Carrownedin APPS 7, 34
Carrowreagh 140
Carrowrory 36n, APP 7
Carter, Oliver APP 37
Carter, Rowland 155n, APP 43
Cartron APP 48
Cary, Bishop Mordecai 137, 138, 140, APP 2
Casey, John APP 48
Cassidy family 57
Cassidy, Jack 79
Castlebar 17, 67, 68, 69, 74, 76, 79, 103, 104, 114, 124, 124n, 151, 152, 186, 187, 225, 258, 277, 278, 296, 315, 351
Castleconnor 74
Castleloye 182, APP 48
Castlemore *see Ballaghaderreen* 16, 142n, 144n, 145, 171n, 227, 288, 292, 322, 324, 345, APPS 5, 8, 10, 34, 48
Castlerea 58, 198, 229, 324, 346
Castlereagh, Lord 81
Caulfield, Adam 144n, 146, 150, APP 37
Caulfield, Bishop James 320
Caulfield, Capt Thomas 149
Caulfield, Tobias 43n, 125, 142n, 144n, 147, 148–50, APP 37
Caulfield, Sir William 149
Chaffpool 95
Charlemont, Lord 21, 149
Charlestown *(Kilbeagh)* 18, 34, 44, 51, 88n,

89n, 115n, 142, 222, 273, 275, 374, APPS 34, 51
Charost 67, 69, 71
Cheevers, Bishop 333
Chidley, Col 38
Church, Thomas APP 46
Clagnagh APP 7
Clare 190, 253, 271
Claregalway 191, 233, 236n
Claremorris 68
Clarinbridge 132
Clark 76
Clarke OP, Albert APP 38
Clarke OP, Edward 231, 366n, APPS 23, 24, 25, 38
Clayton, Bishop Robert 43, 138n, 139, 140, 169, 175, 176, 192, APPS 2, 8
Clondevaddock 142n
Clogher 220, 273, 274
Cloonacool 230, APPS 17, 18, 19, 34
Cloonamahon 88, 131, 155n, 298, APP 42
Cloonbare 202, APP 7
Clooncither APP 7
Cloone 68
Clooneen 305
Cloonfad 47
Cloonfinnish 220
Cloonimighane 155n
Cloonkelagh APP 7
Cloonmore 37, 47, 138, 141, 193, 202, 227, 262, 264, 283, 310, 313, 316, APP 18
Cloonoghill *see Bunninadden* 16, 44, 141n, 142, 294, PPS 5, 6, 7, 8, 17, 18, 19, 34, 40
Cluane OP, Peter 30, 33, 46, APPS 34, 38
Cluane, Richard 46, APPS 5, 6, 7, 34
Cobbe, Bishop Charles 137, 138, 139, 140, APP 2
Coen, Bishop Thomas 353
Cogan, Patrick APP 47
Coleman, James APPS 47
Coleman, John (Darby?) 182, 185, 193, 367, APPS 24, 33, 34, 36, 48
Coleman, Rev APP 33
Collery, Owen 263
Collery, Thomas APP 47
Collins, Andrew 182, APP 48
Collooney 23, 35, 38, 68, 69, 70, 73, 77, 84, 85, 99, 108, 121, 124, 124n, 143n, 144, 148, 149, 150, 167, 168, 171n, 178, 193, 195, 224, 249, 286, 298, APPS 7, 27n, 34, 42, 43, 46

Collooney *(Kilvarnet)* 17, 19, 30, 36, 37, 44, 46, 46n, 48, 51, 52n, 94n, 95, 102, 142, 143, 147, 155n, 273, 360, 367, 368, 369, 373, APPS 38, 48, 51
Collooney, Lord 18, 19
Collracell APP 7
Conane, Edmund APPS 7, 34
Concanen OP, Luke 327, 338, 346
Conelly, Kitty 149
Cong 202, 301, APP 7
Conian OFM, Michael 45n
Conilan, James APP 42
Conlan, Andrew APPS 22, 23, 24, 35
Conmy OSA, James 231, APP 41
Connell, Patrick APP 42
Connellan, Thady 158, 160, 162, 175, 177, 189, 190, 191
Connelly, James APP 46
Connelly, John APP 46
Connemara 74, 135, 157, 262, 283
Connolly, Andy APP 42
Connolly OP, John 338, 345
Connolly, Martin APP 42
Conroy, James 74
Conry, John APP 42
Conry, Maurice APP 42
Conry, Pat APP 42
Conry, Peter 299, 300, 301, APP 42
Conway, Michael 74
Conyngham, Sir Albert 21
Conyngham, Honora 155n
Cooke, John APPS 28, 34
Cooke, Peter APPS 24, 25, 36
Coolaney *(Killoran)* 17, 35, 36n, 44, 46, 51, 52n, 89, 92, 94n, 95, 102, 142, 143, 145, 147, 154, 155n, 158, 162, 182, 184, 223, 224, 273, 372, APPS 7, 34, 37, 40, 43, 46, 48, 51
Coolavin barony 16, 17, 36n, 37, 47, 49, 56, 66, 69, 70, 77, 87, 112n, 128, 131, 161, 198, 256, 346, APPS 7, 51
Coolcarney 76, 80, APP 45
Coolrecul 36n
Cooper Capt Arthur 19
Cooper, Col Joshua Edward 55, 77, 84, 93, 101, 109, 115n, 148, 286
Cooper family 18, 19, 85, 86, 87, 89, 131, 143
Cooper, Nancy 131
Coote family 18
Coote, Hon Chidley 19
Coote, Richard, Lord Collooney 18, 19

Coote, Sir Charles 19
Cootehall *(Ardcarne)* 34, 39
Corcoran 173
Corcoran OP, Cormac APP 38
Corcoran, James APP 47
Corcoran, Peggy 131
Corcoran, Thomas 35, 37, 39, APPS 7, 42
Cordrissagh APP 7
Cormack OFM, fr APP 8
Corr, Peter 96
Corran barony 16, 17, 39, 41, 56, 69, 70, 109, 110, 125, 291, APP 51
Corry OFM, Thomas APP 39
Costello OP, Andrew APP 38
Costello barony 16, 17, 18, 30, 79, 85, 87, 87n, 97, 123, 198, 222, 322, APP 51
Costello, Charles 155, 322, 324, 327, 345, 349, APP 43
Costello, Dudley 36n, APP 7
Costello, Edmund 42, 155, APP 43
Costello, Fr Edmund 217n, APP 29
Costello family 86, 197, 232, 323, 331
Costello OP, John APP 38
Costello, Michael APPS 10, 35, 42
Costello, Mr APP 47
Costello Gallen, Viscount of 19, 24, 25, 30, 37, 48, 78, 86
Costello OP, Peter APP 38
Costello OP, Raymond APP 38
Costello, Richard APP 42
Costello, Bishop Thomas 99, 198, 199, 200, 206, 214, 219, 227, 230, 313, 315, 317, 318, 319, 323, 338, 341-43, 345, 353, APPS 17, 18, 19, 32, 34
Costello, Thomas 200, 347
Costello OP, Thomas 30
Costello, Tomás Láidir 128
Costello, Walter APPS 5, 6, 34
Costello, William 200, 331, 351, 352, 353, APPS 23n, 29, 30
Court Abbey 29, 43, 231, 235, 262, 263, 264, APP 39
Cowley, Bartholomew APP 47
Cowley, Owen 74
Coyne, Bart APP 42
Craughwell, 132
Crawford, Col 70
Crawley, James 220, 238
Crean, James APP 7
Crean, John 36, 37

Crean, Stephen 36, 37
Creary, William APP 47
Creevliagh 176
Cregane 220, 227, 230, 318, APP 18
Creggin 202, 203, 204, APP 7
Croagh Patrick 162, 270
Croghan APP 48
Crofton family 18, 77, 86, 189
Crofton, Henry 19, APP 37
Crofton, Sir Joshua 156, 344
Crofton, Mrs 131
Crofton, Richard 100
Croghan 21
Cromie, John 144, APP 37
Cromwell, Oliver 32
Crosbie, Rev APP 33
Crossmolina 56, 67, 68, 74
Crotty, Bartholomew 347
Cuffe, James 56, 57
Cuffe OFM, John APP 39
Cullen OP, James APP 38
Cully 36n, APP 7
Cumffe (Cuniffe?), Mrs Eleanor 155, APP 43
Cummins OFM, John APP 39
Cunane OFM, Francis APP 8, 39
Cuniffe OFM, Anthony APP 39
Cuniffe, Michael APP 42
Cunnane OFM, Michael APP 39
Cunningham, Thomas APP 44
Curley, Anthony 76n, APP 45
Curragh, The 86
Curraghmore 118
Curry 76, 94n, 104, 132, 152, 228, 230, 270n, 273, 318, 357, APPS 19, 34, 45, 50
Cusack, Jane 328
Dalton, Garret 88n
Dalton, General 198, 336
Dalton, James 197, 200, 353, 356, 359, 360, 361, 367, 368, 370, 371, APPS 22, 23, 24n, 30, 35
Dalton, Thomas 88n
Dalton OP, Thomas 336, 337
Dalton, William 287
Daly, Bishop 211
Daly, Ignatius 216
Daly, Michael 209, 217, APP 29
Daniel, Garret APP 7
Daniel-Rops 152
Darcy, Anastase 301
Daton, Walter 210, 211, 212

INDEX

Davey OFM, Francis 45n, APPS 8, 39
Davey, James APP 45
Davey, Michael 76, APP 45
Davey, Patrick 76, APPS 45, 48
Davey, Peter APP 42
Davey, Teige 39, 43, APPS 7, 8, 10, 34
Davis, E APP 37
Daze (Deasy?) OP, Denis APP 38
Deane, Coll APP 42
Deane, Edward APP 42
Deane, Hugh APP 42
Dease, Bernard 74
De Latocnaye 113n, 147
Devine, Rev APP 33
Devorny, Daniel APP 47
Devlin, M APP 44
Dickens, Charles 285
Dillon, Archbishop Arthur Richard 25, 51
Dillon, Arthur 25, 26
Dillon, Charles I 87
Dillon, Charles II 87
Dillon, Archbishop Edward 62, 278, 324, 326
Dillon family 24, 25, 37, 86, 87, 88
Dillon OFM, Francis 31
Dillon, Henry 87
Dillon, James 88n
Dillon, Col James 25
Dillon, Lord 51, 60, 62, 78, 79, 222, 227, 232, 322
Dillon OFM, Bishop Louis 230
Dillon, Richard 87
Dillon, Robert APPS 21, 22, 34
Dillon, General Theobald 26
Dillon, Thomas 66
Dillon, Viscount Charles 25, 48
Dillon, Viscount Henry 24, 30
Dillon, Viscount Theobald 19, 24
Doddy, John APPS 23, 24, 33, 34, 36
Dogherty, Winifred APP 46
Dohorn APP 20
d'Oisel, Healy 239
Dolan OFM, Laurence APP 39
Dolan, James 35, APP 7
Donamon 149
Donbroy, Bryan 256
Donlevy, Andrew 41, 167, 196, 210, 211, 212, 213, 214, 215, 239, 241, 243, 334n, 335, APP 29
Donlevy PP, Andrew APPS 18, 19, 20, 26, 34
Donlevy, Bernard APP 33

Donlevy, Francis 51n, 202, 315, 318, APPS 18, 19, 34
Donnelan, Matthew 185
Donnelan, Maurice 287
Donnellan, Bishop Andrew 312, 318, 338, 342
Donnellan, Belle 326
Donnellan, Bishop Peter 29, 202, 312, APP 7
Donnellan OFM, Peter APP 39
Donnelly, Bishop Patrick 290
Donoghue, Michael APPS 23, 24, 25, 36
Dooragh 171n, APP 48
Doosey, Charles APP 47
Dorrowne APP 7
Dowell, M 214n, APPS 9, 35
Dowling, Peter 155n, APP 43
Downes, Bishop Henry 138n, 139, APP 2
Doyle, James APP 33
Doyle, Martin 76
Doyle, Matthew APP 45
Dromahair 68
Dromard 116, 275
Dromore-West 36, 74, 192
Drumfin 171n, APP 48
Drumkeeran 68
Drummully 142n
Drumrat *see Keash* 16, APPS 5, 6, 7, 8, 17
Drumshanbo 68
Duany, Patrick 35, APP 7
Duffy, Andrew APP 48
Duffy OP, Andrew 97, 233, APPS 13, 34, 38
Duffy family 166, 167, 263
Duffy OFM, Francis APP 39
Duffy, John 42, 209, 214, 215, 230, 301, 318, 324, APPS 3, 10, 12n, 13, 14, 17, 18, 19, 29, 34
Duffy, Philip APPS 28, 34
Dunbleany 317, 324
Dunboyne, Lord 199
Dunmigan APPS 7, 34
Dunmore 187, 278, 301, 315, 340
Dunn, John APP 42
Dunn, Luke APP 42
Durcan, Maurice 287, 323
Durcan, Patrick 193, APPS 33, 34
Durkan, James 170, APP 48
Durkan, John 38, APPS 7, 17, 23, 24, 25, 33, 34, 35
Durkan, Thomas APP 48
Durkin, Thomas 182, APP 47
Dwyer, James APP 42
Dwyer, Thomas APP 42

Easkey 74, 150, 165
Echlin, James APP 37
Ederieme APP 7
Edgeworth, Abbé 208
Edmondstown 86, 128, 155, 327
Egan, Bishop Boetius 47, 68, 154, 199, 201, 230, 243, 250, 277, 315, 316–9, 320, 322, 324, 325, 330, 331, 332, 333, 336, 337, 339, 343, 344, 351, APPS 1, 19n, 34
Egan, Boetius 68, 225, 277, 278, 326, 351
Egan, Chevalier 336
Egan, Don Demetrio 336
Egan, Francis APPS 24, 36
Egan, John 333
Ellagh 36n, 37, APPS 7, 42
Elphin diocese 17, 28, 34, 36, 45, 74, 80, 95, 96, 105, 114, 136, 138, 139, 141, 149, 153, 178, 198, 199, 200, 206, 217, 219, 267, 287, 289, 290, 291, 299, 300, 301, 303, 304, 314, 315, 319, 320, 337, 339, 341, 343, 345, 347, 348, 351, 353, 361, 364, 365, 366, 368, 369
Elphin village 58, 136
Elwood, James APP 37
Emlefad *see Ballymote* 16, 141n, 142n, 144n, 145, 146, 171n, APPS 7, 8, 13, 20, 34
Enerist, George 36n, APP 7
Erris 140, 175, 262
Everard, J 81
Evelyn, William 144, APP 37
Eyre, Stratford 188
Fairymount *(Tibohine)* 96, 97, 99, 105
Fallon, Bishop 315, 319, 343, 345
Fallon OSA, Edmund 301
Fallon, Thomas 315, APP 42
Farrell OFM, Luke APP 39
Farrell, Michael 227, 256, 322, 327, 344, 345, 347, 349, 356, 359, 360, 367, 368, 371, APPS 20, 22n, 23, 24, 34
Farrell, Thomas 76, APP 45
Farry OFM, Anthony APP 39
Faussett, Robert 43n, APP 37
Feeley, Pat 158, 164, 170, APP 48
Feeny, James APP 42
Feighney, James APPS 23, 24, 26, 34
Ferguson OFM, Francis APP 39
Filan, James 132, 195, 316, 356, 356–71, APPS 3, 23, 24, 33, 34
Filan, Michael APPS 23, 24, 33, 34, 36
Finan, John 76, APP 45
Finan, Laurence APP 45

Finn, Dominick APPS 13, 34
Fitzgerald, Col 158
Fitzgerald OP, Edmund 234, 310, 311, 337, APP 38
Fitzgerald, Lord Edward 25
Fitzmaurice, Edmund APP 33
Fitzmaurice, John 156, 209, 215, 239, 307, 309, 337, 343, 344, APPS 17n, 20, 26, 29, 34
Fitzmaurice, John Petty, Earl of Shelburne 93, 94
Fitzmaurice, Michael APPS 23, 24, 35, 36
Fitzmaurice, Richard 182, APPS 23, 24, 27, 33, 34
Fitzmaurice, Thomas Petty, 94
Fitzpatrick, Stephen APP 42
Fitzsimons OFM, Francis APPS 24, 39
Fitzsimons, Michael APP 33
Fitzsimons, Archbishop Patrick 211, 212, 301n, 332
Flynn, David 212, 335
Foley, Samuel 142n, APP 4
Fox, James APP 44
Foxford *(Toomore)* 17, 18, 28, 34, 43, 51, 56, 57, 59, 61, 67, 68, 69, 74, 76, 85, 94, 104, 111, 119, 122, 124n, 135, 142, 144, 145, 151, 155, 160, 164, 171, 178, 182, 230, 273, 374, APPS 34, 42, 43, 44, 48, 50, 51
Frain, Maurice 38, 233, 288, 289, APPS 5, 7, 34
French OFM, Anthony APP 39
French, Bishop 187
French, Bishop Edmund 319, 320, 341, 345, 346, 348
French, Bishop Patrick 297
French family 49
French, George 102
French, Julia 313
French OP, Martin 312
French, Mary 305
French, Rev William 114
Frenchpark 49, 114
Fuerty 95, 187
Furey, Edward APP 37
Gaffny, Michael APP 42
Gallagher, Bishop 296
Gallagher, James 201, 205, 229, 298–300, 307–10, APPS 11n, 15n, 16n, 23, 24, 28, 34, 36, 42
Gallagher, John 36n, 155, APPS 7, 42, 43
Gallagher, John Fad APP 7
Gallagher, Manus APP 42

Gallagher Mary APP 47
Gallagher, Patrick 170, APP 48
Gallagher, Peter APP 42
Gallagher, Tully APP 42
Gallen barony 16, 17, 18, 79, 87, 120, 121, 122, 124n, 202, 222, APPS 18, 51
Galway 22, 29-30, 40, 46, 51, 102, 113, 115, 119, 122, 126, 132, 147, 165, 199, 200, 202, 203, 204, 206, 243, 267, 274, 275, 281, 284, 293, 301, 304, 305, 311, 313, 335, 337, 341, 351, 353, APP 7
Gannon, Michael 68, 74
Garachloon APP 7
Garacloon 36n
Garrahan OFM, Anthony 365
Garrett, John 95, 144n, 145, 146, APP 37
Garrett, William 144n, 145, 146, 147, APP 37
Garvey OFM, Francis APP 39
Gavin OP, Dominick APP 38
Gaydon, Richard 25
Geraghty, Dominick APP 42
Gethings, Catherine APP 33
Gethings, Capt 34, 35
Gibbons OP, Dr 364, 365, 369
Gillespie, William APP 47
Gilligan OP, Ambrose 45
Givlahan, John APP 33
Glentworth, Lord 138n
Glinsk 347
Glynn, Thady 187
Golden, John APP 47
Golden, Patrick APP 48
Gore family 18, 19
Gore, Francis 20, 21
Gore, Mr 76
Gormley, Denis 300, APPS 11, 13, 35
Gorteen 302
Grady, Michael 88n
Grady, Patrick 80, 82, 239, 251, 330, 349–351, 356, 359, 360, 361, 367, 368, 371–2, APPS 20, 21, 22, 24, 34
Granard 118
Granard, Lord 23
Grange 20
Green OFM, Anthony APP 39
Greenville 95
Grenville, Lord 78
Gunning, Mark APP 33
Gunning, Roderick APP 33
Gurteen 17, 29, 34, 36n, 43, 44, 51, 94n, 142, 143, 171, 198, 230, 233, 244, 272, 273, 275, 276, APPS 34, 37, 48, 51
Gurtogh Mone APP 7, 34
Hagerty, Patrick APP 47
Handcock, Richard 142, APP 4
Handcock, William APP 37
Hanley OFM, John APP 39
Hannan, Andrew APPS 24, 36
Haran, Martin APP 42
Haran, Michael APP 46
Haran, James APP 42
Haran OP, Thomas 33, APP 38
Hart OCD 45n
Hart, Bartholomew 36n
Hart, Bartley 160, 162–4, 167, 177, 181, 185, APPS 48
Hart, Bridget 162
Hart, Con 162
Hart, Edward APP 48
Hart, Elizabeth 162, 164, APP 48
Hart OP, Fr 215
Hart, James 170, APP 48
Hart, John 163, 170, 181, APP 48
Hart, Catherine 163
Hart, Mary 162
Hart (OCD?), Michael APPS 8, 34, 40
Hart, Patrick 155n, 162, 163
Hastings, James 142n, PP 4
Hazelwood 85, 86
Hazlett, J APP 37
Healy, Matthew APPS 25, 36
Healy OP, Thomas APP 38
Henegan OP, Anthony 233, 289, APPS 34, 38
Henegan OP, Raymond APP 38
Henigan, Edmund 300
Henican, Patrick 45, 46, 209, 217, 304, 305, 335, APPS 3, 29, 34
Henry, Brigid APP 33
Henry, David 43, APPS 7, 10, 34
Henry, James 80, 154, 168, 193, 195, 249, 353, 356, 360, 362, 364, 365, 366, 367, 369, 373, APPS 23, 24, 25, 27, 34
Henry OP, John 44, APPS 8, 34, 38
Henry, fr John 46n
Henry, Michael APP 42
Henry, Patrick APPS 5, 7, 27, 33, 34
Henry, Walter 191, 193, 289, APPS 19, 20, 21, 22, 27, 34, 47
Henry, William APP 42
Hepburne, Robert 367, APPS 23, 24, 35, 36

Hern, Josiah 146, 147, APP 37
Hervey, Bishop Frederick Augustus 51
Hester, Owen 274, 282
Higgins, Andrew APP 47
Higgins, John 155n, APP 43
Higgins, Thady 36, 38, 289, APPS 5, 6, 7, 34, 42
Hillas family 150
Hillas, Mr 67
Hillas, Mrs 67
Hills, Francis APP 42
Hopps, William APP 46
Horan OP, John APP 38
Horkan, Seamas Duv 76n, APP 45
Horohy, Roger 36n, APP 7
Howard, Bishop Robert 138n, 139, 140, 141, 152, APP 2
Howley, Edward APP 42
Howley, James 43, 214n, APPS 7, 10, 34
Hebert, Patrick APP 47
Hughes family 57
Hughes, James 88
Hughes, Martin 167
Humbert, General 19, 63, 64, 65, 66, 67, 69, 70, 71, 140, 144, 347
Humes, Parson 149
Hurley, Francis APPS 14, 35
Hurly OSA, William 51, 231, APPS 18, 41
Hurst, Edward APPS 17, 34
Hutchinson, Bishop Samuel 111, 138n, 140, 141n, 146, APP 2
Hutchisson, James APP 37
Ireton, General 32
Irwin, Bishop Alexander 314, 337
Irwin (alias Brett), Anne 155n, APP 43
Irwin, Col 79
Ivemey, Rev 158
Jackson, John 186
Jackson, Laurence 275
Jackson, Col William APP 48
Jennings, James 74
Jobit, Col 67
Johnson, Gideon 145, APP 37
Jones family 86
Jones, Frances 53, 88, 92, 174, 228
Jones, Thomas 35, 36n, APP 7
Jones, Roger 24
Jordan, Canon 315
Jordan OP, Dominick APP 38
Jordan, Edmund 42, 209, 217, APP 29

Jordan family 197, 231
Jordan, Henry APPS 10, 13, 34, 42
Jordan OP, Michael 235, APPS 34, 38
Jordan, Myles APP 42
Jordan OP, Richard APP 38
Jordan, Thady 217n, APP 29
Jordan, Thomas APP 9
Jorges, J APP 37
Jourdan, James APP 42
Jourdan, John 170, APP 48
Joyce, John 200, 304, 324, 326, 337, APPS 3, 30
Joyes, Martin 155n, APP 43
Kearen, Pat 76
Kearney, David APPS 13, 35
Kearney, Dominick 115n, 202, 210, 217, 218, 295, 308, 310, 315, 322, APPS 9, 13, 14, 15, 17, 18, 19, 28, 29, 34
Kearney, Francis 17, 34
Kearns, Bartholomew APPS 23, 36
Kearns, Pat APP 45
Keash *(Drumrat and Toomour)* 17, 34, 36, 41, 44, 94n, 132, 142, 151, 182, 217, 220, 223, 225, 226, 267, 272, 273, 321, APPS 27, 34, 51
Keegan, Patrick APPS 24, 36
Kelly, Andrew APP 42
Kelly, Anthony APP 42
Kelly OFM, Anthony APP 39
Kelly, Daniel APP 42
Kelly OFM, Daniel APP 39
Kelly, David 74
Kelly OP, Dominick 200, APPS 18, 31, 34, 38
Kelly, Edmund 88n, 115n, 208, 210n, 218, APPS 10, 13, 14, 16, 17, 19, 20, 21, 29, 34
Kelly OFM, Edmund APP 23
Kelly, Hugh 39
Kelly, James APPS 42, 48
Kelly, John APP 42
Kelly, Martin APP 42
Kelly, Matthew APP 42
Kelly, Michael APP 42
Kelly, Archbishop Oliver 332, 353, 354, 361, 363, 364, 365, 366, 368, 369, 371, 372
Kelly, Pat APP 42
Kelly OP, Patrick Dominick APP 38
Kelly, William APP 42
Kennedy, William 202, APPS 7, 34
Kenney, Arthur Henry 142n, APP 4
Kent, John 179, 295n
Keoghy, Bishop Teige 202, 203, APP 7

Keregan, Patrick 46, APP 34
Kielly, Pat APP 42
Kilbeagh *see Charlestown* 16, 142n, APPS 8, 13, 34, 37, 48
Kilcolman *see Ballaghaderreen* 16, 275, 288, 322, APPS 5, 7, 8, 10, 15, 18
Kilconduff *see Swinford* 16, 141, 142n, 146, APPS 6, 7, 8, 13, 17, 18, 34
Kilconnell 202, APP 7
Kilcummin 64, 68
Kilfenora diocese 187, 211, 212, 302, 314, 319, 324, 329, APP 7
Kilfree *see Gurteen* 16, 141n, 155n, 349, 373, APPS 5, 7, 8, 13, 17, 19, 20, 23n, 34, 43
Kilgarvan *see Bonniconlon* 16, APPS 7, 8, 17, 18, 34
Kilglass 74
Kilgrellia APP 49
Kilkelly 88
Killahuley, Peter APP 42
Killala diocese 17, 18, 36, 39, 43, 46, 49, 54, 60, 62, 64, 74, 77, 86, 111, 138, 141, 149, 150, 191, 192, 193, 199, 203, 205, 239, 243, 264, 283, 287, 291, 295, 296, 297, 300, 310, 313, 314, 324, 333, 335, 336, 337, 341, 353, 354, 361, 368
Killala town 61, 62, 65, 67, 68, 69, 71, 72, 73, 76, 111, 112, 114, 119n, 139, 140, 146
Killalea, James 76, APP 45
Killaraght *see Gurteen* 16, 142n, 146, 274, 275, PPS 7, 8, 13, 34
Killasser 16, 18, 34, 43, 69, 119, 124, 142, 143n, 164, 170, 171n, 182, 193, 195, 220, 224, 230, 242, 253, 254, 256, 259, 260n, 266, 268, 271, 273, 275, 279, 282, 285, 356, 359, APPS 7, 8, 34, 48, 50, 51
Killedan *see Kiltimagh* 16, 132, 133, 141, 143n, APPS 7, 8, 10, 17, 18, 20, 24, 26, 34, 42
Killery 275
Killevil 318, APPS 18, 34
Killmolass APP 7
Killoran *see Coolaney* 16, 142n, 143, 146, 171n, APPS 5, 6, 7, 8, 17, 19, 20, 34, 46, 48
Killoran, Tim 76, APP 45
Killraine, Jack 79, APP 47
Killvanloon 241
Kilmacduagh 200, 202, 291, 314, 324, 329, 332, 335, 337, 341
Kilmacshalgan 36
Kilmactigue *see Tourlestrane* 16, 59, 75, 111,

112n, 115n, 125, 140, 141, 142, 143, 144, 145, 146, 147, 148, 150, 160, 162, 163, 164, 167, 171n, 172, 177, 181, 182, 185, 189, 193, 202, 220, 234, 242, 248, 249, 252, 254, 264, 275, 285, 286, 315, 326, 357, PPS 5, 6, 7, 8, 15, 17, 18, 20, 28, 34, 35, 37, 48
Kilmartin, Tom 79, APP 47
Kilmore parish 96
Kilmorgan *see Ballymote* 16, 141n, 171n, 182, 275, PPS 5, 7, 13, 19, 20, 34, 48
Kilmovee 16, 18, 88, 88n, 89n, 96, 97, 134, 141, 142, 143, 170, 171n, 200, 217, 224, 233, 235, 260n, 266, 269, 275, 276, 288, 289, APPS 6, 7, 8, 13, 18, 19, 20, 26, 34, 38, 48, 51
Kilmurragh 44, APP 8
Kilshalvey *see Bunninadden* 16, 31, 132, APPS 7, 8, 13, 17, 18, 19, 20, 34, 38
Kiltecolla APP 7
Kilteenane 36n, APPS 7, 34
Kiltimagh *(Killedan)* 18, 34, 38, 43, 115n, 132, 142, 202, 217, 229, 273, 312, 313, 315, 371, 372, 374, APPS 18, 27, 34, 36, 51
Kilturra *see Bunninadden* 16, 141, 155n, 171n, 202, 277, 285, PPS 5, 6, 7, 8, 17, 18, 19, 20, 27n, 34, 48
Kilvarnet *see Collooney* 16, 141n, 142n, 143n, 154, 171n, APPS 5, 6, 7, 8, 20, 27, 34, 48
Kinaffe APPS 17, 20
King family 19
King OFM, Francis APP 8, 39
King junior, Francis 35, 36n, APP 7
King, Gilbert 96
Kingston, Lord 19, 20, 182
Kinlan, Capt 76
Kinturk APP 7
Kivleghan, Robert APP 46
Kirwan, Augustine 313
Kirwan, Christopher 290
Kirwan, James 305
Kirwan, John 313, 335
Kirwan, Bishop Patrick Robert 47, 154, 174, 179, 180, 188, 191, 194, 195, 201, 202, 205, 238, 239, 243, 247, 250, 264, 272, 305–13, 314n, 323, 331, 332, 333, 334, 335, 343, APPS 1, 16n, 26n, 34, 49
Kirwan, Richard 195
Kirwan, Thomas 316
Kirwan, Walter Blake 141
Knavesey, Patrick 115n, 210n, 217, 218, 299, APPS 11, 13, 17, 19, 29, 34, 36

Knockbrack APPS 27n, 34
Knockdaltan 171n, APP 48
Knockmore, Co Mayo 18n
Knockmore, Co Sligo 29, 43, 44, 45, 194, APP 40
Knocknaganny 220, APP 50
Knocknatanvally APPS 7, 34
Knockrany APPS 7, 34
Knockrawer 194
Knott, Capt 70
Lackan 60, 62, 64, 72, 73, 137
Lahardane 67, 68
Lake, General 69, 70
Lally OP, Thomas 235, APP 38
Langdall, Thomas APP 37
Langrishe, James 142n, APP 4
Langton, Zachary APP 37
Larkin, Miss 76n, APP 45
Larkin, Ryan APP 45
Laughnan OP, Peter APP 38
Law, Bishop John 138, APP 2
Lawry, Neal 52n, 155n, APP 43
Lecky, W. E., 240
Leeson, Thomas APP 42
Lehardan APP 48
Leitrim APPS 7, 34, 46
Leonard OSA, Matthew 231, APPS 23, 24, 41
Leonard, Thomas 170, APP 48
Lettice, Mrs 149
Leving, Dorothea 139
Leving, Sir John 139
Leyden OP, Luke 233, APPS 23, 24, 36, 38
Leyny barony 16, 17, 56, 69, 70, 109, 110, 125, 149, 228, 286, APP 51
Linegar, Archbishop 211
Lisballilly 155n
Lishocunian 36n, APP 7
Lislea APPS 7, 34
Lisserightis APP 7
Little, Rev James 60, 61, 62, 64, 72, 73, 137
Lloyd, Robert APP 37
Lloyd, Thomas 21
Lloyd, Bishop William 137, 138, 140, 142n, APPS 2, 4
Lognahaha 182, APP 48
Lomecloon 36n
Longford House 19, 77
Lorin, Thady APP 47
Lough Allen 68
Loughane, Edmund APP 47

Lough Conn 68, 76, 281
Lough Derg 162
Loughgall 56
Lough Gara 17
Lough Gill 68, 126, 275
Loughglynn 66, 86
Lough Key 128, 129
Loughrea 122, 318
Lough Talt 111
Louth, Lord 329, 340
Lovelake, Nicholas 315
Low, John APP 46
Lucan, Lord 79, 225, 344
Lugawarry 79
Lugnadeffa 182, APP 48
Lunchard, Daniel APP 42
Lundy, Col 20
Lunncloo APP 7
Luttrell, Henry 20
Lynagh, Bishop Charles 210, 243, 264, 326–328, 330, 344–347, 351, 360, APPS 1, 29, 34
Lynagh, James 328
Lynagh, Maryann 328
Lynch, Bishop Andrew 202, APP 7
Lynch, Anstace 305
Lynch, Archbishop James 28–29, 202, 289, 290, 330, APP 7
Lynch, Mark 36n, APP 7
Lynsky family 57
Lyons OFM, Anthony APP 39
Lyons, James 215, 216, 218, 219, 229, 285
Lyons OP, Patrick Albert 232, APP 38
MacAlaster, Denis 36n, APP 7
McCann family 57
McCann, Pat APP 44
McCarrick, Miss 249
McCarrick, Thomas APP 46
MacCarthy, Daniel 115n
Macartney, Justice 30, 31
McConville, Charles APP 44
McConville family 57
McConville, M APP 44
McConville, Philip APP 44
McCormack, Mary 52n, 155
McCormack, Peter 92
McCormick OFM, Francis APP 39
McCoy, Denis APP 42
McCoye OFM, fr 46n, APP 39
MacDermot OP, Bishop Ambrose 206, 217, 291

MacDermot, Bernard 347
MacDermot, Bridget *née* O'Conor 47, 48, 49
MacDermot, Charles I 47
MacDermot, Charles II 47, 346
MacDermot family 37, 47, 86, 87, 128, 131, 197
MacDermot, Henry 47, 66
MacDermot, Hugh I 47
MacDermot, Hugh II 47, 66
MacDermot, Bishop Hugh 28, 29, 34, 35, 39-40, 44, 197, 221, 243 287–93, 329, 330, 331, 332, 333, APPS 1, 5N, 6N, 29, 42
MacDermot, Lady Jane 298
MacDermot, Kitty 47
MacDermot, Myles 47, 48, 49, 256
MacDermot OP, Peter 33
MacDermot, Roderick 47
MacDermot, Roger 47, 198, 359, 360, 363, 364, 365, 366, 370, 371, APPS 23, 24, 34
MacDermot, Chevalier Terence 298, 335
MacDermot, Terence I 47
MacDermot, Terence II 47
MacDermot OP, Thomas 292
MacDermot, Tim 88
MacDermot, Una 128
McDermottroe family 130
McDermottroe, Mrs 130
MacDiarmada, Ruaidhrí Ruadh 167
McDonnell, Aeneas 88n
McDonnell OFM, Anthony APP 39
McDonnell OP, Anthony APP 38
McDonnell, Coll APP 42
McDonald OP, Donald 30
McDonnell OP, Daniel (Donald?) 30–31, 33
McDonnell, Francis APP 42, 47
McDonnell, Keadh 88n
McDonnell, James APP 47
McDonnell OP, James APP 38
McDonnell OP, John APP 38
McDonnell, Margaret 88n
McDonnell, Patrick APP 33
McDonnell, Phelim 74
McDonnell, Terence APP 7
McDonnell OP, Terence 199, APP 38
McDonagh, Dolly 131
McDonogh, Capt Andrew 25, 26
McDonogh (OCD?), Anthony APP 40
McDonogh OFM, Anthony 45n, 230, 233, APPS 8, 13, 17, 34, 39
McDonogh, Brian 39, APP 7
McDonogh, Charles APP 42

McDonogh OP, Dominick APP 38
McDonogh family 197
McDonogh, Francis 300, APPS 11, 35
McDonogh OFM, Francis 45n, APP 39
McDonogh OFM, Hugh APPS 8, 39
McDonogh, James 210n, 230, 300, APPS 11, 13, 14, 15, 29, 34, 35
McDonogh, John 36, APPS 5, 6, 7, 34, 42, 46
McDonogh, Luke APP 42
McDonogh, Mark 186
McDonogh (OCD?), Michael 41, APPS 8, 40
McDonogh OFM, Michael APPS 8, 34, 39
McDonogh, Miler APPS 5, 6, 34
McDonogh, Morgan 36, 39, APP 7
McDonogh, Patrick APP 42
McDonogh OP, Patrick 29
McDonogh, Teige 36, 230, APPS 7, 34
McDonogh, Terence 19, 21
McDonogh, Thady 155n, APP 42
McDonogh, Thomas APP 42
McDonogh, William 36, 37, 43, 44, 214n, APPS 7, 10, 34
McEnrea, Patrick APP 47
McGinear, Daniel APP 44
McGowan, Fr 74
McGuan OFM, Terence 233, APPS 13, 34, 39
MacHale OP, Thomas APP 38
McHary, Patrick APPS 13, 34
McHugh OFM, Francis APP 39
McHugh, James 366n, APPS 23, 24, 25, 35, 36, 42
McHugh, John APP 36
McHugh, Michael APP 42
McHugh (McCook?), Peter 203, APPS 9, 13
McHugh, William APPS 24, 36
McKenna, Bishop Matthew 180, 239
McKim, Robert APP 46
McLaughlin, John APP 42
McLaughlin, Pat APP 42
MacLea, Dr Francis 36, APP 7
McManus, James APPS 17, 35
McManus, Patrick 181, APP 48
McManus, Una 41
MacMorrisroe OP, Edmund APP 38
MacMorrisroe OP, Miler APP 38
MacMorrisroe OP, Richard APP 38
McMulrunisin, Thady 263
McNamara, Anthony 202, 228, 230, 318, APPS 16, 17, 18, 19, 20, 26, 34, 36
McNeas (McVeas?) family 57

McNeas, Francis APP 44
McNeas, Henry APP 44
McNeas, John APP 44
McNeven, William James 60, 62
McNicholas, James 372, APP 33
McNicholas OP, Dominick APP 38
McNicholas OP, James 233, 366n, APPS 23, 24, 25, 38
McNicholas, Patrick 312, 353, 356, 359, 362, 365, 366, APPS 18, 20, 21, 23, 24, 25, 34
McNicholas, Bishop Patrick 54, 161, 185, 192, 195, 205, 225, 227, 238, 243, 285, 330, 332, 353, 356, 359–374, APPS 1, 23, 24n, 26n, 33, 34, 38, 42, 48
McNicholas OP, Peter APP 38
McNicholas, Thomas APPS 24, 33, 36
McNicholas OP, Thomas APP 38
McNicholas OP, William APP 38
McNulty, John 164, 182, 353, APPS 23, 24, 25, 33, 34
McNulty, Pat APP 42
McTeere OFM, fr APPS 8, 39
Madden, Anthony 88
Madden, Martin APP 42
Madden, Robert APP 42
Madden, Thomas APP 42
Maddin, Bishop Ambrose 291
Magloin OFM, Daniel APP 39
Magrath OFM, John APP 39
Mahedy, Thomas APP 47
Mahon, Thomas 96
Maitland, Richard APP 47
Maley, John 36, 39, APP 7
Manningham, Thomas 144, 145, 147, APP 37
Mannion OP, James APP 38
Manorhamilton 68
Markrea Castle 19, 77, 84, 84n, 85, 93, 109, 131, 148, 286
Marran, John APPS 7, 34
Martin OFM, Anthony APP 39
Martin OFM, Richard APP 39
Mason, Frank 272
Masshill 220, 222
Maturin, Charles 43n, 145, 146, APP 37
Matthew, Eleanor 87
Maune, James APP 47
Maynooth College 54, 81, 161, 195, 278, 356, 357, 359, 360, 364, 369, 373
Mayo 17, 18, 19, 22, 24, 28, 34, 36, 37, 39, 42, 46, 48, 56, 59, 60, 74, 79, 80, 86, 92, 93, 98, 103, 104, 107, 117, 124, 128, 141, 142, 143, 145, 155, 158, 165, 169, 170, 175, 181, 187, 191, 198, 202, 217, 222, 223, 231, 243, 255, 271, 288, 302, APP 7
Meelick *see* Swinford 38, 128, 141, 142n, 143n, 222, 230, PPS 7, 8, 17, 34, 48, 51
Meemlough 230, 263, APPS 19, 20
Melville, Anne 326
Meredith, Henry APP 46
Meredith, Joseph 88
Merrick, James APP 47
Michelburne, 22, 23
Milleagh APP 7
Mirabeau 58
Mitchel, Peigí 132
Mohill 68
Monasteraden 171, 270n, APP 48
Montbret, Coquebert de 94, 105, 109, 236
Monelly, Thomas 74
Moore, Lady Betty 149
Moore, Michael 208
Moore, Thomas 41, 209, 217n, APP 29
Moore, William 115n, 158–61, 163
Morelly OP, Hugh APP 38
Morgan, Lady (Miss Sydney Owenson) 77, 78, 93, 99, 105, 106, 115, 117, 121, 122, 128, 166, 177, 189, 190, 192, 197, 223, 240, 261, 275, 281, 283, 284
Morgan, Sir Thomas 77
Morley OP, Walter 235
Morris OP, Walter APP 38
Morvornagh, Bernard 208, 215, 217, APP 29
Motherwell, John 95
Moy river 17, 68
Moygara 19, 26
Moylough 324
Moylurg 128, 129
Moyne Abbey 113
Muckross Abbey 263
Mullan, Patrick APP 42
Mullaney, John 181, APP 48
Mullarkey, Daniel 308, APPS 15, 34
Mullet island 63
Mullinabreena 230, 318, APPS 19, 34, 51
Mullingar 186, 226, 227
Mullruniffin, Edmund APPS 8, 10, 34
Mullruniffin, Edward 44, APPS 8, 34
Mullruniffin, James 36, APPS 7, 34
Mullruniffin, Owen 36, APP 7
Munichenolan APPS 7, 34

Murphy OSA 188
Murphy, Richard APP 47
Murray, Archbishop Daniel 348
Murrin, Bryan 52n, 155n, APP 43
Murtagh, John APPS 7, 34
Musgrave, Sir Richard 150
Nall, Michael 206n, 216
Nangle OCD, James 45n, APP 40
Naughtin, Fergus 290
Naughton OFM, James APP 39
Neale, The 74, APP 7
Neligan, Rev James 59, 61, 67, 75, 90n, 102, 108n, 111, 115n, 144, 145, 146, 147, 148, 150–1, 157, 163, 164, 166, 167, 181, 182, 183, 186, 228, 241, 242, 254, APPS 37, 48
Neligan, Maurice 150
Neligan, Michael 145
Nelly OP, Gregory APP 38
Nelly, Peter 38, APPS 5, 7, 34
Newcastle 40
Newport 68, 69, 74, 112n
Nicholson, Arthur APP 42
Nicholson family 19
Nicholson, Parson 149
Nicholson, Thomas APP 42
Ní Chatháin, Úna 132
Ní Eidhin, Máire 132
Nihil, Bishop Laurence 319
Nolan, Patrick 155n, 364, APP 43
Noone OP, James APP 38
Nugent OSA, John 290
Nugent, Mary 346
Nymphsfield 52n, 86, 148, 149, 155, 168
O'Bierne, J APP 42
O'Beirne, Bishop Thomas 240
O'Boyle, James APP 47
O'Boyle, Peter APP 47
O'Brien, Michael 69, APPS 17, 20, 22, 34
O'Burne, James APP 48
O'Carolan, Turlough 130–2, 193, 297
O'Carroll 206
O'Connell, Daniel 82
O'Connell, James 29, 36, 38, 263, APPS 5, 6, 7, 27, 34
O'Connor, Ambrose APP 42
O'Connor OP, Ambrose 30
O'Connor, Charles APP 42
O'Connor, Daniel 89, 154, 184, 185, APPS 21, 22, 24, 42
O'Connor, Denis APP 42
O'Connor, Dermot 156, 320, 340, APP 43

O'Connor family 197
O'Connor, John 40
O'Connor, Laurence APPS 17, 35
O'Connor, Mr and Mrs 92
O'Connor, Owen APP 42
O'Connor, Patrick 315, APPS 17, 18, 19, 20, 21, 22, 34, 42
O'Connor OP, Patrick 30
O'Connor King Roderick 26
O'Connor Sligo family 18, 37
O'Connor, Bishop Thomas 47, 53, 156, 210, 243, 262, 264, 319–326, 327, 329, 330, 331, 339–42, 344, APPS 1, 20n, 21n, 29, 34
O'Conor, Charles 26
O'Conor, Dr Charles 58. 154, 187, 198, 199, 204, 206, 207, 218, 229, 236, 274, 316, 324, 325, 327, 344, 345-48, APP 21n
O'Conor, Charles of Belanagare 26, 27, 47, 49ff, 58, 91, 100, 101, 103, 104, 106, 107, 108, 115n, 127, 167, 176, 177, 185, 193, 226, 234, 242, 246, 260, 268, 290, 297, 316, 332, 333, 337, 338, 346, 348
O'Conor, Denis 176, 177, 198, 218, 291
O'Conor family of Belanagare 47, 131, 186, 262, 276, 282, 351
O'Conor, Mary of Belanagare 185
O'Conor, Matthew 49, 199, 204
O'Conor, Owen 154, 348
O'Cullane OFM, Anthony APP 39
O'Daly, Dermot 293
O'Daly, Bishop Dominick 30, 47, 199, 201, 202, 203, 206, 212, 221, 243, 292, 293–6, 322, 358, APPS 1, 9n, 29
O'Dogherty, Martin APP 42
O'Donnell, Fr 74
O'Donnell, Charles 207
O'Donnell, Hugh 335, 336
O'Donnell, Hugh Baldearg 22, 23
O'Donnell OFM, Hugh APP 39
O'Donnell, James APPS 13, 34
O'Donnell, Manus 36n, APP 7
O'Donnell, Michael APP 42
O'Donnell, Nathaniel APP 42
O'Donnell, Naughten 39, APP 7
O'Donnell, Roger APPS 7, 42
O'Donnell, Terence 36n, 37
O'Donnelly, Terence APP 42
O'Donogher, Bernard 290
O'Donovan, John 278
O'Dowd, David 47
O'Dowd, Dominick 47

O'Dowd family 47, 112
O'Dowd, James 47, 56, 66, 67, 69, 70, 73, APP 45
O'Dowd, Thady 47
Ó Dubhshláine, Liam 132
O'Finan OP, Francis 362
O'Flaherty, Roderick 40, 194
O'Flaherty, Thady 115n, 202, 313, 315, APPS 17, 18, 19, 20, 22, 26, 27, 34
O'Flanagan, Charles APP 42
O'Flynn, Edmund 320
O'Flynn family 197
O'Flynn, John APPS 20, 21, 22, 23, 24, 33, 35
O'Flynn, Bishop John 154, 200, 210, 226, 239, 244, 251, 319, 330, 341, 345, 347, 348, 349–356, 366, 371, 372, APPS 1, 23n, 24, 29, 34
O'Flynn, Mabel 320
O'Flynn, Michael APPS 25, 36
Ó Gadhra, Seán 24, 27, 31, 32, 132, 167, 194, APP 38
O'Gallagher OFM, Bonaventure 300
O'Gara, Archbishop Bernard 188, 295, 296, 305, 334
O'Gara, Count Charles 26
O'Gara, Ever 194
O'Gara family 18, 197
O'Gara, Fergal 26
O'Gara, Francis APP 7
O'Gara, James 36
O'Gara OFM, John APP 39
O'Gara, Archbishop Michael 178, 201, 213, 301, 305, 332, 335, APP 31
O'Gara, Col Oliver 26, 198, 335
O'Gara, Pat 170, 174, APP 48
O'Gara, Phelim 36, APP 7
O'Gara I, Terence 34, 36, 192, 194, 198, 221, 230, 288, 292, APPS 5, 34
O'Gara II, Terence 167, 192, 201, 210, 211, 212, 217, 230, 239, 293, 295, APPS 9, 13, 14, 29, 31, 34
O'Gara OSA, Terence 324
Oghan 36n, APP 7
O'Gorman, Chevalier 167
O'Gorman, Patrick APP 33
O'Grady, Donagh 134
O'Hara, Adam 149
O'Hara, Anne 149
O'Hara, Bryan APP 7
O'Hara, Charles (Lord Tyrawley) 153

O'Hara, Charles MP 52, 53, 54, 55, 56, 59, 62, 69, 70, 79, 80, 81, 87, 143, 147, 148, 154, 168, 183, 184, 185, 249, 263, 329
O'Hara senior, Charles 53, 83, 86, 87, 88, 90, 92, 95, 96, 100, 101, 102, 115n, 143, 186, 263, 298
O'Hara, Dr Charles 34, 35, 44, 47, 197, 208, 215, 230, 293, 294, APPS 7, 29, 34, 40
O'Hara, Charles King 372
O'Hara, Denis 76. APP 45
O'Hara, Dominick 230, APPS 17, 18, 23, 24, 25, 34
O'Hara, Donnell 287, APP 42
O'Hara family, 18, 85, 87, 89, 131, 143, 231, 262
O'Hara OFM, fr APPS 8, 39
O'Hara, Henry 47, 155, APP 43
O'Hara, James 75, APPS 7, 10, 28, 33, 34, 35
O'Hara OFM, James APP 39
O'Hara OSA, John 45, 231, APP 41
O'Hara, Kean 18, 22, 23, 34, 35, 83, 86, 87, 100, 125, 131, 143, 149, 153, 186
O'Hara, Kitty 131
O'Hara, Laurence 309
O'Hara, Mary 47, 155, APP 43
O'Hara, Michael 309, APP 42
O'Hara, Moriarty 230, APP 13
O'Hara, Murtagh 46, APPS 34, 35
O'Hara, Nich 44, APPS 8, 34
O'Hara, Oliver 263
O'Hara, Pat 76, APP 45
O'Hara, Phelim 230, 287, 288, 289, APPS 3, 5, 6, 34
O'Hara, Roger 52n, 155n, APP 43
O'Hara, Thady APP 42
O'Hara, Thady (Charles?) 44, 187, APP 8
O'Hart, Ann 309, APP 42
O'Hart, Charles 287, 298, APP 42
O'Hart, Bishop Eugene 287, 297, 373
O'Hart, John APPS 13, 14
O'Hart, Bishop John 41, 44, 131, 132, 138, 198, 201, 205, 208, 211, 212, 214, 215, 243, 250, 262, 292, 293, 295, 296–300, 301, 308, 329, 331, 335, APPS 1, 3, 9, 10n, 11n, 28, 29, 34, 42
O'Hart family 131, 298
O'Hart, Nancy 131
O'Hart, Teige 287, APP 42
O'Hart OFM, Terence APP 39
O'Heynes OP, Laurence APP 38

O'Heynes OP, Martin APP 38
O'Higgins, Ambrose 26–27
O'Higgins, Bernardo 27
O'Kane, Bernard APP 33
O'Kane, Henry 64, 65, 67, 72, 73, 74
O'Kelly, Carbry 290
O'Kelly OP, Charles 310, 311, 316, 332, 333, 336, 338, 340, 341, 351
O'Kelly, Count 319, 338, 339
O'Kelly OFM, Edmund APP 39
O'Kelly family 197
O'Kelly OFM, John APP 39
O'Kelly, Malachy 364
O'Kennedy OP, Daniel 187
O'Lorcan OFM, Bernard APP 39
O'Malley, Winifred 327
O'Neal, Henry 230, APPS 17, 18, 34
O'Neal, Neal 36n, APP 7
O'Regan, Teague 21, 22, 23
O'Reilly, Archbishop Richard 315, 319, 322, 324, 327, 348
O'Reilly, Luke 216
Ormsby family 18, 19
Ormsby, Elizabeth APP 46
Ormsby, Gilbert 39
Ormsby, John 174, APPS 47, 48
Ormsby, William 20
O'Rorke, Bartley 186
O'Rorke, Bishop Brian 177n, 186, 191, 193, 199, 335
O'Rorke, Connor 176, 248
O'Rorke, James 186
O'Rorke, John 145n, APP 37
O'Rorke, Count Owen 185, 186, 335
O'Rorke, Rev APPS 28, 34
O'Rorke OFM, Bishop Thady 39, 40, 49, 176, 193, 290, 291, 292, 296, 297
O'Ryan, Edmund 336, 337
O'Shaughnessy OP, Colman 296
Owenson, Robert 77, 121
Ox Mountains 17, 97, 159, 189, 283
Paine, Thomas 58
Paley, George APP 37
Parke 40
Parlan, Mark 336, 337
Partry 223, 224
Percival, Col Alexander 55, 58, 79, 80, 87, 95, 154, 158
Percival family 86, 87, 143
Percival, William 186

Perrotin, Philippes Joseph 213
Pery, Bishop William Cecil 138n, 139, APP 2
Phibbs, Patrick APP 46
Philips, Charles 36n, 37, APP 7
Philips, Dominick 353, APPS 22, 23, 24, 35
Philips, Edward 88n
Philips family 47, 87, 197, 262
Philips, James 48, 155n, APP 43
Philips OP, Miler APP 38
Philips, Miles 36n, APP 7
Philips OP, Peter 233, APPS 13, 34, 38
Philips, Bishop Philip 51, 111, 113, 114, 138, 141, 154, 155n, 167, 193, 197, 198, 200, 202, 208, 227, 239, 243, 262, 264, 272, 277, 283, 284, 295n, 303, 305, 307, 310, 311, 313–16, 317, 323, 331, 333, 335, 336, 337, 338, 339, 341, 343, 345, APPS 1, 3, 13n, 14n, 18, 26, 29
Plunkett, Archbishop Oliver 288, 323, 332
Plunkett, Bishop George 331, 353, 361, 362, 363, 364, 366, 369
Plunkett, Bishop Patrick 202, APP 7
Plunkett, General 336
Plunkett, Robert 48, 52n, 155n, APP 43
Plunkett, Rose 26
Plunkett, Walter 88, 227
Pococke, Bishop 144, 178, 280
Ponn, Daniel APP 42
Ponn, Laurence APP 42
Ponn, Terence APP 42
Ponson 67
Poonengane APPS 7, 34
Porter, Bishop John 138n, 139, 141n, APP 2
Prendergast OCD, Henry 44, 45n, APPS 34, 40
Prendergast, John APP 47
Prendergast OSA, Myles 74
Preston, Bishop William 138n, 139, APP 2
Preston, Widow 168
Price, John APP 37
Quigly, Tom 80
Quinan (Cunnane?), Francis APPS 19, 34, 35
Quinn family 57
Quinn, Patrick 89n
Radcliffe, Thomas APP 37
Raftery, Anthony 132–3
Raftery, Siobhán 132
Raghnine, James 100
Rahmine, James APP 7
Rathbarron, 52n, 143, 155n, 249
Rathcormack 259

Rathmore 35, 36n, APP 7
Rathslevin APP 42
Raughnin OFM, fr APPS 8, 39
Read, Patrick APP 37
Reap, Michael APP 47
Reap, Thomas APP 47
Regan, Widow 92
Reilly, Michael 242
Reynolds 59
Rice, John APP 42
Rice, Thomas APP 42
Richardson, Bishop Laurence 302
Roadstown 372
Robinson, Bishop Richard 138, 140, APP 2
Roche OP, Thomas APP 38
Roddy, Edward APPS 24, 36
Roddy, John 38, 230, APP 34
Rogers, Martin APP 45
Rogers, Michael APP 45
Roscommon county 17, 22, 25, 39, 47, 49, 59, 123, 130, 136, 139, 149, 158, 257, 274
Roscommon town 41, 95, 292, 304
Roseturke 36n, APP 7
Rosgrib 36, APP 7
Roughnan, Dan 149
Rowland, Carter 52n
Rowley, James 164, 170, APP 48
Rowley, Máire 164
Ruane, Anthony APPS 17, 35
Ruane OP, Anthony APP 38
Ruane OP, Dominick APP 38
Ruane, John APPS 3, 7, 12, 13, 14, 16, 34, 35
Rush, Mark 80, 320, 344, APPS 3, 17, 18, 19, 20, 21, 22, 23, 34
Ruttledge, James 63
Ryan, Miss 76n
St Sauveur 21
Sarsfield. Patrick 20, 21, 22
Savary, Admiral 63
Scanlan, Brian APP 45
Scanlan, Dudley 76, APP 45
Scanlan, John APP 42
Scanlan, Michael 76, APP 45
Seaview 67, 150
Sessuegarry 36n, APP 7
Seymour, Charles 144n, 145n, 147, APP 37
Seymour, Joseph 144n, APP 37
Shannon river 22, 68
Sharkey OP, Patrick 233, APP 38
Shaw, Robert 102, APP 37

Shaw Mason, William 150
Shelburne, Lord 158
Sheares brothers 25
Shiell, Robert APP 37
Shrule 324
Shyane APP 7
Sills, Lieut 65
Simpson, Edward APP 46
Simpson, James APP 46
Simpson, Veitch APP 37
Skelton, Walter 49, 177n
Skerret, Archbishop Mark 178, 180, 186, 188, 191, 234, 311, 312, 315, 316, 320, 333, 338, 341
Skibbereen 137, 174
Skreen and Dromard 36
Sligo town 17, 18, 19, 20, 21, 22, 23, 29, 30, 33, 35, 36, 37, 39, 41, 46, 70, 76, 79, 81, 84, 93, 95, 104, 105, 110, 117, 123, 124, 151, 152, 158, 162, 186, 187, 195, 206, 214, 215, 222, 224, 229, 231, 233, 268, 285, 303, 304, 315, 319, 345, 348, 349, 356, 367, PPS 7, 38, 42
Smith, William APP 44
Smyth OSA, John 231, APPS 24, 41
Soden, Francis 182
Sotheby, James 43n, 146, APP 37
Spenser, Edmund 121
Spiddal 324
Staunton, Máirín, 132
Stock, Arthur 63, 69
Stock, Edwin 63
Stock, Bishop Joseph 60, 61, 62, 63, 65, 66, 69, 71, 73, 75, 138n, 140, APP 2
Straide (Templemore) 18, 34, 43, 51, 85, 124n, 142, 143n, 230, APPS 8, 34, 37, 51
Straide Friary 29, 30, 43, 187, 199, 231, 232, 235, 268, 289, 359, 360, APPS 23, 24, 38
Strickland, Mr 185
Strokestown 96
Sunvolhane APPS 7, 34
Sweeney, Eugene (Owen) 300, APPS 10, 11, 12, 13, 14, 35
Sweeney OFM, fr 310, APP 39
Sweeney, Manus 74
Sweeney, Michael APP 42
Sweeney, Oliver APP 42
Sweeney, Owen APP 42
Sweeney, Patrick APPS 23, 24, 33, 35, 36, 42
Swift, James APP 48
Swinford (Kilconduff and Meelick) 18, 38,

43n, 57, 68, 69, 74n, 76n, 85, 86, 104, 124n, 131, 142, 145, 151, 155, 171, 174, 182, 185, 193, 230, 233, 273, 288, 289, 315, 367, 374, APPS 18, 34, 36, 37, 42, 43, 45, 48, 50, 51
Symes, Sutton 142, APP 4
Synge, Alicia 106, 114, 139n, 153
Synge, Edward 145, 146, APP 37
Synge, Archbishop Edward 145, 176
Synge, Bishop Edward 96, 106, 114, 136, 138, 139n, 140, 145, 153
Synge, John Millington 145n
Synge, Bishop Nicholas 145
Taaffe, Christopher 48, 88n, 155, APP 42, 43
Taaffe, Edmund 88
Taaffe family 19, 24, 37, 48, 86, 87, 93, 132, 287
Taaffe, Frank 132, APP 42
Taaffe, George APP 42
Taaffe, James 88
Taaffe, Luke APP 42
Taaffe, Michael APP 42
Taaffe, Patrick 88n
Taaffe, Theobald, Earl of Carlingford 18
Taaffe, Thomas APP 42
Taaffe, Viscount Nicholas 24, 49, 50, 87, 197, 222
Taaffe, William APP 42
Tandy, James Napper 58
Taucannanagh APPS 7, 34
Taunagh 147
Tavnagh APPS 7, 34
Tavraun 134
Taylor, General 67
Teeling, Bartholomew 64, 70, 75
Templeboy 36, 189, 272
Templeconny 171n, APP 48
Templehouse 58, 95, 124n, 148, 158, 171n, APP 48
Templemore *see Straide* 16, 142, 143, 144, 145n, 146, APP 7
Templevanny 36, 182, APP 7
Thomas, John 88n
Thompson, John APP 46
Tibohine *see Fairymount* 351
Tiernan, Charles 288
Tighe, James 249
Tialooher APPS 7, 34
Tireragh barony, 17, 100
Tirerril barony 17

Toberbride 267
Tone, Matthew 64
Tone, Theobald Wolfe 58, 64
Tonry, Patrick APP 42
Toomore *see Foxford* 16, 171n, APPS 7, 8, 48
Toomour *see Keash* 16, 220, APPS 7, 8, 17
Tougher, John 289, APPS 5, 6, 7, 34
Touhy OP, Thady APP 38
Tourlestrane *(Kilmactigue)* 17, 34, 36n, 43, 89, 90n, 91, 92, 94n, 95, 96, 97, 98, 99, 102, 103n, 106, 107, 110, 114, 116, 127, 157, 169, 171, 202, 222, 228, 236, 246, 263, 272, 273, 275, 308, 310, 322, 371, APPS 34, 48, 51
Towey, Martin 89n
Trench Power, Maj General 76
Trinity Island 128
Tristan, Margaret 41
Troy, Archbishop John Thomas 51, 52, 58, 81, 82, 167, 315, 316, 319, 320, 324, 330, 339, 341, 342, 348, 353, 357, 358, 364, 368, 369, APP 23n
Truc 67
Tuam 17, 18, 29, 44, 45, 62, 74, 138, 154, 156, 178, 180, 186, 187, 191, 199, 200, 201, 203, 204n, 211, 218, 234, 242, 246, 247, 259, 264, 277, 289, 295, 297, 300, 305, 307, 308, 312, 314, 315, 316, 317, 319, 321, 324, 325, 326, 328, 329, 330, 332, 335, 337, 339, 343, 344, 345, 354, 358, 360, 361, 366, 368, 369, 370, APPS 7, 31, 43
Tubbercurry 51, 59, 68, 69, 70, 76, 99, 124, 124n, 151, 158, 164, 170, 171n, 182, 270n, 275, 318, 374, APPS 13, 34, 45, 46, 48, 50, 51
Tullaghan APP 46
Tullaghanmore *(Edmondstown)* 128
Tullinacorragh 155
Tullycusheen 75
Tullyhugh 47, 155, APPS 7, 34, 43
Tumgesh 171, 174, APPS 48, 50
Turlough 145, 158
Turlow 328
Tymon, James 41, 44, 208, 217, APPS 8, 29, 34
Tyrawley barony 56, 64, 66
Tyrawley, Lord 79, 153, 222
Tyrconnell, Earl of 20
Tyrrell, Edward 40
Urlaur 17, 29, 30, 43, 97, 97n, 134, 135, 138, 166, 167, 171n, 187, 188, 199, 232, 233, 234, 235, 262, 263, 276, 319, 322, 359, 360, 361, 362, 366, APPS 23, 24, 38, 48

Urlure 36n, APP 7
Verdon, Bernard 309, APP 42
Verdon, John 309, APP 42
Vereker, Col 70
Vernon, Rev APPS 28, 34
Verschoyle, Bishop James 138n, 140, APP 2
Verschoyle, Joseph 145, 146, APP 37
Vesey, Thomas 43n, APP 37
Wainright, Mark 145, APP 37
Wakefield, Mr 93, 94
Waldron, Bishop Peter 353, 354
Walker, Henry 186
Waller, Robert 96
Wallis, — APP 42
Walls, Archdeacon 178, APP 37
Walker, Rev Henry 187
Walsh, Andrew 163, 164, 172, 189
Walsh, Pat APP 42
Walsh, Matthew APP 42
Ward, Mathias 155n
Waters, George 334
Weir, George APP 37
Weldridge, Thomas APP 37
Wesley, John 84, 104, 151–2, 258
Westport 56, 68, 69, 84, 88, 93, 103, 108, 109, 110, 111, 118, 243, 264, 283, 326, 327, 345, 347, 364
Whelan, Bishop James APP 7
White, Matthew 217
Whitelaw, Robert APP 37
Whitelock, Edward APP 44
Whoody, Brian APP 45
Whoody, John APP 45
William III 20, 23, 27
Williams OFM, Lewis 51, 315n, APPS 18, 39
Williams, Peggy APP 38
Wilson, Mr 158
Wood, Mr 174, 228
Woodford 281
Wynne, Col 178
Wynne family 85, 86
Ycard, John 142n, APP 4
Yeats, William Butler 298
Young, Arthur 84, 85, 88, 89, 90, 91, 93, 94, 95, 101, 103, 107, 108, 109, 111, 113, 115, 118, 127, 140, 143, 147, 236, 250, 258, 285, 286